# Cisco IP Telephony: Planning, Design, Implementation, Operation, and Optimization

**Ramesh Kaza and Salman Asadullah**

**Cisco Press**

800 East 96th Street
Indianapolis, IN 46240 USA

## Cisco IP Telephony:
## Planning, Design, Implementation, Operation, and Optimization

Ramesh Kaza and Salman Asadullah

Copyright© 2005 Cisco Systems, Inc.

Published by:
Cisco Press
800 East 96th Street
Indianapolis, IN 46240 USA

Printed in the United States of America    2 3 4 5 6 7 8 9 0

Second Printing: April 2005

Library of Congress Cataloging-in-Publication Number: 2003108110

ISBN: 1-58705-157-5

## Warning and Disclaimer

This book is designed to provide information about Cisco IP Telephony. Every effort has been made to make this book as complete and as accurate as possible, but no warranty or fitness is implied.

The information is provided on an "as is" basis. The authors, Cisco Press, and Cisco Systems, Inc. shall have neither liability nor responsibility to any person or entity with respect to any loss or damages arising from the information contained in this book or from the use of the discs or programs that may accompany it.

The opinions expressed in this book belong to the authors and are not necessarily those of Cisco Systems, Inc.

## Trademark Acknowledgments

All terms mentioned in this book that are known to be trademarks or service marks have been appropriately capitalized. Cisco Press or Cisco Systems, Inc. cannot attest to the accuracy of this information. Use of a term in this book should not be regarded as affecting the validity of any trademark or service mark.

## Feedback Information

At Cisco Press, our goal is to create in-depth technical books of the highest quality and value. Each book is crafted with care and precision, undergoing rigorous development that involves the unique expertise of members from the professional technical community.

Readers' feedback is a natural continuation of this process. If you have any comments regarding how we could improve the quality of this book, or otherwise alter it to better suit your needs, you can contact us through e-mail at feedback@ciscopress.com. Please make sure to include the book title and ISBN in your message.

We greatly appreciate your assistance.

## Corporate and Government Sales

Cisco Press offers excellent discounts on this book when ordered in quantity for bulk purchases or special sales.

For more information, please contact: U.S. Corporate and Government Sales 1-800-382-3419
corpsales@pearsontechgroup.com

For sales outside the U.S., please contact: International Sales  international@pearsoned.com

| | |
|---|---|
| Publisher | John Wait |
| Editor-in-Chief | John Kane |
| Cisco Representative | Anthony Wolfenden |
| Cisco Press Program Manager | Jeff Brady |
| Production Manager | Patrick Kanouse |
| Development Editor | Jennifer Foster |
| Project Editor | Marc Fowler |
| Copy Editor | Bill McManus |
| Technical Editors | Niels Brunsgaard |
| | Mark Gallo |
| | Abderrahmane Mounir |
| | Gert Vanderstraeten |
| Team Coordinator | Tammi Barnett |
| Book and Cover Designer | Louisa Adair |
| Compositor | Mark Shirar |
| Indexer | Tim Wright |

**CISCO SYSTEMS**

**Corporate Headquarters**
Cisco Systems, Inc.
170 West Tasman Drive
San Jose, CA 95134-1706
USA
www.cisco.com
Tel: 408 526-4000
   800 553-NETS (6387)
Fax: 408 526-4100

**European Headquarters**
Cisco Systems International BV
Haarlerbergpark
Haarlerbergweg 13-19
1101 CH Amsterdam
The Netherlands
www-europe.cisco.com
Tel: 31 0 20 357 1000
Fax: 31 0 20 357 1100

**Americas Headquarters**
Cisco Systems, Inc.
170 West Tasman Drive
San Jose, CA 95134-1706
USA
www.cisco.com
Tel: 408 526-7660
Fax: 408 527-0883

**Asia Pacific Headquarters**
Cisco Systems, Inc.
Capital Tower
168 Robinson Road
#22-01 to #29-01
Singapore 068912
www.cisco.com
Tel: +65 6317 7777
Fax: +65 6317 7799

Cisco Systems has more than 200 offices in the following countries and regions. Addresses, phone numbers, and fax numbers are listed on the
**Cisco.com Web site at www.cisco.com/go/offices.**

Argentina • Australia • Austria • Belgium • Brazil • Bulgaria • Canada • Chile • China PRC • Colombia • Costa Rica • Croatia • Czech Republic
Denmark • Dubai, UAE • Finland • France • Germany • Greece • Hong Kong SAR • Hungary • India • Indonesia • Ireland • Israel • Italy
Japan • Korea • Luxembourg • Malaysia • Mexico • The Netherlands • New Zealand • Norway • Peru • Philippines • Poland • Portugal
Puerto Rico • Romania • Russia • Saudi Arabia • Scotland • Singapore • Slovakia • Slovenia • South Africa • Spain • Sweden
Switzerland • Taiwan • Thailand • Turkey • Ukraine • United Kingdom • United States • Venezuela • Vietnam • Zimbabwe

# About the Authors

**Ramesh Kaza**, CCIE No. 6207, is a technical leader in the World Wide Voice Practice Group (Customer Advocacy) at Cisco Systems. He has been with Cisco for five years. Ramesh has provided planning, design, and implementation support to many customers in deploying the Cisco IP Communications solutions. Prior to working on IP Communications, he was involved in validating the network designs for enterprise and service provider customers. He is a speaker at the Cisco Networkers event and has presented topics titled "Troubleshooting IPT Networks" and "Designing Large-Scale IPT Networks." Prior to joining Cisco Systems, Ramesh worked for Software Technology Parks of India–Bangalore as a member of the technical staff, and he has played a major role in building the Internet backbone. Ramesh holds a bachelor's degree in electronics and communications engineering.

**Salman Asadullah**, CCIE No. 2240, is a technical leader at Cisco Systems. As a recognized expert within Cisco and the industry, he has been designing and troubleshooting large-scale IP and multiservice networks for more than eight years. Salman represents Cisco in industry panel discussions and technical platforms such as NANOG, APRICOT, SANOG, ASEAN, IETF, IPv6 Forum, Networkers, and so on. Salman influences technology directions and decisions with Cisco business units and the Internet community. He has produced several technical documents and white papers and is a coauthor of *Cisco CCIE Fundamentals: Network Design and Case Studies*. Salman has also developed CCIE exams for IP and multiservice technologies. He holds a bachelor's degree in electrical engineering from The University of Arizona and a master's degree in electrical engineering from Wichita State University.

# About the Technical Reviewers

**Niels Brunsgaard**, CCIE No. 1544, has been with Cisco Systems as a consulting engineer since 1999, specializing in IP telephony. He has been involved in the planning, design, and implementation of a dozen IP telephony networks throughout Asia Pacific and North America. Niels holds a bachelor's degree in electro-mechanical engineering from the Denmark Technical University in Copenhagen, and a master's degree in telecommunications from the University of Colorado. He is a double CCIE, with certification in voice in addition to routing and switching.

**Mark Gallo** is a technical manager with America Online, where he leads a group of engineers responsible for the design and deployment of the domestic corporate intranet. His network certifications include Cisco CCNP and Cisco CCDP. He has led several engineering groups responsible for designing and implementing enterprise LANs and international IP networks. He has a BS in electrical engineering from the University of Pittsburgh. Mark resides in northern Virginia with his wife, Betsy, and son, Paul.

**Abderrahmane Mounir**, CCIE No. 4312, is a network consulting engineer at the Cisco Systems Advanced Services Group in San Jose. He has been working with large-scale IP telephony customers in planning, designing, implementing, and operating IP telephony networks since CallManager release 2.3. He has helped customers to successfully deploy and migrate large IP telephony deployments. He represents Cisco by presenting IPT end-to-end solutions and troubleshooting sessions at Networkers and other internal forums. He has also contributed to the creation and the design of the CCIE voice track. Abderrahmane holds a bachelor's degree in telecommunications engineering and a master's degree in electrical and computer engineering.

**Gert Vanderstraeten** has been working as a telecom/datacom engineer for companies such as Alcatel, Bell, and Lucent Technologies since 1993. Between 1998 and 2002, he was an independent contractor for the Cisco Systems IT department. During this period, his main focus was the implementation, maintenance, and design of VoIP, IP telephony, voice, and video applications, and the integration of Cisco AVVID technologies into large-scale solutions. In September 2002, he became a member of the technical staff and was operating until May 2004 within the Cisco Systems global enterprise architecture solutions team. Gert is currently working in the Advisory Services team as enterprise architect, where he takes on responsibility for large-scale customer deployments.

# Dedications

For my wife for her tireless support and encouragement in this project. Also, for my daughter and son who sacrificed time with dad to make this book happen.

I also dedicate this book to my family for their never-ending support.

—Ramesh

I dedicate this book to:

The people around the world who are suffering and oppressed.

My affectionate parents, who gave me their best, and to my loving wife, for her support and encouragement.

—Salman

# Acknowledgments

**From Ramesh Kaza and Salman Asadullah:**

There are many people who helped us to make this project successful. Please forgive us if we have inadvertently omitted the name of anymore who made such helpful contributions.

Thanks go to the following:

Himanshu Desai, senior manager, Advanced Services; Mike Quinn, VP, technical support; Kadir Koken, director, customer advocacy; and Khalid Raza, Cisco Distinguished Engineer, Cisco Systems, Inc., who encouraged us to write this book and supported us throughout this project.

Abderrahmane Mounir, network consulting engineer, Cisco Systems, Inc., for contributing to Chapter 6, verifying the configuration examples, reviewing the entire book, and providing valuable feedback.

Gert Vanderstraeten, enterprise architect for the Advisory Services team at Cisco Systems, Inc., for contributing to Chapter 7, reviewing the entire book, and providing valuable feedback.

Rajesh Ramarao, technical leader, Cisco Systems, Inc., for his contributions to parts of Chapter 9.

Jake Hartinger, technical leader, Cisco Systems, Inc., for humbly contributing to the valuable questionnaires in Appendixes B and C.

Niels Brunsgaard, technical leader, Cisco Systems, Inc., for reviewing parts of the book and providing valuable suggestions.

Mark Gallo, technical manager, America Online, for reviewing the entire book, helping in content rearrangement, and providing valuable feedback.

Thanks to all our colleagues and friends at Cisco Systems, Inc. whose work has helped us to complete this project. Especially, thanks to the members of the Advanced Services team: Hymed Besrour, Jine-Wen-Kou, Talal Siddiqui, Oludare Odunuga (Tola), Dave Turner, John Vosburg, Alvin Laguerta, Sanjay Jani, Imran Chaudhary, Kathy Decker, and Wesley Shuo.

Thanks to all the customers with whom we have worked over several years and in doing so acquired valuable knowledge and expertise that we have documented in this book.

We would like to express our special thanks to John Kane, editor in chief, for his expert guidance; Andrew Cupp and Jennifer Foster, development editors; Bill McManus, copy editor; Tammi Barnett, editorial assistant; and all other staff at Cisco Press for making this publication possible.

## This Book Is Safari Enabled

The Safari® Enabled icon on the cover of your favorite technology book means the book is available through Safari Bookshelf. When you buy this book, you get free access to the online edition for 45 days.

Safari Bookshelf is an electronic reference library that lets you easily search thousands of technical books, find code samples, download chapters, and access technical information whenever and wherever you need it.

To gain 45-day Safari Enabled access to this book:

- Go to http://www.ciscopress.com/safarienabled
- Complete the brief registration form
- Enter the coupon code P7KR-KEMJ-SV5P-I4JV-ZZTV

If you have difficulty registering on Safari Bookshelf or accessing the online edition, please e-mail customer-service@safaribooksonline.com.

# Contents at a Glance

# Contents

# Foreword

In October, 1998, Cisco took a step forward in its entry into IP Telephony with the acquisition of Selsius Systems, a pioneer and innovator of next generation network PBX systems for high-quality telephony over IP networks. This began the revolution of converged data, voice and video networks rendering separate voice and data networks a thing of the past. Cisco is one of the front runners in changing the way enterprises and service providers deliver converging traditional voice, data, and video applications.

The overall IP communication industry has gained significant momentum. The original Selsius Systems product family acquired by Cisco has expanded and evolved at tremendous speed. Over four million IP phones and over three million Unity seats have been deployed.

In early 1999, I was asked to build a small team of network consulting engineers in order to help Cisco customers and partners with the planning, designing, implementation, operation and optimization (PDIOO) of IP communication networks by providing them with templates, tools and best practices. Salman Asadullah and Ramesh Kaza were among the first few senior engineers who I asked to help with this task. We began working with our customers and during this process we defined the PDIOO processes for core steps that are required for deploying IP communication solutions. These processes and best practices are being shared in this book using hypothetical customer scenarios in the form of a case study. As with any emerging technology, these processes and best practices change over the time, but the approach applied remain the same. Today, our team supports some of largest Cisco IP communication deployments, some with over with 10,000 IP phones. The team, which started with three network consulting engineers, has grown to over 30 engineers in the course of four years.

One day, Salman and Ramesh walked into my office and presented the idea of writing a book based on the experience we acquired on this roller coaster ride. With the strong technical background and experience they gained by working with the largest IP communications networks, it was a valuable idea.

While reviewing their final draft of the book I was impressed to see how beautifully they have made an excellent guide on how to approach the IP communication project using PDIOO life cycle for small-to-medium size deployment. I am confident that the reader will find this book highly valuable and practical because it can be used as a reference guide to create a framework for your IP communication convergence projects.

Regards,
Himanshu Desai
Senior Manager, Advanced Services
IP Communications Services Team

# Introduction

IP telephony (IPT) technology has gained wide acceptance in the industry because it offers new ways to communicate and enables rich media communication capabilities. Recent studies have shown that deployment of IPT also helps improve employee productivity as a result of faster moves, adds, and changes; increased user mobility; and reduction in the time to set up telecommunication infrastructure for new office spaces. These are a few of the many benefits that are motivating organizations to move to IP-based PBX deployments.

Successful deployment of any new technology solution requires thorough understanding of the function of various components involved and the interaction among them. The architects and engineers who are tasked with implementing the IPT solution must ensure that the proposed architecture meets all the requirements and is also scalable in the future. To assist the architects and engineers in accomplishing this task, this book divides the deployment of IPT into planning, design, implementation, operation, and optimization (PDIOO) phases.

This book addresses the most important information that customers, network engineers, and architects should collect in each phase of the PDIOO methodology in deploying Cisco IPT solutions.

## Goals and Methods

The goal of this book is to be a useful guide for network engineers and architects going through the various phases of planning and deploying a Cisco IPT solution. This book helps you to make the decisions that best suit a particular network scenario.

The major tasks involved in each phase of the PDIOO methodology are explained with the aid of a case study that includes the most commonly deployed Cisco IPT architectures, telephony features, and applications. You can use the questionnaires in the appendixes to collect details about the customer's current network and to gather IPT requirements to propose the most suitable IPT network architecture and a detailed design.

To keep this book concise, in-depth discussion of communication protocols is not included because this information is readily available in other books and in Requests for Comments (RFCs).

## Target CallManager Release

The design principles and guidelines discussed in this book are applicable to Cisco CallManager version 3.3.3 and above. With the release of new versions of Cisco CallManager, you might find new features and scalability enhancements. However, the basic design rules and the PDIOO methodology remain the same.

## How This Book Is Organized

This book is organized into three parts.

Part I, "Overview of Technology, Protocols, and the PDIOO Methodology," discusses the VoIP and IPT technology and related protocols, mechanisms, architectures, and basics. It also lays the foundation of the PDIOO methodology and discusses why the PDIOO methodology is critical for successful IPT network implementation. Part I includes the following:

- Chapter 1, "Cisco IP Telephony Solution Overview"

- Chapter 2, "Planning, Design, Implementation, Operation, and Optimization Overview"

Part II, "Large-Scale IPT and Voice-Mail Network," builds on the material discussed in Part I and provides a real-world example with technical details, examples, design tips, and configuration examples at each phase of the

PDIOO methodology on how to build a successful and efficient large-scale IPT network from scratch. Part II includes the following:

- Chapter 3, "Large-Scale Enterprise Requirements for IP Telephony"

- Chapter 4, "Planning Phase"

- Chapter 5, "Design Phase: Network Infrastructure Design"

- Chapter 6, "Design of Call-Processing Infrastructure and Applications"

- Chapter 7, "Voice-Mail System Design"

- Chapter 8, "Implementation"

- Chapter 9, "Operations and Optimization"

The final part includes eight appendixes that comprise questionnaires that enable you to collect the information that you need at different steps of the PDIOO methodology. This information is critical for a successful implementation of an IPT and voice-mail network. The appendixes are as follows:

- Appendix A, "IP Phone Models and Selection Criteria"

- Appendix B, "IPT Planning Phase: Network Infrastructure Analysis Questionnaire"

- Appendix C, "IPT Planning Phase: Telecom Infrastructure Analysis Questionnaire"

- Appendix D, "IPT Design Phase: IP Phone Selection Questionnaire"

- Appendix E, "IPT Design Phase: IPT Requirement Analysis Questionnaire"

- Appendix F, "Ordering T1/E1 PRI from the Carrier Questionnaire"

- Appendix G, "Voice-Mail Design Questionnaire"

- Appendix H, "IPT Implementation Checklist"

## How to Read This Book

This book is organized logically with material advancing gradually. You can reference the various sections and chapters according to your needs and interests. If you have a good understanding of VoIP and IPT technology and tasks involved in PDIOO methodology, you might want to browse through Part I and spend more time on Part II. Part II references the appendix materials as appropriate, so you will have to refer to these appendixes quite often and will find them extremely useful.

This book provides several references and web links to useful material that is readily available and beyond the scope of this book.

# PART I

# Overview of Technology, Protocols, and the PDIOO Methodology

# CHAPTER 1

# Cisco IP Telephony Solution Overview

This chapter provides a high-level overview of legacy networks and the Cisco Architecture for Voice, Video and Integrated Data (AVVID), including its components, underlying protocols, and technologies.

This chapter covers the following topics:

- Legacy voice and data networks and next-generation multiservice networks
- Signaling and transport protocols that are used to build Cisco IP telephony (IPT) networks
- IPT components, applications, and terms used in Cisco IPT solutions
- Components, applications, and terms used in Cisco IPT solutions
- Cisco IPT deployment architectures and the criteria used to choose the deployment model
- How various IPT components and protocols work together, including a look at various call-flow scenarios

The information that is presented in this chapter will help you to understand the operation of legacy voice networks and the evolution of IPT technology. You can use this while doing the planning, design, implementation, operation, and optimization (PDIOO) of Cisco IPT networks.

## Legacy Voice and Data Networks

The term "legacy" refers to networks that have two separate infrastructures to support voice and data network services. A significant portion of many companies' IT budget goes toward maintaining the distinct voice and data networks, which requires one staff dedicated to maintaining the legacy voice infrastructure, including PBXs and voice-mail systems, and another staff dedicated to supporting the data network infrastructure. Two other drawbacks associated with this approach is that these two separate infrastructures cannot share their resources with each other and have to be managed separately, both of which increase IT budgets. Figure 1-1 shows a common example of an enterprise that has separate data and voice networks.

**Figure 1-1**    *Separate Voice and Data Networks*

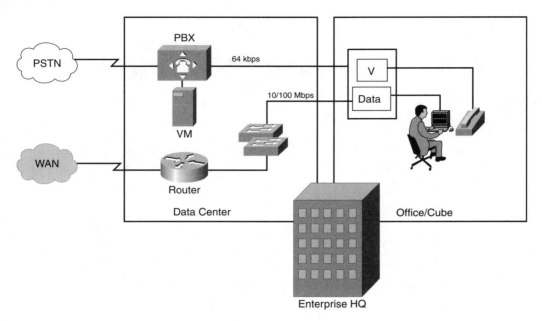

# Next-Generation Multiservice Networks

The desire of industry to combine distinct voice and data networks led to the development of several new concepts and technologies, such as packetized voice. Packetized voice comprises several standards and protocols. Applications use these protocols and standards to provide value-added and cost-effective services to users.

Packetized voice enables a device to send voice traffic (for example, telephone and fax) over an IP/Frame Relay/ATM network. In case of Voice over IP (VoIP), the digital signal processor (DSP) that is located on the voice gateway segments the voice signal into frames. The voice gateway combines these frames to form an IP packet and sends the packet over the IP network. On the receiving end, a reverse action converts the voice information that is stored in the IP packet into the original voice signal.

Across the IP network, these voice packets are transported by using the Real-Time Transport Protocol (RTP) and RTP Control Protocol (RTCP) stack and by using the User Datagram Protocol (UDP) as a transport layer protocol. RTP provides timestamps and sequence numbers in each packet to help synchronize the voice frames at the receiving side. RTCP provides a feedback mechanism that informs session participants of the received quality of the voice call and includes information such as delay, jitter, and lost packets.

It is important to note that most of the real-time applications use UDP as the transport layer protocol rather than TCP, for the following reasons:

- TCP guarantees the retransmission of frames that are lost in the network, which is of no use in a packetized voice network because the late arrival of frames at the receiving end introduces delay. Hence, the capability of TCP to retransmit frames is not useful in packetized voice networks.

- TCP introduces unnecessary delay by waiting for acknowledgements for every packet. This delay is not noticeable in the data networks but causes poor voice quality in packetized voice networks.

In addition to using RTP/UDP/IP as the protocol stack to carry voice calls across the IP network, VoIP networks use VoIP signaling protocols to set up and tear down the calls, carry the information to locate the users/phones, and exchange capabilities such as compression algorithms to be used during the conversation. The commonly used signaling protocols in VoIP networks are H.323, Media Gateway Control Protocol (MGCP), Session Initiation Protocol (SIP), and Skinny Client Control Protocol (SCCP).

Introducing "packetized voice" capability into the router shown in Figure 1-1 turns the router into a voice gateway and enables the router to do the packetization just described along with the duties required as a regular data router. This change allows you to provide additional services such as toll bypass.

Toll bypass enables you to reduce the overall telephony expenditure by routing long-distance interoffice calls over existing packet-based WANs, thus avoiding interexchange carrier (IXC) toll charges. As shown in Figure 1-2, when you make phone calls between the enterprise headquarters and a branch location, you can send the voice calls via the WAN data circuit as opposed to using the Public Switched Telephone Network (PSTN). The connection from the PBX is now terminated on the gateway, allowing the gateway to receive both incoming and outgoing calls. This architecture also allows routing of a voice call over the internal network to the closest gateway to the destination of the call and then connects into the public network as a local phone call. This is called *Tail-End Hop-Off (TEHO)*. You need to be aware that TEHO is not allowed in all countries. Hence, when you are designing a VoIP network with toll bypass or TEHO, you need to check the local government regulations.

To ensure that the design of your toll-bypass application is effective, it must include a voice gateway that is able to support multiple types of call signaling as it interacts with the PSTN, WAN, and existing PBX systems. By maintaining a connection to the PSTN, as shown in Figure 1-2, the gateway can reroute calls to the PSTN if congestion or failure occurs within the packet network.

**TIP**    By having this voice gateway in the network, you eliminate the need to have a separate "tie line" for the voice-only traffic.

**Figure 1-2** *Toll-Bypass Application*

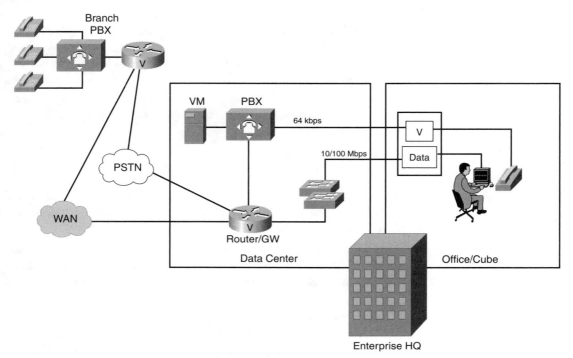

The DSPs that are located on the voice gateways also have the capability to handle different types of compression algorithms, such as G.711, G.723.1, G.726, G.728, and G.729 traffic. These compression algorithms maximize the throughput on the packet network. Compression techniques on gateways, such as compressed RTP (cRTP), reduce the amount of bandwidth per voice call. You should be aware of the side effects of enabling cRTP on the voice gateways. cRTP processing on voice gateways essentially compresses all outgoing voice packets and decompresses the incoming compressed voice packets. Hence, if you have numerous voice calls across the WAN links, the router has to perform many cycles of this task, which can increase the amount of CPU resources consumed for cRTP, thus leaving less CPU cycles for the other tasks.

In traditional voice networks, each call consumes a fixed amount of bandwidth. The PBX does not place more calls than it can handle through the trunks connecting to the PSTN, as shown on the left side of Figure 1-3. In packetized networks, if bandwidth is available to make only two good-quality calls, in the absence of a call admission control (CAC) mechanism, the voice gateway allows the third call to go through, as shown on the right side of Figure 1-3. This third call degrades the quality of the existing two good voice calls. Hence, gatekeepers are deployed in the packetized networks to control the number of calls that can be sent over the WAN links. The CAC mechanism in the gatekeeper ensures that the gateway does not place the third call.

**Figure 1-3**    *Call Control in Circuit- and Packet-Switched Networks*

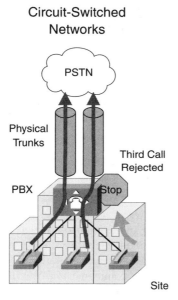
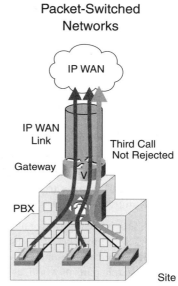

Gatekeepers perform CAC and bandwidth management in VoIP networks. Gatekeepers ensure that enough bandwidth is available before granting permission to a gateway to place a call across the IP WAN. After receiving permission from the gatekeeper, the originating gateway initiates a call setup with the terminating gateway over the packet network.

**TIP**    When you are using IP networks to carry packetized voice traffic, an optional but important consideration is to use proper admission and bandwidth control mechanisms.

Besides performing CAC and bandwidth management, gatekeepers can perform accounting, call authorization, authentication (via RADIUS), address lookup and resolution, and translation between E.164 numbers and the IP addresses.

# Networks Based on Cisco AVVID

Networks no longer are limited to performing toll-bypass call routing. Today, many networks are replacing the legacy PBX systems with IP-based call-processing servers; replacing legacy voice-mail systems with IP-based voice-mail systems; replacing legacy phones with IP phones;

and replacing legacy video transmission with IP-based video transmission. This strategy is also the Cisco AVVID vision of truly converged voice, video, and data networks. In Cisco AVVID, IPT is one of the solutions. If three components of the legacy network previously shown in Figure 1-2 are replaced as described in the following list, the network evolves into the network shown in Figure 1-4:

- Legacy PBXs are replaced by IP-based call-processing servers, such as Cisco CallManager
- Legacy voice-mail systems are replaced by IP-based voice-mail systems such as Cisco Unity
- Legacy phones are replaced by Cisco IP Phones

The migration shown in Figure 1-4 is a big change from a legacy network. These types of migrations have been done on hundreds of networks around the world. Several organizations currently run and manage true IP-based networks for their data and voice traffic or are in the process of migrating to IPT solutions.

Figure 1-5 shows the high-level network architecture of an organization that has transitioned to a Cisco IPT solution. The IPT solution replaced all the legacy PBXs, voice-mail systems, and phones with a true end-to-end IP-based solution. This network supports thousands of users located in different parts of world, using IP-based devices communicating over IP infrastructure. To reach this goal, you have to follow a structured approach; the rest of the chapters in this book discuss the use of PDIOO methodology to build such an end-to-end IP-based telephony network.

**Figure 1-4** *Today's Multiservice Networks*

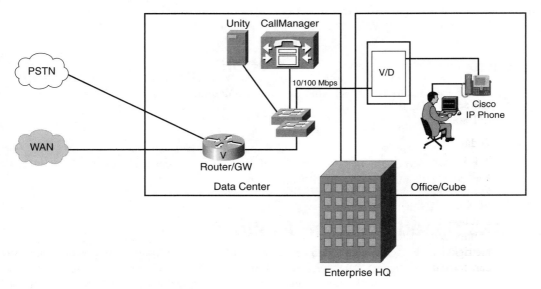

**Figure 1-5**    *End-to-End IPT Network*

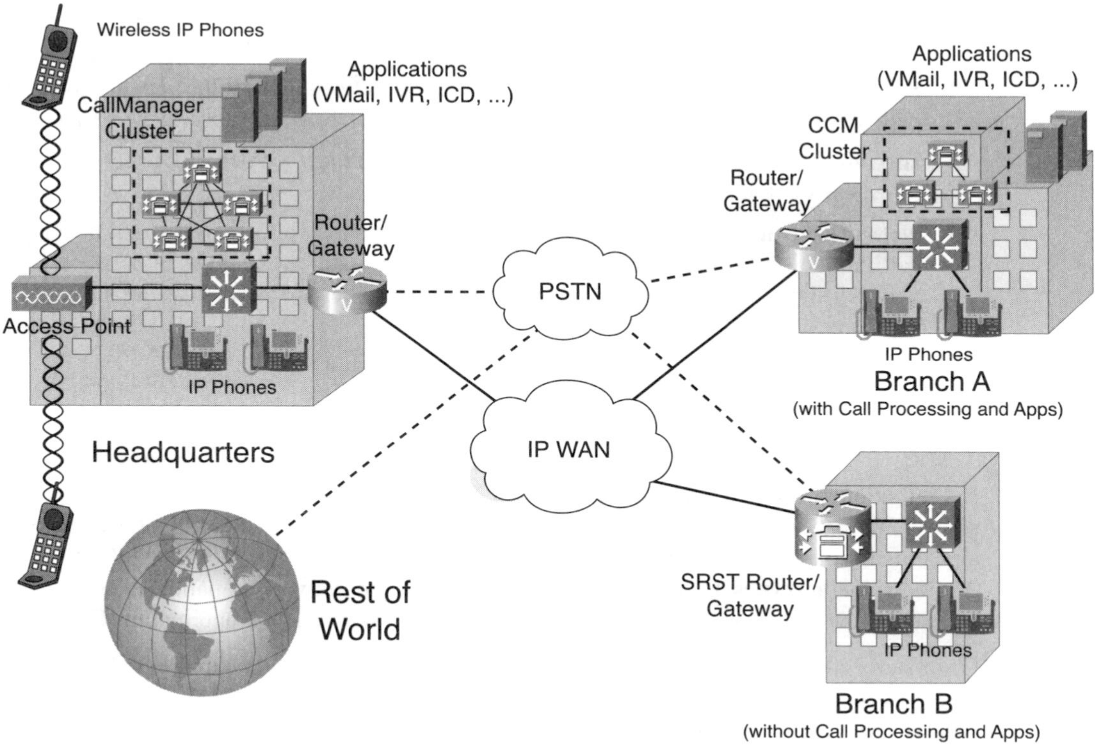

# Signaling and Transport Protocols

Now that you have a good understanding of the evolution of integrated voice and data networks, this section briefly discusses the concepts of different signaling and transport protocols used in IPT solutions.

Today, organizations use a PBX system or a key system as customer premises equipment (CPE) to provide voice services. Key systems are less expensive than PBX systems, but they typically support fewer users and do not have the rich functionality and feature sets available in PBX systems. If there are large numbers of users on the PBX system, it is not possible to forklift the PBX systems and replace them with IP-based call-processing servers. In these scenarios, the IPT solution should provide the integration with the existing PBX or key systems. Knowing the type of interfaces and signaling protocols supported on the PBX or key systems allows you to choose the right hardware and software components on the IPT solution so that the PBX or key systems can coexist with the IPT solution until migration to IPT is completed.

## Telco Signaling Protocols

Conceptually, the signaling protocols that are used in the telco networks can be divided into three categories:

- **Subscriber-to-network signaling**—Used by end users to request the network to set up a call. The telephone companies (telcos) treat these interfaces as subscriber interfaces.

- **Intranetwork signaling**—Used between switches in the telco network to set up and tear down calls between telco switches.

- **Network-to-network signaling**—Used between two networks to set up and disconnect calls and to exchange billing and other related information. The types of network-to-network signaling are not new signaling types but rather are variants of the intranetwork signaling types.

Signaling is further divided into two types: analog and digital.

### Analog Signaling

By definition, analog signals are sent over wires or through air and carry information through some combination of frequency, phase, and amplitude. You can find trunks that use analog signaling in small offices or in offices where the telco switch does not support digital signaling. Analog signaling types usually fall under the subscriber-to-network signaling category. The three common analog trunk types are loop start, ground start, and ear and mouth (E&M).

Loop-start and ground-start trunks use the same wire pair for both audio and signaling. Most of the telephone connections to households around the world use loop-start signaling. E&M uses separate wire pairs for audio and signaling. You can find E&M signaling trunks in older PBX/central office switches.

The telephone system usually uses dual-tone multifrequency (DTMF) or dial pulse/digit transmission methods to transmit the digits that the subscriber dials. DTMF, which is the most popular method, uses two simultaneous voice-band tones for dialing, such as touch-tones. Dial pulse, which is an older method, uses a series of make and brake pulses to represent digits. In pulse dialing, an off-hook state is represented by a make state of the pulse, and an on-hook state is represented by a break state of the pulse.

### Digital Signaling

Analog trunks require a physical set of wires per trunk and thus might not be the best method when provisioning a large number of trunks. Hence, higher-density digital trunks are used in larger organizations that have higher call volumes. There are two varieties of digital signaling trunk types: T1 and E1 circuits. When a network supports voice on T1 and E1 circuits (also used for data transmission), two types of signaling mechanisms are used:

Channel-associated signaling (CAS)

Common channel signaling (CCS)

CAS falls into the subscriber-to-network and CCS into intranetwork signaling.

## CAS

In CAS, signaling information is carried in-band. This means that actual voice conversation travels along with the signaling information on the same circuit. One example of a CAS signaling system is Robbed Bit Signaling (RBS). RBS gets its name from the nature of its operation, in which some of the bits from the payload in each time-division multiplexing (TDM) slot are robbed and reused for signaling.

In the E1 facility, the signaling bits are arranged in time slot 16. CAS on the E1 facility also uses R1 (MF) and R2 (MF Compelled) types of signaling methods.

## CCS

CCS separates signaling information from user data. Two examples of protocols in which you can find CCS signaling are ISDN and Q.SIG.

ISDN permits telephone networks to carry data, voice, and other types of traffic. ISDN has two types of variants:

- **Basic Rate Interface (BRI)**—Composed of two B (bearer) channels (used to carry data and voice traffic) and one D (data) channel (used for signaling), referred to as 2B+D. Each B channel provides 64 kbps, and the D channel provides 16 kbps for signaling. Two B channels combined can provide 128 kbps of bandwidth. Although the signaling is in a separate channel, it travels along with data.
- **Primary Rate Interface (PRI)**—Composed of 23 B channels and one D channel (23B+D) when using a T1 facility, and 30 B channels and a single 64-kbps D channel (30B+D) when using an E1 facility. Each B channel is 64 kbps.

The other example signaling standard that uses CCS, Q.SIG, has many variations in its feature implementations. Q.SIG is used in many PBX systems and in PBX internetworking.

# VoIP Protocols

This section provides a brief overview of the operation of VoIP protocols and explains how these protocols play a role in IPT networks.

Two types of VoIP protocols exist:

- Protocols that provide the call control and signaling
- Protocols that carry voice payload (RTP, RTCP, UDP, and IP)

The job of the call-control and signaling protocols is to set up and tear down the connection between two or more endpoints in a VoIP network. The following is a list of the call-control and signaling protocols commonly found in IPT networks:

- **H.323**—(peer-to-peer model)
- **Session Initiation Protocol (SIP)**—(peer-to-peer model)
- **Media Gateway Control Protocol (MGCP)**—(client/server model)
- **Skinny Client Control Protocol (SCCP)**—(a lighter-weight Cisco proprietary protocol that uses the client/server model)

After the call setup process is complete, the source and destination endpoints can transmit and receive data by using the RTP/RTCP/IP/UDP protocol stack. A typical VoIP network uses any one or a combination of these protocols, depending on the endpoints involved. These protocols are needed at different points in an IPT network. As mentioned before, the gateway is an interface between the IP telephony network and the PSTN or a PBX. On one side, the gateway supports the signaling protocols needed to interface with the PSTN or a PBX. On the other side, the gateway supports the signaling and control protocols needed to interface with the IPT network via the CallManager. The CallManager also acts as a protocol translator. On one hand, the CallManager could be communicating with an IP phone using SCCP, and on the other hand, it could be communicating to the gateway using MGCP, H.323.

The following sections discuss briefly some basic functionality of the call control and signaling protocols that carry voice payload.

## H.323

H.323 is an International Telecommunication Union (ITU) specification to carry real-time voice traffic such as telephone calls, video, and data over an IP network. The H.323 protocol specification describes how a session between two H.323 endpoints is created and maintained. The following are the main components of H.323:

- **H.225**—Scaled-down version of Q.931 to set up an IP connection between two H.323 endpoints.
- **H.245**—Allows H.323 endpoints to negotiate their capabilities (such as codecs available) with each other.
- **RAS**—H.323 endpoints use this protocol to communicate with H.323 gatekeepers to Manage Registration/Administration/Status.

The preceding three components use TCP for transport. The H.323 standard has gone through many revisions. The current standard is H.323 Version 4. Cisco CallManager 4.0 is compliant with H.323 Version 2 standards.

The "Call-Flow Scenarios" section later in this chapter discusses the call flow sequence between the IP phone and a voice gateway using the H.323 protocol.

## SIP

SIP is an RFC standard (RFC 3261) from the Internet Engineering Task Force (IETF), the body responsible for administering and developing the mechanisms that comprise the Internet. SIP is one of the most talked about protocols these days because of its wide interoperability with other products.

SIP is a peer-to-peer protocol. The peers in a session are called user agents (UAs). A user agent can function in one of the following roles:

- **User agent client (UAC)**—A client application that initiates the SIP request
- **User agent server (UAS)**—A server application that contacts the user when a SIP request is received and returns a response on behalf of the user

Typically, a SIP endpoint is capable of functioning as both a UAC and a UAS, but it functions only as one or the other per transaction. Whether the endpoint functions as a UAC or a UAS depends on the UA that initiated the request. From an architectural standpoint, the physical components of a SIP network can be grouped into two categories: clients (endpoints) and servers. Figure 1-6 shows the SIP architecture.

**Figure 1-6**    *SIP Architecture*

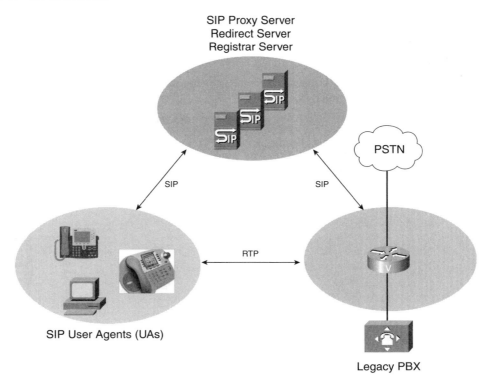

In Figure 1-6, the SIP clients are phones such as Cisco SIP phones (7960, 7940, and ATA-18x can be configured as SIP phones by loading SIP firmware) and SoftPhones that are loaded on the user's PC/laptop. The routing entities within the SIP architecture are called SIP servers. The following are the three types of SIP servers:

- **SIP proxy server**—An intermediate device that receives SIP requests from a client and then forwards the requests on the client's behalf. Basically, proxy servers receive SIP messages and forward them to the next SIP server in the network. Proxy servers can provide functions such as authentication, authorization, network access control, routing, reliable request retransmission, and security. The role of a SIP proxy server is similar to that of a gatekeeper in an H.323 network.

- **Redirect server**—Provides the client with information about the next hop or hops that a message should take, after which the client contacts the next hop server or UAS directly.

- **Registrar server**—Processes requests from UACs for registration of their current location. Registrar servers are often co-located with a redirect or proxy server.

SIP uses six main messages for its basic functionality:

- **Register message**—Sent by the UAs to tell the network where they can be located. The location could be one or more addresses.

- **Invite message**—Sent by a UA to initiate a session.

- **ACK message**—Used to acknowledge that a successful session has been initiated.

- **Bye message**—Used to terminate a session that is already in progress and established.

- **Cancel message**—Used to terminate a session that is not yet established (for example, phone is still ringing).

- **Options message**—Used for an out-of-band mechanism to determine the capabilities of another UA.

Users in the SIP network are identified by a unique SIP address such as an e-mail ID. Figure 1-7 shows the basic call setup diagram of a successful call when a SIP proxy server is present in the network.

**Figure 1-7**    *SIP Call Flow Using SIP Proxy Server*

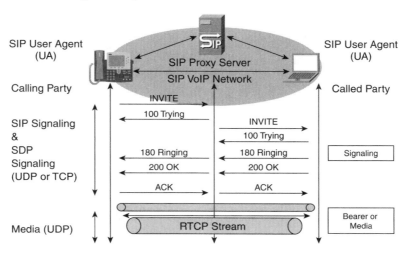

Figure 1-7 shows the following sequence of events:

1    The calling party sends an Invite message to the called party.

2    The SIP proxy server responds to the calling party with the informational response "100 Trying."

3    At the same time, the SIP proxy server sends an Invite message to the called party on behalf of the calling party.

4    The called party responds with two informational responses: "100 Trying" and then "180 Ringing."

5    The SIP proxy server passes the informational response "180 Ringing" to the calling party.

6    The called party responds with the response "200 OK" if the call is successful.

7    The SIP proxy server passes the success response "200 OK" to the calling party.

8    The calling party sends an ACK message.

9    The SIP proxy server passes the ACK message to the called party.

After SIP successfully completes the signaling, a media path between the two endpoints is established.

Starting with CallManager 4.0, CallManager can communicate with SIP endpoints (SIP IP phones, SIP gateways) via SIP Proxy server. This feature, referred to as "SIP Trunk" and shown in Figure 1-8, allows any CallManager-controlled device to communicate with a SIP network.

Future releases of CallManager might include the direct support of SIP so that CallManager can talk to the SIP endpoints directly without the need for a SIP proxy server.

**Figure 1-8**   *SIP Support in CallManager*

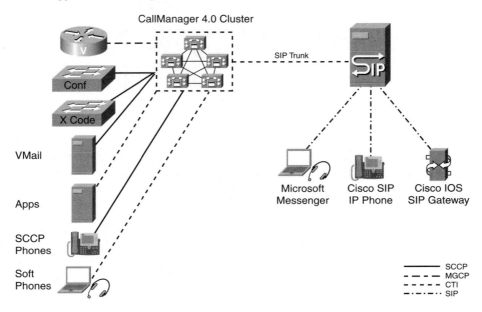

## MGCP

As previously discussed, H.323 and SIP are based on the peer-to-peer model, whereas MGCP is based on a client/server model. As defined in RFC 2705, "MGCP is designed as an internal protocol within a distributed system that appears to the outside as a single VoIP gateway."

MGCP uses the Session Description Protocol (SDP, RFC 2327) to describe and negotiate media capabilities, which is also used in SIP. SDP functionality is similar to H.245 capability in H.323.

There are two main components of MGCP:

- **Media gateway (MG)**—Bridges networks that use different media types, such as circuit-switched, analog, and IP networks. An MG is also referred to as an endpoint (EP). An MG is an interface between a telephony network or a PBX and a VoIP network. Examples of Cisco media gateway products include 26xx/36xx/37xx series routers, Catalyst gateways such as WS-X-6608-T1/E1, and WS-6624-FXS gateways.

- **Media gateway controller (MGC)**—Controls the parts of the call state that relate to connection control for media channels in one or more media gateways. An MGC is also referred to as a call agent (CA) or as the industry term Softswitch. In the IPT networks, CallManager acts as a CA that provides call-processing functions and feature logic and controls the MG.

MGCP messages are sent over UDP/IP between the CA and MG. The client/server relationship is maintained between the CA and MG. Voice traffic (bearer channels) is carried over RTP/UDP/IP or other transmission media (e.g., ATM). MGCP is independent of transport media and can be used to control ATM or circuit-switched gateways.

Similar to H.323, MGCP has undergone several revisions. As of CallManager 4.0, support for MGCP 0.1 is included. The current revision of MGCP is 1.0.

MGCP uses very simple commands in the negotiation process between the MG and CA and uses UDP as a transport layer protocol. The default port is UDP 2427, although it is configurable in the CallManager. Examples of the commands are **CRCX** (**CreateConnection**), **MDCX** (**ModifyConnection**), etc., and every command requires an acknowledgement. The following list describes commonly used MGCP commands, and Figure 1-8 shows the usage of these commands:

- **CRCX**—The CA can use the **CreateConnection** command to create a connection that terminates in an endpoint inside the MG.

- **MDCX**—The CA can use the **ModifyConnection** command to change the parameters associated with a previously established connection.

- **DLCX**—The MG can also use the **DeleteConnection** command to delete an existing connection. The MG can also use the **DeleteConnection** command. This command indicates that a connection can no longer be sustained.

- **RQNT**—The CA can issue a **NotificationRequest** command to a gateway to instruct the gateway to watch for specific events such as hook actions or DTMF tones on a specified endpoint.

- **NTFY**—The MG can use the **Notify** command to inform the CA when the requested events occur.

- **AUEP and AUCX**—The CA can use the **AuditEndpoint** and **AuditConnection** commands to audit the status of an endpoint and any connections associated with it.

- **RSIP**—The MG can use the **RestartInProgress** command to notify the CA that the MG, or a group of endpoints managed by the MG, is being taken out of service or is being placed back in service.

Table 1-1 shows the directions of the signaling messages exchanged between the CA and the endpoint or MG.

**Table 1-1** *MGCP Message Types and Flows*

| MGCP Command Code | MGCP Command Verb | Direction of the Command Flow |
|---|---|---|
| Endpoint Configuration | EPCF | CA -> EP |
| Creation Connection | CRCX | CA -> EP |
| ModifyConnection | MDCX | CA -> EP |
| DeleteConnection | DLCX | CA <-> EP |
| Notification Request | RQNT | CA -> EP |
| Notify | NTFY | CA <- EP |
| AuditEndpoint | AUEP | CA -> EP |
| AuditConnection | AUCX | CA -> EP |
| RestartIn Progress | RSIP | CA <- EP |

The "Call-Flow Scenarios" section later in this chapter discusses the call-flow sequence between the IP phone and a voice gateway using the MGCP protocol.

## SCCP

SCCP is a "lightweight" Cisco proprietary protocol that is based on a client/server model. In this model, all the intelligence is built into the server, which is a CallManager in the Cisco IPT solution. The client, which is a Cisco IP Phone, has minimal intelligence. In other words, the Cisco IP Phones have to do less work, thus requiring less memory and processing power. The CallManager, being the intelligent server, learns client capabilities, controls call establishment, clears calls, sends notify signals (i.e. message waiting indication (MWI), reacts to signals from the client (after the user presses the directory button on the phone), and so forth. CallManager communicates with the IP phones using SCCP and, if the call has to go through a gateway, communicates with the gateway using H.323 or MGCP.

## RTP/RTCP

By now you should have a good operational understanding of signaling protocols such as H.323, SIP, MGCP, and SCCP. These protocols provide call-signaling and control functionality and are responsible for setting up and tearing down the connection between the endpoints. After the connection is set up between the two endpoints, the source and destination endpoints can transmit and receive data by using RTP/RTCP. As discussed in the "Next-Generation Multiservice Networks" section earlier in this chapter, RTP/RTCP uses UDP for transport.

Figure 1-9 shows the IP packet header information that transports the RTP/RTCP packets. As you can see, the IPv4 header is 20 bytes, the UDP header is 8 bytes, and the RTP header is 12 bytes, which means that a total of 40 bytes of header information is required to transport the single RTP packet. After this 40 bytes of IP header information, two 10-byte frames (10 bytes per frame for G.729 codec voice samples) of real voice payload are carried, for a total of 20 bytes of voice payload. (The Cisco implementation puts two frames into one packet.) A simple math calculation shows that the header has twice the number of bytes that are in the real payload. To address this particular issue, you can use RTP header compression technique on point-to-point links. You must apply the RTP header compression on a link-by-link basis. When enabled on a gateway, you can use the RTP header compression technique compresses the 40-byte header into 2 or 4 bytes. However, enabling compression increases the load of the CPU on the router. You need to make a decision based on the number of calls that you need to send out through that gateway.

**Figure 1-9**    *RTP, UDP, and IP Protocol Headers*

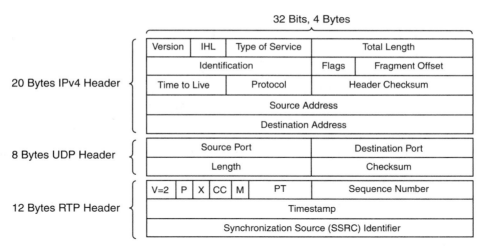

# IP Telephony Components

So far this chapter has focused on analyzing how legacy networks are migrating to integrated voice and data networks and on describing the various protocols used in the new multiservice networks. This section discusses the main components of Cisco AVVID and some of the key areas to look for when deploying the Cisco IPT solution. Key areas include the following:

- Network infrastructure
- Call processing

- CallManager Directory Services
- IPT endpoints
- Call admission control
- Fax
- Media resources
- Applications

Understanding the features and capabilities of these components will help you to design the network that meets the targeted organization's requirements.

## Network Infrastructure

Network infrastructure plays a key role in building multiservice networks such as Cisco AVVID. Integration of data and voice traffic puts strong requirements on packet loss, delay, and jitter (variable delay). When designing IPT networks, you should choose network infrastructure components in the LAN and WAN that support QoS mechanisms, in addition to faster convergence in case of network failures to avoid the delay, jitter, and so forth.

The addition of voice traffic on top of the existing data traffic increases the bandwidth requirements in both LANs and WANs. The bandwidth within the LAN is not a challenging issue because of the availability of the high-speed LAN switching technologies. However, when transporting the voice traffic across the WAN links, you need to ensure that adequate bandwidth is available to support the additional bandwidth required to transport voice calls. If the WAN links do not have adequate bandwidth, you need to increase their bandwidth to support the additional voice traffic. After the bandwidth is available, you can use QoS mechanisms to prioritize the voice traffic and reserve the bandwidth.

Chapter 4, "Planning Phase," discusses the infrastructure requirement analysis in depth.

## Call Processing

CallManager software is the main component of the Cisco IPT solution. CallManager handles all the call-processing requests received from various clients in the IPT network. CallManager software runs on the Microsoft Windows 2000 Server/Windows 2000 Advanced Server operating systems.

CallManager is installed on the Cisco Media Convergence Server (MCS). The selection of the hardware platforms depends on the size of the network in which they are going to be deployed, including its high-availability and performance requirements. Table 1-2 lists the maximum number of devices supported per server platform.

**Table 1-2**    *Maximum Number of Devices per Server Platform*

| Server Platform | Maximum Number of Devices per Server |
| --- | --- |
| Cisco MCS-7845 | 7500 |
| Cisco MCS-7835 | 2500 |
| Cisco MCS-7825 | 1000 |
| Cisco MCS-7815 | 300 |

## CallManager Clustering

CallManager servers are grouped to form clusters to support more devices (IP phones, gateways, and so forth). Starting with CallManager Version 3.3, a CallManager cluster can have up to eight CallManager servers running the CallManager service.

In addition to eight call-processing servers, the cluster can have servers such as a publisher server, a Trivial File Transfer Protocol (TFTP) server, and a Music on Hold (MoH) server. A publisher server has the read/write database of Microsoft SQL that stores the CallManager configuration information. There can be only one publisher server in a cluster. All other servers in the cluster, referred to as subscribers, have the read-only database. Subscribers pull their up-to-date subscriptions from the publisher server. During normal operating conditions, when the publisher server is available, the subscriber database is not used.

If a publisher is offline, you cannot perform updates such as adding new devices, changing user passwords, speed dials, or any other features that require a write operation on the database, because it is the only server that has the read-write database. However, the phones and other devices will continue to function normally.

CallManager stores the configuration of the IP phones in the TFTP server. (The default is to store it in the memory. You can change this default by modifying the service parameters. Chapter 9, "Operations and Optimization," discusses these techniques.) The configuration information is stored in the XML format. The configuration file contains information such as device pool associations, directory URLs, authentication URLs, language-specific information, and so forth. IP phones and many other endpoints in the Cisco IPT network download the firmware and configuration information from the TFTP server.

Failure of a TFTP server is not an issue for the devices that were already configured and functioning before the failure. The devices store the previously loaded configuration and firmware in memory and use the same if they fail to contact the TFTP server during the reboot. However, an update to a phone's configuration information that is stored in the TFTP configuration file will fail if the TFTP server is unavailable. In addition, provisioning of new devices fails if a TFTP server is not available.

For networks that require high availability, you can deploy two TFTP servers to provide redundancy and load balancing in the network. Cisco IP Phones and other Cisco IPT endpoints receive the TFTP server information via the DHCP server in the custom option 150. You can configure an array of IP addresses for option 150 in the DHCP server, instead of one IP address, to communicate to the Cisco IPT endpoints the existence of the secondary TFTP server.

---

**TIP**     In a large IPT deployment, the recommendation is to have a dedicated publisher server that does not participate in the call processing and a separate server that provides TFTP services.

---

## Device Weights

The devices in the IPT network consume different amounts of memory and CPU resources on the CallManager servers. Based on the amount of resource consumption, Cisco has assigned a weight to each device, as shown in Table 1-3. This information is based on CallManager Version 3.3.(3).

**Table 1-3**     *Base Device Weights*

| Device Type | Weight per Session/ Voice Channel | Session/DS0 per Device | Cumulative Device Weight |
| --- | --- | --- | --- |
| IP phone | 1 | 1 | 1 |
| Analog MGCP ports | 3 | Varies | 3 per DS0 |
| Analog SCCP ports | 1 | Varies | 1 per DS0 |
| CTI route point | 2 | Varies | Varies[1] |
| CTI client port | 2 | 1 | 2 |
| CTI server port | 2 | 1 | 2 |
| CTI third-party control[2] | 3 | 1 | 3 |
| CTI agent phone[2] | 6 | 1 | 6 |
| H.323 client | 3 | Varies | 3 per call |
| Intercluster trunk gateway | 3 | Varies | 3 per call |
| H.323 gateway | 3 | Varies | 3 per call |
| Digital MGCP T1 gateway ports | 3 | 24 | 72 per T1 |
| Digital MGCP E1 gateway ports | 3 | 30 | 90 per E1 |
| MoH stream | 10 | 20 | 200[3] |
| Transcoding resource | 3 | Varies | 3 per session |

**Table 1-3**    *Base Device Weights (Continued)*

| Device Type | Weight per Session/ Voice Channel | Session/DS0 per Device | Cumulative Device Weight |
|---|---|---|---|
| Media Termination Point (MTP) (software) | 3 | 24 | $72^4$ |
| Conference resource (hardware) | 3 | Varies | 3 per session |
| Conference resource (software) | 3 | 24 | $72^4$ |

1. Cumulative weight of the CTI (Computer Telephony Integration) route point depends on the associated CT ports used by the application.
2. Includes the associated IP phone.
3. When MoH is installed on the same server as CallManager, the maximum number of media streams is 20.
4. When installed on the same server as CallManager, the maximum number of conference sessions is 24.

The devices that are registered with CallManager consume additional server resources during transactions, which are in the form of calls. A device that makes only 6 calls per hour consumes fewer resources than a device that makes 12 calls per hour. The device weights that are assigned to the devices in Table 1-3 are based on the assumption that the device makes 6 or fewer calls during the busy hour call attempts (BHCA).

BHCA is the number of call attempts made during the busiest hour of the day. Before deploying a Cisco IPT solution, you must determine the busiest hour of the day for an organization and then scale the type of devices that are going to be deployed within the Cisco IPT solution. The BHCA varies from organization to organization and depends on the type of business (which can vary by season) and on the sales/promotional periods. A thorough network audit or analysis of historical call detail records is required to determine an organization's BHCA.

Each device that requires more than six BHCA has a multiplier applied to its base weight. Based on the BHCA multiplier table, Table 1-4, if an IP phone is making 16 BHCA, its multiplier is 3. The total weight of the IP phone with 16 BHCA is equal to its base weight 1 (refer to Table 1-3) multiplied by 3. The multiplier is applied only to station/client devices and not to devices that are a media resource or gateway.

**Table 1-4**    *BHCA Multiplier*

| BHCA | 0–6 BHCA | 7–12 BHCA | 13–18 BHCA | 19–24 BHCA | 25–30 BHCA |
|---|---|---|---|---|---|
| Multiplier | 1 | 2 | 3 | 4 | 5 |
| Example IP phone | 1 | 2 | 3 | 4 | 5 |
| Example CTI client port | 2 | 4 | 6 | 8 | 10 |

The total number of device units that a single CallManager can control depends on the server platform. Table 1-2 gives the details of the maximum number of devices per platform based on CallManager Version 4.0. You have to deploy multiple CallManager clusters if the number of IP phones plus other devices exceeds the device weights limit supported by a single cluster.

---

**TIP**    In Table 1-2, the number provided in the Maximum Number of IP Phones per Server column is based on the assumption that all phones are configured with a single directory number. If the network that you are deploying is complex and involves multiple lines/directory numbers per IP phone or dial plan that includes numerous route patterns and translational patterns, you have to understand the concept of dial plan weights, as discussed in the following section.

---

## Dial Plan Weights

Device weights determine the maximum number of physical devices that can be registered to a CallManager subscriber. Some IP phone models support multiple lines (directory numbers or line appearances). Many IPT deployments have directory numbers that are shared across multiple IP phones and a large number of dial plan entries that include route patterns; translational patterns require an extra amount of resources (CPU, memory) on the CallManager.

Dial plan weights provide the limit on the number of such dial plan entries configured in a CallManager subscriber. Dial plan weight calculations provide guidelines to size the cluster. Two types of dial plan weights are available:

- Subscriber dial plan weights (include line appearances)
- Global dial plan weights (include route patterns and translational patterns)

In larger IPT deployments, you should register all the endpoints to the subscribers and none to the publisher server. That way, you can prevent the publisher server from doing call-processing activity. Subscriber dial plan weights consist of the following main types:

- **IP phone weight**—Associated with the subscriber server to which the IP phone is normally registered. This weight is for the base device. The dial plan weight of an IP phone is independent of its device weight. (See Table 1-3.)
- **Line weight (unique or shared appearance)**—Associated with the subscriber server to which the device is normally registered.
- **Reachability weight**—Associated with all other subscribers in the cluster that have to be able to reach (call) a given line. Consider a CallManager cluster with two CallManager servers: CCM1 and CCM2. An IP phone 'A' is registered to CCM1. Even though the IP phone is registered to CCM1, the CCM2, which is part of the same cluster, needs to know how to reach the phone 'A.' CCM2 keeps this information in the memory. *Reachability Weight* accounts for this memory utilization on CCM2.
- **Global dial plan weights**—Consist of route pattern and translation pattern weights.

In summary, dial plan components contribute the weights outlined in Table 1-5.

**Table 1-5**    *Base Dial Plan Weights*

| Subscriber Dial Plan Componenents | Dial Plan Weight |
|---|---|
| IP phone device (excluding line appearances) | 5 |
| Unique line appearance | 5 |
| Shared line appearance | 4 |
| Reachability per line appearance | 3 |
| **Global Dial Plan Components** | |
| Route pattern | 2 |
| Translational pattern | 1 |

To understand more about the dial plan weight calculations, consider Figure 1-10. When IP phone A (primary extension 2000), which is a unique line appearance, is registered with subscriber CCM A, the dial plan weight on subscriber CCM A is 10 units (5 units for the IP phone and 5 units for the unique line appearance (primary extension 2000). Subscriber CCM B in cluster 1 has a dial plan reachability weight of 3 units to reach extension 2000 on subscriber CCM A.

**Figure 1-10**    *Dial Plan Weight Calculations*

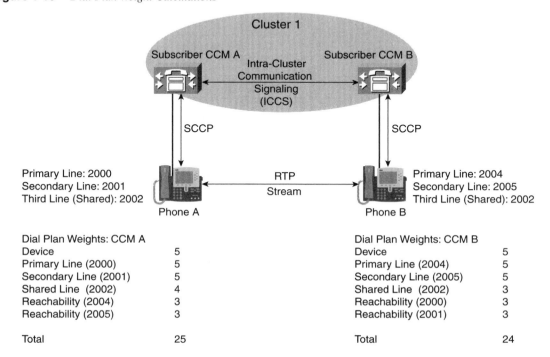

| Dial Plan Weights: CCM A | | Dial Plan Weights: CCM B | |
|---|---|---|---|
| Device | 5 | Device | 5 |
| Primary Line (2000) | 5 | Primary Line (2004) | 5 |
| Secondary Line (2001) | 5 | Secondary Line (2005) | 5 |
| Shared Line  (2002) | 4 | Shared Line  (2002) | 3 |
| Reachability (2004) | 3 | Reachability (2000) | 3 |
| Reachability (2005) | 3 | Reachability (2001) | 3 |
| | | | |
| Total | 25 | Total | 24 |

The secondary unique line appearance on IP phone A (secondary extension 2001) adds a dial plan weight of 5 units to subscriber CCM A and 3 units to subscriber CCM B located in cluster 1. Each shared line appearance (shared extension 2002) on IP phone A adds a dial plan weight of 4 units to subscriber CCM A and 3 units to subscriber CCM B located in cluster 1. A line appearance is called "shared" when the same unique line appears on multiple devices in the same partition.

Figure 1-10 also shows IP phone B with primary extension 2004, secondary extension 2005, and shared extension 2002, registered with subscriber CCM B in cluster 1. Note that shared extension 2002 has a dial plan weight of 4 units on subscriber CCM A and 3 units on subscriber CCM B, since the shared extension 2002 is primarily controlled by subscriber CCM A, thus requiring more resources.

In each cluster, the global dial plan weights apply to all subscriber servers. For example, a route pattern of 9.1xxxxxxxxxx adds a dial plan weight of 2 units to each subscriber server in the cluster (refer to Table 1-5).

Table 1-6 lists guidelines for how much physical memory to install on a subscriber server, based on the number of phones, number of line appearances, and complexity of the dial plan that is configured on that server.

**Table 1-6**    *Server Memory Requirements for Dial Plan Weights*

| Total Dial Plan Weight on a Subscriber | Server Memory Requirements |
|---|---|
| Up to 15,000 | 512 MB of RAM |
| Up to 35,000 | 768 MB of RAM |
| Up to 70,000 | 1 GB of RAM |
| Up to 140,000 | 2 GB of RAM |
| Up to 220,000 | 4 GB of RAM |

**TIP**    When determining the server hardware and number of servers in the cluster, you should choose a server based on the size of the network, performance, and high-availability requirements. A properly sized cluster must satisfy both the device weight and dial plan weight requirements.

Starting with CallManager 4.0, Cisco has introduced a Cisco CallManager Capacity Tool to size the CallManager clusters. This is a web-based tool and is currently not available on Cisco Connection Online (CCO). In the back end, the tool uses device weights, dial plan weights, and the BHCA multipliers concept to calculate cluster sizing. The device weights and BHCA factors could change from one version of CallManager to another, but the concept remains the same.

## CallManager Directory Services

CallManager is bundled with a Lightweight Directory Access Protocol (LDAP) compliant directory called DC Directory (DCD). DCD is a Cisco OEM product from Data Connection Limited.

CallManager stores system and device configurations in a Microsoft SQL database. The application scripts and the following information are stored in DCD:

- User authentication and authorization
- Extension Mobility profiles
- Personal Assistant profiles
- Internationalization information
- Personal Address Book (PAB)
- Spoken name
- Fast dial
- Call Forward All information

The DCD process replicates the information among the members of the cluster, as shown in Figure 1-11. This process is similar to Microsoft SQL replication.

**Figure 1-11**    *DC Directory Replication Within a Cluster*

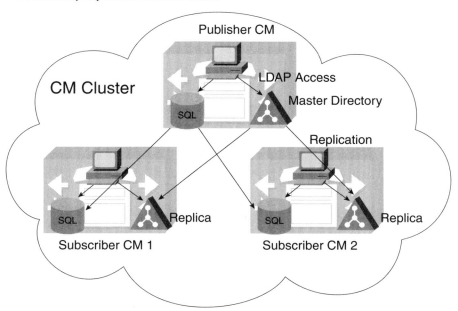

Many organizations have already deployed LDAP-based directories to store the user-related information, such as user ID, password, authentication information, authorization information, e-mail ID, phone number, and address. There are two possible deployment scenarios for the CallManager directory:

- Use the embedded DCD, which is part of CallManager

- Use corporate directory integration, which allows CallManager to store the user-related information in a centralized, existing directory, instead of using DCD. CallManager supports the directory integration with Microsoft Active Directory 2000/2003, Netscape 4.x, iPlanet 4.x, or SunOne 5.x Server.

You do not need to perform additional planning or design tasks when using the embedded DCD. The publisher server stores the master copy of the directory database, and the subscribers have the replica of the publisher server's directory database.

However, if you are considering integration of CallManager with an existing corporate directory, you must take extra care to achieve successful integration and functioning of the CallManager cluster. Corporate directory integration requires schema extensions to the existing corporate directory schema structure. The schema extension creates new objects and attributes in the existing corporate directory schema structure to store CallManager-specific information in the directory. The CallManager schema extensions use official object identifiers (OIDs) that are approved by the Internet Assigned Numbers Authority (IANA).

Many other Cisco IPT applications, such as Cisco Unity, IPCC Express, Personal Assistant (PA), and Cisco Emergency Responder (CER), support directory integration with external directories. Cisco Unity requires a special set of schema extensions when integrated with an external directory, and other applications create special directory trees and attributes in the corporate directory.

---

**NOTE**    The IPT planning team must consult the corporate directory team to discuss the effects of this schema extension and to determine the effects of the extra size of the directory database because of the addition of new objects and attributes. Note that the directory schema extension process requires higher user privileges.

---

CallManager integration with the corporate directory includes the following benefits:

- You do not need to maintain two separate directories (one for the corporate directory and another for the CallManager directory), which results in minimal administration overhead

- When deploying multiple CallManager clusters, you do not need to provide different services to look up users in different clusters.

- Moves, adds, and changes are centralized.

# IP Telephony Endpoints

In a Cisco IPT network, endpoints are the devices that accept or initiate a VoIP session. This section introduces the following endpoints that are used in a Cisco IPT network.

- Cisco IP Phones
- SoftPhones
- Wireless IP Phones
- Voice gateways
- Survivable Remote Site Telephony (SRST)
- CallManager Express (CME)

## Cisco IP Phones

IP phones are one of the endpoints in Cisco AVVID. Various IP phone models are available, the selection of which depends on the end-user requirements and the overall budget for the project. Appendix A, "IP Phone Models and Selection Criteria," provides a list of currently available IP phone models and selection criteria.

IP phones keep the connection to the primary and standby CallManager servers. CallManager redundancy groups (device pools) that are configured on the CallManager administration page provide this feature. Each CallManager redundancy group consists of more than one CallManager. The first CallManager listed in the CallManager redundancy group has the highest priority. IP phones attempt to register with the higher priority CallManager.

Just like any other networking device, IP phones require an IP address, subnet mask, default gateway, DNS server, and TFTP server information to communicate with CallManager. By default, IP phones are configured to obtain the IP address and the other network settings via the Dynamic Host Configuration Protocol (DHCP). This allows mobility and improves IP address manageability. The only downside is that critical IP address allocation information for many nodes is stored within one file or database on the DHCP server. You should have adequate support for DHCP services and treat the DHCP data as highly critical data.

---

**TIP**    Best practice is to keep the DHCP databases mirrored or backed up on a continual basis. In addition, have a plan in case DHCP services fail. In large deployments, separate the DHCP and TFTP server functionality to achieve stability and reliability.

---

If an organization has an existing DHCP server, it can extend the services to IPT endpoints, such as IP Phones. The only requirement is that the DHCP servers should also support adding custom option 150 or 66 for IP phone provisioning. The DHCP server uses one of these option fields to forward to the IP phones information about the TFTP server or array of TFTP servers.

Only option 150 supports specifying an array of IP addresses. Hence, if you are planning to use more than one TFTP server, you should use option 150. Specifying more than one TFTP server allows the endpoints to use the secondary server if the primary server fails. Also, you can achieve load balancing by configuring these TFTP servers in different orders in the DHCP scopes.

The DHCP and TFTP services can be collocated on the CallManager publisher server in a small IPT deployment. However, for larger deployments, separating these services from the publisher server provides greater performance.

---

**TIP**    To build a standalone TFTP server, you simply need to install the CallManager software, as you would do with any other subscriber, but activate only the TFTP and DataBase Layer (DBL) monitor services on that server.

---

Domain Name Service (DNS) is not mandatory in IPT environments. IP phones can use IP addresses to communicate with CallManager. However, DNS is useful for managing the overall network environment and provides redundancy/load balancing for the IP phones that require access to the application servers.

## SoftPhones

SoftPhones are software-based applications that turn your computer into a full-featured Cisco IP Phone, allowing you to place, receive, and otherwise handle calls. These types of applications are useful for telecommuters or users who move within the campus. With the wireless connectivity to the PC, users can freely move to any location within the reach of the wireless and thus carry the phone with them.

Two types of soft phone applications are available:

* Cisco IP SoftPhone
* Cisco IP Communicator

Cisco IP SoftPhone is a Telephony Application Programming Interface (TAPI) application that communicates with CallManager via the Computer Telephony Interface (CTI), whereas Cisco IP Communicator communicates with CallManager via SCCP. The user interface for the Communicator phone looks like a Cisco 7970G IP Phone.

Table 1-7 lists the major differences between Cisco IP SoftPhone and Cisco IP Communicator.

**Table 1-7**    *Differences Between Two Cisco SoftPhone Products*

| Feature | Cisco IP SoftPhone | Cisco IP Communicator |
|---|---|---|
| User interface | PC application look and feel | Cisco IP Phone 7970G look and feel |
| Communication protocol with CallManager | CTI | SCCP |
| Provisioning | Requires creation of CTI port and user association | Just like any other Cisco IP phone |
| Call-control features | Features are limited to the capability of CTI APIs | All features supported in the 7970G Phone, such as multiple lines and access to Cisco IP Phone services, are supported |

As Table 1-7 indicates, Cisco IP SoftPhone uses CTI to communicate with CallManager. When deploying Cisco IP SoftPhone, you need to note the limitations on the number of CTI devices that can be provisioned on the CallManager depending on the hardware platform. Table 1-8 shows the CTI device limitations for CallManager 4.0 and assumes that the Cisco IP SoftPhones are configured with one line appearance, and no more than six BHCAs are made from the Cisco IP SoftPhones.

The maximum CTI limits are shown in Table 1-8 and include any other provisioned CTI devices such as IP-IVR or third-party CTI-enabled applications.

**Table 1-8**    *CTI Device Limitations on CallManager*

| Hardware Platform | Number of CTI Devices per Server | Number of CTI Devices per Cluster |
|---|---|---|
| MCS-7825, MCS-7835 | 800 | 3200 |
| MCS-7845 | 2500 | 10,000 |

Because Cisco IP Communicator uses SCCP, it is treated like any other Cisco IP Phone; hence, you can deploy Cisco IP Communicator phones up to the maximum allowed IP phone device limits per server.

Both Cisco IP SoftPhone and Cisco IP Communicator mark the voice and signaling packets (0xB8/EF for media and 0x60/CS3 for signaling). These applications run on the user's laptop/PC connected to the PC port that is on the back of the IP Phone. Because the packets coming from the PC port on the IP phone are not trusted, when deploying these applications, you need to create the access lists on the access or distribution switches to identify and mark with proper Differentiated Services Code Point (DSCP) values the signaling and media packets coming from these applications. Chapter 4 discusses the QoS and markings in detail.

## Wireless IP Phones

Cisco Wireless IP Phone 7920 works in conjunction with CallManager and Cisco Aironet 1200, 1100, and 350 Series Wi-Fi (IEEE 802.11b) access points.

The planning procedures for deploying wireless voice are different from those used to deploy wired IP phones. Wireless IP phone deployment involves the following major tasks:

- Preparing a site survey to do the following:
    - Determine the location of the access points
    - Identify and eliminate the sources of interference
    - Determine the power levels of the access points
    - Identify and eliminate the rogue access points
- Determining the number of access points required
- Configuring QoS policy on access points
- Configuring security

## Voice Gateways

Voice gateways connect the IPT network to the PSTN or a PBX. CallManager supports a variety of voice gateways. Selection of the gateway depends on the specific site requirements. Geographical placement of the voice gateways determines the type of interfaces and link layer protocol selection.

CallManager communicates with gateways using any of the following protocols:

- MGCP
- H.323
- SIP

MGCP-based gateways provide call survivability and do not require a local dial plan. All the dial plan configurations are required to be made on the CallManager, whereas with H.323 gateways, you need to configure the local dial plan on the router by configuring the voice dial peers.

Cisco offers a variety of voice gateways, which are essentially the routers and switch modules with interfaces that can connect to the PSTN or a PBX. These routers and switch modules support two types of signaling interfaces: analog and digital. Analog signaling interfaces use Foreign eXchange Office (FXO), Foreign eXchange Station (FXS), and E&M signaling protocols. Digital signaling interfaces use T1/E1 Primary Rate Interface (PRI), ISDN Basic Rate Interface (BRI), or T1 CAS. Most of the Cisco IOS voice gateways support H.323, MGCP, and SIP, whereas the majority of the Catalyst voice gateways support MGCP.

## Survivable Remote Site Telephony

Survivable Remote Site Telephony (SRST) provides the fallback support for the IP phones that are connected behind a router running the Cisco IOS software version that supports SRST. This feature enables you to deploy the IPT at small branch offices with a centralized call-processing model. Figure 1-12 depicts a branch office deployment with SRST.

During normal operation, when the CallManager is active and the WAN link is available, IP phones at the branch behave the same way as the IP phones at the central site. The SRST feature on the router becomes active as soon as the IP Phones detect the failure of the WAN link. (The IP Phones miss three consecutive acknowledgements from the CallManager.) The IP phones attempt to register with the other CallManagers in the redundancy group before attempting the registration with the SRST router. So, the fallback process to the SRST router could take longer if other CallManagers are in the IP phone's redundancy group. SRST provides the basic call handling and minimal features to the IP phones during the WAN failure. Without this feature, the IP phone users at these locations would not be able to make outside calls.

**Figure 1-12**  *SRST Operation in a Branch Office*

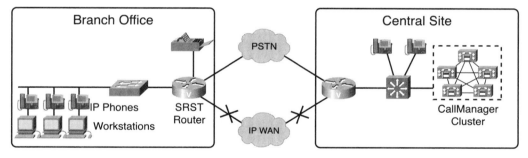

When the WAN link comes back online, IP phones detect the keep-alive acknowledgements from the CallManager and attempt to re-home back to the CallManager servers.

The number of IP phones supported in the SRST mode depends on the router platform, the Cisco IOS version, and the amount of memory. You have to choose the appropriate router model and amount of memory based on the number of phones being deployed at the branch office.

## Cisco CallManager Express

Cisco CallManager Express (CME) is the new name given to the feature formerly known as IOS Telephony Services (ITS) on the Cisco IOS routers. CME is a licensed feature of Cisco IOS software that is available on many router hardware platforms. CME delivers key system functionality for small and midsize branch offices. In the CME solution, IP phones are registered to the CME router all the time. As shown in Figure 1-13, for a branch office/retail store that operates independently, the CME-based solution provides flexibility. Like SRST, the number of phones supported by the CME gateway depends on the router hardware, the Cisco IOS version, and the amount of memory.

**Figure 1-13** *CME Operation in a Branch Office*

Branch Office/Retail Store

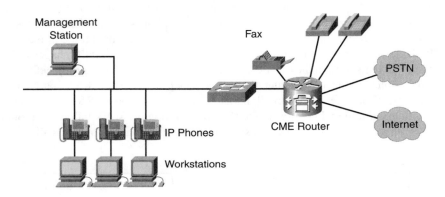

## Call Admission Control

In VoIP networks, CAC does the bandwidth management. CAC ensures that enough bandwidth is available before granting permission to a gateway for placing the call across the IP WAN. When deploying IPT solutions with multiple locations, you have two choices for implementing the CAC:

- CallManager locations-based CAC
- Gatekeeper CAC

### CallManager Locations-Based CAC

CallManager locations-based CAC is one mechanism to limit the calls sent across an IP WAN in a single CallManager cluster deployment. Locations are configured in the CallManager and assigned a maximum bandwidth. The bandwidth assigned per location depends on the number of calls that are allowed to be made to a particular location and the type of codec used for that location. Before placing a new call, CallManager checks its location tables to determine if enough bandwidth is available to place the new call. If enough is available, the call is allowed and CallManager updates the available bandwidth for that location. Locations-based CAC is ideal for centralized call-processing deployments with a hub-and-spoke topology.

CallManager locations-based CAC is not scalable for multicluster CallManager deployments; gatekeeper CAC, discussed next, is recommended for such deployments.

## Gatekeeper CAC

A Cisco IOS gatekeeper in Cisco AVVID networks provides call admission and call routing between the CallManager clusters in distributed call processing deployments. Gatekeeper CAC is suited for deployments that follow the hub-and-spoke topology and does not work with the meshed topologies. The following are some of the advantages of using the gatekeeper:

- It simplifies the dial plan management by enabling you to quickly add or remove routes and devices.

- It provides CAC between calls from different clusters, ensuring that the WAN bandwidth allocation is strictly enforced.

- It reduces configuration overhead by eliminating the need to configure a separate H.323 device for each remote CallManager that is connected to the IP WAN.

- It offers a choice of protocols for communicating with CallManager or H.225 gateways.

- It can perform basic call routing in addition to call admission control.

You have two choices of deploying a gatekeeper with CAC:

- Gatekeepers deployed with the Hot Standby Router Protocol (HSRP)
- Gatekeeper clustering

Gatekeepers in HSRP mode do not share the CAC information, whereas gatekeeper clustering enables true redundancy and load balancing. Gatekeepers that are deployed in a cluster mode exchange the CAC information via the gatekeeper Update Protocol (GUP) and are the recommended deployment method.

# Fax

One of the most important pieces in the transition to converged networks is support for fax communication. As network implementations increasingly provide for e-mail attachments and web-downloadable documents, fax communication nonetheless is still a significant method of immediate document delivery worldwide. Studies have shown that a large portion of long-distance minutes is fax traffic.

The frequent use and customer expectations of fax functionality and reliability demand a support for reliable fax transmissions across a converged network. Most Cisco voice gateways currently support three methods to transmit fax traffic across the IP network:

- **Fax Pass-Through**—In Fax Pass-Through mode, the gateways do not distinguish a fax call from a voice call
- **Cisco Fax Relay**—In Cisco Fax Relay mode, the gateways terminate the T.30 fax signaling.
- **T.38 Fax Relay**—This standard provides standards-based Fax Relay.

Fax Relay mode is the preferred method to transmit fax traffic. Because the T.38 Fax Relay protocol is standards-based, fax gateways that use this protocol can interoperate with third-party T.38-enabled gateways and gatekeepers in a mixed-vendor network. As of CallManager 4.0, T.38 Fax Relay is not supported. When deploying the fax over IP by using the CallManager, Cisco Fax Relay or Fax Pass-Through are the only choices that you can use on the gateways.

Similar to voice traffic, fax traffic is also sensitive to delay, jitter (variable delay), and packet loss. Hence, the network must be QoS enabled.

## Media Resources

The function of media resource devices is to mix the multiple streams into a single output stream, converting the data stream from one compression type to another, and so forth. Examples of media resources are conferencing, transcoding, and MoH.

The media resources can be hardware or software. CallManager has built-in software media resources for conferencing, transcoding, and media termination. The limitation of software media resources is that they can't combine the streams that use different compression techniques.

Hardware media resources have the same features as software media resources with an additional advantage of mixing the streams that use different compression types. Hardware media resources offer good performance and quality because the processing is done in the hardware.

MoH is another example of a media resource. MoH is an application that is installed by default on the CallManager servers (or you can install a standalone MoH server on a dedicated server for large deployments). As the name implies, MoH provides music or announcements when the users are put on hold.

When you are designing the IPT network, one of the tasks is to size the media resources and determine their placement within the network.

## Applications

Cisco has a wide range of applications that can be deployed in an IPT network. These applications are optional, and their deployment adds more features and capabilities to the overall IPT network. Design and deployment of the applications, such as CRS and IP phone services, are discussed in Chapters 6, "Design of Call Processing Infrastructure and Applications," and 7, "Voice-Mail System Design."

### Customer Response Solution

The Customer Response Solution (CRS) platform provides interactive telephony and multimedia services. It provides a multimedia (voice, data, and web) IP-enabled customer-care application environment. The CRS platform uses VoIP technology, so an organization's telephony network can share resources with the data network.

The CRS platform uses an open architecture that supports industry standards. This enables application designers to integrate applications with a wide variety of technologies and products.

The CRS platform includes the following applications:

- Cisco IP Auto Attendant (IP AA)
- Cisco Interactive Voice Response (IP IVR)
- Cisco IP Contact Center (IPCC) Express (formerly known as Integrated Contact Distribution, or ICD)

CRS has add-on components, including Automatic Speech Recognition (ASR) and Text-to-Speech (TTS).

### IVR

IVR queues the callers, accepts the input, and does a database lookup based on the input. The open standards–based design of the CRS platform supports connectivity to various databases, such as Microsoft SQL, Oracle, Sybase, and IBM DB2 via Open DataBase Connection (ODBC) interface.

### IPCC Express

Cisco IPCC Express provides enterprises with a contact management solution that is ideal to implement a small-scale contact center or internal help desk. IPCC Express provides Automated Call Distribution (ACD), IVR, and CTI functionality. The ACD queues and distributes incoming calls that are destined for groups of CallManager users. The IVR gathers caller data and classifies incoming calls based on user-entered information. IPCC Express includes a web-based real-time reporting system that monitors the system performance, Contact Service Queue (CSQ), and resource performance.

A Java Telephony API (JTAPI) connection manages communication between the CRS engine and CallManager Computer Telephony Integration Manager (CTIM) service.

The sizing of the CRS platform depends on the organization's call volume.

## Cisco Unity

CallManager integrates with many existing voice-mail systems that use the Simplified Message Desk Interface (SMDI) standard and other voice-mail systems from Lucent, Avaya, or Nortel that use proprietary protocols. CallManager uses the Cisco Digital PBX Adapter (DPA) 7630 to integrate with Lucent or Avaya voice-mail systems and DPA 7610 to integrate with Nortel voice-mail systems.

Cisco Unity is a voice-mail/unified messaging solution that delivers powerful unified messaging (e-mail, voice, and fax messages sent to one inbox) for Microsoft Exchange or Lotus Domino environments. Cisco Unity can integrate with CallManager and with many legacy PBXs. Cisco Unity communicates with CallManager via SCCP.

Likewise, CallManager server has guidelines on the maximum number of devices that can be registered; Cisco Unity server has guidelines on the number of subscriber accounts per Unity server. The capacity depends on the hardware platforms.

Redundancy is achieved in an IPT network by deploying the CallManagers in cluster configuration. To build the redundancy for Cisco Unity deployment, two Unity servers are deployed. Unlike CallManager, where the load can be shared on all the servers in the cluster, the Cisco Unity servers deployed in the failover model do not share the load. Only one server is active at a time.

## Cisco Emergency Responder

An IPT network provides flexibility to move the IP phones from one location to another location without the involvement of an administrator. This is attractive to many organizations and network administrators because it reduces the cost.

However, careful planning is required, which varies depending on the country where the telephony system is deployed and local government rules and regulations for routing emergency calls.

In the United States and Canada, users dial 911 (in other countries, this number varies) to make emergency calls to get the services of police, ambulance, and fire personnel. In a regular 911 system, also called a Basic-9-1-1 system, the emergency calls are sent to a public safety answering point (PSAP). No mechanism ensures that the call is sent to the correct PSAP, and the PSAP does not receive information about the location of the 911 caller. Enhanced 9-1-1, or E-9-1-1, sends 911 calls to the correct PSAP based on the location of the caller, and it ensures that the PSAP knows where the 911 caller is located (even without the caller providing directions). The location is determined by querying an Automatic Location Information (ALI) database that maps the phone number of the 911 caller to the caller's physical location.

Large organizations that maintain their own phone systems (e.g. key systems, PBXs, and Cisco CallManagers) are responsible for maintaining the ALI database information and providing the updates to the ALI database to the local exchange carrier (LEC) from time to time.

Cisco Emergency Responder (CER) is designed to address the E-9-1-1 functionality requirements for multiline telephone systems (MLTSs) deployed in North America. CER dynamically tracks the device (IP phone or SoftPhone) movements and routes the emergency calls to the right PSAP based on the device's current physical location.

Consider a case in which an employee in New York office location 1 moves the phone to New York office location 2. Assume that these two offices are served by different PSAPs. After the employee moves the phone to New York office location 2, if a user makes an emergency call, the call is routed to the PSAP for location 1. Because the user's phone number originally registered with New York office location 1, the PSAP for location 1 dispatches emergency staff to New York office location 1, and the user at location 2 waits indefinitely for the help.

CER in an IPT network enables emergency agencies to identify the location of callers and eliminates the need for administration when phones or people move from one location to another.

The phone's location is dynamically tracked by CER based on the switch ports to which the phone is attached. CER polls the switches via the Simple Network Management Protocol (SNMP) and updates the location database. Thus, in the previous example, when the phone is moved to New York office location 2, CER detects that the phone is now in New York office location 2, because it is connected to a switch that is in New York office location 2, and it routes the emergency calls to the PSAP that services New York office location 2.

## Cisco Conference Connection

Cisco Conference Connection (CCC) is an application that allows users to schedule conferences. Users can schedule conferences via a simple web-based interface. Conference participants call in to a central number, enter a meeting identification, and are then placed into the conference.

## IP Phone Services

You can provide additional services such as those listed here to the end users from their IP phones:

* Calendar
* Weather information
* Airline information
* Corporate directory lookup
* Stock quotes

Offering these services on the IP phones requires a connection through an external web server such as Microsoft Internet Information Server (IIS) or Apache, as shown in Figure 1-14. The IP phone sends the requests in the HTTP packet to the web server. The request could be to get the latest stock quote, flight arrival/departure information, or some other information. The IP Phone services web server contacts the external web servers and sends the response in XML format back to the IP phones. IP phones parse the information contained within the XML tags and display it on the phone.

**Figure 1-14**   *IP Phone Services*

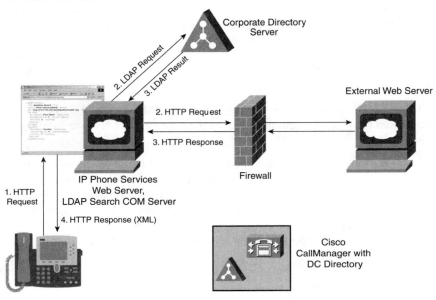

**NOTE**   In the Figure 1-14, "Step 2. HTTP Request" and "Step 3. HTTP Response" are used when accessing the IP phone services that require connection to the external web server. Examples of such services are stock quote and airline information.

The preceding concept can be extended to provide IP phone service to do a corporate directory lookup from the IP phone. The following steps explain how this service works:

1   The IP phone user selects a corporate lookup directory service on the IP phone.

2   The IP phone sends an HTTP request to the IP phone services web server.

3   The IP phone services web server sends an LDAP request to the corporate LDAP server.

4   The IP phone services web server passes the returned LDAP result to the IP phone in XML format.

5   The IP phone parses the information and displays the search results on the IP phone.

For more information on providing such services, refer to the IP phone services Software Development Kit (SDK) documentation, available at http://www.cisco.com/pcgi-bin/dev_support/access_level/product_support.

# IP Telephony Deployment Architectures

By using CallManager, organizations can eliminate PBX and replace it with IPT over a converged network. CallManager provides call-control functionality and, when used in conjunction with IP phone sets or a soft phone application, it can provide PBX functionality in a distributed and scalable fashion. Cisco IPT solution deployment models fall into one of the following categories:

- Single-site deployment
- Centralized call processing with remote branches
- Distributed call-processing deployment
- Clustering over the IP WAN

Selection of the deployment model depends on the organization's requirements, such as the size of the network, features, and availability of the WAN bandwidth. This section provides information on various deployment models at a high level. To get detailed information on the benefits and limitations, refer to the *IP Telephony Solution Reference Network Design for Cisco CallManager 4.0* on Cisco.com, available for download at http://www.cisco.com/go/srnd.

## Single-Site Deployment

In this deployment model, shown in Figure 1-15, CallManager applications such as voice mail, IP-IVR, AutoAttendant (AA), Transcoding, and conferencing resources are located at the same physical location. All the IP phones are located within this single site. The PSTN is used to route the off-net calls.

**Figure 1-15** *Single-Site Deployment Model*

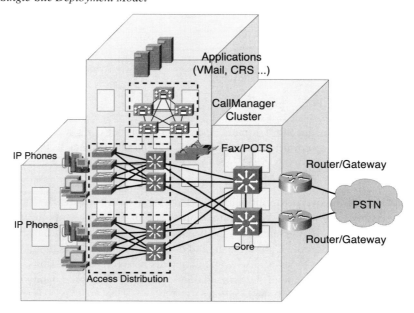

# Centralized Call Processing with Remote Branches

Figure 1-16 shows the centralized call-processing deployment with remote braches. All the call processing is done at the central site. This is suitable for organizations in which the majority of the workforce is concentrated at a single site and small numbers of employees work at the remote branches.

**Figure 1-16**    *Centralized Call-Processing Model*

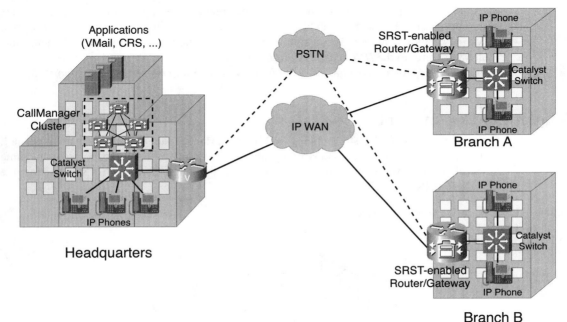

At each remote branch, SRST routers ensure that call processing is preserved in case of WAN link failure. The voice traffic travels via the IP WAN and falls back to the PSTN if not enough bandwidth is available across the WAN link, by using the Automated Alternate Routing (AAR) feature available in the CallManager.

You can avoid the oversubscription of the WAN bandwidth by using the locations-based CAC feature in the CallManager. This feature works for hub-and-spoke topologies. For example, as shown in Figure 1-16, the hub site is the headquarters and the braches are spokes. Each branch is defined as a location in CallManager, and maximum bandwidth is assigned to each location along with the codec to be used when placing calls between two locations. CallManager maintains the current state of the utilized bandwidth and checks the bandwidth availability before placing a new call to the locations.

With this deployment model, you can use the G.711 codec within the LAN. However, when placing the voice calls between the headquarters site and the branch sites or between the branch sites, you can use lower-bandwidth codecs such as G.729. The amount of bandwidth required per voice call depends on the type of codec chosen between the central and remote sites. Remote branch routers running Cisco IOS software along with the CallManager software can provide transcoding and conferencing functions locally. QoS configurations are required on the WAN links between the central site and each of the remote sites to prioritize the traffic. The traffic that requires priority includes the call-control traffic between the IP phones and the CallManager, the gateway signaling protocol (H.323, MGCP) traffic between the remote gateways and the CallManager, and the actual voice traffic.

This deployment model is cost effective and provides many benefits, such as a unified dial plan, less administrative overhead, and potential savings on communications costs as intersite calls use the IP WAN as first choice. The only limitation is that the remote sites will have limited features available if a WAN failure occurs while you are operating in the SRST mode.

## Distributed Call Processing Deployment

In a distributed call-processing deployment, CallManager and applications are located at each site. Device weights and dial plan weight calculations determine the number of IP phones supported at each site.

Figure 1-17 depicts a distributed call-processing model in which headquarters and branch A IP phones are served by separate CallManager clusters and branch B is served by the Cisco CallManager Express (CME) feature that is enabled on the router. CME solution is suitable for a small branch.

Intercluster Trunks link CallManager clusters. The Cisco IOS gatekeeper ensures that only a permitted number of calls are sent across the IP WAN between the CallManager clusters. PSTN connections on the gateways route the local off-net calls from each location and serve as a backup connection to IP WAN when insufficient bandwidth is available to support additional calls.

**Figure 1-17** *Distributed Call-Processing Model*

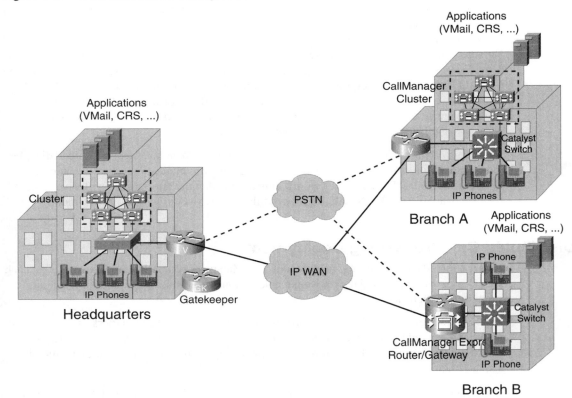

## Clustering over the IP WAN

The vital activities in any business are continuity planning and disaster recovery. Large and small disasters happen all the time. Events ranging from purely local disasters, such as flooding, fire, evacuations caused by a hazardous material spill, or a region-wide blizzard, all have potential impact on the organization's business.

The Cisco IPT solution allows organizations to build disaster recovery sites by separating the single CallManager cluster across the WAN. CallManager servers in a cluster update the configuration information via the Microsoft SQL replication process. To ensure successful SQL replication and propagation of other critical information in real time, the round-trip time (RTT) between any CallManager servers in the cluster should not exceed 40 ms. You need to satisfy many other requirements before selecting this deployment model. Refer to the Cisco document, *IP Telephony Solution Reference Network Design for Cisco CallManager 4.0,* at http:// www.cisco.com/go/srnd.

When using the clustering over the IP WAN deployment model, deploy voice gateways, media resources, and voice mail locally at each site. Essential services such as DHCP, DNS, and TFTP that are critical for the functioning of IP phones and other IPT endpoints must also be deployed locally. This configuration avoids dependency on a single site for crucial resources.

**TIP**    When using centralized DHCP services, you should configure the IP address lease intervals for IPT endpoints for long periods. Otherwise, the DHCP servers are not reachable to respond to the address renewal requests made by the IPT endpoints at the branch sites during a WAN failure.

Clustering over the WAN can support two types of deployments:

* Local failover deployment model
* Remote failover deployment model

## Local Failover Deployment Model

In this model, each site contains a primary CallManager subscriber and at least one backup subscriber. All the servers are part of the same CallManager cluster. As depicted in Figure 1-18, the headquarters has a publisher server, a DHCP and TFTP server, subscriber 1, subscriber 2, and the backup subscriber 12. Branch A houses subscriber 3, subscriber 4, and backup subscriber 34.

**Figure 1-18** *Clustering over the IP WAN—Local Failover Deployment Model*

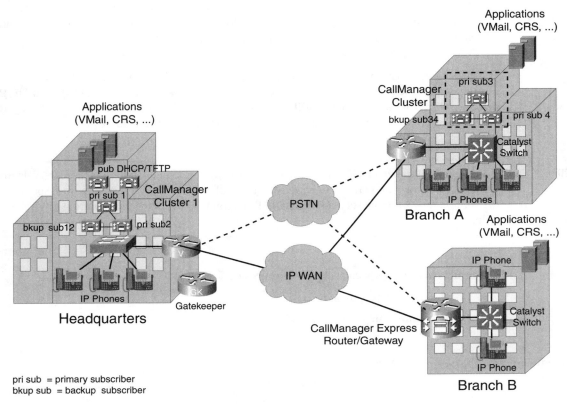

## Remote Failover Deployment Model

In this model, shown in Figure 1-19, each site contains at least one primary CallManager subscriber and might or might not have a backup subscriber. Branch A and branch B have only primary subscribers, and the backup subscriber is not located in each site.

**Figure 1-19**    *Clustering over the IP WAN—Remote Failover Deployment Model*

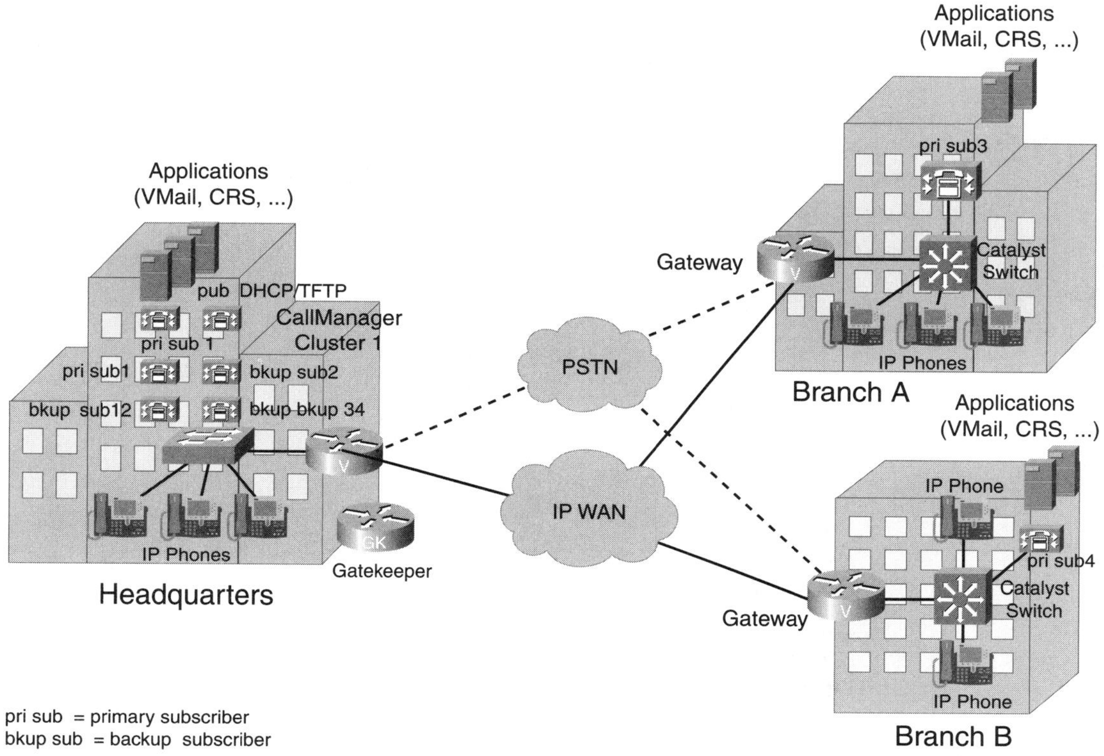

pri sub  = primary subscriber
bkup sub = backup subscriber

# Call-Flow Scenarios

So far, this chapter has discussed call signaling, media protocols, call-processing servers, and other IPT endpoints used in Cisco IPT. To understand how all of these components work together, this section discusses the following call-flow scenarios:

- IP phone to IP phone call
- Intracluster call
- Intercluster call
- Intercluster call with gatekeeper

- Off-net calls
  - Using MGCP gateway
  - Using H.323 gateway with gatekeeper

## IP Phone-to-IP Phone Call

In the first scenario, IP phone 1 and destination IP phone 2 are registered with the same CallManager, CCM1. Figure 1-20 shows the high-level sequence of steps that occur when source IP phone 1 calls destination IP phone 2.

**Figure 1-20**   *IP Phone to IP Phone Call Flow*

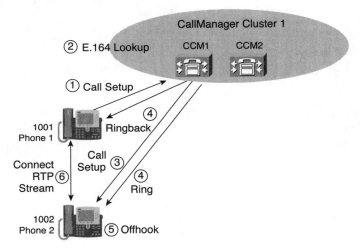

Figure 1-21 shows the sequence of SCCP messages that are exchanged between the phones and the CallManager to establish and tear down the call.

The SCCP messages in Figure 1-21 are grouped together to correlate with the high-level sequence of steps shown in Figure 1-20.

**Figure 1-21**    *IP Phone to IP Phone Call Flow—SCCP Messages*

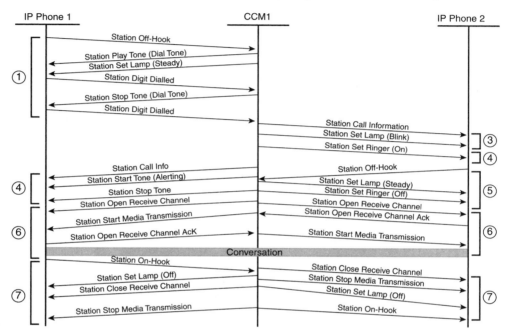

The description of the sequence of steps is given here:

**1**  Phone 1 goes off-hook. This triggers an event to the CallManager, which then instructs the phone to play a dial tone. The user then dials the extension 1002 of Phone 2. As soon as the user dials the first digit, CallManager instructs the phone to stop playing the dial tone. As the user dials the digits, the SCCP messages carry this information from the phone to the CallManager.

**2**  After the user completes dialing the destination number, CallManager looks in its database to see if it can find the dialed destination number. This process is called *digit analysis* and takes place within the CallManager. The digit analysis process is similar to the functionality of a router wherein the router looks into its routing table to see if it has a valid route to forward the received packet to the destination. If CallManager cannot find the dialed number in its database or does not have the information to route the call to the dialed number, it generates a reorder tone to the calling party.

3   After CallManager finds the valid number/destination (phone 2 in this case), it sends the call setup information to Phone 2.

4   CallManager instructs phone 2 to ring and, at the same time, generates the ring-back or alerting tone to the calling party Phone 1.

5   As soon as Phone 2 answers by going off-hook, CallManager sends to each phone a request for the IP address and the UDP port that it is listening to. This information is required to establish the media session between phones. In this step, CallManager also checks for the media capabilities of the phones, such as the codecs supported on each phone, and invokes the transcoder media resource device if both phones talk different codecs. If CallManager fails to invoke the transcoder device because no such device is configured, the users might experience one-way audio.

6   IP Phones respond with IP address and UDP port information to the CallManager. CallManager communicates to each phone about the other phone's IP address and UDP port number. After both phones receive the other phone's IP address and UDP port, they start the media exchange directly between them.

7   After the call is terminated by either phone, CallManager instructs the phone to tear down the RTP channel and updates the call state of the phones and the date and time on the IP phones.

As the preceding steps demonstrate, all the instructions come from the CallManager. The phone has little intelligence. In this scenario, after establishing an RTP stream between the two phones, the communication can continue even if the CallManager server goes down, because the CallManager is not involved in passing the media streams between the phones. However, if the CallManager server to which the phones are registered fails during a conversation, users will not be able to invoke some of the supplementary services—such as hold, park, and mute during the conversation—that require the participation of CallManager in signaling. The phones will be reregistered to the backup CallManager after hang-up of the active call.

## Intracluster Call

In the second scenario, IP phones 1 and 2 are registered with CallManager CCM1, and Phone 3 is registered with CallManager CCM2. Both CCM1 and CCM2 are part of the same CallManager cluster. Figure 1-22 shows the intracluster call scenario when source IP Phone 2 calls destination IP phone 3. In this call scenario, CallManager and IP phone communication is done using SCCP, and CallManager-to-CallManager communication is based on Intra-Cluster Communication Signaling (ICCS). As the name implies, ICCS is a signaling protocol used between the CallManager servers in a cluster. The same sequence of events takes place between the IP phone and CallManager as described in the preceding section, "IP Phone-to-IP Phone Call."

As you can see, the other members of the cluster automatically know about the devices that are registered in the cluster because the database is the same across all the servers.

**Figure 1-22**    *Intracluster Call Scenario*

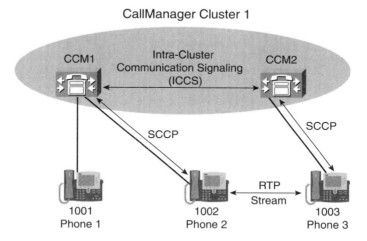

## Intercluster Call

In the third scenario, shown in Figure 1-23, IP Phones 1 and 2 are registered with CallManager CCM1 in CallManager Cluster 1 and destination IP Phone 3 is registered with CallManager CCM2 in CallManager Cluster 2. CCM 1, and CCM 2 are part of different CallManager clusters and an ICT connects the two clusters. The ICT protocol is similar to the H.323 Version 2 protocol with some extensions. CallManager sends ICT protocol signaling directly to the other CallManager in another cluster without the involvement of a gateway and uses a TCP/IP connection path available between the two clusters.

When a phone call is made from Phone 2 to Phone 3, the CallManager node CCM1 establishes a TCP/IP connection to a CallManager node CCM2 in the destination cluster. CCM1 in the originating cluster sends the Setup message, and CCM2 responds with the Call Proceeding, Alerting, and Connect messages, which are similar to the H.323 messages that are exchanged between two H.323 endpoints as the call progresses and is answered.

**Figure 1-23** *Intercluster Call Flow*

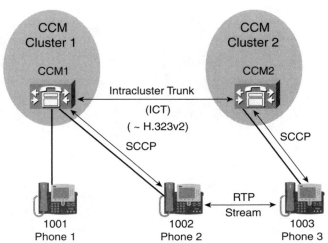

## Intercluster Call with the Gatekeeper

The fourth scenario is similar to the third scenario except for the addition of the gatekeeper for CAC purposes. Gatekeeper-controlled ICTs are required when the clusters are separated by a WAN link and you need to control the number of calls that can go through the WAN link. In a large deployment involving multiple CallManager clusters, the gatekeeper can also perform the call routing via the locally configured dial plan.

Figure 1-24 shows the call flow for this scenario. The IP phones communicate with the CallManager using SCCP. The CallManager communicates with the gatekeeper using the H.323 RAS protocol. CCM A and CCM B are part of CallManager Cluster 1, and CCM C and CCM D are part of CallManager Cluster 2. These two clusters are connected via the ICT through the gatekeeper. Phone 1 is registered with CCMB, and Phone 2 is registered with CCMC.

In Figure 1-24, the following sequence of events takes place:

1  IP phone 1 dials the number of IP Phone 2.

2  CCM B sends an Admission Request (ARQ) message to the gatekeeper.

3  From the dial plan configured in the gatekeeper, the gatekeeper finds that CCM C is registered with prefix 2 and returns the Admission Confirmation (ACF) message to CCM B with an IP address of CCM C.

4  CCM B sends an H.225 call setup message to CCM C with the phone number of Phone 2.

**5** CCM C sends an ARQ message to the gatekeeper asking permission to place the call across the ICT.

**6** The gatekeeper responds with an ACF message to CCMC. Before returning the ACF, the gatekeeper performs checks to ensure that it has enough resources to place the call across the ICT. If no resources such as bandwidth are available, the gatekeeper sends an Admission Reject (ARJ) message.

**7** CCM C initiates the call setup with phone 2 via SCCP.

**8** When phone 2 answers the call by going off-hook, CCM C sends an H.225 Connect message to CCM B and the audio path is made directly between IP phones in different clusters using RTP.

**Figure 1-24**  *Intercluster Call Flow with Gatekeeper*

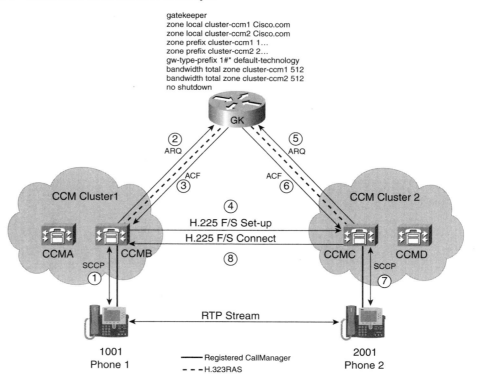

## Off-Net Calls

Any call that is routed outside the CallManager cluster is treated as an off-net call. This section discusses two off-net call-flow scenarios with the following types of gateways:

- MGCP gateway
- H.323 gateway

### Using MGCP Gateway

Before analyzing the off-net call flow with MGCP, it is important to understand how the CallManager achieves call survivability with MGCP-based gateways. CallManager uses the MGCP PRI backhaul mechanism to receive the signaling information from the ISDN PRI gateway to provide the call-control functionality and preserve the D channel (and thus call survivability) during the CallManager failover and switchover event. Figure 1-25 shows this mechanism.

**Figure 1-25** *MGCP PRI Backhaul with CallManager*

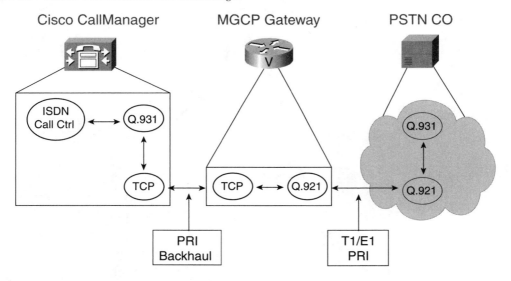

As shown in Figure 1-25, the MGCP PRI gateway terminates the D channel link layer (Q.921) signaling. The Q.931 termination remains in the CallManager. The CallManager backhaul function transports the Q.931 messages over the IP network to and from the gateway.

With this backhaul functionality, during the CallManager switchover, because the Q.921 layer is terminated on the gateway, the D channel stays active during the CallManager failure; hence, the active calls are not dropped on that interface.

A UDP logical (UDP port 2427) connection exchanges MGCP messages, and a TCP connection (TCP port 2428) backhauls the Q.931 messages. The values of both default ports are configurable on the CallManager. The source port from the gateway is randomly chosen.

In Figure 1-25, if the physical interface to the PSTN central office switch on the MGCP gateway is other than PRI, such as T1 CAS, FXS, or FXO, the gateway translates these signaling types into MGCP messages and sends them to CallManager for call control.

You should take into account the call-survivability feature with MGCP gateways when choosing the signaling protocol for the voice gateways.

Now look at a call-flow example from an IP phone to a PSTN phone via an MGCP voice gateway. Figure 1-26 shows the CallManager cluster with a registered IP phone 1 and a MGCP gateway with a PRI interface to the PSTN CO switch. The IP phone user makes an off-net call to a PSTN phone (Phone Z). The CallManager routes the call via the MGCP gateway.

**Figure 1-26**    *Off-Net Call Scenario with MGCP Gateway*

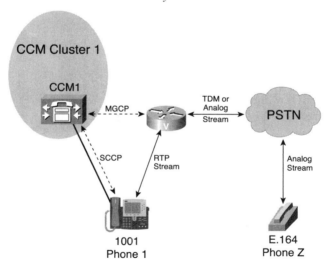

CallManager communicates with IP phones via SCCP and with the gateway via MGCP. Figure 1-27 shows the signaling messages exchanged between the IP phone, CallManager, and the MGCP gateway to route this call.

**Figure 1-27** *Off-Net Call Flow Using MGCP Gateway*

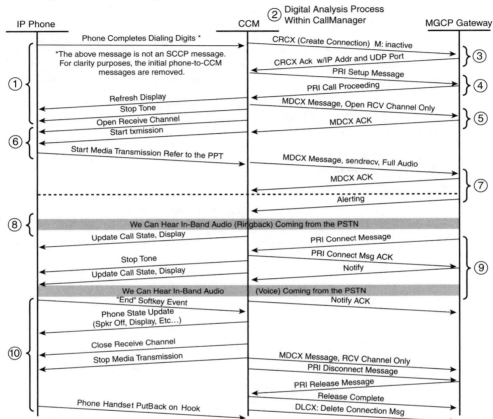

For purposes of clarity, in Figure 1-27, the initial messages from the phone, beginning with the off-hook event until the end of dialing, are not included. These steps are the same as the ones shown in Figure 1-21 that are labeled as Step 1.

The following steps describe the events of messages that take place when IP Phone 1 makes an off-net call through the MGCP gateway:

1 Phone 1 goes off-hook and dials the number of Phone Z.

2 CallManager performs the digit analysis and finds that the call has to be routed via the MGCP gateway.

**3** CallManager sends a MGCP CRCX command with inactive mode to reserve the B channel. The gateway responds with a MGCP CRCX ACK message with the Connection ID in the SDP portion of the MGCP that contains information such as IP address, UDP port number, and codec capabilities.

**4** CallManager sends an ISDN SETUP message to the PSTN switch. In Figure 1-27, the ISDN messages are shown as being sent from the CallManager to the gateway. Actually, these messages are sent to the PSTN through the gateway. CallManager receives an ISDN Call Proceeding message from the PSTN side.

**5** CallManager issues an MGCP MDCX command with recvonly mode to the gateway to open the receive channel and gateway acknowledges the MDCX command by responding with MDCX ACK message.

**6** CallManager sends an SCCP OpenReceiveChannel message to the IP phone. This message requests the phone to send its IP address and the UDP port number. The IP phone responds with its IP address and UDP port number in the OpenReceiveChannelACK message to the CallManager. At the same time, CallManager sends the IP address and UDP port number of the gateway received in Step 2 to the IP Phone via the Start Media Transmission SCCP message.

**7** CallManager sends the IP address and UDP port number of the IP phone to the gateway in another MGCP MDCX command with sendrecv mode to establish a full-duplex connection.

**8** At this moment, the IP phone user can hear the ring-back or alerting tones coming from the PSTN.

**9** After CallManager receives an ISDN PRI Connect message from the PSTN side, it acknowledges with a PRI Connect ACK message, after which a two-way communication path is open between the IP Phone and the PSTN Phone to begin the conversation. CallManager updates the display status on the IP Phone to Connected via the SCCP Update Call State Messages.

**10** After the call is terminated at either end (Figure 1-27 shows that IP Phone user terminated the call by pressing the End Softkey on the IP Phone), CallManager instructs the IP phone and the gateway to close the media channels and sends a DLCX (DeleteConnection) command to the gateway release the channel. At the same time, CallManager also sends PRI Disconnect message to the PSTN via the gateway to inform the PSTN switch the call termination event.

## Using H.323 Gateway

Figure 1-28 shows the CallManager cluster with a registered IP phone 1 and an H.323 gateway. A gatekeeper is also registered with the cluster, and the off-net calls contact the gatekeeper before placing the call. The IP phone user makes an off-net call to a PSTN phone (Phone Z). The CallManager routes the call via the H.323 gateway.

**Figure 1-28** *Off-Net Call Scenario with H.323 Gateway*

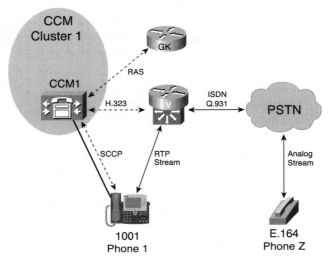

The following steps describe the events of messages that take place when IP phone 1 makes an off-net call via the gatekeeper through the H.323 gateway. Figure 1-29 shows the exact call-signaling sequence.

1 Phone 1 goes off-hook and dials the number of Phone Z.

2 CallManager performs the digit analysis and finds that it has to contact the gatekeeper before placing the call.

3 CallManager sends an ARQ message with the destination phone number. The gatekeeper responds with an ACF message and includes the IP address of the H.323 gateway.

4 CallManager sends an H.225 Setup message to the gateway. This message includes the calling party name, calling party number, and called party number. CallManager receives an H.225 Call Proceeding message from the gateway.

5 The gateway sends a Q.931 Setup message to the PSTN along with the calling party number, called party number, and calling party name and receives the Q.931 Call Proceeding message from the CO switch.

6 The CO switch sends a Q.931 Alerting message to the gateway, and the gateway sends a H.225 Alerting message to the CallManager.

**7**  CallManager and the gateway exchange the media capabilities using H.245. They exchange information such as the codecs supported on both ends; through this negotiation, they choose a common codec for the session.

**8**  Later, CallManager sends a request to the IP phone (via SCCP OpenReceiveChannel message) and the gateway (via H.245 openLogicalChannel message) to respond with their respective IP address and the UDP port number. The IP Phone and gateway responds with IP address and the UDP port number information in the corresponding ACK messages. CallManager communicates to IP phone and the H.323 gateway about the other's IP address and UDP port number. At this point the IP Phone has the IP Address and UDP port number of the H.323 gateway, similarly, the H.323 gateway has the IP Address and UDP port number of the IP Phone. Hence, the IP Phone user can hear the Call Progress tones coming from the PSTN.

**9**  After the called party answers the phone, the CO switch sends a Q.931 Connect message, RTP streams are established between the IP phone and the H.323 gateway, and both parties can begin the conversation.

**10**  A disconnect from either end causes the termination of audio channels, and CallManager sends a Disengage Request to the gatekeeper.

**Figure 1-29**  *Off-Net Call Flow Using H.323 Gateway*

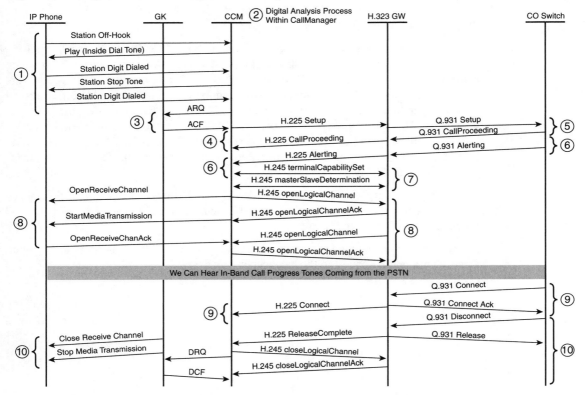

## Summary

This chapter presented a high-level summary of how the legacy voice and data networks have transitioned to new-world multiservice networks and the corresponding evolution of the Cisco AVVID IPT network solution. This chapter provided an overview of telco and VoIP signaling protocols, call processing in Cisco IPT networks, and IPT components and applications. The introduction of the various IPT deployment models and their benefits and the detailed discussion of the call-flow scenarios should prepare you for the deployment of IPT in the real world.

Because this book is about planning, design, implementation, operation, and optimization (PDIOO) of Cisco IPT networks, the next chapter gives you a high-level introduction to different phases and steps of the PDIOO methodology. The next chapter explains how the PDIOO methodology helps you to achieve your goal of deploying a scalable and optimized IPT network in an orderly fashion.

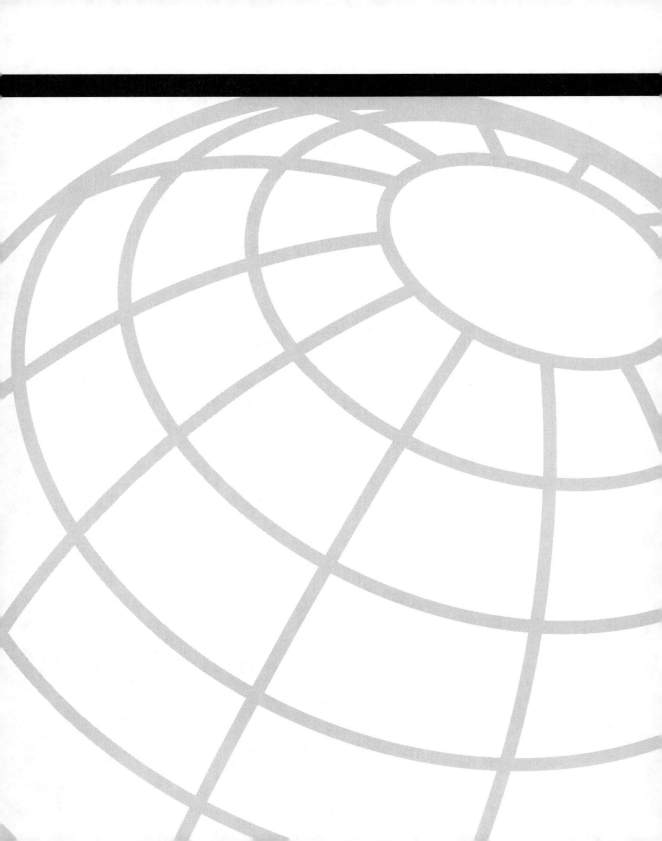

# Planning, Design, Implementation, Operation, and Optimization Overview

The first chapter should have given you an understanding of the evolution of data and voice networks and the various components of IP telephony (IPT) networks. IPT merges separate voice and data networks into a single, converged network. This change requires fine-tuning the existing network infrastructure.

To facilitate a successful IPT rollout in an organization, you should follow the planning, design, implementation, operation, and optimization (PDIOO) methodology. This widely accepted procedure, outlined in this chapter, ensures the smoothest, most efficient path to a successful IPT deployment. In fact, the best practice is to follow the PDIOO methodology while deploying any new technology. Technologies that are deployed without following the PDIOO methodology usually end up in broken, unscalable, and unoptimized networks. To avoid the time delays that increase the total cost of the project, make a decision from day one to follow the PDIOO methodology while deploying IPT.

As a network design engineer who is engaged in the PDIOO of IPT networks, you should have a solid understanding of packetized voice technology, voice products, TDM network inter-actions, and IPT technology and components.

This chapter discusses each stage in the PDIOO methodology and explains how this approach can help you to achieve your goals and smoothly migrate the legacy telephony network to an IPT network. Figure 2-1 shows the complete PDIOO methodology to deploy the IPT network and various subtasks within each phase.

As shown in Figure 2-1, the whole project typically starts with the customer issuing a Request for Proposal (RFP). IPT vendors respond with the IPT network proposal based on the requirements given in the RFP. The planning phase starts immediately after the customer decides on a particular vendor solution. Chapter 3, "Large-Scale Enterprise Requirements for IP Telephony," presents the sample RFP (this task is shown in dotted lines in Figure 2-1) for a fictitious customer, XYZ, Inc. The subsequent chapters in this book cover the various tasks shown in Figure 2-1 within the PDIOO phases to roll out IPT at XYZ, Inc. Figure 2-1 shows the PDIOO tasks for deploying the IPT solution in the dotted lines. Note that Figure 2-1 shows the ommonly followed tasks to deploy IPT by following the PDIOO methodology. However, depending on the type of the business and requirements, you might have to add extra tasks within each phase.

**Figure 2-1** *PDIOO Methodology for Deploying IPT Solution*

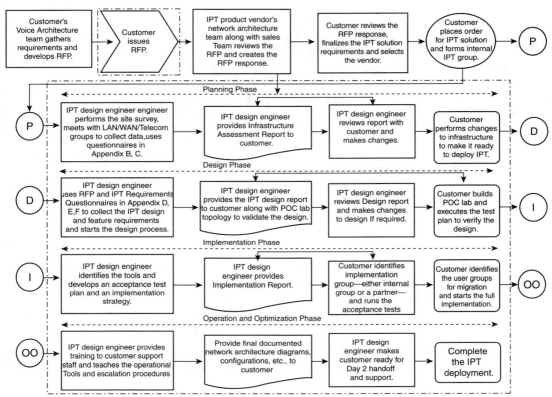

# Planning Phase

Planning is the first phase in the PDIOO lifecycle. A thorough execution of the planning phase tasks lays a solid foundation for the design of an IPT network.

One of the first important tasks in the planning phase is to understand the end customer's expectations and requirements. These fall into two main categories:

- Business expectations and requirements
- Technical expectations and requirements

**NOTE**    The customer usually provides the business and technical expectations and requirements in the RFP document. You should use the information presented in the RFP first and then consult the voice network architecture group, IT groups, or other groups in the customer's organization to obtain additional information.

From the business expectations and requirements point of view, you should understand the company's goals and vision and analyze how these relate to the future IPT network. More particularly, information that might help you to execute the project in a timely manner and complete it within the projected budget includes the company's goals for expansion in the next 4 to 6 years, its capital expenditures (CAPEX), its operational expenditures (OPEX), its return on investment (ROI), and its expectations regarding how long the project should take to plan, design, and implement.

From the technical expectations and requirements point of view, you should understand the company's current and future needs regarding IPT network features and functionality. These expectations and requirements include general features that are required in the IPT network, such as network redundancy, high availability, convergence, security, network management, application requirements, utilization, performance, scaling requirements, and so forth.

After you understand these high-level business and technical expectations and requirements, the next phase is to conduct a site survey. One of the most important tasks in the site survey is to meet the right groups of people (i.e., LAN group, WAN group, IP network group, legacy PBX and voice-mail network group, applications group, etc.). Establishing the right contacts helps you to quickly obtain accurate information pertaining to the network.

While conducting the site survey, you need to obtain details regarding the following:

- Existing LAN infrastructure, such as the LAN topology, equipment deployed, and current LAN QoS policies
- WAN infrastructure, such as the WAN architecture, WAN equipment deployed, existing QoS policies, traffic flows, bandwidth assignments, and link utilizations
- Layer 3 and Layer 2 infrastructure
- IP addressing scheme, including how network services such as Dynamic Host Configuration Protocol (DHCP) and Domain Name System (DNS) are deployed
- Directory and messaging architecture
- Layer 3 routing and routed protocols used in the network
- Legacy telephony and voice-mail infrastructure and telephony features such as paging, operator, night bell, call center, Music on Hold, etc. deployed in the network
- Legacy dial plan configurations
- Current utilization and performance for voice and data networks

- Current network management infrastructure
- Current day 2 support and operations support process

After you collect the information by conducting the site surveys, you should perform a detailed network infrastructure assessment to ensure that the network will support IPT, that new systems and applications will be compatible with existing systems and devices, and that the new IPT system will perform as planned. The infrastructure assessment should include details regarding gaps in the infrastructure that need to be filled to support IPT and recommendations to strengthen the infrastructure to support the converged network.

Proper execution of the planning phase will lead to the following:

- Realistic expectations of the scalability, performance, and features of the new IPT system
- A network infrastructure that is able to support the IPT traffic
- Identification of proper resources to accelerate the rollout of the IPT deployment
- An IPT network that is aligned with business needs
- Successful integration with legacy PBX and voice-mail systems or complete migration to an IPT network
- Deployment of IPT applications and their integration with existing applications

Chapter 4, "Planning Phase," covers the planning phase and various tasks involved. Appendixes B, "IPT Planning Phase: Network Infrastructure Analysis Questionnaire," and C, "IPT Planning Phase: Telecom Infrastructure Analysis Questionnaire," include Network Infrastructure and Telecom Infrastructure Analysis Questionnaires, respectively, that you can use to collect the information required in the planning phase and to perform the network infrastructure assessment and gap analysis.

# Design Phase

After you complete the planning phase, you should begin working on the design phase of the IPT network. The goal of the design phase is to propose an IPT network design by using the information that is collected in the planning phase and the information that is provided by the customer in the RFP. You also need to collect additional information that is specific to IPT feature requirements. (Refer to Appendixes D, "IPT Design Phase: IP Phone Selection Questionnaire," and E, "IPT Design Phase: IPT Requirement Analysis Questionnaire," for the IPT Design Phase Questionnaires).

You should consider several different design alternatives before arriving at the final design. This proposed design should cater to the company's current and future IPT needs.

The design phase consists of the following high-level tasks, through which different critical areas of the network are designed based on IPT network needs:

- Network infrastructure design
- Design of call-processing infrastructure and applications
- Software version evaluation
- Design validation

As shown in Figure 2-1, the goal of the design phase is to complete the preceding four design phase tasks and provide the design document that proposes an IPT network design that satisfies the customer's needs. The design document should include the proposed IPT network architecture diagrams, recommended configurations for voice gateways, QoS recommendations for LAN/WAN, etc. Chapters 5, 6, and 7 cover the preceding four tasks involved in the design phase and explain the individual tasks with the help of the case study.

IPT network designers should review this design document with the voice network architecture team and infrastructure groups in the customer's organization to ensure that the proposed design meets their requirements.

## Network Infrastructure Design

The first task of the design phase is to enable the existing network infrastructure to support IPT. Chapter 5 discusses the network infrastructure design tasks and focuses on the following design areas:

- Choosing the IPT deployment model
- Designing an IP addressing scheme, voice VLANs for IPT network devices, and IP routing
- Evaluating and selecting Cisco IP phone models
- Designing DHCP and TFTP services for Cisco IP phones and other IPT endpoints in addition to the use of DNS services
- Designing quality of service (QoS) in the LAN
- Choosing the in-line power standard and determining the additional hardware needs on the switches and the power requirements
- Designing the LAN and WAN infrastructure for resiliency
- Sizing the WAN links and design of QoS in the WAN

## Design of Call Processing Infrastructure and Applications

The second task of the design phase is to choose and size the IPT components, review and make recommendations to integrate or migrate current telephony applications with or to new IPT applications based on customer's telephony requirements. Chapters 6 and 7 discuss the following design tasks:

- Sizing the CallManager clusters
- Sizing the voice gateways and gatekeeper
- Preparing the IPT system to integrate or access the corporate Lightweight Directory Access Protocol (LDAP) directory

- Designing dial plan

- Choosing the right design steps to migrate or integrate with the legacy systems (PBX, key, voice mail, or unified messaging system)

- Incorporating the fax and modem requirements in the IPT network

- Deploying the conferencing and transcoding resources and sizing them based on the requirements

- Recommending the security and network management solutions

- Customizing and sizing the IPT applications such as Auto Attendant (AA) and call center application IP-ICD (Integrated Contact Distribution)

- Designing and customizing the voice mail system

## Software Version Evaluation

As with any other products, the Cisco IPT products have undergone many software revisions. New versions include bug fixes to the old versions and many new features. The heart of the Cisco IPT solution is Cisco CallManager. It interfaces with other applications as described in the preceding section to provide additional features and capabilities. You should refer to the Cisco CallManager Compatibility Matrix available on Cisco.com to ensure that all the software versions on the other IPT endpoints—such as IP Phones, voice gateways, and applications— are compatible with the CallManager version chosen for the deployment. The Cisco CallManager Compatibility Matrix is available at http://www.cisco.com/univercd/cc/td/doc/ product/voice/c_callmg/ccmcomp.htm.

## Design Validation

The final task of the design phase is to validate the proposed design by building a proof of concept (POC) lab and conducting the acceptance testing. The POC lab topology that you design should emulate the proposed network and must contain all the different IPT components that are proposed in the actual design.

This acceptance testing is necessary for a smooth rollout of IPT throughout the entire network. To ensure this, you, along with the customer technical team, should develop a test plan that clearly defines various unique test scenarios and then execute the test plan. Typical scenarios include testing the following:

- Internal and external phone calls

- Conference calls

- IPT features that are deployed

- Failover scenarios

- Calls between the sites across the WAN

- Call admission control feature
- WAN circuit failure conditions
- Recovery times for failures within the LAN
- Access to voice mail and message notification
- Voice-mail/PBX integration
- Call routing and calling privileges
- System restoration from the backup data

While you are going through this exercise, the time that you devote must be reasonable enough to cover all the test scenarios described in the test plan. Following are some clear advantages of going through this exercise:

- Fix problems such as functionality issues, configuration errors, and design flaws that are discovered during the testing.
- Make necessary changes in the design depending on the types of problems discovered.
- Modify or adjust the procedures used to build the servers, deploy phones, migrate users, etc. based on the results. This ensures that the final deployment process is smooth and helps to make the IPT rollout faster.
- Fine-tune and adjust the server configuration parameters during the testing phase to achieve minimal telephony service disruptions by conducting failover tests.
- Ensure that all the critical elements are in proper working order.
- Ensure smooth transition/migration to the proposed IPT design.

# Implementation Phase

After you have documented the design phase on paper, the next vital phase in the PDIOO lifecycle is implementation. This phase helps to ensure that the deployed network delivers all of its desired functionality. This phase involves developing the implementation strategy and procedures.

In large networks, the company might subcontract some of the implementation tasks, such as physical deployment of IP phones, configuring the IP phones in the CallManager, and so forth. Hence, defining the process is important so that subcontractors can leverage this process and follow the methodology developed. This ensures timely resolution of any problems that are encountered during the implementation.

A good strategy for implementing the IPT rollout in large networks is to divide the whole project into small phases. Choose a small section of the network in the initial phase of the deployment. After you successfully complete the IPT deployment for the first phase, move to the other parts of the network in an orderly fashion.

You should monitor the network utilization statistics and the functionality of the newly deployed network at every stage. Keep a log of the problems reported by the users and modify the implementation procedures to ensure that users of the future IPT rollout do not face the same issues. At any given stage, resolve any unexpected behaviors and conduct thorough research on the root cause of the problems before further deployment.

An implementation strategy should have at minimum the following steps clearly defined and documented:

- Identify the implementation team responsible for provisioning the new IPT system into the production network.

- Identify and standardize the implementation tools that are useful in deploying IP phones and other IPT endpoints.

- Document clearly the installation and configuration steps for various devices.

- Define the migration user groups and timelines for the migration.

- Inform users about the new phone system and plan for end-user training on using the new phone features.

- Communicate routinely with telephone companies (telcos) to coordinate the configuration changes required on the central office switches and the support required for cutover to the new IPT system.

- Provide updates to the PBX/voice-mail system and other telecom engineers and ensure that they perform the changes required on these systems for successful migration/integration of them to/with the new IPT system.

- Prepare a telephone number management system to track the phone number allotments and changes.

- Ensure that constant communication occurs between the implementation team and the design staff to exchange the problems faced in the field and solutions to the problems.

- Define the escalation procedures to address the feature and functionality faults or network tuning requirements as discovered during implementation.

- Provide the organization with a technical review for IPT-related field alerts that might affect the customer's current implementation.

- Communicate to the executive team and to the users if there is any downtime that could be caused by this deployment.

Depending on the customer's organization and type of business, you might need to define additional strategic steps to successfully deploy the IPT network. Chapter 9, "Operations and Optimization," covers the detailed implementation steps for deploying various IPT components and applications and introduces you to some of the implementation tools.

# Operation and Optimization Phase

The last phase of the PDIOO life cycle is operation and optimization.

As opposed to traditional telephony networks, IPT networks have less need for expensive services and provisioning tools for moves, adds, and changes. Nevertheless, a solid support plan is essential to attain operational excellence for high availability and seamless quality.

Operation planning protects the networking investment and provides the operations staff the capability to proactively monitor the network to reduce problems. The following are the important steps that organizations should plan to execute for successful operation of the IPT network:

- Provide training and hands-on expertise to the support staff on the IPT products operational tools, and network management tools.
- Involve the key operational staff in the planning and implementation stage of the IPT project.
- Define escalation procedures and provide resources such as the tools required and product, vendor contacts to troubleshoot user-reported problems and product issues.
- Define a process to perform the software and hardware upgrades. The process should outline when to perform the software/hardware upgrades, who should be notified when performing the upgrades, etc.
- Define procedures for managing configuration change requests.
- Define the backup and restore procedures and backup schedules.
- Establish a service and support contract with the IPT product vendor.

The optimization phase involves executing steps that help the network to deliver the best possible performance, thus decreasing network issues and reducing revenue losses caused by outages.

To optimize the network, the support staff should have a solid understanding of the available operation, monitoring, and optimization tools. Chapter 9 provides detailed information on various tools that are available in Cisco IPT products and optimization techniques.

These tools and procedures simplify network expansion, ensure the quality of the network and its applications, focus staffing and training needs, facilitate problem solving, and lower the total cost of ownership.

# Summary

Following the PDIOO methodology ensures that the converged network solution is successful and cost effective throughout its life cycle.

This chapter briefly introduced you to the PDIOO methodology and tasks performed at every phase. After reading this chapter, you should have a solid understanding of IPT technology and the tasks involved in the PDIOO of an IPT network. Chaper 3, "Large-Scale Enterprise Requirements for IP Telephony," examines the network of an organization that is planning to migrate to an IPT network and describes how to collect its IPT requirements as part of the PDIOO lifecycle.

# Large-Scale IPT and Voice-Mail Network

# CHAPTER 3

# Large-Scale Enterprise Requirements for IP Telephony

The first two chapters provided an overview of the Cisco IP telephony (IPT) solution, a brief introduction to the various components and protocols involved in an IPT network, and a tutorial on the planning, design, implementation, operation, and optimization (PDIOO) methodology to deploy IPT networks. The customer requirements provided in this chapter are used as the basis for the planning activities described in this book.

In this chapter, we consider a large-scale customer named XYZ, Inc., which is pursuing a Cisco IPT solution to replace its existing PBX systems as part of an emerging technology deployment project. The goal of this project is to establish a reliable, manageable, integrated, and scalable IPT solution that meets or exceeds the capabilities of the current voice network that is deployed with the legacy PBX systems.

To achieve this goal as a network engineer, you need to study the existing data, legacy voice network infrastructure and understand the customer's network requirements for the IPT project. This information will help you to properly design the IPT network and enable the infrastructure to carry the integrated data/voice/video traffic smoothly.

The information presented in this chapter is used in subsequent chapters to guide you through the various tasks in the PDIOO methodology, which can help you to deploy IPT in real-world networks. The idea here is not to discuss complex networks and confuse you with a lot of requirements. Instead, you will build the IPT network for XYZ, Inc. with commonly deployed IPT features and applications. You will be able to use the basic principles and design techniques discussed in this book to customize or add more applications to meet your IPT network requirements.

This chapter also serves as a reference to voice architecture teams that are tasked to write a Request for Proposal (RFP). It gives guidance as to what needs to go into the RFP so that IPT product vendors can respond with their proposed architectures.

---

**NOTE**    The information presented in the "Customer Profile" and "Customer Requirements" sections in this chapter is usually provided by customers in the form of an RFP. If you are a network engineer who is responsible for the IPT network design and you do not have this information, you must collect it prior to starting any tasks described in the PDIOO methodology by meeting with the voice network architecture group in the customer organization.

---

# Customer Profile

XYZ, Inc. (hereafter referred to as XYZ) is one of the largest manufacturers of pharmaceutical products in the United States. The company headquarters is located in San Jose, California. The company has grown rapidly and currently has two branch offices in the United States and an international presence in Australia.

The San Jose headquarters location has 1000 employees. Within the United States, the company has two branch sales offices, in Seattle and Dallas. The international headquarters in Sydney, Australia has 500 employees and has two branch sales offices, in Melbourne and Brisbane. Table 3-1 lists the exact number of employees per site.

**Table 3-1**     *Employee Counts for XYZ Offices*

| Site Name | Number of Users |
|---|---|
| San Jose – U.S. Headquarters | 1000 |
| Seattle – branch | 50 |
| Dallas – branch | 15 |
| Sydney – International Headquarters | 500 |
| Melbourne – branch | 40 |
| Brisbane – branch | 10 |

XYZ is looking for ways to improve its customer service. Its goal is to achieve higher customer satisfaction while reducing operational costs. Because telephone communications is one of the primary ways that XYZ does business with its customers, it has decided that it can achieve its goal by deploying a new IPT system and associated applications.

# Data Network Architecture

Figure 3-1 shows the existing data and voice network architecture of XYZ. The voice and data networks are separate and operated independently. The central sites for the XYZ network are San Jose and Sydney. The Seattle and Dallas sites are the remote sites in the U.S. that connect to the San Jose central site. The Melbourne and Brisbane sites are the remote sites in Australia that connect to the Sydney central site. The data traffic from the remote sites traverses across the IP-WAN links to the central sites. A 2-Mbps leased circuit connects the central sites in San Jose and Sydney.

**Figure 3-1**  *XYZ Data and Voice Network Architecture*

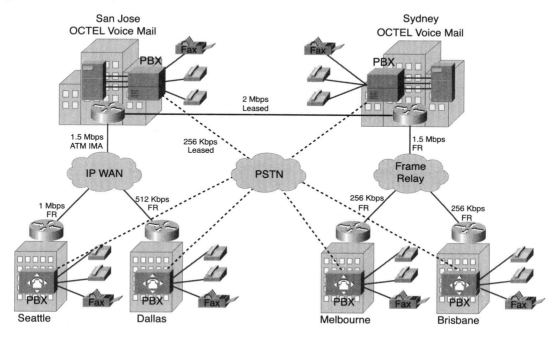

Figure 3-2 depicts the physical LAN architecture at the San Jose and Sydney central sites. The San Jose and Sydney offices have a similar LAN architecture. At XYZ, every desk in the current campuses has a set of two RJ-45 ports for data communications and two RJ-11 ports for connecting telephony devices. With the deployment of IPT, only one of the two RJ-45 ports is required for both data and voice communications.

**NOTE**  At XYZ, most of the LAN switches and WAN routers that are deployed are products from Cisco Systems. However, in some building closets, LAN switches from other vendors are also deployed. Hence, you need to consider these exceptions when proposing the IPT solution, because their presence affects how the power to the IP phones is provided and has quality of service (QoS) implications such as marking and prioritizing voice and signaling packets.

Chapter 4, "Planning Phase," discusses these exceptions and provides recommendations for handling them.

When you are building new cabling infrastructure for future campuses, you need only one RJ-45 port at every desk for both data and voice communications, eliminating the need for extra cabling infrastructure to support voice communications. However, having a second RJ-45 port and connecting to a different switch or to a different module on the same switch chassis provides physical redundancy.

**Figure 3-2**    *XYZ Physical LAN Architecture at Central Sites*

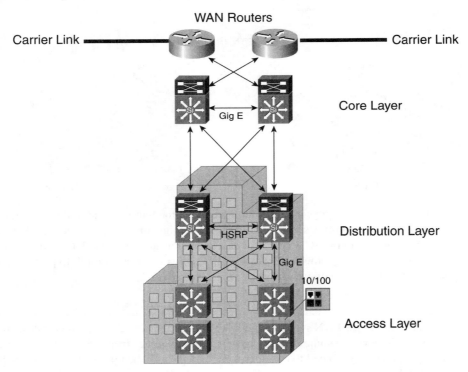

In Figure 3-2, the access layer Catalyst 6500 switches connect via two Gigabit Ethernet fiber links to two Catalyst 6500 switches in the distribution layer. Two distribution layer Catalyst 6500 switches use the Hot Standby Routing Protocol (HSRP) between them for path redundancy. Each distribution layer Catalyst 6500 switch connects back to the two core layer Catalyst 6500 switches via a routed Gigabit Ethernet link. The core layer Catalyst 6500 switches also connect to WAN routers, which connect to the carrier to provide WAN connectivity.

Figure 3-3 shows the physical LAN and WAN architecture at the remote sites.

**Figure 3-3**  *XYZ Physical LAN and WAN Architecture at Remote Sites*

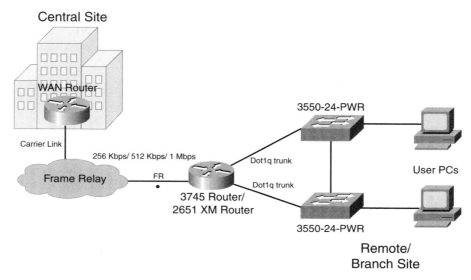

As shown in Figure 3-3, the WAN link from each branch site is the WAN link from each branch site is a Frame Relay IP circuit that connects it to the respective central site. Also, the LAN is a switched network. The branch routers are either Cisco 3745 or Cisco 2651 XM routers, and the LAN switches are Cisco 3550 inline power-capable switches.

## Voice Network Architecture

As shown in Figure 3-1, each site has PBX systems deployed locally. Each site processes its own calls. Failure of the PBX system at any site does not impact other sites.

All the calls that originate from the individual sites are routed via the local PSTN connection. The international calls between the U.S. sites and Australian sites traverse the PSTN and are the major part of the XYZ telecommunications expenditure.

## Data Applications

At XYZ, commonly used applications are e-mail, file transfers, web, and some database applications. No real-time application in the network requires traffic prioritization. However, the QoS policies and configurations must ensure that the performance of existing applications does not degrade because of the traffic prioritization that is required for real-time applications.

## Directory and Messaging Architecture

The XYZ corporate directory architecture is based on Microsoft Active Directory. The messaging environment is based on Microsoft Exchange 2000 on a Windows 2000 Server operating system platform. Users use Microsoft Outlook to retrieve e-mail via Post Office Protocol Version 3 (POP3).

## PBX and Voice-Mail System Features

As shown earlier in Figure 3-1, all the locations have PBX systems today. The PBX systems support the following functions:

- **Call park**—Allows a phone user to "park" a call that is received on their phone, effectively placing the call in a hold state, retrieve the call at another station, and continue the conversation. Another phone user can also retrieve the parked call if notified by the first phone user. This feature provides phone users with mobility and eliminates the need to return calls.

- **Call transfer**—Allows a phone user to transfer the call received on their phone to another phone user within the system or transfer the call to an external phone user. This feature eliminates the need for the calling party to hang up and dial another number to reach the desired party.

- **Call pickup**—Allows a phone user to retrieve and answer a call ringing at another phone, or on any other phone in the phone user's assigned call-pickup group (call pickup). The phone user can also pick up the call that is ringing on another phone that is part of another call-pickup group (group pickup). The phone user dials a preconfigured call-pickup number to take the call.

- **Call back**—Notifies a phone user of the availability of a previously called user phone if that user did not answer the call previously. The phone user who invokes this feature gets an audible or visual notification informing them of the availability of the other phone user.

- **Ad hoc conferencing**—Allows a phone user to add a third user to the existing conversation, effectively making the call a conference call.

- **Class of Restrictions (CoR)**—Allows you to assign calling privileges on a per-phone basis based on the location of the phone or the type of user. For example, you can configure a lobby phone to prevent someone from making long-distance or international calls.

- **Speed dialing**—Allows a phone user to program the buttons on their phone with frequently dialed numbers. The phone user can call the number by pressing the button instead of dialing the whole number.

- **Music on Hold**—Provides a phone user with announcements while their call is placed on hold.

- **Call forwarding**—Allows a phone user to forward calls received on their phone to another phone within the system or to an external phone number. The following functionalities are supported:
  - **Call Forward All (CFwdAll)**—Forward all calls to a programmed destination number
  - **Call Forward Busy (CFB)**—Forward the calls to another number to a voice-mail system if the user phone is engaged in another conversation
  - **Call Forward No Answer (CFNA)**—Forward calls to another number within the system or external to the system if the phone user does not answer the call at their phone
- **Display call history**—Allows a phone user to view the missed calls, previously dialed numbers, and received calls on their phone and to dial the numbers without entering the digits manually.
- **Call waiting**—Provides a visual notification or alert mechanism to the phone user to inform them of other incoming calls arriving at their phone while they are engaged in a conversation on the same line.
- **Site-specific Automated Attendant functionality**—Allows external callers when they dial the branch main number to search the phone directory based on the user's extension number or by their first or last name.
- **Call Detailed Recording (CDR)**—Stores the information about incoming/outgoing calls received or dialed by every phone user in the system. This information is useful in generating department-wide billing reports or doing a study of the calling patterns in the organization.

XYZ's voice-mail systems are currently completely separate from the e-mail environment. The existing voice-mail systems support the following features:

- **Message Waiting Indication (MWI)**—Provides a user with a visual or audible notification on the phone that new voice mails are waiting in the mailbox.
- **Message notifications**—Allows a user to configure the settings on their mailbox to notify them via e-mail, pager, or cell phone whenever they get new voice mails.
- **Alternate greetings**—Allows a user to set up different greetings to inform the calling party that the user is on an extended absence or is out of the office temporarily.
- **Directory service**—Allows an external/internal user to search the company's phone directory by using the extension number or by entering the first or last name of the user.
- **Group mailboxes or distribution lists**—Allows voice-mail users to be grouped so that a voice message sent to such a group is distributed to all users in that group. This feature allows executives or management to send out voice messages to the entire company staff or to a group of people about company events.

- **Storage**—Approximately 20 minutes of storage is available per user mailbox.

- **Remote voice-mail access**—Access to voice mail from remote locations is available via the Telephony User Interface (TUI).

The proposed IPT solution should support at minimum all of the preceding functionalities and features that exist in the current PBX and voice-mail systems.

# Customer Requirements

This section lists the XYZ IPT network requirements. As mentioned at the beginning of this chapter, customers usually provide this information in the RFP.

While reviewing the existing voice network infrastructure, system administrators at XYZ have identified the following limitations in the current system:

- Because of the multivendor PBX systems that exist in the network and the use of non-standard, propriety signaling mechanisms and interfaces on the PBX systems, XYZ cannot interconnect the PBX systems to save the communications costs on the interoffice calls.

- Some PBX systems and key systems are old and lack the functionality and the call features required.

- Nonavailability of empty slots on the PBX systems is preventing the expansion plans.

- Because the equipment is old, cost of replacement parts is high.

- Costs incurred in maintaining the PBX and voice-mail systems by external vendors have increased substantially over the years, resulting in more recurring expenditures.

- Coordinating with external vendors to implement the changes or additions is causing an extra delay and impacting negatively on the company productivity figures.

- Moves, adds, and changes cost $200 to $250 every time a staff member relocates to a new office. This cost is for the PBX engineer to reprogram the PBX systems and the cable contractor to install the new connection. This whole process sometimes takes up to two business days for completion, which impacts overall company productivity.

These system limitations and extra costs have forced the administrators of XYZ to consider the migration to IPT solutions. The following sections provide the minimum requirements for the proposed IPT network.

# System Architecture

XYZ has been expanding its operations rapidly because of growing demand for its products. To protect the investments made and to achieve quicker expansion, XYZ requires a scalable call-processing system that

- Requires minimal redesign in case of an expansion.

- Provides redundancy and load balancing.
- Optimizes bandwidth utilization on the WAN links for voice traffic.
- Supports keeping the call control at the central sites and providing local call processing capability on the WAN routers at the branch sites during WAN link failure.

## IP Phones

At XYZ, the IP phones can be categorized as follows:

- Employee phones
- Assistant/secretary phones
- Conference/meeting room phones
- Lobby/break room phones

The employee and assistant/secretary phones must support headsets. Assistant/secretary phones usually have multiple lines. The phones and headsets are required to work with hearing-impaired users. High-quality conference phones are required in meeting rooms for conference calls. Lobby/break room phones do not require; PC connectivity from the phones.

The phones must obtain power from the wiring closet switches and, if required, must work with other vendors' networking equipment by taking advantage of interoperable standards.

## Integration and Replacement of Legacy PBX Systems

All the sites currently have either PBX systems or key systems. These systems are not interconnected. A phased migration to the new IPT system is required for the San Jose site because of the large user presence. The PBX system at the San Jose site requires integration with the new IPT system. At all other locations, the PBX lease periods are ending; hence, IPT systems can replace legacy PBX systems.

## Integration and Replacement of Legacy Voice-Mail Systems

There are two Avaya Octel voice-mail systems, one each at San Jose and Sydney. The Octel system at San Jose has mailboxes for all the employees in the United States. Similarly, the mailboxes for all the users in Australia reside on the Octel system in Sydney.

As a part of the new technology deployment, XYZ would like to deploy a new voice-mail system that supports unified messaging. The proposed voice-mail system architecture should have high availability and redundancy. The proposed voice-mail system should be able to leverage the already deployed messaging infrastructure.

In the initial deployment, the international office (Sydney, Melbourne, and Brisbane) users' mailboxes are migrated from the Octel system to the new voice-mail system. The Octel voice-mail system at the San Jose Headquarters site will continue to exist.

The new proposed voice-mail system at Sydney must be integrated with the existing Octel voice-mail system at the San Jose central site. The networking of the Octel and new voice-mail systems is a requirement to route voice mails between the two systems.

## Voice Gateways

Every location requires a voice gateway to connect to the local PSTN and must support T1/E1 PRI trunks. Each site routes local calls via a PSTN connection that is terminated on the local gateway.

The remote branch gateways should provide call-processing functionality to the connected devices in case of WAN link failure. The IP phones that are attached to the local voice gateways should use the local conferencing resources as a first preference and the central site conferencing resources as a secondary choice.

XYZ wants to deploy Fax over IP across its entire network. Hence, voice gateways must support analog ports to connect the fax machines.

## Quality of Service

XYZ requires good voice quality with its IPT network. Integrated voice and data networks require an intelligent network infrastructure that can properly interpret the QoS markings set by the IPT endpoints.

The XYZ network does not have QoS enabled currently. The XYZ network requires the following:

- The endpoints that can mark real-time frames and packets for QoS
- The infrastructure that can give preference to the marked frames

## Call Routing

Despite the low cost of national long-distance service charges within the United States, to save costs on the calls made between the offices within the United States, XYZ would like to use the IP-WAN for routing voice calls. The following are the requirements of call routing in the new IPT system:

- Calls should be routed via IP-WAN as the first choice, where available, and then via PSTN trunks if bandwidth is not available or a WAN link has failed.

- Automatic failover must be provided for all IP-WAN routing.
- Within the site, users should use four digits to dial other extensions. Site-to-site dialing also should use four digits.
- Tail-End Hop-Off (TEHO) is enabled where legally allowed and bandwidth permits. Transporting voice calls across the existing WAN links requires additional bandwidth. Hence, the proposed IPT system must clearly specify the amount of additional bandwidth required in such cases and provide an optimized solution to conserve it.

**NOTE**    In certain countries, transporting the voice call across the IP WAN links to another location before terminating the call on a PSTN is illegal.

- The remote sites in each global region must use the local gateways to route the local calls and use the gateways at the central sites as an alternative if the local PSTN connection is not available.
- A mechanism must be included to control the number of calls that traverse the IP-WAN considering the traffic utilization on the WAN links.
- Classes of restrictions must be provided based on the phone type (e.g., a lobby phone versus an employee phone).

For the initial deployment, branch sites will have a single PRI or multiple PRI circuits where needed. The IPT system must be flexible enough to make new changes and must be easy to troubleshoot.

## Emergency Services

All small branch sites have direct connectivity to the PSTN, and the billing number is associated with the street address of each branch site. All the emergency calls need to be routed via the PSTN connections from the branch sites. This avoids the emergency service calls being accidentally routed via the TEHO and connecting to an incorrect public safety answering point (PSAP). All the remote sites have a single T1/E1 PRI connectivity to the PSTN. Where possible, you should provide backup circuits to route the emergency calls if the T1/E1 PRI links are unavailable.

Within the United States, the IPT system must comply with Federal Communications Commission Enhanced 911 (E911) regulations. For more information on E911, go to http://www.fcc.gov/911/enhanced/.

---

**NOTE**   To determine if a particular state's law requires businesses to comply with E911, go to the
following website:

http://www.nena9-1-1.org/9-1-1TechStandards/state.htm

Based on this website, the three states in which the U.S. locations reside—California, Texas,
and Washington—do not require businesses to comply with E911.

---

There are currently no requirements for E911-equivalent functionality in Australia.

## IPT Features and Applications

The "Customer Requirements" section, earlier in this chapter, mentioned the limitations of the
current voice network infrastructure at XYZ. The management staff of XYZ is looking for an
IPT solution that can remove those limitations and provide the following additional features and
applications that were not possible with the legacy infrastructure:

- **Attendant Console**—Provides a centralized attendant operator for each site that has a
  web-based GUI that can be used to answer the incoming calls and direct them to the right
  user within the company.

- **Manager/Assistant (Boss/Secretary) Feature**—Allows assistants to receive/transfer
  calls received for managers. Managers can designate more than one assistant to handle
  their calls.

- **IP phone services**—The following services should be provided:

  — Corporate directory lookup from IP phones

    A corporate directory lookup application allows IP phone users to search
    against the XYZ corporate Active Directory for a user's phone number.
    Applications of this type improve employee productivity.

  — Calendar and other useful services

- **Multiple line appearances**—Provides more than one line appearance on the phone and
  is especially useful for call center agents who need one line that is specifically used for
  handling incoming customer support calls and another line for making other calls.

- **Mobility**—Some users at XYZ frequently travel between the sites, and XYZ company
  policy encourages telecommuters. The IPT system should enable such users to log in from
  any phone and personalize the phone with their extension number, speed dials, and other
  settings. This allows the users to work from any phone and still receive the calls as if they
  were at their desk phone.

- **Help desk support for 25 agents**—XYZ requires the IPT application that provides Automated Call Distribution (ACD), wherein the external/internal callers are directed to the right skill group agent to handle the customer support calls for the following two groups:
  - Internal IT help desk group
  - Customer support group
- **IP SoftPhone support for mobile users**—A SoftPhone is an application that is installed on a user's computer/laptop and emulates the real IP phone. This type of application is especially useful for mobile users because they can carry the phone with them.
- **Conferencing support**—Currently, XYZ uses an external provider to provide the conference bridge services. With the deployment of IPT, XYZ wants to deploy self-manageable conferencing resources that can support up to ten participants per conference call and that enables conference calls to be scheduled and managed via a web-based GUI.

## Security

With the integration of voice and data solutions, the call-processing servers and the telephony endpoints—such as gateways, media resource devices, and IP phones—will be part of the data network. Security plays a critical role in achieving the high availability of the IPT networks. XYZ has the following basic security requirements:

- Multiple administration levels for the administrative and operations staff to configure the call-processing servers
- Intrusion detection system
- Antivirus software support
- Logging of user login attempts and configuration changes
- Secure call-processing and application servers through the use of firewalls

## Redundancy and High Availability

XYZ requires this solution to provide redundancy and fault tolerance at every level. A failure of a server, gateway, gatekeeper, switch, or any other critical resource should not affect end users. The failure must be transparent to end users.

The IPT solution should provide 99.999 percent uptime for all the IPT devices and infrastructure.

# Network Management

XYZ has a global network operations center (NOC) located in San Jose that monitors all the existing networking devices. XYZ is looking for a complete network management solution to monitor the IPT components covering all the following aspects:

- Fault management
- Configuration management
- Accounting
- Performance management
- Security management
- Change management

# Return on Investment

ROI analysis takes into account cost of technology ownership and the strategic value of the IT initiative. For effective maximization of ROI, you need to understand how your overall cost of network ownership (voice, video, and data) will be lower in a converged environment. You have to compare the cost of implementing a converged environment to the cost of having a separate voice, video, and data network infrastructure, which includes expenses for separate IT groups for voice, video, and data networks; license renewal fees for your legacy voice systems; expenses for moves, adds, and changes; and other overhead.

According to a study conducted by Sage Research, Inc. for Cisco Systems (to download the "Sage IPT Productivity Study" presentation, go to http://www.cisco.com/partner/cnic/presentations.shtml), 75 percent of the survey respondents believed that cost savings is the main reason to move to a converged network, whereas 65 percent feel that employee productivity gains is the key driver motivating companies to deploy IPT.

XYZ, similar to other companies, is looking to save costs and at the same time recognizes the potential for a converged network to improve employee productivity, enable new application capabilities, and potentially drive revenues.

---

**TIP**     A detailed white paper, "The Strategic and Financial Justification for IP Communications," is available to provide senior network engineers and managers with the factual support to justify a strategic and financial decision to invest in a converged voice, video, and data network.

This white paper is available for download from http://www.cisco.com/partner/cnic/roi.pdf.

---

# Summary

This chapter provided the requirements of the customer XYZ that will be used in the upcoming chapters to build the IPT network based on the PDIOO approach.

Because it is impossible to cover every case scenario in this book, as mentioned at the beginning of this chapter, the requirements set for XYZ in this chapter are similar to what you commonly see in the majority of the IPT networks that exist today or in the networks that are transitioning to IPT. We feel confident that either you will find all the major requirements of your customer in the scenarios described in this book, or you will meet your customer requirements by slightly modifying the scenarios described in this book.

Chapter 4 discusses the planning phase of the PDIOO model. The goal of the planning phase is to identify the gaps in the existing network infrastructure and provide recommendations and best practices to make the infrastructure scalable and highly available to support the converged data and voice traffic. At the end of the planning phase, you should have a list of equipment required at each site, site-specific QoS policies, WAN bandwidth requirements, and dial plan requirements.

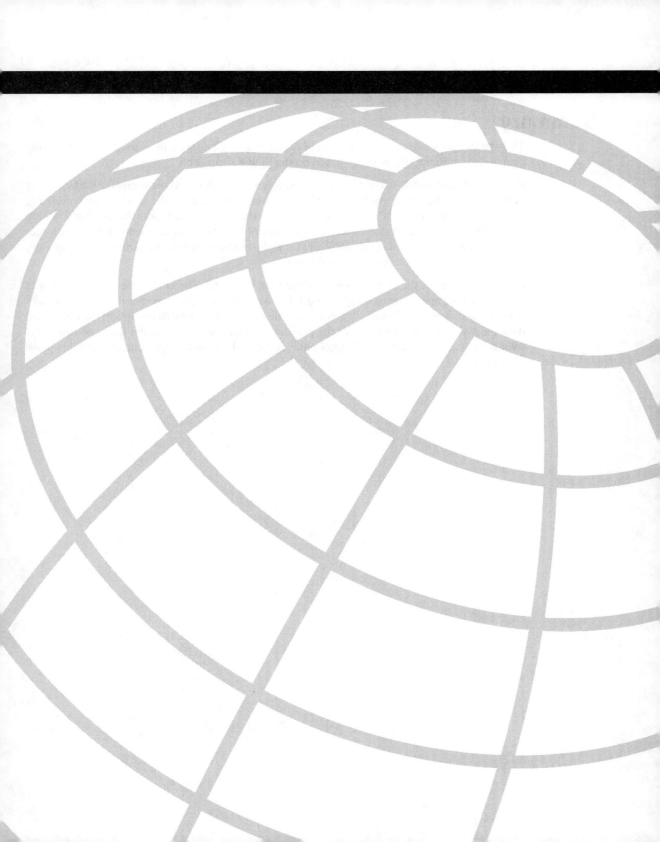

# Planning Phase

Chapter 3, "Large-Scale Enterprise Requirements for IP Telephony," presented the XYZ, Inc. current network scenario and its high-level requirements for its future IPT network. Typically, customers provide these requirements in the Request for Proposal (RFP); otherwise, you can gather the requirements by meeting the voice architecture group in the customer organization. Understanding these requirements is critical to planning and designing a scalable and optimized IPT network.

Before you begin studying the planning phase, you need to understand the approach that we have taken to analyze the network infrastructure of XYZ in the planning phase.

The network infrastructure topologies of XYZ that were presented in Figures 3-2 and 3-3 show that the network is designed with full redundancy, that all network elements are Cisco switches and routers, that all devices understand QoS, etc. This topology is 100 percent ready to deploy IP Telephony (IPT). You will not find a network like this in the real world; instead, you will see networks that pose many challenges. Some of the common challenges are the following:

- Networks that are deployed with non-Cisco switches—you are required to provide a solution to deploy Cisco IPT products
- Switches that do not understand Layer 3 QoS
- Switches that cannot provide inline power to Cisco IP phones
- Networks that are deployed without following the recommended designs/best practices

To provide you with answers to some of the preceding challenges, we could have introduced some of these problems into the XYZ network. However, doing so would have made it harder to keep up with the chapter flow. Hence, the approach taken is as follows:

- Describe the best practices in making the network infrastructure ready to support IPT
- Provide alternate solutions and suggestions for commonly faced problems and challenges, such as those described in the preceding list, at appropriate places in the chapter

This chapter guides you through various tasks involved in the planning phase and discusses the best practices and the steps you need to follow at every layer of the network to make the network infrastructure ready to run the Cisco IPT solution.

To complete the planning phase for XYZ, this chapter uses the information presented in Chapter 3 along with the input provided by the customer to the following two questionnaires:

- Network Infrastructure Analysis Questionnaire found in Appendix B, "IPT Planning Phase: Network Infrastructure Analysis Questionnaire".

- Telecom Infrastructure Analysis Questionnaire found in Appendix C, "IPT Planning Phase: Telecom Infrastructure Analysis Questionnaire".

# Getting Started

The first step in the planning phase is to understand the high-level business and technical expectations and requirements for the future IPT network, which include the following:

- Company vision, goals, and forecasted growth
- The plan for voice and data networks over the next 3 to 5 years
- Solution expectations
- Deployment and timing
- Financial expectations

To simplify the discussion for this case study, assume that XYZ expects its workforce to grow 5 to 10 percent every year. XYZ requires that the new IPT system must emulate the functionality of the current PBX, voice-mail, and application systems, be scalable, and provide additional services and features that improve employee productivity. The new technology update project at XYZ received approval from the company's financial board to support the funding for the IPT project, and there are no major budget constraints.

---

**NOTE**    When you are working with a customer, you might have to study some of these requirements carefully. For example, a customer might have limited funding available for the IPT project, in which case you might have to adjust the hardware needed in the infrastructure and size the other expensive equipment so that the total cost of the project falls within the approved budget. In some cases, you might also have to choose a phased migration to IPT to minimize the costs.

---

After you understand the high-level business and technical expectations of the customer, the next step is to conduct meetings with the engineers and architects in the LAN, WAN, IT, legacy PBX, legacy voice-mail, and applications network groups. During these meetings with the various groups, you should make sure that the high-level requirements that you received from the customer in the RFP are accurate. Most importantly, make sure that you understand how the customer's existing network infrastructure is built so that you can identify the gaps in the infrastructure that need to be filled to support the converged traffic.

# Network Infrastructure Analysis

Appendix B includes a Network Infrastructure Analysis Questionnaire that you can use to complete the network infrastructure analysis. (Another term commonly used for this analysis is IP Telephony Readiness Assessment.) The purpose of this assessment is to check whether the customer's network infrastructure is ready to carry the converged traffic. The assessment covers basic LAN switching design, IP routing including power and environmental analysis, and so forth. As a network engineer, you are required to identify the gaps in the infrastructure and make appropriate recommendations before you move forward with the IPT deployment.

The network infrastructure analysis of XYZ is divided into eight logical subsections:

- Campus network infrastructure
- QoS in campus network infrastructure
- Inline power for IP phones
- Wireless IP phone infrastructure
- WAN infrastructure
- QoS in WAN infrastructure
- Network services such as Domain Name Service (DNS) and Dynamic Host Configuration Protocol (DHCP)
- Power and environmental infrastructure

After reviewing the preceding list, you might be wondering why planning for the IPT network includes analyzing campus infrastructure (Layers 1, 2, and 3), WAN infrastructure, LAN and WAN QoS, and network services. The analysis of the aforementioned network infrastructure components is required during the planning phase of the IPT network deployment to identify the gaps in the current infrastructure to support the additional voice traffic on top of existing data traffic. After identifying the gaps, you need to make the appropriate changes in the network, such as implementing QoS in LAN/WAN, upgrading the closet switches to support QoS, and supporting the in-line power.

Chapter 1, "Cisco IP Telephony Solution Overview," discussed how legacy voice and data networks are migrating to new-generation multiservice networks. Chapter 1 also briefly discussed some of the requirements of the migration to multiservice networks. This section describes the technologies, features, and best practices to design a scalable and optimized infrastructure, which caries in parallel over the same IP infrastructure both real-time, delay-sensitive voice and video traffic and nonreal-time, delay-tolerable data traffic (i.e. FTP, e-mail, and so forth).

When you introduce real-time, delay-sensitive voice and video traffic into ensuring that your infrastructure is hierarchical, redundant, and QoS enabled, it becomes even more important to provide a scalable and redundant network infrastructure with fast convergence. Large network infrastructures use the access, distribution, and core layers at Layer 2 and Layer 3 for isolation, with redundant links and switches at these layers to provide the highest level of redundancy.

This isolation helps you to summarize the IP addresses and traffic flows at different layers and troubleshoot the issues in a hierarchical manner when they occur.

**TIP**   Small networks do not have to have access, distribution, and core layers at Layer 2 and Layer 3. Networks can collapse the core and distribution layer functionality in the same switch, depending on the size of the network. The redundancy and QoS requirements remain the same.

According to the International Telecommunications Union (ITU) G.114 recommendation, you need to achieve 0- to 150-ms one-way delay for the voice packet. You can achieve this delay value only by making sure that your network infrastructure is hierarchical, redundant, and QoS enabled. If you are transporting voice across the WAN links, you also should have adequate bandwidth to carry the additional voice traffic.

# Campus Network Infrastructure

The best way to start the campus network infrastructure analysis of XYZ is by analyzing the XYZ current multilayer infrastructure. Figure 4-1 depicts a well-designed multilayer network, which provides redundancy and high availability. Access to the distribution layer of this network is Layer 2, and access to the rest of the network is Layer 3.

When you analyze this network, one of the main concerns you should have is the number of points of failure in this network. More points of failure in a network translates to a less highly available network.

As you can see in Figure 4-1, this network has one single point of failure, which is the access layer switch. If the access layer switch fails, you lose the devices connected to the access layer switch. On the other hand, if you lose an uplink to a distribution layer switch or if a distribution layer switch fails, you will be fine, because you have redundant links and redundant switches in the distribution layer. If you lose an uplink to the core layer switch or if a core layer switch fails, you can still reach the rest of the network, by using the redundant links and switches at the core layer, and continue the communications.

In IPT applications, voice traffic uses IP. If your primary path fails and you have another path to the destination, you can reroute these VoIP packets to the destination, and you will not necessarily lose the calls. You can achieve this goal if your IP network can converge fast enough and correct itself. The advantage of having an IP network with fast convergence and redundant links is that if someone pulls a link from a distribution layer switch or any other device in the network, IPT users will not notice a difference.

**Figure 4-1**    *XYZ Multilayered Campus Infrastructure*

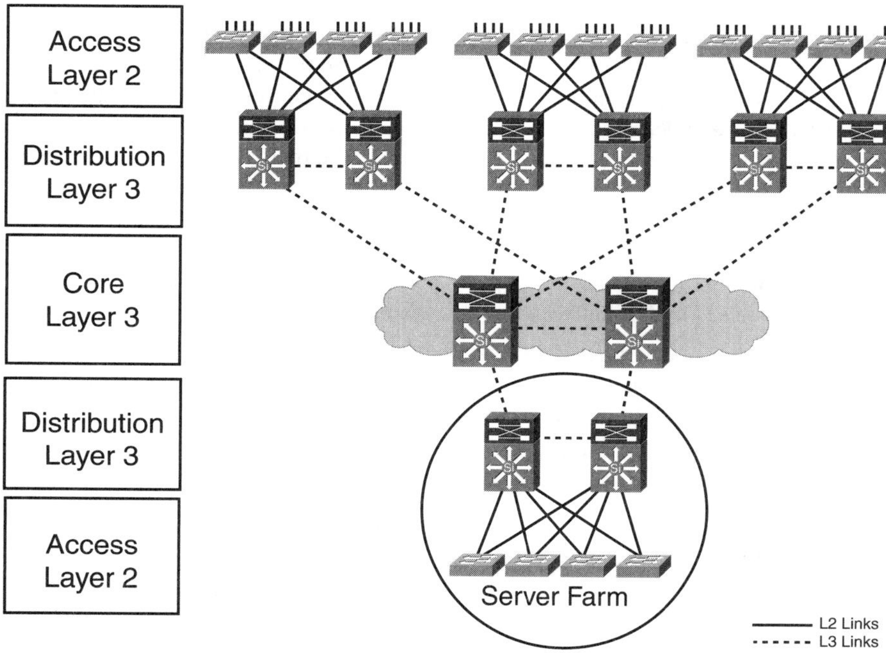

The next few sections examine the access, distribution, and core layers of this network and highlight the key points to remember while planning for each layer.

## Access Layer

The first thing you should plan for at the access layer is the virtual LANs (VLANs) in the network. A single VLAN should not span multiple access layer (wiring closet) switches in your network. You can have multiple VLANs in one wiring closet switch. By prohibiting a single VLAN from spanning across multiple wiring closet switches, you can limit the spanning tree into the wiring closet switch, which results in increased convergence time.

When you have multiple uplinks from the wiring closet switch to different distribution layer switches, you can use these multiple uplinks for faster convergence and load balancing, resulting in maximized use of redundant links.

The following features on the access layer switches help you to make the network infrastructure ready to support IPT.

## Auxiliary VLAN

When you deploy IPT, you connect the IP phones to access layer switches. Some of the Cisco IP Phones also have a PC port on the back of the phone to connect the user workstations. The challenge to address in this scenario is to separate the traffic coming from the IP Phones with the data traffic coming from the user workstations. To address this scenario, Cisco switches support a feature called auxiliary VLAN, or voice VLAN, and the VLAN ID assigned to this voice VLAN is referred to as voice VLAN ID (VVID). In this approach, you create a new voice VLAN on the access layer switch and leave the original data VLAN (access VLAN) untouched.

Some of the clear advantages of implementing separate data and voice VLANs are as follows:

- You can configure the differential treatments such as priority queuing for packets in the voice VLAN within network devices to guarantee the voice quality.

- Because the voice traffic will be on a separate VLAN, IP phones can use a separate IP address space altogether. Hence, you do not need to redesign the existing IP addressing scheme that is already deployed for the data network.

- When troubleshooting problems in the network, you can easily recognize and distinguish between data network and voice network traffic packets.

- Creating security policies and access lists is easy because the voice and data subnets are separate.

- Phones do not have to respond to broadcasts that are generated on the data network.

## IEEE 802.1Q/p Support

The introduction of the IEEE 802.1Q standard (which defines a mechanism for the trunking of VLANs between switches) includes support for priority in an Ethernet frame. IEEE 802.1Q adds 4 bytes into the Ethernet frame, inserted after the MAC Source Address field, as shown in Figure 4-2.

**Figure 4-2** *Layer 2 Classification 802.1Q/p*

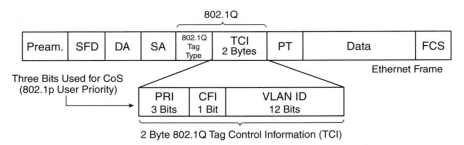

The 4 bytes of the 802.1Q field incorporate a 2-byte Ethernet Tag Type field and a 2-byte Tag Control Information (TCI) field. Within the 2-byte TCI field are 3 bits that set the priority of the Ethernet frame. These 3 priority bits are often referred to as IEEE 802.1p or, more commonly, dot1p. Dot1p is a term used to identify support for this priority mechanism in a switch. Note that this is a MAC layer mechanism and, as such, has significance to all devices connected at the MAC layer (such as in a bridged or Layer 2 switched network segment); it does not imply that end-to-end QoS is supported.

These 3 priority bits, also called Class of Service (CoS) bits, can mirror the 3 bits used as the IP Precedence bits in the ToS (Type of Service) field in the IPv4 header, as shown in Figure 4-3. Because the ToS setting is a Layer 3 setting, it can support end-to-end QoS. Ideally, the matching of these fields will allow end-to-end QoS to be provisioned across a network that incorporates both Layer 2 and Layer 3 technologies by mapping CoS to ToS bits and vice versa.

**Figure 4-3**    *Layer 3 Classification IP Precedence/DSCP*

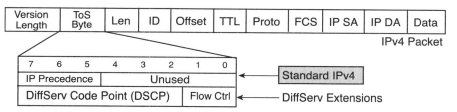

Figure 4-3 also shows Differentiated Services (DiffServ). DiffServ is a new model in which traffic is treated by intermediate systems with relative priorities based on the ToS field. It is defined in RFCs 2474 and 2475. As shown in Figure 4-3, the 6 most significant bits in the ToS byte are called Differentiated Services Code Point (DSCP). The last 2 bits are reserved for flow control and currently are not used. The intermediate devices in the network use the DSCP values set in the IP packet to determine the per-hop behavior (PHB).

When you turn on the auxiliary VLAN feature on an access port on a Cisco switch, two things happen:

1  The switch port is set to an 802.1 Q trunk port.

2  The switch starts sending the VVID information via the Cisco Discovery Protocol (CDP) on the switch port.

If a Cisco IP Phone is connected to a switch port that is configured with auxiliary VLAN, the IP Phone obtains the VVID configured on the switch via CDP. Cisco IP phones store this information in the Operational VLAN ID field.

However, when you are deploying Cisco IP Phones that are connecting to non-Cisco switches that do not have the auxiliary VLAN feature, you have to manually configure the voice VLAN on each Cisco IP Phone. This results in higher administrative and operational overhead and is not scalable for large networks. You can use the Admin VLAN ID field in the Cisco IP Phones to manually assign the VVID.

---

**TIP**       To view the Operational VLAN ID and Admin VLAN ID settings on Cisco IP Phone model 7960G, click the Settings button and select the Network Configuration option. These two values are listed in items 19 and 20, respectively.

---

In many Cisco IPT networks, IP phones are connected to the access layer switches. User workstations are connected to the PC port on the back of the phone. However, you cannot use this method if you are in either of the following two situations:

- Wiring closet switches do not support 802.1p class of service.
- Wiring closet switches do not support 802.1Q VLANs on access ports, and IP address space limitations exist.

Instead of connecting the PC to the PC port on the back of the phone, connect the PC and phone on two separate switch ports. This method consumes additional switch ports in the wiring closet for each IP phone installed but provides a physical delineation between voice and data traffic.

## PortFast

PortFast is a spanning-tree enhancement that is available on Cisco Catalyst switches. PortFast causes a switch or trunk port to enter the spanning-tree forwarding state immediately, bypassing the listening and learning states.

When you connect a Cisco IP Phone to a switch port, enabling PortFast on that port allows the IP Phone to connect to the network immediately, instead of waiting for the port to transition from the listening and learning states to the forwarding state. This feature decreases the IP Phone initialization time because it can send the packets as soon as the physical link is activated.

---

**NOTE**    Do not enable PortFast on a switch port if it is connected to another Layer 2 device. Doing so might create network loops. Enable PortFast only on the ports that are connected to IP phones.

---

Spanning Tree Protocol (STP) is defined in the IEEE 802.1d standard. New standards that are enhancements to IEEE 802.1d are available:

- IEEE 802.1w Rapid Spanning Tree Protocol (RSTP)
- IEEE 802.1s Multiple Spanning Tree (MST)

## UplinkFast

Like PortFast, UplinkFast is the spanning-tree enhancement on Cisco Catalyst switches. Typically, you connect the access layer switch to two distribution layer switches for redundancy and load balancing. When you have two uplinks, one uplink port on the access layer switch is in a blocked state and the other is in an active or forwarding state. If the access layer switch detects a failure on the active uplink (because of the failure of the distribution layer switch or a bad port), use of the UplinkFast feature on the uplink ports immediately unblocks the blocked port on the access layer switch and transitions it to the forwarding state, without going through the listening and learning states. Because of this, the switchover to the standby link happens quickly.

## Deployment Models

Figure 4-4 shows possible deployment models at each layer. The access layer portion of the diagram shows the two models that are available in the access layer.

In the first access layer model, each access layer switch has dual uplinks to distribution layer switches. In this case, we recommend that you split the users among the access switches to address the failure situations.

In the second access layer model, the access switches are daisy chained and do not have dual uplinks to distribution layer switches. You have to be careful for the reasons explained in the next two paragraphs about how many of these low-end switches can be connected in a daisy-chained manner.

Some of the low-end switches include a scheme called "giga-stack," which is a half-duplex environment. A half-duplex environment is bad for voice traffic because it is a collision domain. Because you are compressing voice, you could face voice-quality issues, depending on what kind of compression technique you are using. G.711 is more robust, but if you are using G.729a and lose two consecutive voice packets, the digital signal processor (DSP) will not be able to compensate for this packet loss, and users will likely complain about voice-quality issues.

In a half-duplex environment, you might run into these issues if you have daisy chained too many switches. If you are planning to daisy chain switches, start with a low number. If you have to increase the number of daisy-chained switches, monitor the packet drops and other statistics on the network. Also remember that if any one of the switches in the daisy chain of switches fails, it will cause the subnet to split, and you will run into connectivity issues.

**Figure 4-4**    *Deployment Models*

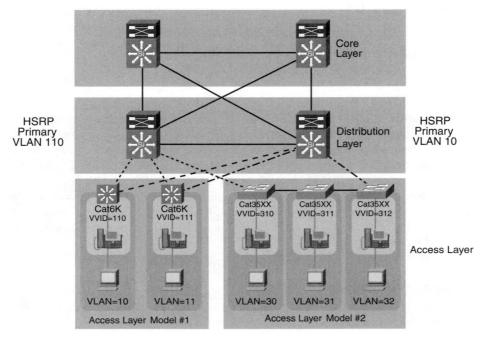

The access layer model 1 is well suited for deploying IPT.

## Distribution Layer

At the distribution layer of the network, you have the following three options for redundancy. You can choose any one or a combination of options, depending on your capabilities and needs.

- Implement redundant distribution layer switches, each with two supervisory modules. In this case, you have two levels of redundancy: switch redundancy and supervisory module redundancy.

- Implement redundant distribution layer switches, each with one supervisory module. In this case, you have only switch redundancy.

- Implement one distribution layer switch with two supervisory modules. In this case, you have supervisory module redundancy.

We recommend that you design the network with redundant distribution layer switches, each with two supervisory modules, as shown in the distribution layer in Figure 4-4, for the highest level of redundancy and load balancing. The network infrastructure below the distribution layer is Layer 2, and it is unaware of Layer 3 information. At the distribution layer, you should implement the Hot Standby Routing Protocol (HSRP) for redundancy between the two distribution layer switches: the primary and secondary switch. You also need to use passive interfaces on distribution layer switches that face the Layer 2 access switches, because they do not require Layer 3 information. Use of passive interfaces stops the propagation of Layer 3 information to Layer 2 switches. With HSRP, you can choose one of the following methods for redundancy:

- Make one switch the primary switch for the whole network and let the network fail over to the secondary switch in case of primary switch failure.

- Make both switches the primary switch for some of the network and the secondary switch for the rest of the network. By using this technique, you can load balance your traffic. One approach is to make one switch primary for the voice VLANs and the second switch primary for the data VLANs.

Because you are now analyzing Layer 3 infrastructure, you should make sure that you follow the Layer 3 guidelines listed here. These guidelines will help you to increase the overall convergence of the network.

- Use Open Shortest Path First (OSPF), Enhanced Interior Gateway Routing Protocol (EIGRP), or Intermediate System-to-Intermediate System (ISIS) Protocol for improved network convergence.

- Follow consistent configuration standards and naming conventions for all routers in the network for better convergence and ease of troubleshooting.

- Implement IP summarization toward the core to reduce routing protocol overhead and to ensure IP scalability.

- Implement stub or default routing in WAN hub-and-spoke environments to reduce routing protocol traffic overhead on WAN links.

- Review routing protocol impact and scalability based on device types, number of routes, and IP routing protocol neighbors.

- Review the timers of your IP routing protocols and tune them as needed for faster convergence only after you have performed thorough testing.

## Core Layer

The core layer of the network should act as a transitory layer. Access switches should not be collapsed on the core layer. With parallel links in the core layer, you can provide redundancy and do load balancing and fast convergence. The core layer is based on Layer 3 protocols. All the guidelines mentioned in the previous "Distribution Layer" section apply to the core layer, too. The top layer in Figure 4-4 depicts the core layer infrastructure.

## Cabling Infrastructure

Different categories of cabling are available when building Ethernet-based networks. Category 5 (Cat 5) cabling is the most commonly used in many networks because it offers higher performance than other categories, such as Cat 4 and Cat 3. Cat 5 cabling supports data rates up to 100 Mbps (Fast Ethernet), whereas Cat 3 cabling supports data rates up to 10 Mbps (Ethernet). The Fast Ethernet specifications include mechanisms for auto-negotiation of speed and duplex.

By default, the switch port and the PC port on the Cisco IP phone are set to auto-negotiate the speed and duplex. Hence, if you are deploying IPT in a network that is built on Cat 3 cabling that supports a speed of only 10 Mbps, you have to manually set the connection between the IP phone and the switch port to 10 Mbps/full duplex to avoid the possibility of this connection negotiating as 100 Mbps/full duplex. This requires manually setting the speed/duplex on every IP phone switch port to 10 Mbps/full duplex, which could become a tedious task and cause administrative overhead in larger deployments.

Also, because the uplink connection from the IP phone to the switch port is 10 Mbps, you need to ensure that users who connect the PC to the back of the IP phone's PC port have their network interface card (NIC) settings set to 10 Mbps/full duplex, and you need to manually set the speed/duplex setting of the PC port on the switch to 10 Mbps/full duplex.

---

**NOTE**     To understand how auto-negotiation works on Ethernet networks, refer to http://www.cisco.com/warp/customer/473/3.html.

---

## Common Guidelines

When you are reviewing the network infrastructure, make sure to provide redundancy at every layer and use standardized software versions throughout the network, to avoid situations in which hardware or software failure impacts the network.

Also, make sure to eliminate single points of failure in all the layers. At the access layer, you have a single point of failure if you do not have two outlets to the desk from two different catalyst switches. This situation applies in all data networks and even in legacy voice networks. If the connection between the IP phone or PC and the access layer switch fails, the device loses the connection. This is also true in legacy phone networks. If the phone line coming to your home fails, you lose the phone connection. The last hop is always a single point of failure, which is unavoidable. We have not seen common scenarios in which two NICs are placed in a PC or two PCs are placed in every office for redundancy, with redundant links from the access layer switch to these devices.

At the distribution layer, you need to make sure that you keep modularity in your network. To do so, plug in these different modules to the distribution layer and keep them separate, as shown in Figure 4-5, where you have WAN, Internet, PSTN, server farm, and internal PC/IP phone users connecting to their own access layer switches. The access layer switches have dual connections to redundant distribution layer switches. The distribution layer switches of each module have dual connections to redundant Layer 3 switches. This strategy provides a robust, highly available, and easy-to-troubleshoot network architecture.

**Figure 4-5**    *Modular Campus Architecture*

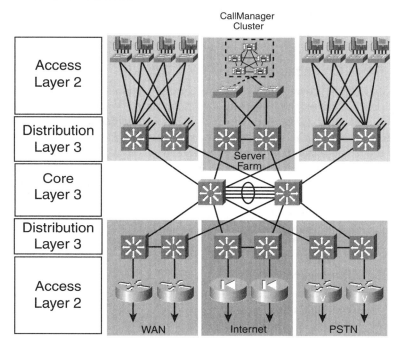

## QoS in Campus Network Infrastructure

Implementing QoS is about giving preferential treatment to certain applications over others during periods of congestion. Which preferential treatments are enabled in a network varies depending on the technology (such as voice and video) and business needs.

QoS is not an effective solution when chronic network congestion occurs. If the network is frequently congested, you need more bandwidth. QoS should be implemented to ensure that critical data is forwarded during occasional brief periods of congestion, such as when there is a link failure and all traffic must traverse the remaining path.

You configure QoS in your network for the times of need. When you are implementing QoS in a network, you need to give voice traffic highest priority, followed by video applications and then data applications. You can divide data applications into multiple classes if necessary, because you might have some data applications that are more critical for your business (such as Systems Network Architecture [SNA] traffic, typically used by IBM mainframe computers) than simple FTP or web applications.

In our experience, voice and data traffic in a network that has not been configured for QoS experiences voice-quality issues because of the differences in the characteristics of traffic and voice traffic.

## Data and Voice Traffic Characteristics

Most data traffic is bursty, delay and drop insensitive in nature (SNA is an exception, which is not drop insensitive), and can always be retransmitted. Voice data, in contrast, is consistent, smooth, and delay and drop sensitive. As mentioned earlier, in the section "Deployment Models," if you are using a G.729a codec and the network drops even two consecutive packets, those drops will result in poor voice quality. There are two types of delay: one-way delay and jitter. The jitter is variation in the delay, which also results in poor voice quality. Voice applications do not retransmit dropped packets, because the retransmission would cause the dropped packets to arrive to the destination even later, resulting in poor voice quality. When you put voice traffic on the same network that is carrying data traffic, you need to make sure that you remember these characteristics of voice and data.

## Oversubscription in Campus Networks

Figure 4-6 shows the access, distribution, and core layers of the network architecture that XYZ built initially for data applications.

**Figure 4-6** *Oversubscription in Campus Networks*

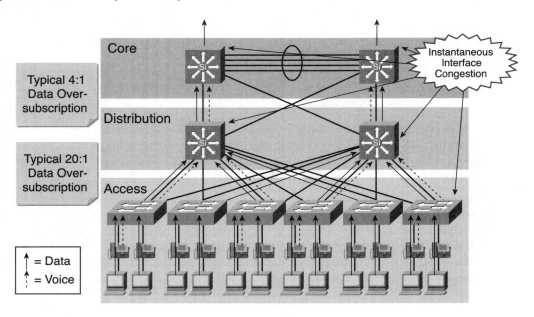

Usually, oversubscription is done at every layer while building the network for data applications. This oversubscription usually works well for data applications because of their nature, as described in the earlier "Data and Voice Traffic Characteristics" section. When adding voice applications to your existing data network, however, you might do either of two things to avoid congestion: redesign your network so that it is less oversubscribed, or add more bandwidth to the network. These two actions by themselves do not provide a voice application–friendly infrastructure. You will encounter interface congestion at the egress interfaces. When you add more bandwidth in the network, the data application characteristics do not change. The data applications have the same bursty nature and try to consume the added bandwidth.

The problem you want to solve is how to eliminate the instantaneous congestion points. When you look at the interface statistics, you might see only 20 percent usage and thus think that no congestion. But you are not seeing the statistics when the congestion occurs, due to some data application that is bursting traffic and consuming the bandwidth of that egress interface, causing the voice packets to drop. This instantaneous congestion in the network introduces bad voice quality. Users might call you at the end of the week and report that this week, they have experienced voice-quality issue twice. Troubleshooting this issue is going to be tough, because your users did not report the problem when they were experiencing the voice-quality issue.

The solution to this problem is to configure QoS in your network. If you have QoS configured in your network, at times of congestion, QoS ensures that voice traffic gets higher priority. QoS is an end-to-end mechanism, which should be configured throughout the network, starting from IP phones, access layer switches, distributions layer switches, and core layer routers.

If you are routing voice traffic over the WAN, you should configure QoS on the WAN routers for the WAN links, too. You should provision your WAN links to carry the additional voice traffic. You need to know how many calls you are sending over your network and how much bandwidth these calls require.

Before enabling end-to-end QoS in your network, you need to define the current and future important and critical applications for your business. Based on the business importance of these applications, you need to find out what the technical requirements are to provide preference to these applications. When planning and reviewing these applications, always keep future applications in mind and leave room in your QoS policy for them. For example, if you are currently planning for data and voice applications, leave room for future video applications in your QoS policy.

## Network Trust Boundaries

The packets that enter your network or hardware can be marked into different classes; you can define the trust boundaries in your network. You can define some devices as trusted devices and some as untrusted devices. The packets that come from trusted devices are considered trusted because the trusted devices classify the packets correctly. The packets that come from untrusted devices are considered untrusted because they might not classify the packets correctly. After you have marked the packets and defined the trust boundaries, you can force the scheduling of the packets into different queues. These queues invoke at the time of congestion.

Defining trust boundaries is important in your network. As shown in Figure 4-7, in the first option, your trust boundary starts from an IP phone. Setting the trust boundary at the IP phone means that you can accept all the IP phone markings into the network without modifications.

In the second option, your trust boundary starts from an access layer switch, which means that the access layer switch is going to be marking the packets.

In the third option, your trust boundary starts from a distribution layer switch, which means that you cannot do anything with your high-priority packets until they reach the distribution layer switch, resulting in possible voice-quality issues.

You should always try to do classification close to the edge of the network, for scalability. This recommendation means that you should choose option one or two while planning for your IPT network. Choosing option one enables the IP phone to queue the packets that it is originating according to their Layer 2 CoS and Layer 3 ToS values.

**Figure 4-7**  *Network Trust Boundaries*

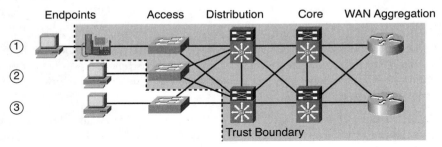

## IP Phone QoS

As mentioned earlier, QoS is an end-to-end mechanism; with IPT networks, QoS starts from the IP phone. As shown in Figure 4-8, a Cisco IP Phone has a built-in three-port 10/100 switch (not all Cisco IP Phones have the PC port on the back of the phone), where port 2 connects to the access layer switch and passes all the traffic to/from ports 0 and 1. Port 0 connects to the IP Phone's application-specific integrated circuit (ASIC) and carries traffic generated from the IP Phone. Port 1 (also called the access port) connects to a PC or any other device and carries traffic generated from there.

**Figure 4-8** *Three-Port 10/100 Switch in IP Phone*

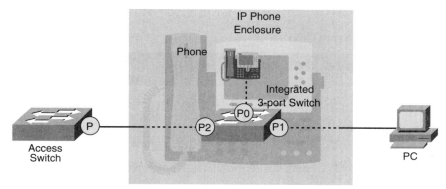

By default, an IP phone marks all the voice-bearer traffic that it generates with a Layer 3 IP precedence value of 5 (DSCP value of 46) and a Layer 2 CoS (802.1p) value of 5. The voice-control traffic is marked with a Layer 3 IP precedence value of 3 (DSCP value of 26) and a Layer 2 CoS (801.p) value of 3.

In Figure 4-8, the untagged data coming from the PC port (with no Layer 2 CoS value) passes through the IP phone unchanged, regardless of the trust boundary. The tagged data (802.1Q/p) from the PC or any other device that is attached to the access port (port P1 in Figure 4-8) of the IP phone can be trusted or untrusted. In trusted mode, the IP phone passes all the data unchanged. In untrusted mode, the IP phone re-marks the Layer 2 CoS value to the new value (if configured on the access layer switch) or changes it to 0, if nothing is configured. The default is untrusted mode, which is the recommend method.

Most of the Cisco switches have support for priority queuing on the egress interfaces. You should perform the configuration on the access, distribution, and core layer switches in such a way that the delay-sensitive packets, such as voice packets and voice-control packets, are placed in the priority queue. If no priority queue exists on the egress interface of a switch that you have in your network, place the delay-sensitive packets in the queue that has the lower drop threshold. Chapter 5, "Design Phase: Network Infrastructure Design," provides some configuration examples of this procedure. If the access layer switch is Layer 3 aware, it can pass the packets marked by the IP phones as unchanged toward the upper layers as long as the access layer switch ports are configured to trust the packets coming from the IP phones.

If the access layer switch is Layer 2 aware, the packets are sent to the next layers unchanged.

When voice packets reach the distribution layer switch (entering the Layer 3 boundary domain), they are mapped to corresponding Layer 3 ToS bits (IP Precedence and DCSP) and shipped to the core layer. The core layer forwards the packets based on the ToS bit values. When packets cross the Layer 3 boundary and enter the Layer 2 domain, you must remap Layer 3 ToS values to Layer 2 CoS values. Layer 2 CoS and Layer 3 ToS values are backward compatible, as shown in Figure 4-9. Figure 4-9 also depicts the use of Layer 2 CoS and Layer 3 QoS values in different applications.

**Figure 4-9**   *Layer 2 CoS and Layer 3 QoS Chart*

| L2 | L3 Classification | | | Application |
|----|----------|-----|------|-------------|
| CoS | IP Prec. | PHB | DSCP | |
| 7 | 7 | - | 56-63 | Reserved |
| 6 | 6 | - | 48-55 | Reserved |
| 5 | 5 | EF | 46 | Voice Bearer |
| 4 | 4 | AF41 | 34 | Video Conferencing |
| 3 | 3 | AF31 | 26 | Call Signaling |
| 2 | 2 | AF2y | 18,20,22 | High-Priority Data |
| 1 | 1 | AF1y | 10,14,16 | Medium-Priority Data |
| 0 | 0 | BE | 0 | Best-Effort Data |

**NOTE**   The new IETF standard recommends that you mark signaling packets with a DSCP value of 24 (PHB value CS3) instead of the currently used value of DSCP 26 (PHB AF31). Only a few endpoints, such as Cisco IP Communicator and Cisco IP SoftPhone products, implemented this new change. Hence, until this new marking takes effect in all the products, reserve both values for signaling in the network.

## Inline Power for IP Phones

The first-generation Cisco IP Phones received power through external power supplies. Later, Cisco invented the concept of supplying inline power to Cisco IP Phones by using the same Ethernet pair used to send data (Power over Ethernet [PoE]). The inline power has two ends. One end is the switch, which sends the 48V DC power on the same Ethernet pair used to send data. The other end is the Cisco IP phone, which can accept power on the same pair used for data or Cisco IP Phones can use the unused pair for accepting the inline power. The reason for supporting these two options on the Cisco IP phones is that some of the switches do not have the capability to provide inline power. In this scenario, you can use a power patch panel—the power comes from the switch to the patch panel, and the patch panel uses the unused Ethernet pair to send the inline power to the IP phone.

Cisco IP Phones are capable of accepting inline power and can inform the switch how much power they need. This allows the switch to allocate the correct amount of power to the Cisco IP Phone without over- or underallocating power. Initially, the switch does not know how much power a Cisco IP Phone is going to need, so it assumes it needs the user-configured default allocation. After the IP phone is booted, it sends a CDP message to the switch with a type, length, value (TLV) object that contains information about how much power it needs. At this point, the switch adjusts its original allocation and returns any remaining power to the system for use on other ports.

**NOTE**    IEEE has recently approved a new inline power standard, IEEE 802.3af. Cisco is complying with this new IEEE standard.

Since the ratification of the Power over Ethernet (PoE) standard IEEE 802.3af, Cisco has shipped the new Cisco IP Phone 7970G, which is compatible with this new standard. The new generation of Cisco IP Phones that will be released in the future will support both Cisco PoE and IEEE 802.3af PoE mechanisms. The Cisco IP Phones shipped prior to the ratification of the standard support only Cisco PoE. Hence, if you are deploying Cisco IP Phones in a network without Cisco switches, your options are as follows:

- Use the Cisco IP Phones that support IEEE 802.3af, provided your switch supports IEEE 802.3af.
- Use the external power patch panel to supply the power to Cisco IP Phones.

High-end catalyst switches such as Cisco 6000 series switches use inline-power daughter cards that sit on the 10/100 modules to provide the power to Cisco IP phones. If your network currently uses Cisco PoE, you can do a field upgrade to replace the Cisco PoE daughter cards with IEEE 802.3af inline-power daughter cards. The new IEEE 802.3af–compliant inline-power daughter cards support both Cisco PoE and IEEE 802.3af PoE. Thus, you can still have the old Cisco IP Phones that use Cisco PoE and also have new Cisco IP Phones that use IEEE 802.3af PoE.

Refer to the "Power and Environmental Infrastructure" section later in this chapter for more information on how to plan for a scalable, highly available, redundant power infrastructure.

## Wireless IP Phone Infrastructure

This section discusses briefly the integration of wireless IP phones in your infrastructure planning, as shown in Figure 4-10. As discussed earlier, in the "Access Layer" section, the purpose of keeping the VLAN in the closet is to limit the spanning tree in the closet. There are some exceptions to this rule; one of them applies when using wireless IP phones. If you want to use wireless IP phones and roaming, you have to do this on Layer 2. You will create a single wireless VLAN for wireless IP phones, which will span the closets. Because you can support spanning tree per VLAN, the wireless VLAN is going to be the only VLAN that is affected with longer convergence times, if there is a problem. Make sure that you allow the wireless IP phones to use only this wireless VLAN (WLAN).

**Figure 4-10** *WLAN Infrastructure*

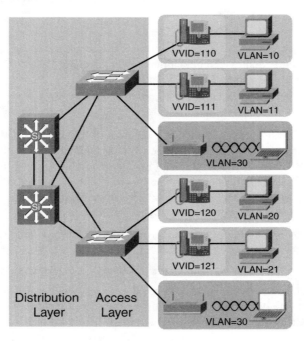

# WAN Infrastructure

To support toll-quality voice traffic over your existing WAN, you have to re-engineer your WAN to support QoS and call admission control (CAC). Traditional telephony networks are connection oriented. If all 23 DS0s are in use, a PBX with a T1-PRI connection to the PSTN rejects the 24th call, because no physical channel is available to place the 24th call. In contrast, IP networks are connectionless in nature. Therefore, if you have a 128-kbps Frame Relay link supporting two good-quality 64-kbps (without considering protocol overhead) G.711 VoIP calls, and a request to place a third call is allowed, this would result in degradation of the voice quality of the existing two calls. To avoid oversubscribing the WAN links, you have to use CAC when transporting voice traffic on the WAN, as discussed in Chapter 1 in the "Next-Generation Multiservice Networks" section.

Based on presently available WAN technologies, you have to deploy a physical or virtual hub-and-spoke topology to make sure that you do not oversubscribe on the WAN links, as shown in Figure 4-11.

**Figure 4-11**    *Hub-and-Spoke WAN Topology*

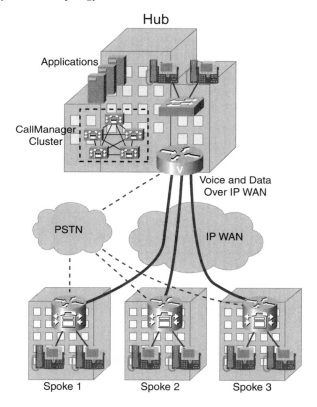

The full or partially meshed topology cannot give the control you need to deploy CAC and QoS. The following are some of the available WAN technologies that can provide QoS:

- Leased lines
- Frame Relay (FR)
- ATM
- ATM/FR service interworking
- Multiprotocol Label Switching (MPLS) VPN
- Voice- and video-enabled IP Security (IPSec) VPN (V3PN)

By using QoS on any of the preceding WAN technologies, you can get guaranteed good-quality voice. Other WAN technologies, such as DSL and cable, can provide best-effort quality voice rather than guaranteed good-quality voice. The reason for this is that the cable/DSL service providers use the public Internet to transport the data and voice packets, which does not guarantee the delay and priority treatments that are required for voice traffic.

In the planning phase of the IPT deployment, you need to first obtain the information about the existing WAN architecture and WAN circuit characteristics. The "Wide Area Network" section in the Network Infrastructure Analysis Questionnaire in Appendix B assists you in gathering the information.

XYZ is currently using a combination of FR and ATM WAN technologies on its WAN. Table 4-1 summarizes the XYZ WAN circuit characteristics.

**Table 4-1**   *XYZ WAN Circuit Characteristics*

| Link Name | WAN Router Model | Speed and WAN Type (ATM, FR, or Leased Line) | Current Utilization | CIR (if ATM or FR) |
|---|---|---|---|---|
| Seattle – San Jose | Seattle Router 3745 | 1 Mbps, FR | 60% | 1 Mbps |
| Dallas – San Jose | 2651 XM | 512 kbps, FR | 50% | 512 kbps |
| San Jose (Headend) | 7200 | 1.5 Mbps, ATM | 50% | 1 Mbps |
| Melbourne – Sydney | Melbourne Router 3745 | 512 kbps, FR | 40% | 256 kbps |
| Brisbane – Sydney | 2651 XM | 256 kbps, FR | 40% | 256 kbps |
| Sydney (Headend) | 7200 | 1.5 Mbps, ATM | 50% | 1.5 Mbps |
| San Jose-Sydney | 7200 | 2 Mbps, leased line | 50% | 2 Mbps |

CIR = committed information rate

## QoS in WAN Infrastructure

Packet loss, one-way delay, and jitter (variation in delay) were discussed earlier in the context of the campus QoS infrastructure. These parameters become even more important in a WAN environment. Although you often hear that bandwidth is getting cheaper, most enterprise networks still have less WAN bandwidth than is actually needed. It is important to understand the various techniques that are available to reduce packet loss, delay, and jitter in the WAN circuits:

- Minimizing delay
- Using traffic shaping
- Provisioning WAN bandwidth

- Using voice compression

Understanding these techniques helps you to properly provision the WAN circuits in the real world.

## Minimizing Delay

Figure 4-12 shows the components that introduce delay and the mechanisms that are available in routers that can minimize these delays to achieve good voice quality. The objective behind using the mechanisms is to achieve the ITU G.114 recommendation of 0- to 150-ms one-way delay for the voice packet.

**Figure 4-12**   *End-to-End Delay Components*

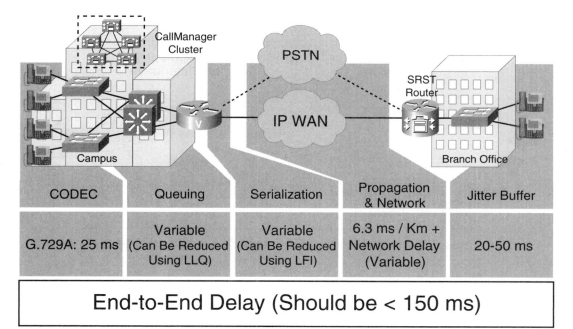

### CODEC Delay

The first delay component is the delay that the voice codec introduces. The codec takes the voice sample, processes it, and creates a voice packet. The time taken for this process depends on the type of codec that is selected. The G.729a codec, shown in Figure 4-12, takes 25 ms to take two voice samples (10 ms for each voice sample plus a 5-ms look-ahead time) and put them into a packet before it can send this packet. Other codec types take about the same time except G.711, which takes less time.

## Queuing Delay

As shown in Figure 4-12, the second component that introduces delay is queuing delay. Congestion in the network invokes the queuing in the routers. At times of congestion, packets start to build up in the queues within the routers. The packets in the queues eventually transmit, when congestion goes away, causing delay. The queuing mechanism you should use on the WAN links to reduce this delay is called Low Latency Queuing (LLQ), also known as Priority Queuing/Class-Based Weighted Fair Queuing (PQ/CBWFQ), as shown in Figure 4-13.

**Figure 4-13** *PQ/CBWFQ and LFI Operation*

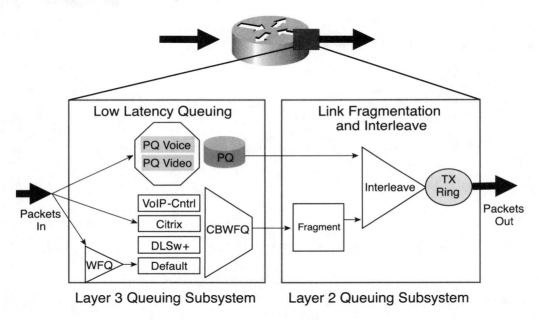

In Figure 4-13, the priority queue holds all the voice and delay-sensitive traffic, such as the following:

- **Voice traffic**—CoS value of 5, IP Precedence value of 5, DSCP value of 46, PHB value of EF

- **H.323 video-conferencing traffic**—CoS value of 4, IP Precedence value of 4, DSCP value of 34, PHB value of AF41

The CBWFQ holds voice-signaling traffic and data traffic:

- **Voice-signaling traffic**—CoS value of 3, IP Precedence value of 3, DSCP value of 26, PHB value of AF31

- **Data traffic**—Different priorities of data traffic

## Serialization Delay

As shown in Figure 4-12, the third component that introduces delay is serialization delay. Table 4-2 shows the serialization delay matrix.

**Table 4-2**    *Serialization Delay Matrix*

| Link Speed | Frame Size | | | | | |
|---|---|---|---|---|---|---|
| | **64 Bytes** | **128 Bytes** | **256 Bytes** | **512 Bytes** | **1024 Bytes** | **1500 Bytes** |
| 56 kbps | 9 ms | 18 ms | 36 ms | 72 ms | 144 ms | 214 ms |
| 64 kbps | 8 ms | 16 ms | 32 ms | 64 ms | 128 ms | 187 ms |
| 128 kbps | 4 ms | 8 ms | 16 ms | 32 ms | 64 ms | 93 ms |
| 256 kbps | 2 ms | 4 ms | 8 ms | 16 ms | 32 ms | 46 ms |
| 512 kbps | 1 ms | 2 ms | 4 ms | 8 ms | 16 ms | 23 ms |
| 768 kbps | 640 µs | 1.2 ms | 2.6 ms | 5 ms | 10 ms | 15 ms |

You derive the delay values in the table by calculating the time it would take to send 1 byte on the circuit for the appropriate speed. The following example illustrates the calculation of serialization delay for a 56-kbps circuit.

56 kbps/8 bits = 56000/8 bits = 7000 bytes per second
1 second/7000 bytes per second = 143 microseconds to transmit 1 byte

You can then extrapolate the serialization delay for various byte sizes by multiplying the time required for 1 byte at a given circuit speed times the frame size to be sent. The following example illustrates the serialization delay for a 1500-byte packet on a 56-kbps circuit:

143 microseconds for 1 byte at 56 kbps × 1500 bytes = 214 ms for a 1500-byte frame at 56 kbps

From the previous calculation, you can see that a 1500-byte packet takes 214 ms to reach from one end to the other end on a 56-kbps link. Therefore, if a 1500-byte packet is in the transmit queue on a router in front of a small voice packet that has a requirement of 0- to 150-ms one-way delay, the voice packet has to wait at least 214 ms before it can be placed on the wire. As the link speed increases, the time required to transmit the 1500-byte packet from one end to the other end decreases. For example, in Figure 4-14, the same 1500-byte packet takes only 15 ms to make it to the other end on a 768-kbps circuit.

When using a 768-kbps or lower-speed link, you always encounter this problem in which you have different large-size packets causing delay to small, constant-size voice packets. The varying sizes of the large packets cause voice packets to arrive at the destination at irregular intervals. This variation in delay is called jitter. You can reduce the delay introduced by the large packets and the jitter condition by using Link Fragmentation and Interleaving (LFI) mechanisms such as Multilink PPP (MLPPP) on point-to-point links, ATM, Frame Relay and ATM Service Inter-Working (SIW) environments, and FRF.12 in Frame Relay environments. When using a

768-kbps or lower-speed link, use LFI mechanisms to fragment the large data packets and interleave small voice packets between the fragmented data packets (refer to Figure 4-13).

## Propagation Delay

As shown in Figure 4-12, the fourth component that is a source of delay is propagation delay. Propagation delay is the amount of time it takes to transmit the bits of packets on the physical wire. The factors that influence propagation delay are the physical circuit distance between the source router and the destination router and the type of circuit media that is used, such as fiber-optic link or satellite link. Propagation delay is generally fixed but grows as the length of travel from source to destination. Consider the propagation delay especially if the connecting media is a satellite link that introduces large amounts of delay. A voice packet traveling across this media might not meet the ITU-T recommendation of less than 150 ms one-way delay if all the other delay factors are combined.

## Jitter Buffer

As shown in Figure 4-12, the fifth source of delay is the jitter buffer. Depending on the type of codec in use, the jitter buffer size could change. The jitter buffer holds about two and one-half voice packets (each voice packet has a couple of 10-ms voice samples) and is dynamic in nature. The rate at which the voice packets arrive at the jitter buffer is uneven. The jitter buffer looks at the time stamps of the arriving voice packets to create a large enough jitter buffer. Then it stores and plays the voice packets to the user in a constant and even manner, so that the user is not interrupted. If you have excessive jitter in your network and the jitter buffer cannot hold that many packets, these packets are dropped. It is important to control the jitter in your network by using a combination of LLQ/PQ-CBWFQ, LFI, and traffic shaping.

# Using Traffic Shaping

The job of a router is to transmit packets as fast as possible and put them on the wire. If you have a 64-kbps link and a Committed Information Rate (CIR) of 32 kbps on your FR or ATM link, the router does not consider the 32-kbps CIR and tries to send the packets at the rate of 64 kbps. More or less, every router tries to transmit more than its respective CIR assigned by the provider on the FR and ATM networks. This causes congestion within the network and eventually results in packet drops. When you want to transmit voice packets over the FR and ATM networks, you have to change the traffic pattern, because you cannot afford the voice packet loss. You have to make sure that the router considers the CIR value.

The traffic-shaping functionality on the router delays the excess traffic in a buffer and shapes the flow to ensure that packets are not transmitted above the CIR values.

You should also make sure that you take care of line-speed mismatch between the central and remote sites. As shown in Figure 4-14, if you have a central site with a T1 link speed and a remote site with a 64-kbps link speed, you should not try to send data at T1 speeds to the remote site, because the remote site is not capable of receiving data at T1 speeds.

**Figure 4-14** *Mismatch of Speeds Between Central and Remote Sites*

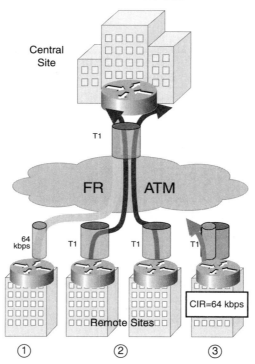

Even if you try to send data at T1 speeds, it will sit in the egress queue of the central site router, causing extra delay for your voice packets. When supporting voice, you cannot use oversubscription between your remote and central sites. Traffic shaping helps you to engineer your network in a way that you do not run into issues related to the following:

- Line-speed mismatch
- Remote site to central site oversubscription
- Bursting above CIR

## Provisioning WAN Bandwidth

After you have deployed QoS in your campus and WAN infrastructure, one of the most important steps is to provision the WAN links in your network. You should make sure that the sum of voice, video, voice-control, video-control, and data traffic does not exceed 75 percent of your link bandwidth. You want to leave 25 percent of the link capacities for the critical traffic such as routing protocol traffic, which keeps your network up and running.

Table 4-3 shows the voice bandwidth consumption based on the choice of codec and the sampling rate. Note that the bandwidth values shown in the rightmost column include only Layer 3 overhead.

**Table 4-3**   *Voice Bandwidth Consumption (Without Layer 2 Overhead)*

| Codec | Sampling Rate | Voice Payload in Bytes | Packets per Second (pps) | Bandwidth per Conversation |
|---|---|---|---|---|
| G.711 | 20 ms | 160 | 50.0 | 80.0 kbps |
| G.711 | 30 ms | 240 | 33.3 | 74.7 kbps |
| G.729a | 20 ms | 20 | 50.0 | 24.0 kbps |
| G.729a | 30 ms | 30 | 33.3 | 18.7 kbps |

You also need to consider Layer 2 overhead when provisioning the WAN bandwidth. Table 4-4 provides the voice bandwidth consumption with Layer 2 overhead taken into consideration.

**Table 4-4**   *Voice Bandwidth Consumption (with Layer 2 Overhead)*

| Codec Sampling Rate | Ethernet 14 Bytes of Header | PPP 6 Bytes of Header | MLPPP 10 Bytes of Header | Frame Relay 4 Bytes of Header | ATM 53-Byte Cells with a 48-Byte Payload |
|---|---|---|---|---|---|
| G.711 at 50.0 pps<br><br>Sampling rate 20 ms | 85.6 kbps | 82.4 kbps | 84 kbps | 81.6 kbps | 106 kbps |
| G.711 at 33.3 pps<br><br>Sampling rate 30 ms | 78.4 kbps | 76.3 kbps | 77.3 kbps | 75.7 kbps | 84.8 kbps |
| G.729a at 50.0 pps<br><br>Sampling rate 20 ms | 29.6 kbps | 26.4 kbps | 28.0 kbps | 25.6 kbps | 42.4 kbps |
| G.729a at 33.3 pps<br><br>Sampling rate 30 ms | 22.4 kbps | 20.3 kbps | 21.3 kbps | 19.7 kbps | 28.3 kbps |

As you can see in Table 4-3, increasing the sampling rate reduces the bandwidth required per conversation, because more voice samples are sent in a single IP packet, thus reducing the protocol overhead. This is especially attractive in ATM networks. Table 4-4 shows that increasing the sampling rate to 30 ms for the G.729a codec reduces the bandwidth utilization by 37 percent compared to using the sampling rate of 20 ms when using ATM. You can change the sampling rate for the codecs in CallManager by modifying the following service parameters:

- PreferredG711MillisecondPacketSize (default 20 ms)
- PreferredG723MillisecondPacketSize (default 30 ms)
- PreferredG729MillisecondPacketSize (default 20 ms)

These parameters are cluster-wide parameters and affect all the IPT devices that are attached to the cluster.

However, before you decide to change the sampling rate, you need to be aware of two factors: This change adds more latency due to packetization and serialization delay, and if you lose one packet, it can affect voice quality because you are losing more information than that contained in a smaller sample. So, when you are doing bandwidth provisioning, you have to keep in mind the voice- and video-control traffic. The voice- and video-control packets are small, but you need to reserve the bandwidth for these call-control packets. Refer to the CallManager Solution Reference Network Design Guide (SRND), *IP Telephony Solution Reference Network Design for Cisco CallManager 4.0,* available on Cisco.com at http://www.cisco.com/go/srnd, to determine the amount of bandwidth that you need to reserve.

## Using Voice Compression

Voice packets are carried using RTP, UDP, and IP as a protocol stack. The IPv4 header is 20 bytes, the UDP header is 8 bytes, and the RTP header is 12 bytes, totaling 40 bytes of header information, as shown in Figure 4-15.

**Figure 4-15**   *RTP Header Compression*

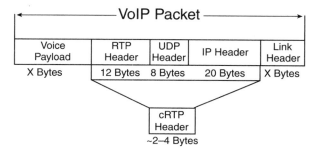

After this 40 bytes of header information, two 10-byte frames (the Cisco G.729a codec implementation) of real voice payload are carried, totaling another 20 bytes of voice payload. Simple math shows that the header is twice the size of the real payload. To address this particular issue, an RTP header compression technique called compressed RTP (cRTP) is used on low-speed point-to-point links. When enabled on a router, cRTP compresses the 40-byte header to 2 or 4 bytes. This dramatically reduces the bandwidth required per call, as shown in Table 4-5. Referring to Table 4-4, a G.729a call at 50 pps on a PPP link requires 26.4 kbps of bandwidth. Referring to Table 4-5, the same call with cRTP requires only 12 kbps, a 45 percent savings in the bandwidth required. This means that you can send more calls within the same WAN link without increasing the bandwidth on the link. However, keep in mind that enabling cRTP on a router requires extra processing power on both ends of the link. One link compresses and the other decompresses, resulting in extra work on both routers.

Hence, you should restrict the use of cRTP on low-speed point-to-point links. On high-speed links, it is better not to use cRTP, because you have enough bandwidth and you can avoid putting extra pressure on both routers of the point-to-point link. However, if your voice traffic on the high-speed links amounts to more than 30 percent of the link capacity, you can enable cRTP to save costs.

**Table 4-5** *Bandwidth Consumption with cRTP (Including Layer 2 Headers)*

| Codec | PPP 6 Bytes of Header | Frame Relay 4 Bytes of Header | ATM 53-Byte Cells with a 48-Byte Payload |
|---|---|---|---|
| G.711 at 50.0 pps | 68.0 kbps | 67.0 kbps | 85 kbps |
| G.711 at 33.3 pps | 66.0 kbps | 65.5 kbps | 84.0 kbps |
| G.729a at 50.0 pps | 12.0 kbps | 11.2 kbps | 21.2 kbps |
| G.729a at 33.3 pps | 10.1 kbps | 9.6 kbps | 14.1 kbps |

**NOTE** An online voice codec bandwidth calculator tool is available on Cisco.com, at http://tools.cisco.com/Support/VBC/do/CodecCalc2.do. This tool calculates the bandwidth requirements per voice call.

To accurately provision the WAN bandwidth, you need to obtain the following information:

- What are the various traffic flows across the WAN link?
- Are there requirements to give priority treatment for a specific traffic flow?
- What is the WAN technology deployed?
- What is the current utilization of the WAN link?
- What is the choice of the codec and the sampling rate?

- How many voice calls are required across the WAN?
- Is RTP compression required to save the bandwidth?

After you have the previous information, with the help of Tables 4-4 and 4-5, you can determine the amount of bandwidth required for the voice traffic.

Figure 4-16 summarizes all the techniques and features discussed and recommended at different layers in the network infrastructure to provide end-to-end guaranteed delivery of your voice traffic.

**Figure 4-16**    *IPT Network with End-to-End Guaranteed Delivery*

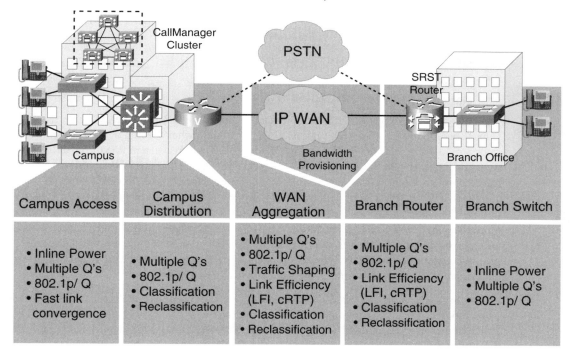

As stated earlier, XYZ is planning to deploy voice applications on its existing data network. To do so, it has to deploy the right set of QoS parameters on its campus and WAN networks. This chapter has provided you the best practices for implementing QoS in the LAN/WAN environments to deploy IPT. Chapter 5 uses these best practices and some of the information collected in this chapter regarding the XYZ network to design its network to support voice applications.

# Network Services

Network services are critical to the overall functionality of IPT environments. The major network services are DHCP, DNS, Network Time Protocol (NTP), and directories and messaging.

## DHCP

All IPT implementations should implement DHCP for IP phone provisioning; otherwise, manual phone configuration is required, which is not a recommended practice. The DHCP service should support adding custom option 150, or you can use option 66 to support Cisco IPT deployment. DHCP uses options to pass IP configuration parameters to DHCP clients. The following are some commonly used options:

- **Option 003**—IP address of the default gateway/router
- **Option 006**—DNS server IP addresses
- **Option 066**—TFTP boot server host name

The custom option types are configurable parameters in the DHCP server, which passes the values specified in these custom options to DHCP clients when leasing the IP configuration information. Most options are defined in DHCP RFC 2132. You can define the custom options based on need. IP phones and other IPT endpoints in a Cisco IPT network can receive the information about the TFTP server via custom option 150 or option 66. The endpoints then contact the TFTP server to download the configuration files. The advantage of using custom option 150 over option 66 is that you can configure an array of IP addresses corresponding to more than one TFTP server in custom option 150, whereas option 66 allows you to configure only one host name. IP phones and other IPT endpoints understand the array of IP addresses listed in custom option 150 and use this multiple TFTP server information to achieve redundancy and load balancing of the TFTP server in the IPT network.

If your network already uses a DHCP server to lease out the IP addresses for the PCs/workstations, you can use the same server to lease out the IP addresses for the IPT endpoints as long as they support custom option 150 or option 66. In small-scale IPT deployments, involving 500 or fewer IP phones, you can enable the DHCP server service on the CallManager Publisher to lease the IP addresses to the endpoints. For larger deployments, you should consider separating the DHCP server function-ality from the CallManager Publisher server to avoid the extra CPU utilization of the DHCP service.

When you are deploying Cisco IPT solutions, use of custom option 150 is recommended because of its ability to send the TFTP server information as an IP address (or as multiple addresses to achieve load balancing and redundancy) instead of as a single host name, as in the case of option 66.

## DNS

DNS translates domain names to IP addresses and vice versa. This process is also referred to as name resolution. You can use the local name resolution methods by using the LMHOSTS/HOSTS file on each server. The following list gives you some of the processes that depend on name resolution when deploying the Cisco IPT solution:

- The SQL replication process keeps the SQL database information synchronized among all the CallManager servers in the cluster. SQL replication processes on each server use the local LMHOSTS/HOSTS file to learn about the other servers in the cluster. Hence, the recommendation is to use the LMHOSTS/HOSTS file resolution method. (See the note following this list.)

- If you are using DHCP option 66, which allows you to configure only the host name, IP phones and other IPT endpoints need to contact the DNS server to resolve the TFTP server name to an IP address. Therefore, you should provision the DNS server to resolve the TFTP server name to an IP address.

- If you are using DHCP custom option 150, use the array of IP addresses for this option rather than the host names, to avoid the dependency on the DNS server. If you choose to use the host name, ensure that the DNS server is provisioned to resolve the TFTP server name(s) to an IP address.

- If you are planning to use MGCP gateways in the IPT network, you have to enter the router/switch host name in CallManager while configuring the MGCP gateway. If the router/switch is configured with the domain name (by using the **ip domain-name** *word* command), you must configure the fully qualified domain name (FQDN) in CallManager instead of just the host name. For example, if your router/switch host name is 3745-GW and you configured the domain name as xyz.com (using the **ip domain-name xyz.com** command on the router/switch), then, in CallManager, when you are configuring the gateway, you should use 3745-GW.xyz.com as the MGCP domain name. In this case, CallManager needs to contact the DNS server to resolve the 3745-GW.xyz.com name to an IP address. You can get away without using the DNS name by configuring the static name resolution entry in the HOSTS file. However, in a network with a large number of gateways, this becomes a tedious task.

- If you are considering CallManager directory integration with an external directory (refer to the "Directories and Messaging" section later in this chapter), you should use the DNS name of the domain controller when configuring and installing the directory plug-in instead of specifying an IP address. You can configure DNS to return more than one IP address for a single host name. That way, CallManager can contact the alternate domain controller if the first domain controller is not reachable.

**NOTE** To use local name resolution using the LMHOSTS/HOSTS file, you need to configure the mapping of host names and IP addresses in each file. These files are located in the C:\WINNT\ system32\drivers\etc directory on CallManager servers and other Cisco IPT application servers. The disadvantage of using this method is that you need to visit each server and update the files whenever you make changes such as adding, deleting, or modifying the name-to-address mappings for the servers. The benefit of using this name resolution method is that you avoid the dependency on the DNS services.

## NTP

NTP service ensures that all the network devices synchronize their clocks to a network time server. If you already have an existing NTP server in the network, you should configure all the IPT devices (such as CallManager servers, voice gateways, and other IPT application servers) to use the same NTP server. Refer to the following Cisco.com web page to find out how to configure CallManager and other IPT application servers to synchronize their time with the NTP server:

http://www.cisco.com/en/US/partner/products/sw/voicesw/ps556/ products_configuration_example09186a008009470f.shtml

## Directories and Messaging

As discussed in Chapter 1, in the "CallManager Directory Services" section, embedded in CallManager is an LDAP-compatible directory called DC Directory (DCD), which can be integrated with corporate directories such as Microsoft Active Directory and Netscape Directory. Directories store employee-related information such as e-mail ID, phone numbers, location, and so forth. Cisco IPT applications use DCD to store user information such as password, PIN number, phone number, speed dials, and so forth.

If your enterprise already has Active Directory or Netscape Directory deployed, you can integrate Cisco IPT applications with such external directories without using the embedded directory. This directory integration reduces the administrative overhead by providing a single repository for all the applications (IPT and enterprise applications). If you are considering directory integration, you need to understand the directory architecture before you proceed with the integration. XYZ uses Microsoft Active Directory and requires corporate directory access from the IP phones. XYZ does not want to use directory integration.

If you are considering deploying unified messaging, you also need to understand the architecture of the existing messaging network. Chapter 7, "Voice-Mail System Design," discusses this in more detail. XYZ uses a Microsoft Exchange–based e-mail messaging application and wants to deploy a unified messaging system.

So far, this chapter has discussed how to analyze the existing LAN/WAN infrastructure and the availability of various network services. The following section looks at the power and environmental infrastructure. This infrastructure plays a major role in IPT deployments, because when you deploy IPT, you need to plan and provision your power infrastructure to handle the power requirements not only for CallManager and other application servers, but also for the numerous endpoints such as the Cisco IP Phones.

## Power and Environmental Infrastructure

Lack of power and environmental reliability can dramatically affect overall IPT network availability. Even short-term outages require rebooting of affected equipment, increasing the length of time that equipment is unavailable.

Deployment of an IPT solution to take advantage of inline power–capable switches and IP phones decreases the cost of maintenance and enables faster deployment. In this method of deployment, IP phones receive power from the attached LAN switches. Hence, deployment of redundant power supplies in the wiring closet switches ensures high availability. In addition, battery power backup systems and generator backup systems make the network highly available.

Power and environmental planning is not unique to IPT deployments. Legacy phones also generally receive power from the legacy switch with UPS and generator power provided for the PBX.

The following factors affect power- and environmental-related availability:

- Availability and capacity of the power backup systems, such as the uninterruptible power supply (UPS) and generators

- Whether or not network management systems are used to monitor UPS and environmental conditions

- Whether recommended environmental conditions such as heating, ventilation, and air conditioning (HVAC) for network equipment are maintained

- Availability and quality of the surge-protection equipment used in the infrastructure

- Natural threats inherent in the geographic location of equipment, such as lightening strikes, floods, earthquakes, severe weather, tornados, or snow/ice/hail storms

- Whether the power cabling infrastructure installed is conformant to National Electrical Safety (NEC) and IEEE wiring standards for safety and ground control

- Whether during power provisioning process factors such as circuit wattage availability and circuit redundancy for redundant equipment and power supplies are taken into consideration

- Reliability of the IPT equipment sourcing the power to the IP Phones

When deploying IPT, calculate the amount of power required ahead of time by taking into consideration the number of in line powered IP phones and the additional number of servers such as CallManager and other application servers. While designing the IPT solution, ensure that, where possible, multiple power drops and redundant power supplies are provisioned in the network to further boost the availability of each device.

Table 4-6, from American Power Conversion (APC), provides power availability estimates with various power-protection strategies.

**Table 4-6**    *Power Availability and Protection Strategies*

|  | Raw AC | 5-Minute UPS System | 1-Hour UPS System | UPS System w/ Generator | Power Array w/ Generator |
|---|---|---|---|---|---|
| Event Outages | 15 events | 1 event | .15 event | .01 event | .001 event |
| Annual Downtime | 189 minutes | 109 minutes | 10 minutes | 1 minute | 6 seconds |
| Power Availability | 99.96% | 99.979% | 99.998% | 99.9998% | 99.99999% |

Source: American Power Conversion, Tech Note #24

From Table 4-6, it is clear that to achieve five 9's of power availability, you need a UPS system with a generator.

When you are deploying an IPT solution with inline power capable switches in the wiring closets, it is essential to calculate the capacity of the power supplies required in each wiring closet. To make this calculation, you need to make a list of the following items:

- The switches and routers in the network that need to provide the inline power to IP phones
- The switch/router hardware platform
- The quantity of IP phones, along with model numbers, that connect to each closet switch (power consumption varies between IP phone models)
- Other modules that are installed in the switch

To determine the power supply requirements of the Cisco switches and routers, to provide inline power to IP phones, use the web-based Cisco Power Calculator, available at http://tools.cisco.com/cpc/launch.jsp.

**NOTE**     At the time of planning, you would not have decided which switches to use to connect the IP phones, or the quantity and type of IP phone models required in the network. Hence, it is impossible at this stage to determine the total power consumption and switch power supply capacity requirements. Typically, you finalize which IP phone models and quantity to use during the design phase. Because power is an infrastructure component, all the information that is required to properly size the power is covered in this chapter, and Appendix B includes the tables to document the switch/router inventory.

# Telecom Infrastructure Analysis

This section examines the XYZ telecom infrastructure. The Telecom Infrastructure Analysis Questionnaire, included in Appendix C, assists you in conducting this analysis. You need to conduct this analysis to understand how the current telecom infrastructure is built and how it operates. Based on this information, you can design the IPT network so that it operates in a similar way, and at the same time introduce new features and services. The information presented in this section uses answers that XYZ provided to the questions in the questionnaire.

## PBX Infrastructure and Migration

XYZ requires replacement of the PBX systems at all the remote branch locations and at the Sydney HQ location, except at the San Jose location, as mentioned in Chapter 3.

The PBX at the San Jose site requires integration with the new IPT system. Table 4-7 provides the details of the PBX systems at the San Jose and Sydney locations. This information helps you to determine what types of gateways are required to achieve the integration, what features in CallManager need to be enabled, etc.

**Table 4-7**     *Details of XYZ PBX Systems*

| Site | PBX Vendor Model Software Version | PSTN Interface Signaling | Interface Type to IPT System | Number of T1 Trunks to PSTN |
|------|-----------------------------------|--------------------------|------------------------------|-----------------------------|
| San Jose | Lucent/Avaya Definity G3Si<br><br>Version 10 | T1-PRI NI 2 | T1-QSIG | 6 |
| Sydney | Lucent/Avaya Definity G3Si<br><br>Version 10 | E1-PRI NET5 | E1-QSIG | 4 |

The large user presence at the San Jose site prevents a complete forklift of the PBX system. Hence, a slow migration is required at this site. A discussion with the PBX staff at San Jose proposed the solution described next for smooth migration of users to the IPT system.

As shown in Table 4-7, the San Jose site has six T1 trunks. At the beginning of the IPT deployment in the San Jose site, only four of the T1 trunks that are currently terminating on the PBX will be moved to voice gateways in the IPT system. In Sydney, you need to plan a complete migration to IPT. All users will retain their old PBX extensions after the migration to the new IPT system. When a user moves to the IPT system, the legacy PBX is configured to forward the calls to their IP phone.

At the end of the complete migration of users to the IPT system, all the remaining T1/E1 trunks will be moved to voice gateways. At this point, the legacy PBX systems might be removed.

## Telephony Numbering Plan

XYZ uses a four-digit dial plan at every central and remote branch location. After the migration to IPT, each user will retain their old extension number on the new IP phones. At all sites, the carrier sends all the digits to the PBX. PBX retains only the last four digits to extend the call to the end station.

Table 4-8 provides information on the PSTN trunk types, Direct Inward Dial (DID) numbering ranges, and numbering plan for each site of XYZ.

**Table 4-8**   *Current Numbering Plan at XYZ*

| Site Name | DID Range | Station Directory Range | Type of PSTN Signaling |
|---|---|---|---|
| San Jose | +1 408 555 3000 to +1 408 555 4999 | IP Phone DNs 3000–4999 | 6 T1 PRI NI2 |
| | +1 408 555 2500 to +1 408 555 2999 | PBX station DNs 2500–2999 | |
| Seattle | +1 206 555 2100 to +1 206 555 2199 | 2100–2199 | 1 T1-PRI |
| Dallas | +1 972 555 5600 (grouped line) +1 972 555 5611 (fax) | 5601–5619 (Non-DID numbers, private numbering plan) | 1 T1-PRI |
| Sydney | +61 2 5555 6000 to +61 2 5555 6999 | 6000–6999 | 4 E1 PRI ISDN Net 5 |
| Melbourne | +61 3 5555 4300 to +61 3 5555 4399 | 4300–4399 | 1 E1 PRI ISDN Net 5 |
| Brisbane | +61 7 5555 8680 (grouped line) | 8681–8699 (Non-DID numbers, private numbering plan) | 1 E1 PRI ISDN Net 5 |

## Voice-Mail Infrastructure and Migration

From the initial requirements given in Chapter 3, XYZ has two voice-mail systems: one at San Jose and the other at Sydney. The Simplified Message Desk Interface (SMDI) integration method integrates the Octel voice-mail system with the PBX systems. The deployment of IPT enables migration of user mailboxes from Octel systems to the Cisco Unity system in a phased manner. As per the XYZ requirements, discussed in Chapter 3, in the "Integration and Replacement of Legacy Voice-mail Systems" section, Cisco Unity will be deployed in Sydney with the unified messaging mode in redundant fashion and the Octel voice mail systems in San Jose will continue to exist.

During the migration, XYZ requires all the users to be able to send and receive between the Octel voice-mail system in San Jose and the Cisco Unity system in Sydney. This requires networking of Cisco Unity and Octel voice-mail systems. The Cisco Unity Bridge application provides intermessaging between Cisco Unity and Octel voice-mail systems.

## Emergency Services

Today, XYZ uses basic 911 service, in which calls are forwarded to a public safety answering point (PSAP). There is no guarantee that the call reaches the correct PSAP, and the PSAP does not get information about the location of the caller.

The Enhanced 911 (E911) solution, an advanced version of basic 911 services in North America, addresses the user mobility issue and provides the following benefits:

* Automatically provides the location of the caller to the PSAP
* Calls reach the right PSAP based on the user location

Cisco Emergency Responder (CER) tracks user movements and sends the user's current location information to the PSAP. CallManager provides the basic functionality required to route the emergency calls.

The XYZ branch offices are located in Seattle, Washington, and Dallas, Texas. As discussed in Chapter 1, in the "Cisco Emergency Responder" section, these two states do not require businesses to comply with E911 (as of the time of writing the design proposal). Hence, you do not need to design the IPT network with CER.

## Telephony Features and Applications

The current PBX systems at the San Jose and Sydney central sites support basic functions, such as call forwarding, call transfer, call conferencing, and the following applications:

* Auto-Attendant
* An internal help desk support group with 10 agents supporting internal IT issues of XYZ
* An external help desk support group with 40 agents supporting XYZ product issues

XYZ requires the future IPT network to migrate all the legacy applications to the IPT system. In addition, XYZ would like to implement the following functionality in the newly built IPT system:

- IP phone services
  - Corporate directory lookup from IP phones
  - Calendar and other useful services
- Extension Mobility feature for mobile users
- Cisco IP SoftPhone support for a few users

# Business Continuity and Disaster Recovery

Before you deploy any new product or system in the network, it is important to understand not only the potential underlying risks and impact of disasters, but also how to quickly recover from such situations and document these procedures by developing a business-continuity or disaster recovery plan.

In legacy voice networks, the central component of call processing are the PBX/key systems. A PBX system comes with dual process cards so that a failure of one card does not affect business operations. In a similar way, the Cisco IPT system offers grouping of CallManager servers to form a CallManager cluster. A cluster offers high availability. A failure of a single server in the cluster does not impact the call processing.

An organization that is looking for a high level of business continuity in case of any disaster should consider splitting a single CallManager between multiple data centers. Refer to the "Clustering over the IP WAN" section in Chapter 1 to understand this design and recommended best practices.

The second factor that affects business continuity is the availability of the backup power, as discussed earlier in this chapter in the "Power and Environmental Infrastructure" section.

You need to include the IPT systems as part of your backup operations and protect the systems from viruses and other security attacks by installing antivirus tools.

# Securing IPT Infrastructure

The Internet has made it easy for anyone to access different denial of service (DoS) tools, viruses, and applications that are used for financial fraud, theft of information, and sabotaging data or networks. Usually, someone writes an application and puts it on the Internet, available for everyone to grab.

Many tools are easily available on the Internet to attack networks. These include, among many others, tools to carry out DoS attacks, VLAN attacks, Address Resolution Protocol (ARP) attacks, MAC attacks, and spanning tree attacks. If you are deploying real-time applications into your data networks, you need to make sure that security breaches are prevented. These security breaches can slow down or bring down the network, causing the network to be unable to support voice calls. You need to make sure that your internal and external network is not misused in any way. For example, if someone tries to introduce large amounts of traffic across your WAN link, it results in  dropped voice calls. This is a potential case of DoS attack and, in this situation, having the right set of QoS policies and CAC in place prevents the excessive traffic and avoids the call drops.

Deciding which security measures to implement requires that you balance how much risk you are willing to accept and how much money you are ready to spend to protect your network against security breaches.

Regardless of your decision, you have to make sure that your network is built following a layered approach and you have taken the necessary measures to secure it at every layer.  This means that compromised security at any one layer does not compromise security at every layer. For example, if someone is able to break the password and get into one of the VLANs, IP phones, CallManager, or any other network component, they should not be able to get into the whole network. PC endpoints usually require user authentication, but typically IP phones do not. You have to realize that if you want to build a secure IPT network, you have to build it on a secure data network. If your data network is not built securely, you will not be able to build a secure IPT network.

Remember that now your voice is traveling over your existing data network. Some of the simple steps to provide security include having separate voice and data VLANs, using access control lists (ACLs), and using firewalls.

Chapter 6 provides security recommendations to protect the XYZ IPT infrastructure.

## Redundancy and High Availability

The key component of network design is redundancy. Redundancy not only prevents equipment failures from causing service outages, but it also provides a means for performing maintenance activities such as upgrades without impacting the service.

The predominant factor that determines the effectiveness of a redundancy scheme is the switchover coverage, defined as the probability of a successful switchover to the standby side whenever needed. Switchover coverage of 0.9 indicates that, on average, when a switchover is required, nine out of ten incidents will be successful. The chart in Figure 4-17 illustrates the impact of switchover coverage on the downtime of a system.

**Figure 4-17**  *Impact of Switchover Coverage*

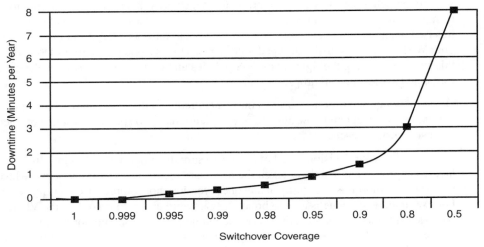

Switchover coverage of 0 is equivalent to a simplex (nonredundant) system, thus rendering the redundancy setup completely ineffective. Switchover coverage of 1 represents an ideal redundancy setup; it reduces the downtime of a simplex system by about four orders of magnitude. Although it is difficult to achieve perfect coverage, a good redundancy design can achieve coverage of 0.99, which offers a downtime improvement over a simplex system by about two orders of magnitude.

Availability refers to the percentage of total time that a network or system is available for use. A network or system that has high availability includes specific design elements that are intended to keep the availability above a high threshold (for example, 99.999 percent).

XYZ requires the highest level of availability at every layer and component of the network. The following is a list of a few design principles to achieve high availability:

- **Maximize the redundancy**—Maximizing the redundancy allows you to provide uninterruptible service to the end users. An example is a CallManager cluster, which contains more than one server and provides call-processing redundancy. Another example is the XYZ LAN infrastructure, which has two distribution layer switches and two core layer switches to provide redundancy.

- **Minimize complexity**—Reducing complexity minimizes the time to rectify problems, thereby increasing the overall availability of the system or device.

- **Minimize points of single failure**—Minimizing single points of failure increases the redundancy in the network. An example is a connection to the PSTN. If you have only a single T1/E1 circuit that, for some reason, goes down, no one from that location can make outbound calls. Hence, you should plan for redundant circuits to minimize these types of single points of failure.

As you have seen in the infrastructure analysis, XYZ has a high level of availability and redundancy in its current infrastructure. Chapter 6 provides recommendations to achieve the same level of high availability and redundancy for the IPT infrastructure of XYZ.

# IPT Network Management System

Each IPT deployment is different, but generally, a Cisco AVVID IPT environment includes a CallManager cluster, IP phones, a PSTN gateway(s), a voice-mail system (Cisco Unity and/or a legacy voice-mail system), L2/L3 switches, routers, and applications such as Automated Attendant, Personal Attendant, Emergency Responder, CCC, CRS, and others.

While you are planning for management and monitoring of an IPT network, the main goal should be to define a list of parameters that can be proactively monitored in an IPT environment. The output of these predefined parameters is intended to establish a set of alarms for spontaneous problems and a proactive early-warning system that is based on comparing baseline data to current conditions.

The following two steps help you to define a solid management and monitoring policy for your IPT network:

- Define a set of parameters that needs to be monitored on every component of your IPT network.

- Select IPT network management and monitoring products and tools that are capable of monitoring the defined set of parameters.

Several products and tools are available to manage and monitor your IPT network. The CiscoWorks IP Telephony Environment Monitor (ITEM) product gives real-time, detailed fault analysis specifically designed for Cisco IPT networks and other products from third-party vendors. It is a proactive tool to evaluate the health of IPT implementations. Cisco ITEM provides alerting and notification of problems and areas that you should address to help minimize IPT service interruption. Cisco ITEM also identifies the underutilized or imbalanced gateway resources, whereas its historical trending and forecasting of future capacity requirements helps you to plan for growth.

Given the type of IPT infrastructure, CallManager server health, CallManager services health, CallManager functionality, IP phones functionality, IP gateway health, QoS monitoring, L2/L3 switches, and applications are some components that we recommended for monitoring your IPT network.

XYZ requires proper network management tools to monitor its IPT infrastructure. Chapter 9, "Operations and Optimization," discusses in detail the parameters, tools, and techniques for managing and monitoring IPT networks.

# Summary

This chapter provided the tasks and best practices involved in the planning phase of the IPT deployment. It used XYZ's answers to the questionnaires provided in Appendixes B and C to plan the IPT network. You have also seen the steps that are required to ensure that the infrastructure is ready to carry the converged traffic. Based on all the information collected and the current state of the XYZ network, Chapter 5 covers the design of network infrastructure, such as enabling QoS in the LAN/WAN, to support the IPT rollout for XYZ.

# Design Phase: Network Infrastructure Design

The design phase is the second step in the planning, design, implementation, operation, and optimization (PDIOO) life cycle. Whereas Chapter 4, "Planning Phase," discussed the best practices in designing the LAN/WAN infrastructure, this chapter provides configuration steps and sample configurations for the devices based on the XYZ, Inc. network topology and requirements. Topics in this chapter include the following:

- Understanding call-processing architecture
- Selecting IP Phones
- Designing network infrastructure:
  - Designing an IP addressing and VLAN scheme
  - Designing DHCP/TFTP services
  - Configuring QoS in LAN/WAN

## Call-Processing Architecture

The proposed call-processing architecture for XYZ, Inc., uses centralized call processing with remote branches model, as discussed in the "IP Telephony Deployment Architecture" section of Chapter 1, "Cisco IP Telephony Solution Overview." This architecture provides telephony services to XYZ, Inc., across the main and remote branch sites. At the Australia location, Cisco Unity Voice Mail deployment is also centralized. Unity is deployed at the main site in Sydney, allowing Australian users to access it remotely.

Based on the information collected in Chapter 3, "Large-Scale Enterprise Requirements for IP Telephony," Figure 5-1 shows the high-level system architecture of the proposed IP Telephony (IPT) solution for XYZ, Inc.

**Figure 5-1** *XYZ IPT Deployment Model*

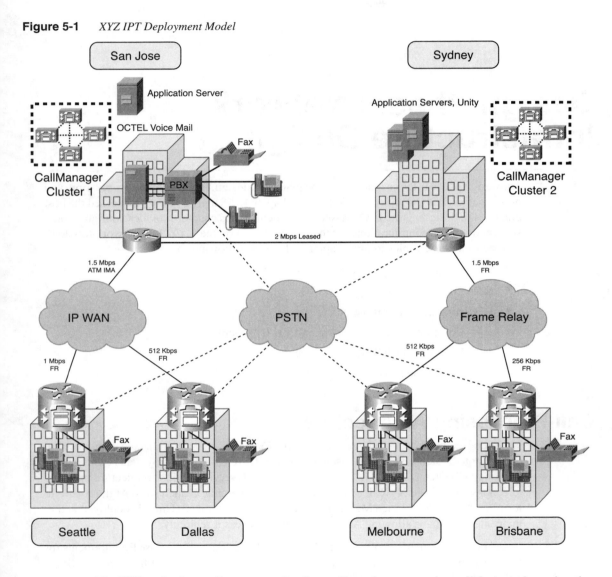

The PBX and voice-mail systems at San Jose will continue to coexist until the complete migration to IPT is completed. IP Phones at the remote sites use the CallManager cluster at the central sites for call processing under normal operations, replacing the PBXs at these remote sites.

The solution proposes to deploy two centralized call-processing clusters to handle the IPT needs of XYZ. The San Jose CallManager cluster provides call processing for the telephony devices in the San Jose, Seattle, and Dallas sites. The Sydney cluster provides call processing for the telephony devices in the Sydney, Melbourne, and Brisbane sites. An IP WAN interconnects all the sites. The PSTN serves as a backup connection between the sites in case the WAN connection fails or does not have enough bandwidth to carry the voice calls.

**NOTE**    XYZ has only one data center, in San Jose, for its entire U.S. operations. In large-scale deployments, if you have multiple data centers, you should split the CallManager cluster to place some servers in the first data center and the remaining servers in the second data center. This design approach provides spatial redundancy. Refer to the "Clustering over the IP WAN" section of Chapter 1 for guidelines on implementing this type of design. In a single data center scenario, place the servers on different switches to improve the redundancy.

# IP Phone Selection

Table 5-1 shows the number of users and IP Phones planned at each site. The number of IP Phones shown includes the user phones and the phones required in the conference rooms, break rooms, lobby, and other common areas.

**Table 5-1**    *Number of Users and IP Phones in Each Site*

| Site Name | Number of Users | Number of IP Phones |
|---|---|---|
| San Jose—headquarters | 1000 | 1100 |
| Seattle—branch | 50 | 56 |
| Dallas—branch | 15 | 24 |
| Sydney—headquarters | 500 | 545 |
| Melbourne—branch | 40 | 52 |
| Brisbane—branch | 10 | 12 |

A large selection of IP Phones is available. Based on the needs and the telephony services required by XYZ, Table 5-2 compiles the models and numbers of end-user terminals that this deployment will use. The 7960s are allocated to managers and assistants. All other workers will use either the 7940 or the 7960. Lobby and common areas are provisioned with 7905 model IP Phones.

**NOTE**    You can use Appendix A, "IP Phone Models and Selection Criteria," and Appendix D, "IPT Design Phase: IP Phone Selection Questionnaire," to gather the end users' IP Phone requirements and to determine which IP Phone models you need for each site.

**Table 5-2** *Number and Type of Devices in Each Location*

| Site Name | Phone Model | Number of Phones |
|---|---|---|
| San Jose—headquarters | 7960G IP Phones | 200 |
| | 7940G IP Phones | 820 |
| | 7905G IP Phones | 30 |
| | 7936 IP Conferencing Stations | 50 |
| | 7914 Expansion Modules | 20 |
| Seattle—branch | 7960G IP Phones | 10 |
| | 7940G IP Phones | 42 |
| | 7936 IP Conferencing Stations | 2 |
| | 7914 Expansion Modules | 2 |
| | 7905G IP Phones | 2 |
| Dallas—branch | 7960G IP Phones | 15 |
| | 7940G IP Phones | 7 |
| | 7914 Expansion Module | 1 |
| | 7936 IP Conferencing Station | 1 |
| | 7905G IP Phone | 1 |
| Sydney—headquarters | 7960G IP Phones | 200 |
| | 7940G IP Phones | 310 |
| | 7936 IP Conferencing Stations | 15 |
| | 7914 Expansion Modules | 10 |
| | 7905G IP Phones | 20 |
| Melbourne—branch | 7960G IP Phones | 40 |
| | 7914 Expansion Modules | 2 |
| | 7940G IP Phones | 10 |
| | 7936 IP Conferencing Station | 1 |
| | 7905G IP Phone | 1 |
| Brisbane—branch | 7960G IP Phones | 2 |
| | 7914 Expansion Module | 1 |
| | 7940G IP Phones | 8 |
| | 7936 IP Conferencing Station | 1 |
| | 7905G IP Phone | 1 |

The "Power and Environmental Infrastructure" section in Chapter 4 provides the information that you need to determine the additional hardware requirements, such as the number of inline power modules and the capacity of the power supplies required in the access layer switches to support the inline power to IP Phones.

In the XYZ network, at the central sites, access layer switches are Catalyst 6500 switches that have inline power capable 10/100 line cards. All IP Phones connect to the access layer switches. The remote-site access devices are either inline power capable or upgradeable to support the inline power. XYZ decided to go with the Cisco inline power standard method to supply the power to IP Phones.

# Network Infrastructure Design Tasks

Chapter 4 discussed the details of the network infrastructure design and requirements to support the converged network. This section applies the design tasks and concepts learned in Chapter 4 to the XYZ network architecture.

To support the converged data and voice traffic, the network infrastructure should have proper quality of service (QoS) mechanisms enabled at the following network infrastructure elements:

- Access, distribution, and core layer switches and routers
- WAN aggregation routers
- Remote-site routers

This section discusses the steps that you need to take to ensure that the XYZ network is ready to support IPT.

## Designing IP Addressing and VLAN Scheme

The existing IP addressing scheme used for the data network at XYZ is collected with the help of Appendix B, "IPT Planning Phase: Network Infrastructure Analysis Questionnaire." With this information, the next step is to design the IP addressing and VLAN scheme for the IPT network throughout the XYZ network. Table 5-3 shows the VLAN and subnet design for the converged network.

You arrive at IP addressing and VLAN scheme shown in Table 5-3 by following these guidelines:

- Use the RFC 1918 address space (nonroutable) to assign the IP addresses to the IPT devices to tighten the security of the telephony network.
- Implement separate VLANs for data and voice networks.
- Do not place all the IPT call-processing servers and application servers in a single VLAN. This approach prevents Layer 2 issues such as a faulty NIC on one server bringing down all servers, thereby causing a major network failure.

- Whenever possible, design the IP addressing scheme so that you can do route summarization to optimize the IP routing table sizes in the routers.

- Establish a standard naming convention to assign the VLAN IDs and IP addresses. This greatly helps later in troubleshooting and managing the network. For example, in Table 5-3, the servers are assigned to a VLAN with the name SJC_SRV1.

**Table 5-3**   *VLAN/Subnet Assignment for XYZ Network*

| Location | VLAN ID | VLAN Name | VLAN Subnet | Description |
|----------|---------|-----------|-------------|-------------|
| San Jose | 3 | SJC_SRV1 | 10.1.1.0/27 <br> GW: 10.1.1.1 <br> HSRP1: 10.1.1.2 <br> HSRP2: 10.1.1.3 | VLAN for publisher server, TFTP server, DHCP[1] server, subscriber 1, IVR[2] 1, and other existing data center servers such as DNS[3] servers, mail servers, and so on. |
| | 4 | SJC_SRV2 | 10.1.1.32/27 | VLAN for subscriber 2, IVR 2, and other exiting data center servers |
| | 5 | SJC_media | 10.1.1.64/27 | VLAN for gateways, conferencing, and transcoding resources |
| | 11 | SJC_voice1 | 10.1.11.0/24 <br> GW: 10.1.11.1/24 <br> HSRP1: 10.1.11.2/24 <br> HSRP2: 10.1.11.3/24 | IP Phones |
| | 12 | SJC_voice2 | 10.1.12.0/24 | IP Phones |
| | 13 | SJC_voice3 | 10.1.13.0/24 | IP Phones |
| | 14 | SJC_voice4 | 10.1.14.0/24 | IP Phones |
| | 15 | SJC_voice5 | 10.1.15.0/24 | IP Phones |
| | 111 | SJC_data1 | 10.1.111.0/24 | User PCs |
| | 112 | SJC_data2 | 10.1.112.0/24 | User PCs |
| | 113 | SJC_data3 | 10.1.113.0/24 | User PCs |
| | 114 | SJC_data4 | 10.1.114.0/24 | User PCs |
| | 115 | SJC_data5 | 10.1.115.0/24 | User PCs |
| Seattle | 21 | SEA_voice1 | 10.2.1.0/24 | IP Phones |
| | 211 | SEA_data1 | 10.2.11.0/24 | User PCs |
| Dallas | 31 | DAL_voice1 | 10.3.1.0/24 | IP Phones |
| | 311 | DAL_data1 | 10.3.11.0/24 | User PCs |

**Table 5-3**    *VLAN/Subnet Assignment for XYZ Network (Continued)*

| Location | VLAN ID | VLAN Name | VLAN Subnet | Description |
|---|---|---|---|---|
| Sydney | 4 | SYD_SRV1 | 10.4.1.0/27<br>GW: 10.4.1.1<br>HSRP1: 10.4.1.2<br>HSRP2: 10.4.1.3 | CallManager publisher server, subscriber 1, and Unity 1 |
| | 5 | SYD_SRV2 | 10.4.1.32/27 | CallManager subscriber 2 and Unity 2 |
| | 6 | SYD_GW | 10.4.1.64/27 | Sydney gateways |
| | 11 | SYD_voice1 | 10.4.11.0/24 | IP Phones |
| | 12 | SYD_voice2 | 10.4.12.0/24 | IP Phones |
| | 13 | SYD_voice3 | 10.4.13.0/24 | IP Phones |
| | 411 | SYD_data1 | 10.4.111.0/24 | User PCs |
| | 412 | SYD_data2 | 10.4.112.0/24 | User PCs |
| | 413 | SYD_data3 | 10.4.113.0/24 | User PCs |
| Melbourne | 51 | MEL_voice1 | 10.5.1.0/24 | IP Phones |
| | 511 | MEL_data1 | 10.5.11.0/24 | User PCs |
| Brisbane | 61 | BRI_voice1 | 10.6.1.0/24 | IP Phones |
| | 611 | BRI_data1 | 10.6.11.0/24 | User PCs |

[1] DHCP = Dynamic Host Configuration Protocol

[2] IVR = interactive voice response

[3] DNS = Domain Name System

# Designing DHCP and TFTP Services

After you finalize the IP addressing and VLAN assignment, the next step in the infrastructure design is to identify how the IP Phones receive the IP addressing information. DHCP provides an easy way to allocate and manage the IP addressing.

For XYZ, a separate DHCP server is provisioned in San Jose to lease out the IP addresses for IPT endpoints that are located in San Jose. In Sydney, the CallManager publisher server acts as the DHCP server for IPT endpoints in Sydney. The remote-site routers in the U.S. and Australian locations lease out the IP address to the endpoints that are located in the remote sites. Table 5-4 summarizes the DHCP servers and various configurations required per site.

As discussed in Chapter 1 in the "CallManager Clustering" section, the TFTP server stores the configuration information and binary loads for the IP Phones and other IPT endpoints. For the San Jose CallManager cluster, the DHCP server also performs the role of a TFTP server. In Sydney, the CallManager publisher server acts as a TFTP server.

In both clusters, the DHCP server is configured to send the TFTP server the IP address in DHCP custom option 150 to Cisco IP Phones and other endpoints. Because each cluster has a single TFTP server, the value of custom option 150 for all the scopes in San Jose points to the TFTP server in San Jose. Similarly, the DHCP option 150 value for all scopes in Sydney points to the IP address of the CallManager publisher server in Sydney, which is performing the job of TFTP server.

---

**NOTE**     The best practice is to off-load the DHCP and TFTP services from the publisher for any IPT deployments that involve more than 500 IP Phones.

---

**Table 5-4**     *DHCP Server Information for the XYZ Network*

| Location | DHCP Server | DHCP Settings |
|----------|-------------|---------------|
| San Jose | Name: *SJCDHCPTFTP*<br>IP addr: 10.1.1.7/27 | **Common Parameters**<br>DNS domain name: XYZ.com<br>Lease interval: 8 hours<br>DNS server: 10.1.1.20<br>Option 150: 10.1.1.8<br>**Scope 1**<br>Address range: 10.1.11.5–254<br>Subnet mask: 255.255.255.0<br>Default GW: 10.1.11.1<br>**Scope 2**<br>Address range: 10.1.12.5–254<br>Subnet mask: 255.255.255.0<br>Default GW: 10.1.12.1<br>**Scope 3**<br>Address range: 10.1.13.5–254<br>Subnet mask: 255.255.255.0<br>Default GW: 10.1.13.1<br>**Scope 4**<br>Address range: 10.1.14.5–254<br>Subnet mask: 255.255.255.0<br>Default GW: 10.1.14.1<br>**Scope 5**<br>Address range: 10.1.15.5–254<br>Subnet mask: 255.255.255.0<br>Default GW: 10.1.15.1 |

**Table 5-4**    *DHCP Server Information for the XYZ Network (Continued)*

| Location | DHCP Server | DHCP Settings |
|---|---|---|
| Seattle | 3745 router in Seattle<br>Name: *R3745-SEA*<br>IP addr: 10.2.1.1 | **Pool: IP_PHONES_SEA**<br>Address range: 10.2.1.5–254<br>Subnet mask: 255.255.255.0<br>Default GW: 10.2.1.1<br>Option 150: 10.1.1.7 |
| Dallas | 2651XM router in Dallas<br>Name: *R2600-DAL*<br>IP addr: 10.3.1.1 | **Pool: IP_PHONES_DAL**<br>Address range: 10.3.1.5–254<br>Subnet mask: 255.255.255.0<br>Default GW: 10.3.1.1<br>Option 150: 10.1.1.7 |
| Sydney | CallManager publisher<br>Name: *SYDCCMA-PUB*<br>IP addr: 10.4.1.5 | **Common Parameters**<br>DNS domain name: XYZ.com<br>Lease interval: 8 hours<br>Option 150: 10.4.1.5<br>**Scope 1**<br>Address range: 10.4.11.5–254<br>Subnet mask: 255.255.255.0<br>Default GW: 10.4.11.1<br>**Scope 2**<br>Address range: 10.4.12.5–254<br>Subnet mask: 255.255.255.0<br>Default GW: 10.4.12.1<br>**Scope 3**<br>Address range: 10.4.13.5–254<br>Subnet mask: 255.255.255.0<br>Default GW: 10.4.13.1 |
| Melbourne | 3745 router in Melbourne<br>Name: *R3745-MEL*<br>IP addr: 10.5.1.1 | **Pool: IP_PHONES_MEL**<br>Address range: 10.5.1.5–254<br>Subnet mask: 255.255.255.0<br>Default GW: 10.5.1.1<br>Option 150: 10.4.1.5 |
| Brisbane | 2651XM router in Brisbane<br>Name: *R2600-BRI*<br>IP addr: 10.6.1.1 | **Pool: IP_PHONES_BRI**<br>Address range: 10.6.1.5–254<br>Subnet mask: 255.255.255.0<br>Default GW: 10.6.1.1<br>Option 150: 10.4.1.5 |

# Central Site LAN Infrastructure

This section discusses the tasks involved in making the central site LAN infrastructure at San Jose and Sydney sites ready to support IPT. Figure 5-2 shows the XYZ LAN architecture at central sites San Jose and Sydney. The central sites use Catalyst 6500 switches at the access, distribution, and core layers.

**Figure 5-2**  *XYZ IPT LAN Architecture at Central Sites*

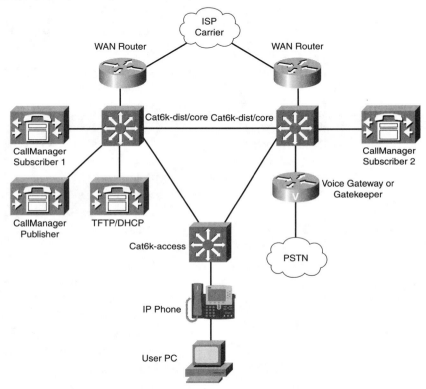

# Central Site LAN QoS Design

Use of the QoS features that are available in the network devices ensures voice quality in a converged network. These features must be enabled end to end in a converged network to provide high-quality voice services.

In high-bandwidth LANs (10/100/1000 Mbps Ethernet networks), the QoS concern is the smaller buffers in the switches rather than bandwidth or transmission delays. Therefore, the main objective becomes protecting time-sensitive traffic from buffer limitations.

Use the following guidelines when designing the LAN QoS for IPT networks:

- Protect the voice traffic against packet drops caused by buffers or queues overflowing.
- Protect video traffic and any other time-sensitive traffic against packet drops caused by buffers or queues overflowing.
- Protect against individuals inadvertently or intentionally configuring their workstations to send packets by setting a high-priority Type of Service (ToS) byte.
- Provide a trusted edge or trust boundary at the LAN edge to help ensure that classification is done specifically for WAN QoS.
- Implement the WAN QoS configuration as accurately as possible, keeping the available bandwidth and traffic flows in mind.

The QoS policies that enforce the trusted edge verify the proper classification of class of service (CoS), ToS, and Differentiated Services Code Point (DSCP) values. LAN switches can trust incoming CoS values, allowing them to queue the traffic based on CoS values. The LAN device hands off Layer 3 IP precedence bits to the WAN device based on the recommended traffic classification for various types of traffic, as shown in Table 5-5. When deploying QoS in the network, you need to identify the number of classes of service (traffic types) that exist in the network and the type of treatment required for each traffic type.

Also refer to Figure 4-9 in Chapter 4, which shows the detailed Layer 2 and Layer 3 classification values for various types of applications.

**Table 5-5**    *Traffic Classification Recommendations*

| Traffic Type | Layer 2 COS | Layer 3 IP Precedence | Layer 3 DSCP (PHB) |
|---|---|---|---|
| Voice RTP[1] | 5 | 5 | 46 (EF[2]) |
| Voice control (SCCP[3], H.323, MGCP[4]) | 3 | 3 | 26 (AF[5]31) 24 (CS3)* |
| Data | 0–2 | 0–2 | 10–22 (0–AF23) |
| Video | 4 | 4 | 34 (AF41) |

[1] RTP = Real-Time Transport Protocol
[2] EF = Expedited Forwarding
[3] SCCP = Skinny Client Control Protocol
[4] MGCP = Media Gateway Control Protocol
[5] AF = Assured Forwarding

**NOTE**    The new Internet Engineering Task Force (IETF) standard recommends that the signaling packets be marked with DSCP value 24 (per-hop behavior [PHB] value CS3) rather than the currently used value DSCP 26 (PHB AF31), as shown in Table 5-5. Only a few endpoints, such as Cisco IP Communicator and Cisco IP SoftPhone products, implement this new change. Therefore, until this new marking is incorporated in all the products, you should reserve both values for signaling in the network.

At XYZ's San Jose and Sydney sites, the campus layer access switches are Catalyst 6500s with Policy Feature Cards (PFCs). The PFC on the Catalyst 6500 is an important component of the switch QoS functionality because it provides the capability to handle classification and marking in the IP packet at Layer 3, instead of being limited to the Layer 2 CoS values learned from 802.1p. When you are working with a Catalyst 6500 switch without a PFC, or any Layer 2 switch that can perform only Layer 2 CoS marking, you have to rely on distribution and core layer switches that can map Layer 2 CoS values to Layer 3 ToS values accurately.

XYZ is using Catalyst 6500 switches at access, distribution, and core layers, so this section covers the configuration details for Catalyst 6500 switches. The QoS Solution Reference Network Design (SRND) that is available on Cisco.com covers the configuration guidelines for other switches.

Note that the concepts and design principles remain the same regardless of the type of switch deployed in the network. The only difference you notice is in the syntax required to configure the switches.

## Access Layer Catalyst 6500 QoS Configuration Guidelines

As mentioned earlier, the classification and honoring of classified packets is an end-to-end process. The first component of this end-to-end topology could be an IP Phone. The Cisco IP Phone sets the Voice over IP (VoIP) traffic (RTP) to CoS 5 and the voice-control traffic (SCCP) to CoS 3.

Access layer switches classify the packets at the edge of the network. This classification helps to identify the type of the packet and special treatment requirements such as priority queuing or routing. IEEE 802.1p is a Layer 2 standard (CoS packet classification methodology) that has the capability to classify packets, as shown in Table 5-5. Figure 5-3 summarizes the QoS configurations that are required at every layer for the XYZ central sites.

Configuration guidelines for the access layer 6500 switches at the central sites are as follows:

**Step 1**   Configure access switch ports where IP Phones are connected.

The following example shows the Catalyst 6500 access switch configuration, where the ports are configured for inline power, speed, voice, and data VLANs. Refer to Table 5-3, and observe the VLAN IDs and subnets that are configured for voice and data VLANs for the San Jose central site.

```
cat6k-access> (enable) set port inlinepower 3/1-48 auto
cat6k-access> (enable) set port speed 3/1-48 auto
cat6k-access> (enable) set port host 3/1-48
cat6k-access> (enable) set vlan 111 name SJC_data1
cat6k-access> (enable) set vlan 11 name SJC_voice1
cat6k-access> (enable) set vlan 111 3/1-48
cat6k-access> (enable) set port auxiliaryvlan 3/1-48 11
```

**Figure 5-3**    *XYZ IPT LAN QoS Configuration Summary*

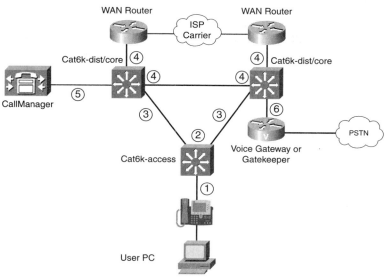

**Step 2**    Enable the QoS capabilities switch wide.

By default, QoS is disabled on the Catalyst switches. When you enable it by using the following command, all the switch ports are set to an untrusted state. This means that the switch rewrites the CoS, ToS, and DSCP values for all incoming packets to 0. (How to enable trusting is described later in this procedure.)

```
Cat6k-access> (enable) Set qos enable
```

**Step 3**    Place voice-control traffic in proper output queues.

The queuing mechanisms that are available in many Cisco switches and routers provide service guarantees such as less drops and less delay to certain types of traffic (for example, voice traffic). The Catalyst 6500 switch, with its queuing capabilities, can provide preferential treatment to voice traffic. Each port on the switch has a series of input (receive, Rx) and output (transmit, Tx) queues that are used as temporary storage areas for data. A certain amount of buffer space is allotted to each queue to store the data. These queues are implemented in application-specific integrated circuit (ASIC) hardware for each port. The number of queues implemented for each port varies depending on the hardware version of the line card.

---

**NOTE**    To determine the number of queues supported on a port, on a Catalyst 6500 switch, you can use the **show port qos** *mod/port* command, where *mod* is the module number and *port* is the port number.

---

The older 10/100 ports on the 6348 line cards used in the Catalyst 6500 switch have a single input queue (Rx queue) with four drop thresholds (1q4t) and two output queues (Tx queue) with two drop thresholds (2q2t). Thresholds define at which point the switch can drop the packets for that queue during the congestion times. Newer line cards have one extra queue each for transmit and receive—thus, two input queues (1p1q4t) and three output queues (1p2q2t). These extra queues are special-priority queues (represented by 1p). The switching engine empties the packets in the priority queues before processing the packets in any other queues. This priority queue is especially useful for voice traffic and signaling traffic, which require less delay.

When you are designing the QoS in the campus switches, you should always place the voice-bearer traffic and voice-signaling traffic in the queue that has higher preference with a lower drop threshold. The switch uses the CoS value in the Ethernet frame to determine in which queue to place the frame and at what point (threshold) during the congestion to drop the frame.

By default, the switch places the voice traffic (RTP traffic, which is marked with CoS 5) coming from the IP Phone in the second output queue in case of 2q2t and in the priority queue in case of 1p2q2t. However, the switch does not put the voice-control traffic in the second output queue in case of 2q2t and into the priority queue in case of 1p2q2t. Manual configuration on the switch is required to accomplish this, as shown in the following example, which illustrates the configuration commands needed to place the voice-control traffic into the second nonpriority queue:

```
cat6k-access> (enable) set qos map 2q2t tx 2 1 cos 3
cat6k-access> (enable) set qos map 1p2q2t tx 2 1 cos 3
```

**Step 4**    Map CoS and IP precedence values to the standard DSCP values.

When QoS is enabled on the switches, the switch configures a series of default QoS mappings. In its default mappings, the traffic that is marked with CoS 5 and ToS (IP precedence bit value) 5 is mapped to a DSCP value of 40, and traffic that is marked with CoS 3 or ToS 3 is mapped to a DSCP value of 24. The CoS-to-DSCP mapping command and IP precedence-to-DSCP command changes these settings to mark the CoS 5 and ToS 5 traffic with a DSCP value of 46 and to map traffic with CoS 3 and ToS 3 to a DSCP value of 26. The default for video traffic is to map to the DSCP value of 32. However, referring to Table 5-5, the recommended DSCP value for video traffic is 34. Therefore, if you are deploying video in your network, you need to change the value from 32 to 34. The following example shows the configuration commands needed to map CoS-to-DSCP and IP precedence-to-DSCP values:

```
cat6k-access> (enable) set qos cos-dscp-map 0 8 16 26 32 46 48 56
cat6k-access> (enable) set qos ipprec-dscp-map 0 8 16 26 32 46 48 56
```

**Step 5**  Apply policies at interfaces that are connected to IP Phones.

The following command allows you to apply access control lists (ACLs) of QoS policy based on VLAN. The default action applies ACLs of QoS policy to a port. This command is applicable to switches such as Catalyst 6500 with PFC cards.

```
Cat6k-access> (enable) Set port qos 3/1-48 vlan based
```

Because it is relatively easy for users to change their IP CoS, ToS, and DSCP values on their desktops, you can use the Catalyst QoS features to rewrite these values based on the port's CoS or re-mark the IP CoS, ToS, and DSCP values to 0.

By setting the port default CoS value to 0 the following occurs:

— The Catalyst switch internally assigns a DSCP value of 0 to any inbound frame that is not tagged with an 802.1p CoS value.

— The trust boundary moves from the Catalyst switch to the IP Phone.

The following example shows the configuration command needed to set the PC port to untrusted:

```
Cat6k-access> (enable) Set port qos 3/1-48 trust-ext untrusted
```

This command effectively resets the IP precedence or DSCP values of the packets that are coming from the PC to 0. This approach does not work in scenarios where you are deploying the Cisco IP SoftPhone application on the users' PCs or you need to keep the prioritizations that were set by certain applications running on the user PCs. In these cases, you need to create ACLs on the access layer switches that identify the RTP traffic that is carried in the UDP packets, the signaling traffic that is coming from the PC, and other application traffic and mark it appropriately before sending it to the distribution and core switches. You can optionally enable the policing feature on the switches to limit the amount of traffic allowed per flow, eliminating possible denial of service (DoS) attacks from the user PCs.

Refer to the following URL to get a list of TCP/UDP ports used in the CallManager. This information is required while creating the ACLs.

http://www.cisco.com/en/US/partner/products/sw/voicesw/ps556/products_tech_note09186a00801a62b9.shtml

Because the IP Phones mark the voice-bearer and -signaling traffic appropriately using both CoS and DSCP, the next command configures the switch port to trust the CoS and DSCP values incoming from the IP Phone. The advantage of trusting CoS rather than DSCP is that it enables ingress scheduling on the switch port.

The following example shows the configuration command needed to set the switch to "trust" the CoS value coming from the IP Phone ports:

```
Cat6k-access> (enable) Set port qos 3/1-48 trust trust-cos
```

The next command configures the Catalyst 6500 switch to apply CoS 0 to each incoming frame without an 802.1p tag. This command is not visible with a **show configuration** command because it is the default.

```
Cat6k-access> (enable) Set port qos 3/1-48 cos 0
```

When you are applying this command, the switch parser might return the following error:

```
>Trust type trust-cos not supported on port(s) 3/1-48
>Receive thresholds enabled on port(s) 3/1-48
>Trust type set to untrusted on port(s) 3/1-48
```

This error indicates that the switch has activated the four receive thresholds for the input queue (1q4t), and discarding will take place according to the received CoS. However, the line card in the switch does not support trusting the CoS for queuing on the transmit side. As a workaround to this issue, apply an ACL to the voice VLAN to force the Catalyst 6500 switch to trust the CoS settings coming from the IP Phones, as shown in the following example. Note that ACLs specified in this example can be applied only on Catalyst 6500 switches with a supervisory module that has a PFC.

```
Cat6k-access> (enable) set qos acl ip ACL_VOICE_VLAN trust-cos ip any any
Cat6k-access> (enable) commit qos acl ACL_VOICE_VLAN
Cat6k-access> (enable) set qos acl map ACL_VOICE_VLAN 11
```

If you do not receive error messages while applying this command, you have new-generation line cards and do not need to apply the ACLs as shown in the example.

Refer to the following URL to obtain more information on the line card limitations:

http://www.cisco.com/en/US/products/hw/switches/ps700/
products_tech_note09186a008014f8a8.shtml#topic5-3

**Step 6**   Restore QoS capabilities on interfaces that are connected to distribution switches.

You need to restore the port-based QoS capabilities on the access switch interfaces (typically the gigabit links) that are connecting the distribution switch and trust the markings coming from the distribution switches. The following example shows the configuration commands needed to configure uplink ports on access switches:

```
Cat6k-access > (enable) set port qos uplink-Port port-based
Cat6k-access > (enable) set port qos uplink-Port trust trust-cos
```

## Distribution and Core Layer Catalyst 6500 QoS Configuration Guidelines

Follow these steps to configure the distribution and core layer Catalyst 6500 switches at the central sites:

**Step 1**   Enable QoS switch wide:

```
Cat6k-dist> (enable) Set qos enable
```

**Step 2**   Place the voice-control traffic into queue 2, as discussed in the previous section:

```
cat6k-dist> (enable) set qos map 1p2q2t tx 2 1 cos 3
cat6k-dist> (enable) set qos map 2q2t tx 2 1 cos 3
```

**Step 3**   Map CoS and IP precedence values to the standard DSCP values:

```
cat6k-dist> (enable) set qos cos-dscp-map 0 8 16 26 32 46 48 56
cat6k-dist> (enable) set qos ipprec-dscp-map 0 8 16 26 32 46 48 56
```

**Step 4**   Configure the interfaces that connect to CallManager servers.

CallManager sets the DSCP value to 46 (ToS 5/PHB EF) for bearer (RTP) traffic (streaming music files, conference bridge streams, and so forth). It also sets the DSCP value to 26 (ToS 3/PHB AF31) for all VoIP-control traffic (such as SCCP, H.323, and MGCP). However, CallManager does not use 802.1q Layer 2 encapsulation.

To ensure that the packets leaving the CallManager are set to the right value, you should configure the switch port connecting to CallManager servers to trust the DSCP/IP precedence. However, due to current limitations on the Catalyst 6500 switch, as explained in Step 5 of the preceding section, the port trust state on 10/100 ports cannot be set to **trust-dscp** or **trust-ipprec**. As a workaround, you need to configure a QoS ACL that trusts DSCP and map the ACL to the CallManager port. The following example shows how to configure QoS settings for ports that connect to CallManager servers:

```
cat6k-dist> (enable) set port qos CM-port trust trust-dscp
! Use the above command if you are using new generation line cards; otherwise,
! use the ACLs as described below. If you use the above command on older
! line cards, returns an error message "Trust type trust-dscp not
! supported on this port"

cat6k-dist> (enable) set port qos CM-port port-based
cat6k-dist> (enable) set qos acl ip ACL_TRUST_DSCP trust-dscp ip any any
cat6k-dist> (enable) commit qos acl ACL_TRUST_DSCP
cat6k-dist> (enable) set qos acl map ACL_TRUST_DSCP CM-port


! The above command maps the ACL named TRUST_DSCP to the CallManager Port.
! CM-Port is the port number where the CallManager server is connected.
```

**Step 5**  Connect the interfaces to the voice gateways.

CallManager, Cisco H.323, MGCP voice gateways, and VG248 gateways can set IP precedence and DSCP values for VoIP-control and bearer traffic. However, because of the same limitations discussed in Step 5 in the preceding section, you should use the ACLs to trust the markings made by the voice gateways.

The following example shows the QoS configurations needed on switch ports connecting to voice gateways at the central site:

```
cat6k-dist> (enable) set port qos VoIPGW-port trust trust-dscp
! Use the above command if you are using new generation line cards; otherwise,
! use the ACLs as described below. If you use the above command on older line
! cards, it returns an error message "Trust type trust-dscp not supported on
! this port"

cat6k-dist> (enable) set port qos VoIPGW-port port-based
cat6k-dist> (enable) set qos acl ip ACL_TRUST_DSCP trust-dscp ip any any
cat6k-dist> (enable) commit qos acl ACL_TRUST_DSCP
cat6k-dist> (enable) set qos acl map ACL_TRUST_DSCP VoIPGW-port
! VoIPGW-Port is the port number where the VoIP gateways are connected.
```

Most of the Cisco voice gateways set the DSCP and IP precedence values for call-control signaling and media (bearer) packets. If you have voice gateways in your network that cannot set the DSCP and IP precedence values for the bearer and call-control traffic, you can use extended access lists to match the packets carrying this type of traffic and rewrite the DSCP and IP precedence values.

**Step 6**   Connect the interfaces to the WAN routers.

This step discusses the configuration needed on the switch ports of the Cisco Catalyst switches that connect to the WAN aggregator routers at the central sites. Configure the ports to trust the DSCP values set by the other routers and switches at the remote sites. If the remote site routers or switches do not set the DSCP value, you need to classify and mark DSCP values for the incoming packets at the WAN aggregation router. The following example shows how to configure trust for the ports of the central site connecting to WAN routers at the central site:

```
cat6k-dist> (enable)  set port qos WAN-port trust trust-dscp
! Use the above command if you are using new generation line cards; otherwise,
! use the ACLs as described below. If you use the above command on older line
! cards it returns an error message "Trust type trust-dscp not supported on
! this port"
cat6k-dist> (enable) set port qos WAN-port port-based
cat6k-dist> (enable) set qos acl ip ACL_TRUST_WAN trust-dscp any
cat6k-dist> (enable) commit qos acl ACL_TRUST_WAN
cat6k-dist> (enable) set qos acl map ACL_TRUST_WAN WAN-port
! Where WAN-port is the port number where the WAN router(s) are connected
```

**Step 7**   Configure unused switch ports.

The distribution and core switches are not supposed to connect any IP Phone or any other device that might affect the QoS configuration. The CoS and ToS values for the switch ports that are in a not-connected state or ports connecting to unknown or untrusted devices should have their CoS and ToS values rewritten to 0. The following example shows the unused switch port configurations:

```
cat6k-dist> (enable) set port qos unused-ports port-based
cat6k-dist> (enable) set port qos unused-ports untrusted
! By default, all ports are in the untrusted state when QoS is enabled.
```

# Remote-Site IPT Infrastructure

With the centralized call-processing model, the IP Phones at the remote (branch) sites depend on the central site CallManager under normal operations. During a WAN failure, the voice gateways at the remote sites handle the call-processing requests received from the IP Phones of their respected sites. The Survivable Remote Site Telephony (SRST) feature on the voice gateways provides this functionality. Figure 5-4 shows the IPT network architecture for the Seattle and Melbourne remote sites.

**Figure 5-4** *Remote-Site IPT Architecture: Seattle and Melbourne*

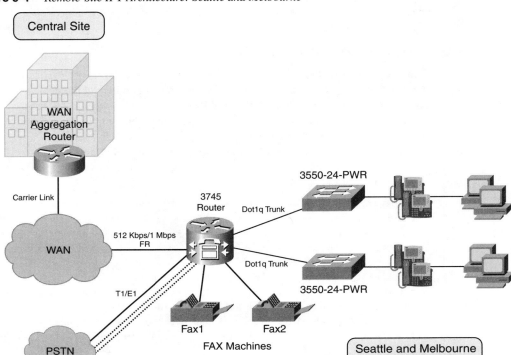

As shown in Figure 5-4, the Seattle and Melbourne sites have two Cisco 3550-24 PWR switches to support 50 and 40 IP Phones, respectively. Cisco 3550-24 PWR switches have 24 inline power ports. The 3745 router at Seattle and Melbourne also has a 16-port Ethernet switch module to support additional phones if required.

Figure 5-5 depicts the remote-site IPT network for the Dallas and Brisbane sites. The Dallas and Brisbane sites use a Cisco 2651XM router as a voice gateway and WAN router.

**Figure 5-5**  *Remote-Site IPT Architecture: Dallas and Brisbane*

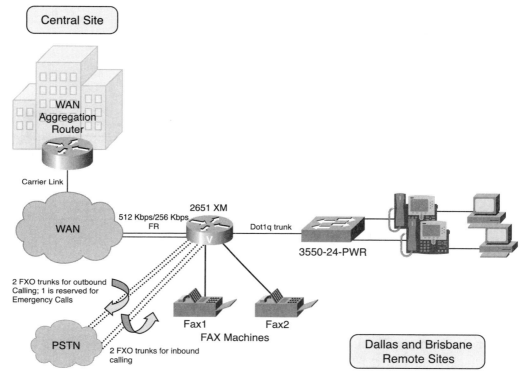

Every remote-site router of XYZ supports the number of IP Phones required in the SRST mode. The number of IP Phones supported per router depends on the router platform and the amount of physical memory installed on the router. Refer to the following URL to access the SRST data sheet that provides the information on the platform support and the maximum number of devices supported:

http://www.cisco.com/en/US/partner/products/sw/voicesw/ps2169/
products_data_sheet09186a00800888ac.html

## Remote-Site LAN QoS Design

The QoS requirements in the LAN at the remote sites are similar to the central site LAN QoS requirements. For smaller remote sites, you can use the low-end LAN switches with fewer capabilities. Therefore, the command syntax for configuring QoS changes slightly. Figure 5-6 summarizes the areas to focus on while configuring the QoS for the remote sites. QoS configuration is required at the LAN switches and the WAN routers.

**Figure 5-6** *Remote-Site QoS Configuration Guidelines*

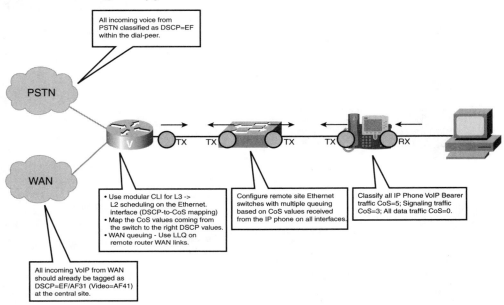

## Configuring the Remote-Site LAN Switches for QoS

Remote sites have Catalyst 3550-24 PWR switches. Catalyst 3550 switches have the following queuing characteristics:

- The receive interface is one standard FIFO (first-in, first-out) queue (1q-FIFO) for both Fast and Gigabit Ethernet interfaces.

- The transmit interface has four queues with two drop thresholds (4q2t) on a Gigabit Ethernet interface. One of the queues can be configured as the priority queue. This is indicated with 1p3q2t (one strict priority queue, three standard queues, and each queue with two configurable drop thresholds). The FastEthernet interface has four queues with no configurable drop thresholds (4q0t). Just like on the Gigabit Ethernet interface, one of the queues can be configured as the priority queue. This is indicated with 1p3q0t.

**NOTE**     For 3550 switches, you can use the **show interfaces** *interface-name x/y* **capabilities** command on the switch to see the number of queues that support the interfaces support.

The scheduling algorithm on the switch services the four transmit queues based on the configured Weighted Round Robin (WRR) weights and thresholds. The scheduling algorithm empties the packets waiting in the priority queue before servicing the other queues. The default scheduling policy is WRR.

Table 5-6 summarizes the queues, CoS values, and default queue assignments based on the CoS value on the Ethernet Catalyst 3550 switch. To see the default queue CoS assignments on a 3550 switch, type the command **show mls qos interface** *interface-number* **queuing**.

**Table 5-6**    *Values for Layer 2 QoS*

| Queue Number | CoS Value |
|---|---|
| 4 | 6, 7 |
| 3 | 4, 5 |
| 2 | 2, 3 |
| 1 | 0, 1 |

Queue 4 is the priority queue. The voice-bearer (RTP) packets coming from the IP Phones, which are marked as CoS 5, should be queued into queue 4. The control packets that are marked as CoS 3 should be queued into queue 3. Table 5-7 summarizes the suitable placement of traffic into various queues based on the CoS values for the IPT deployments when using Catalyst 3550 switches.

**Table 5-7**    *Queue Assignments Based on CoS Values for the Catalyst 3550 Switch*

| Queue Number | CoS Value |
|---|---|
| 4 (priority queue) | 5 |
| 3 | 3, 4, 6, 7 |
| 2 | 1, 2 |
| 1 | 0 |

**NOTE**    If your deployment scenario includes other types of switches, check the product documentation and configure the switches to place the packets coming from the IP Phones tagged with CoS 5 in the priority queue. The packets with CoS 3 should be queued one level below the priority queue. This configuration technique ensures that voice packets get priority treatment over untagged packets, resulting in better voice quality in your network.

Remote sites of XYZ are using Cisco 3550-24 PWR switches. The next few sections discuss the required QoS configurations for the remote sites using Cisco 3550-24 PWR switches.

## Configuring Catalyst 3550 Switches

IP Phones at the remote sites connect to Catalyst 3550-24 PWR switches. To enable QoS on the Catalyst 3550 switches that are located in the Seattle site, you must follow these configuration steps:

**Step 1**  Enable QoS globally on the Catalyst 3550 switch:

```
S3550(config)#mls qos
```

**Step 2**  Modify the default CoS-to-DSCP mapping:

```
S3550(config)#mls qos map cos-dscp 0 8 16 26 34 46 48 56
```

**Step 3**  Modify the default DSCP-to-CoS mapping:

```
S3550(config)#mls qos map dscp-cos 0 8 16 26 34 46 48 56
```

**Step 4**  Turn on priority queuing (which is disabled by default) on the switch interfaces that connect the IP Phones:

```
S3550(config)# interface range fastethernet 0/2 - 24
S3550(config-if-range)#priority-queue out
```

**Step 5**  Place the CoS 5 traffic into the priority queue, which is queue 4, and the CoS 3 traffic into queue 3. Note that CoS 6 and CoS 7 value packets are placed in queue 4, and CoS 4 value packets are placed in queue 3.

```
S3550(config)# interface range fastethernet 0/2 - 24
S3550(config)# no shutdown
S3550(config)# duplex auto
S3550(config-if-range)#wrr-queue cos-map 1 0
R3550(config-if-range)#wrr-queue cos-map 2 1 2
S3550(config-if-range)#wrr-queue cos-map 3 3 4 6 7
! Placing the CoS 3 traffic into queue 3. CoS 4 value packets are
! also placed in queue 3.
S3550(config-if-range)#wrr-queue cos-map 4 5
! Placing the CoS 5 traffic into the priority queue, which is queue 4.
! CoS 6 and CoS 7 values packets are also placed in queue 4.
```

**Step 6**  Enable QoS features on the switch ports connecting the IP Phones:

```
S3550(config)# interface range fastethernet 0/2 - 24
! Select the interfaces where the IP Phones are connected
S3550(config-if-range)# mls qos trust cos
! Trusts the CoS values set by the IP phone
S3550(config-if-range)#switchport voice vlan 21
! Create the Voice VLAN 21
S3550(config-if-range)#switchport access vlan 211
! Create the Data VLAN 211
S3550(config-if-range)#switchport priority extend cos 0
! Untrust the PC port located in the IP phone
```

```
S3550(config-if-range)#spanning-tree portfast
! Disable the spanning tree cycles and bring the port to
! forwarding state immediately
```

**Step 7** Enable QoS features for uplink. In all the branches, the Catalyst 3550 switches connect to the WAN routers. Because the incoming traffic from the central sites has been set with the correct DSCP values, you can configure the uplink switch port connecting to the WAN router at the branch to trust the incoming traffic markings. The following example shows the uplink configurations required on the Catalyst 3550 switch. Here the WAN router is connected to the FastEthernet 0/1 port on the Catalyst 3550 switch.

```
S3550(config)# interface fastethernet 0/1
! Interface connecting to the WAN router
S3550(config)# no shutdown
S3550(config)# priority-queue out
S3550(config-if)#wrr-queue cos-map 1 0
R3550(config-if)#wrr-queue cos-map 2 1 2
S3550(config-if)#wrr-queue cos-map 3 3 4 6 7
S3550(config-if)#wrr-queue cos-map 4 5
S3550(config-if)#mls qos trust dscp
! Trust the DSCP markings coming from the WAN router
S3550(config-if)#switch port mode trunk
! Configure the port connected to the WAN router as a trunk port
S3550(config-if)#switch port trunk encapsulation dot1q
! Configure the trunk as an IEEE 802.1Q trunk
```

**NOTE**     The configurations of the Catalyst 3550 switches in other remote sites such as Dallas, Brisbane, and Melbourne are similar to Seattle except that you need to put in the right data VLAN and voice VLAN numbers in the configurations.

## Configuring the Ethernet Switch Module on the Cisco 3745 Router

The Catalyst 3550-24 PWR switches have 24 inline power ports, 23 of which connect to IP Phones. The remaining port connects to the WAN router.

As shown earlier in Table 5-1, the Seattle and Melbourne remote sites have more than 23 IP Phones. Hence, these sites require two switches, providing 46 ports to connect the IP Phones. However, in Seattle, to support 50 IP Phones, extra inline power Ethernet ports are required. A 16-port Ethernet switch module in the Cisco 3745 router in Seattle provides these additional ports. The Ethernet switch module can function as a Layer 2 switch connected to a Layer 3 router.

To configure an IP Phone port on the Ethernet switch module, follow these steps:

**Step 1**    Include voice and data VLANs in the VLAN database.

With Catalyst 3550 switches, when you configure a port in a VLAN that is not in the switch's VLAN database, the switch automatically adds the VLAN to the database. With Ethernet switch modules, you need to add the VLAN manually to the database. The following example shows the commands that you need to enter the voice and data VLANs manually into the switch's database.

```
R3745-SEA#vlan database
R3745-SEA(vlan)#vlan 211 name SEA-DATAVLAN
R3745-SEA(vlan)#vlan 21 name SEA-VOICEVLAN
```

**Step 2**    Select the interface on the router to connect the IP Phones:

```
R3745-SEA(config)#interface FastEthernet0/1-16
```

**Step 3**    Set the encapsulation format on the port to 802.1Q. With this format, the router supports simultaneous tagged and untagged traffic on a switch port.

```
R3745-SEA(config-if)#switchport trunk encapsulation dot1q
```

**Step 4**    Set the native VLAN to send and receive untagged traffic when the interface is in 802.1Q trunking mode. The traffic coming from the PC that is attached to the data port on the back of the IP Phone goes into the native VLAN.

```
R3745-SEA(config-if)#switchport trunk native vlan 211
```

**Step 5**    Configure the switch port as a trunk port:

```
R3745-SEA(config-if)#switchport mode trunk
```

**Step 6**    Configure the voice VLAN:

```
R3745-SEA(config-if)#switchport voice vlan 21
```

**Step 7**    Set the switch port to override the priority received from a PC or any other attached device to the IP Phone's switch port:

```
R3745-SEA(config-if)#switchport priority extend cos 0
```

**Step 8**    Enable the Port Fast feature on the main interface to disable spanning tree in all its associated VLANs:

```
R3745-SEA(config-if)#spanning-tree portfast
```

# Remote-Site WAN QoS Design

Based on the detailed discussion in Chapters 1 and 4, the VoIP traffic consists of two unique components:

- Bearer or voice (RTP) traffic
- Call-control or signaling traffic

The call-control traffic carries the required signaling for call setup, call teardown, and reporting mechanisms. The bearer traffic is the actual voice conversation.

Although VoIP-control (or call-control) traffic can be UDP-based traffic, it is typically TCP-based traffic. VoIP-bearer traffic is always UDP. Because of the unique requirements of UDP and TCP, the network must treat their associated traffic flows differently.

The VoIP-bearer traffic, composed of many small UDP packets, each carrying a vital piece of the voice conversation, must be queued with an absolute minimum probability of drops or delays within the packet network. On the other hand, VoIP-control traffic is not nearly as delay sensitive as bearer traffic and, because it can be retransmitted by TCP if a packet gets lost, can be treated with less strict queuing policies with the network.

Because each type of VoIP traffic requires different treatment, the network elements must have a method of identifying and separating the flows. The most efficient way to achieve this is to combine the use of a Priority Queuing (PQ) scheme with a Class-Based Weighted Fair Queuing (CBWFQ) scheme to guarantee the required bandwidth for delay- and jitter-sensitive traffic, without starving other traffic types. The combination of PQ and CBWFQ mechanisms is known as Low Latency Queuing (LLQ).

Table 5-8 shows the traffic classifications used in the remote sites for various data flows. The voice-bearer traffic has the highest priority, followed by the VoIP-control traffic.

XYZ also has mission-critical data that requires a higher priority than the other regular data traffic, which is given third priority. In every network, certain data packets are more important and require a higher priority than other, lower-priority data packets. Systems Network Architecture (SNA) protocol traffic is an example of high-priority data traffic, compared to FTP traffic. The low-priority data traffic follows the mission-critical data traffic.

**Table 5-8**    *Traffic Classification for Remote Sites*

| Class Name | DSCP Value |
| --- | --- |
| VoIP-bearer traffic (RTP) | EF (46) |
| VoIP-control traffic | AF31 (26) |
| Mission-critical data | AF21 (18) |

The application of QoS policies requires the following three configuration procedures:

- **Class map**—Defines one or more traffic classes by specifying criteria for classifying the traffic
- **Policy map**—Defines one or more QoS policies to be applied to the traffic defined in the class maps
- **Service map**—Attaches a policy to any specific interface on the router

As depicted in Figure 5-5, designing the QoS on the WAN routers involves three tasks:

- Performing DSCP-to-CoS mappings
- Mapping COS-to-DSCPmapping on remote-site routers
- Configuring WAN interface queuing

## Perform DSCP-to-CoS Mappings

As shown in Figures 5-3 and 5-4, the connection between the remote-site routers and remote-site switches is an 802.1Q trunk. The remote-site WAN routers can trust the DSCP value of all incoming packets from the WAN link. WAN routers are responsible for changing the DSCP-to-CoS mappings before they pass the packets to Layer 2 switches. The DSCP-to-CoS mapping is accomplished by class-based marking. This allows the Layer 2 switch to prioritize the traffic appropriately.

---

**NOTE**    Because the LAN switches proposed in case of XYZ, Inc., are Layer 3-aware (Cisco Catalyst 3550 switches), they can trust the DSCP values. Therefore, there is no need to perform the DSCP-to-CoS mappings on the WAN router, as discussed in this section. This step is required only if you have Layer 2 switches (such as the Cisco 29xx series).

---

Example 5-1 shows the classification of packets by examining the Layer 3 DSCP value. Voice packets have a DSCP value of EF, signaling that traffic packets have a DSCP value of AF31, and mission-critical data packets have a DSCP value of AF21.

**Example 5-1**    *Classifying the Packets Based on Incoming DSCP Values*

```
class-map match-all VOICE
 match ip dscp ef
class-map match-all VOICE-CONTROL
 match ip dscp AF31
class-map match-all MISSION-CRITICAL
 match ip dscp AF21
```

After you have classified the traffic, use the **policy map** commands, as shown in Example 5-2, to set the CoS value. Any packet that has a DSCP value of EF will be marked with a CoS of 5, packets that have a DSCP value of AF31 will be marked with a CoS of 3, and the mission-critical data packets that have a DSCP value AF21 will be marked as CoS 2.

**Example 5-2**    *Setting the CoS Values*

```
policy map DSCP2COS-VOICE
 class VOICE
  set cos 5
 class VOICE-CONTROL
  set cos 3
policy map DSCP2COS-DATA
 class MISSION-CRITICAL
  set cos 2
```

The class map and policy maps are not effective until they are attached to the voice and data subinterface. In this case, the policy map attaches to the voice and data, as shown in Example 5-3.

**Example 5-3**   *Attaching the Policy Map to an Interface*

```
interface fastethernet 0/0.21
! Subinterface for the voice subnet for Seattle remote site
 service-policy output DSCP2COS-VOICE

interface fastethernet 0/0.211
Subinterface for data subnet for Seattle remote site
 service-policy output DSCP2COS-DATA
```

## Map CoS-to-DSCP Mapping on Remote-Site Routers

The remote-site WAN routers must set the DSCP values for the incoming packets from the LAN switches before sending them out on the WAN link. The classification of packets shown in Table 5-8 is used.

Example 5-4 shows the classification of packets by examining the Layer 2 CoS values. Voice packets coming from the IP Phones have a CoS value of 5, and signaling traffic packets have a CoS value of 3. The mission-critical data packets are matched against an access list, because the data applications cannot set the CoS value to 2. Hence, you use the extended access list to identify the mission-critical traffic.

**NOTE**    In Example 5-4, an extended access list identifies the mission-critical data. In your network, you can add more access list statements with varying criteria to match your traffic prioritization needs.

**Example 5-4**   *Classifying the Packets Based on Incoming CoS Values*

```
! Matching all voice-bearer traffic coming from the IP Phones
class-map match-all COS5
 match cos 5
! Matching all voice-control traffic coming from the IP Phones
class-map match-all COS3
 match cos 3
! Matching all mission-critical data based on the access list
class-map match-all COS2
 match access-group 101
! Applying the access list according to mission-critical data criteria
access list 101 permit tcp any host 10.2.11.5 eq 80
access list 101 permit tcp 10.2.11.0 0 0.0.0.255 host 10.1.1.1 eq 80
```

After you have classified the traffic, use the **policy map** commands, as shown in Example 5-5, to set the DSCP values. Packets that have a CoS value of 5 are marked with a DSCP value of EF, packets that have a CoS value of 3 are marked with a DSCP value of AF31, and mission-critical data packets that have a CoS value of 2 are marked as DSCP value AF21.

**Example 5-5**    *Setting the DSCP Values*

```
policy map COS2DSCP-VOICE
 class EF
  set dscp ef
 class AF31
  set dscp af31

policy map COS2DSCP-DATA
 class AF21
  set dscp af21
```

The final step is to attach the policy map to the voice and data subinterface, as shown in Example 5-6.

**Example 5-6**    *Attach the Service Policy to the Voice and Data Voice and Data Subinterfaces*

```
interface fastethernet 0/0.21
 service-policy input COS2DSCP-VOICE

interface fastethernet 0/0.211
 service-policy input COS2DSCP-DATA
```

## Configure WAN Interface Queuing

On the WAN edge router (the WAN aggregator router at the central sites and the WAN router at the remote sites), voice traffic needs to be assigned to an LLQ, and voice-control traffic needs to get a minimum bandwidth guarantee by using CBWFQ mechanisms.

### Voice and FAX Bandwidth Calculations

Referring to Table 4-4 in Chapter 4, you see that the G.729a codec requires approximately 30 kbps (26.4 kbps with PPP as the Layer 2 protocol) of bandwidth per call. XYZ is using a G.711 codec for fax calls, which consumes approximately 90 kbps (82.4 kbps with PPP as the Layer 2 protocol). Keeping these values in mind, Table 5-9 summarizes the bandwidth required by each remote site on the WAN link.

**Table 5-9**    *QoS Bandwidth Calculations*

| Criteria | Seattle | Dallas | Melbourne | Brisbane |
|---|---|---|---|---|
| Number of phones | 50 | 15 | 40 | 10 |
| Bandwidth/media | 1-Mbps FR | 512-kbps FR | 512-kbps FR | 256-kbps FR |

**Table 5-9**    *QoS Bandwidth Calculations (Continued)*

| Criteria | Seattle | Dallas | Melbourne | Brisbane |
|---|---|---|---|---|
| No. of simultaneous voice calls | 10 | 4 | 8 | 3 |
| No. of fax calls | 1 | 1 | 1 | 1 |
| Codec used for voice calls | G.729 | G.729 | G.729 | G.729 |
| Codec used for fax calls | G.711 | G.711 | G.711 | G.711 |
| Bandwidth for voice calls (simultaneous voice calls × 30 kbps per call) | 300 kbps | 120 kbps | 240 kbps | 90 kbps |
| Bandwidth for fax calls (one fax call × 90 kbps per call) | 90 kbps | 90 kbps | 90 kbps | 90 kbps |
| Total voice and fax bandwidth (*ValueVoicefax*) | 390 kbps | 210 kbps | 330 kbps | 180 kbps |
| Voice control (*ValueVoiceControl*) | 10 kbps | 8 kbps | 10 kbps | 8 kbps |
| Mission-critical data (*ValueMissionCritical*) | 200 kbps | 100 kbps | 80 kbps | 40 kbps |

In Table 5-9, the bandwidth that is reserved for the voice control traffic depends on the number of IP phones that are connected at the remote sites. To obtain the recommended bandwidth for voice control traffic, refer to the IP Telephony Solution Reference Network Design (SRND) at the following URL:

http://www.cisco.com/go/srnd

Also in Table 5-9, the bandwidth that is identified for the mission-critical traffic depends on your traffic requirements. You need to identify these requirements during the planning phase of the IPT deployment.

According to Figure 5-1, the Seattle site is connected to the San Jose site via a 1-Mbps Frame Relay circuit (high-speed link), and the Dallas site is connected via a 512-Kbps Frame Relay circuit. The San Jose central site connects to the service provider network with a 1.5-Mbps link. Because there is a mismatch between the link bandwidths of the central and remote sites, Frame Relay Traffic Shaping (FRTS) is required to send the traffic at a consistent rate.

You need to configure the links with the following values:

- Committed Burst Rate $B_c$ = CIR (Committed Information Rate) /100
- Excess Burst Rate $B_e$ = 0
- Minimum CIR (mincir) = CIR

### Seattle Router WAN Queuing and Traffic Shaping

Recall the discussion in Chapter 4, in the "Serialization Delay" section, regarding link fragmentation and interleaving (LFI) and traffic shaping. Because the link from Seattle to San Jose is a high-speed link, you do not need LFI. However, traffic shaping is required because of the mismatch of link speeds at remote and central sites. Example 5-7 shows the configuration of the Seattle router.

**Example 5-7**   *Seattle Router Configuration*

```
interface Serial0/1
! Interface connected to WAN link on Seattle router
no ip address
encapsulation frame-relay
frame-relay traffic-shaping
! This command enables FRTS on the main interface.
interface Serial0/1.50 point-to-point
! FR link to San Jose from Seattle
bandwidth 1000
ip address 10.200.10.1 255.255.255.252
frame-relay interface-dlci 250
class FRTS-1000kbps
! This command applies the FRTS map-class to the DLCI.
map-class frame-relay FRTS-1000kbps
frame-relay cir 1000000
frame-relay bc 10000
frame-relay be 0
frame-relay mincir 1000000
no frame-relay adaptive-shaping
service-policy output Remote-WAN-EDGE
! This command applies the MQC policy to the FRTS map-class.
policy map Remote-WAN-Edge
 class VOICE
   priority ValueVoicefax
 class VOICE-CONTROL
   bandwidth ValueVoiceControl
 class MISSION-CRITICAL
   bandwidth ValueMissionCritical
Class Class-default
   Fair-queue
```

The same classes that were used for DSCP-to-CoS mapping are used again for WAN interface queuing. Refer to Table 5-9 for the bandwidth values for *ValueVoicefax*, *ValueVoiceControl*, and *ValueMissionCritical* in the Seattle branch.

### Dallas Router WAN Queuing and Traffic Shaping

The Dallas site connects to the service provider via a Frame Relay link, and the San Jose site connects to the service provider via an ATM link. The conversion between ATM and Frame Relay is accomplished through Frame Relay-to-ATM Service Interworking (described in the FRF.8 [Frame Relay Forum] implementation agreement) in the carrier network. Because the link between the Dallas and San Jose sites is a low-speed link (512 Kbps), you need to use LFI to fragment the large packets to ensure that voice packets do not experience delay. Multilink PPP (MLPPP) over the ATM to Frame Relay LFI mechanism will be deployed. Example 5-8 lists the configuration required for the Dallas router.

---

**NOTE**    When using a 768-Kbps or lower-speed link, the LFI mechanism fragments the large data packets and interleaves small voice packets between the fragmented data packets. Figure 4-13 shows the LFI process and serialization delay matrix.

---

**Example 5-8**    *Dallas Router Configuration*

```
interface Serial0/1
! Interface connected to WAN link on Dallas router
no ip address
encapsulation frame-relay
frame-relay traffic-shaping
! This command enables FRTS on the main interface.
interface Serial0/1.51 point-to-point
description FR Link to San Jose from Dallas
bandwidth 512
frame-relay interface-dlci 251 ppp virtual-template51
class FRTS-512kbps
! This command applies the FRTS map-class to the DLCI.
interface Virtual-Template51
bandwidth 512
ip address 10.200.60.1 255.255.255.252
service-policy output Remote-WAN-EDGE
! This command applies the MQC policy to the FRTS map-class.
! The service policy is applied to the virtual template

ppp multilink
ppp multilink fragment-delay 10
ppp multilink interleave

map-class frame-relay FRTS-512kbps
frame-relay cir 512000
frame-relay bc 5120
frame-relay be 0
frame-relay mincir 512000
no frame-relay adaptive-shaping

 class VOICE
  priority ValueVoicefax
 class VOICE-CONTROL
  bandwidth ValueVoiceControl
 class MISSION-CRITICAL
  bandwidth ValueMissionCritical
Class Class-default
  Fair-queue
```

The same classes that are used for DSCP-to-CoS mapping will also be used for WAN interface queuing. Refer to Table 5-10 for the bandwidth values for *ValueVoicefax*, *ValueVoiceControl*, and *ValueMissionCritical* in the Dallas branch.

Recall the discussion of cRTP in the "Using Voice Compression" section of Chapter 4. Because sufficient bandwidth exists to send the required number of voice calls on the WAN link, you do not need to enable cRTP on the Dallas router.

---

**NOTE**     The Brisbane and Melbourne router configuration is similar to that of the Dallas router. Look at Table 5-10 for the appropriate values for *ValueVoicefax*, *ValueVoiceControl*, and *ValueMissionCritical*.

---

# Central Site WAN QoS Design

According to Figure 5-1, the San Jose site WAN router has an IMA (Inverse Multiplexing of ATM) card to connect to the service provider network via ATM at 1.5 Mbps. The remote sites connect to the service provider via Frame Relay links. The conversion between ATM and FR and vice versa is done in the carrier network using the FRF.8 standard.

The configurations for the LAN switches described earlier for the San Jose site correctly classify and mark the voice-bearer packets, call-control packets, and mission-critical data packets. Hence, on the WAN routers at the central sites, you need to classify the packets based on the received DSCP values and give the priority using the LLQ.

**Example 5-9**   *San Jose WAN Router Configuration*

```
! The class map "VOICE" matches on all packets with the DSCP value of EF.

class-map match-all VOICE
match ip dscp ef

! The class map "VOICE-CONTROL" matches on all packets with the DSCP
! value of AF31.

class-map match-all VOICE-CONTROL
match ip dscp af31

! The class map "MC-DATA" matches on all packets with the DSCP value of
! AF21.

class-map match-all MC-DATA
match ip dscp af21

! Policy map for packets going to "WAN-EDGE-Seattle"

policy map WAN-EDGE-Seattle
```

**Example 5-9**  *San Jose WAN Router Configuration (Continued)*

```
! For all packets that previously matched on class-map "VOICE" for
! having a DSCP value of EF, 390 kbps is allocated to the priority queue.

class VOICE
priority 390

! For all packets that previously matched on class-map "VOICE-CONTROL"
! for having a DSCP value of AF31, 10 kbps bandwidth is allocated to
! this waited fair queue (WFQ).

class VOICE-CONTROL
bandwidth 10

! For all packets that previously matched on class-map "MC-DATA"
! for having DSCP value of AF21, 200 kbps is allocated to the priority queue.

class MC-DATA
bandwidth 200

! All other traffic is matched to "class-default" and it will be
! treated by a fair queue.

class class-default
fair-queue
random-detect dscp-based

! Policy map for packets going to "WAN-EDGE-Dallas"

policy map WAN-EDGE-Dallas

! For all packets that previously matched on class-map "VOICE" for
! having a DSCP value of EF, 210 Kbps is allocated to the priority queue.

class VOICE
priority 210

! For all packets that previously matched on class-map "VOICE-CONTROL"
! for having a DSCP value of AF31, 10 Kbps is allocated to this
! waited fair queue (WFQ).

class VOICE-CONTROL
bandwidth 10

! For all packets that previously matched on class-map "MC-DATA"
! for having a DSCP value of AF21, 100 Kbps bandwidth is allocated to
! this waited fair queue (WFQ).

class MC-DATA
bandwidth 100

! All other traffic is matched to "class-default" and will be
```

*continues*

**Example 5-9** *San Jose WAN Router Configuration (Continued)*

```
! treated by a fair queue.

class class-default
fair-queue
random-detect dscp-based

policy map WAN-EDGE-Sydney
class VOICE
bandwidth 536
class VOICE-CONTROL
bandwidth 30
class MC-DATA
bandwidth 500
class class-default
fair-queue
random-detect dscp-based

interface ATM3/0
no ip address
no atm ilmi-keepalive

interface ATM3/0.60 point-to-point
pvc DALLAS 0/60
vbr-nrt 512 512
tx-ring-limit 10
protocol ppp Virtual-Template60
interface Virtual-Template60
bandwidth 512
ip address 10.200.60.2 255.255.255.252
service-policy output WAN-EDGE-Dallas
ppp multilink
ppp multilink fragment-delay 10
ppp multilink interleave

interface ATM3/0.61 point-to-point
pvc SEATTLE 0/61
vbr-nrt 1000 1000
tx-ring-limit 28
ip address 10.200.10.2 255.255.255.252
service-policy output WAN-EDGE-Seattle
```

**NOTE**     The Sydney router configuration is similar to that of the San Jose router.

# Summary

This chapter covered the QoS design approach along with detailed configurations for central and remote sites of XYZ. Successful implementation of QoS is key to achieving good voice quality in the IPT network. This chapter used commonly deployed switch and router platforms to explain key design concepts, highlighting the critical areas where QoS is required in the network. If your network uses a different hardware platform than described in this chapter, you need to refer to the appropriate product documentation for exact command syntax. However, the QoS design principles and guidelines remain the same and are independent of the hardware platform.

# CHAPTER 6

# Design of Call-Processing Infrastructure and Applications

This chapter provides a detailed explanation of the tasks and processes involved in designing a call-processing infrastructure and IP Telephony (IPT) applications that meet the requirements of XYZ, Inc. Topics covered in this chapter include the following:

- High-level IPT design
- Low-level design
- Securing the IPT infrastructure

This chapter uses information collected in the design questionnaires listed in Appendixes D, "IPT Design Phase: IP Phone Selection Questionnaire," through F, "Ordering T1/E1 PRI from the Carrier Questionnaire". It also uses the information collected about XYZ in Chapter 3, "Large-Scale Enterprise Requirements for IP Telephony." To review the high-level architecture of the proposed IPT solution for XYZ, which is a multisite WAN with distributed call processing, see Figure 5-1 in Chapter 5, "Design Phase: Network Infrastructure Design."

## High-Level IPT Design

This section covers these high-level design aspects of the proposed IPT system for XYZ:

- Fax and analog terminals
- Voice gateways
- Media resources
- IPT applications

## Fax and Analog Terminals

The VG248 and FXS ports on Cisco IOS routers will handle the fax needs. Three VG248s will be deployed in San Jose to provide a total of $3 \times 48 = 144$ analog ports to connect fax machines and provide modem access to the users. VG248 communicates with CallManager via the Skinny Client Control Protocol (SCCP).

# Voice Gateways

Voice gateways connect the IPT network to the public switched telephone network (PSTN) and the PBX system. This section discusses the voice gateway modules and signaling protocols used to interface the IPT network with the PSTN and PBX system.

## Access to the PSTN

Each site in the XYZ network has direct access to the PSTN. At each site, the primary path to call the PSTN is the local voice gateway. Calls between sites take the IP WAN as a first preference and are rerouted to the PSTN if the IP WAN is down or not enough bandwidth is available to route the call. Detailed call-routing requirements are discussed in the "Dial Plan Architecture" section later in this chapter.

As mentioned in Chapter 4, "Planning Phase," in the "PBX Infrastructure and Migration" section, the San Jose site has six T1 connections. At the beginning of IPT deployment in the San Jose site, only four of the T1s that are currently terminating on the PBX will be moved to voice gateways in the IPT system. The remaining two T1s will stay connected to the PBX. This is required to route the calls between the IP Phones and the phones that are on the PBX (not yet migrated to the IPT network). Table 6-1 shows the different hardware used for PSTN access and the type of PRI signaling used for the trunking.

**Table 6-1**  *Hardware List for PSTN Trunks and Signaling Type*

| Location | Hardware | Port and Signaling Type | No. of Trunks |
|---|---|---|---|
| San Jose | Communications Media Module (WS-SVC-CMM-6T1) | T1 PRI National ISDN (NI2) | 4 |
| Seattle | Cisco 3745 with the High-Density Voice Network Module (NM-HDV) and the Network Voice Module (NM-HDA) | T1 PRI NI2, Analog FXS[1] | 1 |
| Dallas | Cisco 2651XM with the analog NM-HDA | Analog FXS Analog FXO[2] | 4 |
| Sydney | Catalyst 6000 Family Voice E1 WS-X6608-E1 | E1 PRI NET5 | 4 |
| Melbourne | Cisco 3745 with the NM-HDV | E1 PRI NET5 Analog FXS | 1 |
| Brisbane | Cisco 2651XM with the analog NM-HDA | Analog FXS Analog FXO | 4 |

[1] FXS = Foreign Exchange Station

[2] FXO = Foreign Exchange Office

### Access to the PBX

The PBX system will continue to operate in the San Jose office. Table 6-2 shows the location where a PBX will remain connected to the IPT network.

**Table 6-2**  *Hardware List for the PBX Trunks and Signaling Type*

| Location | Hardware | Trunk Type, Signaling | No. of Trunks |
|----------|----------|-----------------------|---------------|
| San Jose | Communications Media Module (WS-SVC-CMM-6T1) | T1 PRI, QSIG | 2 |

---

**NOTE**   In both San Jose and Sydney, for redundancy and high-availability purposes, the Communication Media Module (CMM) and WS-X6608-E1 modules are deployed in two separate Catalyst 6500 chassis. Half of the trunks from the PSTN are connected to one chassis and the other half to the other chassis.

---

## Media Resources

Media resources are the entities that provide resources for media mixing (conferencing), codec conversion (transcoding), Media Termination Point (MTP), and Music on Hold (MoH). These resources, except the transcoding, are available as both software and hardware. Transcoding requires the use of digital signal processors (DSPs), so it is available only as hardware. Every CallManager in the cluster provides conferencing, MTP, and MoH resources by default. The CallManager services that are responsible for providing these resources are Cisco IP Voice Media Streaming Application and Cisco MoH Audio Translator (used only by MoH).

Enabling these software-based resources on the CallManager consumes some part of the system resources. Hence, you need to take into account these services when you calculate device weights, discussed later in this section.

---

**TIP**   Cisco IOS gateways and Catalyst gateways provide the conferencing, transcoding, and media termination resources in hardware. If you have enough hardware equipment to provide these resources, disable these two services on the CallManager to reduce its load.

---

In a multisite IPT deployment, you can deploy all the media resources at a central location or use the distributed approach.

If you choose centralized deployment, for every conferencing or transcoding request, the streams from the remote sites have to traverse to the central site, which is a waste of bandwidth on the WAN link. If the requirement is to use a centralized deployment, make sure that you choose a lower-bandwidth codec to optimize the bandwidth usage on the WAN links by multiple streams.

Distributed media resource deployment conserves the bandwidth, but you might have to spend more money on the hardware. You should compare the cost of the additional hardware required to the cost of additional bandwidth on the WAN links before you make a decision on placing the media resources in the network.

## Conferencing and Transcoding

The following two types of conferencing services are available in CallManager:

- **Ad Hoc conferencing**—The conference call initiator (conference controller) adds the participants to the conference call. IP Phone users press the Confrn softkey on the IP Phone to join the other participants in the existing conversation.

- **Meet-Me conferencing**—All participants are provided with a preconfigured bridge or directory number that they dial to join the conference call. Before users can invoke Meet-Me, the CallManager system administrator must configure the Meet-Me directory numbers in the CallManager as a part of the dial plan configuration and publish these numbers to all the users in the organization.

The transcoding resources convert voice streams from one compression type to another. In a multisite IPT deployment, such as XYZ's, the remote sites typically use the G.729 codec over the WAN to conserve the bandwidth, because G.729 consumes less bandwidth than G.711. Voice applications such as IVR and voice mail can stream either G.711 or G.729. In case of XYZ, these two applications are deployed at the central site to use the G.711 codec only. It is highly recommended not to enable the transcoding features on these applications even if they are available, because it consumes a lot of system resources and generates poor voice quality. Deploying the hardware-based transcoder is the best approach when a user in a remote site needs to access one of these two applications and when a transcoder will be required in the voice path to convert the audio G.729 to G.711 or vice versa.

When an IP Phone (G.729 voice stream) at a remote site connects to IVR or the Cisco Unity server, CallManager invokes the transcoder to transcode the G.729 voice stream to G.711. Chapter 7, "Voice-Mail System Design," covers the Cisco Unity design and deployment.

Two endpoints using different codecs cannot establish a two-way communication if no transcoding devices are available. You can press the *i* button twice on the Cisco IP Phone (7960/7940 models) during the call to see the codec used for the call. The following list summarizes the deployment of transcoding and conferencing resources for XYZ:

- In San Jose, Cisco CMM provides conferencing and transcoding resources using the Ad Hoc Conferencing and Transcoding (ACT) port adapter (WS-SVC-CMM-ACT), which has four DSPs. Each ACT port adapter provides 128 channels (32 channels per DSP) for conferencing and transcoding. A single CMM can have a maximum of four ACT port adapters, providing a maximum of 512 channels. One ACT port adapter in the San Jose

CMM provides the resources for transcoding and conferencing by using the partitioning technique. We will partition the ACT port adapter to use three DSPs to provide a conferencing resource pool of 96 channels and to use one DSP to provide a transcoding resource pool of 32 channels.

- In Seattle and Melbourne, the Cisco 3745 router that is equipped with the NM-HDV provides support for conferencing only, by partitioning the DSP resources. The ACT port adapter in the CMM at San Jose handles all the transcoding requests for Seattle.

- In Sydney, the additional E1 ports on the Catalyst 6000 Family Voice E1 (WS-6608-E1) card provide transcoding and conferencing resources. Two E1 ports provide conference resources, and two E1 ports provide transcoding.

- No local conferencing and transcoding resources are deployed in Dallas or Brisbane. Users in Dallas and Brisbane use the conferencing and transcoding resources at the San Jose and Sydney central sites, respectively.

Table 6-3 shows the hardware deployed in each location for providing conferencing and transcoding resources.

**Table 6-3**    *Hardware Conferencing and Transcoding Device List*

| Location | Hardware |
|----------|----------|
| San Jose | Two ACT port adapters (WS-SVC-CMM-ACT), one ACT per CMM. |
| Seattle | NM-HDV (DSP partitioning) with 4 Packet Voice DSP Modules (PVDMs) for conferencing only |
| Dallas | None |
| Sydney | Catalyst 6000 family voice E1 (WS-X6608-E1) using 4 ports (2 port conferencing and 2 port transcoding) |
| Melbourne | NM-HDV (DSP partitioning) with 5 PVDMs for conferencing only |
| Brisbane | None |

**NOTE**    Cisco CMM and WS-X6608-E1 modules are deployed in two separate Catalyst 6500 chassis—in San Jose and Sydney—for redundancy and high-availability purposes. In each chassis, one port is configured as a conference bridge and one port as a hardware transcoder.

## Music on Hold

Music on Hold, as the name implies, streams the predefined music from an MoH server to the caller when the caller is placed on hold. The MoH feature allows two types of hold:

- **End-user hold**—An IP Phone user presses the Hold key while on the call.

- **Network hold**—An IP Phone user attempts to transfer a call, joins a conference call, or parks the call at a call park number.

MoH supports both unicast and multicast transport mechanisms to transport the audio streams to the endpoints. Unicast MoH consists of streams sent directly from the MoH server to the endpoint requesting an MoH audio stream. With multicast, the MoH server continuously plays the audio stream. Endpoints that request a multicast MoH stream have to join the multicast IP address of the stream. This is similar to a multicast client joining a multicast group.

As discussed in the preceding section, CallManager offers MoH as a software feature. While designing the MoH feature, you need to consider the following:

- Can CallManager servers provide the MoH feature in the network? Alternatively, is a dedicated MoH server needed?
- How many simultaneous MoH requests are required for the planned IPT network?
- Is the MoH feature required for all the sites?
- Should unicast MoH or multicast MoH be used?

Before you choose an MoH model for XYZ, you need to consider some of the MoH design scenarios, described next.

Enabling the MoH feature on the CallManager consumes system resources. If you plan to enable the MoH feature on the CallManager servers in the cluster, ensure that you account for the device weights for the MoH feature when you calculate the device weights. As long as the device weights do not exceed the maximum capacity of the server, you can enable the feature on the CallManager servers. However, in larger IPT deployments, consider separating the MoH feature onto a dedicated server. For instance, you can combine DHCP, TFTP, and MoH functionality into a single server. An MoH server that is co-resident with CallManager supports 20 streams, whereas a dedicated standalone MoH server supports up to 250 streams depending on the server platform. You can install the dedicated MoH server on any approved Media Convergence Server (MCS) platforms.

The industry recommendation to calculate the number of users who will be using the Hold feature in any telephony system is approximately 1 to 2 percent of the total user base. This could be network or end-user hold. Based on the numbers that you derive by using this formula, you can choose either a co-resident or a dedicated MoH server solution.

Another approach to the MoH design is to enable MoH on the CallManager servers and monitor the MoH server performance counters (refer to "Memory Upgrades" in Chapter 9, "Operations and Optimization," for a discussion on Performance Monitor counters and monitoring procedures) to check the MoHOutOfResources performance counter for the Cisco MoH device performance object. If you see this counter going up, you can plan to add the dedicated MoH server to the network.

With multisite IPT deployment models, enabling the MoH feature for the remote branches consumes bandwidth on the WAN links. If you enable MoH, ensure that you provision the Low Latency Queueing (LLQ) for WAN links to include the additional bandwidth required for the MoH streams.

Finally, you have to consider whether you want to enable unicast, multicast, or both for MoH streams. Multicast MoH is attractive especially when streaming the audio files from the central site MoH server. Consider the scenario in which two IP Phones at the remote site place their respective callers on hold. With multicast MoH, only one stream traverses from the MoH server to the remote-site router, whereas with unicast MoH, two separate streams would go from the MoH server to each IP Phone, which consumes twice the bandwidth. In XYZ, the approach taken to deploy MoH across the network is as follows:

- One CallManager in the cluster runs the MoH server, and all the central site users receive the audio streams from this MoH server via unicast.

- In addition to the capability of CallManager to provide centralized MoH, the remote-site routers at Seattle and Melbourne can function as multicast MoH resources. This allows a distributed MoH design. This feature is available on the routers starting with Cisco IOS releases 12.2(15)ZJ2 and 12.3(4)T.

- XYZ has no plans to deploy the MoH feature for the Dallas and Brisbane sites. A Beep/Tone on Hold is played when a user in either of these two locations is placed on hold. The Beep/Tone on Hold replaces MoH when MoH is turned off. Instead of hearing music, the user on hold will hear a beep/tone every 10 seconds (could be more or less depending on the configuration of a service parameter in CallManager)

# IPT Applications

Cisco offers a wide variety of IPT applications that integrate with CallManager. Deploying these applications in the network adds functionality and, in some cases, helps to increase the overall productivity of the organization. Based on the requirements received by XYZ, it requires the following applications:

- AutoAttendant (AA)
- Interactive Voice Response (IVR)
- Call Center

## AutoAttendant

XYZ requires an application that can provide full-time AutoAttendant functionality to take every call on the first ring, present to the caller a menu of options, and provide the following three choices:

- Dial by extension
- Dial by name
- Transfer to the operator

XYZ has a dedicated number for the AutoAttendant. Every external caller who calls this number reaches the AutoAttendant application's main menu and is provided with the preceding three choices.

## Interactive Voice Response

XYZ also has a separate number to reach an IVR system. When external callers call this number, the IVR system provides the caller with the following two options:

- Transfer to the AutoAttendant
- Transfer to the sales and support group

---

**NOTE**    In San Jose, the AutoAttendant application is based on the Cisco Customer Response Server (CRS) engine. In implementation (when users reach the AutoAttendant application in San Jose), the search scope includes all the employees of XYZ in the San Jose, Seattle, and Dallas sites. Note that you can also implement the AutoAttendant application by using Cisco Unity. The Directory Partitioning feature in Cisco Unity allows us to limit the search scope to any branch based on the user's selection. Refer to the "Multiple Directory Handlers" section of Chapter 7 for details on implementing the AutoAttendant feature in Cisco Unity.

---

## Call Center

XYZ needs a call center capability in the IPT network. The XYZ call center group consists of 20 personnel from the sales group and support groups, all of whom are employees of XYZ, USA. These groups are responsible for answering customer calls regarding the new sales and support of existing products.

At any given time, 20 personnel will be servicing the customers. The call center operates from 8 a.m. to 5 p.m., Monday through Friday. The proposed architecture includes a CRS/IP Contact Center (IPCC) Express solution, which is best suited for companies such as XYZ that have a small- to medium-scale call center network.

## Voice Messaging

According to the proposed voice-messaging architecture for XYZ, the present Octel voice-mail system at San Jose integrates with CallManager via the Simplified Message Desk Interface (SMDI). Cisco Unity replaces the voice-mail system at Sydney. The remote locations in Australia will use the Sydney Unity voice-mail system.

Whereas Chapter 7 provides the details of the voice-messaging system design, this chapter covers the configuration and design requirements to configure the CallManager system to support the proposed voice-mail architecture.

# Low-Level Design

Cisco CallManager, which is the key part of Cisco IPT solution, requires configuration and customization to meet specific requirements. When you are designing the IPT solution for large-scale enterprises, it is critical to understand the call-routing, sizing, and future growth requirements and to translate those requirements into CallManager configurations. This section provides the detailed design and configurations based on XYZ's requirements.

## CallManager Cluster Design

The CallManager cluster (cluster 1) in San Jose, shown in Figure 6-1, consists of three CallManager servers: one CallManager publisher, SJCCMA-PUB, and two subscribers, SJCCMB-SUB1 and SJCCMC-SUB2. An additional server, SJCDHCPTFTP, acts as a DHCP and TFTP server. In large deployments, the best practice is to separate the TFTP/DHCP server functionality from the publisher server.

**Figure 6-1**   *U.S. Cluster—Cluster 1 of XYZ*

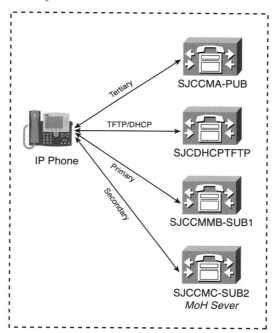

The servers perform the following roles in the U.S. cluster:

- **SJCCMB-SUB1**—Serves as the primary subscriber to which all the IP Phones, voice gateways, and other IPT endpoints register under normal operations.

- **SJCCMC-SUB2**—Serves as the secondary subscriber, which acts as a backup to the primary subscriber.
- **SJCCMA-PUB**—Keeps the read-write master database of the cluster's configuration information. Also acts as a tertiary CallManager to keep the IPT service up and running should both subscribers fail.
- **SJCDHCPTFTP**—Serves the configuration and binary loads for the IPT endpoints in its role as a TFTP server and serves as a DHCP server to lease out the IP addresses for the IP Phones in San Jose.

Table 6-4 shows the CallManager server names, IP addresses, and server roles in the U.S. cluster. You perform CallManager server configuration via the Cisco CallManager Configuration page in Cisco CallManager Administration (choose **System > Cisco CallManager**).

Refer to Table 5-3 in Chapter 5 for the VLAN/IP addressing assignments designed for the XYZ network.

To access the CallManager Administration page from a web browser, use the following URL:

http://*IP_Address_of_Publisher*/ccmadmin

**Table 6-4**   *U.S. CallManager Servers*

| CallManager Server Name | CallManager Server IP Address | Server Role | Auto-Registration Information |
|---|---|---|---|
| SJCCMA-PUB | 10.1.1.5/27 | Publisher | Auto-Registration Disabled on This CallManager: Checked<br><br>Partition: **\<None\>** |
| SJCCMB-SUB1 | 10.1.1.6/27 | Subscriber—primary call processing for all devices | Auto-Registration Disabled on This CallManager: Unchecked<br><br>Partition: **p-autoregphone** |
| SJCDHCPTFTP | 10.1.1.7/27 | DHCP, TFTP server | Not applicable |
| SJCCMC-SUB2 | 10.1.1.36/27 | Subscriber—secondary call processing for all devices; MoH server | Auto-Registration Disabled on This CallManager: Checked<br><br>Partition: **\<None\>** |

The CallManager cluster in Sydney consists of two CallManager servers, as shown in Figure 6-2. Table 6-5 shows the server names, IP addresses, and server roles.

**Figure 6-2**    *Australia Cluster—Cluster 2 of XYZ*

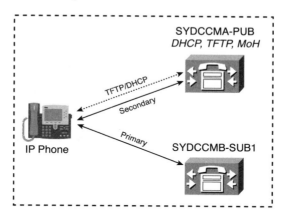

**Table 6-5**    *Australia CallManager Server Function*

| CallManager Name | CallManager IP Address | Server Role | Auto-Registration Information |
|---|---|---|---|
| SYDCCMA-PUB | 10.4.1.5/27 | Publisher, TFTP server, MoH server, and DHCP server | Auto-Registration Disabled on This CallManager: Checked<br><br>Partition: **\<None\>** |
| SYDCCMB-SUB1 | 10.4.1.36/27 | Subscriber—primary call processing for all devices | Auto-Registration Disabled on This CallManager: Unchecked<br><br>Partition: **p-autoregphone** |

From now on, the CallManager cluster in San Jose will be called cluster 1, and the CallManager cluster in Sydney will be called cluster 2.

As shown in Tables 6-4 and 6-5, the XYZ network scenario enables auto-registration only for the primary CallManager servers. Auto-registration enables new phones to register with the CallManager server and get a directory number from the range specified in the CallManager configuration. The partition for the auto-registered phones is the partition (p-autoregphone) specified on the CallManager Configuration page.

You can use this auto-registration feature during the initial phase of the deployment to auto-register the IP Phones. The "Implementation of IP Phones Using BAT" section of Chapter 8, "Implementation," discusses the IP Phone implementation methods using auto-registration and the Tool for Auto-Registered Phones Support (TAPS) service. Disable auto-registration after you complete the deployment, to avoid rogue phones registering to the cluster.

## CallManager Scalability and Sizing

Many types of devices can register with CallManager, such as IP Phones, voice-mail ports, Computer Telephony Integration (CTI) ports, voice gateways, and DSP resources such as transcoding and conferencing. Each of these devices carries a different weight based on the amount of resources it requires from the server platform with which it is registered. The required resources include memory, the processor, and I/O. Each device then consumes additional server resources during transactions, which are normally in the form of calls. For example, a device that makes only 6 calls per hour consumes fewer resources than a device that makes 12 calls per hour. As a common starting point, the base weight of a device is calculated with the assumption that it makes six or fewer calls per hour during its busiest hour, or six busy hour call completions (BHCC). Refer to Table 1-3 in Chapter 1, "Cisco IP Telephony Solution Overview," to get the base device weights for the various device types.

Tables 6-1 and 6-2 outline the hardware deployed in the IPT network. Table 5-1 in Chapter 5 provides the number of IP Phones required at each location. This information is useful in calculating the total device weight of the cluster. Table 6-6 shows the device weight calculation in the U.S. cluster.

**Table 6-6**   *Device Weight Calculation of Cluster 1*

| Device Type | Weight per Session/Voice Channel [b] | Sessions/DS0s per Device [c] | Device Total [d] | Cumulative Device Weight at XYZ Cluster 1 e = b × c × d |
|---|---|---|---|---|
| IP Phone | 1 | 1 | 1180 | 1180 |
| Analog SCCP ports (3 VG248s, 48 analog ports each) | 1 | 48 | 3 | 144 |
| Analog MGCP ports (FXO/FXS) | 3 | 1 | 10 (10 FXO + FXS ports) | 30 |
| CTI route point | 2 | 1 | 5 (5 CTI route points: AA, IVR, IP-ICD, IPMA, and TAPS) | 10 |
| CTI client port | 2 | 1 | 60 CTI ports | 120 |
| ICT gateway | 3 | 1 | 1 | 3 |
| Digital MGCP T1 | 3 per DS0 | 23 | 7 T1s (6 in San Jose, 1 in Seattle) | 483 |

**Table 6-6**    *Device Weight Calculation of Cluster 1 (Continued)*

| Device Type | Weight per Session/Voice Channel [b] | Sessions/DS0s per Device [c] | Device Total [d] | Cumulative Device Weight at XYZ Cluster 1 e = b × c × d |
|---|---|---|---|---|
| Conferencing resource (hardware) | 3 per session | 96 conferencing channels per ACT | 2 ACTs (one in each CMM Module deployed with separate chassis) | 576 |
| | | 36 conference channels (NM-HDV) in Seattle | 1 | 108 |
| Transcoding resource (hardware) | 3 per session | 32 transcoding channels per ACT | 2 ACTs (one in each CMM Module deployed in separate chassis) | 192 |
| Total | | | | 2846 |

**NOTE**    Starting with CallManager 3.3, Cisco has a Cisco CallManager Capacity tool to size the CallManager clusters. This is a web-based tool and is currently not available on Cisco.com. The calculations shown in Tables 6-6 and 6-7 are valid for CallManager versions prior to 3.3. Because the CallManager Capacity tool is not available on Cisco.com, we have used the old method (by using device weights) to size the CallManager cluster. Until the tool is available on Cisco.com (when you are dealing with complex Cisco IPT deployments involving large number of IP Phones, gateways, multiple lines per IP Phone and so forth), contact your local Cisco sales team to help size the CallManager cluster(s) for your IPT deployments.

The total number of device units that a single Cisco CallManager can control varies, depending on the server platform. The Media Convergence Server model MCS-7835 supports up to 5000 device weight units. From Table 6-6, with a total device weight of 2846, the CallManager cluster designed with MCS-7835 servers can handle the load of all the registered devices and also gives enough room for future expansion of the IPT network.

Similarly, Table 6-7 shows the device weight calculation for cluster 2. A cluster of two MCS-7835 servers can handle the calculated load.

**Table 6-7** *Device Weight Calculation in Cluster 2*

| Device Type | Weight per Session/ Voice Channel [b] | Sessions/ DS0s per Device [c] | Device Total [d] | Cumulative Device Weight at XYZ Cluster 2 e = b × c × d |
|---|---|---|---|---|
| IP Phone (includes Unity ports) | 1 | 1 | 609 | 609 |
| Analog SCCP ports (2 VG248s; 48 analog ports each) | 1 | 48 | 2 | 96 |
| Analog MGCP ports (FXO/FXS) | 3 | 1 | 10 | 30 |
| CTI route point | 2 | 1 | 2 (2 CTI route points: AA, IVR) | 4 |
| CTI client port | 2 | 1 | 40 (CTI ports) | 80 |
| ICT gateway | 3 | 1 | 1 | 3 |
| Digital MGCP E1 | 3 per DS0 | 30 DS0s per E1 port | 5 (4 E1s in Sydney, 1 E1 in Melbourne) | 450 |
| Conference resource (hardware) | 3 per session | 32 per port | 2 E1 ports | 192 |
| | | 36 conference channels (NM-HDV) in Melbourne | 1 | 108 |
| Transcoding resource (hardware) | 3 per session | 32 per port | 2 E1 ports | 192 |
| Total | | | | 1764 |

# Customer Response Solution Server Scalability and Sizing

The Customer Response Solution (CRS) server is deployed to roll out a small call center and an AA. The call center script application uses the default icd.aef script provided with the CRS platform plus other additions that consist of including the time of the day and the day of the week routing.

| NOTE | Effective with release 3.0, Cisco Customer Response Application (CRA) has been renamed Cisco Customer Response Solution and, effective with release 3.1, the CRS product is marketed under the names IPCC Express and IP IVR. |
|------|---|
| | In this chapter and the rest of the book, the names CRS, CRA, and IPCC Express are used interchangeably. |

Sizing a call center consists of sizing the following items:

- **Number of agents**—Agents that handle incoming calls
- **Number of IVR ports**—Ports that handle sessions such as prompting and collecting information at the front end of a call center system
- **Number of gateway/PSTN trunks**—Ports handling calls originating from the PSTN

To size the call center parameters, two types of traffic models are used (which are named after A. K. Erlang, a Danish scientist):

- **Erlang-B**—Use to size IVR ports and gateway trunks. This model assumes the following:
  - Calls arrive randomly into the network.
  - A percentage of calls is lost or blocked if the trunks are busy. This percentage is not queued.
- **Erlang-C**—Use to size the number of agents in call centers in which calls are queued before being presented to agents. This model assumes the following:
  - Calls are presented randomly to the servers.
  - Callers who find all agents busy are queued, not blocked.

## Sizing the Number of Agents

The first step to size a call center is to determine the number of agents using the Erlang-C traffic model. This model relies on the following parameters:

- **Busy hour call attempts (BHCA)**—The number of calls received in the busy hour
- **Average handle time (AHT)**—The average duration (talk time) of the call
- **Average work time (AWT)**—The average agent wrap-up time after the caller hangs up
- **Service level goal**—The percentage of the calls to be answered within a certain number of seconds

Table 6-8 shows the values of these parameters as provided by XYZ. The telecom department provided these numbers by analyzing the historical reports from the legacy call center.

**Table 6-8**    *Erlang-C Value Parameters for Agent Sizing*

| Parameter | Value |
|---|---|
| BHCA | 200 |
| AHT | 180 seconds |
| AWT | 30 seconds |
| Service-level goal | 90% of calls answered within 15 seconds |

To determine the number of agents and other parameters, insert the values in Table 6-8 in the Call Center Calculator, available at http://www.erlang.co.uk/ccc.htm.

As the highlighted row in Figure 6-3 shows, the service-level goal that is nearer to the requirement of 90 percent (refer to Table 6-8) is 93 percent. This requires 17 agents, and XYZ already plans to have 20 agents in the call center. Table 6-9 lists other parameters and values that resulted from this calculation.

**Figure 6-3**    *Call Center Calculator*

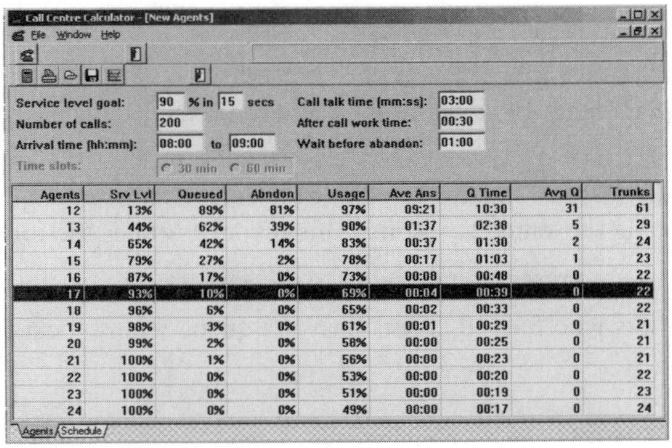

**Table 6-9**    *Call Center Calculator Results*

| Parameter | Description | Value |
|---|---|---|
| Agents | Number of agents needed to meet the service-level goal | 17 |
| Srv Lvl | Percentage of the calls that will be answered within the service level time | 93% |
| Queued | Percentage of calls that will have to queue for a period of time before being answered by an agent | 10% |
| Q Time | The average time spent in the queue for those calls that have to queue (when no agents are available) | 39 seconds |

**NOTE**    In Figure 6-3, the Trunks column shows the number of PSTN trunks required for this call center. This number is irrelevant in this calculation because sizing the PSTN trunks uses the Erlang-B model, not the Erlang-C model. This calculator is based on the Erlang-C model used for call center sizing.

## Sizing the Number of IVR Ports

The second step is to determine the number of IVR ports needed for the XYZ call center. In the case of the Cisco IPT solution, IVR ports are the CTI ports. A CTI port is a computer telephony logical device that handles telephony devices, such as ports used for queuing and handling IVR sessions.

Use the Erlang-B model to calculate the IVR ports. This model relies on the following parameters:

- **BHCA**—Number of calls received in a busy hour.
- **AHT**—The average duration of the call for self-service applications, which includes both the initial treatment or information gathering and the queuing time:
  - **Initial waiting period when a caller reaches the system**—In the case of XYZ, the only call treatment done when a caller enters the application script is in the prompt time, which lasts 15 seconds. Hence, initial treatment time + information gathering time = 15 seconds
  - **Wait time in the IVR queue**—The number of seconds the user has to wait in the queue. The percentage of queued calls must also be considered, because this affects the number of IVR ports required. The average queue time (Q Time) is taken from the Erlang-C calculation in Table 6-9. This time equals 39 seconds.
- **Busy hour traffic (BHT) in Erlangs**—Each subcategory of the AHT is calculated through the following formula:

BHT = (BHCA × AHT seconds) ÷ 3600

In calculating the BHT for the wait time in the IVR queue, a BHCA of 20 is used in Table 6-10 because with the 17 agents (refer to Table 6-9), only 10 percent of the total calls is queued (10 percent of 200 is 20).

- **Blockage or grade of service**—The percentage of calls that is blocked due to unavailability of IVR ports.

Table 6-10 shows the values of BHCA, AHT, BHT, and blockage for XYZ.

**Table 6-10**   *Erlang-B Values for IVR Sizing*

| Parameter | Value |
|-----------|-------|
| BHCA | Total BHCA: 200 |
| | Queued BHCA: 20 (10%, taken from Table 6-9) |
| IVR AHT | Call treatment: 15 sec |
| | Average queue time: 39 sec |
| BHT in Erlangs | BHT1 = 200 × 15 ÷ 3600 = 0.833 |
| | BHT2 = 20 × 39 ÷ 3600 = 0.216 |
| | Total IVR BHT = 1.049 |
| Blockage | 0.1% |

To determine the number of IVR ports, use one of the Erlang-B calculators available at these URLs:

http://www.erlang.com/calculator/erlb/
http://mmc.et.tudelft.nl/~frits/Erlang.htm

Figure 6-4 shows that the number of IVR ports required for the call treatment is 5.9, or 6. As mentioned earlier, in the Cisco IPT solution, the IVR ports are equivalent to CTI ports. Hence, a minimum of six CTI ports is required for the call center solution.

**Figure 6-4**   *Erlang-B Calculations for IVR Ports*

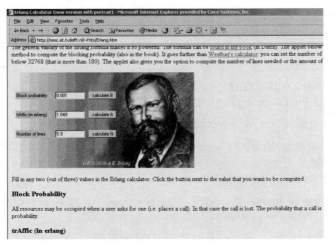

## Sizing the Gateway Trunks for the Call Center

The third step is to determine the number of PSTN trunks needed for the XYZ call center. As mentioned earlier, you use the Erlang-B model to size the gateway trunks.

This model relies on the following parameters:

- **BHCA**—The number of calls received in a busy hour.
- **AHT**—The average time of a call for IVR treatment, queuing, and agent talk time. Wrap-up time is not included in the calculation because a PSTN trunk is not used.
- **BHT in Erlangs**—BHT = (BHCA × AHT seconds) ÷ 3600.
- **Blockage or grade of service**—The percentage of calls that will get a busy tone (because no trunks are available) out of the total BHCA.

Table 6-11 shows the values of BHCA, AHT, BHT, and blockage for XYZ.

**Table 6-11**  *Erlang-B Values for PSTN Trunk Sizing*

| Parameter | Value |
|---|---|
| BHCA | 200 |
| AHT | 180 seconds |
| BHT in Erlangs | BHT3 = 200 × 180 ÷ 3600 = 10<br>BHT = IVR BHT + BHT3 = 11.049 |
| Blockage | 1% |

To determine the number of PSTN trunks, use one of the Erlang-B calculators available at the following URLs:

http://www.erlang.com/calculator/erlb/
http://mmc.et.tudelft.nl/~frits/Erlang.htm

As shown in Figure 6-5, the number of PSTN trunk ports required for the XYZ call center is 18.8, or approximately 19. XYZ already has six PRIs in which the required trunks for the call center have been included. When you are sizing call center IVR ports and PSTN trunks, it is better to over-provision; cost of extra capacity is much cheaper than loss of revenue.

**Figure 6-5**  *Erlang-B Calculations for the PSTN Trunk Ports*

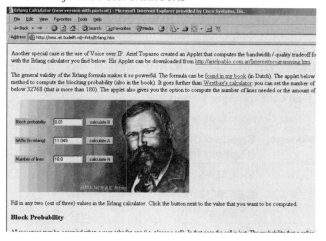

**NOTE**     Cisco has introduced Cisco IPC Resource Calculator to size the contact center resources such as number of agents, IVR ports, PSTN trunks and so forth. This calculator is an integrated tool that uses the call center calculator, Erlang B and Erlang C calculators discussed in this section and provides you with the same results with a single click of a button.

This calculator is currently available on Cisco.com and is currently accessible by only Cisco partners. Cisco is working on making this tool available to all other Cisco customers. Cisco Partners can use the following URL to access the Cisco IPC resource calculator:

http://tools.cisco.com/partner/ipccal/index.htm

## CallManager Group Configuration

The CallManager group lists the CallManager servers in the order of priority. IP Phones and other endpoints attempt to register with the first CallManager server specified in the CallManager group. If the first server is not available, the group attempts to register with the second server, followed by the tertiary server.

Tables 6-12 and 6-13 show the CallManager group naming convention and server priority within the CallManager group for XYZ. As shown, auto-registration for these CallManager groups is enabled. As discussed earlier in the "CallManager Cluster Design" section, the auto-registration feature enables new phones to register with the CallManager server and get a directory number. To enable auto-registration at the CallManager group level, you must enable it on at least one CallManager in the group.

To avoid rogue phones registering to the cluster, you should either turn off auto-registration for the CallManager group at the end of the initial phase of IP Phone deployment or configure the CallManager such that auto-registered phones cannot make calls other than to a security number. Refer to the "Auto-Registration" section in Chapter 9, "Operations and Optimization," for more information on restricting calling from auto-registered phones.

From Table 6-12, you can see that all the IPT endpoints, such as IP Phones and voice gateways, register to the SJCCMB-SUB1 server, which is the primary subscriber. If SJCCMB-SUB1 is not reachable, the IPT endpoints attempt to register with SJCCMC-SUB2. If both SJCCB-SUB1 and SJCCMC-SUB2 are not reachable, the devices attempt to register with the publisher server, SJCCMA-PUB, as a last resort. To define or modify CallManager group configurations, go to the Cisco CallManager Group page. (From Cisco CallManager Administration, choose **System > Cisco CallManager Group**.)

**Table 6-12**  *CallManager Group Configurations in Cluster 1*

| Cisco CallManager Group | Selected Cisco CallManagers (Ordered by Highest priority) | Priority | Auto-Registration Cisco CallManager Group |
|---|---|---|---|
| SJ-GRP-1 | SJCCMB-SUB1 | 1 | Checked |
|  | SJCCMC-SUB2 | 2 |  |
|  | SJCCMA-PUB | 3 |  |

Table 6-13 shows the CallManager group configurations for the Sydney cluster, which has two CallManager servers. Because the SYDCCMB-SUB1 server is listed as the first priority in the CallManager group definition, IPT endpoints attempt to register with this server. If they fail, they attempt to register with the SYDCCMA-PUB server.

**Table 6-13**    *CallManager Group Configurations in Cluster 2*

| Cisco CallManager Group | Selected Cisco CallManagers (Ordered by Highest Priority) | Priority | Auto-Registration Cisco CallManager Group |
|---|---|---|---|
| SYD-GRP-1 | SYDCCMB-SUB1 | 1 | Checked |
|  | SYDCCMA-PUB | 2 |  |

# CallManager Date/Time Configuration

Several CallManager Date/Time groups must be configured, as shown in Tables 6-14 and 6-15, to accommodate the geographically distributed locations.

To perform the date/time group configuration, go to the Date/Time Group page. (From Cisco CallManager Administration, choose **System > Date/Time Group**.)

CallManager synchronizes the date/time settings on the IP Phones every time the user goes off-hook/on-hook on the IP Phone. If the phone is not in use, by default, CallManager sends an SCCP message to update the phone's date/time every day at 3 a.m.

**Table 6-14**    *Date/Time Group Configurations in Cluster 1*

| Group Name | Time Zone | Date Format | Time Format |
|---|---|---|---|
| PST | (GMT-08:00) Pacific Time | M/D/Y | 12-hour |
| CST | (GMT-06:00) Central Time | M/D/Y | 12-hour |

**Table 6-15**    *Date/Time Group Configurations in Cluster 2*

| Group Name | Time Zone | Date Format | Time Format |
|---|---|---|---|
| AEST[1] | (GMT+10:00) Melbourne, Sydney | D/M/Y | 12-hour |
| AEST-QLD[2] | (GMT+10:00) Brisbane | D/M/Y | 12-hour |

[1] AEST = Australian Eastern Standard Time

[2] QLD = Queensland

| | |
|---|---|
| **NOTE** | Table 6-15 lists two different date/time group names but only one time zone. The reason is that Brisbane does not observe daylight savings but Melbourne and Sydney do. |

# CallManager Region Configuration

Regions in CallManager let you specify the voice codec that can be used for calls between devices within that region and between that region and other regions. After regions are configured, each device is assigned to a region via the Device Pool Configuration page. (Refer to "Device Pool Configuration" later in this chapter).

For XYZ, calls within the same location are set to use the G.711 codec. Calls traversing the WAN use the G.729 codec type to conserve the bandwidth across the WAN links. There are three regions:

- One region per physical location in each cluster.

- An additional region per cluster for the remote cluster.

- An additional region called MoH-FAX. The "Music on Hold" and "Fax and Modem" sections explain why this extra region is needed. The MoH-FAX region is configured to use the G.711 codec when communicating with any other region.

To perform the region configuration, go to the Region page. (From Cisco CallManager Administration, choose **System > Region**.) Tables 6-16 and 6-17 show the region definitions for cluster 1 and cluster 2, respectively. As an example of how to read these tables, Table 6-17 lists G.729 in the cells in which Brisbane and Melbourne intersect, meaning that an interregion call between Brisbane and Melbourne is based on the G.729 codec scheme. In the cell in which Brisbane intersects with itself, G.711 is listed, indicating that an intraregion call in the Brisbane region is based on the G.711 codec scheme.

**Table 6-16**  *Regions Matrix in Cluster 1*

| Regions | San Jose | Seattle | Dallas | Australia |
|---------|----------|---------|--------|-----------|
| San Jose | G.711 | G.729 | G.729 | G.729 |
| Seattle | G.729 | G.711 | G.729 | G.729 |
| Dallas | G.729 | G.729 | G.711 | G.729 |
| Australia | G.729 | G.729 | G.729 | G.711 |
| MoH-FAX | G.711 | G.711 | G.711 | G.711 |

**Table 6-17**  *Regions Matrix in Cluster 2*

| Regions | Sydney | Melbourne | Brisbane | U.S. |
|---------|--------|-----------|----------|------|
| Sydney | G.711 | G.729 | G.729 | G.729 |
| Melbourne | G.729 | G.711 | G.729 | G.729 |
| Brisbane | G.729 | G.729 | G.711 | G.729 |
| U.S. | G.729 | G.729 | G.729 | G.711 |
| MoH-FAX | G.711 | G.711 | G.711 | G.711 |

## CallManager Location Configuration

Locations work in conjunction with regions to define the characteristics of a network link. Regions define the type of compression (G.711, G.723, or G.729) that is used on the link, and locations define the amount of available bandwidth for the link.

Locations in the CallManager are used to implement call admission control (CAC) in a centralized call-processing model. Before permitting a call to a location, the CallManager looks up the Locations database to see if there is an available bandwidth to that location. CallManager rejects the call when there is not enough bandwidth to place the call to a location and, if Automated Alternate Routing (AAR) is configured, it routes the call through PSTN.

Figure 6-6 depicts the regions, locations, CODECs used for the calls within each region, CODECs used for the calls between the regions, and bandwidth required for the voice calls between all the sites of XYZ in cluster 1. You need to define one CallManager location per physical site within each cluster.

**Figure 6-6**    *Summary of XYZ Locations and Regions*

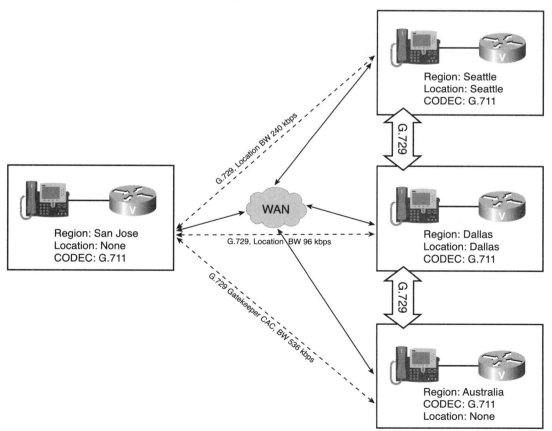

Tables 6-18 and 6-19 show the amount of bandwidth to be provisioned for each location based on the maximum number of calls allowed inbound and outbound. You can obtain the maximum number of calls to each site from the customers by using Table E-6 in Appendix E, " IPT Design Phase: IPT Requirement Analysis Questionnaire." To determine these values, during the busy hour, measure the total number of calls (both inbound and outbound) from the central site and analyze how many calls were destined for any particular branch. This information gives the busy hour traffic for a site. Based on the available bandwidth for that particular branch, you can determine the maximum number of calls allowed over the IP WAN.

As Table 6-18 indicates, we will allow a maximum of ten calls over the WAN link; the eleventh call is rejected and will be routed via the PSTN using the AAR mechanism. A G.729 call consumes 24 kbps and a G.711 call consumes 80 kbps. The fax endpoints at the branches will have their own locations, because we will be deploying fax pass-through without the up-speed feature. These types of calls are considered G.711 calls.

---

**NOTE**   The calculations used in Tables 6-18 and 6-19 are for CallManager and are based on bandwidth consumption of 24 kbps per call for G.729 and 80 kbps per call for G.711. These numbers do not include the overhead values. However, when engineering the WAN links to ensure QoS, you must consider the overhead. Observe Table 5-9 where 30 kbps and 90 kbps of bandwidth are used for the G.729 and G.711 codec types, respectively. These values include the overhead.

---

To perform the location configuration, go to the Location page. (From Cisco CallManager Administration, choose **System > Location**.)

**Table 6-18**   *CallManager Location Settings in Cluster 1*

| Location | Max. Calls | Bandwidth (kbps) |
|---|---|---|
| Seattle | 10 | $10 \times 24 = 240$ |
| Dallas | 4 | $4 \times 24 = 96$ |
| Seattle—fax | 1 | $1 \times 80 = 80$ |
| Dallas—fax | 1 | $1 \times 80 = 80$ |

**Table 6-19**   *CallManager Location Settings in Cluster 2*

| Location | Max. Calls | Bandwidth (kbps) |
|---|---|---|
| Melbourne | 8 | $8 \times 24 = 192$ |
| Brisbane | 3 | $3 \times 24 = 72$ |
| Melbourne—fax | 1 | $1 \times 80 = 80$ |
| Dallas—fax | 1 | $1 \times 80 = 80$ |

## Device Pool Configuration

A device pool is a grouping of common parameters such as region, CallManager group, date/time group, and so forth that can be applied to a group of devices. Some of these parameters are also configurable at the device level. The parameters that are configured at the device level take precedence over the parameters that are configured at the device pool level.

Each cluster has four device pools. For example, device pool DP-SanJose includes all the devices in San Jose, such as IP Phones and gateways.

To perform the device pool configuration, go to the Device Pool Configuration page. (From Cisco CallManager Administration, choose **System > Device Pool**.) Tables 6-20 and 6-21 list the field names and the values to enter for each of the device pools.

**Table 6-20**    *Device Pool Settings in Cluster 1*

| Device Pool Name | Cisco CallManager Group | Date/Time Group | Region | Calling Search Space for Auto-Registration |
|---|---|---|---|---|
| **DP-SanJose** | SJ-GRP-1 | PST | San Jose | CSS-taps |
| **DP-Seattle** | SJ-GRP-1 | PST | Seattle | CSS-taps |
| **DP-Dallas** | SJ-GRP-1 | CST | Dallas | CSS-taps |
| **DP-MOH-FAX** | SJ-GRP-1 | PST | MoH-FAX | CSS-taps |

**Table 6-21**    *Device Pool Settings in Cluster 2*

| Device Pool Name | Cisco CallManager Group | Date/Time Group | Region | Calling Search Space for Auto-Registration |
|---|---|---|---|---|
| **DP-Sydney** | SYD-GRP-1 | Sydney | Sydney | CSS-taps |
| **DP-Melbourne** | SYD-GRP-1 | Sydney | Melbourne | CSS-taps |
| **DP-Brisbane** | SYD-GRP-1 | Brisbane | Brisbane | CSS-taps |
| **DP-MOH-FAX** | SYD-GRP-1 | Sydney | MoH-FAX | CSS-taps |

The "Calling Search Space Design" section later in this chapter discusses the details of the calling search space (CSS) and partitions. At this point, simply note that the auto-registered phones do the following:

- Obtain the CSS specified in the Calling Search Space for Auto-Registration field in the Device Pool Configuration page.

- Obtain the directory number and the partition information from the information specified on the CallManager Configuration page.

# Media Resources Configuration

Media resources provide resources for media mixing (conferencing), codec conversion (transcoding), MTP, and MoH. This section discusses the design of these media resources for the XYZ network.

## Conferencing

As mentioned in the "High-Level IPT Design" section, the conferencing resources exist only in San Jose, Sydney, Seattle, and Melbourne. This section looks into the configuration steps required to set up the conference resources for these sites.

As previously discussed, enabling any feature, such as the software conference bridge feature, on the CallManager adds to the device weights. Based on the device weights in Table 6-6, you can see that the San Jose cluster has not reached its capacity.

Even though the CallManager servers have enough capacity to host software conferencing resources, they are disabled in both clusters. The reason for this is that a misconfiguration of the media resource groups and media resource group list can lead to their usage affecting the server performance.

### Conferencing Resources in San Jose

The ACT port adapter in the Cisco CMM will provide conferencing resources for the San Jose site. The ACT port adapter contains four DSPs. We will use the DSP partitioning technique to register the DSPs as two separate resources in the CallManager. We will partition the DSPs in the ACT port adapter between two resource pools:

- **Conferencing pool**—Assign three DSPs: $3 \times 32 = 96$ channels
- **Transcoding pool**—Assign one DSP: $1 \times 32 = 32$ channels

To configure the ACT module in this fashion, perform the following procedures:

**Step 1** Add the conference bridge. (From the Cisco CallManager Administration page, choose **Service > Media Resource > Conference Bridge**.)

Table 6-22 shows the conference bridge settings to configure on the Conference Bridge page for the San Jose site.

**Table 6-22** *San Jose ACT Port Adapter on CMM Conference Bridge Settings*

| Parameter | Value |
|---|---|
| Conference Bridge Type | Cisco IOS Conference Bridge |
| Conference Bridge Name | CFB001122334455<br>001122334455 is the MAC address of the Ethernet interface that is associated with the ACT module. |

**Table 6-22**  *San Jose ACT Port Adapter on CMM Conference Bridge Settings (Continued)*

| Description | Cat6k-SJ-1 CMM ACT Media Card (slot 3) |
|---|---|
| Device Pool | DP-SanJose |
| Location | <None> |

**NOTE**  In Tables 6-22 and 6-24, the location of the conference bridge is configured as <None> because the resources are located at the central sites.

**Step 2**  Configure the CMM from the CLI.

```
version 12.2
!
hostname Gateway
!
!
ms dsp firmware 0 bundled
ms dsp firmware 1 bundled
ms dsp firmware 2 bundled
!
! Gigabit Ethernet interface on the CMM module
interface GigabitEthernet1/0
 ip address 10.1.10.10 255.255.255.0
!
! Internal Ethernet interface on the ACT module.
! This interface connects the ACT module to the Switch backplane
interface Ethernet2/0
 ip address 10.1.1.11 255.255.255.255
!
! ACT module is in slot3 of the CMM module
mediacard 3
! 3 DSPs will be assigned to a pool called SanJoseCFB
resource-pool SanJoseCFB dsps 3
!
! Define the IP addresses of the CallManagers in cluster 1
sccp ccm 10.1.1.6 identifier 1
sccp ccm 10.1.1.36 identifier 2
sccp ccm 10.1.1.5 identifier 3
sccp
!
! Order in which the SCCP endpoint should register
sccp ccm group 1
```

```
   associate ccm 2 priority 1
   associate ccm 3 priority 2
   associate ccm 1 priority 3
   associate profile 1 register CFB001122334455
   !
  dspfarm
  ! List all the CODECS supported by this conference pool
  dspfarm profile 1 conference adhoc
   codec g711ulaw packetization-period 30
   codec g711alaw packetization-period 30
   codec g729r8 packetization-period 30
   codec g729ar8 packetization-period 30
   codec g723r63 packetization-period 30
   codec g723r53 packetization-period 30
  ! Associate the resource pool previously defined to the conferencing
    function
   associate resource-pool SanJoseCFB
```

## Conferencing Resources in Seattle

In Seattle, the NM-HDV module provides conferencing resources. The NM-HDV module is deployed with four PVDMs. Each PVDM contains three DSPs. The number of calls that can terminate on a DSP depends on the codec complexity. Codec complexity is the grouping of different codec types according to their processing overhead. For instance, G.711 and G.729a are considered medium-complexity codecs, whereas all the flavors of the G.723.1 codec are considered high-complexity codecs.

The T1-PRI circuit from the PSTN terminates on the NM-HDV module. DSP modules on NM-HDV convert the voice-call information received from the PSTN into the IP packet format. Two PVDMs are required for the T1 circuit, based on the following calculations: Under the medium-complexity codec mode, one DSP can provide four channels, so two PVDMs provide $2 \times (3 \text{ DSPs} \times 4 \text{ channels per DSP}) = 24$ channels.

The two remaining PVDMs are assigned to the conferencing function. Each DSP has the capacity to handle one conference call of up to six participants. With the two PVDMs, this site can hold up to six conference calls, which is 36 sessions.

To configure the DSP partitioning, perform the following procedures:

**Step 1**   Add the conference bridge. (From the Cisco CallManager Administration page, choose **Service > Media Resource > Conference Bridge**.)

Table 6-23 shows the conference bridge settings to configure in the CallManager for the Seattle site.

**Table 6-23**  *Seattle NM-HDV Conference Bridge Settings*

| Parameter | Value |
|---|---|
| Conference Bridge Type | Cisco IOS Conference Bridge |
| Conference Bridge Name | CFB00AABBCCDDEE<br><br>00AABBCCDDEE is the MAC address of the configured SCCP interface in the Cisco IOS router. |
| Description | Seattle Cisco 3745 NM-HDV |
| Device Pool | DP-Seattle |
| Location | Seattle |

**Step 2**  Configure the NM-HDV module on the 3745 routers from the CLI.

```
voice-card 1
 dspfarm
 dsp services dspfarm
!
sccp local Loopback0
sccp
sccp ccm 10.1.1.6 priority 1
sccp ccm 10.1.1.36 priority 2
!
! This command sets the IP Precedence value to be used by SCCP
sccp ip precedence 5
sccp switchback timeout guard 180
! Two PDVMs are assigned to the conferencing function for a total of 6 DSPs.
dspfarm confbridge maximum sessions 6
dspfarm
```

**NOTE**

The hardware conference bridge configuration in Melbourne is identical to Seattle's configuration. Because the E1 span requires five DSPs, you have to deploy five PVDMs in the NM-HDV.

## Conferencing Resources in Sydney

In San Jose, the ACT port adapter in the CMM module provides the conferencing resources. In Sydney, the WS-X6608-E1 card in the Catalyst 6500 switch is the DSP resource used for conferencing. Referring to Table 6-1, Sydney has four E1 trunks connecting to the PSTN to route incoming and outgoing calls. We will deploy two WS-X6608-E1 modules in two different 6500 chassis to achieve redundancy and terminate two E1 trunks in each module from the

PSTN. The WS-X6608-E1 module has eight E1 ports. Each port can be configured as conference, transcoder, or MTP resource.

In each WS-X6608-E1 module, port 3 is provisioned in the CallManager as a conferencing resource. In addition to provisioning the ports as hardware conference bridges on the CallManager Administration page, the only other configuration requirement in the Catalyst OS is to put the port in the right VLAN and enable DHCP.

Each port on the WS-X6608-E1 card can handle 32 participants in G.711 mode, with a maximum of 6 participants per conference call. In G.729 mode, the port can handle only 24 participants.

To provision the port on the WS-X6608-E1 card as a conference bridge, from the CallManager Administration page, choose **Service > Media Resource > Conference Bridge** and add the conference bridge with the settings shown in Table 6-24.

**Table 6-24** *Sydney WS-X6608-E1 Conference Bridge Settings*

| Parameter | Value |
| --- | --- |
| Conference Bridge Type | Cisco Conference Bridge Hardware |
| Conference Bridge Name | CFB00EEDDCCBBA9 |
| Description | Sydney Cat6k-1 6608 Port 4/3 |
| Device Pool | DP-Sydney |
| Location | <None> |

## Conferencing Resources in Melbourne

The Melbourne configuration is identical to Seattle's configuration. We will be using the DSP partitioning technology in the NM-HDV module. In the CallManager Conference Bridge Configuration page, this conference resource belongs to the device pool DP-Melbourne and the Melbourne location. It is important to configure the device pool and location so that the right codec is chosen and the right amount of bandwidth is deducted for the CAC.

## Transcoding

Cisco IPCC Express and IP IVR version 3.1 and higher support the G.711 codec and the G.729 codec. You have to choose one or the other, because deployment in a mixed-codec mode is not an option currently. If you deploy using the G.711 codec, all the prompts in the server are stored in the G.711 format. If a device across the WAN needs to establish a G.729 media stream to IPCC Express server, the stream has to go through a transcoder to convert the media to G.711 format. Because the IPCC Express server is collocated with the main PSTN gateway from which most of the calls will be coming, it makes more sense to deploy the server using the G.711 codec.

In addition to supporting both codec types, Cisco Unity can be deployed in a mixed-codec mode. Unity can handle the transcoding in software. We have observed that, in most cases, the quality of a stream transcoded with a hardware transcoder is much better than a stream transcoded in software. Hence, Unity will be deployed using G.711 prompts, and the transcoding capability to G.729 will be turned off to force the G.729 media streams to go through a hardware transcoder.

Transcoding devices will be deployed only in the central sites (San Jose and Sydney) because they need to be collocated with the Cisco IPCC Express and Unity server.

### Transcoding Resources in San Jose

Recall the previous discussion of partitioning the ACT port adapter resources. The fourth DSP in the ACT module will be used for transcoding. The one that DSP configured for transcoding can handle 32 channels. Because each session uses two channels, the total number of transcoding resources is 16.

To configure the ACT module for transcoding, perform the following steps:

**Step 1**   Add the transcoder on Transcoder page. (From the Cisco CallManager Administration page, choose **Service > Media Resource > Transcoder** and choose **Add a New Transcoder**.) Table 6-25 shows the transcoder settings to configure in the CallManager to add this transcoder for the San Jose site.

**Table 6-25**   *San Jose ACT Port Adapter on CMM—Hardware Transcoder Settings*

| Parameter | Value |
| --- | --- |
| Transcoder Type | Cisco IOS Media Termination Point |
| Device Name | MTP001122334455 <br><br> 001122334455 is the MAC address of the Ethernet interface that is associated with the ACT module. |
| Description | Cat6k-SJ-1 CMM ACT Media Card (slot 3) |
| Device Pool | DP-SanJose |

**Step 2**   Configure the Cisco CMM from the CLI.

```
version 12.2
!
hostname Gateway
!
!
ms dsp firmware 0 bundled
ms dsp firmware 1 bundled
ms dsp firmware 2 bundled
!
interface GigabitEthernet1/0
 ip address 10.1.10.10 255.255.255.0
```

```
!Internal Ethernet Interface on the ACT Module.
! This interface connects the ACT module to the Switch backplane
interface Ethernet2/0
 ip address 10.1.10.11 255.255.255.0
 !
! ACT Module is in slot3
mediacard 3

! One DSP will be assigned to a pool called SanJoseXcode
resource-pool SanJoseXcode dsps 1

! Define the IP addresses of the CallManagers in San Jose cluster 1
sccp ccm 10.1.1.6 identifier 1
sccp ccm 10.1.1.36 identifier 2
sccp ccm 10.1.1.5 identifier 3
sccp

! Order in which the SCCP endpoint should register.
sccp ccm group 1
 associate ccm 2 priority 1
 associate ccm 3 priority 2
 associate ccm 1 priority 3
 associate profile 2 register MTP001122334455
 !
dspfarm
 !
 !
! List all the CODECS supported by this conference pool
dspfarm profile 2 transcode
 codec g711ulaw packetization-period 30
 codec g711alaw packetization-period 30
 codec g729r8 packetization-period 30
 codec g729ar8 packetization-period 30
 codec g723r63 packetization-period 30
 codec g723r53 packetization-period 30

! Associate the resource pool previously defined to the transcoding function
associate resource-pool SanJoseXcode
```

## Transcoding Resources in Sydney

The WS-X6608-E1 card in the Catalyst 6500 switch is the DSP resource used for transcoding in Sydney. Port 4 in each chassis will be provisioned in the CallManager as a transcoding resource. The only other configuration requirement in the Catalyst OS is to put the port in the right VLAN and enable DHCP. Note in the WS-X6608-E1 module that each port can handle 24 transcoding sessions.

Add the transcoder on the Transcoder page. (From the Cisco CallManager Administration page, choose **Service > Media Resource > Transcoder** and choose **Add a New Transcoder**.) Table 6-26 shows the transcoder settings to configure in the CallManager to add this transcoder for the Sydney site.

**Table 6-26**   *Sydney Transcoder Settings*

| Parameter | Value |
|---|---|
| Transcoder Type | Cisco Media Termination Point Hardware |
| MAC Address | 00EEDDCCBBA0 |
| Description | Sydney Cat6k-SYD-1 6608 port 4/4 |
| Device Pool | DP-Sydney |

## Music on Hold

According to the XYZ requirements, the central and remote locations will use the MoH integrated feature with CallManager in the following manner:

- San Jose users will use the second CallManager subscriber (SJCCMC-SUB2) as the MoH server.

- Sydney users will use the CallManager publisher (SYDCCMA-PUB) as the MoH server.

- Seattle and Melbourne will use the Cisco IOS MoH feature in the router. That will prevent MoH streams from traversing the WAN and will save bandwidth.

- Brisbane and Dallas users will not use the MoH feature. Instead, users of Brisbane and Dallas will hear a Beep/Tone on Hold.

XYZ will deploy MoH using a single audio file stored in the MoH server. The default audio file that ships with the CallManager will be used in this case study.

To enable MoH for the San Jose and Sydney users, on the CallManager side, we need to configure the integrated MoH server on the backup subscribers in San Jose and on the publisher in Sydney.

To enable MoH for the Seattle and Melbourne branches, the local Cisco IOS gateway/router (3745) will be configured to stream permanently multicast RTP packets from an audio file stored locally in the Flash memory of the router. This feature is available in Cisco IOS versions 12.2.15ZJ2 and above.

The CallManager does not control the streaming part of the Cisco IOS router. The trick is to configure the Cisco IOS router to multicast the audio stream to the same IP multicast address and port as the one configured for the CallManager MoH server. When a phone in the remote site is placed on hold, the CallManager instructs that phone to join a multicast group to receive the audio. Because the multicast address to which the router is multicasting is identical to the one configured on the CallManager, the phone will start listening to the audio (MoH) sourced by the router that is sending this multicast stream.

Of course, you need to ensure that the multicast stream from the CallManager MoH server does not reach the remote sites via the IP WAN links. To achieve this, set the max hops parameter to 1 while configuring the MoH server, as shown in Table 6-27. The maximum hops parameter indicates the maximum number of routers that an audio source is allowed to cross. If the max hops parameter is set to 0, the audio source will remain in its own subnet. If max hops is set to 1, the audio source can cross up to one router to the next subnet.

To take advantage of this design, you have to do the following:

- Configure the MoH server in the cluster and enable multicasting.
- Configure the audio source file for multicasting.
- Configure the remote-site router for MoH.
- Configure the media resource groups (MRGs) and media resource group lists (MRGLs).

The next few sections cover the procedures to complete the preceding tasks.

### Configuring the MoH Server

To configure the MoH server in the San Jose CallManager cluster, from CallManager Administration, choose **Service > Media Resources > Music On Hold Server**. Use the values in Table 6-27 to configure the MoH server.

---

**NOTE**   All the servers in the CallManager cluster have the MoH server enabled by default. To disable this service on the CallManager servers other than the servers designated as MoH servers, set the Run flag to No.

Another way to deactivate the MoH server is to deactivate IP Voice Media Streaming Service and MoH Audio Translator Service on the CallManager Serviceability page. However, disabling IP Voice Media Streaming Service also disables the software conferencing and MTP services. Setting the Run flag to No is a good option if you just want to disable the MoH server and keep the software conference and MTP resources running on the CallManager servers.

---

**Table 6-27**   *MoH Server Configuration in Cluster 1*

| Parameter | Value |
|---|---|
| **Device Information** | |
| Host Server | IP address of the second subscriber: 10.1.1.36 |
| Music on Hold Server Name | Generic name of the MoH entity: MOH-SJCCMC |
| Device Pool | DP-MOH-FAX |
| Location | <None> |
| Max Half Duplex Streams | 30 (Recommended value for MoH collocated with CallManager) |
| Run Flag | Yes |
| **Multicast Audio Source Information** | |
| Enable Multicast Audio Sources on This MoH Server | Checked |
| Base Multicast IP Address | 239.1.1.1 |
| Base Multicast Port Number | 16384 |
| Increment Multicast On | IP Address |
| **Selected Multicast Audio Sources** | |
| Audio Source Name | SampleAudioSource |
| Max Hops | 1 |

Note that even though the multicast MoH is turned on, unicast can still be used. Whether a device uses unicast or multicast depends on how the MRG and MRGL options are configured.

Another important point to discuss is the effect of the Increment Multicast On option. This setting affects the configuration required on the Cisco IOS router at the remote site. The result of setting this option to Increment Multicast on IP Address is that each MoH audio source and codec combination are multicasted to a different IP address but uses the same port number. The result of setting this option to Increment Multicast on Port Number is that each MoH audio source and codec combination is multicasted to the same IP address but uses a different destination port number. Table 6-28 illustrates this distinction, assuming base IP address 239.1.1.1 and base port 16384.

**Table 6-28**    *Effect of Increment Multicast On Option*

| Audio Stream | Codec | Increment Multicast on IP Address | | Increment Multicast on Port Number | |
|---|---|---|---|---|---|
| | | Dst. IP Address | Dst. Port | Dst. IP Address | Dst. Port |
| 1 | G.711 ulaw | 239.1.1.1 | 16384 | 239.1.1.1 | 16384 |
| 1 | G.711 Alaw | 239.1.1.2 | 16384 | 239.1.1.1 | 16386 |
| 1 | G.729 | 239.1.1.3 | 16384 | 239.1.1.1 | 16388 |
| 1 | Wideband | 239.1.1.4 | 16384 | 239.1.1.1 | 16390 |
| 2 | G.711 ulaw | 239.1.1.5 | 16384 | 239.1.1.1 | 16392 |
| 2 | G.711 Alaw | 239.1.1.6 | 16384 | 239.1.1.1 | 16394 |
| 2 | G.729 | 239.1.1.7 | 16384 | 239.1.1.1 | 16396 |
| 2 | Wideband | 239.1.1.8 | 16384 | 239.1.1.1 | 16398 |

It is important to know exactly which audio stream and codec CallManager will choose when you are placing on hold a device that will receive Cisco IOS MoH. After these are known, you specify the correct multicast IP address and port number when configuring the Cisco IOS router at the remote site.

**NOTE**    MoH on Cisco IOS routers supports G.711 only. Therefore, you have to make sure that the MoH server is situated in a region that is configured to open a G.711 MoH connection when a device at the Seattle site is placed on hold. Table 6-20 defines a separate device pool called DP-MOH-FAX for this purpose. As Table 6-27 indicates, the MoH server is in the device pool DP-MOH-FAX.

## Configuring the Audio Source

By default, the audio sources are configured for unicast only. To configure the audio source file for multicast, go to the MoH Audio Source page. (From CallManager Administration, choose **Service > Media Resource > Music on Hold Audio Source**.) Choose **Allow Multicasting** to enable the multicasting for the audio source.

Table 6-29 shows the other settings for configuring the MoH audio source.

**Table 6-29**  *MoH Audio Source Configuration Settings*

| Parameter | Value |
|---|---|
| MoH Audio Stream Number | 1 |
| MoH Audio Source File | SampleAudioSource |
| MoH Audio Source Name | SampleAudioSource |
| Play Continuously (repeat) | Checked |
| Allow Multicasting | Checked |

**Assigning the Audio Source to the Devices**    After configuring the audio source, you need to assign it to the devices. As mentioned before, CallManager supports two types of hold: Network Hold and User Hold. You can specify the same or different audio source files for each type of hold. In the CallManager, there are four ways to assign the audio source file to the devices:

- Directory number level
- Device level
- Device pool level
- Cluster-wide default setting; two parameters define the default values:
  — Default Network Hold MoH Audio Source ID (Default 1)
  — Default User Hold MoH Audio Source ID (Default 1)

CallManager chooses the audio source specified at directory number level as a first choice. If none is specified, it checks at the device level. If none is found at this level, it moves to device pool level. If no audio sources are specified in any of these three levels, CallManager chooses the audio source specified in the service parameters.

To access the default settings, from the CallManager Administration page, choose **Service > Service Parameters**. The default value 1 means play Audio Source File 1.

The best practice is to assign the audio sources to the device pool level. Tables 6-20 and 6-21 define the device pools configured for both clusters. We will assign the SampleAudioSource ID 1 for the Network Hold MoH audio source and User Hold MoH audio source options.

## Configuring the Remote-Site Router for MoH

After you configure the MoH server and the audio source, the next step is to configure the remote-site router to stream the audio file from Flash memory.

Example 6-1 shows an example of the Cisco IOS router configured for multicast MoH.

**Example 6-1** *Multicast MoH Cisco IOS CLI Configuration*

```
ccm-manager music-on-hold

interface Loopback0
 ip address 10.2.11.1 255.255.255.255

interface FastEthernet0/0.33
 ip address 10.2.1.1 255.255.255.0

call-manager-fallback
 ip source-address 10.2.1.1 port 2000
 max-ephones 48
 max-dn 96
 ! Defining the filename in the flash to be played
 moh music.au
 ! Defining the multicast base address.
 ! It has to match the one configured in the CallManagerRefer to Table 6-27.
 multicast moh 239.1.1.1 port 16384 route 10.2.1.1 10.2.11.1
```

**NOTE**    In Sydney, the CallManager publisher (SYDCCMA-PUB) is the MoH server. The configuration of the Sydney cluster is similar to that of the San Jose cluster. Ensure that the multicast address used is different from the one used in San Jose, to avoid address conflict.

## Configuring the MRGs and MRGLs

A *media resource group* is a group of media resources (conference bridges, transcoder, and MoH server), possibly of different types, that is logically bundled for load-sharing purposes. A *media resource group list* is an ordered list of MRGs used for redundancy purposes.

In XYZ, different media resources are deployed throughout the network. To ensure the right media resources are selected, we will design different MRGs and MRGLs.

### Designing MRGs and MRGLs for Cluster 1

Before you design the MRGs and MRGLs, you need to understand the media resource access requirements per site. For cluster 1, the requirements are as follows:

- San Jose local endpoints should use the following:
    - Conferencing resources in San Jose
    - Transcoding resources in San Jose
    - MoH resources in San Jose—unicast

- Seattle endpoints should use the following:
  - — Conferencing resources on the local router as a primary choice, resources in San Jose as a backup if the primary resources on the local router are unavailable or exhausted
  - — Transcoding resources in San Jose
  - — MoH streamed from the local Cisco IOS router—multicast
- Dallas endpoints should use the following
  - — Conferencing resources in San Jose
  - — Transcoding resources in San Jose
  - — No MoH; instead, play a Beep on Hold/Tone on Hold

Tables 6-30 and 6-31 show the design details of the MRGs and MRGLs, respectively, to meet the cluster 1 requirements.

To configure the MRGs, from CallManager Administration, choose **Service > Media Resource > Media Resource Group**.

**Table 6-30**    *MRG Settings in Cluster 1*

| Media Resource Group Name | Devices for This Group – Selected Media Resources | Description/Comment |
|---|---|---|
| MRG_SJ | CFB001122334455(CFB) | Cat6k-SJ-1 CMM ACT CFB |
| | CFB001122334456(CFB) | Cat6k-SJ-2 CMM ACT CFB |
| | MOH-SJCCMC(MOH) | MOH Server (Use Multicast for MoH Audio—unchecked) |
| MRG_Seattle | CFB00AABBCCDDEE(CFB) | 3745 NM-HDV |
| | MTP001122334455(XCODE) | Cat6k-SJ-1 CMM ACT MTP |
| | MTP001122334456(XCODE) | Cat6k-SJ-2 CMM ACT MTP |
| | MOH-SJCCMC(MOH) | MOH Server (Use Multicast for MoH Audio—checked) |
| MRG_Xcode | MTP001122334455(XCODE) | Cat6k-SJ-1 CMM ACT MTP |
| | MTP001122334456(XCODE) | Cat6k-SJ-2 CMM ACT MTP |
| MRG_CFB_SJ | CFB001122334455(CFB) | Cat6k-SJ-1 CMM ACT CFB |
| | CFB001122334456(CFB) | Cat6k-SJ-2 CMM ACT CFB |

To configure the MRGLs, from CallManager Administration, choose **Service > Media Resource > Media Resource Group List**.

**Table 6-31**    *MRGL Settings in Cluster 1*

| Media Resource Group List Name | Media Resource Groups for This List - Selected Media Resource Groups | Endpoints That Use This MRGL |
|---|---|---|
| MRGL_SJ | MRG_SJ | San Jose |
| MRGL_Seattle | MRG_Seattle<br>MRG_CFB_SJ | Seattle |
| MRGL_Dallas | MRG_Xcode<br>MRG_CFB_SJ | Dallas |

Table 6-31 indicates that the devices in Dallas do not have access to any MRGs that contain an MoH resource, per XYZ's requirements. As a result, when Dallas users are placed on hold, they hear beeps only.

---

**NOTE**    If a user in Dallas initiates an Ad Hoc conference call, all the media streams are moved to the central site. In the worse-case scenario, all participants are in Dallas, which results in most if not all the bandwidth allocated to this site being used; consequently, no one can call out of the site while the conference is in progress. If this becomes an issue, deploy local conferencing resources at the Dallas site. This also applies to the Brisbane site.

---

## Designing MRGs and MRGLs for Cluster 2

The design of the MRGs and MRGLs for cluster 2 is similar to that of the design of cluster 1. The only difference is that in cluster 2, we use E1 ports on the 6608 module as conferencing and transcoding resources, whereas for cluster 1, the conferencing and transcoding resources reside on the ACT port adapter on the CMM module. The configuration of MRGs and MRGLs is the same regardless of the use of different hardware.

The following are the requirements for cluster 2:

- Sydney local endpoints should use the following:
    - Conferencing resources in Sydney
    - Transcoding resources in Sydney
    - MoH resources in Sydney—unicast
- Melbourne endpoints should use the following:
    - Conferencing resources on the local router as a primary choice, resources in Sydney as a backup if the primary resources on the local router are either unavailable or exhausted
    - The transcoding resources in Sydney
    - MoH streamed from the local Cisco IOS router—multicast

- Brisbane endpoints should use the following:
  - Conferencing resources in Sydney
  - Transcoding resources in Sydney
  - No MoH; instead, play a Beep on Hold/Tone on Hold

Tables 6-32 and 6-33 show the design details of the MRGs and MRGLs, respectively, to meet the cluster 2 requirements.

**Table 6-32**  *MRG Settings in Cluster 2*

| Media Resource Group Name | Devices for This Group - Selected Media Resources | Description/Comment |
|---|---|---|
| MRG_SYD | CFB00EEDDCCBBA9(CFB) | Cat6k-SYD-1 6608 4/3 |
| | CFB01EEDDCCBBA9(CFB) | Cat6k-SYD-2 6608 4/3 |
| | MOH-SYDCMA(MOH) | MOH Server (Use Multicast for MoH Audio—unchecked) |
| MRG_MEL | CFB01AABBCCDDEE(CFB) | 3745 NM-HDV |
| | MTP011122334455(XCODE) | Cat6k-SYD-1 6608 4/4 MTP |
| | MTP011122334456(XCODE) | Cat6k-SYD-2 6608 4/4 MTP |
| | MOH-SYDCMA(MOH) | MOH Server (Use Multicast for MoH Audio—checked) |
| MRG_Xcode | MTP011122334455(XCODE) | Cat6k-SYD-1 6608 4/4 MTP |
| | MTP011122334456(XCODE) | Cat6k-SYD-2 6608 4/4 MTP |
| MRG_CFB_SYD | CFB00EEDDCCBBA9(CFB) | Cat6k-SYD-1 6608 4/3 |
| | CFB01EEDDCCBBA9(CFB) | Cat6k-SYD-2 6608 4/3 |

To configure the MRGLs, from CallManager Administration, choose **Service > Media Resource > Media Resource Group List**.

**Table 6-33**  *MRGL Settings in Cluster 2*

| Media Resource Group List Name | Media Resource Groups for This List - Selected Media Resource Groups | Endpoints That Use This MRGL |
|---|---|---|
| MRGL_SYD | MRG_SYD | Sydney |
| MRGL_MEL | MRG_MEL | Melbourne |
| | MRG_CFB_SYD | |
| MRGL_BRI | MRG_Xcode | Brisbane |
| | MRG_CFB_SYD | |

## Assigning MRGs and MRGLs to the Devices

After designing the MRGs and MRGLs, you need to assign the MRGLs to endpoints. MRGLs determine what MRGs the device will access when requesting the media resources. The MRGLs can be assigned at the following levels:

- Device level
- Device pool level
- Default MRGL—Contains the media resources that are not assigned to an MRG

CallManager chooses the MRGL at the device level if specified, and then checks at the device pool level. If no MRGL is specified at either level, it chooses the MRGs in the default MRGL list.

---

**NOTE**     If you are not planning to use media resources, a best practice is to put them in an MRG and MRGL and not assign that MRGL to a device. Leaving the media resources without putting them in an MRG puts them into the default MRGL, where they remain accessible by the devices as a last resort.

---

The best practice is to apply the MRGL at the device pool level, so that all the devices using that device pool use the same MRGL. Tables 6-34 and 6-35 update Tables 6-20 and 6-21, respectively, by adding the settings of the Network Hold MoH Audio Source, User Hold MoH Audio Source, and MRGL fields to the device pool definitions. To configure or update the device pools, from CallManager Administration, choose **System > Device Pool**.

**Table 6-34**  *Updated Device Pool Settings in Cluster 1*

| Device Pool Name | Cisco CallManager Group | Date/Time Group | Region | Calling Search Space for Auto-Registration | MRGL | Network Hold MoH Audio Source; User Hold MoH Audio Source |
|---|---|---|---|---|---|---|
| DP-SanJose | SJ-GRP-1 | PST | San Jose | CSS-taps | MRGL_SJ | 1-SampleAudio Source; 1-SampleAudioSource |
| DP-Seattle | SJ-GRP-1 | PST | Seattle | CSS-taps | MRGL_Seattle | 1-SampleAudio Source; 1-SampleAudioSource |
| DP-Dallas | SJ-GRP-1 | CST | Dallas | CSS-taps | MRGL_Dallas | 1-SampleAudio Source; 1-SampleAudioSource |
| DP-MOH-FAX | SJ-GRP-1 | PST | San Jose | CSS-taps | None | \<None\> |

**Table 6-35** *Updated Device Pool Settings in Cluster 2*

| Device Pool Name | Cisco CallManager Group | Date/Time Group | Region | Calling Search Space for Auto-Registration | MRGL | Network Hold MoH Audio Source; User Hold MoH Audio Source |
|---|---|---|---|---|---|---|
| DP-Sydney | SYD-GRP-1 | Sydney | Sydney | CSS-taps | MRGL_SYD | 1-SampleAudio Source; 1-SampleAudioSource |
| DP-Melbourne | SYD-GRP-1 | Sydney | Melbourne | CSS-taps | MRGL_MEL | 1-SampleAudio Source; 1-SampleAudioSource |
| DP-Brisbane | SYD-GRP-1 | Brisbane | Brisbane | CSS-taps | MRGL_BRI | 1-SampleAudio Source; 1-SampleAudioSource |
| DP-MOH-FAX | SYD-GRP-1 | Sydney | Sydney | CSS-taps | None | <None> |

## Gateway Selection and Sizing

Each site within the U.S. and Australian clusters has a local gateway to access the PSTN. Each gateway is deployed for different purposes. Tables 6-36 and 6-37 show the function of each gateway in both clusters. These same tables show the signaling protocol used on the gateways to communicate with CallManager.

A centralized Cisco IOS gatekeeper is deployed to provide call routing and CAC between the U.S. and Australia clusters. Calls between the two countries are routed primarily across the IP WAN and considered on-net calls. Under a WAN failure or insufficient bandwidth, calls are routed through the PSTN gateway in the central site.

To configure a gateway, from CallManager Administration, choose **Device > Gateway**. Click the **Add New Gateway** option on the Gateway configuration page. On the Add a New Gateway page, select the gateway type and device protocol used for signaling.

As an example, to add a T1/E1 port on a CMM module, choose Communication Media Module as the gateway type. To add a T1/E1 port on a WS-6608 module, choose Catalyst 6000 T1 (E1) VoIP Gateway. The preceding example is to configure the gateways to use the MGCP protocol. To configure a gateway to use the H.323 protocol, choose the H.323 gateway from the Gateway Type drop-down menu.

**Table 6-36** *Cluster 1 Voice Gateways—Functions and Signaling*

| Location | Endpoint Name | Function | Signaling and Other Configuration Parameters |
|---|---|---|---|
| San Jose | S1/DS1-0@SJ-CMM1<br>S1/DS1-1@SJ-CMM1<br>S1/DS1-0@SJ-CMM2<br>S1/DS1-1@SJ-CCM2 | PSTN access for San Jose users<br>PSTN access for Dallas users (except 911 calls)<br>Backup PSTN access for Seattle | Signaling: MGCP<br>Device Pool: DP-SanJose<br>Location: San Jose<br>AAR Group: San Jose<br>MRGL: MRGL_SJ |
| | S1/DS1-2@SJ-CMM1<br>S1/DS1-2@SJ-CMM2 | Access to the PBX for all sites | |
| | Gatekeeper | Intercluster calls | ICT |
| Seattle | S1/DS1-0@R3745-SEA | PSTN access for Seattle users | MGCP with H.323 Fallback<br>Device Pool: DP-Seattle<br>Location: Seattle<br>AAR Group: Seattle<br>MRGL: MRGL_Seattle |
| | AALN/S2/SU0/0@R3745-SEA<br>AALN/S2/SU0/1@R3745-SEA | Fax machines | |
| Dallas | AALN/S1/SU0/4@R2650-DAL<br>AALN/S1/SU0/5@R2650-DAL<br>AALN/S1/SU0/6@R2650-DAL<br>AALN/S1/SU0/7@R2650-DAL | FXO: PSTN emergency<br>FXO: All PSTN calls under SRST | MGCP with H.323 FallBack<br>Device Pool: DP-Dallas<br>Location: Dallas<br>AAR Group: Dallas<br>MRGL: None |
| | AALN/S1/SU0/0@R2650-DAL | Fax machine | |

In Table 6-36, S1/DS1-0@SJ-CMM1 represents the MGCP digital endpoint for the T1 controller T1 1/0. Because the signaling protocol in use is MGCP and the T1 trunk is digital, these endpoints are called *MGCP digital endpoints.*

SJ-CMM1 is the Domain Name field configured when configuring the CMM module. This domain name must match the host name configured on the CMM module. The naming convention SJ-CMM1 indicates that this DS1 is located on the Cisco Communication Media Module CMM1, in a Cisco Catalyst 6500 switch located in San Jose.

S1/DS1-1@SJ-CMM1 represents the MGCP digital endpoint for the controllers T1 1/1.

AAL/S1/SU0/4@R2650-DAL represents the MGCP analog endpoint for the analog port 1/0/4. S1/SU0/4 represents the analog port 1/0/4 located in the NM-HDA of Cisco 2651XM. @R2650-DAL indicates that this is a Cisco 2651XM router located in Dallas.

These endpoints are called MGCP analog endpoints, because MGCP is the signaling protocol and the port is an analog port.

**Table 6-37**    *Cluster 2 Voice Gateways—Functions and Signaling*

| Location | Name | Function | Signaling |
|---|---|---|---|
| Sydney | S0/DS1-0@SDA00EEDDCCBBA7<br>S0/DS1-0@SDA00EEDDCCBBA8<br>S0/DS1-0@SDA01EEDDCCBBA7<br>S0/DS1-0@SDA01EEDDCCBBA8 | PSTN access for Sydney<br>PSTN access for Brisbane<br>Backup PSTN access for Melbourne | Device Pool: DP-Sydney<br>Location: Sydney<br>AAR Group: Sydney<br>MRGL: MRGL_SYD |
| | Gatekeeper | Interclustrer calls | ICT |
| Melbourne | S0/DS1-0@R3725-MEL | PSTN access for Melbourne users | MGCP with H.323 Fallback |
| | AALN/S2/SU0/0@R3725-MEL<br>AALN/S2/SU0/1@R3725-MEL | Fax machines | |
| Brisbane | AALN/S1/SU0/4@R2650-BRI<br>AALN/S1/SU0/5@R2650-BRI<br>AALN/S1/SU0/6@R2650-BRI<br>AALN/S1/SU0/7@R2650-BRI | FXO: PSTN emergency<br>FXO: All PSTNs under SRST | MGCP with H.323 FallBack |
| | AALN/S1/SU0/0@R2650-BRI | FXS Fax machine | |

One of the naming conventions used in Table 6-37 differs from Table 6-36. In Table 6-37, the gateways use a different naming pattern. The reason is that the T1 gateways in San Jose are provisioned via the CMM module, and the E1 gateways in Sydney are provisioned using the WS-X6608-E1 module.

S0/DS1-0@SDA00EEDDCCBBA7 represents the MGCP digital endpoint for the T1 controller T1 1/0, where 00EEDDCCBBA7 is the MAC address of the T1 port. SDA stands for Selsius Digital Access.

Refer to Appendix F to order new T1/E1 circuits or modify the configurations on the existing circuits if required for deploying IPT.

All the PRI trunks in the U.S. and Australia are provisioned for ISDN User side, and the clocking is provided from the telco or the PBX.

The line coding in the U.S. is set to B8ZS and the framing to Extended Super Frame (ESF). In Australia, the line coding is set to HDB3 and the framing to CRC4.

The detailed configuration of the Cisco IOS router is provided, in the next section. The detailed configuration of the Cisco IOS voice gateways is provided in the "Survivable Remote Site Telephony" section, later in this chapter.

The other important parameters when designing the gateways are the inbound call routing settings such as significant digits, CSS, AAR CSS, and prefix DN. These parameters are discussed in the "Inbound Call Routing" section later in this chapter.

---

**NOTE**   MGCP with H.323 Fallback in Tables 6-36 and 6-37 means that the MGCP gateway falls back to an H.323 session application when the WAN TCP connection to the primary Cisco CallManager server is lost and no backup Cisco CallManager server is available. When the WAN link is functional, the gateway communicates with CallManager via MGCP. During the WAN failure, the gateway loses the connectivity with the CallManager at the central site and acts as an H.323 gateway to route the calls.

An ICT is an H.323 connection that connects two Cisco CallManager clusters.

---

## Dial Plan Architecture

As you know, the XYZ IPT design consists of two CallManager clusters: cluster 1 and cluster 2. In this section, while discussing the dial plan architecture for XYZ, we focus specifically on cluster 1, and generally on cluster 2 only for clarity and simplicity. The dial plan architecture topics and detailed dial plan presented in Tables 6-38 to 6-53 cover all aspects of the dial plan for cluster 1. After you understand the methodology used in building the dial plan for cluster 1, building the dial plan for cluster 2 is not difficult, which is why the dial plan for cluster 2 is not presented specifically.

The CallManager dial plan architecture handles two general types of calls:

- Internal calls to IP Phones and other devices registered to the CallManager cluster
- External calls through a PSTN or PBX gateway to another Cisco CallManager cluster over the IP WAN

The dial plan for internal calls registered with CallManager is simple. Configuring CallManager to handle external calls requires the use of a route pattern. In most cases, CallManager matches the dialed number against a route pattern for directing calls out to a PSTN gateway.

## Numbering Plan

Before designing a dial plan, you need to obtain the existing numbering plan. The numbering plan provides the following information:

- The Direct Inward Dial (DID) ranges per site
- The length of the phone number extensions that are used internally
- The number of digits forwarded by the local telephone company
- If implementing Tail-End Hop-Off (TEHO), the local calling area codes for each site

| | |
|---|---|
| **NOTE** | In a private enterprise network, TEHO is the routing of a voice call over the internal network to the closest gateway to the destination of the call, and then connecting into the public network as a local phone call. In the XYZ network scenario, consider an employee in San Jose making a call to a phone number that is local to the Seattle office. With TEHO implementation, this call would go over the internal IP WAN from San Jose to Seattle to reach the PSTN gateway in Seattle. This makes the call a local call instead of a long-distance call. This solution eliminates long-distance calls between offices and achieves significant savings on telecom bills. |

XYZ currently uses a four-digit numbering plan at every site, and the new IPT design keeps the same scheme. All the locations except for Dallas and Brisbane have DID numbers. This means that a call coming from a PSTN cannot directly reach the IP Phone or any other application without going through an operator.

Because Dallas and Brisbane sites do not have DID numbers, a private numbering scheme is required for these two locations. These two sites have four FXO trunks for inbound calling and for routing the outbound emergency calls. Table 6-38 provides the information on the existing DID and station-numbering plan collected during the planning phase through the questionnaire in Appendix C, "IPT Planning Phase: Telecom Infrastructure Analysis Questionnaire," in the section "Telephony Numbering Plan."

**Table 6-38**  *DID and Numbering Plan at XYZ*

| Site Name | DID Range | Station Directory Range |
|---|---|---|
| San Jose | +1 408 555 3000 to +1 408 555 4999 | IP Phone DNs<br>3000–4999 |
| | +1 408 555 2500 to +1 408 555 2999 | PBX stations DNs<br>2500–2999 |
| Seattle | +1 206 555 2100 to +1 206 555 2199 | 2100–2199 |

*continues*

**Table 6-38**   *DID and Numbering Plan at XYZ (Continued)*

| Site Name | DID Range | Station Directory Range |
|-----------|-----------|-------------------------|
| Dallas | +1 972 555 5600 (Grouped line) +1 972 555 5611 (Fax) | 5601–5619 (non-DID numbers, private numbering plan) |
| Sydney | +61 2 5555 6000 to +61 2 5555 6999 | 6000–6999 |
| Melbourne | +61 3 5555 4300 to +61 3 5555 4399 | 4300–4399 |
| Brisbane | +61 7 5555 8680 (Grouped line) | 8681–8699 (non-DID numbers, private numbering plan) |

For XYZ, we will design the TEHO calling between the San Jose and Seattle locations. To design the TEHO, you need to obtain the local area codes for each site, as shown in Table 6-39. The San Jose site has three in-state local area codes, and you need to dial 11 digits to reach these numbers. Similarly, Seattle has two local area codes, and 11 digits are required to dial these numbers.

**Table 6-39**   *Local Calling Area Codes*

| Site Name | Local Calling | | In-State Toll Calling | |
|-----------|---------------|--|------------------------|--|
| | Area Code/ Exchange | Number of Digits to Dial | Area Codes/ Exchange | Number of Digits to Dial |
| San Jose | 408 | 10 | 650 510 925 | 11 |
| Seattle | 206 | 10 | 425 253 | 11 |

Besides the station numbering, you need another range of internal directory numbers for any device that does not require direct access from the PSTN. These can be CTI ports, CTI route points, Meet-Me conferences, Group Pickup, and Call Park numbers. Table 6-40 provides the details of the internal dial plan of cluster 1.

**NOTE**    You need to add a CTI port for each active voice line that you intend to use on an IP SoftPhone. The CTI port is actually a virtual device that allows you to create a virtual line.

**Table 6-40**  *Internal Dial Plan in Cluster 1*

| Station DN | Device Type | Description |
|---|---|---|
| 3101-3999 | IP Phones | San Jose IP Phones |
| 4000–4199 | IP Phones | San Jose main extension for managers |
| 4800–4899 | IP Phones | San Jose proxy lines for managers |
| 4201–4299 | VG248 | San Jose fax machines |
| 2101–2150 | IP Phones | Seattle IP Phones |
| 2151–2152 | MGCP FXS | Seattle fax machines |
| 2100 | IP Phone | Seattle operator |
| 5602–5610 | IP Phones | Dallas IP Phones |
| 5601 | IP Phone | Dallas operator |
| 7XXX | ICD lines, intercom lines for managers and assistants | Secondary line for an ICD agent, an intercom line for a manager or assistant, or a proxy line for a manager; XXX is the last three digits of the main number |
| 5611 | MGCP FXS | Dallas fax machine |
| 3555 | voice mail pilot | Voice mail pilot number to reach the Octel voice-mail system |
| 1999 | MWI on | Turns the MWI on |
| 1998 | MWI off | Turns the MWI off |
| 1900–1997 | Voice-mail ports | Voice-mail ports |
| 1601–1610 | CTI ports | CTI ports for ICD |
| 1611–1630 | CTI ports | CTI port for AA |
| 3877 | CTI route point | AutoAttendant |
| 3888 | CTI route point | IP ICD |
| 3800 | CTI route point | IP IVR General number |
| 3889 | CTI route point | TAPS number |
| 40XX, 41XX, 210[1-4] | CTI route point | IPMA-Manager extensions in San Jose and Seattle locations |
| 1701–1720 | Meet-Me | Meet-Me conference |
| 1721–1740 | Call Park | Call Park |
| 1741–1760 | Group Pickup | Group Pickup |
| 80000-81000 | Auto-registered DN range | DN range for auto-registered phones |

| NOTE | Cisco IP Interactive Call Distribution (ICD) is an application that runs on Cisco CallManager to offer queuing and dispatch services for a call center or help desk environment. ICD can be used as part of IP Contact Center (IPCC) Express, but IPCC is not required to use ICD. In normal use, agents log into ICD using an application on their PC that signals to Cisco CallManager that they are ready to accept calls from a shared call-in number. |
| --- | --- |

## Call-Routing Requirements

You are ready to begin designing the dial plan for cluster 1. The first step is to identify the types of calls in the network and come up with call-routing requirements. Cluster 1 has three kinds of calls:

- **Cluster 1 internal calls**—Internal calls originating from an IP Phone in one location calling to any other internal location reach the called party's IP Phone directly (IP Phone-to-IP Phone calls within cluster 1). These types of calls must use IP WAN as the first preference and then use the local PSTN trunks to route the calls transparently to the user if the WAN link is not available or bandwidth is too exhausted to route the new calls.

- **Cluster 1 external calls**—Calls to any external numbers that are not part of the CallManager numbering plan.

   **San Jose Site:**

   — External calls that are local to Seattle use the PSTN trunks in Seattle but fall back to the San Jose gateway as a long-distance call if all the Seattle trunks are busy or unavailable (TEHO implementation).

   — All other external calls (local, long distance, international) use San Jose PSTN trunks.

   — All emergency calls use local PSTN trunks in San Jose.

   — Incoming calls to the San Jose site arrive on the PSTN trunks in San Jose and reach any IP Phone or extension directly, because San Jose numbers are DID numbers.

   — TEHO calls originating from Seattle and bound for the San Jose area are routed out via the PSTN trunks in San Jose.

   — Calls that are not answered by IP Phone users are forwarded to voice mail.

   — Calls made to the San Jose main number are forwarded to an AutoAttendant application on the CRS server.

   — Calls made to reach the contact support personnel are forwarded to an IP-ICD application on the CRS server.

**Seattle Site:**

— External calls that are local to San Jose use the PSTN trunks in San Jose but fall back to the Seattle gateway as a long-distance call if all the San Jose trunks are busy or unavailable (TEHO implementation).

— All other external calls (local, long distance, international) use Seattle PSTN trunks as first preference and use San Jose trunks as a backup.

— All emergency calls use local PSTN trunks in Seattle.

— Incoming calls to the Seattle site arrive on the PSTN trunks in Seattle and reach any IP Phone or extension directly, because Seattle numbers are DID numbers.

— TEHO calls originating from San Jose and bound for the Seattle area are routed out via the PSTN trunks in Seattle.

— Calls that are not answered by IP Phone users are forwarded to voice mail.

**Dallas Site:**

— All external calls (local, long distance, international) use San Jose PSTN trunks to route the calls. If San Jose PSTN trunks are busy or unavailable (including WAN failure), no external calls can be made from the Dallas site.

— All emergency calls use local PSTN trunks in Seattle (two FXO trunks).

— Incoming calls to the Dallas site arrive on the PSTN trunks in Dallas (two FXO trunks). Because Dallas numbers are non-DID, the incoming calls are forwarded to the operator. The extension for the operator is 5601. Refer to the section "SRST for Dallas and Brisbane Remote Sites," later in this chapter, to see which configuration is needed on the SRST-enabled Dallas router for this functionality.

— Calls that are not answered by IP Phone users are forwarded to voice mail.

● **Intercluster calls between cluster 1 and cluster 2**—Intercluster calls use IP WAN, using ICT as the first preference and PSTN trunks as the second preference.

## CallManager Route Plan

The route plan determines all aspects of call handling. Many elements, as shown in Figure 6-7, define the route plan in CallManager. A brief description of all these elements follows:

● Route patterns identify different groups of telephone numbers. For example, a route pattern of 3xxx matches any digits from 3000 to 3999. A route pattern of 3000 matches exactly the number 3000.

● Route lists provide multiple paths to route a call. It is an ordered list of route groups. You associate a route pattern with a route list. When a dialed number matches a route pattern, CallManager routes the call via the route groups that are specified in the route lists.

- A route group is an ordered list of devices/gateways that can route the call to different destinations. The route group can direct all calls to the primary device and then use the secondary devices when the primary device is unavailable. One or more route lists can point to the same route group. Because a gateway can be assigned to only one route group, the best practice is to assign each gateway to one route group if you want to use this gateway more than once in your dial plan or within different route patterns.

**Figure 6-7**   *Hierarchical Route Plan Elements in CCM*

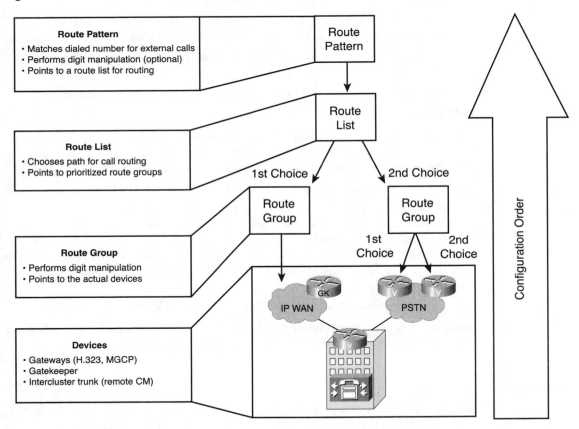

As shown in Figure 6-7, when you are configuring the route plan elements, the configuration order is a bottom to top approach, which means that the devices and gateways are configured first, followed by the route group, route list, and route patterns. On the other hand, CallManager process the call in a top to bottom approach. For example, when a user dials a number, CallManager checks whether it matches a route pattern. If there is a match, CallManager sends the call to the route list. CallManager checks the list of route groups in the route list. If there are multiple route groups, it sends the call out via the first route group. If the call cannot be completed (because no trunks are available in the devices in the route group), CallManager selects the second route group to route the call.

## Partition Design

After you identify the call routing paths, the next step in designing the dial plan is to devise the partitions. A *partition* is a group of devices with similar reachability characteristics. The entities that you can place in partitions are the route patterns and directory numbers of IP Phones, voice-mail ports, CTI route points, CTI ports, messaging waiting indicator (MWI) On/Off devices, and so forth. The route patterns can match internal or external PSTN destinations.

We will define the partitions that group the route patterns that match the following criteria:

- All internal numbers, CTI ports, and voice-mail ports
- Special partitions required by applications such as Cisco IPMA
- Emergency numbers per site
- Local calling (within the same area code) per site
- Long-distance calling per site
- International dialing per site
- Toll-free numbers per site
- TEHO numbers per site

Because each site has local gateways that connect to the PSTN, you need to define the same route patterns per each site. For example, to route 911 calls, you need three route patterns in three different partitions, one per site. This allows you to route the 911 calls through the local gateways.

Also, note that in the previous classification, local, long-distance, and international route patterns are separated, which provides more flexibility in defining classes of restrictions (CoRs) on the end-user phones. As an example, to give an IP Phone access to call local numbers only, you would include only the local calling partition in the phone's CSS. To give both local and long-distance access, you include the local and long-distance partitions in the CSS. The next section describes CSSs in greater detail.

Referring to Table 6-38, you can see that XYZ has nonoverlapping station directory ranges. The last four digits used for numbering the IP Phones for each site are unique. If you are designing a multisite network, you might be in a situation in which the last four digits are the same for two or more sites. To avoid the overlapped numbers, you should consider increasing the number of digits used for internal IP Phone numbering. For example, you should consider using four digits instead of three digits or using five digits instead of four digits to represent the directory numbers for the phones. If you still see overlaps, you cannot assign all the IP Phone numbers a single partition, as shown in Table 6-41; instead, assign the phones within each site to a different partition. If you put two or more lines that have the same directory number in a single partition, those numbers become shared lines.

Table 6-41 provides the partitions created in the XYZ for the U.S. cluster to accommodate the dial plan.

To add partitions, from CallManager Administration, choose **Route Plan > Partition** and click the **Add a New Partition** option.

**Table 6-41** *Partitions in Cluster 1*

| Partition Name | Description |
|---|---|
| P-Internal | Contains all IP Phones, fax machines, CTI ports, CTI route points, voice-mail ports, and Group Pickup |
| P-Internal-Managers | Contains all managers' directory numbers; needed to implement IPMA |
| P-IPMA | Contains IPMA CTI route point |
| P-Emergency-SJ | E911 dialing in San Jose |
| P-Emergency-SEA | E911 dialing in Seattle |
| P-Emergency-DAL | E911 dialing in Dallas |
| P-TEHO-SJ | Contains area codes that are local to the San Jose office to implement TEHO calling for other sites |
| P-TEHO-SEA | Contains area codes that are local to the Seattle office to implement TEHO calling for other sites |
| P-Local-SJ | Contains local calling area codes in San Jose |
| P-Local-SEA | Contains local calling area codes in Seattle |
| P-LD-SJ | Contains long-distance area codes in San Jose |
| P-LD-SEA | Contains long-distance area codes in Seattle |
| P-INT-SJ | International calling in San Jose |
| P-INT-SEA | International calling in Seattle |
| P-Block | Blocked numbers, if any |
| P-Block-Local | Block local calling |
| P-Block-LD | Block long-distance calling |
| P-Block-INT | Block international calling |
| P-LD-AAR-SEA | Long-distance AAR for Seattle |
| P-INT-AAR-SEA | International AAR for Seattle |
| P-LD-AAR-DAL | Long-distance AAR for Dallas |
| P-INT-AAR-DAL | International AAR for Dallas |
| P-Autoregphone | Partition for the Autoregistered Phones and the TAPS CTI route point |
| P-TollFree-SJ | Partition for toll free number access for San Jose users |
| P-TollFree-SEA | Partition for toll free number access for Seattle users |

**NOTE**    Observe in Table 6-41 that Dallas has its own partitions even though the PSTN trunks in San Jose are used to route local and long-distance calls originating from Dallas. This is required because we are routing the calls to different route lists depending on whether the call originates from Dallas or San Jose. Calls originating from San Jose use the San Jose partitions, whereas calls originating from Dallas use the Dallas partitions.

## Calling Search Space Design

A CSS is an ordered list of partitions that a user's phone searches before being allowed to place a call. CallManager uses CSS to define CoR levels. CSSs are assigned to devices that can initiate calls. These include IP Phones, Cisco SoftPhones, and gateways. Dialing restrictions are simple to invoke because users can dial only the partitions in the CSS to which they are assigned. Dialing a directory number outside an allowed partition causes the caller to receive a fast busy tone.

To reach a certain destination, the called party's partition must be part of the calling party's CSS.

With the help of the questionnaire in Appendix E, specifically the "Class of Restrictions Requirements" section, XYZ requires the four levels of CoRs listed in Table 6-42 in the IPT network.

**Table 6-42**    *Classes of Restrictions Required*

| Class of Restriction Level | Which Calls Are Users Allowed to Make? | Which User Phones Require this CoR? |
|---|---|---|
| 1 (Default) | Calls to all IP Phones, 911 and other services like 611, toll-free numbers (800, 866, 877), and voice mail<br><br>Not allowed to dial 900 numbers | Lobby phones |
| 2 (Default + Local) | Level 1 access, plus local calls and TEHO calls to other locations | Break room phones |
| 3 (Default + Local + LD) | Level 2 access, plus long-distance calls | All employee phones, conference room phones |
| 4 (No restriction) | Level 3 access, plus international calls | All executives phones |

In CallManager, for an IP Phone, you can assign the CSS at two levels:

- Line level (directory number level)
- Device level (on the IP Phone itself)

When you define a CSS at both levels, as shown in Figure 6-8, CallManager does the following:

- Combines the list of partitions at the line level and the device level.

- Places the list of partitions in the line level ahead of those listed in the device level (beginning with CallManager release 3.1). In prior releases, the partitions in the device level are placed ahead of the partitions in the line level. CTI ports still use the old method. Therefore, if you are deploying applications such as IP SoftPhone, you should note this behavior.

- Selects the best match from the combined list.

**Figure 6-8**    *Combining Line- and Device-Level CSSs on an IP Phone*

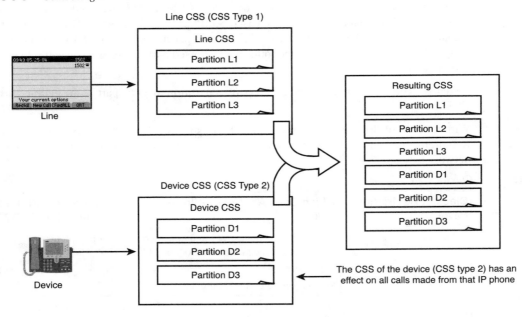

We will use this feature of combining the line- and device-level CSSs in CallManager to define the CoRs required for XYZ. For that, we define three types of CSSs, as follows:

- **CSS type 1**—Attached to line level. It gives the line a certain class of service. You need one CSS type 1 for each type of CoR required.

- **CSS type 2**—Attached to device level. It gives the device access to the local resources to reach the PSTN. You need one CSS type 2 for each branch.

- **CSS type 3**—A general type, assigned to resources suh as CTI ports, voice-mail ports, and the call-forwarding CSSs at the line level.

Table 6-43 outlines the list of CSSs to be provisioned, with a brief description for the U.S. cluster.

To add CSSs, from CallManager Administration, choose **Route Plan > Calling Search Space**.

**Table 6-43**  *Calling Search Space in Cluster 1*

| CSS Name | Selected Partitions (Ordered by Highest Priority) | Description | CSS Type |
|---|---|---|---|
| CSS-Line-Default | P-Block-Local<br><br>P-Block-LD<br><br>P-Block-INT | CSS to be attached to every line not allowed to call the PSTN except 911 and toll-free numbers. Example of such lines are in the lobby phones and IP Phones that support hot desking (enables users to "log on" to any IP Phone with just a PIN number). | 1 |
| CSS-Line-Local | P-Block-LD<br><br>P-Block-INT | CSS to be attached to every line that can make local calling only in addition to 911 and toll-free numbers. | 1 |
| CSS-Line-LD | P-Block-INT | CSS to be attached to lines that can make any PSTN call except international calls. | 1 |
| CSS-Line-Managers | P-Internal-Managers | CSS to be attached to the assistants' lines. | 1 |
| CSS-SJ | P-Block<br><br>P-Internal<br><br>P-IPMA<br><br>P-Emergency-SJ<br><br>P-TollFree-SJ<br><br>P-Local-SJ<br><br>P-LD-SJ<br><br>P-INT-SJ<br><br>P-TEHO-SJ | CSS to be attached to any device in San Jose. | 2 |
| CSS-SEA | P-Block<br><br>P-Internal<br><br>P-IPMA<br><br>P-Emergency-SEA<br><br>P-TollFree-SEA<br><br>P-Local-SEA<br><br>P-LD-SEA<br><br>P-INT-SEA<br><br>P-TEHO-SEA | CSS to be attached to any device in Seattle. | 2 |

*continues*

**Table 6-43** *Calling Search Space in Cluster 1 (Continued)*

| CSS Name | Selected Partitions (Ordered by Highest Priority) | Description | CSS Type |
|---|---|---|---|
| CSS-DAL | P-Block<br>P-Internal<br>P-IPMA<br>P-Emergency-DAL<br>P-TollFree-SJ<br>P-Local-SJ<br>P-LD-SJ<br>P-INT-SJ | CSS to be attached to any device in Dallas. | 2 |
| CSS-Restricted | P-Internal<br>P-Block-Local<br>P-Block-LD<br>P-Block-INT | CSS that can reach the partition P-Internal only. This partition will be assigned to CTI ports and to CFB, CFNA, and CFA fields on the IP Phone's directory numbers. | 3 |
| CSS-AAR-SEA | P-LD-AAR-SEA<br>P-INT-AAR-SEA | CSS to be assigned to AAR CSS in Seattle. | 3 |
| CSS-AAR-DAL | P-LD-AAR-DAL<br>P-INT-AAR-DAL | CSS to be assigned to AAR CSS in Dallas. | 3 |
| CSS-Gateways | P-Internal<br>P-Internal-Managers<br>P-IPMA | CSS to be assigned to gateways so that they can reach the devices to extend the calls coming from the PSTN to the IPT devices. | 3 |
| CSS-taps | P-autoregphone | This CSS is assigned at the device pool level. The autoregistered phones receive this CSS. | 1 |

According to Table 6-43, you should do the following:

- At the line level, assign CSS type 1 to each line depending of the class of service.
- At the device level, assign CSS type 2 to each device depending on the location. For example, the device CSS for all IP Phones in San Jose will have CSS-SJ, in Seattle CSS-SEA, and in Dallas CSS-DAL.
- Do not assign CSS (no CSS) for a line that has an unrestricted CoR. Such a device will inherit its calling privileges from the CSS configured at the device level (CSS type 2).

To see how the CSSs that are defined in Table 6-43 work, consider an IP Phone in San Jose that requires access only to dial 911 calls, toll-free calls, and local numbers. Figure 6-9 depicts the CSSs that are assigned to such an IP Phone at the line level and the device level to achieve the desired CoR for that IP Phone.

**Figure 6-9**    *Two Calling Search Spaces from Table 6-43*

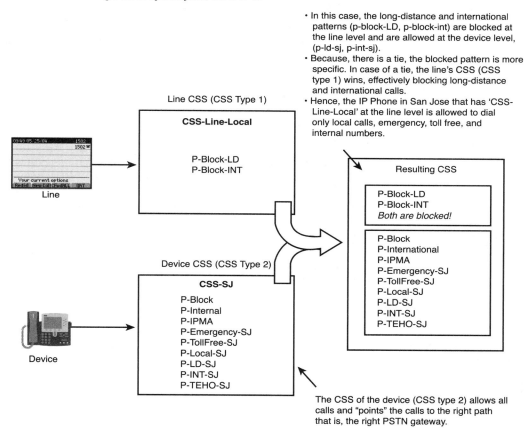

- In this case, the long-distance and international patterns (p-block-LD, p-block-int) are blocked at the line level and are allowed at the device level, (p-ld-sj, p-int-sj).
- Because, there is a tie, the blocked pattern is more specific. In case of a tie, the line's CSS (CSS type 1) wins, effectively blocking long-distance and international calls.
- Hence, the IP Phone in San Jose that has 'CSS-Line-Local' at the line level is allowed to dial only local calls, emergency, toll free, and internal numbers.

The CSS of the device (CSS type 2) allows all calls and "points" the calls to the right path that is, the right PSTN gateway.

The line-level CSS is CSS-Line-Local, which is CSS type 1. It consists of two partitions, P-Block-LD and P-Block-INT, which comprise route patterns that block the long-distance and international dialing patterns.

The device-level CSS is CSS-SJ, which is CSS type 2. It consists of all the other partitions that permit various calls, including-long distance and international calls.

The resulting CSS includes all the partitions from the line level and the device level. If the same route pattern appears in both the line level and the device level, the partition listed in the line level takes precedence. Hence, in the example shown in Figure 6-9, the IP Phone is blocked from making any long-distance and international calls because these partitions appear before the partitions that allow the long-distance and international calls.

On the IP Phone line level, you can configure three types of call-forward settings: Call Forward Busy (CFB), Call Forward No Answer (CFNA), and Call Forward All (CFA). Table 6-43 indicates that CSS-restricted CSS is applied to all three call forward settings. CSS-restricted allows calls only to internal numbers. Thus, users cannot forward their calls to external PSTN numbers. If your company policy allows you to forward the calls to external PSTN numbers, you can add the partition that allows reaching the external numbers to the CSS-restricted calling search space.

"Enabling the AAR Service Parameter," later in the is chapter, discusses the CSS-AAR-SEA and CSS-AAR-DAL CSSs.

## Route Groups

A route group is analogous to a trunk group in traditional PBX terminology. Each route group is a prioritized list of gateways to which a route pattern sends the call (through a route list). Refer to Figure 6-7 for a visual depiction of this process. A route group directs all calls to the primary device and then uses the subsequent devices when the primary device is unavailable or its resources are exhausted. All devices in a route group have the same characteristics, such as discard and digit manipulation. Table 6-44 provides the details of the route group to be created to accommodate XYZ's dial plan.

To add route groups, from CallManager Administration, choose **Route Plan > Route/Hunt > Route Group**.

**Table 6-44**  *Route Groups in Cluster 1*

| Route Group Name | Selection Order | Gateways/Devices (Route Group Members) | Description |
| --- | --- | --- | --- |
| RG-GW-PSTN-SJ | 1 | S1/DS1-0@SJ-CMM1 | PSTN gateway in San Jose |
| | 2 | S1/DS1-1@SJ-CMM1 | |
| | 3 | S1/DS1-0@SJ-CMM2 | |
| | 4 | S1/DS1-1@SJ-CMM2 | |
| RG-GW-PBX-SJ | 1 | S1/DS1-2@SJ-CMM1 | PBX gateway in San Jose |
| | 2 | S1/DS1-2@SJ-CMM2 | |
| RG-GW-PSTN-SEA | 1 | S1/DS1-0@R3745-SEA | PSTN gateway in Seattle |
| RG-GW-911-DAL | 1 | AALN/S1/SU0/4@R2650-DAL | 911 gateway in Dallas |
| | 2 | AALN/S1/SU0/5@R2650-DAL | |
| RG-GW-PSTN-DAL | 1 | AALN/S1/SU0/6@R2650-DAL | AAR trunks in Dallas |
| | 2 | AALN/S1/SU0/7@R2650-DAL | |
| RG-Gatekeeper | 1 | Gatekeeper | ICTs between cluster 1 and cluster 2 |

Figure 6-10 graphically depicts the list of route groups defined in Table 6-44.

**Figure 6-10**    *Route Group Definitions*

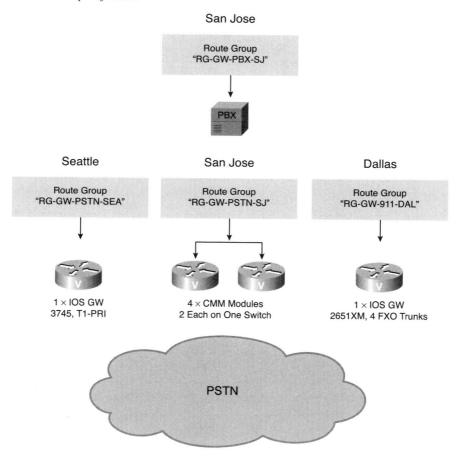

## Route Lists

A route list defines the way that a call is routed. Route lists are configured to point to one or more route groups, which effectively serve the purpose of trunk groups. The route list sends a call to a route group in a configured order of preference, as shown in Figure 6-7. Table 6-45 shows the details of the route lists configured for the U.S. cluster.

To add route lists, from CallManager Administration, choose **Route Plan > Route/Hunt > Route/Hunt List**.

**Table 6-45**   *Route Lists in Cluster 1*

| Route/Hunt List Name | Selection Order | Route Groups | Description |
|---|---|---|---|
| RL-PSTN-SJ | 1 | RG-GW-PSTN-SJ | All PSTN calls going through San Jose PSTN trunks |
| RL-PBX-SJ | 1 | RG-GW-PBX-SJ | All calls to extensions on PBX |
| RL-TEHO-SJ | 1 | RG-GW-PSTN-SEA | All PSTN calls originating from San Jose site to PSTN numbers that are within the Seattle local calling area |
|  | 2 | RG-GW-PSTN-SJ | |
| RL-PSTN-No911-SEA | 1 | RG-GW-PSTN-SEA | All PSTN calls originating from Seattle site, except 911 and AAR calls |
|  | 2 | RG-GW-PSTN-SJ | |
| RL-PSTN-911-AAR-SEA | 1 | RG-GW-PSTN-SEA | 911 and AAR calls originating from Seattle site |
| RL-TEHO-SEA | 1 | RG-GW-PSTN-SJ | All PSTN calls originating from Seattle site to PSTN numbers that are within San Jose local calling area |
|  | 2 | RG-GW-PSTN-SEA | |
| RL-PSTN-No911-DAL | 1 | RG-GW-PSTN-SJ | All PSTN calls originating from Dallas site, except 911 and AAR calls |
| RL-PSTN-911-AAR-DAL | 1 | RG-GW-911-DAL | 911 and AAR calls originating from Dallas site |
| RL-ICT-Sydney | 1 | RG-Gatekeeper | ICT calls to Sydney originating from cluster 1 |
|  | 2 | RG-GW-PSTN-SJ | |
| RL-ICT-Brisbane | 1 | RG-Gatekeeper | ICT calls to Brisbane originating from cluster 1 |
|  | 2 | RG-GW-PSTN-SJ | |
| RL-ICT-Melbourne | 1 | RG-Gatekeeper | ICT calls to Melbourne originating from cluster 1 |
|  | 2 | RG-GW-PSTN-SJ | |

To understand how the route list design is achieved, recall the XYZ call-routing requirements. One of the requirements is that the Seattle site should primarily use the trunks in the local T1 circuit to reach a PSTN destination. When local trunks are busy or unavailable, CallManager should reroute the call via central site trunks in San Jose. Route list RL-PSTN-No911-SEA, listed in Table 6-45, satisfies this requirement. This route list consists of two route groups: RG-GW-PSTN-SEA (priority 1) and RG-GW-PSTN-SJ (priority 2). RG-GW-PSTN-SEA represents PSTN trunks in Seattle, and RG-GW-PSTN-SJ represents PSTN trunks in San Jose.

Another route list, RL-PSTN-911-AAR-SEA for Seattle, routes the emergency calls and AAR calls only. This route list includes only the trunks on the Seattle T1 circuit and does not include the San Jose trunks for the following reasons:

- Routing the emergency calls originating from Seattle via the San Jose trunks results in emergency calls reaching the San Jose Public Safety Answering Point (PSAP).

- CallManager invokes the AAR feature when there is not enough bandwidth across the WAN link to send the call to San Jose. Hence, there is no point in routing the call via the San Jose trunks for the AAR scenario.

The Seattle site also requires TEHO implementation for calls to San Jose. This means that all PSTN calls originating from the Seattle site to PSTN numbers that are within the San Jose local calling area (refer to Table 6-39) use route list RL-TEHO-SEA, which consists of RG-GW-PSTN-SJ (first priority) and RG-GW-PSTN-SEA (second priority). Using this route list, TEHO calls from Seattle use the IP WAN to reach the San Jose site and then use San Jose local PSTN trunks to reach San Jose local calling numbers, falling back to Seattle trunks if no bandwidth is available to place the call across the WAN.

With the TEHO feature, XYZ does not have to pay for long-distance PSTN calls from Seattle to the San Jose local calling area.

The requirements for the Dallas site are to route all the calls via the San Jose trunks only and never use local trunks; therefore, route list RL-PSTN-No911-DAL includes only San Jose trunks. The emergency calls are routed via the local FXO trunks using the route list RL-PSTN-911-AAR-DAL.

Route lists RL-ICT-Sydney, RL-ICT-Melbourne, and RL-ICT-Brisbane route the intercluster calls that are destined to Sydney, Melbourne, and Brisbane (cluster 2) from any site in cluster 1. These route lists consist of two route groups: RG-Gatekeeper and RG-GW-PSTN-SJ. This indicates that calls are routed via the IP WAN after checking the availability of the bandwidth with the gatekeeper as the first preference. If there is not enough bandwidth on the IP WAN, the calls are routed through the PSTN trunks in San Jose as a second preference.

## Route Patterns

Route patterns primarily serve the following three functions:

- Match dialed number for internal/external calls
- Perform digit manipulation (optional)
- Point to a route list for routing

Refer to Figure 6-7 for a visual representation of route patterns and their order in the hierarchy of call routing.

Before going into the route pattern design for XYZ, the next few sections discuss the important concepts regarding route patterns, such as wildcards, route filters, digit discarding instructions, and digit transformations. Understanding these concepts is important in designing a trouble-free dial plan.

## Wildcards

In CallManager, every directory number or phone number is a route pattern. You can use wildcard characters to define the route patterns that match a group of dialed numbers. Table 6-46 shows the list of wildcard characters supported in CallManager, and Table 6-47 shows examples of defining route patterns using wildcard characters.

**Table 6-46**  *Wildcard Characters*

| Wildcard | Description |
|---|---|
| 0, 1, 2, 3, 4, 5, 6, 7, 8, 9, *, # | Match exactly one digit |
| X | Any single digit in the range 0–9 |
| [xyz…] | One occurrence of any of the digits in the brackets |
| [x-y] | One occurrence of any digit from x to y |
| [^x-y] | Any digit that is *not* between x and y |
| ! | One or more digits in the range 0–9 |
| wildcard? | Zero or more occurrences of the previous wildcard |
| wildcard+ | One or more occurrences of the previous wildcard |
| @ | Matches the North American Numbering Plan (NANP) |

**Table 6-47**  *Examples of Route Patterns with Wildcard Characters*

| Route Pattern Definition | Description |
|---|---|
| 2222 | Matches 2222 |
| *2*2 | Matches *2*2 |
| 14xx | Matches numbers between 1400 and 1499 |
| 15[25-8]6 | Matches 1526, 1556, 1566, 1576, 1586 |
| 13[^3-9]6 | Matches 1306, 1316, 1326, 13*6, 13#6 |
| 13!# | Matches any number that begins with 13, is followed by one or more digits, and ends with #, such as 135# and 13579# |

The . and @ are special wildcard characters:

- . denotes a portion of a route pattern that can be stripped when the pattern matches.
- @ is a macro for many patterns that encompass the NANP or the numbering plan that is installed on the CallManager.

## Route Filters

Route filters are applicable only when you are designing the route patterns using the @ macro. CallManager understands NANP by default. This means that CallManager knows all the elements of the NANP dial plan, so you can use the @ wildcard to design the route patterns. The NANP dial plan includes approximately 166 route patterns that are specific to NANP.

---

**NOTE**      To see all the route patterns that are included when using the @ wildcard, refer to the NANP dial plan file located in C:\Program Files\Cisco\Dial Plan\NANP on the CallManager server.

---

If you define a route pattern 9.@ without associating it with a route filter, CallManager checks the dialed number against all the route patterns included in the NANP dial plan file. Table 6-48 shows some route patterns in NANP that match the route pattern 9.@ when defined without a route filter.

**Table 6-48**    *9.@ Route Pattern Without a Route Filter*

| No. | Route Pattern | Description |
|-----|--------------|-------------|
| 1 | 9.[2-9]11 | 311, 611, 911 SERVICEs |
| 2 | 9.[2-9]XX XXXXXXX | 7-digit dialing by OFFICE CODE |
| 3 | 9.[2-9]XX [2-9]XXXXXX | 10-digit local dialing by LOCAL AREA CODE |
| 4 | 9.1[2-9]XX [2-9]XXXXXX | 11-digit long-distance dialing by AREA CODE |
| 5 | 9.011! | International dialing by COUNTRY CODE |

You can use route filters to select fewer route patterns to match against, rather than matching against all the route patterns defined in the NANP dial plan file. For example, if you intend to define a route pattern that matches the dialed numbers for service calls only, you can define a route pattern 9.@ with a route filter SERVICE EXISTS.

To define route filters, from CallManager Administration, choose **Route Plan > Route Filter**.

After defining a route filter, you associate it with a route pattern to limit the number of route patterns you need to match against the dialed number.

## Digit Transformations

A *digit transformation* in CallManager is a process wherein the modifications are made to calling party and called party numbers before handing over the call to the next system. Three types of digit transformations are available:

- Calling party transformations
- Connected party transformations
- Called party transformations

In CallManager, you can do these digit transformations at the following levels:

- Route pattern level
- Route group level within a route list

The digit transformations that are done at the route group level within a route list override those that are defined at the route pattern level. The best practice is to do the manipulations at the route group level within a route list, to avoid configuration mistakes.

Figure 6-11 shows the digit transformation options available in each type of transformation at a route pattern level.

**Figure 6-11**   *Digit Transformations at Route Pattern Level*

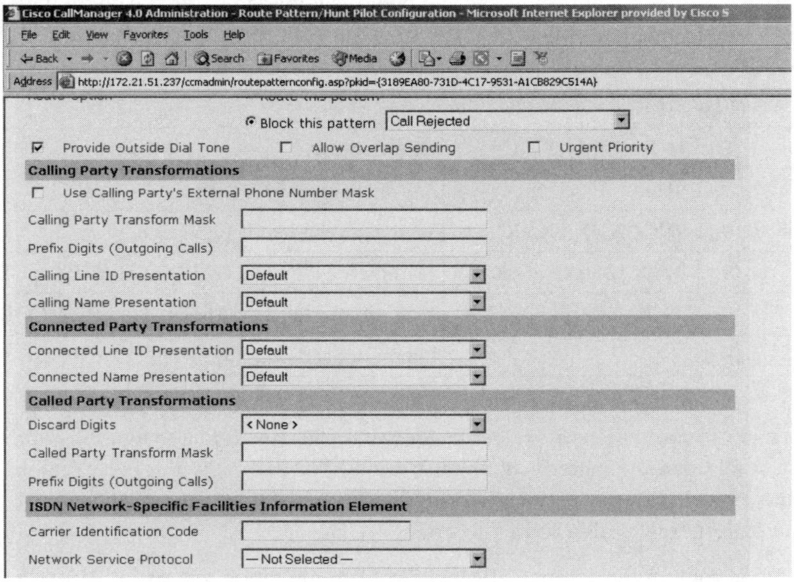

Figure 6-12 shows the digit transformation options available in each type of transformation at a route group level within a route list.

**Figure 6-12**    *Digit Transformations at Route Group Level*

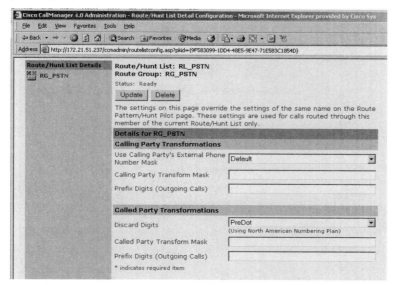

## Calling Party Transformations

Transformations that are made to the calling party change the caller ID. The following list explains some of the important settings shown in Figure 6-11:

- **Use Calling Party's External Phone Number Mask**—Checking this box tells CallManager to use the value in the External Phone Number Mask field on the IP Phone Directory Number Configuration page, shown in Figure 6-13. On this page, you can also define in the Display (Internal Caller ID) field the name that identifies the user of the phone. The AAR feature (discussed later in this chapter) in CallManager uses the value in the External Phone Number Mask field to route the call via PSTN when a location's CAC rejects placement of the call over the IP WAN because of lack of bandwidth. If this field is blank or configured with a wrong number, AAR fails.

- **Calling Party Transform Mask**—Use this field to mask the calling party number before sending out the call. A mask can contain digits 0 to 9, *, X, and #.

- **Prefix Digits**—The field allows you to prefix digits to the calling number.

To understand when to use the calling party transformations, consider the Dallas site-numbering plan described in Table 6-38. Dallas does not have a range of valid DID numbers to be assigned to IP Phones. Instead, the Dallas site has a single DID number, 1-972-555-5600. Internally, a four-digit private numbering plan is implemented to assign the directory numbers to IP Phones. The private directory numbering range is 5601 to 5619 (refer to Table 6-40).

**Figure 6-13** *Calling Party Transformations at Directory Number Level on IP Phone*

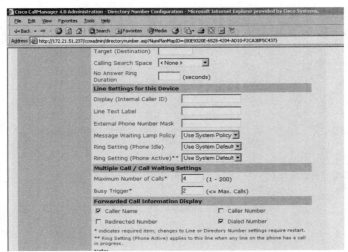

When an IP Phone in Dallas with a directory number of 5601 makes an outgoing call to an external PSTN number, CallManager should send the valid DID number (1-972-555-5600) to the PSTN as the calling party number and not 1-972-555-5601.

You can accomplish this in either of two ways:

1  For all the IP Phones in Dallas, enter **1-972-555-5600** in the External Phone Number Mask field of the Directory Number Configuration page (refer to Figure 6-13) and check the Use Calling Party's External Phone Number Mask box on the Route Pattern/Hunt Pilot Configuration page (refer to Figure 6-11).

2  Enter **19725555600** in the Calling Party Transform Mask field at the route group level in the route list (refer to Figure 6-12); the resulting number will match the DID number as shown here:

Caller ID
5601

Calling party transformation mask
197255555600

Resulting number
197255555600

The first option is used for the Dallas site IP Phones, because the AAR feature requires configuration of the external phone number mask. The Seattle and San Jose sites have valid DID numbers, so the External Phone Number Mask field on the IP Phones Directory Number Configuration page for Seattle and San Jose can be set to their actual DID number. At the route group level within the route list, check the option to use the e-Calling Party's External Phone Number Mask.

## Connected Party Transformations

In Figure 6-11, the Connected Party Transformations section allows you to choose whether you want Cisco CallManager to allow or restrict the display of the connected party's phone number on the calling party's phone display for this route pattern.

## Called Party Transformations

Under the Called Party Transformations sections in Figure 6-11 or 6-12, the Called Party Transform Mask and Prefix Digits fields serve the same function as the corresponding fields discussed for the Calling Party Transformations section. The additional field shown in Figure 6-12, Discard Digits, is discussed next.

## Digit Discarding Instructions

CallManager uses the value chosen in the Discard Digits field of Figure 6-11 or Figure 6-12 to modify the digits in the called number before routing the call to the next system.

CallManager provides you with many digit discarding instructions (DDIs). The DDIs, with the exception of NoDigits and PreDot, work only with route patterns that are defined using the @ wildcard, placed in the NANP dial plan or any other installed international dial plan combined with route filters.

To understand the importance of the DDIs, consider Table 6-49. The number before . in each route pattern defines the access code. In North America, the access code 9 is used; in some other countries, 0 is used. You can define any access code you like. You simply need to configure the route patterns accordingly.

Typically, route patterns that have access codes point to external numbers. If the access code is not part of the actual dialed number, you have to discard it before sending out to the PSTN. You can select the appropriate DDIs listed in the *Digit Discards* option under the Called Party Transformations section shown in Figure 6-11 or Figure 6-12 to achieve this.

With XYZ, the DDI that is selected for the route patterns that begin with 9. is PreDot. This discards 9 and sends the remaining number to the gateway that is specified in the route list. Digit 9 is the access code used to make the external calls.

As mentioned earlier in this section, one reason for not recommending the use of digit manipulation at the route pattern level is that if you dial a number (for example, 91408...) and the Discard Digits option is set to PreDot, the number that is stored in the Placed Calls list in the IP Phone is the number after 9 is stripped. If you want to redial the number on the same IP Phone, the 9 will not be included and the redial operation will fail to complete the call. This is why you should do the digit manipulation at the route group level within a route list instead of at the route pattern level.

When designing a dial plan in CallManager, you can either use explicit route patterns or use the @ macro with route filters. In designing the route patterns for XYZ, the explicit route patterns are defined instead of using the @ macro with route filters, because the dial plan is easy to read and follow.

To implement the call-routing requirements and restrictions of XYZ described previously, you can use the route patterns defined in Tables 6-49 and 6-50 in the U.S. cluster.

To add route patterns, from CallManager Administration, choose **Route Plan > Route Pattern/ Hunt Pilot**.

**Table 6-49**  *Route Patterns in Cluster 1*

| Route Pattern | Partition | Route List | Description |
|---|---|---|---|
| 2[5-9]XX | P-Internal | RL-PBX-SJ | PBX calls in San Jose |
| 6XXX | P-Internal | RL-ICT-Sydney | On-Network to Sydney<br><br>Apply called party transformation mask of 910116125555XXXX at the RG-GW-PSTN-SJ level |
| 43XX | P-Internal | RL-ICT-Melbourne | On-Network to Melbourne<br><br>Apply called party transformation mask of 91011613555543XX at the RG-GW-PSTN-SJ level |
| 86[89]X | P-Internal | RL-ICT-Brisbane | On-Network to Brisbane<br><br>Apply called party transformation mask of 9101161255558681 at the RG-GW-PSTN-SJ level |
| 9.911 | P-Emergency-SJ | RL-PSTN-SJ | 911 calls for San Jose users |
| 9.911 | P-Emergency-SEA | RL-PSTN-911-AAR-SEA | 911 calls for Seattle users |
| 9.911 | P-Emergency-DAL | RL-PSTN-911-AAR-DAL | 911 calls for Dallas users |
| 9.[2-9]XXXXXX | P-Local-SJ | RL-PSTN-SJ | Local calling in San Jose |
| 9.1425[2-9]XXXXXX<br>9.1253[2-9]XXXXXX | P-Local-SJ | RL-TEHO-SJ | Local calling in Seattle |
| 9.[2-9]XXXXXX | P-Local-SEA | RL-PSTN-No911-SEA | Local calling in Seattle; prepend 1 at the RG-GW-PSTN-SJ |
| 9.1408[2-9]xxxxxx<br>9.1510[2-9]xxxxxx<br>9.1650[2-9]xxxxxx<br>9.1925[2-9]xxxxxx | P-Local-SEA | RL-TEHO-SEA | Local calling within San Jose |

**Table 6-49**    *Route Patterns in Cluster 1 (Continued)*

| Route Pattern | Partition | Route List | Description |
|---|---|---|---|
| 9.[2-9]XXXXXX | P-Local-DAL | RL-PSTN-No911-DAL | Local calling in Dallas; prepend 1 plus the area code 972 at the RG-GW-PSTN-SJ |
| 9.1[2-9]XX[2-9]XXXXXX | P-LD-SJ | RL-PSTN-SJ | LD calls for San Jose |
| 9.1800[2-9]XXXXXX 9.1866[2-9]XXXXXX 9.1877[2-9]XXXXXX 9.1888[2-9]XXXXXX | P-TollFree-SJ | RL-PSTN-SJ | Toll-free calls for San Jose and Dallas |
| 9.1800[2-9]XXXXXX 9.1866[2-9]XXXXXX 9.1877[2-9]XXXXXX 9.1888[2-9]XXXXXX | P-TollFree-SEA | RL-PSTN-No911-SEA | Toll-free calls for Seattle |
| 9.1[2-9]XX[2-9]XXXXXX | P-LD-SEA | RL-PSTN-No911-SEA | Long-distance calls for Seattle |
| 9.1[2-9]XX[2-9]XXXXXX | P-LD-DAL | RL-PSTN-No911-DAL | Long-distance calls for Dallas |
| 9.1[2-9]XX[2-9]XXXXXX | P-LD-AAR-SEA | RL-PSTN-911-AAR-SEA | Long-distance AAR for Seattle |
| 9.1[2-9]XX[2-9]XXXXXX | P-LD-AAR-DAL | RL-PSTN-911-AAR-DAL | Long-distance AAR for Dallas |
| 9.011! | P-INT-SJ | RL-PSTN-SJ | International calls for San Jose |
| 9.011!# | P-INT-SJ | RL-PSTN-SJ | International calls for San Jose |
| 9.011! | P-INT-SEA | RL-PSTN-No911-SEA | International calls for Seattle |
| 9.011!# | P-INT-SEA | RL-PSTN-No911-SEA | International calls for Seattle |
| 9.011! | P-INT-DAL | RL-PSTN-No911-DAL | International calls for Dallas |
| 9.011!# | P-INT-DAL | RL-PSTN-No911-DAL | International calls for Dallas |
| 9.011! | P-INT-AAR-SEA | RL-PSTN-911-AAR-SEA | International AAR calls for Seattle |
| 9.011! | P-INT-AAR-DAL | RL-PSTN-911-AAR-DAL | International AAR calls for Dallas |

---

**NOTE**     Set the Urgent Priority flag to all the 9.911 route patterns. When this flag is set, CallManager routes the call immediately after the user dials 9911 even if there is another potential match in the digit analysis table.

---

Figure 6-14 shows the complete dial plan, including route patterns, route lists, and route groups for the San Jose site. CallManager matches against a list of the route patterns based on the dialed number. For an IP Phone to match a route pattern, the partition of that route pattern should be included in the phone's CSS. Route patterns point to route lists, which point to route groups. Based on the route pattern, CallManager selects a route list and routes the call via the gateways that are specified in the route group based on the priority order.

Figures 6-15 and 6-16 show the complete dial plan, including route patterns, route lists, and route groups, for the Seattle site and Dallas site, respectively.

Figure 6-17 shows the dial plan to route the calls from the San Jose cluster to the Australia cluster. CallManager selects a different route list based on the dialed number. San Jose users dial four digits to reach the IP Phone users in the Australian cluster. No digit manipulations are necessary if the call goes through the IP WAN. However, to route the call via PSTN, you have to send the full E.164 number based on the phone location within Australia. You can accomplish this by applying the called party transformation mask specific to the site on the RG-GW-PSTN-SJ route group within each route list. For example, in Figure 6-17, 910116125555XXXX is applied on the RG-GW-PSTN-SJ route group within the route list RL-ICT-Sydney to route the call via PSTN. Because the IP Phone numbers at the Brisbane site are non-DID numbers, the mask 9101161255558681 is used. This routes the call to the operator number in Brisbane.

Figure 6-18 shows the call flow for a TEHO call originating in Seattle and going to a PSTN user in San Jose.

**Figure 6-14**  *Complete Dial Plan for San Jose Site*

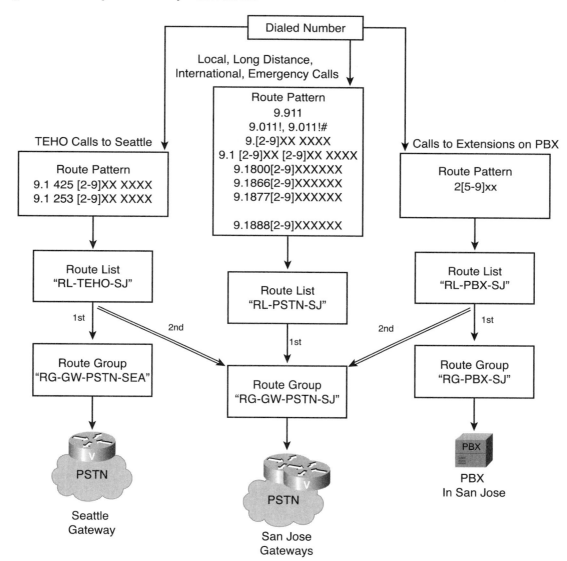

**Figure 6-15** *Complete Dial Plan for Seattle Site*

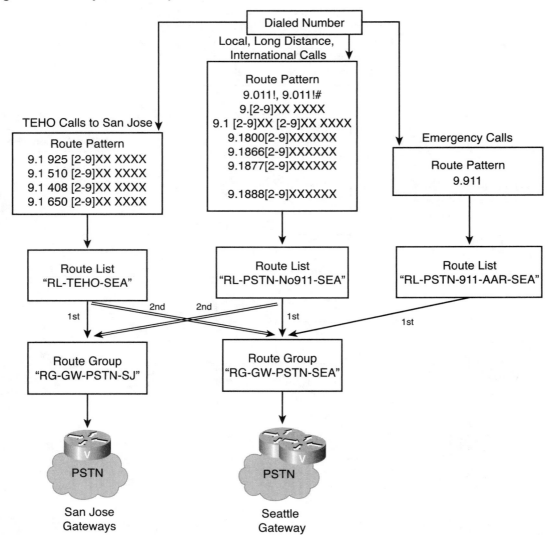

**Figure 6-16**   *Complete Dial Plan for Dallas Site*

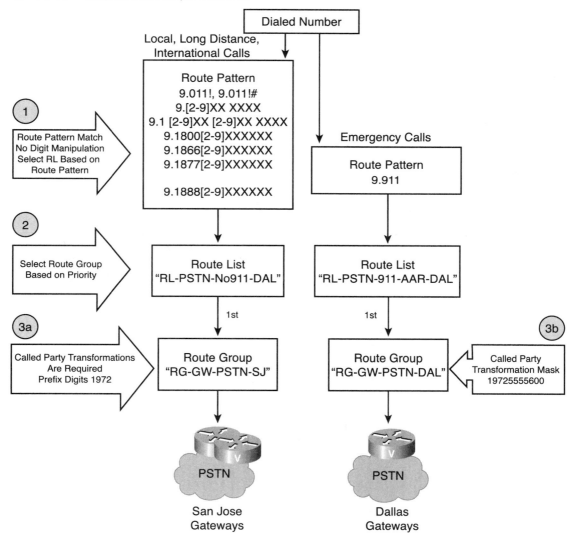

**Figure 6-17** *Dial Plan for Intercluster Calls Between U.S. Cluster and Australian Cluster*

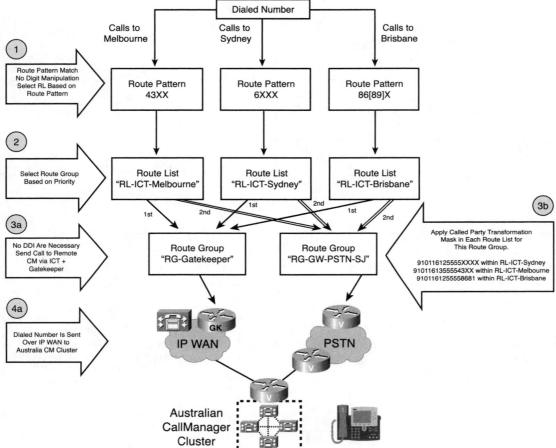

**Figure 6-18**    *Dial Plan for TEHO Calls from Seattle to San Jose*

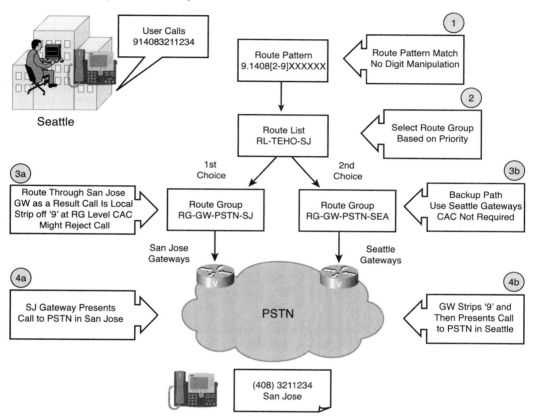

Table 6-50 shows the blocked route patterns for cluster 1. (The partition names are from Table 6-41.)

**Table 6-50**    *Blocked Route Patterns in Cluster 1*

| Route Pattern | Partition |
|---|---|
| 9.[2-9]XXXXXX | P-Block-Local |
| 9.1[2-9]XX[2-9]XXXXXX | P-Block-LD |
| 9.011! | P-Block-INT |
| 9.011!# | P-Block-INT |

## Gatekeeper

Intercluster trunks connect two or more CallManager clusters. These are virtual trunks. Typically, a WAN connection exists between clusters that are distributed across multiple locations. To control the number of calls across the ICT via the IP WAN, you can use a gatekeeper. Cisco CallManager uses the H.323 protocol to communicate with the gatekeeper.

For XYZ, one cluster is located in San Jose and the other is in Australia. Deploying a gatekeeper to perform CAC in a CallManager environment requires the following steps:

1  Select the gatekeeper hardware platform and deployment mode.

2  Configure the gatekeeper in the CallManager.

3  Configure the trunk in the CallManager.

4  Configure the gatekeeper.

Using a gatekeeper in the intercluster communications provides the following advantages:

- Increased scalability, by reducing the number of ICTs required to communicate between clusters

- Ease of management, enabling quick addition and removal of routes and devices

- CAC between calls from different clusters, ensuring that the WAN bandwidth allocation is strictly enforced

- Reduced configuration overhead, by eliminating the need to configure a separate H.323 device for each remote Cisco CallManager that is connected to the IP WAN

- Ability to perform basic call routing in addition to CAC

The gatekeeper is a software feature in Cisco IOS software and runs on most of the routers. The selection of the hardware platform depends on the following factors:

- Number of calls per second (CPS) that the gatekeeper needs to process.

- Gatekeeper deployment model deploys a gatekeeper in clustering mode that reduces the performance hit and provides load sharing and redundancy in the network.

### Defining a Gatekeeper in CallManager

In Cisco CallManager 3.3 and above, to configure the gatekeeper, the first step is to define the gatekeeper. To define a gatekeeper, from the CallManager Administration page, choose **Device > Gatekeeper**. Table 6-51 shows the configuration parameters that you need to enter when defining the gatekeeper in CallManager.

**Table 6-51**  *Gatekeeper Configuration Parameters*

| Host Name/IP Address | Description | Registration Required Time to Live | Registration Retry Timeout | Enable Device |
|---|---|---|---|---|
| IP Address of GK | Gatekeeper | 60 | 300 | Checked |

### Defining a Gatekeeper Trunk

After you configure the gatekeeper information, the next step is to define the trunk. From the CallManager Administration page, choose **Device > Trunk** and click the **Add New Trunk** option. Choose the Trunk Type as **Inter-Cluster Trunk (Gatekeeper Controlled)** and the Device Protocol as **Inter-Cluster Trunk**.

Table 6-52 shows the configuration parameters that you need to enter when defining the gatekeeper trunk in CallManager.

**Table 6-52**  *Gatekeeper Trunk Configuration Parameters*

| Parameter | Value |
|---|---|
| **Device Information** | |
| Device Name | AS_GKTrunk |
| Description | Gatekeeper Trunk |
| Device Pool | DP-SanJose |
| MRGL | MRGL_SJ |
| Location | San Jose |
| AAR Group | None |
| MTP Required | Unchecked |
| Retry Video Call as Audio | Unchecked |
| **Call Routing Information—Inbound** | |
| Significant Digits | All |
| Calling Search Space | Css-gateways |
| AAR Calling Search Space | |
| Prefix DN | |
| Redirecting Number IE-Delivery—Inbound | Checked |
| **Gatekeeper Information** | |
| Gatekeeper Name | Name Configured in Table 6-49 |
| Terminal Type | Gateway |
| Technology Prefix | 1# |
| Zone | Cluster 1 |

## Gatekeeper Configuration

Example 6-2 shows the gatekeeper configuration at the San Jose site in cluster 1 according to the XYZ requirements. The configuration at the San Jose gatekeeper is simple, and similar configuration guidelines will be followed for the Sydney gatekeeper.

**Example 6-2** *San Jose Gatekeeper Configuration*

```
Gatekeeper
! Split the GK into multiple local zones
! Define one zone for the U.S. cluster
zone local Cluster1 xyz.com 10.1.19.1
! Define one zone for the Australia cluster
zone local Cluster2 xyz.com
! To prevent any other device than the U.S. CallManagers from registering
zone subnet Cluster1 10.1.1.5/27 enable
zone subnet Cluster1 10.1.1.6/27 enable
zone subnet Cluster1 10.1.1.36/27 enable
no zone subnet Cluster1 0.0.0.0/0 enable
! To prevent any other device than the Australia CallManagers from registering
zone subnet Cluster2 10.4.1.5/27 enable
zone subnet Cluster2 10.4.1.36/27 enable
no zone subnet Cluster2 0.0.0.0/0 enable
! Define the prefixes for the U.S. zone
zone prefix Cluster1 3...
zone prefix Cluster1 4...
zone prefix Cluster1 21..
zone prefix Cluster1 560.
zone prefix Cluster1 561.
! Define the prefixes for the Australian zone
zone prefix Cluster2 6...
zone prefix Cluster2 43..
zone prefix Cluster2 868.
zone prefix Cluster2 869.
! Maximum of 20 G.729 interclusters calls.
! We need to provision 16k for each call.
bandwidth interzone Cluster1 320
bandwidth interzone Cluster2 320
! Defines the default technology prefix that is necessary for routing decisions
gw-type-prefix 1#* default-technology
arq reject-unknown-prefix
no shutdown
```

## Inbound Call Routing

The incoming calls for the San Jose and Seattle sites come in via the PRI trunks. The PSTN trunks in San Jose terminate on T1 PRI ports on the CMM modules, and in Seattle they terminate on the T1 PRI port on the Cisco 3725 router. All the voice gateways are configured to use MGCP. The voice gateways receive all the digits from the PSTN. You need to set the Significant Digits field on the Gateway Configuration page for the San Jose and Seattle gateways to 4. This setting instructs the CallManager to use only the last four digits to route calls. Because the San Jose and Seattle sites have DID numbers, using the last four digits, CallManager extends the call to the IP Phone or to the CTI route point. We do not need to set this field on the PRI trunks that are connected to the San Jose PBX. The PBX is configured to forward four digits for the IPT network.

Another setting that is important to discuss is the CSS. To successfully route the call from the gateway to an IP Phone or to a CTI route point, the CSS on the gateway should include the partitions that contain IP Phones and CTI route points. Hence, set the CSS field on the gateway to CSS-Gateways (refer to Table 6-43).

When configuring the gateway for the Dallas site, where the numbers are non-DID numbers, you should set the Attendant Directory Number field on the Gateway Configuration page for the Dallas gateway to match the directory number of a local IP Phone in Dallas. Typically, it will be the IP Phone of the person who is fulfilling the role of the operator.

## Automated Alternate Routing

AAR is a mechanism that allows the call path for an intracluster call to be reestablished through the PSTN when the location-based CAC denies the call because of insufficient bandwidth. Remember that AAR is an intracluster feature. This means that AAR does not work between two CallManager clusters.

Configuring AAR involves the following steps:

1  Enable the AAR service parameter.

2  Define the external phone number mask.

3  Configure AAR groups and assign IP Phone directory numbers and gateways to the AAR groups.

4  Define AAR CSSs and assign them to IP Phone devices and gateways.

### Enabling the AAR Service Parameter

The first step in configuring AAR is to enable AAR on the CallManager. To enable AAR from the CallManager Administration page, choose **System > Enterprise Parameters** and set the Automated Alternate Routing parameter to **True**.

### Defining the External Phone Number Mask

Figure 6-19 shows the AAR call-rerouting process. A Seattle user makes a call to a Dallas user by dialing four digits. However, because the bandwidth is not available, CallManager CAC denies access to route the call via the IP WAN. CallManager invokes the AAR mechanism to route the call via PSTN to reach the Dallas user.

**Figure 6-19** *AAR Implementation and Functionality in Cluster 1 of XYZ*

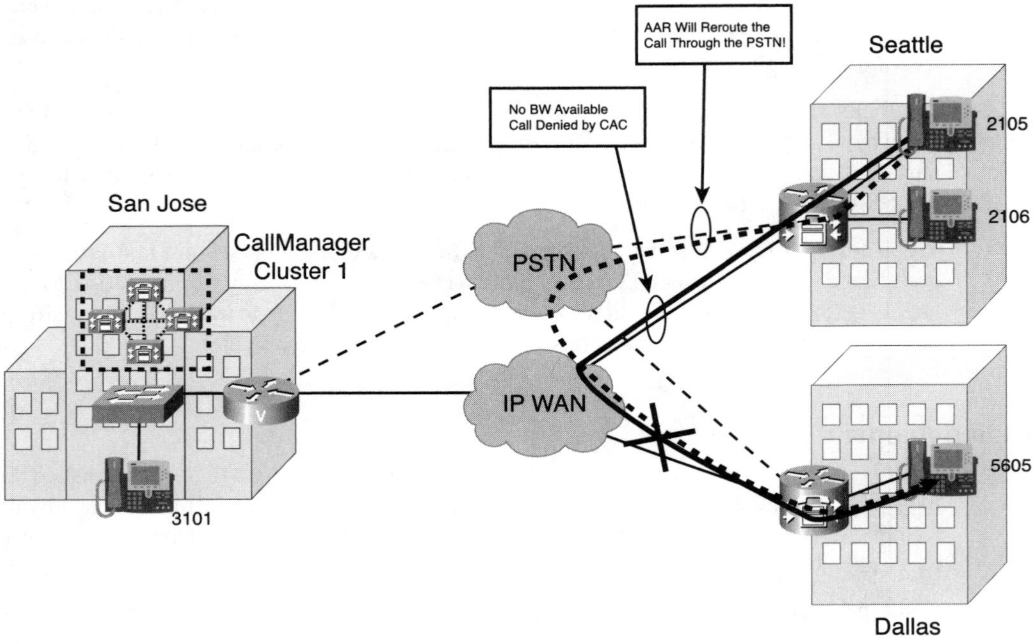

Based on the implementation shown in Figure 6-19, you might wonder how CallManager knows what is the full E.164 number to dial to reach the Seattle user. The answer is that CallManager refers to the External Phone Number Mask field on the IP Phone Directory Number Configuration page. Configuring this field is mandatory for AAR to work. Table 6-53 shows the external phone number masks for each location for XYZ. Note that for the Dallas and Brisbane locations, the external phone number mask is configured to match the single DID number for those locations. All other locations of XYZ have valid DID number ranges for IP Phones.

**Table 6-53** *External Phone Mask Applied at the Line Level*

| Site | External Phone Number Mask |
| --- | --- |
| San Jose | 408 555 XXXX |
| Seattle | 206 555 XXXX |
| Dallas | 972 555 5600 |
| Sydney | 02 5555 XXXX |
| Melbourne | 03 5555 XXXX |
| Brisbane | 07 5555 8680 |

### Configuring AAR Groups

Another question that you might have based on the implementation shown in Figure 6-19 is how CallManager knows what access code to dial to reach the destination via PSTN. The answer to this question is AAR groups. AAR groups specify the access code plus any long-distance code that needs to be added to the external phone number mask before making the call to the PSTN.

To configure AAR groups, from CallManager Administration, choose **Route Plan > AAR Group**. You need to define one AAR group (for example, AAR group name as AAR_cluster1) in cluster 1 so that CallManager prepends 91 to the external phone number mask before placing an AAR call. 9 is the PSTN access code and 1 is the prefix for the long-distance call.

In cluster 2, configure a single AAR group (for example, AAR group name as AAR_cluster2) such that CallManager prepends 0 when calling any location within Australia, where 0 is the access code used to reach the PSTN numbers.

After defining the AAR groups, you need to assign them to the directory numbers on each IP Phone. All directory numbers in cluster 1 will have AAR_cluster1 as their AAR group, and all directory numbers in cluster 2 will have AAR_cluster2 as their AAR group. The AAR groups in both clusters are simple because the length of telephone numbers across the country is the same. You might end up with multiple AAR groups if your sites use variable-length area codes.

### Defining AAR Calling Search Spaces

The final step in configuring the AAR is to define a separate AAR CSS and assign it at the device level for gateways and for the IP Phones. The AAR CSS is used when placing the call through the PSTN. The AAR CSS was already defined in Table 6-43. The dial plan route patterns (refer to Table 6-49) and route lists (refer to Table 6-45) have been designed to accommodate AAR. The dial plan is designed to utilize the local gateway under AAR.

## Survivable Remote Site Telephony

Survivable Remote Site Telephony (SRST) provides the CallManager with fallback support for the Cisco IP Phones that are attached to routers on the local Ethernet. SRST enables the routers to provide call-handling support for the IP Phones when the IP Phones lose connection to the remote primary, secondary, or tertiary CallManager or when the WAN connection is down. SRST will be deployed for every remote site in the XYZ network in cluster 1 and cluster 2 to support the IP Phones in the remote sites in case of a WAN failure.

Under SRST mode, the IP Phone users cannot use four digits to dial the other IP Phones at a different site. For example, during the failure of a WAN link between the San Jose and Seattle sites, a user in Seattle who is calling another user in San Jose with four digits hears a reorder tone. In this case, the user in Seattle must dial the full telephone number to reach the user in San

Jose or any other user in any site. However, you can overcome this limitation by placing translation rules in the SRST router, as shown in the next section in Example 6-3.

If the WAN link is available but no bandwidth is available on the WAN link to route a call across the WAN, CallManager uses AAR to automatically route the call via the PSTN. This process is transparent to the user. The important point to note is that AAR kicks in only if the CallManager is unable to route the call because of CAC and the unavailability of bandwidth. It does not kick in if the WAN link fails.

Under SRST mode, all inbound calls from the PSTN to the remote sites are routed to the end stations if they have a valid DID number. The H.323 session on the remote-site routers handles the call routing under the SRST mode. Also in the SRST mode, users can access the voice-mail messages via the PSTN; however, the MWI will not work. As a workaround, users will have to call the voice-mail server to check for messages. When users press the Messages button on the IP Phone, the gateway automatically dials the voice-mail system via the PSTN. Example 6-3, discussed in the next section, shows the commands to achieve this.

In the Dallas and Brisbane sites, which have FXO trunks that are non-DID trunks, inbound calls are routed to the operator. The Dallas and Brisbane sites have only four analog connections on the routers. Under SRST mode, call routing from these sites is limited as follows:

- Only two ports are allowed to route the outbound calls.
- One port is always reserved for routing emergency calls.
- One port can dial local, long-distance, or international calls.

## SRST for Seattle and Melbourne Remote Sites

Example 6-3 shows the CLI configuration for the Seattle router to support SRST. Besides the E1 PRI configuration for the Melbourne router, the rest of the Melbourne SRST configuration is identical to that of the Seattle router.

**Example 6-3** *Seattle Router SRST Configuration*

```
hostname R3745-SEA
!
!
! Translation rule that converts the user extensions in San Jose
! and Dallas to a full E.164 number.
voice translation-rule 1

! Rule 1 converts any number beginning with 5 to the
! Dallas site DID number 17325555611

 rule 1 /^5\(...\)/ /17325555611/

! Rules 2 and 3 convert the 4-digit number beginning with 3 or 4 to a full E.164
! number to match the DID numbers in the San Jose site.
 rule 2 /^4\(...\)/ /14085554\1/
```

**Example 6-3**  *Seattle Router SRST Configuration  (Continued)*

```
rule 3 /^3\(...\)/ /14085553\1/

voice-card 1
 dspfarm
 dsp services dspfarm
! Define the translation profile and attach Rule 1
voice translation-profile 4Digits2E164
 translate called 1

! Enables the DHCP on the router
ip dhcp
isdn switch-type primary-ni
ip dhcp excluded-address 10.2.1.1 10.2.1.5
! Router acts as DHCP server for IP Phones in Seattle
ip dhcp pool Seattle-IPPhones
   network 10.2.1.0 255.255.255.0
   default-router 10.2.1.1
   option 150 ip 10.1.1.7
!
ccm-manager fallback-mgcp
! CallManager backup call agent in cluster 1
ccm-manager redundant-host 10.1.1.6
ccm-manager mgcp
ccm-manager music-on-hold
!
controller T1 1/0
 framing esf
 linecode b8zs
 pri-group timeslots 1-24 service mgcp
!
interface Loopback0
 ip address 10.2.11.5 255.255.255.0
!
interface FastEthernet0/0
 no ip address
 duplex auto
 speed auto
!
interface VLAN 21
 description voice subnet
 ip address 10.2.1.1 255.255.255.0
!
interface VLAN 211
 description data subnet
 ip address 10.2.11.1 255.255.255.0
!
interface Serial1/0:23
 no ip address
 no logging event link-status
 isdn switch-type primary-ni
 isdn incoming-voice voice
```

*continues*

**Example 6-3** *Seattle Router SRST Configuration (Continued)*

```
! Backhaul the D channel to the CallManager
 isdn bind-l3 ccm-manager
 no cdp enable
!
call application alternate DEFAULT
! Use H.323 under FallBack mode
!
voice-port 1/0:23
!
voice-port 2/0/0
 description FAX MACHINE 2065552151
!
voice-port 2/0/1
 description FAX MACHINE 2065552152
!
mgcp
! Define the primary call agent
mgcp call-agent 10.1.1.6 service-type mgcp version 0.1
mgcp dtmf-relay voip codec all mode out-of-band
mgcp rtp unreachable timeout 1000 action notify
mgcp package-capability rtp-package
mgcp package-capability sst-package
no mgcp timer receive-rtcp
mgcp sdp simple
mgcp fax t38 inhibit
no mgcp explicit hookstate
! Define the interface from where the signaling and
! audio packet will be sourced.
mgcp bind control source-interface Loopback0
mgcp bind media source-interface Loopback0
mgcp rtp payload-type g726r16 static
!
mgcp profile default
!
! Define local conferencing resources in Seattle
sccp local Loopback0
sccp
sccp ccm 10.1.1.6 priority 1
sccp ccm 10.1.1.36 priority 2
!
sccp switchback timeout guard 180
dspfarm confbridge maximum sessions 6
dspfarm

!
dial-peer voice 1 pots
! Port MGCP controlled when CallManager is up and running or WAN is available
 application mgcpapp
 incoming called-number
 direct-inward-dial
 port 1/0:23
```

**Example 6-3**  *Seattle Router SRST Configuration  (Continued)*

```
!
dial-peer voice 911 pots
! Explicit dial-peer for 911 under SRST mode
 destination-pattern 911
 port 1/0:23
 forward-digits all
!
dial-peer voice 100 pots
! Explicit dial-peer for local calling under SRST mode
 destination-pattern 9[2-9]......
 port 1/0:23
 forward-digits 7
!
dial-peer voice 101 pots
! Explicit dial-peer for long distance calling under SRST mode
 destination-pattern 91[2-9]..[2-9]......
 port 1/0:23
 forward-digits 11
!
dial-peer voice 102 pots
! Explicit dial-peer for international calling under SRST
! mode destination-pattern 9011.T
destination-pattern 9011.T
 port 1/0:23
 prefix 011
!
dial-peer voice 20 pots
 application mgcpapp
! Fax machine1
 destination-pattern 2151
 port 2/0/0
!
dial-peer voice 21 pots
 application mgcpapp
! Fax machine2
 destination-pattern 2152
 port 2/0/1
! This dial peer matches the 4-digit extension numbers for the
! San Jose and Dallas sites, Invokes the translation profile
! to translate the called numbers to valid DID numbers
dial-peer voice 200 pots
 translation-profile outgoing 4Digits2E164
 destination-pattern [3-5]...
 port 1/0:23

call-manager-fallback
 ip source-address 10.2.11.5 port 2000
 max-ephones 48
 max-dn 96
! Provide secondary dial tone to IP Phone users when
! users dial 9 in SRST mode
```

*continues*

**Example 6-3**   *Seattle Router SRST Configuration  (Continued)*

```
 secondary-dialtone 9
 ! For inbound calls, use the last 4 digits and then route the call.
 dialplan-pattern 1 206555.... extension-length 4
 ! To access the OCTEL voice mail system in San Jose when users
 ! press Messages button on the Cisco IP Phone
 voicemail 914085553555
 ! The following two commands forward the calls to a voice-mail system
 ! if the Cisco IP Phone user extension is busy or the call is not answered.
call-forward busy 914085553555
call-forward noan 914085553555 timeout 10
 ! Provide MoH to Seattle phones. Use the audio file from the local router flash
moh music.au
 multicast moh 239.1.1.1 port 16384 route 10.2.11.1 10.2.1.1
```

## SRST for Dallas and Brisbane Remote Sites

Example 6-4 shows the CLI configuration for the Dallas router to support SRST. The Brisbane router SRST configuration will be identical to that of the Dallas router SRST configuration.

In Example 6-4, two POTS dial peers, 200 and 201, are matched when Dallas IP Phone users dial 4-digit numbers during the SRST mode to reach the San Jose and Seattle site users. The called numbers are modified by prefixing the right digits to make the called number a valid E.164 number. The same result is accomplished in Example 6-3 by using the translation rules.

**Example 6-4**   *Dallas Router SRST Configuration*

```
hostname R2600-DAL
!
ccm-manager fallback-mgcp
 ! CallManager backup call agent in cluster 1
ccm-manager redundant-host 10.1.1.6
ccm-manager mgcp
ccm-manager music-on-hold
!
interface Loopback0
 ip address 10.1.64.1 255.255.255.0
!
interface FastEthernet0/0
 no ip address
 duplex auto
 speed auto
!
interface FastEthernet0/0.65
 description voice subnet
 encapsulation dot1Q 65
 ip address 10.1.65.1 255.255.255.0
!
interface FastEthernet0/0.66
 description data subnet
 encapsulation dot1Q 66 native
 ip address 10.1.66.1 255.255.255.0
```

**Example 6-4**   *Dallas Router SRST Configuration (Continued)*

```
!
call application alternate DEFAULT
! Fallback to H.323 when MGCP is down.
!
voice-port 1/0/0
! Fax Machine

voice-port 1/0/1
!
voice-port 1/0/2
!
voice-port 1/0/3
!
voice-port 1/0/4
! Outbound 911 only. No inbound
!
voice-port 1/0/5
! FXO outbound 911 calling under SRST and inbound fax
connection plar opx 5611
!
voice-port 1/0/6
! FXO outbound and inbound PSTN.
! Inbound calls routed to the operator in the site.
 connection plax opx 5601
!
voice-port 1/0/7
! FXO outbound and inbound PSTN.
! Inbound calls routed to the operator in the site.
connection plax opx 5601
!
mgcp
mgcp call-agent 10.1.1.6 service-type mgcp version 0.1
mgcp dtmf-relay voip codec all mode out-of-band
mgcp rtp unreachable timeout 1000 action notify
mgcp package-capability rtp-package
mgcp package-capability sst-package
no mgcp timer receive-rtcp
mgcp sdp simple
mgcp fax t38 inhibit
no mgcp explicit hookstate
mgcp bind control source-interface Loopback0
mgcp bind media source-interface Loopback0
mgcp rtp payload-type g726r16 static
!
mgcp profile default
!
! This dial peer is used to match the 4-digit numbers dialed by
! Dallas IP Phone users in the SRST mode. The called number is
! prefixed with 1408555 to make it a valid E.164 number and route the call.
dial-peer voice 200 pots
 destination-pattern [3-4]...
```

*continues*

**Example 6-4**  *Dallas Router SRST Configuration (Continued)*

```
 port 1/0:23
 forward-digits all
 prefix 1408555
! This dial peer is used for the same reason as above dial peer
! but to match the 4-digit extensions for Seattle users.
dial-peer voice 201 pots
 destination-pattern 2...
 port 1/0:23
 forward-digits all
 prefix 1206555
dial-peer voice 9111 pots
! Explicit dial peer for outbound 911. Dedicated port for 911 and inbound fax
 application mgcpapp
 destination-pattern 911
 port 1/0/4
 forward-digits all
!
dial-peer voice 9111 pots
! Explicit dial peer for outbound 911. Dedicated port for 911 and inbound fax
 application mgcpapp
 destination-pattern 911
 port 1/0/5
 forward-digits all
!
dial-peer voice 1001 pots
! Explicit dial peer for local calling. First port
 application mgcpapp
 destination-pattern 9[2-9]......
 port 1/0/6
 forward-digits 7
!
dial-peer voice 1002 pots
! Explicit dial peer for local calling. Second port
 application mgcpapp
 destination-pattern 9[2-9]......
 port 1/0/7
 forward-digits 7
!
dial-peer voice 1011 pots
! Explicit dial peer for LD calling. First port
 destination-pattern 91[2-9]..[2-9]......
 port 1/0/6
 forward-digits 11
!
dial-peer voice 1012 pots
! Explicit dial peer for LD calling. Second port
 destination-pattern 91[2-9]..[2-9]......
 port 1/0/7
 forward-digits 11
!
dial-peer voice 1021 pots
```

**Example 6-4**  *Dallas Router SRST Configuration (Continued)*

```
! Explicit dial peer for international calling. First port
destination-pattern 9011.T
 port 1/0/6
 prefix 011
!
dial-peer voice 1022 pots
! Explicit dial peer for international calling. Second port
 destination-pattern 9011.T
 port 1/0/7
 prefix 011
!
dial-peer voice 100 pots
! Fax machine
 application mgcpapp
 destination-pattern 5611
 port 1/0/0
!
call-manager-fallback
 ip source-address 10.1.65.1 port 2000
 max-ephones 12
 max-dn 24
 voicemail 914085553555
! The following two commands forward the calls to the
! voice-mail system if the Cisco IP Phone
! user extension is busy or the call is not answered.
call-forward busy 914085553555
call-forward noan 914085553555 timeout 10
```

# Fax and Modem

Two mechanisms are available to deploy fax and modem services over an IP network: fax and modem relay and fax and modem pass-through. The support varies from one Cisco platform to another and is highly dependent on the underlying voice-signaling protocol, whether it is SCCP, MGCP, or H.323.

Fax and modem pass-through capabilities are supported in all the gateways deployed in the XYZ network. Also with this model, pass-through V.34 modem speed can be guaranteed. Refer to the following URL for more details on fax support on various voice gateways:

> http://www.cisco.com/en/US/tech/tk652/tk777/
> technologies_tech_note09186a0080159cf3.shtml

While using fax and modem pass-through, you have to force the codec to be G.711. XYZ will not be able to use the up-speed feature of the pass-through mode because the CAC mechanism that is currently available in CallManager cannot dynamically adjust the bandwidth that is deducted. All fax and modem endpoints will belong to the device pool DP-MOH-FAX (refer to Table 6-20). That will force the call to be negotiated as a G.711 call from the start of the call and deduct the right amount of G.711 bandwidth from the CAC mechanism.

| NOTE | Implementing fax up-speed allows the use of high-compression codecs (such as G.729) for voice calls. However, when certain fax tones are detected, the codec is "up-speeded" or changed to G.711. |
|------|------|

With XYZ, at the central sites in San Jose and Sydney, the incoming fax call from the PSTN comes from the WS-X6608-T1 and WS-X6608-E1 gateways. The fax machines are connected to the VG248 gateways. At the remote sites, the incoming fax calls arrive on the MGCP gateways.

Example 6-5 shows the configuration required for the MGCP Cisco IOS voice gateway to support the fax and modem pass-through features. This configuration is required on all the remote-site gateways.

**Example 6-5**  *Cisco IOS MGCP Gateway Configuration for Fax and Modem Pass-Through Features*

```
Mgcp
 ! Enables MGCP support on the gateway
mgcp call-agent 10.1.2.1 service-type mgcp version 0.1
 ! Point the MGCP daemon on the gateway to a call control agent i.e. CallManager
no ccm-manager fax protocol cisco
mgcp modem passthrough voip mode nse
 ! Enables peer-to-peer RTP NSE (Named Signaling Events) to coordinate
 ! the following between the originating and terminating gateways:
 ! codec switchover and the disabling of
 ! the echo canceller and voice activity detection (VAD).
mgcp modem passthrough voip codec g711ulaw
no mgcp timer receive-rtcp
mgcp sdp simple
mgcp fax t38 inhibit
 ! This is used to disable MGCP support for T.38 fax.
 ! By default, T.38 is enabled.
 !
mgcp profile default
ccm-manager fallback-mgcp
ccm-manager mgcp
 ! This command is required for the CallManager
 ! to be able to control the gateway.
 !
dial-peer voice 100 pots
 ! Fax machine
 application mgcpapp
 ! This voice port is controlled by CallManager via MGCP
 destination-pattern 5611
 port 1/0/0
```

After you configure the fax settings on the MGCP gateway for fax pass-through, you can verify the settings by using the **show mgcp** command on the voice gateway, as shown in Example 6-6.

**Example 6-6**    *Verifying the Fax Pass-Through Configurations on the Cisco IOS MGCP Gateways*

```
#Show mgcp
MGCP voip modem passthrough mode: NSE, codec: g711ulaw, redundancy: DISABLED,
MGCP voaal2 modem passthrough disabled
MGCP voip modem relay: Disabled.
MGCP T.38 Fax is DISABLED
MGCP T.38 Fax ECM is DISABLED
MGCP T.38 Fax NSF Override is DISABLED
MGCP T.38 Fax Low Speed Redundancy: 0MGCP T.38 Fax High Speed Redundancy: 0
MGCP Upspeed payload type for G711ulaw: 0, G711alaw: 8
```

Figure 6-20 shows the configuration of the Catalyst WS-X6608 gateway, which is a non-IOS-based MGCP gateway to enable fax pass-through. The same configuration settings are required even with the 6624 FXS card.

**Figure 6-20**    *Fax Pass-Through Configuration on Catalyst WS-X6608 Gateways*

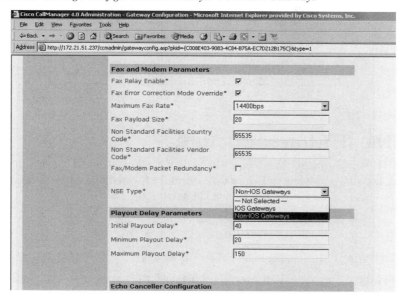

Figure 6-21 shows the configuration of VG248, which is an SCCP-based gateway to enable fax pass-through. When configuring the VG248 for fax, observe the following:

- If Cisco fax relay is enabled on the VG248 and the far-end gateway supports only fax pass-through, the VG248 can negotiate fax pass-through.
- Disable call waiting on the port that is enabled for fax.

- The VG248 has a legacy mode setting for fax pass-through so that it is backward compatible with old devices. If the other end gateway is a Cisco IOS router, change the pass-through signaling parameter to IOS Mode (refer to Figure 6-21 ). Maintain the pass-through signaling as IOS Mode throughout the network on all non–IOS gateway configurations— that is,VG248, 6608, and 6624 if all the other voice gateways in your network are based on Cisco IOS.

**Figure 6-21**  *SCCP Gateway—VG248*

| Cisco VG248 (VGC10101010AA) | |
|---|---|
| Advanced settings | |
| Allow last good configuration | (enabled) |
| SRST policy | (disabled) |
| SRST provider | ( ) |
| Call preservation | (enabled: no timeout) |
| Media receive timeout | (disabled) |
| Busy out of hook ports | (disabled) |
| DTMF tone duration | (default: 100ms) |
| Echo cancelling policy | (alternate: use DSP) |
| **Passthrough signalling** | **(IOS mode)** |
| Hook flash timer | (<country default>) |
| Hook flash reject period | (none) |
| Fax relay maximum speed | (default: 14400 bps) |
| Fax relay playout delay | (default: 300) |

# Securing the IPT Infrastructure

XYZ will be taking different security measures at every layer and at every different component of the network, as shown in Figure 6-22. With the layered approach, if the security is compromised, the problem is contained at one level.

The next few sections examine the following components of the network and security measures that you can implement in the IPT network:

- Securing CallManager and application servers
- Using a firewall and access control lists (ACLs)
- Securing the IPT network from the outside world
- Securing IPT endpoints
- Securing campus network devices
- Securing voice gateways
- Establishing physical security
- Installing host-based intrusion detection

**Figure 6-22**  *Multilayered Secured IPT Infrastructure*

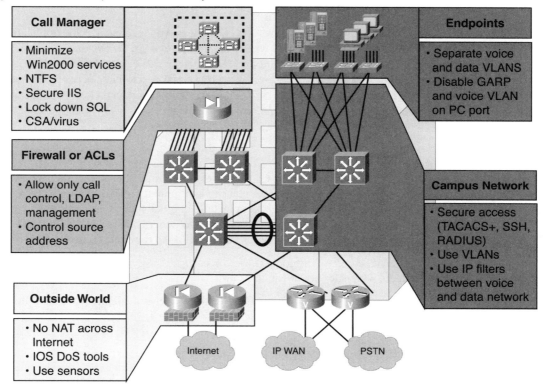

## Securing CallManager and Application Servers

You can secure the CallManager operating system by disabling the Windows services that are not used, disabling Internet Information Services (IIS) on subscribers, and so forth. Beginning with CallManager OS upgrade release 2.6, an optional security script, CCM-OS-OptionalSecurity.cmd, is provided in the C:\Utils\SecurityTemplates\ directory on the CallManager servers. When this script is executed, it runs predefined commands to perform all of these tasks automatically to secure the OS. You should read the instructions from the file CCM-OS-OptionalSecurity-Readme.htm, located in the same directory, before you run the security script.

You should also install the operating system updates on CallManager, Unity, and other application servers regularly. Refer to the "Software Upgrades" section in Chapter 9 for more information on operating system upgrade procedures and best practices.

Antivirus software is not bundled with the CallManager software. Third-party virus-scanning products such as McAfee or Norton AntiVirus are currently supported, and Cisco recommends that you install one of these antivirus products on CallManager and other application servers and schedule them to run during nonpeak hours.

You should also place the CallManager servers, IP Phones, voice gateways, and application servers on different subnets. In addition, when you are deploying a CallManager cluster, you should consider separating the members of the CallManager cluster into different VLANs and thus into different IP subnets. That way, even if a virus attack or DoS attack occurs in one subnet, affecting the functioning of servers in that subnet, the servers in the other subnet are not affected, and you will not experience a major network outage.

## Using a Firewall and ACLs

Use of a firewall and ACLs in front of the CallManager cluster and other IPT application servers adds an extra layer of security. For instance, you can configure the ACLs to allow only known traffic to reach the servers in the CallManager cluster and block the rest of the traffic from reaching the servers. Refer to the following URL on Cisco.com to obtain a list of TCP and UDP ports used by the CallManager. This list helps you to build the required ACLs.

http://www.cisco.com/en/US/products/sw/voicesw/ps556/
products_tech_note09186a00801a62b9.shtml

The list of TCP and UDP ports used by the Cisco Unity server is available from the following URL:

http://www.cisco.com/en/US/products/sw/voicesw/ps2237/
products_white_paper09186a00802077c0.shtml

When you place a firewall in front of your voice network, make sure that it supports stateful inspection of the voice-signaling protocol. Voice can run on any UDP port that ranges between 16384 and 32767, and you need to make sure the firewall opens only the ports needed to support that particular application. Make sure that the firewall you are using supports Application Layer Gateway (ALG) capabilities. ALG inspects signaling packets to discover what UDP port the RTP stream is going to use and dynamically opens a pinhole for that UDP port.

## Securing the IPT Network from the Outside World

While using private addressing (RFC 1918) for your IP Phones (recommended), do not use Network Address Translation (NAT) to translate these private addresses. When you are deploying IP Phone eXtensible Markup Language (XML) applications, you should use proxy servers to reach the Internet to provide the content rather than allow your CallManager servers to reach the Internet directly.

As an example, consider the stock quote application that gets stock quotes from the Internet. In this example, the application server is running on a separate server and you have an XML application running on an IP Phone. When you use your IP Phone to select the ticker symbol CSCO within the stock quote application to get the stock quote update, that request does not go directly to the Internet. Instead, the request goes to the application server, which gets the information for you by using a proxy server. Hence, the IP Phones do not need to reach the Internet directly.

## Securing IPT Endpoints

In the Cisco IPT solution, endpoints are Cisco IP Phones, voice gateways, media resource devices, and so forth. In addition to protecting the critical servers, you should take necessary steps to secure these endpoints. You should completely isolate the data and voice networks by using separate voice and data VLANs. Using this type of separation increases the security of your voice network.

Several security features are available to protect the IP Phones. You can configure all of these features in the CallManager Administration page for each Cisco IP Phone device, shown in Figure 6-23, by setting the following fields to **Disabled**:

- **Gratuitous ARP**— By default, Cisco IP Phones accept Gratuitous Address Resolution Protocol (GARP) packets. Some devices use GARP to announce their presence on the network. However, attackers can also use GARP to spoof a valid network device. For instance, an attacker could send out a GARP message claiming to be the default router. Setting this field to Disabled makes Cisco IP Phones ignore the GARP packets.

- **PC Voice VLAN Access**—By default, Cisco IP Phones pass all packets received on the switch port (the port connected to the upstream switch) to the PC port, including 802.1q tagged packets that are destined for the Cisco IP Phone. Setting this field to Disabled makes the Cisco IP Phone stop forwarding the packets tagged with the voice VLAN to the PC port and prevents the attached PC from sending and receiving data on the voice VLAN. You should enable this feature only if you want to capture the voice packets sent on the voice VLAN by using the capture application that is being run on the PC for troubleshooting and monitoring purposes.

- **PC Port**— You should disable the PC port on the back of the Cisco IP Phone for those IP Phones that are in the common areas, such as the lobby or break rooms.

- **Settings Access**—Disabling this field prevents users from viewing or modifying the network configuration values on the IP Phones.

**Figure 6-23** *Product-Specific Configurations for Cisco IP Phones*

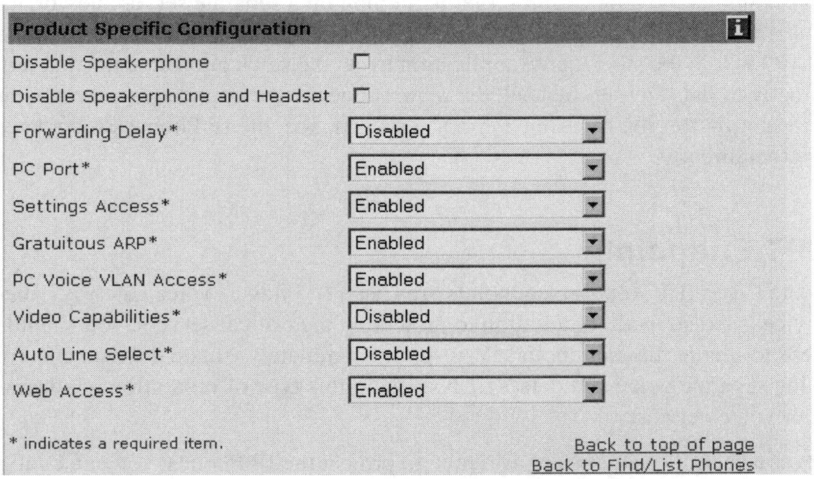

## Securing Campus Network Devices

Secure the access to campus network devices such as switches and routers by using TACACS+ and RADIUS authentication methods in your campus network. You can perform configurations for your campus network devices from the CLI via Telnet sessions, but you should use Secure Shell (SSH) to access these devices. Disable unused switch ports on the LAN switches and place them in unused VLAN so that they are not misused. Use Spanning Tree Protocol (STP) attack mitigation tools such as BPDU Guard and Root Guard. Refer to the following URL to get more information on securing the routers in your network:

http://www.cisco.com/warp/public/707/21.html

## Securing Voice Gateways

You can increase the security for voice gateways by accepting VoIP call-control messages only from CallManager servers that are members of the CallManager cluster, and block such messages from all other sources. Also, the VoIP gateways should deny H.323, MGCP, Skinny, or SIP connection attempts from the data network. If any PC can use VoIP gateways for calling, it will be hard for you to enforce a centralized dial plan. Lack of this policy can cause a possible DoS vulnerability.

## Establishing Physical Security

Physical security is sometimes taken lightly, but permission to access network equipment should be given in a controlled manner. Network equipment should be well within recommended environmental limits. All the mission-critical resources might require dispersion to provide effective redundancy. Turning off power is an effective DoS attack; give controlled and limited access to power switches.

## Installing Host-Based Intrusion Detection

In addition to deploying the firewall, you should install Cisco Security Agent (CSA) software on the CallManager, Unity, and other application servers to ensure security and integrity of the server applications.

Instead of focusing on attacks, CSA focuses on preventing malicious and undesired activities on the host. CSA detects and blocks the damaging activities, regardless of the attack. CSA ships with predefined policies that prevent most types of malicious activity from occurring. You can download the CSA standalone-installation version for CallManager, Unity, CRS, and other applications at no charge from Cisco.com.

For more in-depth information on securing IPT networks, refer to the white paper "SAFE: IP Telephony Security in Depth" (Jason Halpern, primary author):

> http://www.cisco.com/en/US/netsol/ns340/ns394/ns171/ns128/
> networking_solutions_white_paper09186a00801b7a50.shtml

Cisco posts security advisories and notices as and when vulnerabilities are detected in Cisco products. You can access this information from the following URL:

> http://www.cisco.com/en/US/products/products_security_advisories_listing.html

# Summary

This chapter provided detailed information about designing the call-processing architecture for XYZ. The detailed configurations and configuration procedures should help you to apply to real-world networks based on the example design discussed. Your requirements might be different from what was described in this chapter, but the methodology and processes described should still apply to all IPT designs.

The next chapter takes you through the Cisco Unity design steps for XYZ.

# CHAPTER 7

# Voice-Mail System Design

The previous chapter discussed the design of the call-processing architecture for XYZ, Inc. This chapter addresses the design and customization of Cisco Unity as an IP-based voice-mail system for XYZ and focuses on the following topics:

- Defining the voice-mail system architecture
- Designing the Cisco Unity system
- Installing Cisco Unity
- Integrating voice mail
- Understanding the Cisco Unity networking
- Networking Octel and Cisco Unity
- Customizing the Cisco Unity system
- Designing multiple directory handlers
- Improving the user experience during migration

Based on the information provided about XYZ in Chapter 3, "Large-Scale Enterprise Requirements for IP Telephony," XYZ uses Microsoft Exchange and has deployed Active Directory (AD) throughout the organization. Therefore, the discussion in this chapter is based on a network using AD and the Exchange message store.

You can use Appendix G, "Voice-Mail Design Questionnaire," to collect the customer requirements and design the voice-mail system accordingly.

## Defining the Voice-Mail System Architecture

Figure 7-1 shows the proposed voice-mail architecture for XYZ. The Cisco Unity system that is deployed in Unified Messaging mode replaces the Octel voice-mail system in Sydney. In the San Jose location, the Octel voice-mail system will remain. The Seattle and Dallas sites use the existing Octel voice-mail system in San Jose.

**Figure 7-1** *Voice-Mail Deployment Model of XYZ*

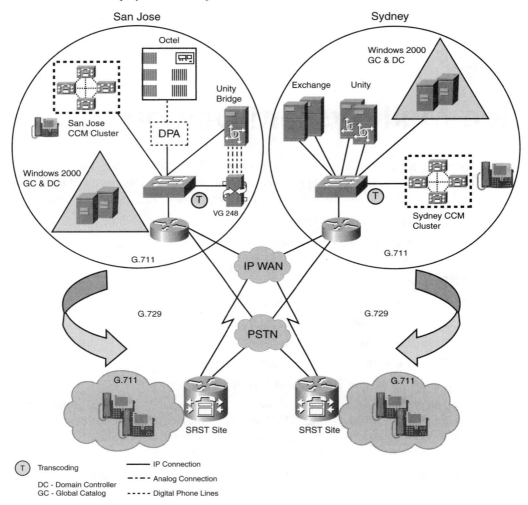

Integration between the CallManager cluster in San Jose and the Octel voice-mail system in San Jose is done by using a Cisco Digital Port Adapter (DPA - 7630). The Cisco DPA-7630 communicates with the Octel voice mail system using 24 digital phone lines. DPA-7630 uses the Skinny Client Control Protocol (SCCP) to communicate with CallManager. Because XYZ uses the voice-mail system as a networking service (meaning all employees can network messages to each other via direct addressing or by using voice-mail distribution lists) integration and interoperability between the Octel network and the Cisco Unity environment needs to be maintained. Therefore, use of the Cisco Unity Bridge is necessary in this setup. The communication between the Cisco Unity server in Sydney and the Unity Bridge in San Jose uses a Simple Mail Transfer Protocol (SMTP) connection, and the communication between the Unity Bridge and the Octel system in San Jose is via an analog connection.

The call flow for messages addressed from a Unity-user in Sydney to an Octel-user San Jose is as follows: The voice mail message addressed in the Unity system in Sydney to an Octel subscriber in San Jose, travels via the internal IP network over an SMTP connection and reaches the Unity Bridge in San Jose. The Unity Bridge will then package this voice mail message as an Analog OctelNet message and place a call, via the VG248, to the Octel system in San Jose. This call will go through the DPA (which is the interface between the CallManager and the Octel system) to reach the Octel System and complete the analog networking call.

The call flow for the opposite is similar. When a voice mail message is addressed from an Octel user in San Jose to a Unity-user in Sydney, the Octel System places a call to the Unity Bridge. The call goes from the Octel system ports that are connected to the DPA and reaches the VG248 which houses the analog extensions for the Unity Bridge. The Unity Bridge then repackages the OctelNet messages to an SMTP message and sends it over the internal network to the Unity server in Sydney.

Unity subscribers in the Sydney, Melbourne, and Brisbane sites can access voice-mail messages via their IP Phones, cell phones, or any other external phone. In addition, Unity will activate the message waiting indicator (MWI) on the phone of the related subscriber and process the Outcall notifications to a pager, cell phone, or home phone, whichever is configured by the subscriber. Subscribers can also access voice-mail messages via a web browser and can customize their mailbox settings, such as greetings, Outcall notifications, and so on.

In the Unified Messaging environment, the voice-mail message is delivered to the subscriber in their common (e-mail and voice-mail) inbox.

## Microsoft Active Directory and Exchange

Unity integrates with AD and heavily relies on the messaging infrastructure. Unity supports Microsoft Exchange 2000 or 2003 and IBM Lotus Notes as the message store. Therefore, understanding the messaging architecture is important when you are designing the Unity system.

A prerequisite for deploying Unity in a Unified Messaging mode is that the AD domain and Exchange 2000/2003 or IBM Lotus Notes environment is set up and working properly. Exchange 5.5 support is not an option with Unity versions 4.0 and above.

Unity can answer calls and take voice-mail messages just like the Octel voice-mail systems that are partially replaced in this case study. The subscriber can retrieve their messages through any of the following choices:

- By using the phone
- By using Microsoft Outlook
- By accessing the Cisco Unity Inbox via the web interface

| NOTE | Because XYZ uses Microsoft Exchange as a message store, use of IBM Lotus Notes is not applicable for this case study. |

Unity requires extensions to the AD schema. Unity uses AD to service subscribers whose mailboxes reside on Exchange 2000. Unity does this by extending the schema with the addition of the Unity attributes for the following objects:

- User
- Group
- Contact
- Unity Location (newly created object)

Unity Location is a special object that allows Unity servers to identify themselves to other Unity servers in the enterprise. It is used only by Unity servers.

To view the list of attributes added for each object, their values, and the impact on the size of the AD database, use the following URL:

> http://www.cisco.com/en/US/partner/products/sw/voicesw/ps2237/
> prod_technical_reference09186a00800e4535.html

To see the changes made to the AD schema, browse to the directory Schema\LdifScripts on Cisco Unity CD 1, and view the file Avdirmonex2k.ldf. If the extension of the AD schema is not acceptable, deploy a new AD and Exchange environment and deploy Unity as a voice-mail-only solution. After the IT team or the enterprise messaging/directory team is comfortable in extending the schema, it is possible to migrate to Unified Messaging and use the corporate messaging infrastructure.

## Active Directory Architecture

A key requirement before you design a Unity system and deploy it into a network is to understand the existing AD and messaging architecture (Microsoft Exchange/Lotus Domino). Figure 7-2 shows the AD architecture for XYZ. You can see that XYZ has a single AD forest for the entire organization. From the AD point of view, there are two sites—San Jose and Sydney—each of which has a domain controller (DC) and a Global Catalog (GC) server, as shown previously in Figure 7-1.

**Figure 7-2**  *Active Directory Architecture of XYZ*

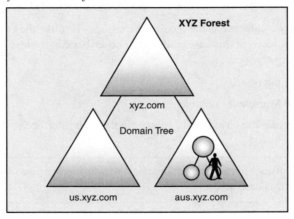

## Exchange 2000 Messaging Architecture

As Figure 7-3 shows, the Exchange 2000 messaging architecture for the XYZ San Jose and Sydney sites has Exchange 2000 servers. The San Jose site has three Exchange servers, and the Sydney site has two Exchange servers.

**Figure 7-3**    *Exchange 2000 Messaging Architecture of XYZ*

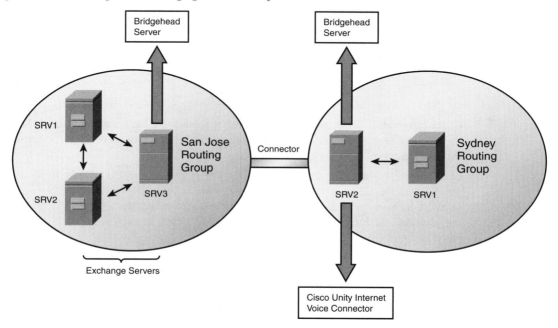

XYZ defined routing groups on a per-site basis, one for San Jose and one for Sydney. Groups of servers running Exchange 2000 form routing groups. Typically, permanent high-speed links connect the servers within the same routing group. A routing group connector connects two different routing groups. Microsoft Exchange uses routing group connectors and Bridgehead servers to route the messages between different routing groups. Bridgehead servers run Exchange 2000 and host routing group connectors.

In the XYZ environment, a message from a user in San Jose to a user in Sydney travels via the routing group connector. Messages between the servers within the same routing group are sent directly from the source server to the destination server using SMTP.

# Unity Deployment Model

After you understand the AD and messaging architecture deployed at XYZ, the next step is to choose the Unity deployment model. Three types of deployment models are available when deploying Unity:

- **Centralized**—Unity servers are collocated with the message store servers and the phone system.

- **Distributed**—Unity servers are not collocated with the message store servers and the phone system.

- **Hybrid**—This is a mix of the centralized and distributed models. Unity servers can be deployed at a central location and at remote sites that have numerous users.

When choosing the deployment model consider the following factors:

- **Unity integration with the phone system**—If the integration is analog, such as SMDI, cable length requirements might force you to have Cisco Unity servers collocated with the phone system.

- **Location of the message store**—If the message store is centralized, place the Unity servers with the message store servers at the same location. To deploy Unity servers in a different location from the message store servers, ensure that there is a LAN connection that connects the locations and that is highly reliable, has less round-trip delay time, and has high bandwidth to avoid synchronization issues.

For XYZ, because the message store servers and CallManager system are in Sydney, deploying Unity servers in Sydney is ideal. A centralized Unity deployment model suits this location because the remote sites in Melbourne and Brisbane have fewer users and do not have significant bandwidth implications. The users at Sydney, Melbourne, and Brisbane access the Unity system in Sydney for their voice mails.

# Physical Placement of Unity Servers

The best practice is to deploy the Unity and Exchange servers on the same subnet in a LAN environment, for the following reasons:

- Unity uses Mail Application Programming Interface (MAPI) to communicate with Exchange.

- MAPI uses remote-procedure call (RPC) as a transport protocol.

- RPC is a chatty protocol, so it can introduce delays over slow-speed links and cause problems while passing through firewalls.

XYZ has an already operational Exchange 2000 environment in its regional hub of Sydney. Therefore, the Sydney data center is the ideal place to deploy the Unity server.

# High Availability

Many organizations rely on networked voice mail as an essential business tool to enable a caller to leave a message if the employee whom they are calling is unavailable to pick up the phone or to send messages directly to another employee's mailbox. Therefore, the high availability of the voice-mail system is critical.

Clustering is not currently available on the Unity servers. To achieve high availability, deploy Unity servers in active/standby pair, whereby one server is sitting idle until the active one fails.

For XYZ to achieve high availability, it will deploy two Unity servers in Sydney.

# Securing Unity Servers

As discussed in Chapter 6, "Design of Call-Processing Infrastructure and Applications," XYZ has good practices in place for securing the CallManager servers. To protect the Unity servers similarly, XYZ plans to do the following:

- Install the virus-scanning software and the Cisco Secure Agent (CSA) for intrusion detection on the Unity and Unity Bridge servers.

- Apply all Cisco-recommended settings, security patches and operating system service packs to the servers from the moment they become available.

- Implement the physical security for the computer room in Sydney where Unity servers are placed.

# Backup of Unity Servers

The procedure to back up the AD forest and the Exchange 2000 environment is already in place in the XYZ network. Add the Unity servers to the list of servers and perform the regular backups. Unlike CallManager software, which bundles the backup utility, Unity does not include a backup utility. Cisco recommends using VERITAS NetBackup software (http://www.veritas.com/).

After every major configuration change to a Unity system, use Disaster Recovery Tool (DiRT), part of the Cisco Unity tools depot, to backup the Unity server database and store the backup data on central file server in Sydney.

# Voice-Mail Access Options

The users of XYZ in Australia will be able to access their voice mail via the following methods (see Figure 7-4):

- Telephone User Interface (TUI)
    - IP Phone or PBX extension
    - User's cell (mobile) phone

- Graphical user interface (GUI)
  - Cisco Unity Inbox (a web interface that is part of Cisco Personal Communications Assistant [PCA])
  - Microsoft Outlook e-mail application
  - Outlook Web Access (OWA)

**Figure 7-4**  *Voice-Mail Access Options*

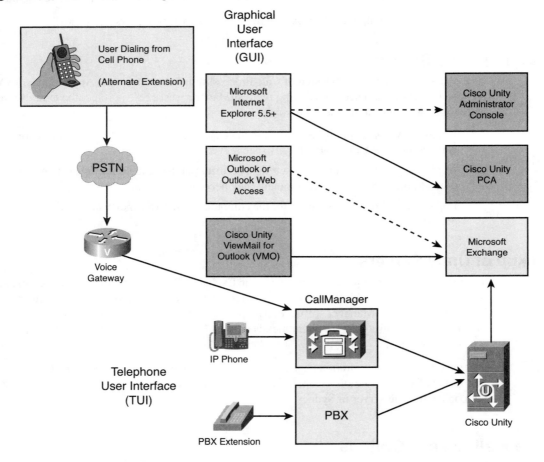

## Telephone User Interface

Accessing voice mail using the TUI is the same as accessing voice mail on the Octel system.

## Accessing Voice Mail from IP Phone or PBX Extension

By dialing into the Unity server, users can access their voice-mail messages via the IP Phone or via a PBX extension, if Cisco Unity integrates with the PBX. Via this method, users can listen to their voice-mail messages, to the headers of e-mail messages, and to the body of e-mail messages. This method embodies the definition of Unified Messaging.

The default order in which Unity plays the messages to the user is as follows: urgent voice mails, normal-priority voice mails, urgent e-mails, and normal-priority e-mails. This order of access can be changed by the Australian employees of XYZ in Cisco PCA. When a user dials in from their car in the morning, they might want to hear urgent e-mails, before urgent voice mails. This characteristic depends on how the mails are handled in the XYZ environment and what privileges are given to users, based on their role and position in the company.

Listening to e-mails when calling the voice mailbox over the TUI requires the license for text-to-speech (TTS) sessions on the Unity servers.

## Accessing Voice Mail from a User's Mobile Phone

All users from XYZ will also have their mobile phone numbers configured in Unity as an alternate extension (as discussed later, in the "Customizing the Cisco Unity System" section). As a result, it will be easy for them to call their inbox when they are not at their desk phone in the office. The system will recognize the calling line ID (CLID) from the mobile phone and immediately prompt the user for their personal identification number (PIN) rather than his mailbox number.

# Graphical User Interface

Cisco Unity also provides a GUI so that you can access voice-mail messages from your desktop/PC by using Cisco Personal Communications Assistant.

## Cisco Unity Inbox

The Australian users will also be able to access their messages via the Cisco Unity Inbox, a web application that is part of Cisco PCA. The Cisco Unity Inbox allows users to browse to a web page and retrieve their messages, greetings, and so on. Users can also use this web page to change their alternate greetings.

Cisco PCA enables Unity subscribers to access the following two applications in Unity:

- Cisco Unity Assistant (also called Active Assistant [AA]), which lets subscribers do the following:
  - Customize how they and callers to their mailbox interact with Unity by phone
  - Personalize Unity settings, including their recorded greetings and message-delivery options
  - Set up message-notification devices and create private lists

- Cisco Unity Inbox (formerly known as Visual Messaging Interface [VMI]), which allows subscribers to listen to, compose, reply to, forward, and delete voice-mail messages. Cisco Unity Inbox is a licensed feature.

To access Cisco PCA, subscribers use the following URL from the Internet Explorer web browser:

http://*IP_Addr_Unity*/ciscopca

Figure 7-5 shows the Cisco PCA application.

**Figure 7-5** *Cisco PCA Interface to Access Unity Inbox and Unity Assistant*

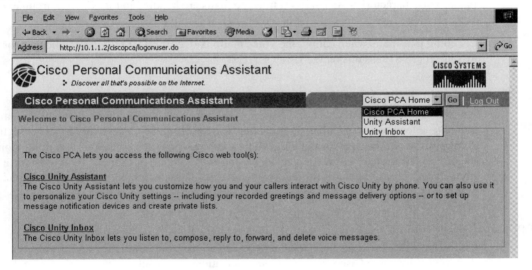

## Microsoft Outlook E-Mail Application

It is also possible to use Microsoft Outlook to read e-mails, receive voice mails as a WAV attachment, and retrieve voice mails by using View Mail for Outlook (VMO). VMO is a plug-in application, added to the user's PC, that enables the user to retrieve voice mails from their laptop or desktop.

With this VMO component added to Outlook, it is possible to receive a voice mail from a peer and reply as a voice mail to the originating party. Without VMO, this reply is always sent as a WAV file attachment in an e-mail. Also, the originating party who receives the reply will not be able to handle this message as a voice mail (in Unity) without VMO.

The advantages of VMO are seen only when both the sender and receiver of the voice mail use Unity system. For XYZ, because in US location, users have Octel system and Australian users have Unity system, whenever a user from Australia sends a voice mail to a user in San Jose using VMO, San Jose user will always receive the voice mail as an e-mail with a WAV attachment.

### Outlook Web Access

Another method of accessing the voice messages is through OWA. To access the messages, type the following URL from your Internet Explorer:

http://*IP_Addr_of_Exchange_Server*/exchange

When you use OWA, voice mails are shown as e-mails, with the actual voice message as a WAV attachment.

# Designing a Cisco Unity System

As discussed in the preceding sections, XYZ uses Exchange 2000 as the e-mail system for all the users in Australia. The AD forest (domain controller/Global Catalog) is fully deployed and operational in Australia. A stable working AD domain and Exchange 2000 network is the key to the success of this Unified Messaging rollout.

For the purpose of this case study, the Unity system replaces the Octel voice-mail system in Sydney. In the San Jose location, the Octel voice-mail system will stay in place and integrate with the CallManager cluster in San Jose.

Because XYZ already has a stable infrastructure, the Unity design and deployment for XYZ does the following:

* Uses the existing Windows 2000 domain infrastructure to house the Unity servers
* Uses the existing Exchange 2000 messaging infrastructure to service as a back-end message store
* Requires installation of Unity on a separate server and not on any of the existing AD/ Exchange infrastructure

The hosting team within XYZ feels comfortable extending the scope of Exchange 2000 to accomplish a Unified Messaging setup. In addition, the additional MAPI connections to the server are not expected to cause issues. MAPI functions as the primary means by which Exchange and Outlook communicate with one another.

To XYZ, whether San Jose users are also using Exchange 2000 or are still using another e-mail infrastructure with plans to move to Exchange in the future before implementing Cisco Unity is unimportant, because San Jose users will continue to use their current Octel voice-mail system. The e-mail system that is used in San Jose is important only after San Jose users start to move to Unity/Unified Messaging. For now, the voice-mail environment is not affected if San Jose users are on Exchange 2000.

## Message Store Options and Sizing

The Unity server can store the messages either in G.711 or G729a format. Selecting the codec format depends on the availability of hardware resources such as hard disk sizes and hardware transcoder devices if the IPT network that is deployed uses multiple codecs. Based on XYZ's requirements, G.711 is the choice of codec to store messages on the Unity server.

Before you size the hard disk, you need to study the use of the existing voice-mail system. Investigating the system statistics from the Octel messaging system in Sydney reveals that it is sufficient to provision the Sydney user mailboxes to store 1 hour's worth of voice messages. According to Table 7-1, G.711 uses 8 KB of hard disk space to record a 1-second voice message. To store voice messages of up to 1 hour (3600 seconds), you need approximately 3600 × 8 KB, which is 28.8 MB for each Exchange mailbox.

**Table 7-1**  *Unity Hard Disk Sizing Guide*

| Users | Messages | Codec Type and Sampling Rate | Average Message Size in Seconds | Storage Size for G.711 in Bytes |
|---|---|---|---|---|
| 1 | 15 | G.711 @ 8 Kbps | 40 | 4,800,000 |
| 10 | 15 | | 40 | 48,000,000 |
| 100 | 15 | | 40 | 480,000,000 |
| 500 | 15 | | 40 | 2,400,000,000 |
| 1000 | 15 | | 40 | 4,800,000,000 |
| 1500 | 15 | | 40 | 7,200,000,000 |
| 2000 | 15 | | 40 | 9,600,000,000 |
| 5000 | 15 | | 40 | 24,000,000,000 |
| 7500 | 15 | | 40 | 36,000,000,000 |
| 10,000 | 15 | | 40 | 48,000,000,000 |
| Users | Messages | Codec Type and Sampling Rate | Average Message Size in Seconds | Storage Size for G.729a in Bytes |
| 1 | 15 | G.729a @ 8 Kbps | 40 | 600,000 |
| 10 | 15 | | 40 | 6,000,000 |
| 100 | 15 | | 40 | 60,000,000 |
| 500 | 15 | | 40 | 300,000,000 |

**Table 7-1** *Unity Hard Disk Sizing Guide (Continued)*

| Users | Messages | Codec Type and Sampling Rate | Average Message Size in Seconds | Storage Size for G.729a in Bytes |
|---|---|---|---|---|
| 1000 | 15 | | 40 | 600,000,000 |
| 1500 | 15 | | 40 | 900,000,000 |
| 2500 | 15 | | 40 | 1,500,000,000 |
| 5000 | 15 | | 40 | 3,000,000,000 |
| 7500 | 15 | | 40 | 4,500,000,000 |
| 10,000 | 15 | | 40 | 6,000,000,000 |

**NOTE**     If you cannot obtain the statistics from the existing voice-mail system or no voice-mail system existed before, use Table 7-1 to calculate the hard disk size required.

XYZ corporate policy is to retain the deleted voice messages for up to 7 days. To account for this, the storage requirements per user mailbox are expanded to 56 MB.

Taking into account the 550 employees that use the Unity system in Sydney, Melbourne, and Brisbane, the additional requirement for voice-mail storage increases to a minimum of approximately 56 MB × 550 = 30 GB. From the current standards regarding disk space, this is not an issue for XYZ, because it has performed decent sizing of its Exchange 2000 environment from the beginning.

To accommodate the additional storage requirements to store the voice messages, the Exchange system administrator of XYZ will expand the storage limits on an individual mailbox basis to reflect these previously mentioned requirements.

Using the class of service (CoS) feature in Unity, a user or group of users can get additional hours of storage to retain their voice mails. You can define a separate CoS with more hours and assign this CoS to the users who need extra storage.

## Sizing Unity Ports and Sessions

The number of Unity ports in a system determines the number of simultaneous callers who can call into the Unity system. Because ports or sessions are licensed components in Unity, XYZ has to pay a license for each. Therefore, proper sizing of the Unity ports/session is important to avoid paying for unneeded ports/sessions.

There are two different approaches to doing port sizing. The first approach, adopted by XYZ, is to use a port-to-user ratio of 1:20 to determine the number of ports or sessions required on the Octel voice-mail system. Using the same approach, for 550 users (including the users at Melbourne and Brisbane), 28 ports are needed on the Unity server. In Unity, you also need a few ports exclusively reserved for lighting the MWI on the handsets of IP Phones and a few ports exclusively reserved for Outcall notification purposes. Therefore, after reserving two ports each for these purposes, XYZ requires a Unity system with 32 port/sessions.

In the second approach to port sizing the Unity system, the number of ports required depends on the following parameters:

- Average calls per hour to the voice-mail system
- Average length in seconds

If you have an existing voice-mail system, these parameters are available in the system reports. After you have these parameters, to calculate the number of ports required, use the following formula:

Number of ports or sessions = Average calls per hour ÷ average length in hours

As an example, assume that a customer has on average 200 calls per hour into the system with an average length of 4 minutes (240 seconds) for voice-mail messages. Based on this information, this customer requires a Unity system with 13 ports. Taking into consideration the additional ports that must be reserved for MWI and Outcall notifications and future expansion possibilities, the customer could deploy one primary Unity server with 20 ports and one standby Unity server with 20 ports for failover situations.

# Unity Server Hardware

Various Cisco-certified hardware platforms are available to run the Unity software. Selection of the hardware depends on the following factors:

- Number of ports or sessions
- Number of users
- Number of TTS sessions
- Message store location
    - An external message store requires less hard drive capacity on the Unity server.
    - A message store on the Unity server requires more hard drive capacity.
- Number of slots required on the Unity system
- Data protection requirements

Refer to the following URL to obtain the complete Cisco Unity Supported Platforms List:

http://www.cisco.com/en/US/products/sw/voicesw/ps2237/
products_data_sheets_list.html

XYZ is opting for the higher-end servers because they offer more redundancy. The MCS-7845I has a dual power supply, and each of the power supplies is on isolated, redundant circuits that can handle a minimum of 350W.

Because the Sydney office is a regional hub site, it has good backup processes in place and usually stores the backups on a network backup server. That is why the servers do not need a DAT tape drive to perform backups.

## Data Protection

System administrators commonly implement redundant array of inexpensive disks (RAID) to provide a reliable, redundant means of protecting critical data on a server. RAID is a method whereby information is spread across several disks, using techniques such as disk striping (RAID level 0) and disk mirroring (RAID level 1) to achieve redundancy, lower latency, and higher bandwidth for reading and writing and recoverability from hard-disk crashes. Six different types of RAID configurations are "available", RAID 1 is the most inexpensive method to protect the data.

At XYZ, Unity servers will use a RAID 1 array to protect the data, because voice-mail messages are essential to users and often contain sensitive and important information.

## Exchange Software Licensing

The prerequisite for the Unified Messaging rollout in this case study is a fully established and working AD forest and Exchange 2000 organization. For Unified Messaging deployment using Unity, Cisco does not ship licenses to use Microsoft Exchange server software or Client Access Licenses (CALs) for accessing the Microsoft Exchange server.

Count the Microsoft Exchange 2000 server software and CAL against the corporate software licensing agreement that XYZ has with Microsoft. XYZ's corporate messaging team should verify this with the vendor management office to ensure full licensing.

If numerous Unity servers and bridges are connected to the network, a specific naming convention has to be put in place that clearly identifies the function and location of the server. This is just a naming convention and should be used only to make future troubleshooting tasks easier.

## Unity Software Licensing

With the design steps covered so far, enough information is available to decide on the required number of Unity licenses. Each Unity server will have its license configured as follows. XYZ must submit a license request to Cisco Systems with the MAC address of each server in the node.

- Unity version 4.0.3
- 600 Unified Messaging for Exchange user licenses

- 32 ports per server
- 600 VMI or Unity Inbox user licenses
- 16 RealSpeak TTS sessions
- 16 additional language licenses if not all subscribers on the Sydney Unity will use the same language
- Unity Bridge 4 port license
- Failover enabled (Product ID: UNITY-FOVRSVR33-UP)

---

**NOTE**    You obtain these license files directly from Cisco Systems. Go to the Cisco Unity Licensing FAQ site to learn how to obtain the licenses for the Unity system:

   http://www.cisco.com/en/US/products/sw/voicesw/ps2237/
   products_qanda_item09186a0080094ce5.shtml

Refer to the following URL to get more information on how licensing works in Unity:

   http://www.cisco.com/en/US/products/sw/voicesw/ps2237/
   products_white_paper09186a008019c743.shtml

The Cisco Unity license ties to the MAC address for the network interface card (NIC) in the Cisco Unity server that Cisco Unity will be run on. To find the MAC address on the Unity server after installing the operating system but before installing Cisco Unity, follow these steps:

1. On the server where Cisco Unity will be installed, on the Windows Start menu, click **Programs > Accessories > Command Prompt**.

2. In the Command Prompt window, enter **ipconfig/all** and press Enter.

3. Select the value for Physical Address and press Enter (This copies it to the Windows clipboard.) For multiple MAC addresses, select the first one only.

4. Paste the value of the MAC address and remove the hyphens (for example, 00-A1-B2-C3-D4-E5 should be entered as 00A1B2C3D4E5) when submitting for a license to Cisco.

5. If you are deploying Unity with dual NICs, use the virtual MAC address when obtaining the license file.

6. If you replace the NIC on the servers, you have to resubmit the request to obtain the new license files.

---

## Extending the Schema for Unity and Unity Bridge

As discussed in the "Microsoft Active Directory and Exchange" section earlier in this chapter, extending the AD schema is an important and mandatory task prior to installing Unity or the Unity Bridge. The extension of the AD schema allows a proper installation and integration of the Unity and Bridge systems.

Active Directory supports the use of LDAP Data Interchange Format (LDIF) scripts to extend the schema. Therefore, you need to run on the AD DC the executable called ADSchemaSetup.exe, located on the Unity installation DVD/CD-ROM, and the LDIF script files. Although there are two DCs, one in San Jose and one in Sydney, there is only one common schema. When you run the ADSchemaSetup.exe program, shown in Figure 7-6, the schema is extended and Unity-specific attributes are added into the AD. When you run ADSchemaSetup.exe, check the **Exchange 2000 or Exchange 2003 Directory Monitor** and **Exchange 2000 or Exchange 2003 Bridge Connector** check boxes to extend the schema required by Unity and the Unity Bridge.

**Figure 7-6**  *Active Directory Schema Setup Window*

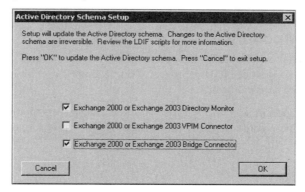

Follow the guidelines exactly as addressed in the *Cisco Unity Installation Guide* (discussed next) and *Cisco Unity Bridge Installation Guide*, both of which are available on Cisco.com. A domain administrator who has access rights to the Active Directory (for example, as a member of the AD Schema Admin group) must perform the schema extension operation.

# Installing Cisco Unity

The steps to install Cisco Unity are listed in the *Cisco Unity Installation Guide* on Cisco.com:

http://www.cisco.com/univercd/cc/td/doc/product/voice/c_unity/unity40/inst/inst403/ex/index.htm

You should ensure that you fulfill the physical requirements of the Unity server before you install Unity. The IT team of XYZ has verified the following with the employees who are responsible for the computer room and buildings in Sydney:

- Enough free rack space is available.
- Data connections are available.
- The UPS can handle the additional load.

On one of the Exchange 2000 servers in Sydney, the Cisco Unity Internet Voice Connector (IVC) has to be installed. It is up to the Exchange 2000 administrator to determine which server can best handle this functionality. In the case of XYZ, this is the exchange@XYZ.com server, which handles all user accounts for Australia.

As mentioned earlier, the Unity server will handle only messages that are using the G.711 codec. If XYZ discovers after installation that the G.729a codec is required over the WAN for capacity reasons, XYZ will rely on hardware transcoding in DSP farms to perform these conversions. You have to take into account that too much iteration between the G.711 and G.729a codecs can eventually degrade the voice quality. As a rule of thumb, try to limit the number of conversions of a single message to two.

## Unity Installation Account

The staff who is responsible for the operation and maintenance of the Unity server will use the administrator account of the Unity server. This account is used to install the server and allows all maintenance activities on the server.

The first-line support staff will get base access on the servers to administer subscribers. The administrator passwords are distributed only to senior Unity support staff.

## End-User Interaction

End users can interact with the Unity system by using their phone, Outlook client, or Cisco PCA. When using Cisco PCA, the user credentials are sent in clear text across the network when Secure Sockets Layer (SSL) protocol is not enabled on Unity. In case of XYZ, as an added security measure, Unity will be set up to support the SSL protocol to avoid the security risk.

For security reasons, the administrator of the Unity server will not use the same account and password to log in to Cisco PCA as he uses to log in to the administration web pages.

The official business language within XYZ is English. Two language packages will be installed. U.S. English (Windows locale is required) and Australian English. The Australian subscribers will be configured for the Australian English option.

The TTS language will be based on the user's location. Because all the Unity users in this case study are based in Australia, only one option will be selected for now.

# Integrating Voice Mail

XYZ requires voice-mail integration at two locations:

- The CallManager in Sydney
- The Octel system with CallManager in San Jose

# Unity Integration with CallManager

Unity integrates seamlessly with CallManager by using SCCP. The next few sections discuss the configurations required to complete the Unity integration with CallManager.

- Configuring partitions and CSS in CallManager
- Changing service parameters in CallManager
- Defining MWI on and off numbers in CallManager
- Defining voice-mail ports in CallManager
- Defining the voice-mail pilot number in CallManager
- Defining the voice-mail profile in CallManager
- Reserving ports for MWIs and outcall notifications in Unity
- Making changes to the Octel access numbers
- Configuring the AutoAttendant functionality in Unity

## Configuring Partitions and CSS in CallManager

This section discusses the design of partitions and the calling search space (CSS) for voice-mail ports, MWI On/Off numbers, and voice-mail pilot numbers. Because voice-mail ports appear to CallManager as any other IP phone, the concept of partitions and CSS also applies to these ports. Unity uses voice-mail ports for two purposes:

- To turn on and off MWI lamps on the phones
- To send call notifications

Tables 7-2 and 7-3 list the partitions and CSS configurations, respectively, required on IP Phones, MWI On/Off numbers, and voice-mail ports in the Sydney CallManager cluster.

**Table 7-2**  *List of Partitions*

| Partition Name | Description |
|---|---|
| Pt_allphones | All IP Phones' DN[1]s are included in this partition |
| Pt_mwi | MWI On/Off number partition |
| Pt_vmpilot | Voice-mail pilot number partition (first voice-mail port) |
| Pt_vmpilot1 | Partition that includes all other voice-mail ports |
| Pt_local | Partition that contains route patterns that provide local access |

[1] Directory Number

**Table 7-3**  *List of Calling Search Spaces*

| CSS Name | List of Partitions | Description |
|---|---|---|
| Css_local | Pt_allphones<br><br>Pt_mwi<br><br>Pt_vmPilot<br><br>Pt_local | IP Phones that have access to local calling |
| Css_mwi | Pt_allphones | CSS on MWI On/Off numbers |
| Css_vmports | Pt_mwi<br><br>Pt_allphones<br><br>Pt_local | CSS on the voice-mail ports |
| Css_CFBCFNAvmports | Pt_vmpilot1 | CSS for the Call Forward Busy (CFB) and Call Forward No Answer (CFNA) on the voice-mail ports |

## Changing Service Parameters in CallManager

By default, CallManager hops to a maximum of 12 voice-mail ports. Because the Unity system at XYZ has 32 ports, the following two service parameters for CallManager service have to be set on the Sydney CallManager cluster accordingly. To access the service parameters, from the CallManager Administration page, choose **Service > Service Parameters > CallManager Service**.

- Set the Voice Mail Maximum Hop Count to **28** (because XYZ has a maximum of 32 ports, the last 4 of which are assigned to MWI and Outcall notifications).

- Set the Advanced CallForward Hop Flag to **True** (to immediately jump to the first available port).

Both parameters are cluster-wide parameters.

## Defining MWI On and Off Numbers in CallManager

An MWI lamp lighted on the IP Phone indicates to the user that new voice-mail messages are waiting in the mailbox. Before you define the MWI On/Off numbers, it is helpful to understand how Unity and CallManager turn on/off MWI lamps on the phones. To turn on the MWI for extension 6200, for example, Unity goes off hook on one of its ports and dials the MWI On number. However, Unity sets the calling party extension as 6200. CallManager looks at the calling party number and lights the lamp for extension 6200. Similarly, to turn MWI off, Unity dials the MWI Off number.

Hence, you need one MWI On and one MWI Off number per CallManager cluster. To define these numbers in the CallManager from the CallManager Administration page, choose **Feature > Voice Mail > Message Waiting**. On this page, you have an option to configure a partition and

CSS for MWI On and Off numbers. Table 7-4 shows the configuration settings for the MWI On/Off numbers in the Sydney CallManager cluster.

**Table 7-4**  *MWI On/Off Settings*

| MWI Number | MWI Type | Partition | Calling Search Space |
|---|---|---|---|
| 5600 | ON | Pt_mwi | Css_mwi |
| 5601 | Off | Pt_mwi | Css_mwi |

The CSS on the MWI On/Off numbers helps CallManager to determine which phones' MWI to turn on and off. Assume that two phones with the same directory number 6200 exist, one in Partition_X and the other in Partition_Y. If the CSS for the MWI On/Off numbers contains Partition_X alone, it can turn on and off the MWI for the phone with extension 6200, which is in Partition_X. The opposite is true if the CSS includes only Partition_Y. If the CSS contains both partitions, the partition order that is defined in the CSS comes into effect, because there is a tie in the pattern, which in this case is 6200. Hence, the rule is that the CSS on the MWI On/Off numbers should include the partitions in which IP Phone directory numbers reside.

As mentioned earlier, Unity goes off hook on one of the voice-mail ports and dials the MWI On/Off number to turn on or off the MWI lamp. This means the following:

- The CSS that is configured on the voice-mail ports should include the partition in which MWI On/Off numbers reside. Without this, Unity cannot set the MWI On/Off for the phones.

- The CSS that is configured on the IP Phones should also include the partition in which MWI On/Off numbers reside.

## Defining Voice-Mail Ports in CallManager

To configure the voice-mail ports in CallManager, you can use the Voice Mail Port Wizard that is available specifically for Unity. To access this wizard from the CallManager Administration page, choose **Feature > Voice Mail > Cisco Voice Mail Port Wizard**.

As stated in the "Sizing Unity Ports and Sessions" section earlier in this chapter, the Unity system at XYZ requires 32 ports. Hence, the number of ports that has to be configured on the CallManager is 64: 32 for the primary Unity server and 32 for the failover Unity server. Each set of ports matches to a voice-mail pilot number. The primary Unity server uses the same voice-mail pilot number as used in the past for the Octel system in Sydney, which is 5000.

Table 7-5 shows the voice-mail port settings required in the Sydney CallManager cluster. The table shows samples that you can follow for all 32 ports.

**Table 7-5** *Voice-Mail Port Settings*

| Voice-Mail Port in CallManager | Partition | Device Pool | Calling Search Space | Directory Number | CFB | CFNA |
|---|---|---|---|---|---|---|
| PriUM-VI1 | Pt_vmpilot | DP-SYDNEY | Css_vmports | 5000 | 5001 | 5032 |
| PriUM-VI2 | Pt_vmpilot1 | DP-SYDNEY | Css_vmports | 5001 | 5002 | 5032 |
| PriUM-VI28 | Pt_vmpilot1 | DP-SYDNEY | Css_vmports | 5027 | 5000 | 5032 |
| PriUM-VI31 | Pt_vmpilot1 | DP-SYDNEY | Css_vmports | 5030 | 5000 | 5000 |
| PriUM-VI32 | Pt_vmpilot1 | DP-SYDNEY | Css_vmports | 5031 | 5000 | 5000 |
| SecUM-VI1 | Pt_vmpilot1 | DP-SYDNEY | Css_vmports | 5032 | 5033 | 6002 |
| SecUM-VI28 | Pt_vmpilot1 | DP-SYDNEY | Css_vmports | 5058 | 6002 | 6002 |
| SecUM-VI31 | Pt_vmpilot1 | DP-SYDNEY | Css_vmports | 5062 | 5032 | 5032 |
| SecUM-VI32 | Pt_vmpilot1 | DP-SYDNEY | Css_vmports | 5063 | 5032 | 5032 |

Note the following from Table 7-5:

- The CFNA setting for all the voice-mail ports on the first Unity server is configured with the directory number of the first voice-mail port on the secondary Unity server (5032). A CFNA situation arises only if the Unity server is not responding, which indicates a failure in the system and that the call should be forwarded to the secondary Unity server.

- The directory number for the first voice-mail port is 5000. In Sydney, the DID number to access the voice mail from the public switched telephone network (PSTN) is 555-6000. A CTI route point/CTI port will be created and Call Forward All (CFA) will be set to forward to DN 5000. The Unity call-routing rules will be modified as discussed in the "Multiple Directory Handlers" section later in this chapter to play the opening greeting for the Sydney office.

- The voice-mail pilot number on the primary server is in a different partition compared to the other voice-mail ports. The partition pt_vmpilot1 is not visible to any other device, which means that users cannot dial these ports directly from their phones. This gives the impression of a single voice-mail number to the whole system. The partition pt_vmpilot1 will only be part of the CSS that is configured on the CFB and CFNA on the voice-mail ports.

- The CFB and CFNA on the last two voice-mail ports on the secondary server are set to forward to the operator (60002). In Table 7-5, Unity Ports 1 to 28 (thatr is. ports PriUM-VI1 through PriUM-VI28 on the primary server and ports SecUM-VI1 through SecUM-VI28 on the secondary server) are used for accessing the voice mail. The last four ports on each server are used for the MWI notifications.

When defining the Unity voice-mail ports in CallManager, you have an option to configure the CSS at the device level and at the voice-mail port directory-number level. At the directory-number level, you can configure the partition in which the directory number resides.

You must set the access restrictions on the voice-mail ports by assigning a restricted CSS in CallManager for voice-mail ports, to avoid the expensive telephone charges. The best practice in configuring the voice-mail ports is to limit the CSS of these ports to allow national calls but to block international dialing. This also avoids toll fraud via the voice-mail system that can occur due to message notifications (user configurable) being sent to international numbers.

It is better to keep the restrictions centralized on the CallManager. That way, you need to make sure only that they are really applied on the CallManager ports; otherwise, you are going to open a door for toll fraud. On the other hand, it is not a good design to build part of the restrictions into the Unity configuration and another part into the CallManager dial plan. To summarize, the following are the rules for the CSS and partitions for the voice-mail ports:

- The CSS for the Unity voice-mail ports should contain the partition in which the MWI On/Off numbers reside.

- If you would like Unity to notify external phone numbers, the partition to reach the external numbers should also be part of this CSS.

- To enable users to call the voice mail directly to log in to their mailbox or press the * key to call another extension, the CSS on the line or the device should include the voice-mail ports.

## Defining the Voice-Mail Pilot Number

The voice-mail pilot number is what the phone dials when the user presses the Messages button on the Cisco IP Phone or forwards the call to voice mail. CallManager uses the CSS that is defined for the voice-mail pilot numbers when the phone is forwarded to voice mail. If the CSS on the voice-mail pilot number is set to None and the voice-mail port directory numbers are configured to be in a partition, the forward operation will fail even if the line can call the voice-mail directory numbers.

To configure the voice-mail pilot from CallManager Administration, choose **Feature > Voice Mail > Voice Mail Pilot**. Table 7-6 shows the configuration settings for the voice-mail pilot number in the Sydney CallManager cluster.

**Table 7-6**    *Voice-Mail Pilot Number Settings*

| Pilot Number | Description | CSS | Make This Default |
|---|---|---|---|
| 5000 | Pilot for Sydney | Css_local | Yes |

## Defining the Voice-Mail Profile

The last step is to configure a voice-mail profile. To access the configuration page, from CallManager Administration, choose **Feature > Voice Mail > Voice Mail Profile**. The voice-mail profile is the link between the phone configuration and the voice-mail pilot. Each voice-mail pilot is assigned to a voice-mail profile. The voice-mail profile is in turn assigned to each line or directory number on the phone. Table 7-7 shows the configuration settings for the voice-mail profile in the Sydney CallManager cluster.

**Table 7-7**    *Voice-Mail Profile Settings*

| Voice-Mail Profile Name | Description | Voice-Mail Pilot | Voice-Mail Box Mask | Make This Default VM Profile |
|---|---|---|---|---|
| VM Profile1 | Voice Mail Profile1 | 5000/Css_local | None | Yes |

## Reserving Ports for MWIs and Outcall Notifications in Unity

Some ports on the Unity system must be configured exclusively for the MWIs. These ports will be able to send a message to CallManager indicating when to turn off or on the MWI lamp on the handset of IP Phones. In addition, these ports will allow for notifications when the users of XYZ receive new messages. Users can choose the time intervals and type of messages (normal, urgent, and so on) for which they want to be notified.

## Making Changes to the Octel Access Numbers

Some changes are required in the Octel system with the introduction of the Unity server in Sydney and the Unity Bridge in San Jose. Before the introduction of Unity in the network, if a user in San Jose addressed a message to a user in Sydney, a digital (over TCP/IP) comm-unication occurred between both Octel systems to get the messages across (using digital OctelNet). In addition, as a failover or backup, there was an analog communication whereby the Octel system in San Jose would call the Octel system in Sydney, and the messages would be delivered via the analog OctelNet protocol.

The phone numbers used for communicating the analog OctelNet messages from San Jose now have to be directed to the Unity Bridge in San Jose instead of the destination in Sydney. The reason for this redirection is that the analog OctelNet destination is now the Unity Bridge in San Jose instead of the Octel system in Sydney. As a result, the Octel voice-mail administrator has to change the voice-mail access number in the San Jose server. For the users, nothing changes; a translation pattern will be in place to translate the local Sydney number to the first Unity port.

## Configuring the AutoAttendant functionality in Unity

Because the Octel system in Sydney offers integrated AutoAttendant (AA) functionality, you need to design the Unity system with similar functionality. The requirement for this feature to work properly is a uniform dial plan, which means that every user who has a mailbox on this Unity system must have a unique extension number within the dialing domain. The easiest way to think about this is to compare the Unity port with a regular IP Phone. As long as the extension number assigned in Unity to the subscriber redirects the call to the subscriber IP Phone, the AA feature will work fine.

Because XYZ has a unique four-digit extension number for every subscriber in Australia, this functionality will be available upon activation of the Unity server without additional programming. Also, because everybody who has a voice-mail account on the Sydney Unity server has a unique four-digit extension number, only one dialing domain will be configured on the Unity server.

XYZ will also verify that the Unity server is within the acceptable boundaries regarding jitter and delay in relation to all users and applications. If an end user picks up the phone and dials the Unity main number, they can listen to messages, record greetings, and perform other functions. The maximum delay between the user's IP Phone and the Unity system must be within the 150-ms boundary. Because both the Unity server and the CallManager cluster are based in Sydney, delay and jitter are not issues.

The built-in AutoAttendant and the stringent jitter and latency requirements offer an additional advantage. Because the Brisbane users for example, do not have DID number, they have to rely on an AA solution. In this directory, they only want to find the Brisbane users.

Therefore, a call to the AA number in Brisbane is forwarded to the Unity system in Sydney over the WAN link. Refer to the "Remote-Site WAN QoS Design" section in Chapter 5, "Design Phase: Network Infrastructure Design," to understand the necessary QoS configurations that have to be made for this forwarding to be successful and offer a good voice quality. The calling party connects to the AA in Sydney and Unity system guides the caller through the menu prompts. Based on the user input, Unity system will release the call to the corresponding called party in Brisbane. This avoids the need for a dedicated AA in the other Australian offices. You have to make sure that the necessary bandwidth and failover mechanism are in place via the PSTN.

| NOTE | Another possibility for small remote offices is to use Cisco Unity Express (CUE) and the built-in AA functionality. This is currently a standalone solution, which can be seen as a local answering machine. In combination with the Tool Command Language (Tcl) IVR on the Cisco IOS gateways, it is possible to offer local scripting if the WAN does not have enough capacity available. |
|------|---|

## Octel Integration with CallManager

The type of communication, analog or digital, determines the integration type used between the CallManager and the Octel system. In its San Jose location, XYZ plans to maintain its existing analog integration between the Lucent time-division multiplexing (TDM) PBX and the voice-mail system.

There are three different ways to integrate the CallManager with the Octel voice-mail system in an analog fashion:

- Use SMDI between CallManager and the Octel voice-mail system
- Use a VG248
- Use digital integration with Digital Port Adapter (DPA)

### SMDI Integration

SMDI integration is required if you want to continue to offer existing features and functionalities to the users when they migrate from the Lucent TDM PBX to the CallManager. In fact, this SMDI integration will make it possible for the users to see no change with regards to their voice mail when they move from a Lucent phone to a Cisco IP Phone. This is, of course, only the case when their mailbox stays on the TDM system and is not converted to a Unity mailbox.

When using SMDI integration, there is a serial cable between the CallManager and the serial port (RS-232) of the Octel system. The analog ports used to transfer the voice traffic between both systems can be provided by using a router that has analog ports. The disadvantage of this type of integration is the physical cable between the CallManager and the voice-mail system, as shown in Figure 7-7. If the CallManager at which this physical cable terminates experiences a problem, the voice-mail system will be disconnected from the CallManager. In addition, physical requirements (such as, the length of the serial cable) are related to this setup.

**Figure 7-7**    *Simplified Message Desk Interface*

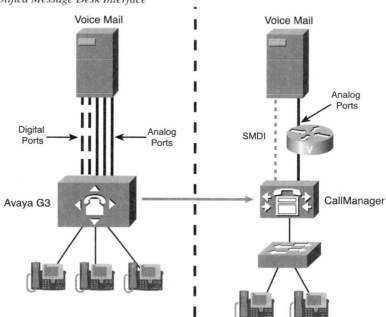

## Integration Using VG248

VG248 communicates using SCCP with the CallManager cluster. VG248 offers failover and redundancy, like any other SCCP device. This method of integration does not require involvement from the Octel voice-mail system either. It is possible to simply unplug the cables from the voice-mail system and plug them into the VG248—no recabling is required.

Figures 7-8 and 7-9 show how this integration looks and how to scale this integration further, respectively. Another possibility is to implement a hybrid solution whereby the CallManager and TDM PBX can coexist and use the same voice-mail system. However, XYZ has chosen to do a full transition to the IP-based PBX systems in San Jose.

**Figure 7-8** *Use of Single Voice-Mail System with VG248*

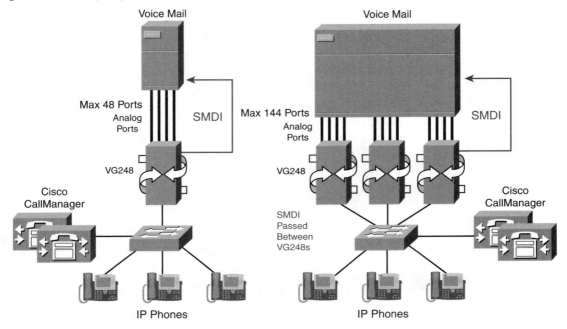

**Figure 7-9** *Use of Multiple Voice-Mail Systems with VG248*

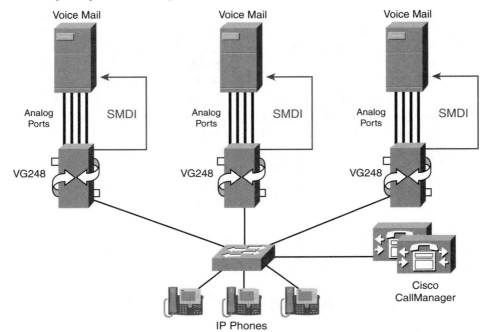

### Digital Integration Using DPA

There is also a digital integration method available between the CallManager and the Octel voice-mail system by using the Digital Port Adaptor 7630 (DPA-7630), as shown in Figure 7-10. The functionality of this device is comparable to the VG248, because it translates SCCP messages to DCP, the proprietary protocol used by the digital Lucent handsets. The digital integration method has the same advantages as the VG248 related to failover and physical requirements.

**Figure 7-10**    *Use of Voice-Mail System with DPA*

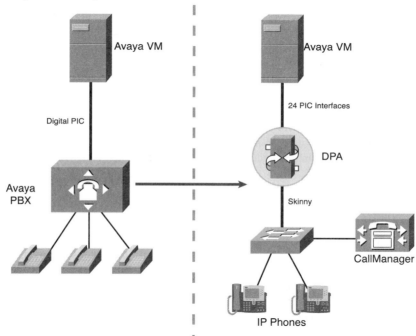

XYZ has chosen the digital integration method to integrate the Octel voice mail system in San Jose with the San Jose CallManager cluster because XYZ has the required hardware on the Octel voice mail system to support the integration with DPA-7630.

## Designing the Cisco Unity Networking

The Networking feature in Cisco Unity is used to deliver the messages from a Unity server to a target voice-mail system and from the target voice mail system to Unity server. The target voice-mail system could be another Unity server or any other supported vendor's voice mail system. The following networking options are discussed in the next few sections:

- Digital Networking
- Bridge Networking

- AMIS Networking
- VPIM Networking

## Digital Networking

Digital Networking allows messaging between two or more Unity servers provided they share the same global directory.

Because XYZ's setup has only one Unity server site (Sydney), it is not necessary to address specifically the Unity networking connections between different Unity servers. In brief, if in the future the San Jose site is also converted to Unity, the digital networking can be performed by the Exchange 2000 organization, by the message transport agent (MTA). This is true if both Unity servers are part of the same AD forest.

## Bridge Networking

Bridge Networking allows messaging between the Unity server and Octel voice-mail system by using Cisco Unity Bridge. In the current case study, the Unity system in Sydney has to be able to communicate with the Octel system in the San Jose site. Unity Bridge will network the two systems.

## AMIS Networking

Unity also supports the Audio Messaging Interchange Specification–analog (AMIS-a) networking protocol, which can be made available on the Octel system depending on the options purchased for the Octel system. However, AMIS-a offers fewer features than the analog OctelNet protocol. In fact, the analog OctelNet protocol is an improved version of AMIS-a. Avaya (or better, the part of Avaya that used to be Octel before Avaya acquired them) originally developed the analog OctelNet protocol as a common denominator between the Aria and Serenade systems. It then made improvements based on the AMIS-a foundation. The Aria platform is a voice-mail product line from Avaya that is used mainly in the United States, whereas the Serenade product line is used mostly in Asia Pacific and Europe.

One example of this feature difference between AMIS-a and Analog OctelNet is the use of multiple/single-source delivery. When a message is sent using AMIS-a between two voice-mail systems and the message has to reach five different recipients at the destination site, the message is sent across (played back between both systems) five times. This is known as multiple source delivery. With the analog OctelNet protocol (also used by the Unity Bridge), single source delivery is used—namely, the message is sent over only once and is distributed accordingly in the destination voice-mail system. Signaling between both systems is carried as DTMF signals over analog phone lines.

### VPIM Networking

Another possibility for voice-mail networking is the Voice Profile for Internet Messaging (VPIM) networking protocol. VPIM allows communication between voice-mail systems to exchange voice and fax messages over the Internet or any TCP/IP connection. VPIM is based on SMTP and the Multipurpose Internet Mail Extensions (MIME) protocol.

VPIM can be used under different circumstances. In certain voice-mail networks, an Intuity Interchange is present. This Interchange product was developed by Avaya and is in fact a protocol converter to link voice-mail systems from different vendors. As a result, these disperse systems can look as one voice-mail network with limited functionality. An example of this limited functionality is the forwarding of messages between two systems from different vendors. Both Unity and Intuity Interchange support VPIMv2.

Another use of VPIM is to integrate Unity and another vendor's voice-mail system that supports the same flavor of VPIM. This allows messages and some other advanced features to be exchanged between two systems.

VPIM can also be used between Unity systems that do not share the same AD and Exchange 2000 infrastructure. In this case, VPIM can be a solution to network these different systems together, which makes it look like one virtual voice-mail system to the users. The directory synchronization is still a manual process, but that is no different from directory synchronization in AMIS-a or Unity Bridge. In earlier releases of Unity, where VPIM was not available, SMTP could be used to bridge two Unity systems located in different AD forests and Exchange 2000 organizations. For every possible destination subscriber on the other system, an Internet subscriber account had to be defined in the local Unity server. Per definition, an Internet subscriber does not have a mailbox in the Exchange 2000 server of the organization that this Unity server integrates. The users do have an entry in the AD forest, which identifies them as Internet subscribers. This entry can hold information such as spoken name, greetings, and so on.

# Networking Octel and Unity

As previously discussed in the "Bridge Networking" section, Cisco Unity Bridge acts as a networking gateway between Cisco Unity and an Octel system on an Octel analog network. This case study addresses the use of the Unity Bridge as a means to allow users to move to a Unity system without having to lose their voice-mail networking capabilities. This section discusses the following topics:

- Deployment architecture with Unity Bridge
- Unity Bridge software
- Unity Bridge hardware
- Configuring Unity Bridge
- Unity Internet Voice Connector

# Deployment Architecture with Unity Bridge

Figure 7-11 depicts the logical deployment architecture with the Unity Bridge for XYZ. The Unity Bridge will allow messaging between the Unity server in Sydney and the Octel system in San Jose via the analog OctelNet protocol. The Unity Bridge acts as a networking gateway between Unity and the Octel system, and it allows the systems to exchange voice messages. Messaging between the Unity server in Sydney and the Unity Bridge in San Jose is carried over the internal network using a digital networking protocol, which is based on the VPIM protocol, with proprietary extensions.

**Figure 7-11**    *Deployment Architecture with Unity Bridge for XYZ*

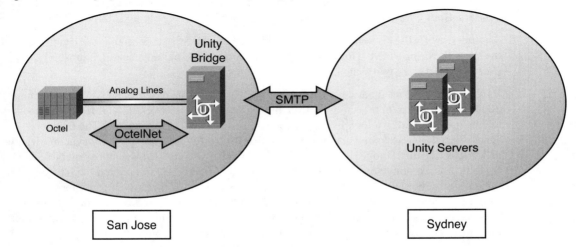

Messaging between the Octel system and the Unity Bridge in San Jose happens using the analog OctelNet protocol. It does not matter whether the Octel system is an Aria platform or a Serenade platform, because the analog OctelNet protocol is the same for both product lines.

Because the communication between the Unity Bridge and the Octel server is analog (in other words, phone calls with DTMF signaling), it is recommended that you keep the connection between them as short as possible. Because the Unity Bridge talks to the Unity server via TCP/IP, distance is not a concern between San Jose and Sydney. In addition, you can administer the Unity system from a web browser via HTTP. Therefore, to avoid possible problems such as DTMF distortion because of a transatlantic analog connection, it is better to place the Unity Bridge in San Jose than in Sydney.

The analog OctelNet protocol works comparably to the AMIS-a standard. An analog phone call is placed to transfer the messages between the servers. Upon answering the incoming call, DTMF handshaking occurs while determining the call is an analog OctelNet call.

The major element in this handshaking is the serial number of the system. When the serial number of the destination system does not match the serial number in the database of the originating server, the call is disconnected. That is why it is important to collect the serial number of the Octel voice-mail system in Sydney and assign the same serial number to the Unity Bridge. Reprogramming of this parameter is not needed in the Octel system in San Jose.

After this verification, both systems start the signaling for the message exchange. Both systems send, receive, and confirm the existence of certain mailboxes on their respective systems. The message is played back from the originating server to the destination server.

Because XYZ has only a single Unity Bridge in San Jose, using a Unity Bridgehead server as a central management entity is not an advantage. If XYZ had to administer a whole range of Bridges, the use of the Bridgehead could simplify the design.

---

**NOTE**     Unity and Exchange both use the term *Bridgehead server.* An Exchange Bridgehead is a route point for routing messages between route groups within an Exchange organization. Typically, this is between different sites of an organization. A Unity Bridgehead is a single place to maintain bridge locations, bridge subscribers, and distribution lists.

---

## Unity Bridge Software and Hardware

Unity Bridge software runs on a separate and dedicated platform. For the list of supported hardware platforms for Unity and Unity Bridge, refer to the following URL on Cisco.com:

> http://www.cisco.com/en/US/partner/products/sw/voicesw/ps2237/
> products_data_sheet09186a008009267e.html

As shown in Figure 7-11, the communication between the Unity Bridge and the Octel system in San Jose happens via an analog connection. On the Unity Bridge server, these analog ports are provided by the Brooktrout cards, which you need to order specifically. Refer to the following URL for ordering information on these cards:

> http://www.cisco.com/en/US/products/sw/voicesw/ps2237/
> prod_system_requirements_hardware09186a00801b91cc.html

The ports on the Brooktrout cards work the same as analog phones. That is why you need a VG248 or an FXS card (for example, WS-X-6624) controlled by CallManager to establish the connection between the Unity Bridge in San Jose and the Octel system. This effectively makes it possible to establish communication between the analog extension and the Octel voice-mail system. XYZ decided to deploy the VG248 to provide the analog ports to the Unity Bridge (refer to figure 7-1). Because the Brooktrout card that will be installed on the Unity Bridge server only has 4 analog ports, the remaining 44 ports on the VG248 can be used for other analog extensions such as faxes and POTS-phones in San Jose.

The Unity Bridge software should be licensed for at least four ports per server. This means that one four-port Brooktrout card in the server can do the conversions from analog to digital signals. This also means that there can be a maximum of four simultaneous calls between the

Bridge and the Octel system in San Jose. Therefore, a maximum of four messages can be delivered simultaneously from one system to the other.

Based on traffic reports from the Octel systems (from the voice-mail networking, confirmed by traffic-flow analysis on the TCP/IP network), the majority of the messages is exchanged in the local hubs in San Jose and Sydney. There is far less traffic flow between San Jose and Sydney; therefore, having the capacity to handle four parallel calls between these systems is sufficient. It is always possible, through future expansions, to add additional Brooktrout cards in the server and increase the capacity.

The Unity Bridge hardware selected for XYZ consists of the following components:

- IBM MCS-7845I-2.4-ECS2 server, with IBM RSA-II adapter which provides the remote management to the Unity Bridge server.

- Four-port voice/fax ports (UNITY-TR114U-US).

The Bridge, regardless of the power supply configuration, requires two power connections. The power connections should be on isolated, redundant circuits and rated to handle a minimum of 350W. Also, the Bridge requires a minimum of two 10/100/1000 copper Ethernet connections. Three connections are preferred:

- One connection for the RSA-II adapter (assigned in DNS as using the format hostname-r).

- Two connections for the built-in Ethernet ports. The network connections must be rated at 100-Mbps full duplex as a minimum.

If you are deploying Unity Bridge in the network, you need to extend the AD schema for Unity Bridge (refer to Figure 7-6). The next steps are to install the Cisco Unity IVC on the Exchange server and configure the Cisco Unity server for Bridge networking before configuring the Unity Bridge.

# Configuring Unity Bridge

Most of the pages available from Cisco Unity Bridge Administration have default settings. This section describes the steps to follow to configure the Unity Bridge and customize the default settings. To access the Bridge Administration page on the browser, type the following URL:

http://*Bridge_server_IP_ADDR*/Bridge

Figure 7-12 shows the Unity Bridge Administration page and the various configuration options that are available. The following sections describe the first four configuration options in the list on the left side of the Bridge Administration page.

**Figure 7-12**    *Unity Bridge Administration Page*

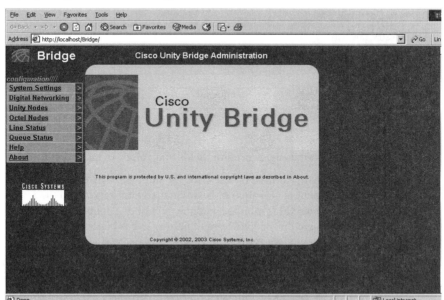

## System Settings

To access the System Settings page, click **System Settings** on the Bridge Administration page. The System Settings page allows you to configure how the Unity Bridge server handles retries when a call delivers a failure message. There are separate settings for busy, no answer, and failed call conditions.

Table 7-8 lists the various fields on the System Settings page and the appropriate values for XYZ.

**Table 7-8**    *Unity Bridge—System Settings Page for XYZ*

| System Settings Field | Value |
|---|---|
| Attempts if Busy | 15 |
| Attempts on No Answer | 15 |
| Attempts on Bad Connection | 100 |
| Interval if Busy | 5 minutes |
| Interval if No Answer | 5 minutes |
| Name Aging (Recorded/Text Name) | 90 days |
| Name Retrieval Retries | 0 |

*continues*

**Table 7-8**   *Unity Bridge—System Settings Page for XYZ (Continued)*

| System Settings Field | Value |
|---|---|
| Name Retry Interval | 1 |
| Queued Call Threshold | 10 |
| Max. Ports per Node | 2 |
| Call Log Retention | 7 days |
| Call Tracing Level | Verbose |

The following list describes the preceding fields and values in more detail:

- **Attempts and Interval fields**—Describe the number of analog call attempts and the interval of each analog call attempt between the Octel server and the Unity Bridge. The unit used for an interval is minutes, and the default of 1 minute is used. If the systems are busy in an extensive meshed voice-mail network, it is better to increase the interval, to avoid excessive call charges over the PSTN.

- **Name Aging**—Set to 0 to avoid name aging. Setting this field to zero retains the spoken name that is used for confirmation of the destination.

- **Name Retrieval Retries**— Indicates for how many days the Unity Bridge will try to obtain the spoken names at a specific time (midnight) from the Octel system in San Jose and store them in AD for use by the Australian users. Once done successfully, the users who have a mailbox in Sydney can address a message to a user in San Jose and hear the user's spoken name confirmation.

- **Name Retry Interval**—The Retry Interval is expressed in days. It is used to launch a call every day until all names are retrieved or until the maximum retrieval retries are used. These calls are made at no cost, because the Bridge and Octel server are located in the same room and are connected via a direct analog connection.

- **Queued Call Threshold**—Indicates the number of messages that must be waiting in the queue before another port initiate's a call from the Unity Bridge to the Octel server located in San Jose via the analog connection. Note that XYZ has only two destinations, and the value will be lowered to 2 automatically. Based on availability, this will always open an additional channel when messages are queued. This implementation has no cost implications because the Bridge is located in San Jose next to the Octel server.

- **Max. Ports per Node**—Indicates how many ports can be used in parallel between the Unity Bridge and the Octel server located in San Jose. Because XYZ has only two voice-mail systems, it can allocate the maximum number of ports. If you have a mesh of voice-mail systems, it is important not to assign too many ports for communication between any two nodes. Take into account that the maximum number of ports in use between any two nodes can be doubled when urgent messages need to be transferred. The maximum number of ports is determined by the licenses purchased from Cisco. In this example, the number of ports purchased in the maximum capacity is 48.

- **Call Log Retention**—Indicates the number of days that call logs are retained. The default is 7, which XYZ will use.

- **Call Tracing Level**—The choices are None, Basic, or Verbose. XYZ chose Verbose to facilitate initial troubleshooting after the setup. Afterward, you can set it to Basic to limit the impact on the Bridge server. Choosing None is not recommended. Doing so makes obtaining any information that is related to a problem difficult, resulting in a lack of troubleshooting capabilities.

## Digital Networking

The Digital Networking page provides settings that allow you to record error and status messages in a log file and allow you to view outbound messages that are retained in SMTP format. To access the Digital Networking page, choose **Digital Networking** on the Bridge Administration page.

Table 7-9 lists fields on the Digital Networking page and the values used for XYZ.

**Table 7-9**  *Unity Bridge—Digital Networking Page for XYZ*

| Digital Networking Field | Value |
|---|---|
| ESMTP Server | Exchange@xyz.com |
| Cisco Unity Bridge Domain Name | Bridge@xyz.com |
| Tracing Level | Flow |
| Retention Days for Temporary SMTP Messages | 2 days |
| SMTP Port | 25 |

The following list explains a few of the Digital Networking page fields and values in more depth:

- **ESMTP Server**—exchange@XYZ.com is a fully qualified domain name (FQDN) of the Exchange server. If your Exchange organization relies on a relay server for the routing of messages (ESMTP e-mail host), specify that server here. Contact your Exchange 2000 administrator for confirmation.

- **Tracing Level**—Choosing Flow enables you to see detailed information flows and examine all the parameters before you declare that everything is working fine. After you make sure that everything is working fine, you can change this parameter to Error, which will show only the errors and prevent the hard disk from storing unrelated information.

- **Retention Days for Temporary SMTP Messages**—Helps you to keep track of all incoming and outgoing messages. After a first week of problem-free production, you can set this value to 0. However, if enough disk capacity is available and the traffic is not high, leave this parameter on 2 for troubleshooting purposes.

## Unity Nodes

The Unity Nodes page displays information about the Unity node. You create and configure a Unity node through the Bridge Administrator to communicate with the Cisco Unity server. You must set up the Cisco Unity server for networking with the Bridge before you enter information on this page. Although the Unity Nodes page allows you to create multiple Unity nodes, currently only one Unity node is supported. To access the Unity Nodes page, choose **Unity Nodes** on the Bridge Administration page.

Table 7-10 shows the Unity Nodes page settings used for XYZ.

**Table 7-10**    *Unity Bridge—Unity Nodes Page for XYZ*

| Unity Nodes Field | Value |
|---|---|
| Serial Number | 27975 |
| Name | UnitySydney |
| Unity Computer Name | Unity |
| Unity SMTP Mail Suffix | Mail@xyz.com |
| Codec | G.711 |

The following list explains three fields on the Unity Nodes page:

- **Serial Number**—Must match exactly the serial number of the Octel server replaced in Sydney to avoid Octel reprogramming in San Jose, and must be different from the serial number used by the Octel server in San Jose.

- **Unity SMTP Mail Suffix**—Identifies the SMTP e-mail address of the mail system that supports Cisco Unity. This information is provided by the Exchange 2000 administrator.

- **Codec**—Determines the codec used for traffic flows from the Bridge to the Unity server. The Unity server can perform the transcoding function in software. However, XYZ decided not to perform this conversion in software because it has a negative impact on the voice quality. As discussed in the "Transcoding" section of Chapter 6, DSP farms deployed in Catalyst WS-X6608-E1 card are used to convert the G.729a codec streams to G.711. Hence both Unity and Unity Bridge will be configured to send and receive all the traffic in G.711.

Note that you can click the Directory button to see a list of subscribers associated with this Unity node.

## Octel Nodes

Each Octel server represents a node in the Octel analog network. In Octel analog networking, each node is assigned a unique serial number that identifies the node. The Bridge and Cisco Unity Bridgehead servers must be configured with information about the Octel nodes on the network. The Octel Nodes page displays information about the Octel nodes. You create and configure an

Octel node through the Bridge Administrator. To access the Octel Nodes page, choose **Octel Nodes** on the Bridge Administration page.

Tables 7-11 and 7-12 show the Octel Nodes page fields and the settings for the XYZ network in Unity Bridge.

**Table 7-11** *Unity Bridge—Octel Nodes Page for XYZ*

| Octel Nodes Field | Value |
|---|---|
| Serial Number | 24555 |
| Name | San Jose Octel |
| Phone Number | 1000 |
| Extension | <Leave Blank> |
| Dial Sequence | P91000 |

**Table 7-12** *Unity Bridge—Octel Nodes Message Delivery Windows Values for XYZ*

| Message Type | Enabled | Begin | End | Interval |
|---|---|---|---|---|
| Normal | Checked | 00:00 | 23:59 | 15 |
| Urgent | Checked | 00:00 | 23:59 | 5 |
| Administration | Checked | 00:00 | 23:59 | 120 |

The following list explains various Octel Nodes page fields:

- **Serial Number**—The serial number of the Octel system in San Jose.
- **Name**—Included to make the window easier to read.

  **Phone Number**—The number to be dialed by the Bridge in San Jose to reach the Octel server in San Jose, which is why it is a local San Jose number.

  Note that the CallManager in San Jose is providing analog lines via a module in the Catalyst 6000. This allows the transformation of this number to the internal four-digit number according to the dial-plan standard of XYZ.

- **Extension**—Stays blank because the Octel server in San Jose is equipped with DID lines.
- **Dial Sequence**—The dial sequence for the United States is 9 (access code) followed by the number defined in the Phone Number field. The CallManager dial plan for XYZ has to consider # as the end of the dialing string. In addition, it is best to start the dial sequence with a pause (P).
- **Message Delivery Windows**—Specify begin and end times and the interval, in minutes, for normal, urgent, and administrative calls. As indicated in Table 7-12, normal calls go through 24 hours a day with short time intervals; this allows the fastest delivery of messages and the highest degree of service to users of XYZ. As mentioned earlier, the

communication between the Unity Bridge in San Jose and the Octel server does not traverse the PSTN, so XYZ does not incur telephone charges for these calls. If the calls are going over PSTN, you can change these times and intervals to be more conservative.

We will not add names to the Octel directory on the Bridge. Instead, because of the addressing of messages and the involved automatic NameNet feature, this directory will be populated over time. This will require proper user communication to set the right user expectations. NameNet update is used when one node in an OctelNet network makes a call to another node in the OctelNet network (which can be a Unity Bridge) to retrieve the spoken name of one or more subscribers on that system. Such communication is referred to as an administrative call. This mechanism to retrieve the spoken names is to offer name confirmation to the users when they address messages to users on another system in the network. NameNet updates can also be part of a "regular" OctelNet communication or can be launched separately, depending on the configuration of the Bridge (time window and intervals).

By clicking the Directory button in this menu, you can see a list of mailboxes that exchanged messages with the Bridge. This information is retrieved via OctelNet NameNet.

This is also true in the opposite direction. The Octel system in San Jose will lose the spoken names (NameNet information) for Sydney users after Sydney migrates to Unity. This information will be propagated, as messages are exchanged or forced, as configured in the Bridge. An alternative—which is not recommended from a cost perspective and is not done for XYZ—is for the Octel system administrator in San Jose to populate the NameNet information in the San Jose system manually.

None of the other voicemail functionalities and habits will change for the users who are located on the Octel server in San Jose. They will not notice a difference in the way they interact with users from Australia.

# Unity Internet Voice Connector

The purpose of the Internet Voice Connector (IVC) is to preserve key properties as messages are routed between Unity and third-party messaging systems. IVC interacts with other Microsoft Exchange components to send and receive messages for Unity subscribers from third-party messaging systems and vice versa.

For the Unity server to communicate with the Unity Bridge, you need to install one instance of IVC on the Exchange server in each routing group. IVC stores its data in the Windows registry of the Exchange server. With Unity 4.x and above, it is not possible to integrate with Exchange 5.5, so you must use the correct version of IVC.

As shown in Figure 7-3, one routing group and one Bridgehead server are located in the Sydney site. The Sydney Bridgehead Exchange server will have the Unity IVC.

To see the call-flow and message-routing steps that occur when a subscriber on a Unity server leaves a voice mail for a subscriber on an Octel server, suppose that there is a message flowing from Octel subscriber 1000 in San Jose to subscriber 2000 in Sydney.

Via the analog OctelNet protocol, the message is delivered to the Unity Bridge. From the Unity Bridge server, the message is sent to the IVC in the following format:

FROM: 1000 @ 24555 (Mailbox 1000 – Serial Number 24555)
TO:   2000 @ 27975 (Mailbox 2000 – Serial Number 27975)

The IVC has to translate the address in the TO field to a format that can be understood by Exchange and Unity. IVC queries AD with parameters of Mailbox 2000 and Serial Number 27975. The return is the Exchange alias that Exchange and Unity understand. Therefore, the message addressing looks as follows:

FROM: 1000 @ 24555
TO: Alias_For_Mailbox_2000

The next task is to do something useful with the FROM address so that it can be understood by Exchange. Therefore, the IVC is going to query AD again with a parameter, the Serial Number 24555 (as remoteNodeId). It finds the corresponding DTMF-Id (being 152, San Jose), after which the addresses are changed as follows:

FROM: OMNI:152_1000 (LocationDialId_Extension)
TO:   Alias_For_Mailbox_2000

This processing does not resolve the FROM address, but it does put the addresses in a format that Exchange can understand. Identifying and resolving the sender of this message is the next step.

The IVC will query the AD again with the DTMF-Id and try to find a match. If the IVC finds a match, the alias is returned and it replaces the 152_1000. Now, the addresses look as follows:

FROM: Alias_For_Mailbox_1000
TO:   Alias_For_Mailbox_2000

The recipient now hears the name confirmation of the sender in the TUI and sees in the GUI the display name.

If AD cannot respond to the IVC query, the TUI and GUI indicate that this message came from an unidentified caller, without name confirmation in the TUI or display information in the GUI.

# Customizing the Cisco Unity System

Customization of the Unity system is required to meet the specific customer requirements. This section discusses commonly used customization areas in Unity, such as the Class of Service (CoS), Subscriber Template, Account Policy, Subscribers, Public Distribution Lists, Call

Management, Call Handlers, Network, and Reports pages that are accessed from the Cisco Unity System Administration (SA) page. This section gives you a better understanding of how various options work and provides customization examples for XYZ that enable you to develop settings based on your needs.

To configure Cisco Unity, go to the Unity SA page, shown in Figure 7-13, by following this URL:

http://*IP_address_of_Unity_Server/web/sa.*

**Figure 7-13**   *Unity System Administration Page*

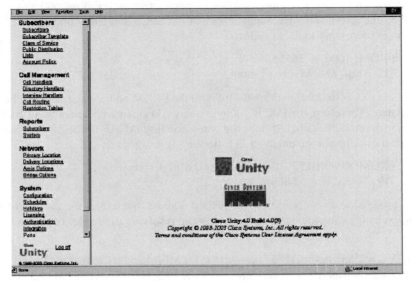

The Unity SA page is divided into the following five categories, and each category is further divided into many subcategories (see the following list). Depending on the type of Unity licenses purchased for your system, you might see some additional or fewer subcategories under each main category. For example, if you have not purchased Bridge licensing and AMIS licensing options for your Unity server, you will not see these two options listed under the Network category.

- Subscribers
- Call Management
- Reports
- Network
- System

# Subscribers

The Subscribers category under the SA page is divided into the following subcategories:

- Subscribers
- Subscriber Template
- Class of Service
- Public Distribution Lists
- Account Policy

The next few sections cover the customizations required for the previous subcategories for deploying the Unity at XYZ Inc. In the following sections, the subcategories are not covered in the order they appear in the SA page. They are covered in the order that simplifies the customization of Unity.

## Class of Service

To access the CoS settings from the SA page, click the **Class of Service** option to open the Class of Service page, shown in Figure 7-14.

The first step in the customization of the Cisco Unity system is to define the CoS, which specifies the level of access granted to the end users. This access includes what features subscribers can use and the different levels of access that an administrator might have within the Unity System Administrator.

After you define the CoS settings, assign them to the corresponding subscriber templates that will be used as default settings for the different users.

**Figure 7-14** *CoS Page Configuration Options*

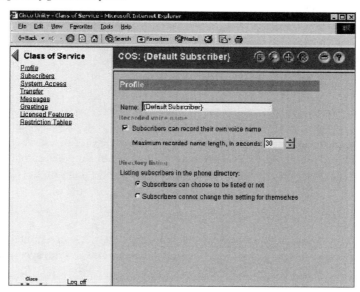

The following sections describe in turn each of the options in the list on the left side of the Class of Service page.

## Profile

For XYZ, CoS profiles are required for the following types of users:

- Managers
- Employees
- Tier 1 support group

The Tier 1 support group members provide first-level support and escalate problems to the system administrator, who takes care of Tier 2 support. To access CoS profiles, click **Profile** on the Class of Service page.

Table 7-13 shows the CoS profiles and the settings for each CoS that is required by XYZ.

**Table 7-13** *CoS—Profile Page for XYZ*

| Profile Page | Value | Value | Value |
|---|---|---|---|
| Name | Employees_CoS | Managers_CoS | SupportTier1_CoS |
| **Recorded Voice Name** | | | |
| Subscribers Can Record Their Own Voice Name | Checked | Checked | Checked |
| Maximum Recorded Name Length, in Seconds | 30 | 30 | 30 |
| **Directory Listing** | | | |
| Subscribers Can Choose to Be Listed or Not | Not clicked | Not clicked | Not clicked |
| Subscribers Cannot Change This Setting for Themselves | Clicked | Clicked | Clicked |

## Subscribers

The Subscribers menu option is useful for verifying the CoS that is assigned to different users. It is also used to reassign a CoS to a user, such as when a regular employee moves to a "manager" status. To configure subscribers, click **Subscribers** on the Class of Service page.

## System Access

The System Access option allows you to define the level of access granted to users to administer the entire Unity system or parts of the system. To configure system access, click **System Access** on the Class of Service page.

XYZ users who are members of SupportTier1_CoS require access to some parts of the Unity Administration windows. For the CoS profiles Managers_CoS and Employees_CoS, do not check the Cisco Unity Administrator Application Access check box. For the CoS profile SupportTier1_CoS, the access permissions are set as shown in Table 7-14.

**Table 7-14**   *CoS—System Access Page for SupportTier1_CoS for XYZ*

| System Access Page | Value |
| --- | --- |
| Cisco Unity Administrator Application Access | Checked |
| Class of Service; Class of Service Access | Read |
| Directory Handlers; Directory handlers Access | Read |
| Subscribers; Subscribers Access | Read, Edit, Add, Delete |
| Can unlock Subscriber Accounts and Change Passwords | Checked |
| Lists; Public Distribution Lists | Read, Edit |
| Schedules and Holidays | Unchecked |
| **Call Management** | |
| Restriction Tables Access | Unchecked |
| Routing Tables Access | Unchecked |
| Call handlers Access | Unchecked |
| **Troubleshooting and Administration** | |
| Status monitor Access | Checked |
| Reports Access | Checked |
| Network Access | Checked |
| Diagnostics Access | Checked |
| Technician Functions Access (Configuration, Licensing, Ports, and Switch Pages) | Unchecked |

**NOTE**   The Unity system administrator must take care of all other administration tasks that are not assigned to SupportTier1_CoS. To achieve this, you can either define another CoS Unity Administrator and grant all permissions on the System Access page or assign the Default Administrator CoS to those users who are responsible for the administration of Unity.

## Transfer

Enabling the Transfer page settings allows subscribers to change their call-screening and call-holding options. However, if too many subscribers use these features, the Unity ports will be kept busy too long. The best practice is to enable them for selected groups of subscribers only when needed. To configure transfer options, click **Transfer** on the Class of Service page.

The call-screening and call-holding options are not enabled for all three CoS profiles in XYZ, as shown in Table 7-15.

| NOTE | The transfer option does not work when the CallManager has control over the call. This option is influential only when the Unity System handles call control, such as when somebody dials the company's general number and uses the AutoAttendant to reach a certain person. When someone dials the DID extension, such as the call, CallManager controls and these values and settings do not come into play. |
|---|---|

**Table 7-15**   *CoS—Transfer Page for XYZ*

| Transfer Page | Value |
|---|---|
| Subscribers Can Change Call Screening Options | Unchecked |
| Subscribers Can Change Call Holding Options | Unchecked |

## Messages

The maximum length of the message that callers can record for subscribers is configurable through the options on the Messages page. To configure messages, click **Messages** on the Class of Service page.

At XYZ, the maximum length of recorded messages for managers is set to 600 seconds, to allow them to send company announcements of up to 10 minutes. For all other users, the length of recorded messages is limited to 300 seconds. These values are shown in Table 7-16, along with the other values on the Messages page.

**Table 7-16**   *CoS—Messages Page for XYZ*

| Messages Page | Employees_CoS | Managers_CoS | SupportTier1_CoS |
|---|---|---|---|
| Maximum Length of Message Subscribers Can Record, in Seconds | 300 | 600 | 300 |
| Subscribers Can Send Messages to Public Distribution Lists | Checked | Checked | Checked |
| Deleted Messages Are Copied to the Deleted Items Folder | Unchecked | Unchecked | Unchecked |
| Live Reply; Subscribers Can Reply to Messages from Other Subscribers by Calling Them | Checked | Checked | Checked |

The following list provides a few more details about three of the Messages page settings:

- **Maximum Length of Message**—Refers to the length of the message that subscribers who are assigned to this CoS can record for any other subscriber in Unity.

- **Deleted Messages Are Copied to the Deleted Items Folder**—XYZ will check this box to allow maximum flexibility and cover mistakes by end users (and limit the number of support calls). Most Outlook clients are configured to empty the Deleted Items folder upon exiting. XYZ is not concerned about hard disk capacity because the price per gigabit of hard disk is low compared to the problems related to unexpected loss of important information. Other mechanisms are in place at XYZ to control the amount of disk space used and to avoid running out of storage capacity.

- **Live Reply**—Check this box to allow users to reply to a caller who has left a message. This is mainly useful for internal callers, because the CLID representation depends on the local telephone company.

## Greetings

The Greetings page parameter sets the greeting recording length allowed for the subscribers who are assigned to this CoS. To configure greetings, click **Greetings** on the Class of Service page. Leave the Maximum Greeting Length field at 90 seconds (default) for all the CoS profiles.

## Licensed Features

The Licensed Features page allows you to configure and control how licensed features can be assigned to users. To configure licensed features, click **Licensed Features** on the Class of Service page.

For XYZ, configure the Licensed Features page for the Unity system, as described in Table 7-17. The following list explains the reasons for choosing these values:

- **Fax Mail**—None of the third-party fax servers is integrated with the Unity server for XYZ, so do not check this box.

- **Text-to-Speech for E-Mail Messages**—Because the number of TTS sessions is limited, XYZ will offer this feature only to managers (Managers_CoS profile) and not to the rest of the staff.

- **Cisco Unity Assistant**—This is checked for all three profiles to offer web-based administration of mailbox settings to all users.

- **Cisco Unity Inbox (VMI)**—This is checked to allow users to work with their inbox even when they are not connected with their own personal laptop.

**Table 7-17** *CoS—Licensed Features Page for XYZ*

| Licensed Features Page | Employees_CoS | Managers_CoS | SupportTier1_CoS |
|---|---|---|---|
| **Phone Conversation Features** | | | |
| Fax Mail | Unchecked | Unchecked | Unchecked |
| Text to Speech for E-Mail Messages | Unchecked | Checked | Unchecked |
| **Cisco PCA Features** | | | |
| Cisco Unity Assistant | Checked | Checked | Checked |
| Cisco Unity Inbox (Visual Messaging Interface) | Checked | Checked | Checked |

**NOTE**    Before you enable the licensed features, ensure that the Unity license keys purchased allow the use of any of the previous enabled features for all users, to avoid inconvenience to the users.

## Restriction Tables

Restriction tables are extremely important to prevent toll fraud in the Unity system. The settings on the Restriction Tables page (click **Restriction Tables** on the Class of Service page) depend on the local dial plan. You can build different restriction tables to restrict or limit the Unity notification destinations. For example, you can allow managers to set up notifications to be sent to their cell phone when a new voice mail is waiting in their inbox, but limit employees' notification destination to internal phone numbers. To achieve this, you have to configure the CSS on the voice-mail ports (refer to Table 7-3, definition of Css_vmports) in the CallManager to reach internal and local telephone numbers and configure separate restriction tables for managers and employees in Unity. The restriction table for managers is configured to allow them to set a local phone number as the notification device, whereas the restriction table for employees is configured to allow them to set only an internal phone number as the target notification device.

The disadvantage of this approach is that you have to configure and maintain the restrictions at the CallManager level (using the CSS on the voice-mail ports) and in Unity by using restriction tables. The best practice is to set these restrictions in CallManager so that, for any trouble-shooting issues, you can focus only on CallManager and do not have to deal with both systems.

Because the XYZ policy allows notifications to be set to local and internal numbers and this is already taken care of in the CallManager, you do not need to define restriction tables.

## Subscriber Template

The Subscriber Template page, accessed by clicking **Subscriber Template** on the Cisco Unity SA page, allows you to create different templates, where each template identifies a certain group of mailboxes with its own specific features, such as password restrictions, call-transfer settings, conversation settings, and so forth.

Templates can be used to create a group of users who have specific features, whereas individual users can still be adapted on a per-user basis after the template has been used for individual user creation. The next few sections introduce you to the various options available in the Subscriber Template page and the customization performed on the Unity servers at XYZ, Inc.

### Profile

The Profile page settings define how Cisco Unity identifies a subscriber. To configure profiles, click **Profile** on the Subscriber Template page. The settings on the Profile page for subscriber templates are explained here:

- **Name**—This defines the name of the template. You need three subscriber templates for XYZ to differentiate three different types of subscriber classes—employees, managers, and support tier 1 group.

- **Class of Service**—The options available here are the ones described and configured in the "Class of Service" section earlier in this chapter. You need to choose the appropriate option from the drop-down list.

- **Active Schedule**—This enables you to define the regular business hours. This setting determines the out-of-office hours, during which Unity plays the Closed Greeting. If the company policy is flexible regarding working hours and days, set this option to All Hours – All Days.

- **Self-Enrollment at Next Login**—If this option is checked, when the new user signs into the Unity system for the first time, they are asked to change the initial password, record their first and last name, record their personal greeting, and so on.

- **List in Phone Directory**—The user is not listed in the directory unless this option is checked. This option is useful if a company has some people who are not on site but have a local mailbox to receive networked messages from other people (for example, the Australian office).

- **Show Subscriber in E-Mail Server Address Book**—Unless this check box is checked, the subscriber is not listed in the address book. This means, for example, that users who are addressing messages in Outlook will not find the subscriber. You can uncheck this option if you are not using Unified Messaging but voice mail only. This is also a viable option for Internet subscribers,.

- **Exchange Alias Generation**—This default alias can be overwritten when a subscriber is added or defined. If the company is deploying Unified Messaging and already has an Exchange server and AD in place, this field is irrelevant. (All users exist in the AD and in the Exchange server.)

Table 7-18 lists the entries required on the Profile page for XYZ to create the subscriber templates.

**Table 7-18** *Subscriber Template—Profile Page for XYZ*

| Profile Page | Value | Value | Value |
|---|---|---|---|
| Name | Emp_Template | Mgr_Template | Sup_Template |
| **New Cisco Unity Subscribers** | | | |
| Class of Service | Employees_CoS | Managers_CoS | SupportTier1_CoS |
| Active Schedule | Weekdays | Weekdays | Weekdays |
| Time Zone | GMT+10:00 (Sydney/Australian time) | GMT+10:00 (Sydney/Australian time) | GMT+10:00 (Sydney/Australian time) |
| **Display Name Generation** | | | |
| Display Name Generation; First Name Then Last Name (Jessie Smith) | Clicked | Clicked | Clicked |
| Display Name Generation; Last Name Then First Name (Smith, Jessie) | Not Clicked | Not Clicked | Not Clicked |
| Set Subscriber for Self-Enrollment at Next Login | Checked | Checked | Checked |
| List in Phone Directory | Checked | Checked | Checked |
| Show Subscriber in E-Mail Server Address Book | Checked | Checked | Checked |
| New Windows and Exchange Users | First Letter of First Name + Last Name | First Letter of First Name + Last Name | First Letter of First Name + Last Name |

## Account

You can use the settings on the Account page to lock out all the user accounts that are associated with the template and define a billing ID for the user accounts. To configure the user accounts, click **Account** on the Subscriber Template page.

The Account page enables you to set the following options:

- **Locked**—Check this box to lock the newly created subscriber account.

- **Billing-ID**—Fill in the department code of the employee to whom this mailbox is assigned. This is useful when generating department-wide billing reports.

Table 7-19 shows the Account page settings used for XYZ for subscriber templates.

**Table 7-19**  *Subscriber Template—Account Page for XYZ*

| Account Page | Value for Emp_Template | Value for Mgr_Template | Value for Sup_Template |
|---|---|---|---|
| Cisco Unity Account Status | Unchecked | Unchecked | Unchecked |
| Billing ID (Optional) | Leave Blank | Leave Blank | Leave Blank |

## Passwords

The settings on the Passwords page control the password policies for the voice mailbox. To configure passwords, click **Passwords** on the Subscriber Template page. The following options are available:

- **User Cannot Change Password**—The best practice is to force users to change passwords once a month, which is accomplished by leaving this box unchecked, the default. This allows the users to change the passwords.

- **User Must Change Password at Next Login**—Check this box for initial installation to force users to change their passwords and not enable them to leave it on the default value, which is the same for everybody.

- **Password Never Expires**—Leave this box unchecked (default setting) for security reasons.

- **Phone Password for New Subscribers**— The default password is 12345. If you change this default value, you need to communicate this password to all users who need to access the Unity system for the first time. Users use this first-time password to log in and complete the self-enrollment process. By checking the User Must Change Password at Next Login check box, Unity forces the user to change the password.

- **Password for New Windows Accounts**— The default password is 12345678. Unity can create the account in the AD for the user during the user account creation in Unity. The password entered in this field is used to set the initial Windows password for the user. In a Unified Messaging deployment, this field is irrelevant, because the users already exist in the AD.

For XYZ, Table 7-20 lists the configured Passwords page values. All the subscriber templates have the same password policies. This is typical, because the security policy is the same for the entire company and does not differ from one employee type to another.

**Table 7-20** *Subscriber Template—Passwords Page for XYZ*

| Passwords Page | Value for Emp_Template | Value for Mgr_Template | Value for Sup_Template |
|---|---|---|---|
| **Phone Password Settings** | | | |
| User Cannot Change Password | Unchecked | Unchecked | Unchecked |
| User Must Change Password at Next Login | Checked | Checked | Checked |
| Password Never Expires | Unchecked | Unchecked | Unchecked |
| Phone Password for New Subscribers | 12345 | 12345 | 12345 |
| Password for New Windows Accounts | Changeme | Changeme | Changeme |

## Conversation

The Conversation page settings allow you to configure and customize the way that Unity interacts with the subscribers. To configure the Conversation page, click **Conversation** on the Subscriber Template page. The following is a list of various options and their recommended settings:

- **Menu Style**—Choosing Full (default) provides extended menus for all new users.

- **Volume**—This field is applicable only for analog integrations/DTMF.

- **After Logging On Play**—Checking Subscriber's Recorded Name enables users to hear their spoken name after logging in. Also, if you check Alternate Greeting Notification, Unity notifies the user whether the alternate greeting is enabled. (See the upcoming "Greetings" section.)

- **Before Playing Messages Play**—Checking Message Type Menu enables users to hear the number of voice/e-mail messages they have, before they start to listen to their messages. This gives them an option to jump straight to their e-mails if they want during a phone conversation.

- **New Message Play Order**—The order is determined by the way your company uses the messaging environment. Voice mails routinely contain sensitive information, so the best practice is to put them at the top of the list, followed by e-mails, faxes, and finally receipts and notices.

- **Saved Message Play Order**—Follow the best practices described for the New Message Play Order option.

- **Before Playing Each Message, Play:**
  - Checking Sender's information announces the originator of the message. This will be the phone number of the party that left the voice mail if the PSTN was able to deliver that message. If another Sydney-based employee from XYZ leaves a message, the spoken name will be heard here instead of the phone number.

— Checking Message number announces the number.

— Checking Time that the message was sent indicates when the message was sent to the mailbox.

• **After Playing Each Message, Play**—Do not choose Time the Message Was Sent, because this information is announced before each message is played. (See the previous bullet.)

Table 7-21 lists all the settings and the values selected for XYZ for all three types of subscriber templates: Emp_Template, Mgr_Template, and Sup_Template.

**Table 7-21**  *Subscriber Template—Conversation Page for XYZ*

| Conversation Page | Value |
|---|---|
| Menu Style | Full |
| Volume | Medium |
| Language | Australian English |
| Time Format | System Default |
| Conversation Style | Standard Conversation |
| When Exiting the Conversation, Send the Subscriber To | Call Handler – Opening Greeting |
| Identify a Subscriber By | Spelling the Last Name, then First Name |
| **After Logging on Play** | |
| Subscriber's Recorded Name | Checked |
| Alternate Greeting Notification | Checked |
| **For New Messages Play** | |
| Message Count Totals | Checked |
| Voice Messages Counts | Checked |
| E-Mail Message Counts | Checked |
| Fax Counts | Checked |
| For Saved Messages Play | |
| Saved Message Count | Checked |
| **Before Playing Messages, Play** | |
| Message Type Menu | Unchecked |
| **New Message Play Order** | |
| Sort by message Type | Urgent VM, Normal VM, Urgent E-Mail, Normal E-Mail, Receipts and Notices |
| Then By | Oldest First |

*continues*

**Table 7-21** *Subscriber Template—Conversation Page for XYZ (Continued)*

| Saved Message Play Order | |
|---|---|
| Sort by Message Type | Urgent VM, Normal VM, Urgent E-Mail, Normal E-Mail, Receipts and Notices |
| Then By | Oldest First |
| **Before Playing Each Message, Play** | |
| Sender's Information | Checked |
| Message Number | Checked |
| Time the Message Was Sent | Checked |
| **After Playing Each Message, Play** | |
| Time the Message Was Sent | Unchecked |

## Call Transfer

The Call Transfer page allows you to configure how calls are handled when coming from the Unity AutoAttendant and going to the subscriber. To configure the Call Transfer page, click **Call Transfer** on the Subscriber Template page. The settings are explained here:

- **Transfer Incoming Calls to Subscriber's Phone?**—Choose Yes, Ring Subscriber's Extension to transfer incoming AA calls to that user's phone.

---

**NOTE**  The default option, No (Send Directly to Subscriber's Greeting), transfers calls to the user's greeting. It never rings the user's phone, so make sure to change this setting from its default value.

---

- **Transfer type**—Checking Supervise Transfer and specifying three rings causes Unity to keep control of the call when it is not answered within three rings.
- **If the call is busy**—Checking No Holding avoids taking up too many voice ports on the Unity system.
- **Gather calling information**—Checking boxes such as Ask Caller's Name and Confirm are useful in highly secured environments such as federal investigatory agencies and others. XYZ does not need these options, so they are not checked. Do not check Introduce unless it is for a call center environment, which is not relevant for XYZ.

Table 7-22 lists the Call Transfer page values selected for XYZ for all three types of subscriber templates (Emp_Template, Mgr_Template, and Sup_Template).

**Table 7-22** *Subscriber Template—Call Transfer Page for XYZ*

| Call Transfer Page | Value |
|---|---|
| **Transfer Incoming Calls to Subscriber's Phone?** | |
| No (Send Directly to Subscriber's Greeting) | No |
| Yes, Ring Subscriber's Extension | Yes |
| Yes, Ring Subscriber at This Number | No |
| **Transfer Type** | |
| Release to Switch | Unchecked |
| Supervise Transfer | Checked |
| Supervise Transfer Rings to Wait For | 3 |
| **If the Call Is Busy** | |
| Always Hold | Unchecked |
| No Holding | Checked |
| Ask Caller | Unchecked |
| **Gather Caller Information** | |
| Announce | Unchecked |
| Introduce (Call for *Name*) | Unchecked |
| Confirm (Call Can Be Accepted or Refused) | Unchecked |
| Ask Caller's Name | Unchecked |

## Greetings

Each subscriber can have up to five types of greetings. To configure the greetings, click **Greetings** on the Subscriber Template page.

The Greetings page allows you to configure the following settings for each greeting type:

- **Greeting**—Enables you to choose one of the available five types of greetings.
- **Status**—Enables you to disable or enable the selected greeting; for example, when you want to play the closed hours greeting on the active schedule as the working hours greeting, disable the 'closed' greeting. You cannot disable the standard greeting.
- **During Greeting (Allow/ Caller Input)**—By checking this option, you can control whether the user enters any digits, such as an extension number of a user or a digit to reach a call handler.

The settings for all the greetings are the same in XYZ for all three types of subscriber templates (Emp_Template, Mgr_Template, and Sup_Template).

Subscribers can enable any of the greetings, record the messages, and perform many other customizations to their mailboxes by accessing Cisco PCA. To access Cisco PCA from any web browser, enter the following URL:

http://*UNITY_SERVR_IP_ADDR*/ciscopca

As an example of the Cisco PCA interface, refer to Figure 7-5. Figure 7-15 shows the Greetings window in the Unity Assistant. Users can enable and record their greeting preferences from this page.

**Figure 7-15**   *Cisco PCA Unity Assistant: Greetings Page*

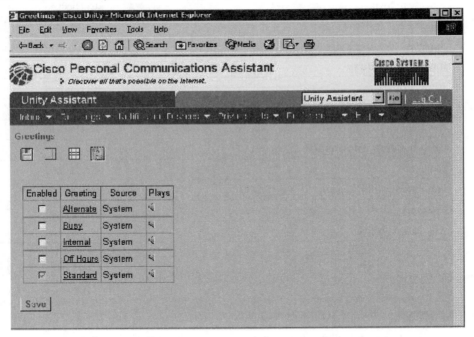

Standard Greeting   Standard Greeting is the default greeting that is played all the time until another greeting overwrites it. Table 7-23 shows the Standard Greeting page settings for XYZ. For Source, System is checked because every user of XYZ will be asked to record their own personal greeting. For general mailboxes, the system administrator will set this to Recording and record a corresponding greeting for this mailbox.

**Table 7-23**  *Subscriber Template—Greetings Page (Standard) for XYZ*

| Greeting Page (Standard) | Value |
|---|---|
| **Status** | |
| Enabled | Clicked |
| Disabled | Not Clicked |
| **Source** | |
| System | Clicked |
| Recording | Not Clicked |
| Blank | Not Clicked |
| **During Greeting** | |
| Allow Caller Input | Checked |
| **After Greeting** | |
| Take Message | Clicked |
| Send Caller To | Not Clicked |
| Reprompt User After This Many Seconds of Silence | Unchecked |
| Number of Times to Reprompt | Default |

**Closed Greeting**    Unity plays the Closed Greeting to callers after business hours. The period that is considered after business hours depends on the schedule configured in Unity, which you can check by clicking **Schedules** on the Cisco Unity SA page. The Closed Greeting overrides the Standard Greeting. XYZ has the Closed Greeting disabled.

**Busy Greeting**    The Busy Greeting is played to callers when the extension is busy, such as when a user is on another call. Because XYZ has flexible hours for its employees, the Busy Greeting is disabled.

**Internal Greeting**    Unity plays the Internal Greeting for internal users only. For example, the Internal Greeting is played when an employee calls another employee and the called employee is not available to answer the call. This greeting is disabled for XYZ.

**Alternate Greeting**    Subscribers can use the Alternate Greeting to announce to callers their out-of-office notification greeting when they go on vacation or are away from the office for a long time. You should leave the Alternate Greeting disabled when you create user accounts. The Alternate Greeting overrides all other greetings.

Table 7-24 shows the Alternate Greeting settings configured for XYZ.

**Table 7-24**  *Subscriber Template—Greeting Page (Alternate) for XYZ*

| Greeting Page (Alternate) | Value |
|---|---|
| **Status** | |
| Enabled | Clicked |
| Disabled | Not Clicked |
| **Source** | |
| System | Not Clicked |
| Recording | Clicked |
| Blank | Not Clicked |
| **During Greeting** | |
| Allow Caller Input | Checked |
| **After Greeting** | |
| Take Message | Clicked |
| Send Caller To | Not Clicked |
| Reprompt the User After This Many Seconds of Silence | Unchecked |
| Number of Times to Reprompt | Default |

## Caller Input

The Caller Input page options allow callers to enter the digits during the greeting. Unity forwards the calls to a call handler or to any other configured action. Users cannot configure these menu options. Only an administrator has access to configure the keys. To configure the Caller Input page, click **Caller Input** on the Subscriber Template page. Table 7-25 gives the settings configured for XYZ.

The settings for the Caller Input page are the same in XYZ for all three types of subscriber templates (Emp_Template, Mgr_Template, and Sup_Template).

**Table 7-25**  *Subscriber Template—Caller Input Page for XYZ*

| Caller Input Page | Value |
|---|---|
| Allow Callers to Dial an Extension During Greeting | Checked |
| Milliseconds to Wait for Additional Digits | 1500 |

## Messages

The settings on the Messages page (click **Messages** on the Subscriber Template page) allow you to set the following options:

- **Maximum Message Length**—Limits the length of the message that an outside caller can leave to a subscriber, created with this subscriber template. Note that this option is different from the one of the same name that appears in the **Class of Service > Messages** page that controls the length of the message that a subscriber can leave for another subscriber.

- **After Message Action**—Designates a subsequent action after an outside caller leaves a message to a subscriber. The default action is to send a Say Goodbye call handler. You also have an option to send the call to any other configured call handler. Leave this setting at its default value.

- **Callers Can Edit Messages**—Allows outside callers to review and re-record their messages.

- **Mark Messages as Urgent**—The options under this setting determine whether a caller can mark the message as urgent. Many implementations choose the Ask Callers for Their Preference option to allow a caller to make a decision.

- **Language that Callers Hear**—The Inherited option means the language that the caller hears is based on the call handler that receives the call for XYZ. This will be Australian English, but the Inherited option allows users to select different languages when they are installed in the future.

- **Use MWI for Message Notification**—Choose Use MWI for Message Notification, and as MWI Extension, configure the value 'X' to allow integration with CallManager for all extensions in the system.

Table 7-26 shows the Messages page settings for XYZ for all three types of subscriber templates (Emp_Template, Mgr_Template, and Sup_Template).

**Table 7-26** *Subscriber Template—Messages Page for XYZ*

| Messages Page | Value |
|---|---|
| Taking Messages from Outside Callers | |
| Maximum Message Length, in Seconds | 300 |
| **After Message Action** | |
| Say Goodbye | Clicked |
| Send Caller To (Select the Call Handler) | Not Clicked |
| Callers Can Edit Messages | Checked |
| **Mark Messages as Urgent?** | |
| Always | Not Clicked |
| Never | Not Clicked |

*continues*

**Table 7-26** *Subscriber Template—Messages Page for XYZ (Continued)*

| Messages Page | Value |
|---|---|
| **Mark Messages as Urgent?** | |
| Ask Caller for Their Preference | Clicked |
| Language that Callers Hear | Inherited |
| **Message Waiting Indicators (MWIs)** | |
| Use MWI for Message Notification | Checked |
| Extension | X (The default value is X) |

### Distribution Lists

The Distribution Lists page allows you to select public distribution lists to which the newly created users who have this template are added. To configure distribution lists, click **Distribution Lists** on the Subscriber Template page.

Table 7-27 shows the settings for the Distribution Lists page in XYZ for all three types of subscriber templates (Emp_Template, Mgr_Template, and Sup_Template). Note that the settings here are different for different classes of users. Users are added to different distribution lists based on their level in the company.

**Table 7-27** *Subscriber Template—Distribution Lists Page for XYZ*

| Distribution Lists Page | Value for Emp_Template | Value for Mgr_Template | Value for Sup_Template |
|---|---|---|---|
| Distribution Lists the Users Get Added To | All Subscribers – Unity<br>Employees-DL<br>Australia-Users-DL | All Subscribers – Unity<br>Managers-DL<br>Australia-Users-DL | All Subscribers – Unity<br>Employees-DL<br>Australia-Users-DL |

As you can see in Table 7-27, all users are added to three distribution lists. The managers are added to a separate distribution list. This allows the top executives in the company to address their voice mails to all managers.

In addition to the preceding distribution lists, three other distribution lists are created: SydneyEmp-DL, MelbourneEmp-DL, and BrisbaneEmp-DL. Subscribers working in the respective branches are assigned to the corresponding distribution lists. This is helpful if you want to limit the directory searches to a particular branch. (Refer to the "Multiple Directory Handlers" section later in this chapter for more information.)

Before you add users to the preceding distribution lists, the administrator has to create the distribution lists from the Cisco Unity SA page (by clicking **Public Distribution Lists**). If you are deploying Unity in Unified Messaging mode, you can use the distribution lists that are already created in the AD/Exchange environment.

## Message Notification

The Message Notification page settings allow subscribers to configure various destinations, such as their home phone or pager, as notification devices on which they should be notified about the arrival of new voice mail. To configure the Message Notification page, click **Message Notification** on the Subscriber Template page.

With XYZ, you do not need to configure the Message Notification page, because all users of XYZ will be encouraged to select their work phone as the main notification device from the Cisco PCA application. This will result in (toll-free) internal calls that do not need public PSTN connectivity. This is a per-user setting (each user has their own personal phone number); therfore, these parameters are left blank in the profiles.

## Account Policy

The settings that you make on the Account Policy page (accessed by clicking **Account Policy** on the Cisco Unity SA page) determine telephone password restrictions and account lockout policies.

Each of these parameters indicates the setting that influences the security of the Unity system. These settings affect only telephone access to the subscriber's account for the Unity system—that is, how they gain access to their Unity voice mailbox over the telephone. The settings have no effect on account policy for accessing the user pages, for example (AD passwords). Changes made on these pages take effect immediately.

## Phone Password Restrictions

The options on the Phone Password Restrictions page allow you to configure restrictions on the phone's password, such as the length of the password, the password age, and so forth. Choose the appropriate values based on your company's password policy. To set phone password restrictions, click **Phone Password Restrictions** on the Account Policy page.

Table 7-28 lists the Phone Password Restrictions page options selected for XYZ.

**Table 7-28**  *Account Policy—Phone Password Restrictions Page for XYZ*

| Phone Password Restrictions Page | Value |
|---|---|
| **Maximum Phone Password Age** | |
| Password Never Expires | Not Clicked |
| Days until Password Expires | 30 |
| **Phone Password Length** | |
| Permit blank Password | Not Clicked |
| Minimum Number of Characters in Password | 5 |

*continues*

**Table 7-28** *Account Policy—Phone Password Restrictions Page for XYZ (Continued)*

| Phone Password Restrictions Page | Value |
|---|---|
| **Phone Password Uniqueness** | |
| Do Not Keep Password History | Clicked |
| Number of Passwords to Remember | Not Clicked |
| Check Against Trivial Passwords for Extra Security | Clicked |

### Phone Lockout Policies

The options on the Phone Lockout Policies page allow you to configure the lockout policy that prevents the user from logging into the voice-mail system via the TUI after making a certain number of unsuccessful login attempts. This page also enables you to configure when to reset or change the lockout policy and other options. To set phone lockout policies, click **Phone Lockout Policies** on the Account Policy page.

Table 7-29 lists the options selected for XYZ. As you can see, the lockout policy is set to Forever after three invalid attempts. Users are required to contact the support group staff and identify themselves to get the account unlocked.

**Table 7-29** *Account Policy—Phone Lockout Policies Page for XYZ*

| Phone Lockout Policies Page | Value |
|---|---|
| No Account Lockout | Not Clicked |
| Account Lockout | Clicked |
| Lock Account After # Invalid Attempt | 3 |
| Reset Count After # Minutes | 60 |
| **Lockout Duration** | |
| Forever (Until the System Administrator Unlocks the Account) | Clicked |
| Minutes | Not Clicked |

## Subscribers

The Subscribers page allows you to create the subscribers in the Unity system. In a large-scale deployment, use the Unity Bulk Import Tool shipped with Unity to create users in bulk. All the Unity tools are accessible from the Unity server via the Cisco Unity Tools Depot. To configure subscribers, click **Subscribers** under the Subscribers category (not under the Reports category) on the Cisco Unity SA page.

The next few sections explain the different fields that you can modify when you are creating a single user, such as password settings, notification devices, and so forth.

**NOTE**    Many of the settings on the various pages under the Subscribers page, such as Profile page, Account page, Phone Password page, and Conversation page, are the same as those that appear on the Subscriber Template > Profile page, discussed earlier in the "Subscriber Template" section. The values for the fields within these pages default to the values that are configured on the Subscriber Template page. Therefore, this section and the following sections explain only the fields that are new.

**NOTE**    To create multiple users who share many common settings, apply a subscriber template. After you create the users, you can change these common settings on a per-user basis. Keep in mind that changing the settings in the template affects the newly created user accounts. User accounts that were created earlier keep all the settings of the template before it was changed. You can rely on bulk change tools (such as the Bulk Edit Tool available in the Cisco Unity Tools Depot) for mass changes.

## Profile

To set the subscriber profiles, click **Profile** on the Subscribers page. The following list explains the additional parameters for XYZ on this Profile page that do not appear on the Profile page for subscriber templates:

- **Extension**—Enter the proper four-digit extension for this user.
- **Fax-ID**—Leave this field empty, because faxes are not an offered service within XYZ.
- **Recorded Voice**—That is used for the end user to record their spoken name.
- **Unity Node Serial Number**—This was assigned during the Analog OctelNet Protocol setup.
- **Legacy Mailbox ID**—This was used before the Sydney users who were on the Octel system.

## Account (Defaults to the Template Settings)

The Account page allows the Unity administrators or support tier 1 group staff to see whether the subscriber phone and Unity GUI account are locked or unlocked. They can unlock the account if the user account has been locked because of too many unsuccessful login attempts. To configure the account, click **Account** on the Subscribers page.

## Phone Password (Defaults to the Template Settings)

The options on this Phone Passwords page are similar to the options that are available on the Passwords page under the Subscriber Template menu option on the SA page. The only difference is that this Phone Passwords page allows administrators to reset the phone password if the user forgets their password. To configure the password options, click **Phone Password** on the Subscribers page.

## Private Lists

The Private Lists page is not available in the Subscriber Template page. Private lists, unlike public distribution lists, are personal to individual users and are not accessible to users other than the owner. Through the Private Lists page, administrators can create private distribution lists for high-profile users. To configure private lists, click **Private Lists** on the Subscribers page.

As an example of how to configure the Private Lists page, the following shows the settings for the direct staff of the CEO of XYZ:

- **Name of List**—CEO direct staff.
- **Recorded Name**—Record the name as "CEO direct staff."
- **Members**—Add members to the list who are part of this group.

Everyone who has access to the CEO's mailbox can add members to or create members for this list. The CEO can also access the web-based Cisco PCA. In addition, users can create private lists through Cisco PCA.

## Conversation (Defaults to the Template Settings)

The settings on the Conversation page are the same as those described in Table 7-21 for the Conversation page available under the Subscriber Template menu option on the SA page. You can change the default conversation settings, created through the subscriber template, for a specific user based on the user's requirements. To configure the Conversation page, click **Conversation** on the Subscribers page.

## Call Transfer (Defaults to the Template Settings)

The settings on the Call Transfer page are the same as those described in Table 7-22 for the Call Transfer page available under the Subscriber Template menu option on the SA page. You can change the default call-transfer settings, created through the subscriber template, for a specific user based on the user's requirements. To configure the Call Transfer page, click **Call Transfer** on the Subscribers page.

## Greetings (Defaults to the Template Settings)

The settings on the Greetings page are the same as those described in Tables 7-23 and 7-24 for the Greetings page available under the Subscriber Template menu option on the SA page. You can change the default greeting settings, created through the subscriber template, for a specific user based on the user's requirements. Individual users can change or record their own greetings through the Cisco PCA interface, as shown in Figure 7-15. To set the greeting, click **Greetings** on the Subscribers page.

## Caller Input (Defaults to the Template Settings)

The settings on the Caller Input page are the same as those described in Table 7-25 for the Caller Input page available under the Subscriber Template menu option on the SA page. You can change the default caller input settings, created through the subscriber template, if a specific subscriber wants a specific call handler to act on an input key during the greeting (that has to be adapted accordingly). To access the Caller Input page, click **Caller Input** on the Subscribers page.

This feature can be implemented on a user-by-user basis, but it requires specific customization per mailbox, which can only be done by the administrator and is time-consuming (one-off solutions per user).

## Messages

The settings on the Messages page are the same as those described in Table 7-26 for the Messages page available under the Subscriber Template menu option on the SA page. You can change the default Messages settings created through the subscriber template. On a per user basis, you can customize any parameter related to a subscriber that is set through a Class of Service.

You can also synchronize the MWI lamp on the subscriber phone through this page. The default value of the MWI Extensions field is X, which lights the MWI lamp on the subscriber extension. If a subscriber needs to light the MWI lamp on a different phone or more than one phone whenever a new voice mail arrives, you can configure the list of such extensions on the Messages page. When you configure multiple extensions, Unity informs the phone system to send the MWI notifications to all the configured extensions. To configure the message settings, click **Messages** on the Subscribers page.

## Message Notification

The options on the Message Notification page allow subscribers to configure various message notification devices to notify them of new voice messages.

The Message Notification page also appears under the Subscriber Template menu option on the SA page. The best practice is to set the values on a per-user basis. Users can configure the message notification and add their devices via the web-based Cisco PCA interface. To set message notifications, click **Message Notification** on the Subscribers page.

With XYZ, all users are encouraged to select their work phone as the main notification device, because that will result in (free) internal calls only.

Table 7-30 shows various parameters on the Message Notification page.

**Table 7-30**  *Subscriber—Message Notification Page for XYZ*

| Message Notification Page | Value |
|---|---|
| **Notification Device** | |
| Work Phone | Selected |
| **Work Phone** | |
| Phone Number | Four-digit extension |
| Extra Digits | Leave blank |
| **Dialing Options** | |
| Try to Detect Connection | Checked |
| Seconds to Wait Before Dialing Extra Digits | Unchecked |
| **Status** | |
| Enabled | Clicked |
| Disabled | Not Clicked |
| **Notify Subscriber Of** | |
| All Messages, Only if Urgent | Unchecked, unchecked |
| Voice Messages, Only if Urgent | Checked, checked |
| Fax Messages, Only if Urgent | Unchecked, unchecked |
| E-Mail Messages, Only if Urgent | Unchecked, unchecked |
| **Notification Schedule** | |
| Working Days | Checked |
| 8AM-5PM | Checked |
| **Notification Options** | |
| Send initial Notification After How Many Minutes | 0 |
| Restart Notification Each Time a New Message Arrives | Clicked |
| Repeat Notification if There Are Still New Messages After This Many Minutes | Not Clicked |

**Table 7-30**   *Subscriber—Message Notification Page for XYZ (Continued)*

| Message Notification Page | Value |
|---|---|
| **Notification Options** | |
| If Device Does Not Answer | |
| Wait for How Many Rings Before Hanging Up | 4 |
| Try Again How Many Times | 10 |
| How Many Minutes to Wait Between Tries | 15 |
| **If Device Is Busy** | |
| Try Again How Many Times | 4 |
| How many minutes to wait between retries | 5 |
| If Notification Fails, Send Notification To | None |

## Alternate Extensions

Unity distinguishes between an internal caller (subscriber) and an external (outside) caller based on the CLID. When you call a Unity system from an internal extension, Unity prompts for the password. When called from an outside phone such as a cell phone or an extension that is not assigned to a subscriber in Unity, Unity plays an external greeting.

To configure Unity to recognize as an internal number other phone devices, such as a subscriber's cell phone or home phone number, and prompt for a PIN instead of playing the external greeting, configure such devices as alternate extensions. This saves time when an internal user is on business travel and wants to check their voice mail; they do not need to enter their extension number followed by a PIN to authorize to the Unity system. Unity automatically recognizes the phone number, provided the local telephone company presents the digits to Unity, and prompts for the password. Unity supports configuring up to nine unique alternate extensions per subscriber. To configure alternate extensions, click **Alternate Extensions** on the Subscribers page.

Follow these steps to add an alternate extension:

**Step 1**   Click the Add button.

**Step 2**   Check the Alternate Extensions check box.

**Step 3**   Enter the Extension—1234567890 (10-digit mobile phone number of the user).

When configuring alternate extensions for a subscriber, such as a cell phone number, you need to know how the PSTN delivers the subscriber number to the Unity system, and use the same number to configure the alternate extension.

## Public Distribution Lists

Clicking **Public Distribution Lists** on the Cisco Unity SA page enables you to create public distribution lists that every user of the Unity system can access. The following sections describe the options on the left side of the Public Distributions Lists page.

### Profile

The Profile page lets you create the public distribution list. To create distribution lists, click **Profile** on the Public Distribution Lists page. The following list describes some of the parameters on the Profile page:

- **Recorded voice**—Record a spoken name so that users receive confirmation when addressing a message to this list.

- **Extension**—Assign an extension that fits the dial plan. Use an extension that is a non-DID number. Subscribers can dial the extension number to address the message to this distribution list. The extension numbers must be unique throughout the Unity system.

- **Show Distribution List in E-Mail Server Address Book**—Choose this option to allow access/confirmation from Outlook.

Table 7-31 shows the settings for one distribution list for XYZ. Refer to Table 7-27 for a list of the distribution lists needed for XYZ. If you are deploying into an existing AD/Exchange network, you do not need to create new distribution lists. You can use the existing distribution lists in the AD/Exchange network.

**Table 7-31**  *Public Distribution Lists—Profile Page for XYZ*

| Profile Page | Value |
|---|---|
| Name | Employees-DL |
| Owner | Unity Installer Account |
| Owner Type | Subscriber |
| Recorded Voice | Record a spoken name |
| Extension (Optional) | 5001 |
| Show Distribution List in E-Mail Server Address Book | Checked |

### Members

The Members page allows you to add, delete, or verify the membership of users in a distribution list. To configure the members in a distribution list, click **Members** on the Public Distribution Lists page.

# Call Management

You can use the options under the Call Management category on the SA page to create different call handlers with specific functions. The most important and useful handlers are in effect by default and do not have to be created again. The Call Management category has the following subcategories available:

- Call Handlers
- Directory Handlers
- Interview Handlers
- Call Routing
- Restriction Tables

The next few sections discuss the subcategories used in deploying the Unity at XYZ, Inc.

## Call Handlers

Call handlers answer calls, greet callers with recorded prompts, provide callers with information and options, route calls, and take messages. Call handlers are a basic component of Cisco Unity and provide one-key routing through the Unity system. Your plan for call handlers can be simple, using only the predefined Cisco Unity call handlers, or you can create an unlimited number of new call handlers. To configure call handlers, click **Call Handlers** on the Cisco Unity SA page.

The following are three default call handlers that are preconfigured in Unity:

- **Opening Greeting**—Used with the Unity AA application
- **Operator**—Forwards the calls to the operator
- **Goodbye**—Unity says "Goodbye" and disconnects the call

Figure 7-16 shows the call management map required for XYZ. Before you design the call handlers, the best practice is to map the call flow, as shown in Figure 7-16.

**Figure 7-16** *Call Management Map for XYZ*

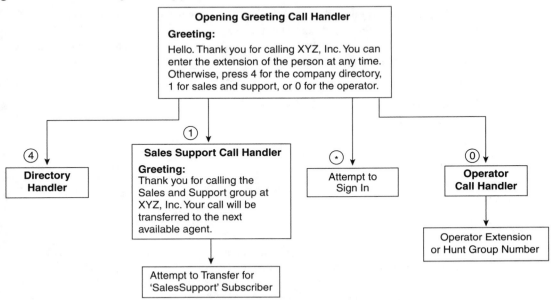

In Figure 7-16, when the external caller reaches the Unity AA application (that is the Opening Greeting call handler, the default), they have three choices:

- Press 1 to reach the sales and support group (call handler).

- Press 4 to reach the employee directory (directory handler).

- Press 0 to reach the operator. This operator extension can be a single phone number or the hunt group number (operator call handler).

- Press *, in which case Unity prompts for the extension number followed by the PIN. This option allows internal subscribers to check their voice mail. (This is the default.)

The steps required to configure the call management plan depicted in Figure 7-16 are as follows:

1  Create a new call handler named SalesSupport and record the call handler greeting.

2  Make the following modifications to the Opening Greeting call handler:

   a  Record a customized opening greeting to reflect the company name and options available to the caller (refer to Figure 7-16).

   b  Modify the caller input for the Opening Greeting call handler to accept the input for pressing the digit 1 and send the caller (all other keys are configured by default) to the SalesSupport call handler configured in step 1. When configuring the action, you should select Attempt to transfer for the SalesSupport option.

The sections that follow discuss the settings required for the SalesSupport call handler on the following pages, which are accessible from the Call Handlers page:

- Profile
- Call Transfer
- Greetings
- Caller Input
- Messages

## Profile

The Profile page allows you to create the new call handler. To access the Profile page, choose **Profile** on the Call Handlers page. Table 7-33 shows the settings required for the new call handler SalesSupport.

**Table 7-32** *Call Handlers—SalesSupport Profile Page for XYZ*

| Profile Page | Value |
| --- | --- |
| Name | SalesSupport |
| Owner | Unity Installer Account |
| Owner Type | Subscriber |
| Recorded Voice | Record the spoken name "Sales Support Call Handler" |
| Active Schedule | All Hours-All days |
| Extension | Leave blank |
| Language | Inherited |

## Call Transfer

The Call Transfer page options specify the call treatment for the call after it reaches the call handler. For the SalesSupport call handler, the call is transferred to the Call Handlers greeting. This option plays the SalesSupport Call Handler greeting before transferring the call to the Sales and Support personnel at XYZ.

For general call handlers, only the Standard condition has to be configured. If this call handler gets another setup during Alternate conditions, for example, also configure the Alternate parameters. To access the Call Transfer page, choose **Call Transfer** on the Call Handlers page.

Table 7-33 shows the parameters on the Call Transfer page for the SalesSupport call handler.

**Table 7-33** *Call Handlers—SalesSupport Call Transfer Page for XYZ*

| Call Transfer Page | Value |
|---|---|
| **Status** | |
| Enabled | Clicked |
| Disabled | Not Clicked |
| **Transfer Incoming Calls?** | |
| No (Send Directly to This Handlers Greeting) | Clicked |
| Yes, Message Recipients Extension | Not Clicked |
| Yes, Ring a Subscriber at This Extension | Not Clicked |
| **Transfer Type** | |
| Release to Switch | Clicked |
| Supervise Transfer | Not Clicked |

## Greetings

To access the Greetings page, choose **Greetings** on the Call Handlers page. The following list explains the parameters on the Greetings page:

- **Status**—Check Enabled for the greeting that is being configured here.
- **Select Source Recording**—The system administrator for Unity records a spoken name for this call handler, which callers who are connected to this call handler will hear. The recording is "Thank you for calling the Sales and Support group at XYZ, Inc. Your call will be transferred to the next available agent."
- **During Greeting**—Check Allow Caller Input.
- **After Greeting**—Choose the destination for the caller, after the greeting is heard:
  - **Take Message**—Select this option to allow to the caller to leave a message. Unity delivers the message to the subscriber or to a distribution list that is configured on the Messages page under the Call Handler page.
  - **Send Caller To**—This option allows moving toward another call/interview handler, subscriber or to the Hang Up handler, which disconnects the caller. With XYZ, the call has to be transferred to the Sales and Support group extension number. The Unity administrator will create a subscriber named "SalesSupport" with a specific assigned extension number, which can be a shared line on multiple user phones that are part of the Sales and Support group. When selecting SalesSupport, two options are available: Send to Greeting For and Attempt to Transfer For. Choosing Send to Greeting For will forward the call directly to the greeting instead of ringing the Sales Support group extension number.

Table 7-34 shows the Greetings page settings configured for the SalesSupport call handler.

**Table 7-34**   *Call Handlers—Greetings Page for XYZ*

| Greetings Page | Value |
|---|---|
| **Status** | |
| Enabled | Clicked |
| Disabled | Not Clicked |
| **Source** | |
| System | Not Clicked |
| Recording | Clicked |
| Blank | Not Clicked |
| **During Greeting** | |
| Allow Caller Input | Checked |
| **After Greeting** | |
| Take Message | Unchecked |
| Send Caller To | Checked, Subscriber *Attempt to transfer for* **"SalesSupport"** <br> This option rings the phone number for the Sales Support group. |
| Reprompt the User After This Many Seconds of Silence | Unchecked |
| Number of Times to Reprompt | Unchecked |

## Caller Input

The Caller Input page allows callers to enter digits during the greeting to transfer out of the call handler and reach another place in the CallManager tree. To access the Caller Input page, click **Caller Input** on the Call Handlers page.

Table 7-35 lists the values that need to be configured on the Caller Input page for the SalesSupport call handler. The other settings on this page are left to their default values. You can expand the tree depicted in Figure 7-16 to include more user options here.

**Table 7-35**   *Call Handlers—SalesSupport Caller Input Page for XYZ*

| Caller Input Page | Value |
|---|---|
| Allow Callers to Dial an Extension During Greeting | Checked |
| Milliseconds to Wait for Additional Digits | 1500 |

## Messages

The options configured on the Messages page are applicable only if the Take Message check box is checked on the **Call Handlers > Greetings** page (see Table 7-34). You can configure the subscriber mailbox or a public distribution list as a message recipient. The settings configured on the Messages page are not applicable for the call management plan depicted in Figure 7-16, because the call is transferred to the SalesSupport group extension.

To configure messages, click **Messages** on the Call Handlers page. Some of the parameters available on the Messages page are described next. Table 7-36 shows the settings required for XYZ:

- **Maximum Message Length**—Enables you to specify the length of the message that callers can leave for this call handler.
- **After Message Action**—Check Say Goodbye to have the line hang up after the message. It is also possible to select another call handler if applicable.
- **Callers Can Edit Messages**—Checking this option allows callers to review and rerecord their messages.
- **Mark Messages as Urgent**—Checking Ask Callers for Their Preference allows callers to mark their messages as urgent.

**Table 7-36**  *Call Handlers—Messages Page for XYZ*

| Messages Page | Value |
|---|---|
| Message Recipient | Subscriber or public distribution list |
| **How to Take Messages** | |
| Maximum Message Length in Seconds | 300 |
| **After Message Action** | |
| Say Goodbye | Clicked |
| Callers Can Edit Messages | Checked |
| **Mark Messages as Urgent?** | |
| Always | Not clicked |
| Never | Not clicked |
| Ask Caller for Their Preference | Clicked |

## Directory Handlers

The Directory Handler call handler allows callers to find a person who is present in the Unity directory. It is part of the Unity AA setup. It is also possible for XYZ to create customized directory handlers, which can be accessed from a certain extension number to limit or expand the search scope or to change the search options. Refer to the "Multiple Directory Handlers" section to see how to use various search options in a centralized call-processing and voice-mail messaging deployment to provide customized site-specific opening greetings and directory handlers.

To configure the directory handlers, click **Directory Handlers** from the SA page. The options on this page are described in the following sections.

## Profile

Unity creates a default directory handler that you can use without modifications. To access it, click **Directory Handlers > Profile** on the Call Handlers page. Table 7-37 shows the settings for the default directory call handler.

**Table 7-37**   *Directory Handler—Profile Page for XYZ*

| Profile Page | Value |
|---|---|
| Name | Choose a relevant name |
| Owner | Example Administrator |
| Owner Type | Subscriber |
| Recorded Voice | Directory Call Handler XYZ |
| Active Schedule | All Hours-All Days |
| Extension | Leave blank |
| Language | Inherited |
| Play All Names | Unchecked |

## Search Options

To access the Search Options page, click **Directory Handlers > Search Options** on the Call Handlers page. The following are the parameters on the Search Options page. The values for XYZ are shown in Table 7-38.

- **Search In**—Check Dialing Domain. (For XYZ, this is the same as selecting Local Server because XYZ does not define dialing domains.)
- **Search By**—Check Last Name/First Name.

**Table 7-38**   *Directory Handlers—Search Options Page for XYZ*

| Search Options Page | Value |
|---|---|
| **Search In** | |
| Local Cisco Unity Server Only | Not Clicked |
| Location | Not Clicked |

*continues*

**Table 7-38** *Directory Handlers—Search Options Page for XYZ (Continued)*

| Search Options Page | Value |
|---|---|
| **Search In** | |
| Class Of Service | Not Clicked |
| Dialing Domain | Clicked |
| Public Distribution List | Not Clicked |
| **Search By** | |
| First Name/Last Name | Not Clicked |
| Last Name/First Name | Clicked |

## Match List Options

The Match List Options page settings specify whether, on a unique match, Cisco Unity routes the caller to the extension automatically or first asks the caller to confirm the match. This page also specifies how Cisco Unity presents directory matches to callers—either by stating the extensions ("for Ramesh Kaza, press 321; for Jon Doe, press 234...") or by offering a menu of choices ("for Ramesh Kaza, press 1; for Jon Doe, press 2..."). Table 7-39 lists the settings used for XYZ. To configure the Match List Options page, click **Directory Handlers > Match List Options** on the Call Handlers page.

**Table 7-39** *Directory Handlers—Match List Options Page for XYZ*

| Match List Options Page | Value |
|---|---|
| **On a Unique Match** | |
| Route Automatically | Not Clicked |
| Request Caller Input First | Clicked |
| **Announce Matched Names Using** | |
| Extension Format | Not Clicked |
| Menu Format | Clicked |
| Announce Extension with Each Name | Not Clicked |

The Caller Input page settings specify what Cisco Unity should do if the user does not enter digits and the expiration time for entering a digit. To configure caller input settings, click **Directory Handlers > Caller Input** on the Call Handlers page. Table 7-40 lists the settings configured for XYZ.

**Table 7-40**   *Directory Handlers—Caller Input Page for XYZ*

| Caller Input Page | Value |
|---|---|
| Timeout if No Input, in Seconds | 5 |
| Timeout After Last Input, in Seconds | 4 |
| Times to Repeat Name Entry Prompt | 1 |
| **If Caller Exists, Send To** | |
| Call Handler | Choose the appropriate call handler, such as the Opening Greeting |

## Interview Handlers

Interview handlers provide a list of questions to an outside caller and, after each list, a beep tone that allows a response. This response is sent to the mailbox or a public distribution list specified in the configuration. Note that the questions are not recorded with the answers, so the only thing that is going to be received by the mailbox recipient is a list of answers without the questions. To configure interview handlers, click **Interview Handlers** on the Call Handlers page.

XYZ is not going to create customized interview handlers to collect customer information for incoming calls, either during or after business hours. Its experience is that collecting information from customers via the phone is not always reliable. For example, if a customer calls using a cell phone and has a bad connection, the customer might leave his name and phone number, but it might not be audible to XYZ, preventing a follow-up call to the customer; thus, the customer will think that XYZ has not returned his call, resulting in an unhappy customer.

## Call Routing

The Call Routing page information is used to direct calls into the system. There is a difference between direct calls into the system and calls that are forwarded from an employee's station because they did not answer the phone. These two types of calls are described next. To access call-routing information, click **Call Routing** on the Call Handlers page.

### Direct Calls

If you make a call from a subscriber phone to the Unity system, Unity treats that call as a direct call. To configure direct calls, click **Call Routing > Direct Calls** from the SA page.

The default settings are not changed for XYZ. The following call handlers handle users dialing into the main Unity access number:

- **Attempt Sign-In**—The system will try to associate the caller with a subscriber on the system.
- **Default Call Handler**—This connects the call to the opening greeting to allow AA functionality, sign-in from a nonsubscriber phone, and so forth.

### Forwarded Calls

Forwarded calls are calls that are forwarded to the Unity system after a caller has dialed a subscriber's extension but the subscriber hasn't picked up. This type of call is directed to the call handlers that are specified in the Forwarded Calls page. (Click **Call Routing > Forwarded Calls** from the SA page.)

The following default settings for the forwarded calls are not changed for XYZ:

- **Attempt Forward to Greeting**—The system will try to associate the called party with a subscriber and play back the corresponding greeting to the calling party.

- **Default Call Handler**—This connects the caller to the opening greeting to allow AA functionality, connection to the operator, and so on.

## Restriction Tables

Settings for the Restriction Tables page are the same as those discussed in the "Restriction Tables" section, earlier in the chapter, with regard to the Class of Service option on the SA page. Refer to that section for more information.

# Network

The Network category on the SA page includes the configuration pages for the following subcategories:

- Primary Location
- Delivery Locations
- Amis Options
- Bridge Options

Configuring the various settings available on these configuration pages is required to enable the networking feature in Unity. To access the Network menu, click **Network** on the SA page.

## Primary Location

Locations are Cisco Unity entities that contain the addressing information needed by Unity to send and receive messages, for any transport mechanism in use. Each Unity server is associated with one location (referred to as the default or primary location), which is created during installation and cannot be deleted. The primary location uniquely identifies the Unity server. Creation of additional delivery locations is required when setting up a Unity bridge. To configure primary locations, click **Primary Location** on the Network page.

All the subscribers of XYZ from Sydney are identified with the Unity server in Sydney through this primary location. The next sections cover the following configuration options in the Primary Location subcategory:

- Profile
- Addressing Options

## Profile

Table 7-41 shows the settings on the Profile page (click **Primary Location > Profile** on the SA page) for XYZ. The Dial ID is used to call anyone in Australia from any other XYZ site in the world. Recording the spoken name for the Sydney site is important because when you are in a later phase, multiple sites are online. This allows the users from San Jose to hear confirmation when addressing a message to a user in Sydney that they are really addressing a message to the subscriber who resides on the Sydney system. The SMTP domain name is used if Unity is networked with other Unity systems or with other voice-mail systems via SMTP or VPIM.

**Table 7-41**   *Primary Location—Profile Page for XYZ*

| Profile Page | Value |
| --- | --- |
| Display Name | Sydney |
| Dial ID | 611 |
| Recorded Name | The system administrator will record a spoken name |
| Dialing Domain | XYZ |
| SMTP Domain Name | XYZ.com |

## Addressing Options

The primary location addressing options allow you to control the scope of the search that Cisco Unity performs when searching for a matching extension when a subscriber addresses a message. To access this page, click **Primary Location > Addressing Options** on the Network SA page.

Because XYZ intends to move toward a networked Unity system for its worldwide operation in the future, the settings in Table 7-42 were chosen to allow maximum flexibility to the users who are addressing messages across the different sites. XYZ has only one dialing domain (no partitioning) because every user has a unique extension number across the globe. With that set, the Limit Searches To setting can indicate Dialing Domain instead of Global Directory.

**Table 7-42** *Primary Location—Addressing Options Page for XYZ*

| Addressing Options Page | Value |
|---|---|
| **Subscriber Searches** | |
| Limit Searches To | Dialing Domain |
| Include Locations in Searches | Checked |
| **Blind Addressing** | |
| Allowed Locations | Dialing Domain |

## Delivery Locations

Delivery locations are Cisco Unity objects that contain the addressing information that Cisco Unity needs to send messages to and receive messages from other voice-mail systems. The other voice-mail systems might or might not be Unity. One delivery location is required that corresponds to each remote messaging system that the local Cisco Unity server communicates with. To access the Delivery Locations page, click **Delivery Locations** on the SA page.

XYZ requires one delivery location for the Unity system to communicate with the Octel system in San Jose via Unity Bridge networking. To configure the delivery location destination type Bridge, the Unity system must have the Bridge Option license.

The next sections cover the following configuration options in the Delivery Location subcategory:

- Profile
- Prefixes
- Subscriber Creation

### Profile

The Profile page defines the remote Octel system for the local Australian users. The DialID before the four-digit extension number to address a message to a San Jose user is 152, and the mailbox length is four digits (so that the Octel system receives the last four digits only). To access the Profile page, click **Delivery Locations > Profile** on the SA page. The values for XYZ are listed in Table 7-43.

The Remote Mailbox Length field is not relevant for XYZ, as explained in the next section, "Prefixes."

**Table 7-43** *Delivery Locations—Profile Page for XYZ*

| Profile Page | Value |
|---|---|
| Display Name | San Jose |
| Dial ID | 152 |
| Destination Type | Bridge |
| Octel Node Serial Number | 24555 |
| Bridge Full Computer Name | Bridge |
| Remote Mailbox Length | N/A |
| Recorded Name | The system administrator will record a spoken name "San Jose Octel Voice-Mail Server" |

## Prefixes

Because XYZ has a well-planned dial plan, the Prefixes option is not important here. There is a unique Dial ID for the San Jose destination from the Australian Unity system. you do not need to decouple the Octel dial plan from the Unity/Bridge dial plan.

If there is an overlap in the voice-mail dial plan Dial ID, prefixes can help in setting up network messaging. The Remote Mailbox Length in the Profile page settings is optional when not using Dial ID but is mandatory when Dial ID is used.

For XYZ, the situation is as follows:

* **Sydney**—Dial ID = 611, mailbox length is four digits
* **San Jose**—Dial ID = 152, mailbox length is four digits

To configure prefixes, click **Delivery Locations > Prefixes** on the SA page.

## Subscriber Creation

The Subscriber Creation page settings are applied to all auto-created subscribers on the Bridge that represent users on the Octel system in San Jose. These settings reflect how Octel text names that do not contain commas should be parsed into first and last names for auto-created Bridge subscribers. Unity stores the first name and last name in two different fields, which allows users to search based on either first or last name, whereas Octel stores the name in a single field. Therefore, when you are creating the subscribers in the Bridge, the Bridge system must know how to treat the single name received from Octel.

The system administrator for the Unity system must talk to the service organization that is managing the Octel system before arriving at the settings required for the Subscriber Creation page. To access this page, click **Delivery Locations > Subscriber Creation** on the SA page.

Table 7-44 shows the Subscriber Creation page settings used for the San Jose Octel delivery location for XYZ.

**Table 7-44**  *Delivery Locations—Subscriber Creation Page for XYZ*

| Subscriber Creation Page | Value |
| --- | --- |
| **Bridge Subscriber Auto-Creation, If the Octel Text Name Has No Comma:** | |
| Treat as "FirstName LastName" <br><br> If the Octel system sends the name as "Ramesh Kaza," the Bridge creates a subscriber with First Name = Ramesh and Last Name = KAZA | Clicked |
| **Mapping Octel Text Names to Cisco Unity Bridge Subscriber Names** | |
| Mapping Octel Text Names Directly to Cisco Unity Bridge Subscriber Display Names | Clicked |
| Include Location Dial ID in Primary Extension on Auto-Created Bridge Subscribers | Checked |

## Bridge Options

The settings that are configured on the Bridge Options page apply to all auto-created Bridge subscribers created on the Bridgehead server. These options include the following:

- Subscriber Creation
- Synchronization
- Unknown Caller

To access the Bridge settings, click **Bridge Options** on the SA page.

### Subscriber Creation

Because the Unity environment fully integrates within the AD forest, all employees of XYZ are known in the AD environment. That is why XYZ is not going to do an auto-creation or modification of users who reside on the Octel system. In addition, by not allowing changes automatically, it is easier to keep the environment under control. This is a good idea, because AD is the backbone for all other IT-related infrastructure.

The only thing that is not available in AD is the spoken name option, because that gets stored on the local Octel server in San Jose. Retrieving those names is advantageous. The users from Sydney, when addressing a message to somebody in San Jose, will hear name confirmation by the voice of the addressed person.

These names are exchanged via the NameNet protocol as part of the analog OctelNet communication between the Bridge and the Octel server in San Jose. Table 7-45 lists the

Subscriber Creation page settings (click **Bridge Options > Subscriber Creation** on the SA page) that are used to create the subscribers for XYZ.

**Table 7-45**    *Bridge Options—Subscriber Creation Page for XYZ*

| Subscriber Creation Page | Value |
|---|---|
| **Bridge Server Subscriber Creation Options** | |
| Subscriber Template | San Jose Octel Subscribers |
| Allow Automatic Creation of Bridge Subscribers | Unchecked |
| Allow Automatic Deletion of Bridge Subscribers | Unchecked |
| Allow Automatic Modification of Bridge Subscribers Names | Unchecked |
| Allow Automatic Modification of Bridge Subscriber Recorded Voice Name | Checked |

## Synchronization

At this point in the Unity system configuration, the system administrator of XYZ will see the node-id (27975) and the name of the Bridge. When you click the Synchronize button, the information for all Unity subscribers who are currently configured on the server will be sent to the Bridge and can be used in a consecutive NameNet session with the Octel server in San Jose.

Under normal circumstances, when you are initially creating all the Unity subscribers and then creating the Unity node on the Bridge, forced directory synchronization is not necessary. To access the Synchronization page, click **Bridge Options > Synchronization** on the SA page.

## Unknown Caller

Because Bridge subscribers are not listed in the phone directory, this information is not relevant to XYZ. To access these settings, click **Bridge Options > Unknown Caller** on the SA page.

# System

The System category, accessed by clicking **Reports > System** on the Cisco Unity SA page, includes general settings to configure and administer the Unity system, available on these pages:

- Configuration
- Schedules
- Holidays
- Licensing

- Authentication
- Integration
- Ports

## Configuration

Configuration settings contain general Cisco Unity settings such as the default schedule, system security, and the cleanup interval for log files, in addition to information about the Cisco Unity server.

To access these settings, click **Configuration** on the SA page.

### Settings

The Settings page options allow you to set basic schedules and to specify the number of days to keep the log and report files. Understanding these settings is important, because higher values require larger amounts of available hard disk space. The Settings page also displays the available hard disk space on all the configured drives in the Unity system.

Enabling the RSA (Rivest-Shamir-Adelman) factor increases the security when accessing the voice mail through the TUI. By checking the RSA Two Factor check box, Unity contacts an external authentication server before granting the access to the phone user.

To access the Settings page, choose **Configuration > Settings** on the SA page. Table 7-46 shows the settings used for XYZ.

**Table 7-46** *Configuration—Settings Page for XYZ*

| Settings Page | Value |
|---|---|
| Default Schedule | Weekdays |
| Use 24-Hour Time Format for Conversation and Schedules | Unchecked |
| Enable Spell Name Search | Checked |
| RSA Two Factor | Unchecked |
| Display Fields Required for Cisco Unity Bridge Networking on Subscribers Profile Page | Unchecked |
| Subscribers Are Identified as Message Senders Only if They Log On | Unchecked |
| Cleanup Interval for Logger Data Files, in Days | 7 |
| Cleanup Interval for Logger Diagnostic Files, in Days | 7 |
| Cleanup Interval for Reports Files, in Days | 7 |

## Software Version

The Software Version page displays the current Unity version and the versions of other software components within the Unity system. This information is useful when working with the Cisco Technical Assistance Center (TAC) to resolve issues. To access this page, choose **Configuration > Software Version** on the SA page.

## Recordings

The parameters on the Recordings page allow you to configure various recording features. The DTMF Clip Length setting indicates how much to truncate at the end of a recording when a message is terminated with a touchtone. To access this page, choose **Configuration > Recordings** on the SA page.

Table 7-47 shows the other settings used in XYZ.

**Table 7-47**  *Configuration—Recordings Page for XYZ*

| Recordings Page | Value |
|---|---|
| DTMF Clip Length, Allowed Time for Recording in msec | 170 |
| Record Short Trail Limit, Allowed Time for Short Recording in Seconds | 10 |
| Before a Recording, Allow How Much Silence Before Timeout in Seconds | 5 |
| During a Recording, Discard Any Recording Less Than, in Seconds | 2 |
| **Stop Recording After How Many Seconds of Silence** | |
| Short Recording (Short Recording Trail Limit or Less) in Seconds | 3 |
| Long Recording (Long Recording Trail Limit or Less) in Seconds | 5 |

## Contacts

The Contacts page lets you put in the name and phone numbers of the person who is responsible for maintaining the Unity system. This helps the support tier 1 group users to contact the Unity system administrators if required. To access this page, choose **Configuration > Contacts** on the SA page.

Table 7-48 lists various settings available on the Contacts page and the settings used for XYZ.

**Table 7-48**  *Configuration—Contacts Page for XYZ*

| Contacts Page | Value |
|---|---|
| Site Name | XYZ, Inc. |
| Cisco Unity Administrator | Mr. John D |
| Customer Contact | Mr. Kane C |
| Customer Phone Number | xxx-xxx-xxxx |
| Alternate Contact | Mr. Don G |
| Alternate Phone Number | Yyy-yyy-yyyy |

## Phone Languages

Unity uses one of the loaded languages for doing phone conversations with the user. If you have multiple languages loaded on the Unity system, you can specify the user's phone language preference on the **Subscriber Template > Conversation** page.

The Phone Languages page displays available languages based on the language licenses purchased. If you do not see the language that you expect to use, ensure that you have purchased the license to use that language. To access this page, choose **Configuration > Phone Languages** on the SA page.

Table 7-49 shows the phone language settings used at XYZ.

**Table 7-49**   *Configuration—Phone Languages Page for XYZ*

| Phone Languages Page | Value |
| --- | --- |
| Loaded Phone Languages | Australian English |
| Default Phone Language | Australian English |
| Default Test-To-Speech Language | Australian English |

## GUI Languages

The GUI Languages page settings determine the language page used to display the Cisco Unity Administration window and other applications, such as Cisco PCA. To access this page, choose **Configuration > GUI Languages** on the SA page.

Table 7-50 shows the GUI Languages page settings used at XYZ.

**Table 7-50**   *Configuration—GUI Languages Page for XYZ*

| GUI Languages Page | Value |
| --- | --- |
| Load GUI Language | Australian English |
| Default GUI Language | Australian English |

## Schedules

Because XYZ will have All Hours – All Day schedule settings, it will leave the Schedules page settings to the defaults. In the future, when working hours become more fixed, Out-of-Office and Closed conditions will be used for certain greetings. The future schedule changes will be made accordingly. To access this page, click **Schedules** on the SA page.

## Holidays

The system administrator inputs all public holidays for the upcoming year on the Holiday page. System administrators should put a reminder on their calendar to update this page at the beginning of each year. By default, the Unity system has only January 1 and December 25 configured as holidays.

Unity checks the Holidays page data entered with the current system date. If a caller calls into the Unity system on one of the holidays, the Unity system plays the Closed Greeting. To set the holidays, click **Holidays** on the SA page.

Table 7-51 lists the holidays observed at XYZ.

**Table 7-51**    *Holidays Observed at XYZ Australian Office*

| Month | Day | Year | Comments |
|-------|-----|------|----------|
| January | 1 | 2005 | New Year |
| January | 26 | 2005 | Australia Day |
| March | 25 | 2005 | Good Friday |
| April | 25 | 2005 | Anzac Day |
| December | 25 | 2005 | Christmas |
| December | 26 | 2005 | Boxing Day |

## Licensing

The information on the Licensing page displays the number of licenses purchased (Licensed Features) that allow the use of certain features, such as multiple languages. It also displays the number ports and so forth.

System administrators need to monitor this page to upgrade the licensees, if the system is getting close to its maximum allowed licenses. To access this page, click **Licensing** on the SA  page.

## Authentication

Subscribers need to supply the Windows logon account information to successfully access the Cisco PCA. The Windows logon information is stored in the subscriber's computer as encrypted cookies in the browser cache.

You can avoid storing this information on the subscriber's computer to prevent unauthorized access to Unity Active Assistant. More importantly, you can prevent unauthorized access to the Unity SA interface by configuring the Unity system not to remember the logons, as shown in Table 7-52. To access this page, click **Authentication** on the SA page.

**Table 7-52**    *Security Measures Through System—Authentication Page at XYZ*

| Authentication Page | Value |
| --- | --- |
| **Cisco Unity Administrator and Status Monitor Settings** | |
| Remember Logons For | Unchecked |
| Remember Passwords For | Unchecked |
| Session Duration | 0 Seconds |
| Disallow Blank Password | Checked |
| **Cisco Unity Administrator and Status Monitor Lockout Policies** | |
| Lockout Account Status | Checked |
| Accounts Are Locked Out For | 60 Minutes |
| Accounts Will Lock Out After | 3 Attempts |
| Reset Account Lockout Counter After | 60 Minutes |

## Integration

The Integration page (click **Integration** on the SA page) displays the Unity integration settings with other systems. The Cisco CallManager option is a read-only window that indicates the Cisco CallManager settings as they relate to Unity. The information on this page is useful when troubleshooting the Unity integration with Cisco CallManager.

The other options for Session Initiation Protocol (SIP) and Circuit-Switched Integration are grayed out if Unity has no such integrations, which is the case with XYZ.

## Ports

Ports or sessions are a licensed feature in Unity. The ports are used not only to accept incoming calls, but also to light the MWI lamp on the IP Phone headset, to send notification about new voice mails to subscribers who configured the Message Notification settings, and to handle outgoing transfers. Therefore, the Unity system administrator must distribute the licensed ports based on the calling needs of the organization. Consider the following factors when distributing the ports:

- Number of subscribers who use the message notification feature and the frequency of the notifications
- Business dependency on the voice-mail system

The extension numbers that are displayed on the Ports page are the voice-mail port numbers configured in the CallManager server. Both should match.

In the Sizing Unity Ports and Sessions sections described earlier in this chapter, XYZ requires a 32-port Unity system. The secondary Unity server will also have 32 ports configured with the same extension numbers. To configure the ports, click **Ports** on the SA page.

The approach followed in distributing the Unity ports for XYZ is as follows:

- Because XYZ employees (other than the executive team) rely heavily on e-mail and less on voice-mail messaging, a ratio of 27:5 (roughly 20 percent) is used to determine the number of ports assigned to incoming/outgoing traffic.

- Twenty-eight ports are dedicated for answering calls.

- The other four ports are used for outgoing traffic, so the Enabled, Message Notification, Dialout MWI, and Trap Connection check boxes are checked.

- The system administrator always assigns the last four ports to calls that have to go out from Unity to the CallManager; this is to avoid as much as possible clashes between an incoming call and the Unity system trying to initiate an outgoing call or message on the same port.

Table 7-53 shows the voice message port settings and their functions.

**Table 7-53**  *Unity Ports Distribution Setup for the XYZ*

| Port Number Range | Number of Ports | Status | Port Reserved For |
|---|---|---|---|
| 1–28 | 28 | Enabled | Answer Calls |
| 29–32 | 4 | Enabled | Message Notification, Dialout MWI, TRAP Connection |

You can use the Ports Usage Analyzer Tool, available in the Unity Tools Depot, to monitor the port-utilization status. If you determine that not enough ports are available for incoming calls (queuing of calls on the CallManager is currently not possible), you can increase the number of ports assigned to incoming calls to more than 28.

# Multiple Directory Handlers

Cisco Unity supports the use of multiple directory handlers that have differing search scopes by enabling you to select different search options on the Directory Handlers page (accessed by clicking **Call Management > Directory Handlers** on the SA page). By using this feature in a headquarters/branch office environment—such as the XYZ Australia region, shown in Figure 7-17, where call processing and messaging are centralized at the headquarters location—external callers to a branch office can access the name of a subscriber for the particular branch office without searching the entire company directory. In addition, external callers can access the operator for the local branch office, rather than being routed to the operator who resides at the headquarters location.

**Figure 7-17** *XYZ Australian Network Layout*

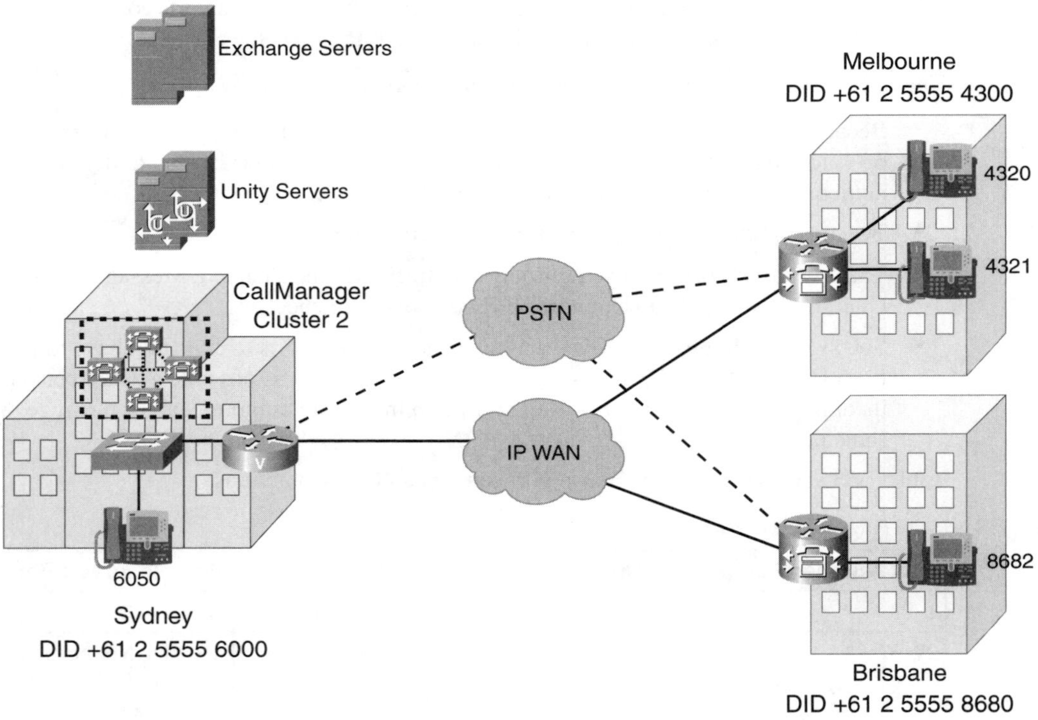

To understand the multiple directory handler feature, consider the XYZ Australian network layout shown in Figure 7-17. The XYZ headquarters is located in Sydney with branch offices in Melbourne and Brisbane. The entire IT department is located in Sydney. As such, all call processing, messaging (e-mail), and Unified Messaging applications for the entire company are managed from the company headquarters in Sydney. Each of XYZ's offices has a group of DID phone numbers. Company headquarters all branch offices have a receptionist. All branch offices and company headquarters have local employees.

In addition to Unified Messaging functionality, XYZ wants Unity to support the following specific requirements:

- All administration of Unity is under the control of the IT department that is located at the company headquarters.

- Subscribers should not have Unity Administration access.

- Although company headquarters and all branch offices have a receptionist, the receptionists have other administrative duties. To help free up the receptionists for other tasks, the Unity system must provide AA services for all offices.

- Outside callers to each branch office should hear a greeting customized for the specific office.

- If an external caller to company headquarters or a branch office needs to search for a subscriber by name, the directory should be filtered to include only the names of subscribers for the specific office.

- During normal working hours, if a caller presses 0 to talk to an operator, the call should be routed to the operator of the specific office. (It is not acceptable for a caller who is calling the Brisbane office to be routed to the operator in Sydney.)

- If a caller to the toll-free phone number for Sales needs to search for a subscriber by name, the directory should be filtered to include only the names of all the sales managers and sales associates for the entire company.

By supporting the use of multiple directory handlers, Unity will be able to meet all the needs of XYZ identified in the preceding list.

The following are the tasks that the Unity administrator must perform to configure Unity to meet the customer needs stated earlier.

1    Assign the Default Administrator CoS (the default) or the Unity Administrator CoS (which you need to define; refer to the note following Table 7-14) and grant system access to the Unity administrators for the Directory Handler SA pages. Grant all privileges (read, create, edit, and delete).

2    Verify that the Employee_CoS denies system access to the Directory Handler SA pages. The Employee_CoS, described in the "System Access" section earlier in the chapter, does not give this access.

3    Create a public distribution list (PDL) for each office (SydneyEmp-DL, MelbourneEmp-DL, and BrisbaneEmp-DL). The membership of each of these PDLs comprises all of the subscribers associated with the particular office, as shown in Table 7-54. Refer to the "Distribution Lists" section earlier in this chapter to understand the procedure to create the distribution lists and the required settings.

**Table 7-54**    *Public Distribution List Settings*

| Distribution List | Members |
|---|---|
| SydneyEmp-DL | All Sydney employees |
| MelbourneEmp-DL | All Melbourne employees |
| BrisbaneEmp-DL | All Brisbane employees |

4    For each specific office's PDL, create a directory handler with the Search Options setting (Directory Handlers> Search Options page, accessed from the SA page) set to the designated office PDL, as shown in Table 7-55.

**Table 7-55** *Directory Handlers and Search Options*

| Directory Handler | Search Options |
|---|---|
| Sydney-DH | Public Distribution List – SydneyEmp-DL |
| Melbourne-DH | Public Distribution List – Melbourne-DL |
| Brisbane-DH | Public Distribution List – BrisbaneEmp-DL |

**5** Create one Opening Greeting call handler for each office. For each Opening Greeting call handler, do the following:

**a** Record a custom greeting for the specific office.

**b** Configure the After Greeting action to send the caller to the Goodbye call handler.

**c** Configure the 4 key to send the caller to the directory handler for the designated office.

Table 7-56 shows the required configuration settings for the opening greetings.

**Table 7-56** *Opening Greeting Settings*

| Opening Greeting Call Handler | Configuration Options |
|---|---|
| Sydney-Opening | Caller Input – Key 4 – Send to Sydney-DH |
| Melbourne-Opening | Caller Input – Key 4 – Send to Melbourne-DH |
| Brisbane-Opening | Caller Input – Key 4 – Send to Brisbane-DH |

**6** Create three Operator call handlers, one for each office, as shown in Table 7-57.

For each Operator call handler, configure the Call Transfer setting to transfer the call to the specified extension of the local operator.

**Table 7-57** *Operator Call Handler Settings*

| Operator Call Handler | Configuration Options |
|---|---|
| Sydney-Operator | Caller Transfer – Yes, Ring Subscriber at This Extension – enter four-digit operator or hunt group number extension for Sydney |
| Melbourne-Operator | Caller Transfer – Yes, Ring Subscriber at This Extension – enter four-digit operator or hunt group number extension for Melbourne |
| Brisbane-Operator | Caller Transfer – Yes, Ring Subscriber at This Extension – enter four-digit operator or hunt group number extension for Brisbane |

**7** Create three call-routing rules (forwarded calls) in Unity that take a call coming to each DID number and forward it to the Opening Greeting call handler that is specific to the site, as shown in Figure 7-18.

**Figure 7-18**  *Unity Call-Routing Rules*

| Routing Table: Forwarded Calls | | | | | | | Change rule order | | |
|---|---|---|---|---|---|---|---|---|---|
| Rule | Status | Call Type | Forwarding Station | Dialed Number | Calling Number | Schedule | Send call to | Language |
| Brisbane | On | Both | 8680 | Any | Any | Always | Send to greeting for Brisbane-Opening | Inherited |
| Melbourne | On | Both | 4300 | Any | Any | Always | Send to greeting for Melbourne-Opening | Inherited |
| Sydney | On | Both | 6000 | Any | Any | Always | Send to greeting for Sydney-Opening | Inherited |

Attempt Forward

**8** Create three CTI route points or CTI ports in CallManager in the Sydney cluster, as follows:

   **a** Match the directory numbers on the CTI route points or CTI ports to the last four digits of the DID number for the site. For Sydney, the CTI RP DN is 6000; for Melbourne, it is 4300; and for Brisbane, it is 8680.)

   **b** Set the CFA on these CTI route points or CTI ports to the first voice-mail port number of the Unity system.

By configuring these settings, you can achieve the desired requirement of XYZ. Figure 7-19 shows the call flow for a call that reaches the Sydney DID number.

**Figure 7-19** *XYZ Australian Network Layout*

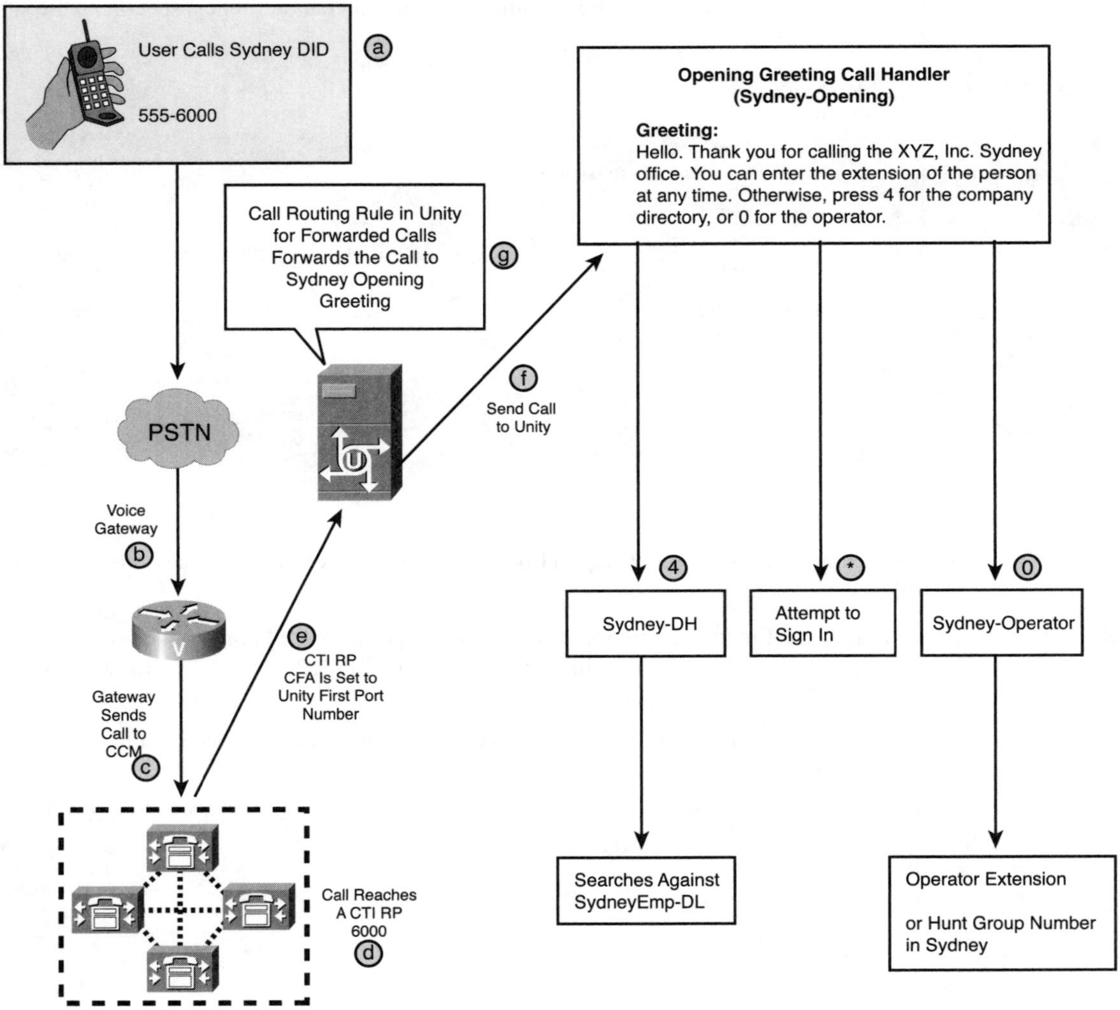

The following are the steps that take place when a call is made to the Sydney DID number:

1 The external caller dials the DID number for Sydney.

2 The call reaches the voice gateway.

3 The voice gateway forwards the call to CallManager.

**4**  CallManager keeps the last four digits in the DID number and finds the matching CTI route point/CTI port 6000.

**5**  The CFA on the CTI route point/CTI port is forwarded to the Unity port.

**6**  The call reaches Unity.

**7**  The Unity call-routing rule (forwarded calls) triggers because the call is forwarded from number 6000, which is configured to send the call to Sydney opening greeting.

**8**  If the user selects option 4, the call is forwarded to Sydney-DH, which searches for employees in the Sydney office only.

It is important to understand that each call made to the branch site DID numbers has to reach via IP WAN to reach the Unity system. Take into account the additional bandwidth requirement for this type of traffic. Also, while sizing the Unity ports, you must take into consideration the use of the AA feature in Unity.

# Improving the User Experience During Migration

This section describes the following two strategies that can be used to improve the user experience during the migration from the Octel voice-mail system to the Unity system in the Sydney location:

- Export the spoken names of the Sydney users from the Octel system to Unity.

- Pre-enroll users before bringing the Unity system live into the network.

## Export Spoken Names from Octel to Unity

It is possible to transfer the spoken names of the users as used in the Octel system before the migration to Unity. This will improve the experience for the Sydney users when they move to Unity, because each Sydney user's spoken name will already be present when they first connect to their new Unity mailbox, and they will get a spoken name confirmation when addressing messages to other users within the company.

For this spoken name confirmation to happen, you need to obtain from the Octel system a list of all the users' mailboxes that are in use. You can get this report from the Octel system administrators. This is a standard monthly report, referred to as the called utilization report, that gives an overview of the active mailboxes for the past period.

This report can be obtained or transformed via import/export in Microsoft Excel to a comma-delimited format (CSV). That file can be used as input for a Cisco tool called Cisco Unity Mailbox Import Tool—MBUpload.exe. This tool is part of the Cisco Unity Tools Depot and can be accessed from the Unity server by double-clicking the Unity Tools Depot icon on the desktop.

This tool allows bulk editing of the Octel node directories on the Cisco Unity Bridge. All the entries created this way are permanent entries on the Unity Bridge and are not subject to name aging, which is inherently present in Avaya's OctelNet protocol. More detailed information can be found on Cisco.com related to this tool:

> http://www.cisco.com/en/US/products/sw/voicesw/ps2237/
> products_tech_note09186a008011c805.shtml

You can get the complete list of tools available for Cisco Unity from http://www.ciscounitytools.com/.

The Unity Bridge will create all Unity Bridge subscribers by this upload. Because there is no spoken name associated with these Bridge subscribers, the Unity Bridge will launch an administration call to the Octel nodes to retrieve the spoken names and then store them. These spoken names will be populated to the Unity servers accordingly via the Bridgehead server in AD and cached in SQL.

It is important to verify that the DTMF-Id is consistent with the designed dial plan for your voice-mail networking and that it matches the expected digit string as it will be known and used by the Sydney users. Changing the DTMF-Ids afterward is a time-consuming activity for all the imported subscribers.

To avoid this manual change of DTMF-Ids it is possible to use the Cisco Unity ExternalUserImport utility to create all Bridge subscribers on the Unity Bridgehead server with the corresponding DTMF-id that will be used to address messages by the Sydney users of the Unity system. After the Bridge has retrieved the spoken names, it will send the spoken name to Unity and the spoken name will be linked with the corresponding user. This prevents the administrator from having to manually change all subscribers.

# Pre-Enrollment Procedures

It is a good practice to familiarize the Sydney users with their new voice-mail system before the actual cutover date. This has a lot of advantages. For the users, it guarantees a smooth transition to the new system without interruption of their normal work rhythm. For the IT personnel, it helps to avoid support calls and, consequently, escalations on the first day of production. Dealing with user problems during the pre-enrollment, whether real problems or just user-manipulation errors and knowledge gaps, is much easier than dealing with them when the system is in full production and used as a daily business tool.

It is also recommended that you give users some sort of training. If classroom training is not practical, you could provide an interactive web tutorial, for example, that allows users to try out the different functionalities. On the first day of production, you can have class-based training for users, at which time they can ask questions. This also benefits people who did not take part in the pre-enrollment. The idea behind this web-based training before the go-live date is obviously that the power users in Sydney recognize that keeping their voice mail going is important and will make the effort to pre-enroll to guarantee a smooth transition. Users who do not recognize the necessity of pre-enrollment are normally those who do not rely on voice mail for their day-to-day job. A special treatment with additional training to explain in more detail the features for power users will be established for VP-level employees and their associated admins working from the Sydney office during the pre-enrollment period.

Pre-enrollment also allows the Sydney users to customize their mailbox with their PDLs, personal greeting, and so on. so that when the IT department switches them over on a Friday evening, for example, their greeting is personalized immediately and external (or internal) callers who are forwarded to voice mail won't get a general system greeting telling them that "Extension 1234 is not available." Instead, callers will hear a personalized greeting, or at least the former Octel-retrieved spoken name if the person did not perform pre-enrollment activities.

When a partial migration is needed—suppose the Sydney office is migrating in different steps over the course of a few weekends—users who are migrating to Unity are changed from Bridge subscribers to full Unity subscribers (and thus get an Exchange mailbox assigned) sometime during one weekend (and before their calls are redirected to Unity, obviously). In the case of XYZ, where all Sydney employees are transferred over to Unity all at once, all Bridge subscribers are changed to full Unity subscribers during the cutover weekend.

# Summary

This chapter discussed the details of Cisco Unity design and customization. Understanding the existing Enterprise Directory and Messaging architecture is important for a successful Unity rollout in the network.

There are many Cisco Unity white papers available on the Cisco.com website from the following URL that you should refer to while doing the design of the Unity system:

http://www.cisco.com/univercd/cc/td/doc/product/voice/c_unity/whitpapr/index.htm

These white papers contain different types of information:

- Active Directory planning and impact
- Unity networking capabilities and features
- Unity backup and restore best practices
- Unity physical storage best practices
- Unity life reply capabilities
- Unity security best practices

The next chapter discusses the implementation phase of the IPT network in general. It focuses on high-level implementation tasks that can be useful when you are dealing with implementation in a real network.

# CHAPTER 8

# Implementation

The actual process of replacing or migrating from a legacy telephony system to a new-world Cisco IP Telephony (IPT) system can be a challenging task if you do not have the proper tasks, tools, and processes in place.

Whereas the previous chapters provided the design and configuration parameters required for actual implementation of the Cisco IPT solution, this chapter helps you to smoothly and successfully complete the IPT implementation phase by discussing in detail implementation tasks, tools, processes, common problems, and possible causes and resolutions of those problems. CallManager provides various tools that assist you in the implementation and in day-to-day operations. Identify which tools you need to use and learn how and when to use them during the implementation. This chapter discusses some of these tools that are applicable in the implementation phase of IPT. Some tools discussed in this chapter can be used in both the implementation phase and the operations and optimization phase. Chapter 9, "Operations and Optimization," discusses the tools that are not covered in this chapter.

A detailed implementation plan will help you to deploy the IPT solution within the estimated time and without facing major hurdles. The following are the major tasks involved in the implementation of IPT networks:

- Complete preimplementation tasks.
- Perform implementation readiness analysis.
- Implement IPT components.
- Identify the implementation tools.
- Deploy IPT solution pilot.
- Develop IPT acceptance tests.
- Complete postimplementation documentation.
- Develop a support strategy.
- Develop a training plan for end users and network administrators.

In large IPT deployments, it is common to subcontract the actual deployment of IP Phones to a partner. In this case, you should review the implementation plan with the partner's IPT deployment team to make sure that all the preceding tasks are covered in detail. This ensures successful deployment of an IPT network that conforms to the proposed design.

# Complete Preimplementation Tasks

The preimplementation tasks include the following subtasks. Appendix H, "IPT Implementation Checklist," includes tables that assist you in collecting the information required to complete the following tasks:

- Develop a project plan.
- Collect site information.
- Build an implementation team.

A project plan itemizes the sequence of steps involved in the IPT solution implementation. Good project management smoothens the implementation process by keeping track of all the tasks and making sure they are being performed in a timely fashion by all parties involved.

For a large-scale deployment, you should have a project manager who can be a single point of contact for the entire IPT implementation project and who has all the current information about the implementation phase. The responsibilities of the project manager should include the following:

- Plan the implementation task schedule, including the resource allocation, and build the implementation team.
- Coordinate with IPT network design engineers, facilities engineers, integration consultants, and other specialists.
- Coordinate the arrival of deliverables from multiple locations with engineers and installers and oversee communication among all parties.
- Interact with external vendors such as telephone companies, to place the order for the voice trunks, and Internet service providers, to order additional bandwidth on WAN links.

# Perform Implementation Readiness Analysis

The second major task in implementation is to perform readiness analysis, which includes the following checks:

- Site readiness
- Voice network readiness
- Data network readiness
- IPT readiness

Appendix H contains the checklists of the steps that the deployment team needs to perform to complete the implementation readiness analysis.

## Site Readiness

The site readiness checklist included in Appendix H covers the following tasks:

- Determine IPT/network component placement.
- Evaluate rack space and cabling requirements.
- Evaluate power and HVAC requirements.

The deployment team needs to review each of these readiness checklists and tighten up the loose ends where needed. You might have covered some of these tasks in the planning phase of the IPT network. The checks are included here to ensure that the steps recommended in the planning phase have been implemented and the basic infrastructure is ready to employ IP Telephony.

You should check the power requirements before deploying the IPT network, especially when you are using inline power features to provide the power to IP Phones. Based on the IP Phone model, quantity, and placement, the capacity of power supplies required at the LAN switches varies. In addition, each device in the network has a different power requirement. For instance, the power requirement of Catalyst switches varies depending on the model number and type of line cards used. Therefore, when evaluating the additional power requirements for IPT solutions, include all of these devices in your calculations. Use the IPT power calculator that is available on Cisco.com to calculate the power supply requirements for the switches:

> http://www.cisco.com/go/powercalculator

An uninterrupted power backup system ensures high availability of the IPT network. Analyze the HVAC requirements for the additional IPT network components that are going to be deployed in the server/data centers. Confirm with facility management that the building where the IPT equipment will be installed has enough air conditioning capacity to meet the IPT equipment cooling requirements.

## Voice Network Readiness

Assessing the voice network consists of examining the legacy PBX, voice-mail system, ACD systems, voice circuits, extension numbers, dial plan, and various call features. To successfully integrate the legacy equipment with the IPT network, you might need to purchase additional hardware or software licenses for the legacy equipment. The readiness process ensures that you are equipped with all such interfacing equipment before you move the users from the legacy system to the new-world IPT system. You can identify these types of special requirements during the planning phase of the IPT project, as discussed in Chapter 4, "Planning Phase," and with the help of the questionnaires in Appendix B, "IPT Planning Phase: Network Infrastructure Analysis Questionnaire," and Appendix C, "IPT Planning Phase: Telecom Infrastructure Analysis Questionnaire."

## Data Network Readiness

A stable, reliable, highly available data network architecture is essential for the success of the converged network deployment. This requires LAN/WAN support teams to complete the preconfiguration tasks discussed in Chapters 4 and 5, "Design Phase: Network Infrastructure Design," such as configuring the switch ports where IP Phones, gateways, and IPT servers terminate, and configuring the quality of service (QoS) on WAN links. The data network readiness includes analysis of the LAN/WAN infrastructure readiness to ensure that all the prerequisite changes are implemented.

## IP Telephony Readiness

The IPT readiness check verifies that the design is completed for the call-processing servers (such as the CallManager server), the voice-mail system, IPT applications, and all the devices supporting the IPT network. Directly diving into the implementation phase without completing the proper design introduces delays and might prevent you from meeting all the requirements of the new IPT system.

During the design phase of the IPT solution, you should select the equipment and CallManager software version that you need in the network, depending on the features required. Before you deploy the IPT solution, to ensure interoperability, you need to consider the software versions for the other applications, such as Unity and IPCC Express, that need to interact with CallManager and the software versions on the voice gateways.

Refer to the Cisco CallManager Compatibility Matrix on Cisco.com before you make a decision regarding the software versions for the other applications:

> http://www.cisco.com/univercd/cc/td/doc/product/voice/c_callmg/ccmcomp.htm

# Implement IPT Components

After you complete the implementation readiness analysis, you can proceed with the actual implementation of various IPT components. Chapters 5, 6, "Design of Call Processing Infrastructure and Applications," and 7, "Voice-Mail System Design," covered various design aspects of the network infrastructure, call processing, enabling features, and voice-mail system. This section covers the basic implementation steps and introduces you to some tools that you can use to verify whether the implementation of the IPT components is successful.

## CallManager and Application Server Implementation

This section covers the high-level implementation steps involved in building the CallManager and application servers. Because the installation procedures might vary from one version to another, you should refer to the installation guides and release notes provided with the CallManager for detailed installation procedures.

## Operating System Installation

The first step in setting up the CallManager or any other application server is to install the operating system on the servers via the Cisco-provided OS CD-ROM/DVD-ROM. You can perform this operation in parallel if you have to build a large cluster with many servers. Collect the information specified in the "Configuration Checklist for Installation of CallManager and Other Application Servers" section of Appendix H before you install any server.

**NOTE**    Use the Cisco-provided OS installation CD-ROM/DVD-ROM to install the operating system on Unity systems. Cisco supplies these discs if you purchase the hardware directly from Cisco. You should use original Microsoft Windows 2000/2003 Server CD-ROMs to install the OS on Unity systems that Cisco does not directly supply.

## Installing CallManager and Other Applications

After you install the OS on all the servers, follow these steps to complete the CallManager installation in the entire cluster:

1  Verify that all servers are running the same base OS version. (Refer to the "Checking CallManager  Version" section later in this chapter for the procedure.)

2  Install operating system updates on all the servers.

3  Update the C:\Winnt\System32\Drivers\etc\hosts and LMHOSTS files on all servers with all the server entries in the cluster and run the **nbtstat -R** command from the DOS command prompt.

4  Install the CallManager software on the publisher server by following the instructions given in the installation guides on Cisco.com.

5  By default, on the CallManager servers, no CallManager-related services are activated except for the Database Layer Monitor service. To enable other services that you need, choose **Tools > Service Activation** on the CallManager Serviceability page.

6  Install CallManager software on other subscribers sequentially; use the same passwords for all the servers in the cluster and activate the necessary services.

7  Check the SQL subscriptions and ensure that the replication process is working properly. (Refer to the "Database Layer Tool to Check SQL Subscriptions" section later in this chapter for the detailed procedure for doing this task.)

---

| NOTE | After you install the CallManager, log in to the CallManager Administration page and choose **System > Server**. By default, you will see the name of the server you entered during the installation. Change this to the IP address of the corresponding server if you are not using DNS. If you are using DNS, ensure that the DNS server has the entry for all the servers in the cluster. Without this, IP Phones will fail to resolve the CallManager DNS name, and IP phones will fail to register with CallManager. |
|------|---|

---

You can install applications such as IP Contact Center Express (IPCC Express) and Cisco Emergency Responder (CER) after you complete the CallManager installation. During the installation of these applications, you might have to provide the IP address or host name of the CallManager publisher and subscriber servers so that the applications can establish the communication with the CallManager servers. It is essential that you build the CallManager servers and make them available on the network before you proceed with the installation of other applications.

### Installing Tools and Third-Party Applications

After you complete the basic installation of CallManager servers and other application servers, perform the following tasks:

- Install the antivirus software and Cisco Security Agent software on all the servers.
- Install tools such as Bulk Administration Tool (BAT), Tool for Auto-Registered Phones Support (TAPS), and Dialed Number Analyzer (DNA) on the CallManager publisher server.
- Install the Backup and Restore System (BARS) software to back up the CallManager database on the CallManager publisher server.

## Implementing Voice Gateways

Voice gateways in the IPT network provide public switched telephone network (PSTN) access to the IP Phones. The following list gives the general implementation tasks that are applicable to all voice gateways:

- Install and configure the gateway or voice network module in the network/device. Refer to the installation and configuration documentation on Cisco.com for the model of gateway that you are configuring.
- Configure the trunk interface on the gateway to the PSTN and configure dial peers if required. Refer to the voice-feature software configuration documentation or Cisco IOS documentation for the model of the gateway you are configuring.
- Add and configure the gateway in CallManager.

- Configure the dial plan for the gateway for routing calls out to the PSTN or other destinations.
- Configure a route group, route list, and route pattern in CallManager.
- Reset the gateway in CallManager to apply the configuration settings.
- Verify the connectivity by making test calls.

This section describes the steps involved in configuring two different types of voice gateways proposed for the XYZ IPT network and provides troubleshooting tips. Because there is a wide selection of voice gateways, refer to the documentation on Cisco.com to configure the other types of gateways that are not described here. The following gateways are described in this chapter:

- Cisco Catalyst WS-X6608-T1 gateway
- Cisco Catalyst Communication Media Module (CMM) gateway

## Implementing Catalyst T1 Voice Gateways Using the WS-X6608-T1 Module

This section covers the steps involved in configuring the Cisco Catalyst WS-X6608-T1 gateway module in Cisco CallManager, procedures to verify the gateway registration status in CallManager, and some common troubleshooting steps.

### Step 1: Obtain the MAC Address of the Voice Port

Before you configure a T1/E1 port on a Catalyst WS-X6608-T1/E1 or WS-SVC-CMM module, you need to obtain the MAC address of the voice port. You can do this on Catalyst 6xxx series switches by running the **show module** command, as shown in Example 8-1. From the output, you can see that the module in slot 4 is a WS-X6608-T1 module and has eight MAC addresses assigned, which are in the range 00-01-64-11-c6-7c to 00-01-64-11-c6-83. The MAC address of the first port 4/1 is 00-01-64-11-c6-7c, the second port 4/2 is 00-01-64-11-c6-7d, and so forth, with the MAC address of the port 4/8 being 00-01-64-11-c6-83.

**Example 8-1**  *Obtaining the MAC Address of the T1/E1 Port*

```
cat6k-voice> (enable) show module
Mod Slot Ports Module-Type            Model               Sub Status
--- ---- ----- -------------------------  -------------------- --- --------
1   1    2     1000BaseX Supervisor   WS-X6K-SUP1A-2GE    yes ok
15  1    1     Multilayer Switch Feature WS-F6K-MSFC      no  ok
3   3    48    10/100BaseTX Ethernet  WS-X6348-RJ-45      no  ok
4   4    8     T1                     WS-X6608-T1         no  ok
5   5    24    FXS                    WS-X6624-FXS        no  disable
6   6    5     Communication Media Mod. WS-SVC-CMM        no  ok
7   7    5     Communication Media Mod. WS-SVC-CMM        no  ok
9   9    8     T1                     WS-X6608-T1         no  ok
```

*continues*

**Example 8-1** *Obtaining the MAC Address of the T1/E1 Port (Continued)*

```
Mod Module-Name          Serial-Num
--- -------------------- -----------
1                        SAD04480PZW
15                       SAD04480KXC
3                        SAL05031N6H
4                        SAD04320KZA
5                        SAD04430ASH
6                        SAD075303F1
7                        SAD0640008A
9                        SAD04450DS1

Mod MAC-Address(es)                           Hw    Fw           Sw
--- --------------------------------------- ------ ---------- ----------------
1   00-02-7e-26-06-a2 to 00-02-7e-26-06-a3 7.0    5.3(1)       8.1(3)
    00-02-7e-26-06-a0 to 00-02-7e-26-06-a1
    00-d0-03-14-74-00 to 00-d0-03-14-77-ff
15  00-02-7e-26-06-a4 to 00-02-7e-26-06-e3 1.4    12.1(1)E,    12.1(1)E,
3   00-04-6d-44-80-c0 to 00-04-6d-44-80-ef 1.4    5.4(2)       8.1(3)
4   00-01-64-11-c6-7c to 00-01-64-11-c6-83 1.1    5.4(2)       8.1(3)
5   00-d0-d3-3e-9d-34                       2.0    5.4(2)       8.1(3)
6   00-03-fe-ad-d9-6a to 00-03-fe-ad-d9-73 2.2    12.2(13)ZP 12.2(13)ZP2,
7   00-02-7e-e4-a2-de to 00-02-7e-e4-a2-e7 2.1    12.2(13)ZP 12.2(13)ZP,
9   00-01-c9-6b-33-20 to 00-01-c9-6b-33-27 1.1    5.4(2)       8.1(3)

Mod Sub-Type             Sub-Model            Sub-Serial  Sub-Hw Sub-Sw
--- -------------------- -------------------- ----------- ------ ------
1   L3 Switching Engine  WS-F6K-PFC           SAD045007LA 1.1
```

## Step 2: Assign the IP Address for the Voice Port

To assign the IP address for the voice port, the best practice is to assign the static addresses for the critical components such as servers, gateways, and gatekeepers. Example 8-2 shows the Catalyst 6xxx command to configure the static address for the port 4/1. You can see that Dynamic Host Configuration Protocol (DHCP) is disabled and the IP address configured for the port is 172.21.54.90 with a subnet mask of 255.255.255.128. The switch port is on VLAN 401. Because DHCP is disabled, the TFTP server address, which in this example is 172.21.51.237, should be configured manually.

**Example 8-2** *Assigning a Static IP Address for the T1/E1 Port*

```
cat6k-voice> (enable) set port enable 4/1
Port 4/1 enabled.
cat6k-voice> (enable) set port voice interface 4/1 dhcp disable 172.21.54.90 255
.255.255.128 vlan 401 tftp 172.21.51.237 gateway 172.21.54.2
Port 4/1 DHCP disabled.
System DNS configurations used.
cat6k-voice> (enable)
```

**NOTE**   You need to obtain the MAC address and configure the switch ports in a similar way to that described earlier for Catalyst 6xxx–based Media Gateway Control Protocol (MGCP) gateway WS-X6624. Note that a single MAC address is assigned to the whole WS-X6624-FXS module.

### Step 3: Configure the Gateway on the CallManager

To configure a gateway on the CallManager Administration page, choose **Device > Gateway** and click the **Add a New Gateway** option on the Gateway page. On the Add a New Gateway page, select the gateway type and device protocol used for signaling.

To add a T1 port on a WS-X6608-T1 module and configure the T1 port for PRI protocol, choose the Cisco **Catalyst 6000 T1 VoIP** gateway as a gateway type and **Digital Access PRI** as the device protocol in the Add a New Gateway Page, and click the Next button. This brings up the Gateway Configuration page, as shown in Figure 8-1. You need to type the MAC address of the port. In Figure 8-1, the MAC address entered is for port 4/1.

**Figure 8-1**   *Adding a T1/E1 Port on a Catalyst WS-X6608-T1 (E1) Module*

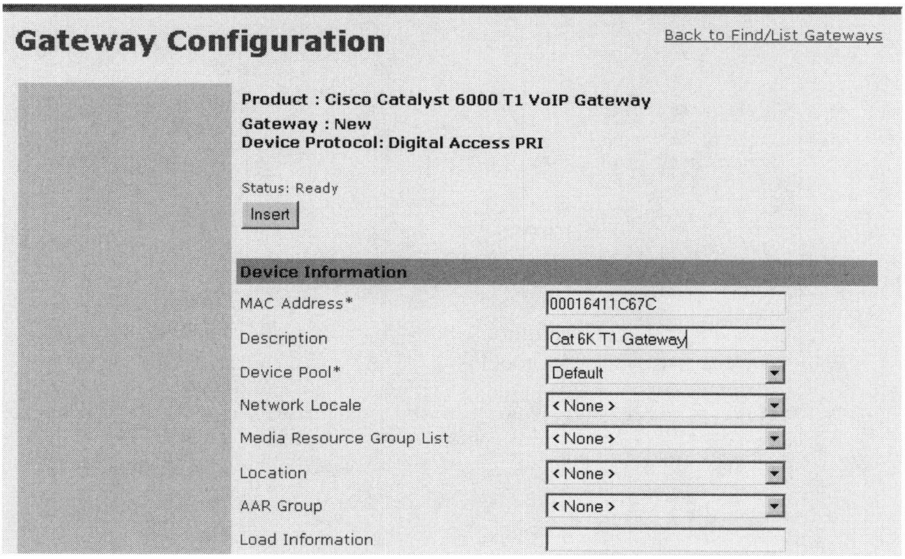

You need to provide values for the fields such as Device Pool, Interface parameters for the T1/E1, calling search space (CSS), and so forth. These values depend on the design. Refer to the "Gateway Selection and Sizing" section in Chapter 6 to understand the importance of the other parameters.

## Step 4: Verify the Gateway Registration Status on the Switch

After configuring the gateway on the CallManager, you can check the status of the gateway registration, as shown in Example 8-3. If the port is successfully registered, you should see the word "registered" under CallManagerState, as shown in Example 8-3.

**Example 8-3** *Verifying the Gateway Registration Status on the Switch*

```
cat6k-voice> (enable) show port 4/1
* = Configured MAC Address

Port  Name                Status      Vlan       Duplex Speed Type
----- ------------------- ----------- ---------- ------ ----- ------------
 4/1  Connection-to-PSTN  connected   401               full 1.544 T1

Port    DHCP    MAC-Address        IP-Address        Subnet-Mask
------- ------- ------------------ ----------------- ---------------
 4/1    disable 00-01-64-11-c6-7c  172.21.54.90      255.255.255.128

Port    Call-Manager(s)   DHCP-Server      TFTP-Server      Gateway
------- ----------------- ---------------- ---------------- ---------------
 4/1    172.21.51.237     -                172.21.51.237    172.21.54.2

Port    DNS-Server(s)     Domain
------- ----------------- -----------------------------------------------------
 4/1    -                 -

Port    CallManagerState DSP-Type
------- ---------------- --------
 4/1    registered       C549

Port  NoiseRegen NonLinearProcessing
----- ---------- -------------------
 4/1  enabled    enabled

Port   Trap     IfIndex
-----  -------- -------
 4/1   disabled 43

Port  Status      ErrDisable Reason   Port ErrDisableTimeout Action on Timeout
----  ----------- ------------------- ---------------------- -----------------
 4/1  connected                     - Enable                 No Change

Idle Detection
-------------

cat6k-voice> (enable)
```

### Step 5: Verify the Gateway Registration Status on the CallManager

You can verify the gateway registration status from the CallManager Gateway Configuration page, as shown in Figure 8-2.

**Figure 8-2**    *Verifying the Registration Status of a T1/E1 Port*

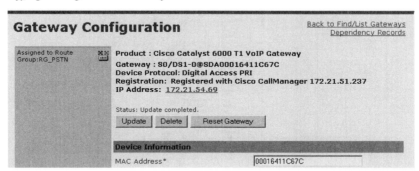

You can also use Windows 2000 performance counters or Real-Time Monitoring Tool (RTMT) to view the gateway registration status. Chapter 9 discusses these tools in detail.

Figure 8-3 shows the performance counters on a CallManager server for the performance object MGCP PRI device. To access the Performance Monitor application on a CallManager server, click **Start > Programs > Administrative Tools > Performance**. Figure 8-3 shows the status of the 23 B channels (channels 1 to 23) and the D channel (channel 24) of the selected MGCP PRI gateway. The status code for channel 23 is 3 (Busy—indicates an active call on the channel), whereas the status code for all the other B channels is 2 (Idle—not in use).

As you can see in Figure 8-3, after registering the gateway with the CallManager, you can check the channel status through the performance counters and monitor the change in the status code after placing the calls. Figure 8-3 shows one active call on the PRI on channel 23. The gateway selected channel 23 because, in the CallManager configuration for this gateway, the channel selection order was configured as bottom up.

A status code of 0 (Unknown) indicates that the status of the channel could not be determined; 1 (Out of service) indicates that this channel is not available for use; 4 (Reserved) indicates that this channel has been reserved for use as a D channel or for use as a synchronous channel for E-1.

**Figure 8-3** *Performance Monitor Counters for MGCP Voice Gateway*

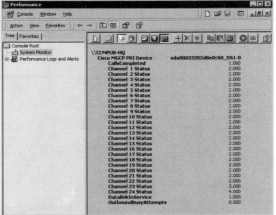

## Implementing a Catalyst T1/E1 Voice Gateway by Using a CMM Module

Implementing a voice gateway using a T1/E1 port on a CMM slightly differs from the procedure followed for the WS-X6608-T1 (E1) module. As mentioned in Chapter 6, the CMM module has four slots. One slot is an internal slot and is not available to plug in any T1/E1 module. The internal slot can only accept an Ad Hoc Conferencing and Transcoding (ACT) adapter. The three other slots can be filled either with three T1/E1 modules each with 6 T1/E1 ports (18 total) or any combination of T1/E1 modules and ACT adapters.

With WS-X6608-T1 (E1) modules, unused T1/E1 ports can be configured as conferencing and transcoding resources. This is not the case with T1/E1 ports on the CMM module. You require the ACT adapter for conferencing and transcoding purposes. Another difference between the WS-X6608-T1 module and CMM is that CMM supports both H.323 and MGCP protocols , besides supporting Survivable Remote Site Telephony (SRST). The following steps cover how to provision the CMM module.

### Step 1: Access the CMM

The CMM module has its own Cisco IOS image. To access the CMM module from the Catalyst switch running the Cat OS and Multilayer Switch Feature Card (MSFC) running the IOS code, enter the **session** *mod_num* command on the switch console, as shown in Example 8-4. The *mod_num* is the module number where CMM is installed. From Example 8-1, the CMM modules are available in modules 6 and 7 on the Cat6k-voice switch used in this configuration.

**Example 8-4** *Accessing CMM from the Switch Console*

```
cat6k-voice> (enable) session 6
Trying VOICE-GATEWAY-6...
Connected to VOICE-GATEWAY-6.
Escape character is '^]'.
User Access Verification
Password:
```

**Example 8-4**  *Accessing CMM from the Switch Console (Continued)*

```
SJ-CMM1>en
Password:
SJ-CMM1#
```

Note that the host name used for the CMM is SJ-CMM1. You have to input this host name when configuring the CMM in CallManager Administration.

## Step 2: Configure the T1/E1 Port

The CMM runs the Cisco IOS image. Therefore, the configuration steps for T1/E1 ports are similar to those for any T1/E1 port on a Cisco IOS router. Example 8-5 shows the configuration for a T1 port. The configuration for the E1 port is similar except that you select the E1 port and configure different line code and framing.

**Example 8-5**  *Configuring the T1/E1 Port*

```
SJ-CMM1# conf
Configuring from terminal, memory, or network [terminal]?
Enter configuration commands, one per line.  End with CNTL/Z.
! Configure the ISDN Switch type
SJ-CMM1(config)#isdn switch-type primary-ni
! Enable the MGCP process on the CMM
SJ-CMM1(config)#mgcp
! Specify the MGCP Call Agent address, which is, the IP address of the primary
! CallManager. You can specify backup CallManager's by using the command
! ccm-manager redundant-host command

SJ-CMM1(config)#ccm-manager mgcp
SJ-CMM1(config)#mgcp call-agent 172.21.51.237

! Configure the Gigabit ethernet interface. This is the interface through
! which the T1/E1 ports communicate with CallManager

SJ-CMM1(config)#int gigabitEthernet 1/0
SJ-CMM1(config-if)#ip address 172.21.54.89 255.255.255.128
SJ-CMM1(config-if)#no shutdown
SJ-CMM1(config-if)#ip default-gateway 172.21.54.5

! Configure the T1 port with correct line code and framing
SJ-CMM1(config)#controller t1 1/0
SJ-CMM1(config)#no shutdown
SJ-CMM1(config-controller)#linecode b8zs
SJ-CMM1(config-controller)#framing esf
SJ-CMM1(config-controller)#pri-group timeslots 1-24 service mgcp

! After configuring the pri-group command under the T1/E1 controller,
! router adds the D channel interface.
! The ISDN bind command configures the ISDN-PRI back-haul to the CallManager
```

*continues*

**Example 8-5**   *Configuring the T1/E1 Port (Continued)*

```
SJ-CMM1(config)#interface serial 1/0:23
SJ-CMM1(config-if)#isdn  bind-l3 ccm-manager

Configure the POTS dial peer and associate the voice port 1/0:23 to this dial peer. The
application command informs the CMM that the voice port 1/0:23 is controlled by MGCP.

SJ-CMM1(config)#dial-peer voice 1 pots
SJ-CMM1(config-dial-peer)#application mgcp
SJ-CMM1(config-dial-peer)#port 1/0:23
```

Because this is an MGCP gateway, the entire dial plan configuration is configured in the
CallManager. If you are configuring the T1/E1 port as an H.323 gateway, an additional step here
is to configure the local dial plan on the router. Refer to the Chapter 6 section "Survivable
Remote Site Telephony" to see a sample configuration of a local dial plan on routers. When the
router is in SRST mode, the gateway falls back to H.323 mode and uses the local dial plan to
perform the call routing.

### Step 3: Configure the Gateway on CallManager

To configure a gateway on the CallManager Administration page, choose **Device > Gateway**.
Click the **Add New Gateway** option on the Gateway page. On the Add a New Gateway page,
choose **Communication Media Module** as the gateway type and click **Next**. In the Domain
Name field, enter the host name of the CMM module and select the interface cards inserted into
the modules, as shown in Figure 8-4. Click **Insert** to insert the gateway into the CallManager.

**Figure 8-4**   *Adding the CMM Module as a Gateway in CallManager*

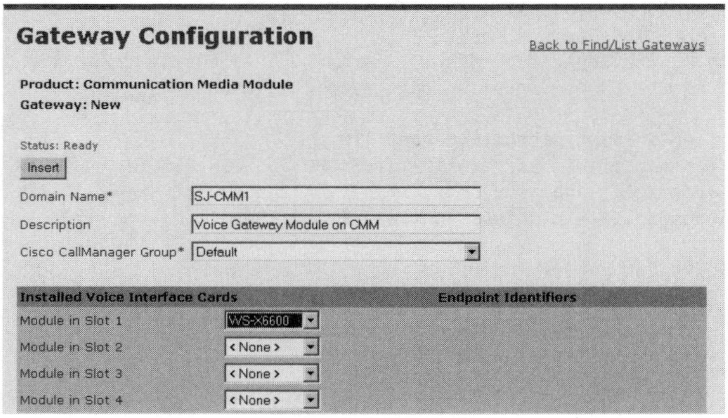

After you insert the CMM module, you need to specify the subunits that are inserted in the
CMM module. In Figure 8-5, the T1 card WS-X6600-T1 is selected.

**Figure 8-5** *Adding Subunits to the CMM Module*

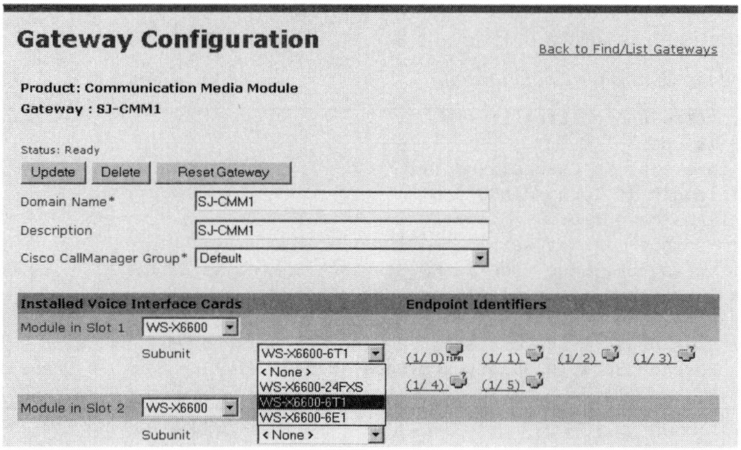

After you insert the subunits and update the configuration, click the T1 port that you want to configure. The configuration of the T1 port is similar to that of the T1 port configuration on the 6608, as shown in Figure 8-5. You need to provide values for the fields such as Device Pool, Interface parameters for the T1/E1, calling search space, and so forth.

## Step 4: Verify the Connectivity Status

After completing the configuration, you need to verify whether the physical connection to the PSTN is up. You can use the **show isdn status** command, as shown in Example 8-6. The Layer 2 status should report MULTIPLE_FRAME_ESTABLISHED.

**Example 8-6** *Verifying the T1/E1 Port Connectivity Status on the CMM*

```
SJ-CMM1#show isdn status
Global ISDN Switchtype = primary-ni
ISDN Serial1/0:23 interface
        dsl 0, interface ISDN Switchtype = primary-ni
        L2 Protocol = Q.921  L3 Protocol(s) = CCM-MANAGER
    Layer 1 Status:
        ACTIVE
    Layer 2 Status:
        TEI = 0, Ces = 1, SAPI = 0, State = MULTIPLE_FRAME_ESTABLISHED
    Layer 3 Status:
        0 Active Layer 3 Call(s)
    Active dsl 0 CCBs = 0
    The Free Channel Mask:  0x807FFFFF
    Number of L2 Discards = 0, L2 Session ID = 3
    Total Allocated ISDN CCBs = 0
SJ-CMM1#
```

If you do not see the successful connectivity status, verify that line code, framing, and clocking are configured correctly. You can use the **show controllers t1 1/0** command to verify these configurations, as shown in Example 8-7.

**Example 8-7**  *Verifying the Controller Configuration*

```
SJ-CMM1#show controllers t1 1/0
T1 1/0 is up.
  Applique type is Channelized T1
  Cablelength is long gain36 0db
  No alarms detected.
  alarm-trigger is not set
  Framing is ESF, Line Code is B8ZS, Clock Source is Line.
  Data in current interval (15 seconds elapsed):
     0 Line Code Violations, 0 Path Code Violations
     0 Slip Secs, 0 Fr Loss Secs, 0 Line Err Secs, 0 Degraded Mins
     0 Errored Secs, 0 Bursty Err Secs, 0 Severely Err Secs, 0 Unavail Secs
SJ-CMM1#
```

## Step 5: Verify the Registration Status

To verify the T1/E1 port registration status on the CMM, use the **show ccm-manager** command, as shown in Example 8-8. The output should show Registered if the port is successfully registered to the CallManager.

**Example 8-8**  *Verifying the Registration Status of the T1/E1 Port on the CMM*

```
SJ-CMM1#show ccm-manager
MGCP Domain Name: SJ-CMM1
Priority        Status                  Host
============================================================
Primary         Registered                172.21.51.237
First Backup    None
Second Backup   None


Current active CallManager:    172.21.51.237
Backhaul/Redundant link port:  2428
Failover Interval:             30 seconds
Keepalive Interval:            15 seconds
Last keepalive sent:           23:24:31 UTC Mar 22 1993 (elapsed time: 00:00:09
)
Last MGCP traffic time:        23:24:31 UTC Mar 22 1993 (elapsed time: 00:00:09
)
Last failover time:            None
Last switchback time:          None
Switchback mode:               Graceful
MGCP Fallback mode:            Not Selected
Last MGCP Fallback start time: None
Last MGCP Fallback end time:   None

PRI Backhaul Link info:
    Link Protocol:      TCP
    Remote Port Number: 2428
```

**Example 8-8**    *Verifying the Registration Status of the T1/E1 Port on the CMM (Continued)*

```
        Remote IP Address:  172.21.51.237
        Current Link State: OPEN
        Statistics:
            Packets recvd:    463
            Recv failures:    76
            Packets xmitted: 390
            Xmit failures:    0
        PRI Ports being backhauled:
            Slot 1, port 0
Configuration Error History:
FAX mode: cisco
SJ-CMM1#
```

## Troubleshooting Gateway Connectivity and Registration Issues

This section provides troubleshooting tips if you are having trouble completing the gateway registration, confronting issues with port status, or experiencing unsuccessful inbound/outbound calls for Catalyst-based voice gateways.

To determine whether the problem is related to a registration issue, do the following:

- Check the basic network connectivity by pinging the TFTP server and the CallManager from the gateway module.

- Check whether the port that is configured for the voice gateway is enabled.

- Check whether the correct IP address, subnet mask, gateway, and VLAN are configured for the port.

- If you are not using DHCP, ensure that the DHCP helper address is configured on the routed interface that is directly connected to the subnet where the gateway port resides.

- Check whether the correct TFTP server is configured.

- If you are using the DNS name for the TFTP server, ensure that the switch can resolve the TFTP server name to the IP address.

- If all of the previous points are correct, check that the MAC address entered in the CallManager matches the MAC address of the port.

To determine whether the problem is related to a connectivity issue, check whether the port status is Connected; refer to Example 8-3. If it is not, check that the interface parameters such as the isdn switch-type, line code, and framing configured on the gateway are set according to the values required by your local telco; refer to Example 8-5.

To determine whether the problem is related to unsuccessful calls (made to and from a Cisco IP Phone through the gateway), verify the following:

- If you cannot make outbound calls from a Cisco IP Phone, check the dial plan configurations and Cisco IP Phone's CSS configuration.

- If you are not able to receive incoming calls from the gateway, check the values in the Inbound Calls section of the Gateway Configuration page in the CallManager, such as the Calling Search Space and Significant Digits fields.

If you still have problems, look into the TFTP traces or CallManager traces to resolve the issue.

The preceding paragraphs discussed the implementation procedures and troubleshooting procedures for commonly used gateways. If your network uses other gateways, refer to the Cisco.com product-specific documentation for configuration and troubleshooting assistance.

# Implementing IP Phones

You can deploy IPT components such as IP Phones and gateways either manually or by using automated tools such as BAT. Use of the automated tools makes the IPT implementation more robust and smooth. These tools can assist you in speeding up the IPT implementation process in most cases, but using them is not mandatory for the IPT implementation process. The following sections describe the implementation of IP Phones using BAT and the physical installation of IP Phones.

## Implementation of IP Phones Using BAT

To enable you to configure or update your CallManager database faster and with less manual entry for larger systems, CallManager ships BAT. By using BAT, you can perform bulk add, update, and delete operations of phones, users, and gateways. The export feature in BAT comes in handy when you are consolidating multiple CallManager clusters into a single CallManager cluster. By using the export feature, you can export the configuration information of phones and users from a CallManager cluster into a CSV file and import the contents of the CSV file into the new CallManager cluster.

BAT is available on the CallManager Install Plugins page. You can install BAT only on a CallManager publisher server. After you install BAT, you can access it by entering the following URL:

http://*CCM_PUBLISHER_IP_ADDRESS*/bat

A complete installation and configuration guide for BAT is available at the following URL:

http://www.cisco.com/en/US/partner/products/sw/voicesw/ps556/
products_user_guide_book09186a0080212686.html

The next two sections discuss the procedures and tools that you can use to provision Cisco IP Phones in the CallManager.

## Barcode Scanners

When you are using BAT to add the MAC address of the IP Phones for a large-scale IPT deployment, you need to type each MAC address, one by one, into the Bat.xlt (BAT Microsoft Excel Template) file, which is a tedious process.

Use of bar-code scanners greatly reduces the chance of human error in entering the MAC addresses while configuring the IP Phones in CallManager and helps you to accelerate large-scale IP Phone deployments.

The back of the IP Phone has a barcoded MAC address. Barcode vendors offer a wide variety of models. The scanner you choose needs to scan the MAC address and put it in the database efficiently. Here is a brief list of barcode scanner manufacturers:

- **Socket Communications**—http://www.socketcom.com/
- **Symbol Technologies**—http://www.symbol.com
- **Wasp Technologies**—http://www.waspbarcode.com

While choosing among different scanner models, the following are features to look for:

- It can read and insert the barcode value into any type of application that is running on the workstation OS that you are using.
- It can write the decoded value into any standard application without the need to install special software on the workstation.
- It is easy to hook up with your workstation, such as via a keyboard interface or USB interface.

After you connect the scanner to your workstation, open the Bat.xlt file (you can copy this file from C:\CiscoWebs\BAT\ExcelTemplate directory on the CallManager publisher server to your location workstation) and scan the barcode of the MAC address on the back of the IP Phone. Repeat this process for all the IP Phones. The scanner records the value of the cell to which the pointer is pointing. The pointer moves automatically to the next row or to the next cell after scanning each input. After scanning the MAC address of the IP Phone, you can input the rest of the phone configuration information, such as the extension number, number of lines on the phone, number of speed dials, and so forth, into the BAT Excel template.

When you are ready with all the information for the IP Phones that need to be deployed, export the data in the BAT Excel template file into a CSV file. You can then import this CSV file via the BAT application to configure the IP Phones in the CallManager.

## Tool for Auto-Registered Phones Support

An alternate approach to the barcode scanners is to use TAPS in conjunction with BAT to update auto-registered phones and replace phones that have a predefined device configuration. TAPS is available on the CallManager Install Plugins page. You can use TAPS to avoid manual entry of the MAC addresses of the IP Phones in the database.

TAPS requires the Customer Response Solution (CRS) server to execute a script that plays prompts and receives the digits from the user to configure the IP Phones. If you have not purchased CRS server software, you can download the optional, free-of-charge software called Cisco CallManager Extended Services, which is available on Cisco.com on the CallManager software downloads page, to provision the IP Phones using TAPS. The Cisco CallManager Extended Services includes the CRA engine that can use applications such as TAPS and Cisco Auto Attendant (AA) can use. The CRA engine that is included with Extended Services comes with a limited number of ports and does not offer you the CRA editor utility to create or modify the application scripts.

The TAPS installation process copies the TAPS script (TAPS.aef) to the C:\Program Files\Wfavvid directory on to the CRA or Extended Services server.

If you have a co-resident CallManager and CRS/Extended Services application installation, you need to install the TAPS only once on the CallManager publisher server. If you have CRS installed on a separate server, you need to install TAPS both on the CallManager publisher server and on the CRS server.

Refer to the BAT user guide on Cisco.com for instructions on installing and using TAPS:

http://www.cisco.com/en/US/partner/products/sw/voicesw/ps556/
products_user_guide_book09186a0080212686.html

## Physical Phone Installation

Install Cisco IP Phones in your network by connecting the Ethernet wire coming from the Ethernet jack in the wall to the back of the IP Phones. IP Phones obtain the DHCP address and TFTP server information and attempt the registration with CallManager.

A complete IP Phone implementation guide is available on Cisco.com:

http://www.cisco.com/en/US/partner/products/hw/phones/ps379/
products_administration_guide_chapter09186a0080080680.html

To troubleshoot issues with Cisco IP Phone registration during implementation and operation, refer to the following document on Cisco.com:

http://www.cisco.com/en/US/partner/products/hw/phones/ps379/
products_administration_guide_chapter09186a0080080689.html

# Implementing the Dial Plan

The "Dial Plan Architecture" section in Chapter 6 discussed the steps involved in designing the dial plan. The implementation of the dial plan consists of configuring the following dial plan components in the CallManager:

- Partitions
- Calling search spaces
- Route groups
- Route lists
- Route patterns
- Translational patterns

Configure your dial plan based on the final design. The next section introduces the Dialed Number Analyzer tool and explains how this tool can help you verify whether the dial plan configured in the CallManager is working according to the design.

## Dialed Number Analyzer

If you have a large dial plan and complex call-routing requirements, you end up with a huge number of dial plan components. The DNA tool helps you to troubleshoot issues when you have such complex dial plans.

From the CallManager perspective, you can make different types of calls, such as IP Phone-to-IP Phone calls, gateway-to-IP Phone calls, IP Phone-to-gateway calls, gateway-to-gateway calls, and calls to feature-specific patterns. The DNA tool recognizes all of these types of calls to display end-to-end details pertaining to the call. In CallManager, the calling and called party transformations affect the calling and called number. The tool considers all of these transformations configured under various dial plan elements and shows the final transformed number.

The DNA tool compares the dialed digits with the list of route patterns specified in the CSS for the device selected (IP Phone, gateway, trunk) and shows you the call flow path. If the call flow path shown by the DNA tool does not match what you thought it would, you can go back, change your dial plan, and rerun the DNA tool.

As discussed in the next section, you do not have to look at CallManager traces to know whether the call flow is correct. After verifying from the DNA tool that the call flow is as per your design, you can make a real call to check whether the call goes through. If you still have problems, the problem could be configurations on the terminating device or the devices outside the CallManager's control. For example, if you have an H.323 gateway, the DNA tool can show you the call reaching the H.323 gateway. The configurations on the H.323 gateway are not known to CallManager; therfore, they are not known to the DNA tool.

The DNA tool is available for installation on the Cisco CallManager Install Plugins page. You can also download the tool from Cisco.com:

http://www.cisco.com/cgi-bin/tablebuild.pl/callmgr-40

### Analyzing the DNA Tool Output

Recall from the discussion in the "Calling Search Space Design" section in Chapter 6 that you can configure the CSS for an IP phone device at the device level, at the line level, or at both places. If you configure CSS at both places, CallManager places the partitions that appear in the line-level CSS on the top of the list and selects the best match.

Assume that you wanted the IP Phone 2001, with the following configuration, to make only local, long-distance, toll-free, and emergency calls, but no international calls:

- The IP phone, 2001, is in partition pt_internal.
- The device-level CSS is css_SJ.
- The line-level CSS is css_line_LD.

The partitions that CSS references are the same as the ones described in Tables 6-41 to 6-43.

To test the configuration, in DNA, select **Analysis > Phones** and select the IP Phone whose line is 2001. Enter an international number as the dialed digits 90119187724436598. Figure 8-6 shows the output of the DNA tool.

**Figure 8-6**  *Using the DNA Tool Example*

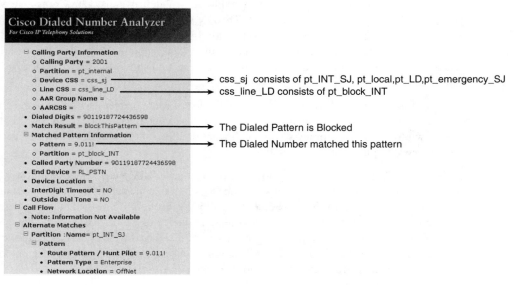

As shown in Figure 8-6, the device-level CSS, css_SJ, has a partition (pt_INT_SJ) that allows international calls. The css_line_LD CSS has a partition that blocks international calls (pt_block_INT). Based on the CSS combination rule discussed in the "Calling Search Space" section of Chapter 6, the partition at the line level comes first. Hence, the international call from the IP Phone 2001 is blocked, which is the desired result.

You can analyze any dialed digits this way and test your dial plan before deploying it in the production server. In addition, before making major changes to the dial plan in the production servers, configure the changes in the lab servers and use the DNA tool for verification. If you are satisfied with the results, make the changes in the production server.

## Implementing Cisco IP AutoAttendant

The IPCC Express standard solution will be deployed to use the AutoAttendant (AA) functionality to meet XYZ's requirements. This is in addition to the call center previously sized in Chapter 6 for XYZ. As mentioned in Chapter 6, in the "Customer Response Solution Server Scalability and Sizing" section, there will be a general phone number to reach a Cisco IP Interactive Voice Response (Cisco IP IVR) menu. This IP IVR menu gives the caller the choice to transfer to either the AutoAttendant or the sales support queue. The AA application is one of the application scripts available in the CRS server. The CRS server communicates with CallManager (specifically, the CTI Manager service) via the Java Telephony API (JTAPI).

Applications such as AA and IP Integrated Contact Distribution (IP ICD) execute steps configured in the application scripts. The application script that is responsible for the AutoAttendant is aa.aef, and it is stored in the CRS server.

Figure 8-7 shows the call flow that describes the sequence of steps involved in invoking AA. In Figure 8-7, the Computer Telephony Integration (CTI) route point is a virtual device that can receive multiple simultaneous calls for application-controlled redirection. In this case, the application is AA. Multiple simultaneous users, up to the configured number of CTI ports for the application, can dial the number assigned to IP AA and have their calls routed to a user's extension or the operator's phone.

**Figure 8-7**   *AA Call Flow*

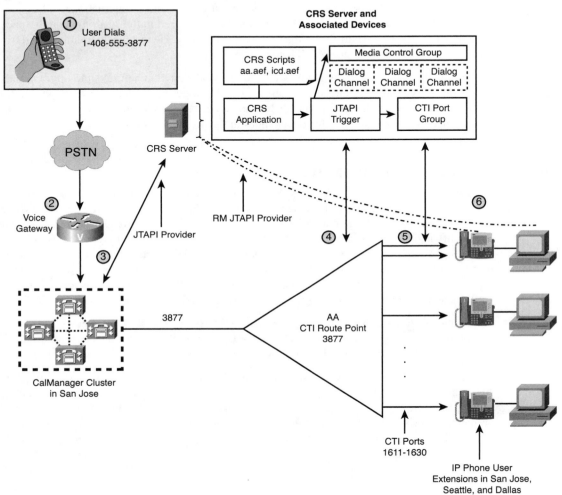

The CTI route point and CTI ports behave like a hunt group. All the calls for the applications enter via the CTI route point and are then handed off to another phone (CTI port) for additional processing. This frees up the original CTI route point number to accept the next call.

In the example shown in Figure 8-7, the following sequence of steps takes place:

1   An external user dials 408-555-3877 from the phone.

2   The PSTN sends the last ten digits of the Direct Inward Dial (DID) number (4085553877) to the gateway, which is configured to present the last four digits to CallManager.

3 The call reaches CallManager on the CTI route point DN 3877. This CTI route point is assigned to the JTAPI trigger in the CRS server.

4 The route points and CTI ports are configured in the CRS server such that all calls received at the CTI route point number are routed through the CRS server's JTAPI subsystem to its application script—in this case, aa.aef.

5 The CRS server uses the available CTI port to accept the incoming call.

6 The CTI port performs a consultative transfer to an IP phone or to an operator based on the user's response to the application prompts.

Every application has one CTI route point and a few CTI ports associated with it. The call center application will have a CTI route point, and the IP IVR application will have another CTI route point.

Design and implementation of AA involves the following tasks:

- Identify the number of CTI ports required.
- Identify the CTI route point number.
- Identify the operator extension.

The "Customer Response Solution Server Scalability and Sizing" section in Chapter 6 covered the sizing of CTI ports required for the call center. Additional CTI ports are required to handle AA calls.

In Figure 8-6, in addition to a CTI port group, you need to provision media control groups on the CRS server. While designing the CRS server, you have three choices regarding the provision of media:

- Cisco Media Termination
- Nuance Asynchronous Speech Recognition (ASR)
- None (media-less calls)

When determining the number of licenses required for the CRS server, note the following:

- All calls configured to use media are counted against the number of licensed IVR ports.
- All calls configured to use ASR are counted against the number of licensed ASR ports.
- Calls configured to use no media are not counted against media licenses and are free to be processed.

A media-less call is a call for which no media interaction is expected. Examples of applications that require no media are E.911 redirect and simple queuing. Examples of calls that require media interaction are calls that prompt the user to enter digits, calls that get DTMF digits, and calls that use speech recognition.

You can put a media-less call on hold and play Music on Hold (MoH) for the caller. CallManager plays the MoH stream for the caller while the caller is waiting in the queue.

The CRA server does not generate or play the music stream for the caller. The media-less call does not use as much CPU as the other types of calls that require access to media. Hence, avoiding media allows you to increase the capacity of the CRA platform.

Refer to the following URL to find out how to play MoH to IP ICD callers in a queue:

> http://www.cisco.com/en/US/partner/products/sw/custcosw/ps1846/
> products_configuration_example09186a0080159eb5.shtml

## Configuration Steps for AA

The AA will be deployed using the aa.aef script provided with the IPCC Express standard server. Configuration of AA involves the following:

- Configurations in the CallManager
- Configurations in the CRS server

Detailed steps of installing and configuring the applications are available on Cisco.com. The following sections discuss only high-level configuration steps.

### Configurations in the CallManager for AA

The following three configuration steps are required to configure the AutoAttendant. The prerequisite for executing these steps is to complete the initial CRA setup. (Refer to the product documentation on the initial setup.)

1  Configure the CTI route point. On the CallManager Administration page, choose **Device > CTI Route Point**. (Refer to Table 6-40 in Chapter 6 for the CTI route point that is assigned to the AA application.)

2  Configure the CTI ports. On the CallManager Administration page, choose **Device > Phone**. Select **Add a New Phone** and select the phone type as **CTI Port**. (Refer to Table 6-40 in Chapter 6 for the directory numbers assigned to CTI ports used for the AA application.)

3  Create a user in the DC directory. On the CallManager Administration page, choose **User > Add a New User** to create the user and associate the CTI route point and the CTI ports with the user.

Table 8-1 lists the settings for the CTI route point, CTI ports, and JTAPI user information that need to be configured in the CallManager server to set up the AA application.

**Table 8-1**  *Configuration Settings in CallManager for AA*

| Step Number | Configured Device | Field | Value |
|---|---|---|---|
| 1 | **CTI Route Point** | Device Name | AARP |
| | | Description | AA Route Point |
| | | Device Pool | DP-SanJose |

**Table 8-1**   *Configuration Settings in CallManager for AA (Continued)*

| Step Number | Configured Device | Field | Value |
|---|---|---|---|
| | | CSS | CSS-SJ |
| | | Location | SanJose |
| | **CTI Route Point DN** | Directory No | 3877 |
| | | Partition | P-Internal |
| | | CSS | Css-Restricted |
| | | Display (Internal Caller ID) | AutoAttendant |
| | | External Phone Mask | 408555xxxx |
| 2 | **CTI Port Device**<br><br>You need to create multiple CTI ports. Each device will have a unique name (CTIPort1, CTIPort2, and so on). | Device Name | CTIPort# |
| | | Description | CTI Ports |
| | | Device Pool | DP-SanJose |
| | | CSS | CSS-SJ |
| | | Location | SanJose |
| | | AAR CSS | None |
| | **CTI Port DN**<br><br>Each CTI port will have a unique directory number (1611, 1612 .. 1630).<br><br>The CFB and CFNA of the first CTI port, 1611, will be set to the 1612, and the CFB and CFNA of the second CTI port, 1612, will be set to 1613.<br><br>The CFB and CFNA for the last CTI port will be set to the first one, 1611. | Directory No | 1611–1630 |
| | | Partition | P-Internal |

*continues*

**Table 8-1** *Configuration Settings in CallManager for AA (Continued)*

| Step Number | Configured Device | Field | Value |
|---|---|---|---|
| | | CSS | CSS-Restricted |
| | | AAR Group | None |
| | | Call Waiting | OFF |
| | | CFB | 1612 |
| | | CFNA | 1612 |
| | | Display (Internal Caller ID) | AA CTI Port |
| | | External Phone Mask | |
| 3 | **JTAPI User** When associating devices, ensure that the No Primary Extension and No ICD Extension check boxes are checked. | First Name | Jtapi |
| | | Last Name | User |
| | | User ID | Jtapiuser |
| | | PIN | 12345 |
| | | Password | Cisco123 |
| | | Enable CTI Applications Use | Checked |
| | | Device Association | 3877, 1611–1630 |

## Configurations in the CRS/CRA Server for AA

The following configurations are required on the CRS/CRA server to enable the AutoAttendant application. Refer to Figure 8-7 to understand how the following configuration steps fit into the overall call flow. These steps require use of the CRA Admin page, which you can access at the following URL:

http://*IP_ADDR_OF_CRA_SERVER*/appadmin

1 Configure the AutoAttendant application. On the CRA Admin page, choose **Applications > Configure Applications**.

2 Configure the JTAPI provider. On the CRA Admin page, choose **Subsystems > JTAPI > JTAPI Provider**.

**3**  Configure the CTI port group and JTAPI call control group that consist of CTI ports that are defined in Table 6-40 (DN 1611 to 1630). On the CRA Admin page, choose **Subsystems > JTAPI > CTI Port Groups**.

**4**  Configure one media group consisting of 20 media ports. On the CRA Admin page, choose **Subsystems > Cisco Media**.

**5**  Configure the CTI route point trigger with DN 3877. On the CRA Admin page, choose **Subsystems > JTAPI > JTAPI Triggers**.

Table 8-2 lists the configuration settings that correspond to the preceding five configuration steps that need to be performed in the CRS server to set up the Cisco IP AA application.

**Table 8-2**    *Configuration Settings in CRS Server for AA*

| Step Number | Configured Device | Field | Value |
|---|---|---|---|
| 1 | **Application**<br>You can customize the welcome prompt by recording your own and uploading it into the CRS server directory. | Application Type | Cisco Script Application |
| | | Name | AA |
| | | Description | AutoAttendant |
| | | ID | 0 |
| | | Maximum No. of Sessions | 20 |
| | | Enabled | Yes |
| | | Script | aa.aef |
| | | Welcome Prompt | AAWelcome.WAV |
| | | Max Retry | 3 |
| | | Operator Extension | 3000 |
| | | Default Script | System Default |
| 2 | **JTAPI Provider**<br>The JTAPI Provider list comprises the IP addresses of the CallManager servers (Subscriber 1, Subscriber 2). | JTAPI Provider (s) | 10.1.1.6, 10.1.1.7 |
| | | User ID | Jtapiuser |

*continues*

**Table 8-2**  *Configuration Settings in CRS Server for AA (Continued)*

| Step Number | Configured Device | Field | Value |
|---|---|---|---|
| | | Password (Password is case sensitive) | Cisco123 |
| 3 | **CTI Port Groups** | Group ID | 0 |
| | | Description | AA-CTI Port Group |
| | | Associated CTI Ports | 1611–1630 |
| | | CSS for Redirect | Redirecting Party |
| 4 | **Cisco Media** | Group ID | 0 |
| | | Description | AA-Media Port Group |
| | | No. of Channels | 20 |
| 5 | **JTAPI Trigger** | CTI Route Point DN | 3877 |
| | | Language | System Default |
| | | Application Name | AA |
| | | Maximum No. of Sessions | 20 |
| | | Idle Timeout | 5000 ms |
| | | Enabled | Yes |
| | | Call Control Group | AA-CTI Port Group |
| | | Primary Dialog Group | AA-Media Port Group |
| | | Secondary Dialog Group | AA-Media Port Group |

# Implementing IP ICD

IP ICD is an IP-based Automated Call Distribution (ACD) system. IP ICD queues and distributes incoming calls destined for a group of CallManager users, which are also call center agents. Forty agents will have the capability to log in to the queue to take calls from the IP ICD.

However, based on the XYZ call center sizing, only 20 agents need to be logged in at any one time. The majority of the agents will be in San Jose. Seattle will have two agents, and Dallas will have one agent. At each shift, one supervisor agent will be logged into the queue.

Similar to the AutoAttendant script (aa.aef), IP ICD has a default script, icd.aef. You can customize the default script to your needs by using the CRA Application Editor, shown in Figure 8-8, that comes with CRS. The CRA Application Editor provides a drag-and-drop interface and several steps (including accepting the call, transfering the call, and so on.) that make it user friendly for developers.

To access the CRA Application Editor, on the CRA server, choose **Start > Programs > Cisco CRA Administrator > Cisco CRA Editor**.

You can also install the CRA Application Editor on your local workstation, create the scripts, and then upload the scripts to the CRA server. To install the CRA Application Editor locally on your workstation, open a web browser, access the CRA Admin page, and choose **Tools > Plug-ins > Cisco CRA Editor**.

All the application scripts are stored in the CRA server in the C:\Program Files\Wfavvid directory. Back up the original scripts before you modify them.

**Figure 8-8**    *CRA Application Editor*

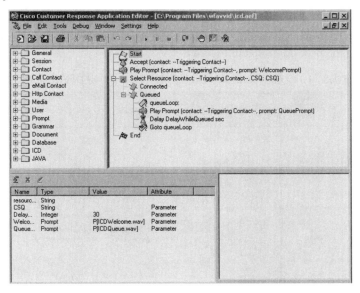

For XYZ, the default call center script, icd.aef, will be customized to add the time-of-day and day-of-week routing steps. Figure 8-9 shows the call-flow diagram for the modified script icd1.aef that queues the calls to the sales support queue of XYZ.

**Figure 8-9** *Sales Support ACD Call Flow of XYZ*

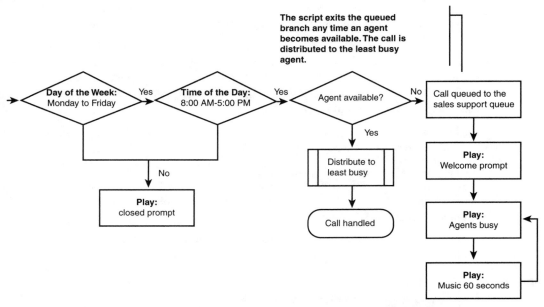

Figure 8-10 shows the modified icd.aef script deployed for the sales support group of XYZ based on the flow described in Figure 8-9.

**Figure 8-10** *Modified icd.aef Snapshot to Include Day of Week and Time of Day Routing*

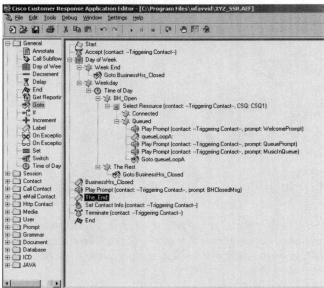

## Configuration Steps for IP ICD

IP ICD will be deployed using the modified icd1.aef script, as shown in Figure 8-10. Configuration of IP ICD involves configuration of the following:

- CallManager
- CRS server
- CRS server that is specific to IP ICD

The detailed steps that you need to follow to install and configure the applications are available on Cisco.com. The following sections discuss only high-level configuration steps.

### Configurations in the CallManager for IP ICD

The steps in the CallManager for configuring IP ICD are similar to those for configuring the AutoAttendant. Table 8-3 explains the various configuration steps specific to IP ICD.

**1** Configure the CTI route point. On the CallManager Administration page, choose **Device > CTI Route Point**. (Refer to Table 6-40 for the CTI route point assigned to IP ICD.)

**2** Configure the CTI ports. On the CallManager Administration page, choose **Device > Phone**. Select **Add a New Phone** and select the phone type as **CTI Port**. (Refer to Table 6-40 for the directory numbers assigned to the CTI ports to be used by IP ICD.)

**3** Associate the CTI route point and the CTI ports with the Jtapiuser created in Table 8-1. On the CallManager Administration page, choose **User > Global Directory**. Search for the Jtapiuser and complete the device association.

**4** Create an RM JTAPI provider in the CallManager. This is a user account in the CallManager. All the IP Phone users that are call center agents are associated with this user. On the CallManager Administration page, choose **User > Add a New User**. The RM JTAPI user is another provider (refer to Figure 8-6) that monitors the following devices:

  — The agent phone devices, such as IP Phones

  — CTI ports that are configured for Cisco IP SoftPhones only

  — Media-terminated desktop devices

Through this interface, the CRA server learns about the agent states such as work, reserved, ready, and not ready.

**5** Identify the call center agents and, in the CallManager directory in the device association, click the ICD Extension radio button for those users. On the CallManager Administration page, choose **User > Global Directory** and update the ICD extension for all the call center users.

Notice that in Table 8-3, ICD has been assigned ten CTI ports. In Chapter 6, in the "Customer Response Solution Server Scalability and Sizing" section, the call center sizing calculation (see Figure 6-4) resulted in six IVR/CTI ports. However, ten CTI ports are provisioned so that the system can handle more callers.

**Table 8-3** *Configuration Settings for CTI Route Points and CTI Ports, and JTAPI User for ICD*

| Step Number | Configured Device | Field | Value |
|---|---|---|---|
| 1 | **CTI Route Point** | Device Name | ICDRP |
| | | Description | ICD Route Point |
| | | Device Pool | DP-SanJose |
| | | CSS | CSS-SJ |
| | | Location | SanJose |
| | **CTI Route Point DN** | Directory No. | 3888 |
| | | Partition | P-Internal |
| | | CSS | CSS-Restricted |
| | | Display (Internal Caller ID) | ICD |
| | | External Phone Mask | 408555xxxx |
| 2 | **CTI Port Device**<br><br>You need to create multiple CTI ports. Each device will have a unique name (CTIPort1, CTIPort2, and so on). | Device Name | CTIPort# |
| | | Description | CTI Ports |
| | | Device Pool | DP-SanJose |
| | | CSS | CSS-SJ |
| | | Location | SanJose |
| | | AAR CSS | None |
| | **CTI Port DN**<br><br>Each CTI port will have a unique directory number (1601, 1602 .. 1610).<br><br>The CFB and CFNA of the first CTI port, 1601, will be set to 1602, and the CFB and CFNA of the second CTI port, 1602, will be set to 1603.<br><br>The CFB and CFNA for the last CTI port will be set to the first one, 1601. | Directory No. | 1601–1610 |
| | | Partition | P-Internal |

**Table 8-3**   *Configuration Settings for CTI Route Points and CTI Ports, and JTAPI User for ICD (Continued)*

| Step Number | Configured Device | Field | Value |
|---|---|---|---|
| | | CSS | CSS-Restricted |
| | | AAR Group | None |
| | | Call Waiting | OFF |
| | | CFB | 1602 |
| | | CFNA | 1602 |
| | | Display (Internal Caller ID) | ICD CTI Port |
| 3 | **Associate ICD CTI Route Points and CTI Ports to the JTAPI User**<br><br>When you are doing device association, ensure that the No Primary Extension and No ICD Extension check boxes are checked. | User ID | jptapiuser |
| | | Device Association | 3888, 1601–1610 |
| 4 | **Add an RM JTAPI User**<br><br>When you are doing device association, ensure that the No Primary Extension and No ICD Extension check boxes are checked. | First Name | rmjtapi |
| | | Last Name | user |
| | | User ID | rmjtapiuser |
| | | PIN | 12345 |
| | | Password | Cisco123 |
| | | Enable CTI Applications Use | Checked |
| | | Device Association | Associate the call center agent phone DNs. |
| 5 | **Assign ICD Extension to Call Center Agent Users**<br><br>Click the ICD Extension radio button on the CallManager Device Association page for all call center agent users. | Device Association | For all the call center users, click the ICD Extension and Primary Extension radio buttons. The Primary Extension radio button can be clicked for all other users. |

## Configurations in the CRS Server for IP ICD

The following configurations are required on the CRS/CRA server to enable IP ICD:

1 Configure ICD. On the CRA Admin page, choose **Applications > Configure Applications**.

2 Configure a CTI port group and JTAPI call control group that consists of CTI ports that are defined in Table 8-3 (DN 1601 to 1610). On the CRA Admin page, choose **Subsystems > JTAPI > CTI Port Groups**.

3 Configure one media group consisting of ten media ports. On the CRA Admin page, choose **Subsystems > Cisco Media**.

4 Configure the CTI route point triggers with DN 3888. On the CRA Admin page, choose **Subsystems > JTAPI > JTAPI Triggers**.

Table 8-4 lists the settings for the preceding four configuration steps that need to be performed in the CRS server to set up the IP ICD application.

**Table 8-4** *Configuration Settings on the CRS Server for IP ICD*

| Step Number | Configured Device | Field | Value |
|---|---|---|---|
| 1 | **Configure Application** You can customize the welcome prompt and ICD queue prompts by recording your own and uploading it into the CRS server. | Application Type | Cisco Script Application |
| | | Name | ICD |
| | | Description | ICD Application |
| | | ID | 1 |
| | | Maximum No. of Sessions | 10 |
| | | Enabled | Yes |
| | | Script | Icd1.aef |
| | | Welcome Prompt | ICDWelcome.WAV |
| | | Queue Prompt (prompt played while waiting in the queue) | ICDQueue.WAV |

**Table 8-4**  *Configuration Settings on the CRS Server for IP ICD (Continued)*

| Step Number | Configured Device | Field | Value |
|---|---|---|---|
| | | Delay While Queued (specifies time between prompts) | 30 |
| | | CSQ | SalesQ |
| | | Default Script | System Default |
| 2 | **CTI Port Groups** | Group ID | 1 |
| | | Description | ICD-CTI Port Group |
| | | Associated CTI Ports | 1601–1610 |
| | | CSS for Redirect | Redirecting Party |
| 3 | **Cisco Media** | Group ID | 1 |
| | | Description | ICD-Media Port Group |
| | | No. of Channels | 10 |
| 4 | **JTAPI Trigger** | CTI Route Point DN | 3888 |
| | | Language | System Default |
| | | Application Name | ICD |
| | | Maximum No. of Sessions | 10 |
| | | Idle Timeout | 5000 ms |
| | | Enabled | Yes |
| | | Call Control Group | ICD-CTI Port Group |
| | | Primary Dialog Group | ICD-Media Port Group |
| | | Secondary Dialog Group | ICD-Media Port Group |

## Configurations in the CRS Server That Are Specific to ICD

Follow these steps to configure the ICD subsystem:

1 Configure the RM JTAPI provider. On the CRA Admin page, choose **Subsystems > ICD > RM JTAPI Provider**.

2 Add a new skill SK-Sales. On the CRA Admin page, choose **Subsystems > ICD > Skills**.

3 Add a new resource group RG-Sales. On the CRA Admin page, choose **Subsystems > ICD > Resource Groups**.

4 Assign the skills to resources and the resources to resource groups. The resources here are the users. The skills indicate the users' specialties and expertise level. With XYZ, only one type of skill level—SK-Sales—is assigned to the users, and all agents are assigned to resource group RG-Sales. On the CRA Admin page, choose **Subsystems > ICD > Resources** and assign the skills and the resource group to the available resources. All the call center agents appear on the Resources page. If you do not see a user, ensure that in the CallManager that particular user has checked the ICD Extension check box.

5 Add a new Contact Service Queue (CSQ) CSQ-Sales. On the CRA Admin page, choose **Subsystems > ICD > Contact Service Queues**.

Table 8-5 shows the configuration settings that need to be performed on the CRS server for the ICD subsystem.

**Table 8-5**  *Configuration Settings on the CRS Server for the ICD Subsystem*

| Step Number | Configured Device | Field | Value |
|---|---|---|---|
| 1 | **Configure RM JTAPI Provider**<br><br>This is the user ID configured in CallManager in Table 8-3, Step 4. | RM JTAPI Provider (s) | 10.1.2.1, 10.1.3.1 |
| | | User ID | rmjtapiuser |
| | | Password | Cisco123 |
| 2 | **Skills** | Skill Name | SK-Sales |
| 3 | **Resource Group** | Resource Group Name | RG-Sales |
| 4 | **Assign Skills to Resources and Group the Resources into Resource Groups** | Resource Group | Assign all the resources to RG-Sales. |
| | | Assigned Skills | Assign the users to SK-Skills. |
| | | Competence Level | Varies from user to user. |
| | | Automatic Available<br><br>(Enabling this field makes the user immediately ready after finishing the current ICD call.) | Enabled |

**Table 8-5** *Configuration Settings on the CRS Server for the ICD Subsystem (Continued)*

| Step Number | Configured Device | Field | Value |
|---|---|---|---|
| 5 | **Contact Service Queue (CSQ)** Setting the CSQ service level to 5 does not display the agents whose competency levels are below 5 on the CSQ Configuration page. | CSQ Name | CSQ-Sales |
| | | Contact Queuing Criteria | FIFO |
| | | Automatic Work | Enabled |
| | | Resource Pool Selection Model | Resource Group |
| | | Service Level | 5 |
| | | Service Level Percentage | 70 |
| | | Resource Selection Criteria | Longest Available |
| | | Resource Group | RG-Sales |

## Call Center Agent and Supervisor Login Options

Agents can log in to the ICD queue in any of the following ways:

- Using the Cisco IP Phone Agent service on the IP Phone
- Using the Cisco Agent Desktop on the hard IP Phone
- Using the media termination desktop on the IP SoftPhone

Refer to the *Cisco Desktop Product Suite Installation Guide* for instructions on how to configure various agent login applications:

http://www.cisco.com/application/pdf/en/us/guest/products/ps1846/c1097/ccmigration_09186a00801f028a.pdf

The supervisor agents will use the Supervisor desktop agent.

# Implementing IP IVR

In addition to the AA and IP ICD published DID numbers, XYZ has another DID number (408-555-3800) to an IVR system that offers the following three menu choices:

- Transfer to an AutoAttendant
- Transfer to sales service support
- Transfer to an operator

Figure 8-11 shows the XYZ-IVR.aef script deployed to fulfill the main menu function.

**Figure 8-11** *Snapshot of XYZ-IVR.aef Script*

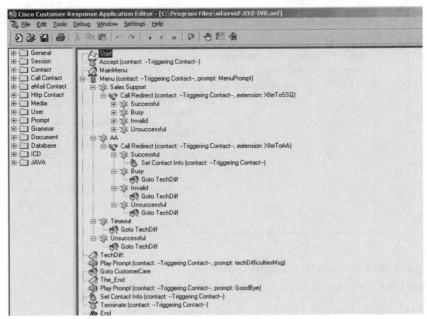

The menu application will be deployed using the following parameters for XYZ:

- One JTAPI call control group of 20 dedicated CTI ports (DN 1611 to 1630—refer to Table 6-40 in Chapter 6 for the internal numbering plan). The JTAPI call control group is shared with the AA application. This JTAPI call control group has already been created (refer to Table 8-2, Step 3).

- One media group of 20 media ports. The media group is shared with the AA application (refer to Table 8-2).

- The CTI route point triggers with DN 3800 (refer to Table 6-40 in Chapter 6).

# Implementing IP Phone Services

Cisco IP Phone models such as 7960, 7940, and 7970 have the ability to access diverse information such as weather, stock quotes, news updates, or any other information received in eXtensible Markup Language (XML) format. You can access these additional services by pressing the Services button on the Cisco IP Phone. You need a web server to host these services that can accept and process the HTTP requests coming from the Cisco IP Phones and send the response in XML format.

The Cisco IP Phone Services SDK provides sample software libraries and scripts that you can deploy readily in your IPT network. You can download the SDK free of charge from the following URL:

http://www.cisco.com/cgi-bin/dev_support/access_level/product_support

Cisco does not recommend installing this SDK on the CallManager servers. You can use a dedicated web server to host this application along with other IP Phone services such as weather, stock lookup services, and so forth. The next section looks at implementing the corporate directory access from Cisco IP Phones using the LDAP Search COM Server, which is bundled in the SDK.

## Corporate Directory Access Through IP Phones

Chapter 1, "Cisco IP Telephony Solution Overview," provided information on the CallManager directory architecture and described the two possible scenarios when working with the CallManager directory—directory access and directory integration—and the pros and cons of each approach.

There are limitations on the type of directories supported for integration (currently, Microsoft AD and Netscape iPlanet), but no such limitations apply for providing directory access to the endpoints such as IP Phones and SoftPhones. To provide directory access to the corporate directory from IP Phones, you do not need to integrate CallManager with the corporate directory. By using LDAP queries, users can obtain the information about the other users from the existing LDAPv3-complaint directory through the IP Phones and SoftPhones.

XYZ already has a corporate Active Directory deployment in its enterprise. It requires the directory access/lookup to the existing AD from the IPT endpoints and wants to enable only a few IP Phone services in the network.

Figure 8-12 illustrates directory access. (In this example, the access is provided to a Cisco IP Phone). The IP Phone user performs a user search against an LDAP directory (such as a corporate directory) by pressing the Directories button or Services button on the Cisco IP Phone, and receives numerous matching entries. From the results of the search, the IP Phone user selects a person and presses the Dial softkey on the Cisco IP Phone to make a call.

**Figure 8-12**    *Directory Access for IP Phones*

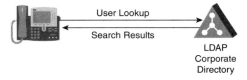

## Implementing Directory Access for IP Phones

Figure 8-13 shows how the directory access setup works. The web server is the machine that is running the LDAP Search COM Server application for the directory access and that hosts other IP Phone services. The IP Phones use HTTP to send requests to the web server. The responses from the web server contain some specific XML objects that IP Phones interpret and display on the screen.

**Figure 8-13**   *IP Phone Directory Access Through LDAP COM Server Access*

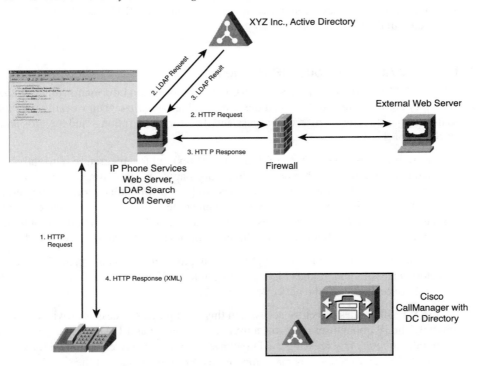

In a corporate directory search, the web server operates as a proxy by receiving the request from the IP Phone and translating it into an LDAP request, which in turn is sent to the corporate directory server such as XYZ Inc., Active Directory server as shown in Figure 8-13. The web server receives the response from the corporate directory server and sends the information back to the IP Phone in the form of XML objects.

## Installing and Configuring the LDAP Search COM Server

The sample IP Phone services scripts that are provided in the SDK are Active Server Pages (ASP) scripts. Hence, the web server must be running on Microsoft Internet Information Services (IIS). To build a new web server, select any server hardware platform. Install Windows

2000, IIS, and all the latest service packs and security hot fixes. Follow these steps to install and configure the LDAP Search COM Server:

1  Run the downloaded installation program, CiscoIPPS_SDK_v3.3.3.exe, on the web server. As previously cited, the SDK download page is http://www.cisco.com/cgi-bin/dev_support/access_level/product_support. You should stop the IIS service on the web server prior to the installation of the SDK to avoid copy violation errors. You have to restart the IIS service after completing the installation of SDK.

2  The installation program copies DLL files to the C:\WINNT\System32 directory and creates a new directory, C:\CiscoIPServices. It also copies a few sample IP Phone services scripts written in ASP to C:\CiscoIPServices\ASP.

3  The installation program copies the LDAP Search COM Server into the C:\CiscoIPServices \COMservers\LDAPSearch directory. This directory contains the ldapsearch.dll and the ASP script ldapsearch.asp that do the lookups to the external LDAP directory.

4  Move the C:\CiscoIPServices\COMServers\LDAPSearch directory under the C:\CiscoIPServices\ASP directory.

5  To install the LDAP Search COM Server:

   — Open a command prompt on the web server and change the directory to C:\CiscoIPServices\ASP\LDAPSearch.

   — Register the COM server by entering **regsvr32 LDAPSearch.dll**.

   Figure 8-14 shows the procedure for installing the LDAP Search COM Server.

**Figure 8-14**   *Installing the LDAP Search COM Server*

6  The installation program creates in IIS a virtual directory with the name CiscoIPServices that points to the C:\CiscoIPServices\ASP directory.

To see the virtual directory on the IP Phone services web server, choose **Start > Programs > Administrative Tools > Internet Services Manager**. Under Default Web Site, you can see the virtual directory CiscoIPServices, as shown in Figure 8-15.

**Figure 8-15** *CiscoIPServices Virtual Directory in IIS*

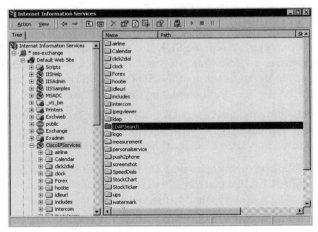

The virtual directory consists of all other directories in which sample scripts are stored for other IP Phone services. You can either create your own virtual directory or, if you already have an existing virtual directory, move the scripts to that directory. However, this requires modifications to the virtual directory path in all the scripts. Therefore, the easiest way is to use the default virtual directory. You can use this virtual directory as the base directory to reference the other scripts.

### Modifying the ldapsearch.asp Script

The next step is to modify the C:\CiscoIPServices\ASP\LDAPSearch\Ldapsearch.asp script and configure it to look up the corporate directory.

Figure 8-16 shows the parameters that require modification in the ldapsearch.asp file. As you can see, the password is in clear-text format. Therefore, the best practice is to create a separate user account for the directory search lookup instead of using an administrator account or any other account that has higher privileges. Table 8-6 describes the parameters in detail.

**Figure 8-16** *Modifying the Parameters in ldapsearch.asp*

```
//Modifications to ldapsearch.asp file

var ldapserver = "ldap.xyz.com";
var ldapport = "389";
var ldapuserid = "IPT Diruser";
var ldappasword = "cisco123";
var ldapsearchbase = "CN=Users, dc=xyz, dc=com"
```

**Table 8-6**  *Parameters in ldapsearch.asp*

| Attribute | Value | Description |
|---|---|---|
| ldapserver | ldap.xyz.com or the IP address of the corporate directory server. | Enter the IP address or host name of the corporate directory server. If you are using a DNS name, ensure that phones can resolve the name to the IP address. |
| ldapport | Default port that the corporate directory server will be listening on for LDAP queries. | You can obtain this information from your corporate directory team. For Microsoft AD, the port number is 389. |
| ldapuserid | Enter the user ID. This is required to authenticate to the corporate directory. Do not use the Administrator or equivalent ID. Create a new user that requires far fewer privileges. | For AD, the user ID is the display name. If you create a user with first name IPT and last name DirUser, AD puts the display name as "IPT DirUser" with a space in between. Ensure that you include the right display name here.<br><br>Some directories require a full canonical name, which has the format CN=Administrator, dc=xyz,dc=com |
| ldappassword | Password. | Enter the password required along with the user ID to authenticate to the LDAP server and obtain the LDAP queries. |
| ldapsearchbase | The user search base for the directory search. | Modify this to match the directory structure that is defined in the corporate directory server.<br><br>The full canonical name can be written as "cn=Users, dc=xyz, dc=com";<br><br>If you have users at multiple containers or multiple organizational units (OUs), set ldapsearchbase to point to the highest level. This ensures that the search includes all OUs. |

## Configuring IP Phone Services on the CallManager

After you modify the ldapsearch.asp file, the next step is to define the Directory Lookup service in the CallManager. To define a new IP Phone service, on the CallManager Administration page, choose **Feature > Cisco IP Phone Services** and click **Add New IP Phone Services**. This opens the Cisco IP Phone Services Configuration window, shown in Figure 8-17.

**Figure 8-17** *Defining IP Phone Services in CallManager*

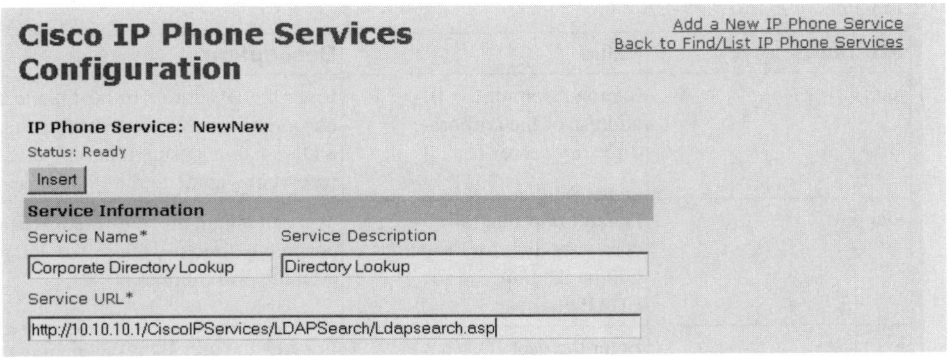

You can enter a meaningful service name in the Service Name field. The Cisco IP Phone displays the name you enter here when the user presses the Services button.

For the Service URL field, enter the following value:

http://*IP_ADDR*/CiscoIPServices/ldapsearch/ldapsearch.asp

You can use the IP address or host name of the web server. If you are using a host name, ensure that IP Phones can communicate with the DNS server to resolve the name-to-IP address mapping.

As mentioned earlier in this section, Directory Lookup is one of the services that is bundled in the IP Phone Services SDK. Other services include Calendar, Measurement conversions, and World Clock. A few services, such as Stock Ticker and World Clock, require access to the Internet for proper functioning.

Table 8-7 describes the URLs required to enable some of these services.

**Table 8-7** *Defining IP Phone Services*

| Service Name | Service URL |
|---|---|
| Directory lookup | http://*IP_ADDR*/CiscoIPServices/ldapsearch/ldapsearch.asp |
| Measurement conversions | http://*IP_ADDR*/CiscoIPServices/measurement/measurementmenu.asp |
| Calendar | http://*IP_ADDR*/CiscoIPServices/Calendar/cal.asp |
| Clock | http://*IP_ADDR*/CiscoIPServices/clock/clock.asp |

By default, the Directory button on Cisco IP Phones 7960, 7940, and 7970 points to the CallManager DC directory:

http://CallManager_IP_ADDRESS/CCMCIP/xmldirectory.asp

To access the previous setting, on the CallManager Administration page, choose **System > Enterprise Parameters**.

The parameter that points to the directories is URL Directories. You can change this URL and point it to the Directory Lookup service URL shown in Table 8-7. If you change it at this level, when users press the Directory button, the queries for the directory lookup refer to the corporate directory instead of the CallManager DC directory.

If you want to keep both DC directory lookup and corporate directory lookup, you have to create IP Phone Directory lookup service, as described in Table 8-7. This enables users to view the CallManager DC directory by pressing the Directory button on the IP Phone. To view the corporate directory listing, users press the Services button and choose the Directory Lookup service.

### Subscribing Users to IP Phone Services

After you define the IP Phone services, subscribe the users to the services by using any one of the following options:

- Ask users to go to the CCMuser page (http://*CallManager_IP_Address*/ccmuser) and subscribe themselves.
- Use the BAT to update the subscriptions on all phones.
- Manually update the subscriptions on all phones.

## Troubleshooting IP Phone Services

If you get errors on the IP Phone when you press the Directory button to access the corporate directory lookup or any other IP Phone services, review the IIS log file stored in the IP Phone services web server under the C:\Winnt\System32\LogFiles\w3svc1 directory.

Following are some common problems and possible resolutions:

- The most common problem encountered when troubleshooting the corporate directory access is that someone has entered invalid credentials in the ldapsearch.asp file, as shown in Figure 8-16. If you encounter this problem, you can find the following lines in the log file:

  2004-02-05 17:37:07 10.17.168.73 - 172.21.51.217 80 GET /CiscoIPServices/ Ldapsearch/ldapsearch.asp action=list|128|800a0031|**Invalid_credentials** 500 Allegro-Software-WebClient/3.12

  This error message clearly indicates that the supplied credentials entered in the ldapsearch.asp file are insufficient for the web server to contact the corporate LDAP server. Possible problems are entry of the wrong username, password, or IP address of the LDAP server. Check the settings and correct any issues.

- When you press the Services button on the IP Phone, if you get a Host Not Found error, check the URL Services service parameter on the CallManager Administration page. To access this parameter, on the CallManager Administration page, choose **System > Enterprise Parameters**. The typical value of this parameter is as follows

  http://*CallManager_Name*/CCMCIP/getservicesmenu.asp

  If you are using a name instead of an IP address in this URL, ensure that phones can resolve the name by contacting the DNS server. Otherwise, use the IP address.

- After you press the Services button on the IP Phone and the phone displays the list of subscribed services, if you get the Page Not Found error when you select a service, check whether the URL that is configured for the IP Phone services in the CallManager is correct. To test whether this URL is correct, open a web browser and type the same URL that you defined in the IP Phone Services page. If the web browser also reports that the page is not available, check the IIS log file and see whether the URL is right. If you are entering a wrong URL, the log file will have the following entry:

  2004-02-05 20:12:54 10.17.168.73 - 172.21.51.217 80 GET /CiscoIPServices/
  Ldapsearch/ldapsearc.asp l-l0l404_Object_Not_Found 404 Allegro-Software-WebClient/
  3.12

  As you can see, an attempt was made to access URL that does not exist on the server. In this example, the ASP filename entered was wrong. It should have been ldapsearch.asp instead of ldapsearc.asp. Correct this URL error in the CallManager in the IP Phone Services Definition page, and update the subscriptions.

- If you still have problems, try restarting the IIS service on the CallManager and on the IP Phone services web server.

- Some older ldapsearch.asp and other scripts have a known bug, which should be fixed in the next release of the SDK. The scripts mistakenly reference version 1 of the LDAP Search COM Server, but it cannot be found because the new SDK ships with version 2.

  Edit the ldapsearch.asp script and change the following line:

  var s = new ActiveXObject("LDAPSEARCH.LDAPSearchList.1");

  to

  var s = new ActiveXObject("LDAPSEARCH.LDAPSearchList");

  Removing the .1 causes IIS to load the latest version (which is 2) of the LDAP Search COM Server.

- The older ldapsearch.asp file also has another problem in which the *ldapsearchbase* variable is not included. Add the *ldapsearchbase* variable line in two places:

```
var ldapserver = "10.1.1.1";
var ldapport = "389";
var ldapuserid = "IPT User";
var ldappassword = "cisco123";
var ldapsearchbase = "CN=Users,dc=xyz,dc=com"
```

```
s.server = ldapserver;
s.port = ldapport;
s.AuthName = ldapuserid;
s.AuthPasswd = ldappassword;
s.searchbase = ldapsearchbase;
```

**NOTE**    Cisco TAC does not provide support for problems with the scripts in the Cisco IP Phone
Services SDK. If you still have problems, you can open a case with Developer Support Central:

http://www.cisco.com/en/US/products/svcs/ps3034/ps5408/ps5418/serv_how_to_order.html

# Identify the Implementation Tools

All the CallManager servers in a cluster must have the same CallManager OS version,
CallManager application version, and SQL server version for successful operation. In a large
network deployment, in the initial stages of implementation or during major upgrades, you
could miss upgrading one server or applying a hot fix on one or more servers. This section
discusses how to check the CallManager OS, CallManager, operating system, and SQL server
versions and identify inconsistencies in software versions.

## Checking the CallManager OS Version

To check the CallManager OS that is running on the CallManager servers, choose **Start > Cisco
OS Version**. The MCS Version Utility displays the CallManager OS version, as shown in
Figure 8-18. Notice that the base OS version is 2000.2.4 and that it has been upgraded to
2000.2.6.

**Figure 8-18**    *Checking the Cisco CallManager OS Version*

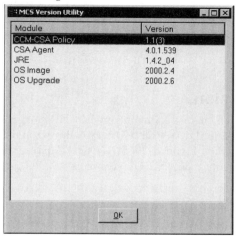

## Checking the CallManager Version

To check the CallManager version that you are running in the cluster, on the CallManager Administration page, click the **Details** button. Figure 8-19 shows the dialog box displaying the CallManager version, 4.0(1), and the active CallManager database name in use, which is CCM0300. You need to provide this information to Cisco personnel when you report problems with CallManager.

**Figure 8-19**   *Checking the Cisco CallManager Version*

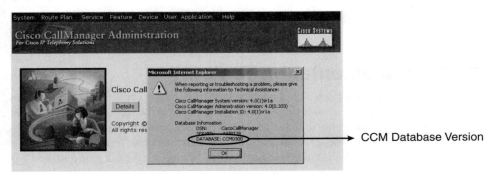

The replication process between the CallManager publisher and subscribers within a cluster ensures that the database is consistent across all the servers. If you see errors reported by the SQL service in the application event log, check the CallManager database version in the error message. CallManager makes a copy of the current database before any major upgrades. Therefore, there could be more than one version of the database in SQL, but at any point in time, only one database is active—the one that is specified in the DATABASE field in Figure 8-19.

If the database version reported in the event log is different from the version you see in the database information, you can neglect those types of events because the error indicates a problem with an old or unused version of the database. If the version is the same in both places, you should investigate the issue and see whether reestablishing the SQL replication resolves the issue.

## Checking the SQL Version

To check the SQL version that is running on the CallManager servers, choose **Start > Programs > Microsoft SQL Server > Query Analyzer** and enter the query statement **select @@version**, as shown in Figure 8-20. SQL Query Analyzer displays the SQL version in the result window. In Figure 8-20, the SQL version is 8.00.760.

Whenever you apply a SQL service pack or hot fix, make sure that you apply it to all the servers in the cluster and check the version on all the servers to ensure that all of them are running the same version.

**Figure 8-20** *Checking the Cisco CallManager SQL Version*

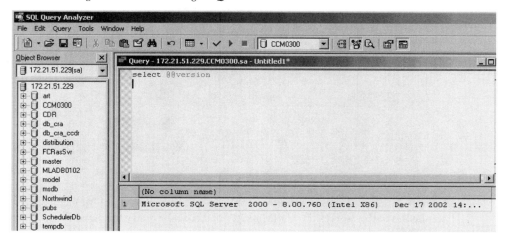

## Database Layer Tool to Check SQL Subscriptions

The DBL Helper tool diagnoses problems and restores replication in the CallManager database. To run the DBL Helper tool, run the DBLhelper.exe file located in the C:\Program Files\Cisco \Bin directory on the publisher server.

---

**NOTE**    If you do not have this tool installed on the publisher server, contact Cisco TAC to obtain this tool and copy it into the previously mentioned folder.

---

Figure 8-21 shows the interface for the DBL Helper tool. The tool has four tabs:

- SQLReplication
- NameResolution
- Compare DB
- Export/Import Data

**Figure 8-21** *DBL Helper Tool*

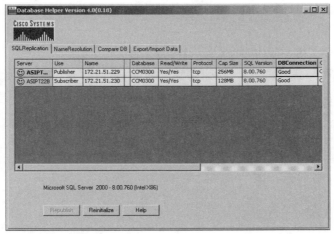

As shown in Figure 8-21, the CallManager cluster consists of two CallManager servers. The SQLReplication tab displays the CallManager database currently used and the SQL server version. You should check these fields whenever you perform CallManager or SQL upgrades to ensure that all the servers in the cluster have the same version of the software.

You can republish or reinitialize SQL subscriptions from the DBL Helper tool. Note that the Republish option is a powerful command, and it takes a considerable amount of time to republish the database. The Republish operation deletes the exiting subscriptions and re-creates them.

The Reinitialize option reinitializes all subscriptions, starts the snapshot agent, and attempts to rebuild the subscription with the current database. If the status column (not shown in Figure 8-21) on any particular CallManager subscriber reports errors, you can select that CallManager and click the Reinitialize button to establish the SQL subscription.

The NameResolution tab checks the name resolution and displays the name of the server in the database, the IP resolved name, the IP address, and the ping time.

The Compare DB tab allows you to compare two databases on the CallManager server. As mentioned before, whenever you perform a major version upgrade to a CallManager server, the old database is stored in the SQL server.

The Export/Import Data tab allows you to export all the data from the CallManager SQL database (or data from selected tables) into a CSV file. The import option does the reverse function. This feature is useful to make any bulk modifications to the database. However, do not make any modifications to the database using this tool unless you are directed to do so by Cisco support personnel. You should use BAT tool to make any bulk changes to the CallManager database.

## Checking Inconsistencies in the Software Versions Within the Cluster

To check for inconsistent versions of different components within a CallManager cluster, on the CallManager Administration page, choose **Help > Component Versions** and click the **Out of Sync** link. If you see inconsistencies, you should examine the files that are not consistent and resolve the issue.

## Multi-Level Administration Tool

The CallManager Multi-Level Administration (MLA) tool provides different levels of permission and access privileges to CallManager Administration and Serviceability pages. Prior to the release of the MLA tool, access to the CallManager Administration and Serviceability interfaces was global in nature and used basic Windows NT authentication. With this authentication method, all pages were available to anyone who logged in. There was no way of providing the granular access to these pages to classify administrators based on their responsibilities.

In large-scale IPT deployments, companies typically subcontract the deployment of IP Phones to other vendors. Using the MLA tool, the CallManager administrator can create different users and assign privileges to those users that limit them to just configuring and managing the IP Phones. The CallManager administrator can also use the MLA tool to track the changes made by the implementation team.

The MLA tool offers the following benefits:

- Keeps a log of changes made by different administrators
- Maintains audit logs and login attempt logs:
  - The audit logs keep track of the configuration changes to the CallManager Administration page and Serviceability page.
  - The login attempt logs keep track of authentication attempts.

For CallManager versions prior to 4.0, MLA was available in a separate software package. Starting with CallManager 4.0, MLA is included in the CallManager software, and no separate installation is required.

To enable the MLA feature in CallManager 4.0, on the CallManager Administration page on the publisher server, choose **User > Access Rights > Configure MLA Parameters** and set the Enable MultiLevelAdmin parameter to **True**. When you set the parameter to True, the web page prompts you to set the CCMAdministrator password. After you enable the MLA feature, use the user ID CCMAdministrator and the password you have entered to access the CallManager Administration pages.

You have to restart the web service on all the servers in the cluster after enabling the MLA feature. Use the CCMPwdChanger.exe tool discussed in Chapter 9 to reset the password for the CCMAdministrator user.

## Functional Groups

The functional groups in MLA comprise different CallManager administration functions. The standard functional groups predefined are as follows:

- Standard Plug-In
- Standard User Privilege Management
- Standard User Management
- Standard Feature
- Standard Service Management
- Standard Service
- Standard Serviceability
- Standard Gateway
- Standard Route Plan
- Standard Phone

These standard functional groups contain predefined menu pages that users can access. For example, users who have full access to the Standard Plug-In group have permissions to access the CallManager Install Plugins pages; users who have full access to the Standard Phone functional group have access to all the pages in CallManager Administration that allow them to modify, create, and add phones.

You can create new functional groups based on the predefined functional groups. However, you cannot modify the predefined functional groups.

## User Groups

User groups define the access privileges to various functional groups and users who have access to the functional groups. The following user groups are predefined:

- Gateway Administration
- Phone Administration
- Read Only
- Server Maintenance
- Server Monitoring
- Super User Group

You can assign a user to multiple user groups; the users in the Super User Group have full access. You cannot delete the Super User Group.

### Access Levels

By using the MLA authentication method, any user who attempts to access a CallManager menu or web page will be allowed one of three access levels:

- **Full Access**—Can perform all functions
- **Read Only Access**—Cannot make any changes
- **No Access**—Cannot even view the page

You can assign these access privileges to the functional groups.

The View Privileges Report prints all the user groups that are defined with their associated functional groups and privileges. This report will assist in troubleshooting problems with access privileges to different functional groups.

### MLA Logs

By default, the debug level in MLA is set to None. To enable full logging so that you can see the changes that the other administrators are making to the system, change the debug level to Debug. To access the debug level parameter, on the CallManager Administration page, choose **User > Access Rights > Configure MLA Parameters**.

MLA stores the log files in the C:\Program Files\Cisco\Trace\MLA directory. The PermissionsXXXXXX.txt file contains debug information. The AccessXX.log file contains login attempts of users and changes made by these users while they are logged in to CallManager web pages.

## Deploy IPT Solution Pilot

Before deploying the IPT solution for the entire organization, you should consider deploying an IPT solution pilot. The IPT solution pilot might be the initial deployment of the solution at a site or set of sites that is representative of the final deployed architecture. The goal of conducting a solution pilot is to gather the real world/real user performance feedback that will allow engineering or process changes to be made prior to a full rollout of the IPT solution throughout the organization.

During the deployment of the IPT solution pilot, you will gain experience with the deployment and operations of the solution. This is an opportune time to develop and tune methods and procedures for installation, configuration and operations of the components and systems, and support and training requirements.

## Implementation Acceptance Tests

It is important to verify the functionality of the IPT network after completing the actual deployment or after deploying the IPT solution pilot. Implementation engineers should conduct different acceptance tests (listed in Appendix H) to verify that the IPT system is functioning as per the requirements.

# Post-Implementation Documentation

After you complete IPT implementation, the project management team should document all equipment for asset-tracking purposes. The deployment team should complete documentation that includes the following items. Proper documentation helps in maintaining and operating the network.

- Updated IPT network topology diagram
- Serial numbers of all IPT devices
- CallManager/application server configurations, software versions, and passwords
- Call-processing backup or failover strategy
- Ethernet switch and router configurations
- IP address plan and VLAN assignments
- Carrier and circuit ID of all WAN links
- Gatekeeper or bandwidth control mechanism
- Asset tagging
- Cable labeling
- Customer acceptance certification and sign-off

# Day 2 Support

Supporting the converged network requires an organization to build a strong support team that has all the required expertise and to develop an escalation procedure. The support team should know the various tools available and how and when to use them.

Unlike the other support teams, the team that supports the converged network has to interact with other groups in the organization, which typically include the following:

- LAN/WAN group
- Enterprise messaging group
- Enterprise directory group
- Enterprise security group

Therefore, a strong working relationship among the groups is required. To manage the network, the support team must also understand the following:

- Networking, including routing and switching technologies, various routing protocols, and QoS
- Cisco CallManager and other deployed Cisco AVVID applications
- How to configure and troubleshoot voice gateways
- Microsoft OS operation and configuration

## Escalation Procedures

In an IPT network, the end customers are users of the IP Phones. By educating users on how to use the new IP Phones and phone features, you can eliminate most basic questions and cases that might otherwise be opened by the users.

Defining clear escalation procedures for handling problems related to the IPT network reduces the problem-resolution times and increases employee productivity.

One suggested approach is to use a four-tier model:

- **Tier 0: end user**—Refers to the user-facing FAQs and tutorials posted on the internal website.

- **Tier 1: voice help desk**—Handles the basic user issues even after the user has gone through tier 0.

- **Tier 2: voice network administration staff**—Handles escalations from tier 1. This group of users has higher-level access privileges to the systems than tier 1 staff and can add new phones and handle moves, adds, and changes (MACs), adding new services based on tier 3 group decisions. This group also gathers information related to a user-reported issue or a network outage issue to pass along to tier 3.

- **Tier 3: voice network design/architecture staff**—Responsible for network expansions, design changes, and capacity planning. Works with vendors such as Cisco to further investigate and troubleshoot issues.

# Training

The goal of many businesses today is to improve employee productivity and reduce costs by deploying new-world technologies such as IP Telephony, wireless, and storage area networking. To successfully deploy the new technologies and gain acceptability within the organization, it is necessary to educate the end users and the support and administration staff.

Following are some tips that can reduce the most basic support calls from the users:

- Build an internal website and post all the presentations, FAQs, and videos that teach how to use various features on the IP Phones. You can download the Cisco IP Phone tutorials on Cisco.com from the following URL:

  http://www.cisco.com/warp/public/779/largeent/avvid/products/clients.html

- Provide training to help desk staff on how to handle basic issues.

- Educate users and help desk staff on the escalation procedures.

# End-User Training

When switching from analog phones to Cisco IP Phones, end users require minimal training. End users do not have to do anything differently to use the basic phone features, such as making on-net and off-net calls, listening, deleting and leaving voice-mail messages, placing the call on hold, making conference calls, transferring a call, forwarding a call, and so forth. You can retain the same level of functionality in the Cisco IPT solution by designing the dial plan to meet these requirements. For example, if an end user is accustomed to dialing 9 to make off-net calls, configure CallManager to do the same. Also, you can plan to use the available features and buttons on the IP Phones that are similar to the features of the legacy phones, such as hold, transfer, and other functionality.

When end users see a Cisco IP Phone on their desks, they find it similar to legacy phones as far as the basic operation is concerned, with the exception of an LCD screen. This LCD screen is used to show several menus, options, outputs, and enhanced features, and to customize the IP Phone settings.

Cisco IP Phones ship with concise end-user guides, which are also available on Cisco.com. Armed with these guides and the online tutorials mentioned in the previous section, users will quickly feel comfortable using the new phone system.

# Help Desk Staff Training

The IPT support staff requires formal training regarding how to support the deployed IPT solution. Several IPT training courses are available through Cisco Systems training partners all over the world. There are also several IPT certifications available to test the efficiency of the IPT support staff.

The following training and exams are recommended for becoming a Cisco IPT support specialist. Completing this training and the exams enables the support staff to provide tier 1 support to end users when they report a problem.

- Cisco Voice over IP (CVOICE) course and CVOICE 642-432 exam
- Cisco IP Telephony (CIPT) course and CIPT 642-443 exam
- Deploying QoS for Enterprise Networks (DQOS) course and QoS 642-642 exam
- IP Telephony Troubleshooting (IPTT) course and IPTT 642-425 exam

# Voice Network Administration Staff Training

In the four-tier support model described earlier, the help desk staff will not have access to the IPT systems to make configuration or design changes to the IPT architecture. The administration staff includes the users who control and manage the IPT network components. The administration staff is responsible for making design and configuration changes in IPT components. The training that is required for administration staff is similar to the IPT support staff training. Usually, administration staff has senior engineers who have prior experience designing, deploying, configuring, troubleshooting, and managing IPT networks.

## Voice Network Design/Architecture Staff Training

The network design/architecture staff consists of engineers who are involved from the planning stages of the IPT network. This group typically handles the following:

- Proactive monitoring of the network and execution of optimization steps
- Critical service failures
- Scalability- and performance-related issues
- Ongoing network expansion/design projects
- Adding products that contribute features to the existing IPT network

This group also interfaces with product vendors such as Cisco during critical problem escalation. Prior to contacting Cisco to report issues, this group should organize and collect the following information:

- Clear and concise problem description
- What hardware platform(s) are involved
- What software version(s) are involved
- What network topology is involved (in case of reactive requests)
- If more than one Cisco product is involved, an accurate topology diagram, including device names, locations, and IP addresses
- Dial-in details (for reactive requests)
- Hardware and software configuration(s)

# Summary

This chapter provided various steps and best practices involved in implementing the IPT solution. For detailed configuration steps and troubleshooting methods, refer to the product-specific documents and configuration guides available on Cisco.com.

Chapter 9 explains the various operational tasks involved in IPT networks and introduces you to some of the commonly used tools and optimization techniques.

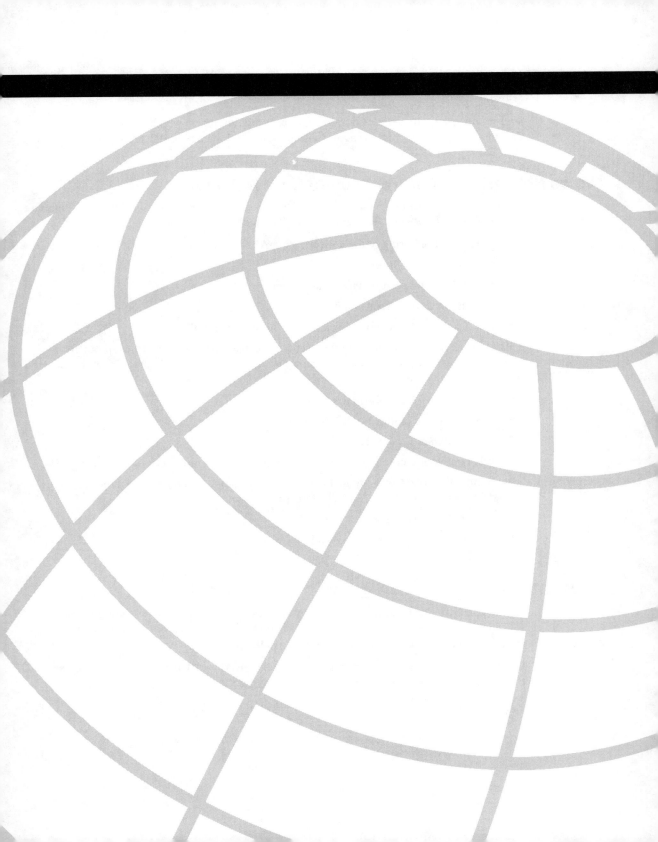

# Operations and Optimization

Network administrators perform daily operations and optimization procedures on their networks. The types of operations and optimization procedures that they perform, the tools that they use, and the methodology that they follow vary from one technology to another.

This chapter discusses the operations and optimization tasks involved in Cisco IP Telephony (IPT) networks and introduces various tools and best practices in this final phase of the planning, design, implementation, operation, and optimization (PDIOO) life cycle. Topics discussed in this chapter include the following:

- Software upgrades
- Hardware upgrades
- CallManager operating and monitoring tools
- Optimization tips
- Day 2 monitoring and management tasks
- IPT network management tools

## Software Upgrades

Upgrading existing software applications from time to time incorporates new features and fixes any defects that existed in the earlier software versions. The upgrade planning and procedures vary from one IPT component to another. Hence, you should read the upgrade documentation and release notes for new versions thoroughly before you perform an upgrade.

Also, before you perform upgrades in the production network, test the new software versions in the lab network to ensure that you do not encounter new problems, such as lack of interoperability with other products in the network.

You can make the following types of upgrades in Cisco IPT solutions:

- Upgrade the operating system
- Upgrade application software, such as Cisco CallManager, Cisco Unity, and Cisco Customer Response Applications (CRA)
- Upgrade the software on IPT endpoints, such as gateways and Cisco IP phones

The next few sections provide the best practices and recommendations for performing various software upgrades.

# Operating System Upgrades

Again, a general rule is to test any OS upgrades or application software upgrades in the lab network prior to applying them in the production network. This section describes the following recommended practices for OS upgrades:

- Subscribe to notification alerts from Cisco Systems.
- Stop services such as antivirus scanning and monitoring tools.
- Use recommended server access methods to perform upgrades.
- Schedule the upgrade.
- Document registered device counts.

## Subscribe to Notification Alerts

It is important to ensure that all the people in the organization who are responsible for managing the IPT network are notified of new software releases related to voice products as and when they become available. You can sign up for the Cisco Voice Technology Group subscription tool, available at the following URL, to receive notifications on the new OS service releases, CallManager, and other applications availability:

http://www.cisco.com/cgi-bin/Software/Newsbuilder/Builder/VOICE.cgi

You also should sign up to receive security field notices from Cisco. For procedures on subscribing, refer to the following URL:

http://www.cisco.com/en/US/products/
products_security_vulnerability_policy.html#SecurityInfo

## Stop Services

Before you perform software upgrades on CallManager servers or any other Cisco AVVID application servers, such as Cisco Unity or CRA, stop the antivirus software scanners and third-party monitoring tools and disable Cisco Security Agent (CSA) if it is running.

Use the following steps to disable CSA:

**Step 1**  Right-click the **CSA** icon on the program bar and click **Suspend Security**. Click **OK** when asked whether you want to suspend it.

**Step 2**  Go to the Start > Programs > Administrative Tools > Services menu option on the CallManager or on the application server. From the list of services, select the Cisco Security Agent Service and click the Stop Service button to stop the service.

To disable McAfee VirusScan:

**Step 1**    Double-click the **VirusScan** icon on the program bar.

**Step 2**    Click the **<Disable>** button.

---

**NOTE**    You must complete both of the steps described to disable CSA. Otherwise, CSA prevents the installation process from stopping IISADMIN or any other required services and installation fails. If you are using a virus scanner other than McAfee, follow the vendor instructions to disable it.

---

## Use Recommended Server Access Methods to Perform Upgrades

Cisco recommends that you not perform upgrades via Microsoft Terminal Services Client. Instead, perform upgrades via Virtual Network Computing (VNC) or directly from the console. VNC software is bundled along with CallManager. It is available under the C:\Utils\VNC directory on the CallManager servers. For security reasons, you should disable VNC during normal operations. When you need to perform upgrades, use Windows Terminal Services to enable VNC and then disable it after the upgrade is complete. For upgrades, or whenever a reboot is required, always make sure to have a local resource around to work directly on the server console, if required.

## Schedule the Upgrade

In most cases, software upgrades to servers require a reboot. This causes some interruptions to the call processing. Therefore, make sure to do the following:

- Plan to do the upgrades during off-peak hours.
- Notify your management, network operations center (NOC) staff, and end users about the anticipated service disruptions and the upgrade timeframe.
- Prepare a backout plan so that you can quickly revert to older versions if the upgrade fails.

## Document Registered Device Counts

The server reboots during upgrades cause devices such as IP phones, gateways, and media resource devices to unregister and reregister with the servers. Therefore, before you begin the upgrade, make a note of the number of devices registered to each CallManager server by monitoring the following performance counters, the names of which are self-explanatory:

- FXOPortsInService
- FXSPortsInService
- RegisteredHardwarePhones

- RegisteredMGCPGateway
- RegisteredOtherStationDevices
- TranscoderResourcesTotal
- PRISpansInService
- T1SpansInService

You can use either the Performance Monitor application that comes with Windows 2000/2003 or the Real-Time Monitoring Tool (RTMT; refer to the "Real-Time Monitoring Tool" section, later in this chapter) to collect this information. The registered device counts taken after the upgrade should closely match the counts taken before the upgrade.

To run Performance Monitor on CallManager servers, select **Start > Programs > Administrative Tools > Performance**. After the application opens, as shown in Figure 9-1, you can add the counters in the preceding list and any other counters by selecting the appropriate performance object. After you add all the desired counters to monitor, you can save the view as a Microsoft Management Console (MMC) file by selecting Save from the Console menu. Running this saved MMC file before you perform an upgrade opens the Performance Monitor screen with all the configured counters.

**Figure 9-1** *Monitoring Performance Counters*

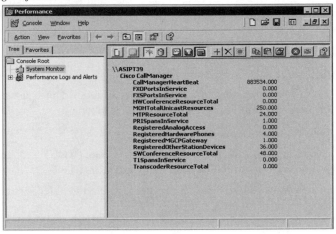

# Windows Operating System Upgrade

CallManager and many other IPT applications run on the Microsoft Windows 2000 Server platform. To install any of these IPT applications (except Cisco Unity) on the Windows 2000 Server, you use special Windows installation CD-ROMs (Media Convergence Server [MCS] Operating System [OS] CD-ROM) with special installation screens that prompt for user input and configure the IPT applications during the installation.

On the second Tuesday of every month, Microsoft releases security hot fixes to resolve defects in any of the windows operating system versions. This does not apply to critical fixes, which are released immediately after the vulnerability is reported and the fix is available. Do not install the hot fixes for IPT application servers by directly downloading them from the Microsoft website unless Cisco recommends doing so.

For critical hot fixes released by Microsoft, Cisco policy is to test and then post them on Cisco.com within 24 hours. Cisco consolidates the noncritical fixes in the form of Operating System Upgrade Service Releases and posts them on Cisco.com on the third Tuesday of every month.

Because Cisco Unity servers are loaded with regular Windows 2000/2003 OS CD-ROMs, you can load the hot fixes or apply the OS service packs that are available from Microsoft. Check the following URL for the recommended way to apply these service packs for Cisco Unity and Cisco Unity Bridge products:

http://www.cisco.com/univercd/cc/td/doc/product/voice/c_unity/cmptblty/msupdate.htm

---

**NOTE**    Cisco does not modify the actual security hot fix released by Microsoft, although Cisco might add its own wrapper to simplify the installation and provide a consistent user interface to the CallManager administrator for all OS upgrades.

---

The following URL provides the CallManager security patch process:

http://www.cisco.com/application/pdf/en/us/guest/products/ps556/c1167/ccmigration_09186a 0080157c73.pdf

The best practice is to apply the OS hot fixes and OS upgrade service releases at a regular interval on all servers. You should apply the critical hot fixes immediately after the patch is available. This process aids in hardening the OS. In most cases, the OS patches are independent of the application running on the servers. Hence, the changes in the hot fix will not affect the application.

# CallManager Software Upgrade

In the Cisco IPT solution, CallManager is the heart of the network, and the availability of the IPT system depends on the uninterrupted running of the CallManager servers. Thus, the major task in software upgrades is to upgrade the software on the CallManager servers. This section covers the following information that you need before you can perform the CallManager software upgrade:

- Upgrade planning and impacts
- Failover procedure
- Recovery methods

## Upgrade Planning and Impacts

Before you decide to upgrade the CallManager software version, ask yourself the following questions:

- Does the current version have any critical defects?
- What defects are fixed in the new version? Do these defects apply to the existing network?
- Does the new version include any new features or support for additional hardware that would be useful to deploy in the existing network?
- Did Cisco announce the End of Life for the current version?

If no critical defects are affecting your existing deployment and product support is continued for your deployment, you do not need to rush for the upgrade. You also need to consider the amount of time and resources required to complete the upgrade before you make a decision.

As mentioned earlier, if you do decide to upgrade, you should perform the upgrade in the lab network before you apply it in the production cluster. You should develop a test plan to test the features and full functionality that deployed in your production environment. Document any changes that end users will notice because of the upgrade, and communicate this information to them ahead of time. If necessary, develop a plan to educate or train the users on new features that you want them to know about.

## Failover Procedure

All software upgrades require that you reboot the servers at the end of the process. This causes some interruptions to call processing. However, you can minimize these interruptions by following this failover procedure:

**Step 1**  Back up the Publisher database before you attempt an upgrade.

**Step 2**  Perform the upgrades on the Publisher server and reboot.

**Step 3**  Perform the upgrades on the TFTP server and reboot.

**Step 4**  Upgrade the backup subscriber and reboot. Fail over all devices to the backup subscriber, leaving the primary subscriber idle, and perform upgrades.

**Step 5**  Set the startup type for the Cisco CallManager service (ccm.exe) to Manual on the primary subscribers. This ensures that the CallManager service does not start automatically after a reboot. This avoids phones cycling between primary and backup subscribers if the upgrade requires multiple reboots.

**Step 6**  Perform the upgrade on the primary subscriber and reboot. Start the CallManager service and set it to start automatically if you have set it to start manually in the previous step. Fail over the devices back to the primary subscriber after the upgrade is complete and successful.

You should perform the upgrades sequentially, one at a time in the cluster. In a Cisco CallManager cluster, you must upgrade all the servers in the cluster to ensure that all of them run the same CallManager version, OS version, and SQL version. Ensure that you reboot the server after the upgrade.

## Recovery Methods

You should plan for the restoration of the system to its original state in case you encounter any problems during the upgrades. The following are the three methods to speed up the recovery:

- Use backup data.
- Use mirrored hard drives.
- Uninstall newly installed software.

The following sections describe these recovery procedures.

### Recovery Using Backup Data

Before you make changes to the system, make sure the Backup and Restore System (BARS— the software component that runs on CallManager servers to back up and restore the data) has successfully completed the backup of data. Store the backup data on a tape drive or a network drive. Successful backup helps you to restore the system to the same state that it was in before the upgrade. Remember that BARS does not back up the OS files or the data files of other, third-party applications.

Recovery using the backup data requires more time because it involves many steps, as described here:

- You have to build the server freshly starting with the operating system install and bring it to the same level as the system from which the backup was taken. The IP address and server name of this new server should match with the old system.
- Install the CallManager application and install any additional service packs to bring it up to the same version level as the old system.
- Install the BARS application and start the data restoration process.
- After successfully restoring the data, install the tools and any other products that existed on the old system, such as Bulk Administration Tool (BAT), CDR Analysis and Reporting (CAR), antivirus software, and CSA.

### Recovery Using Mirrored Hard Drives

A few Cisco Media Convergence Server (MCS) platforms, such as 7835 and 7845, are equipped with two or more hard drives configured with redundant array of independent disks (RAID) 1, also called drive mirroring. In the second method of recovery, you can pull the mirrored hard drive on each machine before you make the upgrade. This recovery method takes less time than using backup data, but it requires spare hard drives.

This process requires careful planning. If you have a server with two hard drives (one in slot 0 and the other in slot 1), remove the drive in slot 1 before starting the upgrade. Label the drive with the machine name and the slot number from which it was taken out. Keep the removed drive in a safe place. If you need to use it for recovery, follow these steps:

**Step 1**    Power off the server.

**Step 2**    Remove the hard drive from slot 0.

**Step 3**    Insert into slot 1 the hard drive that was pulled before the upgrade.

**Step 4**    Power on the server. The server will boot from the drive in slot 1.

**Step 5**    At the bootup screen, press **F2** to select the Interim Recovery mode option.

After the system successfully boots up, insert the drive in slot 0. The system starts mirroring the data from slot 1 to slot 0. You can monitor the progress of mirroring through the HP Array Configuration Utility on the CallManager servers. To access this utility, select **Start > Programs > HP System Tools > HP Array Configuration Utility**.

### Recovery by Uninstalling the Software

After you perform the upgrade to the latest version, if you notice any issues, you can uninstall the recently installed software upgrades by using Add/Remove Programs, accessed from the Control Panel. You should also refer to the release notes or installation instructions for the software to get the exact steps that are required to uninstall the software.

# Application Software Upgrades

CallManager integrates with many other Cisco IPT applications IPT applications and third-party third-party products. Before you make an upgrade decision about CallManager or any application software, you should check whether the new version of the CallManager software is compatible with the other software products that are running in the cluster. Refer to the Cisco CallManager Compatibility Matrix on Cisco.com before you make an upgrade decision:

http://www.cisco.com/univercd/cc/td/doc/product/voice/c_callmg/ccmcomp.htm

Cisco certifies the third-party products that work with Cisco CallManager and other Cisco AVVID applications through its Cisco AVVID certified partner program. Before you purchase third-party software or perform an upgrade, ensure that the partner product is certified by going to the following URL:

http://www.cisco.com/en/US/partners/pr46/pr13/partners_program_solution09186 a00800a3807.html

## Upgrade Planning and Impacts

Because OS installation steps are the same for the majority of the Cisco AVVID applications and CallManager, the best practices recommended performing OS upgrades for CallManager that also apply to the application servers.

However, the process of upgrading software versions for each application varies from one product to another. Refer to the specific product documentation and release notes before the upgrade.

The list that follows includes a few commonly omitted tasks after a CallManager upgrade affects the functioning of the application servers:

* Whenever you upgrade the CallManager version, download the new version of the JTAPI plug-in from the Cisco CallManager Plug-Ins page on the application servers that use a JTAPI connection to communicate with CallManager. For CRA servers, you can use the JTAPI Update tool to upgrade the JTAPI version. To access this tool, on the CRA server, select **Start > Programs > Cisco CRA Administrator > JTAPI Update Tool**. Examples of such applications are CRA servers (Cisco IP-IVR, Cisco IPCC Express), Cisco Conference Connection (CCC), Cisco Emergency Responder (CER), and CallManager Peripheral Gateway (PG) devices in a Call Center network deployed using Intelligent Contact Management (ICM).

* Download the new version of TAPI Service Provider (TSP) from the CallManager Plug-Ins page to the application servers that use a TAPI connection to communicate with CallManager. Examples of such applications are third-party voice mail, Cisco IP SoftPhone, or other applications that use TSP drivers.

* If you have deployed Cisco Unity in the network, you might have to upgrade the Cisco Unity-CM TSP drivers on the Unity servers. Check the Cisco CallManager Compatibility Matrix, download the recommended version onto Unity servers, and perform the upgrade. TSP upgrade on the Unity servers requires reboot of Unity servers. Check the latest Unity TSP Compatibility Matrix with CallManager versions on Cisco.com at

  http://www.cisco.com/univercd/cc/td/doc/product/voice/c_unity/cmptblty/tspmtrx.pdf

* If you have integrated CallManager with a corporate Lightweight Directory Access Protocol (LDAP) directory such as Microsoft Active Directory or Netscape Directory Server, check the CallManager documentation and perform the schema updates on the directory servers if required. Changes made to the directory schema cannot be reverted. Hence, the best practice is to take a backup of the corporate directory database before you upgrade the schema. CallManager schema updates are backward compatible, so after you update the schema, even if you downgrade the CallManager version, it still works with the new schema.

* Sometimes new CallManager versions also include updates to the applications, such as BAT, CAR, and RTMT. Make sure to check the release notes and update these applications accordingly.

# IP Phone and Gateway Upgrades

IP phones and gateways are the other components in the Cisco IPT solution that might require change in the firmware loads to fix some defects or implement new feature functionality. Typically, a CallManager upgrade also upgrades the firmware on the IP Phones and on the Catalyst MGCP–based voice gateways. Thus, you do not have to follow separate installation procedures.

The next section discusses the following three topics:

**Step 1**   Understand the procedure to upgrade the firmware on a few Cisco IP phones or on a few gateways.

**Step 2**   Discuss the planning steps to perform the phone/gateway loads and impact of the upgrade process.

**Step 3**   Identify the steps to revert back to the old firmware in case the upgrade operation fails.

## Upgrading the Firmware on a Few Cisco IP Phones or Gateways

You might need to upgrade the firmware on some Cisco IP Phones or Gateways to test the functionality and features in the new firmware versions before rolling out the changes to all the Cisco IP Phones and Gateways in the production network. The best practice when upgrading the firmware is to load it on a few devices and run it for a few days. If the results are good, you should proceed with upgrading the firmware on all devices.

You can specify the device firmware loads in two places in CallManager. One is on the Device Defaults page. To access this page from the Cisco CallManager Administration page, select **System > Device Defaults**. Before performing the upgrade, make a note of the device load versions specified in this page. The second place is at the individual IP phone or the gateway level. The device firmware specified at the individual device level takes precedence over the specified firmware on the device defaults page.

To perform a selective upgrade of firmware on devices, download the latest firmware and copy the binary files onto the TFTP server. The default path is C:\Program Files\Cisco\TFTPPath. If you are downloading an executable wrapper that contains the loads, the wrapper automatically copies the files to the TFTP server and updates the Device Defaults page with the latest load information. To perform the selective upgrade, you need to update the Device Defaults page configuration that points back to old load IDs.

To upgrade the load on a Cisco IP phone, from the Cisco CallManager Administration page, search for the IP phone for which you want to perform the upgrade and, in the phone device configuration, specify the IP phone Load ID, as shown in Figure 9-2, and reset the phone. After the Cisco IP Phone reboots, verify that the Cisco IP Phone has the latest phone load. On 7960/7940 Cisco IP Phone models, to verify the load, press the Settings button on the Cisco IP Phone and then choose **Status > Firmware Versions** menu options to verify that the App Load ID displayed matches the configured Load ID on the Cisco IP Phone device page, as shown in

Figure 9-2. After the Cisco IP Phone registers with CallManager, make a note of the IP address from the CallManager Administration page and browse to the phone to check the software version when you are not local to the IP phone.

**Figure 9-2**    *Selective Upgrade of Firmware on Cisco IP Phones and Gateways*

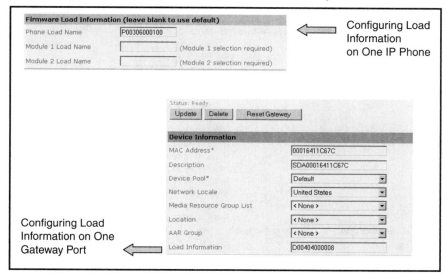

To upgrade the load on a few gateways, configure the load on the gateway configuration page and reset the gateways. Figure 9-2 shows the specific load ID being configured for a WS-6608 MGCP T1 PRI gateway. To verify the load ID on the Catalyst 6608 gateway port, use the **show version** command on the switch, as shown in Example 9-1. Looking at the highlighted portion of the example, port 4/1 has a different load (D00404000008) than the rest of the gateway ports (D00404000007). Ports 4/4 to 4/7 are configured as conference bridges in CallManager and have a different load ID, C00103010014.

**Example 9-1**    *Verifying the Gateway Load on a Catalyst WS-6608-T1 Gateway Port*

```
cat6k-voice> (enable) show version
WS-C6509 Software, Version NmpSW: 8.1(3)
Copyright © 1995-2003 by Cisco Systems
NMP S/W compiled on Oct 10 2003, 12:38:01

System Bootstrap Version: 5.3(1)
System Boot Image File is 'bootflash:cat6000-supk8.8-1-3.bin'
System Configuration register is 0x2

Hardware Version: 2.0   Model: WS-C6509   Serial #: SCA0443045D

PS1  Module: WS-CAC-1300W      Serial #: SON04472655

Mod Port Model                 Serial #     Versions
```

*continues*

**Example 9-1** *Verifying the Gateway Load on a Catalyst WS-6608-T1 Gateway Port (Continued)*

```
--- ----  ---------------------  ---------- ------------------------------------
1   2     WS-X6K-SUP1A-2GE       SAD04480PZW Hw : 7.0
                                             Fw : 5.3(1)
                                             Fw1: 5.4(2)
                                             Sw : 8.1(3)
                                             Sw1: 8.1(3)
          WS-X6K-SUP1A-2GE       SAD04480PZW Hw : 7.0
                                             Sw :
3   48    WS-X6348-RJ-45         SAL05031N6H Hw : 1.4
                                             Fw : 5.4(2)
                                             Sw : 8.1(3)
4   8     WS-X6608-T1            SAD04320KZA Hw : 1.1
                                             Fw : 5.4(2)
                                             Sw : 8.1(3)
                                             HP1: D00404000008; DSP1: D0054133 (4.1.33)
                                             HP2: D00404000007; DSP2: D0054133 (4.1.33)
                                             HP3: D00404000007; DSP3: D0054133 (4.1.33)
                                             HP4: C00103010014; DSP4: C002E031 (3.3.2)
                                             HP5: C00103010014; DSP5: C002E031 (3.6.15)
                                             HP6: C00103010014; DSP6: C002E031 (3.6.15)
                                             HP7: C00103010014; DSP7: C002E031 (3.6.33)
                                             HP8: D00404000007; DSP8: D0054133 (3.6.33)
6   5     WS-SVC-CMM             SAD075303F1 Hw : 2.2
                                             Fw : 12.2(13)ZP2,
                                             Sw : 12.2(13)ZP2,
7   5     WS-SVC-CMM             SAD0640008A Hw : 2.1
                                             Fw : 12.2(13)ZP,
                                             Sw : 12.2(13)ZP,
15  1     WS-F6K-MSFC            SAD04480KXC Hw : 1.4
                                             Fw : 12.1(1)E,
                                             Sw : 12.1(1)E,

       DRAM                   FLASH                 NVRAM
Module Total   Used    Free   Total   Used    Free   Total Used  Free
------ ------- ------- ------- ------- ------- ------- ----- ----- -----
1      65408K  48723K  16685K  16384K  11459K  4925K  512K  280K  232K

Uptime is 88 days, 0 hour, 22 minutes
cat6k-voice> (enable)
```

## Upgrade Planning and Impacts

After you have successfully tested the new loads on a few devices and are ready to upgrade the firmware for the entire cluster, follow these steps:

**Step 1**   Update the Device Defaults page to reflect the new firmware load ID.

**Step 2**   Remove the device-specific load information from the phones or the gateways, as configured in Figure 9-2. If you do not perform this step, when you later upgrade the whole cluster with new device loads, these devices will still have the old load.

**Step 3**  Reset the phones or gateways based on device pools to minimize the number of TFTP requests sent to the TFTP server. In a CallManager cluster with many IP phones, performing a firmware upgrade on all the devices at once affects the performance of the TFTP server. This results in connection timeouts for TFTP requests.

### Failover Procedures and Recovery Methods

You can always revert to the old device loads if you have to do so. The old firmware images still exist in the TFTP server. Hence, all you need to do is update the Device Defaults page to point back to the old firmware load ID and reset the phones and gateways based on the device pool.

---

**NOTE**    Starting with CallManager 3.3.3 Software Release 1, Cisco has added image authentication to its various IP Phone protocols. This prevents tampering with the binary image prior to its being loaded into the phone. Any tampering with the image causes the phone to fail the authentication process and reject that image. The image authentication occurs through signed binary files. After the phones are loaded with the signed binary loads, you cannot revert to unsigned loads.

If you want to load the unsigned loads on a phone that was previously booted with signed binary loads, you are out of luck. Your only option is to send the phones back to Cisco and receive replacements.

---

# BIOS Upgrades

The BIOS contains all the code required to control the keyboard, display screen, disk drives, serial communications, and several miscellaneous functions. Server vendors release upgrades to the BIOS to add additional functionality into the BIOS. Cisco posts on Cisco.com the upgrades to the BIOS for various server platforms. Upgrading the BIOS requires rebooting the servers. Hence, you should follow the same guidelines described earlier in the "Operating System Upgrades" section to reduce the impact on the call processing.

# Hardware Upgrades

Along with software upgrades, you might have to upgrade the hardware components in the IPT network. The hardware upgrades include upgrading the memory on the servers, voice gateways, and routers, and upgrading the server platform. This section discusses the upgrades to the server platform.

# Memory Upgrades

Three critical pieces of server resources are CPU, memory capacity, and hard disk size. Monitoring these resources should be a part of the day-to-day monitoring task for the CallManager administrators. Use RTMT in CallManager 4.0 and above to monitor the performance counters listed in Table 9-1. If you are using older versions of CallManager, include the performance counters listed in Table 9-1 in your monitoring list. Also, remember that you have to monitor these parameters for all the CallManager servers in the cluster.

**Table 9-1** *Performance Counters to Monitor on CallManager Servers*

| Performance Object | Counter |
|---|---|
| Memory | Available Kilobytes |
| | Available Megabytes |
| | Cache Bytes |
| | Demand Zero Faults/sec |
| | Page Faults/sec |
| | Page Reads/sec |
| | Page Writes/sec |
| | Pages Input/sec |
| | Pages Output/sec |
| | Pages/sec |
| Paging file | % Usage - _Total Instance |
| | % Usage Peak - _Total Instance |
| Logical disk (all instances) | % Disk Read Time |
| | % Disk Time |
| | % Disk Write Time |
| | Current Disk Queue Length |
| | Disk Read Bytes/sec |
| | Disk Write Bytes/sec |
| | Free Megabytes |
| Physical disk (all instances) | % Disk Read Time |
| | % Disk Time |
| | % Disk Write Time |
| | Disk Read Bytes/sec |
| | Disk Write Bytes/sec |
| | % Disk Read Time |

**Table 9-1**    *Performance Counters to Monitor on CallManager Servers (Continued)*

| Performance Object | Counter |
| --- | --- |
| | % Disk Time |
| | % Disk Write Time |
| Processor (all instances) | % Processor Time |
| Cisco CallManager | CallManagerHeartBeat |
| | CallsActive |
| | CallsInProgress |
| | FXOPortsActive |
| | FXOPortsInService |
| | FXSPortsActive |
| | FXSPortsInService |
| | PRIChannelsActive |
| | PRISpansInService |
| | RegisteredHardwarePhones |
| | RegisteredMGCPGateway |
| | TranscoderOutOfResources |
| | TranscoderResourceActive |
| | TranscoderResourceAvailable |
| Process (instance CCM) | Private Bytes |
| | Virtual Bytes |
| | Virtual Bytes Peak |
| | Working Set |
| | Working Set Peak |

When you are monitoring the performance counters, if you notice too many peaks for page faults and page writes/reads, the server needs more RAM (provided that you have ruled out the possibility of memory leaks with other applications). As long as you have provisioned the system within the Cisco guidelines of device weights and dial plan weights, you should not encounter resource issues.

## Server Hardware Upgrades

A replacement to server hardware is required in the following cases:

- If the server reaches its End of Service (EoS) period as specified by Cisco or the hardware vendor
- If a nonrectifiable component failure occurs on the server
- If the call-processing capacity of the server needs to be increased

In all three cases, you can replace the hardware without issues if you have a full data backup available. Follow the same procedures described earlier in the " Recovery Using Backup Data" section to recover the data onto the new server.

# CallManager Operation and Monitoring Tools

This section discusses the various tools available in CallManager that assist you in performing day-to-day operations and monitoring tasks.

## Multilevel Administration

Chapter 8, "Implementation," discussed the use of the Multilevel Administration (MLA) tool during the IPT deployment. In day-to-day operations, you can use MLA to create different support groups and assign different access privileges. For example, you can give the tier 1 support group privileges to access the IP Phone configuration pages, and User management pages to troubleshoot basic end-user problems. You can give the tier 2 support group full privileges to add new gateways, new devices, and so forth. Finally, you can give the tier 3 support group, which is responsible for the complete system administration, full access to all the elements of the CallManager Administration and Serviceability pages.

## Quality Reporting Tool

The Quality Reporting Tool (QRT), as the name indicates, helps users to report voice-quality problems and many other common problems with IP phones as soon as they experience them. This tool enables users to flag the following events:

- Poor voice-quality calls
- Phone reset events
- Problems making outside calls

QRT depends on the Cisco Extended Functions (CEF) service, which you must activate to use the QRT feature. You can activate CallManager service(s) by selecting Tools > Service Activation menu option from the CallManager Serviceability page. Users access the QRT feature by using a softkey on the IP Phone, as shown in Figure 9-3.

**Figure 9-3**  *QRT Options*

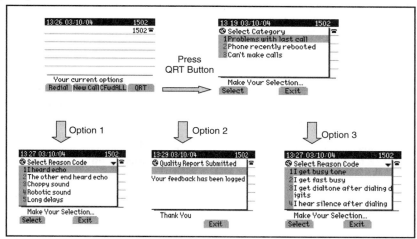

By default, this softkey is not available in the Standard softkey template. You must configure a new softkey template that includes a QRT softkey and assign this template at the device pool or at the individual phone level. To define a new softkey template from the CallManager Administration page, select **Device > Device Settings > Softkey Template**.

The user can select the QRT softkey in four different call states: Connected, Connected Conference, On Hook, and Connected Transfer. In the On-Hook state, pressing the QRT softkey presents three problem categories:

- Problems with last call
- Phone recently rebooted
- Can't make calls

As shown in Figure 9-3, each of these problem categories has reason codes associated with it, to simplify the problem-reporting task for users. When you select the QRT softkey on the Cisco IP Phone in any other state other than On-Hook, you will be asked to report the problem against one of the displayed reason codes, and you are not provided with the problem category choices.

You have the choice to deploy the QRT feature in either of two different modes:

- Silent mode (default)
- Interview mode

To set the QRT feature to interview mode, change the Display Extended QRT Menu Choices service parameter service parameter for the Cisco Extended Functions service to true. To access this service parameter from the CallManager Administration page, select **Service > Service Parameters** to bring up Service Parameters Configuration page. From this page, choose Cisco Extended Functions service for the Service option.

In interview mode, while you are on the call (Connected State), pressing the QRT softkey on the Cisco IP Phone presents various reason codes for the call. Users can select the right reason code (for example, I heard echo or Long delays) when reporting the problem for the current call. In silent mode, in the Connected State, QRT does not present the reason codes to users.

### QRT Viewer

QRT Viewer enables administrators to view the problems that are reported by the IP phone users through the QRT feature. Administrators should run these reports at least twice a week and take proactive measures to reduce the problems before they get out of control.

To access the report in CallManager 4.0, from the CallManager Serviceability page, select **Tools > QRT Viewer**. (In CallManager 3.3.3, select **Tools > Phone Problem Reports Viewer**.)

QRT Viewer provides many filters to pick the records for report generation and provides a variety of fields to include in the generated report. Figure 9-4 shows a sample report generated with QRT Viewer.

**Figure 9-4** *Sample QRT Viewer Report*

IP Phone Problem

Back to Selection    Right Click here to Save in CSV

| SeqId | Category | Reason Code | Source Device DN | Dest. Device DN | Date |
|---|---|---|---|---|---|
| 1 | Problems with last call | Call dropped | 1502 | | 02/26/04 16:36:00 |
| 2 | Problems with current call | | 1502 | 1503 | 02/26/04 16:42:57 |
| 3 | Problems with current call | Other end can't hear me | 1502 | 1503 | 02/26/04 16:47:28 |
| 4 | Phone recently rebooted | | 1502 | | 02/26/04 16:59:11 |
| 5 | Problems with last call | I heard echo | 1502 | 1503 | 02/26/04 17:39:33 |

## Real-Time Monitoring Tool

Real-Time Monitoring Tool (RTMT) assists you in monitoring real-time information of IPT components in a Cisco CallManager cluster. RTMT, a plug-in that is accessible from the CallManager Plug-Ins page, runs on the client workstation as a standalone Java application. Do not install the RTMT client application on CallManager servers. The RTMT client application uses HTTP to communicate with the CallManager server.

RTMT provides monitoring and reporting functionality. RTMT monitoring features provide information about the health of IPT components. RTMT reporting features provide trending analysis. RTMT polls the real-time information database that receives alerts from CallManager; it also polls the performance counters.

RTMT has predefined monitoring parameters. Thresholds can be set on these parameters to alert the administrator via e-mail or page. You can change the polling interval from the default value of 30 seconds. To do so, from the CallManager Administration page, select **Service > Service Parameters**, and then choose the Cisco RIS Data Collector (RISDC) service. Modify the Data Collection Polling Rate service parameter value to the desired polling interval. The predefined monitoring parameters and alerts are sufficient to monitor the health of the IPT system. RTMT provides flexibility to add more performance counters if needed.

RTMT provides the following seven different views. To access any view, click the desired view button on the left side in the RTMT application. Each view displays information about a similar group of objects. For example, Device view displays information about all the devices in the CallManager. The following sections describe the important objects that you need to monitor in each view.

- Summary
- Server
- CallProcess
- Service
- Device
- CTI
- Perfmon

This section also discusses two other important features of RTMT. They are

- RTMT alerts
- RTMT reports

## Summary View

Summary view displays information about CPU usage, memory usage, the number of registered phones, the number of calls in progress, and the number of active gateway ports/channels. This is useful information to monitor on a daily basis. A sudden decrease in the number of registered phones, for example, could indicate a problem with the server or with the switch/module on a particular segment. You should note the statistics on this page before performing an upgrade and run RTMT to ensure that the same numbers of IP phones and gateway ports are available after the upgrade.

During a busy period, monitor the CPU and memory usage. A value above 80 percent is not a good indication. Possible reasons for higher usage are that the server is overloaded with too many devices or a service is malfunctioning because of a memory leak. You should examine the reason for this high usage and act appropriately to reduce the usage values. High CPU usage could introduce call-processing delays.

## Server View

Server view displays information about CPU, memory, and disk usage and the status of critical services.

The CPU and Memory page displays in graphical format the various processes that are currently running on the system and their corresponding memory and CPU usage. Whenever you notice higher CPU or memory usage, you can see which service is taking up maximum resources. This information will help you to troubleshoot issues such as a slow dial tone, CallManager not responding, and so on. You also can view the memory and CPU usage of another server in the cluster.

Enabling detailed tracing levels for the signal distribution layer (SDL) and system diagnostic interface (SDI) traces is often required during troubleshooting. Detailed tracing occupies a lot of disk space. If the level of trace remains at Detailed, you might run out of disk space. The information gathered from disk usage will help to prevent such scenarios.

The Critical Services page lists all the CallManager-related services, including the status and uptime of the service.

## CallProcess View

CallProcess view displays information about call activity, gateway activity, trunk activity, and SDL queues. The information displayed under Gateway Activity assists you in evaluating the capacity of the PRI usage and assists you in troubleshooting issues with PRI when the channel is activated but not operating.

Selecting SDL Queue from the CallProcess view displays the number of signals and requests in various SDL queues and the number of processed requests. To understand the importance of the SDL queue parameters, you need to know about the call-throttling feature in CallManager. Call-throttling protects CallManager from high CPU usage caused either by a burst of call attempts that exceeds the threshold that the CallManager can support or by a call routing loop. In addition, a faulty hardware or faulty firmware could send too many events to CallManager, forcing CallManager to process all the faulty requests, thereby reducing the CPU cycles available for other devices.

To protect from such events, CallManager places the incoming messages and signals into four different SDL priority queues:

- High priority
- Normal priority
- Low priority
- Lowest priority

CallManager processes messages in the high-priority queue before messages in the normal-priority queue, processes messages in the normal-priority queue before messages in the low-priority queue, and so forth. The types of messages that go into the normal-priority queue are the initial call setup messages. Whenever CallManager receives a new message request, it calculates the expected delay to complete the request. The expected delay depends on the number of messages in the queue and the number of messages processed.

The higher the number of signals waiting in the queue, the higher the delay is. If the delay is more than the configured threshold values (configured via the Cisco CallManager (CCM) Call Throttling service parameters), the call-throttling feature denies the incoming requests.

Figure 9-5 shows the CCM Call Throttling service parameters for the CallManager service.

**Figure 9-5**  *CallManager Service Parameters—CCM Call Throttling*

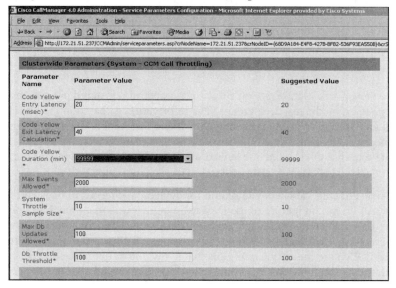

Do not change the default values of the parameters shown in Figure 9-5 unless directed to do by Cisco support personnel.

In Figure 9-5, entering 0 for System Throttle Sample Size disables the call-throttling feature. The call-throttling mechanism applies to incoming calls from phones, Cisco IOS gateways, MGCP gateways, and MGCP back-haul PRI gateways. Whenever the call-throttling feature is called for, the IP phone devices making calls display the message "Too Much Traffic Try Again Later."

## Service View

Service view displays information about the Cisco TFTP service, directory server, and Heartbeat for critical services.

The information gathered for the TFTP service includes total TFTP requests, total TFTP requests not found, and total TFTP requests aborted. This information helps you to troubleshoot TFTP-related issues during the initial phone registrations with CallManager. A higher number for TFTP requests not found indicates that many devices are attempting to download the configuration file or firmware from the TFTP server but are unable to find the specified file. This clearly indicates that you must have specified a device load in the Device Defaults page that does not exist in the TFTP server.

The Directory Server window displays information about the status of the replication; this helps you to troubleshoot issues related to directory replication.

The HeartBeat window shows the HeartBeat count for CallManager service, Cisco TFTP service, and Cisco Telephony Call Dispatcher (TCD) services. The HeartBeat is an incremental count that indicates which service is alive and running. If the count for a service does not increment, you can consider the service dead, and you should take immediate action to analyze the reason for the failure of the service.

## Device View

Device view displays information about the number of registered phones, registered gateways, and registered media resource groups. The information gathered in the Device Summary view assists you during a CallManager upgrade, where the number of devices registered before the upgrade must be equal to the number of devices registered after the upgrade. It also gives you the data required to calculate the device weights or dial plan weights for the CallManager cluster.

The Device Search view lets you search for devices, such as IP Phones and gateways, in the cluster. An important feature of the Device Search view is that it enables you to search for devices based on their status, such as registered, unregistered, or registration rejected, as shown in Figure 9-6. RTMT and the IP Phone Information Facility option in the IP Telephony Monitor (part of ITEM) are the only Cisco tools that allow you to query the devices based on the real-time status. You can use this search filter to determine the number of phones that are in the unregistered status before or after an upgrade or during the deployment of IP Phones in the network.

**Figure 9-6**  *RTMT Device Search Filter—Registration Status*

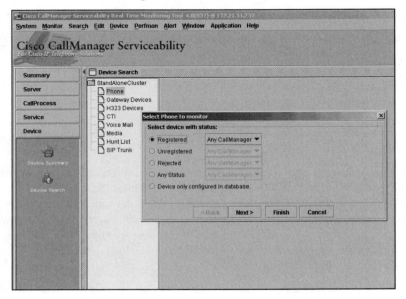

The filter in the Device Search that is of most interest in day-to-day operations is the search based on the IP address or IP subnet, as shown in Figure 9-7. You might want to search using these filter options if multiple users report problems with their IP phones. If you can narrow down the problems to a group of users based on an IP subnet, you can focus on troubleshooting only within that network segment or device pool.

**Figure 9-7** *RTMT Device Search Filter—Cisco IP Phone Characteristics*

## CTI View

The Computer Telephony Integration (CTI) view provides the status of the registered CTI applications and their connection status.

## Perfmon View

Perfmon view displays all the counters available in Windows Perfmon. To meet your requirements, you can select a particular counter that is not available in default monitoring and add it. You can also set alerts for the new counter, as discussed in the next section.

## RTMT Alerts

There are two kinds of RTMT alerts. The first set is preconfigured, and the second set is user defined. You can customize both of them. The main difference is that you cannot delete preconfigured alerts, whereas you can add and delete user-defined alerts. However, you can disable both preconfigured and user-defined alerts. To view the preconfigured alerts, from the RTMT client application, select the **Alert > Alert Central** menu option.

The preconfigured alerts are enabled by default. In most cases, you do not have to change the default threshold settings configured for the preconfigured alerts. However, you have an option to change the threshold settings to meet your requirements. The notification can be an e-mail or a pager. To set up e-mail notification, you should specify the SMTP server name and port number. You can do this in the RTMT client application by selecting the **Alert > Configure E-Mail Server** menu option.

To set a new alert, select the Perfmon Monitoring in PerfMon view, select any performance counter that you want to monitor, and right-click the graph to configure the alert settings, as shown in Figure 9-8.

**Figure 9-8**  *Defining New Alerts in RTMT*

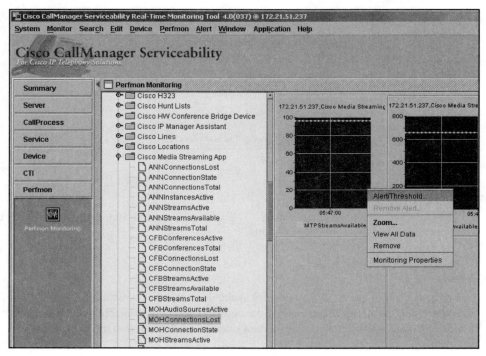

Example 9-2 shows a few sample alert messages sent by RTMT via e-mail.

**Example 9-2**  *Sample RTMT Alert Messages Sent via E-Mail*

```
From: RTMT_Admin@xyz.com
Sent: Friday, February 27, 2004 1:47 AM
To: ccmadmins@xyz.com
Subject: [RTMT-ALERT] CallProcessingNodeCpuPegging

At 01:46:03 on 02/27/2004 on cluster StandAloneCluster.
Number of registered phones in the cluster drops 10 Percent.
Current monitored precanned object has decreased by 100 percent.

This is alert from CallManager 4.0 server At 01:46:33 on
    02/27/2004 on node 10.1.3.1. Processor load over 90 Percent.
    Ccm (91 percent) uses most of the CPU.
```

**Example 9-2**   *Sample RTMT Alert Messages Sent via E-Mail (Continued)*

```
At 21:01:03 on 02/27/2004 on node 10.1.3.1.
Directory connection failed .
Monitored precanned object has value of 0.

At 18:12:27 on 02/26/2004 on cluster StandAloneCluster.
Number of registered gateways increased.
Current monitored precanned object has increased by 1.
```

## RTMT Reports

RTMT reporting functionality provides predefined reports that include the information collected during the monitoring process. To access the RTMT reports, from the CallManager Serviceability page, select **Tools > Serviceability Report Archive**. There are five predefined reports:

- Alert report
- Call Activities report
- Device Statistics report
- Server Statistics report
- Service Statistics report

The service parameter RTMT Report Deletion Age for the Cisco Serviceability Reporter service defines the age of the report. This parameter specifies the number of days that must elapse before reports are deleted. For example, if this parameter is set to 7 (default value), reports that were generated 7 days ago are deleted on the eighth day. A value of 0 disables report generation, and any existing reports are deleted.

These reports aid you in analyzing the capacity of the system and troubleshooting problems. More importantly, careful interpretation of the reports will help you to identify the problems in advance and take appropriate measures to prevent them from happening again.

The service that is responsible for generating the reports is Cisco Serviceability Reporter service. Set the service parameter RTMT Report Deletion Age for this service to 30 and keep the reports for 30 days. At the end of 30 days, copy the reports onto the network share server so that the trending analysis covers a longer period, resulting in meaningful data.

# CallManager Traces

CallManager traces aid you in troubleshooting various issues with CallManager. CallManager logs every incoming and outgoing message in the trace files. Table 9-2 lists the location of the trace files for various applications. This information helps you when you are working on troubleshooting issues. All the trace directories are located under the C:\Program Files\Cisco\Trace directory.

**Table 9-2**    *CallManager Trace File Locations*

| Directory Name | Stores |
| --- | --- |
| BARS | Trace files for BARS. Every day, check the log file to ensure the backup process was successful. |
| CCM | Cisco CallManager traces. CCM traces are the files that you refer to most of the time when troubleshooting the majority of issues. |
| CEF | Log files for CEF services such as Cisco Callback and QRT. |
| CMI | Cisco Message Interface service logs. |
| CMS | Music on Hold trace files. |
| CTI | CTI application services traces. |
| CTL Provider | Certificate Trust List (CTL) Provider service traces. CTL Provider provides added security to IP phones while downloading the configuration information from CallManager. |
| CULS | Trace information for Cisco User Logout Service, the service that runs to log out extension mobility users. |
| DBL | Various traces that log the activities that read and write information into the database. |
| DNA | Log files for the Dialed Number Analyzer tool. |
| MA | Traces for the Cisco IP Manager Assistant. |
| MLA | Traces for the MLA tool. |
| ProgLogs | Current version of the dynamic link library (DLL) running on the system. |
| RIS | Logs related to Real-Time Information Server service. |
| SDL | SDL traces. |
| TCD | Traces related to Web Attendant service. |
| TFTP | TFTP traces. |
| WebDialer | Traces for the WebDialer application. |

## Trace Configuration

To configure the level of tracing for the available services, select **Trace > Configuration** on the CallManager Serviceability page. The default tracing level for all the services is Error. Enabling the Detailed tracing level for any of the services logs huge amounts of data in the log files.

## The Troubleshooting Trace Settings Page and Cisco CallManager Trace Collection Tool

The Troubleshooting Trace Settings page provides a one-stop shop for enabling the traces required to troubleshoot a problem. This page offers you the option of selecting the service on a particular CallManager or on the entire cluster. This page has predefined trace levels to capture sufficient information needed by Cisco TAC and engineering teams to investigate deep into the problems. To access the Troubleshooting Trace Settings page from the CallManager Serviceability page, go to **Trace > Troubleshooting Trace Settings**.

The client portion of this tool, CallManager Trace Collection Tool, sits on a desktop running Windows XP or Windows 2000. With this tool, you can connect to any CallManager from your desktop or laptop and collect all the required traces. The client version of this tool is available as a plug-in on the CallManager Administration page. To access the tool after the installation from your workstation, select the Trace Collection Tool menu option from **Start > Programs > Cisco CallManager Serviceability > Trace Collection Tool**.

This tool gathers log files that are associated with various CallManager services, CallManager applications, system traces. System traces include Event Viewer logs, Dr. Watson logs, Microsoft IIS logs, SQL logs, Directory logs, System Performance logs, and Prog logs.

Refer to the following URL for more information on the Trace Collection Tool and Troubleshooting Trace Settings page:

http://www.cisco.com/en/US/partner/products/sw/voicesw/ps556/
products_configuration_example09186a00801f3b4d.shtml

## Bulk Trace Analysis Tool

The Bulk Trace Analysis Tool assists you in troubleshooting a problem that requires you to analyze logs collected over a period of time. Enabling the Detailed level traces on CallManager uses a lot of CPU and memory resources. Furthermore, analyzing such a large amount of data on CallManager requires more resources. By using the Bulk Trace Analysis Tool, you can analyze the trace files from a standalone workstation. This tool reads the SDI and SDL trace files stored in XML format. By default, all CallManager traces are stored in plain text files. To generate SDI and SDL trace files in XML format, you should enable XML tracing from the Trace Configuration page for the services. The limitation of logging traces in XML format is that it reduces the number of lines stored per log file and increases the amount of processing power required to analyze and display the contents. Hence, avoid using XML logging whenever possible.

You can install the Bulk Trace Analysis Tool on your workstation by downloading the Bulk Trace Analysis Tool plug-in from the CallManager Plug-ins page. Do not install the tool on the CallManager Publisher or Subscriber servers because analyzing a large number of trace files consumes CPU and memory resources. You can copy the XML trace files that you need to analyze from the CallManager server to your workstation and open them in the Bulk Trace Analysis Tool.

Figure 9-9 shows the sample output of an analysis of XML trace files by using the Bulk Trace Analysis Tool.

**Figure 9-9**    *Bulk Trace Analysis Tool Output*

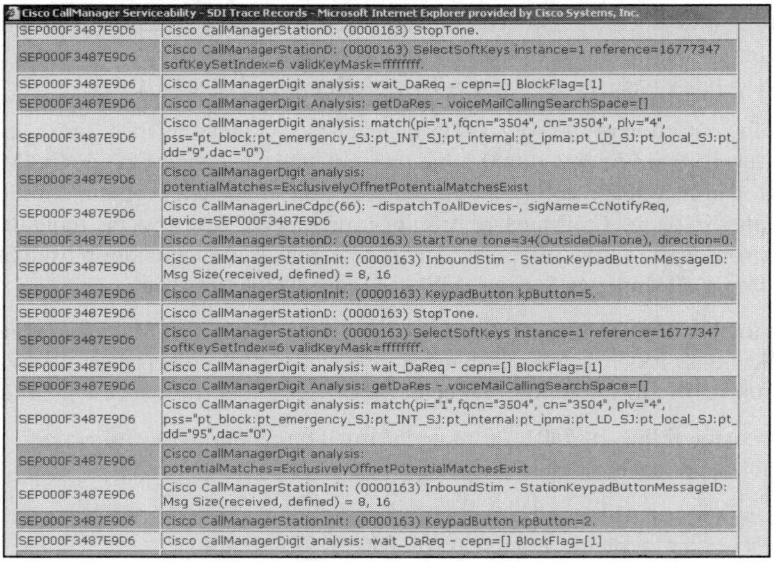

# CDR Analysis and Reporting

CDR Analysis and Reporting (CAR) reads the records stored in the CallManager Call Detail Record (CDR) and Call Management Record (CMR) databases and provides basic billing reports and an interface to search the CDRs. CAR stores all the extracted information from the CDR and CMR databases in a separate database file called ART in SQL (also referred to as the CAR database). By default, this process runs at midnight every day. The amount of time required to complete this process depends on the number of records in the CDR database, which again depends on the call volume in the cluster.

You have to set to True the following three CallManager service parameters to enable logging of CDR and CMR data:

- CDR Enabled Flag
- CDR Log Calls with Zero Duration Flag
- Call Diagnostics Enabled

Note that CAR is not full-fledged billing software, because it contains only raw data. There is no link between the minutes, time of day, destination/called number, and related costs.

You can install CAR on the CallManager Publisher. The installation file is available on the CallManager Plug-Ins page. After CAR is installed, you can access the application from the CallManager Serviceability page by selecting CDR Analysis and Reporting from the Tools menu.

You can generate three types of reports using CAR:

- User reports
- System reports
- Device reports

## User Reports

User reports can provide billing information about an individual user or a whole department. You can determine who the top users are based on several categories, including usage duration, number of calls, and amount of charges. This information helps you to identify users in the cluster who have a heavy call volume.

The CDRs do not contain cost information, by default. However, in the CAR application, you can select Rating Engine from the Report Config menu to configure the costs associated with calls and define the cost factors based on time of day. After you configure these values, the reports you generate through CAR will have cost information.

When you log in to the CAR application, if your user ID is assigned as a manager for some users in the CallManager user pages, you can generate a report for all the users who are reporting to you.

## System Reports

The system reports provide information about QoS, traffic, and malicious calls, and provide a system overview. The QoS reports help you to troubleshoot voice-quality issues; they contain information about jitter and packet loss. The Call Management Record database stores the information about QoS parameters.

The traffic report identifies traffic patterns, provides information about the call activities during the day, and identifies the peak time and lean time. This report helps in capacity planning of the gateways and circuits.

## Device Reports

The device reports help in capacity planning of gateways, Conference Bridge resources, and voice mail. The route plan report provides information about the use of the route pattern, route list, and route group. The route plan report helps you to optimize the dial plan.

The CDR search tool helps you to pull a CDR for a particular call that experiences problems; the details in the record help you to troubleshoot issues with one-way audio, duplex mismatch, and so on.

## Q.931 Translator

The Q.931 Translator tool decodes the ISDN messages by reading the CallManager trace files. You should enable Detailed tracing and Q.931 tracing on the CallManager service to log the messages in the trace files. To access the Q.931 Translator, go to the CallManager Serviceability page and select **Trace > Q.931 Translator**. Figure 9-10 shows the Q931 Translator application.

Alternatively, you can copy to your laptop or PC, along with the trace files, the q931Translator.exe program stored in the C:\Program Files\Cisco\bin directory on the CallManager server. After you have the executable file and the trace files on your PC or laptop, you can run Q.931 Translator locally to analyze the traces. This also avoids the extra CPU time required on the CallManager to run the tool and analyze a large number of traces.

**Figure 9-10**  *Q.931 Translator*

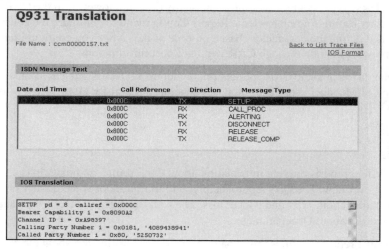

## Alarm Configurations and Definitions

CallManager logs alarms in the Windows Event log, SDI/SDL traces, or syslog. You can also specifically choose the destinations in which to log the alarms. For example, you can configure the alarm settings, so that CallManager logs all emergency alarms in the event log and all alarms with error level in the SDI/SDL logs. You can log the alarms to an external syslog server by specifying the IP Address of the syslog server in the Alarm configuration page.

To get the meaning of these alarms and recommended actions, you can search in the alarm definitions. To access the alarm definitions, from the CallManager Serviceability page, select **Alarm > Definitions**.

# Backup and Restore System

The availability of the IPT network relies mainly on the availability of the CallManager cluster, which controls the call processing and call routing. A strong backup and restore policy enables the organization to restore the database and bring up the CallManager cluster quickly in case of a disaster, such as failure of hard disks, a fire, or a natural disaster (for example, a flood). A good backup also helps in recovering the data in case of an unsuccessful CallManager upgrade.

High-end CallManager servers have mirrored hard drives. Hence, failure on one hard drive does not affect the functioning of CallManager.

During the installation of the BARS application, you configure the backup server and backup target, the backup server performs all the backup operations, and the backup target contains information to back up. Usually, the backup server resides on CallManager Publisher.

In a CallManager cluster, the Publisher contains a read-write database and the Subscribers contain a read-only database. The Publisher database, which is also called the master database, holds all the changes made to a cluster; thus, you do not have to back up the data on Subscribers.

The CallManager application bundles the Cisco IP Telephony Applications Backup Utility software for backing up and restoring the data. Cisco does not support the installation of any third-party backup application to take the backup of the CallManager data. The BARS application allows you to store the backup data on a tape, a network drive, or a local drive. The best practice is to back up the data to a tape or network drive; avoid using the local drive as the backup destination.

If you are using a network drive as the backup destination, ensure that the network drive share is configured and that the CallManager hosts and LMHOSTS files contain the name and IP address of the network share server.

The backup utility archives the configuration data into a single file. The filename format is backupmm-dd-yy.tar. The backup utility truncates the transaction logs for the CallManager database and the ART database.

A good backup strategy requires CallManager administrators to perform the following tasks:

- Schedule the time and day for running the backup. Because the backup process is CPU intensive, schedule the backups during off-peak hours.

- Check for errors after every backup. The log file is available under C:\Program Files\Common Files\Cisco\Logs on the backup server.

- Validate and check the data integrity of the backup data once a month by restoring the data onto a lab server.

- Perform the backup operation when you make major changes to the production cluster, such as numerous configuration changes or a CallManager version upgrade.

Sometimes Cisco releases upgrades to the backup software application alone. Check for the latest upgrades and perform them. After performing an upgrade, make a backup with the new version of the software and ensure that you can restore the data successfully.

To access BARS in CallManager 3.3(3) and above, select **Start > Programs > Cisco BARS > BARS Admin.** This is a web-based utility that allows you to configure the backup and restore the data.

In addition to running the backup utility to back up the data, you can pull one drive from the server spare drives to mirror the data on each server. This requires you to have an additional hard disk for each server. With this method, you can rebuild a cluster in less time. There are three imperative steps in mirroring:

1 Select the option to enable interim recovery mode during the reboot of the server, when you pull the drive. After the server boots up, insert the spare hard drive.

2 Label the drive that is pulled out from the server with the machine name, slot number, current version of Cisco CallManager, and operating system version.

---

**NOTE**     This section discussed the backup and restore operations for CallManager cluster only. You should also include other servers such as Unity, Personal Assistant, Cisco Emergency Responder, voice gateways, and other network devices in your backup schedule.

---

# Password-Changing Tools

Because the interoperability relationships of Cisco CallManager are so complex, Cisco recommends that administrators and installers not change CallManager passwords or services manually. The following two tools are available to change the passwords used by Cisco CallManager:

- Cisco CallManager Admin Utility (adminutility.exe)

- Cisco CallManager Password Changer (ccmpwdchanger.exe)

### Admin Utility

Starting with CallManager 3.3(2), Cisco has modified the way passwords are used for various services in the CallManager cluster to increase the security for the Windows Services that comprise the system. Many of the services that were running as Local System in prior releases have been changed to run as Local Windows user accounts and services. The services that use these accounts are listed in Table 9-3.

**Table 9-3**    *CallManager Service and Account Settings*

| Name of Account | Services that Run with Account |
|---|---|
| CCMServiceRW | ART Scheduler |
| | Cisco CallManager |
| | Cisco CTI Manager |
| | Cisco CTL Provider |
| | Cisco TAPS |
| | Cisco Tomcat |
| | CDR Analysis and Reporting Scheduler |
| CCMService | Cisco Extended Functions |
| | Cisco IP Voice Media Streaming Application |
| | Cisco Messaging Interface |
| | Cisco MoH Audio Translator |
| | Cisco Serviceability Reporter |
| | Cisco Telephony Call Dispatcher |
| | Cisco TFTP |
| CCMEML | Cisco Extension Mobility Logout |
| CCMCDR | Cisco CDR Insert |
| SQLSVC | Cisco Database Layer Monitor |
| | Cisco RIS Data Collector |
| | MSSQLServer |
| | SQLServerAgent |
| CCMUser | This account is used to access the CCMUser virtual directory. |

During installation, by default, the accounts shown in Table 9-3 are created (without Log on Locally access) and the local Windows password is generated by an algorithm based on the NetBIOS name of the CallManager Publisher server as the seed  for each account within the Cisco CallManager cluster. After entering the private password phrase during the Publisher installation, the passwords for the service accounts are regenerated and modified. When you are installing the Subscriber servers, you should enter the same password phrase that you used when building the Publisher.

Because all the servers in the cluster must be able to communicate with Publisher to keep the database up to date, it is critical that the passwords for the service accounts shown in Table 9-3 are identical among all the servers in the cluster. If you decide to change passwords for any of these service accounts, you should use the Cisco-provided Admin Utility. The Admin Utility program is in the C:\Program Files\Cisco\Bin directory on the CallManager servers. You should run this utility on the CallManager publisher server only. Refer to the AdminUtility-Readme.html file located in the C:\Program Files\Cisco\Bin directory on the CallManager servers before running this utility.

As with any installation or upgrade, Cisco recommends that you execute this utility during off-peak hours. This utility will change the affected local Windows account, services, and virtual directories.

If you choose to change all accounts on all systems within the cluster, all call processing will be terminated until the entire cluster is updated. Depending on the number of servers within the cluster and the call volume at the time this utility is executed, the upgrade process could take several minutes per server.

The steps to run the Admin Utility to set a new password are as follows:

**Step 1**   Log on as the local Administrator on the Publisher.

**Step 2**   Using Windows Explorer, browse to C:\Program Files\Cisco\Bin and launch AdminUtility.exe.

**Step 3**   In the CallManager Admin Utility login window, within the User Password field, input the local Administrator password and click OK. If the password entered is valid, the Admin Utility application is launched. Figure 9-11 shows the Admin Utility interface; it shows two servers: Publisher (IP address 172.21.51.229) and Subscriber (IP Address 172.21.51.230). The first item in the tree ASIPT22A is the name of the Publisher.

**Step 4**   Select the check box at the top of the tree next to the globe icon, which should correlate to the DNS name/IP address of the Publisher (in this example, ASIPT22A).

**Step 5**   Select **Options > Set New Password**.

**Step 6**   A new dialog box, Set All Service Accounts Password, appears. Input your alphanumeric password phrase (1 to 15 characters) that will be used to generate the complex passwords for each local account and service. Re-enter the string within the next field for verification and click **OK**.

**Step 7**   A new dialog box, Update Passwords for CallManager Servers, appears. Highlight all systems within the cluster and click **Update Server Password**. You will receive a warning message informing you that this will take down all systems with the cluster and could take a significant amount of time. Click **OK**.

**Step 8**    When completed for each system, you will see that the update was successful. Click **EXIT** after all systems within the cluster have successfully updated.

**Step 9**    Close the Admin Utility window.

**Figure 9-11**    *Admin Utility Interface*

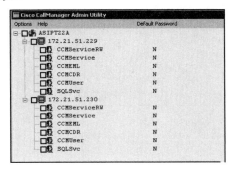

## Cisco CallManager Password Changer

You can use CCM Password Changer to change the password of special CCM users, such as the following:

- Directory Manager (user account for DC Directory)

- CCMSysUser (account used for CTI applications, such as QRT, CRA, and Callback)

- CCMAdministrator (account used by MLA)

- IPMASysUser (account used by IPMA)

CCM Password Changer works with all supported directory servers, which include DC Directory, Active Directory, and Netscape directory. This utility updates the passwords on all the CallManager servers in the cluster and in the registry. You have to reboot the CallManager servers any time you change the passwords.

To launch CCM Password Changer, using Windows Explorer, browse to C:\Program Files\Cisco\Bin and launch ccmpwdchanger.exe. Figure 9-12 shows the CCM Password Changer interface. Use the local Administrator password to log in to the CCM Password Changer.

**Figure 9-12** *CCM Password Changer Interface*

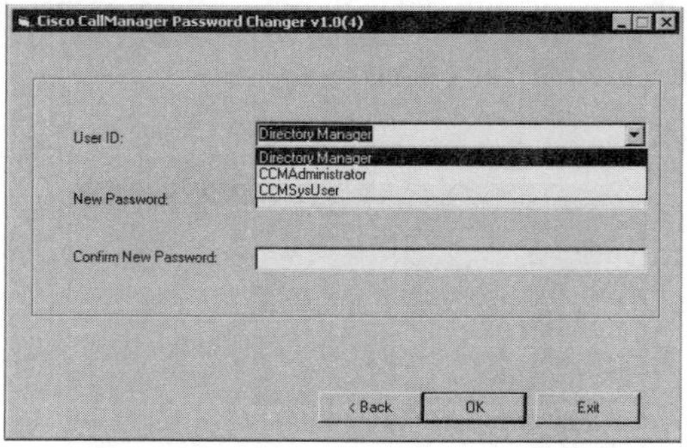

# Event Viewer

Windows Event Viewer is a useful monitoring tool for implementation and troubleshooting. You need to check Event Viewer periodically for errors; specifically, look for several events that occur at the same time. For instance, it is unusual to see a bunch of IP phones reporting transient connections or resetting at the same time; this can happen by pure coincidence, or it could indicate a problem with the switch module or a power failure for that physical location.

CallManager logs all events in the Windows Event Viewer application. Event Viewer records the errors in three kinds of logs. They are System log, Security log, and Application log. CallManager logs all errors under the Application log. If a service (including TFTP) cannot read the database (where it gets the trace configuration), it logs errors to Event Viewer. Event Viewer is the only place where these types of errors appear unless you have configured a syslog server. Figure 9-13 shows an error generated by the Cisco CallManager service in Event Viewer.

**Figure 9-13** *Snapshot of Event Viewer Application Logs Window*

To open Event Viewer on CallManager or any other application servers, including Cisco Unity, select **Start > Programs > Administrative Tools > Event Viewer**.

# Bulk Administration Tool

Bulk Administration Tool (BAT) is bundled with CallManager software and is available on the Cisco CallManager Plug-Ins page. BAT is a useful tool during implementation and in performing day-to-day operations. You have to install BAT on CallManager Publisher. To access the BAT application from Internet Explorer, type the URL http://IPADDROFPUBLISHER/bat.

Some of the day-to-day operations involved in IPT networks are the following:

- Adding new IP Phones
- Changing settings on IP Phones, such as changing calling privileges (changing partitions, CSS), or changing the number of lines configured on the phones
- Subscribing IP Phones to new services
- Migrating users from one cluster to another cluster
- Consolidating two CallManager clusters into a single cluster

BAT allows you to do all of the above and many other tasks. When you are moving users between clusters, you can use the BAT export feature to export the user or phone information into a file and use this file to import the same users or phones into the new cluster. When configuring the users in the CallManager directory, populate all the fields, including Manager Name and Department Name. This helps later when you have to manage the users in bulk, because you can base search criteria on the Manager Name field or Department Name field.

BAT writes the configuration changes directly into the SQL database. To avoid having end users experience call-processing delays because of high CPU usage, perform bulk changes using BAT after hours.

# DHCP Management

IP Phones receive the IP addressing information and TFTP server information via custom Option 150 or Option 66 from the DHCP server. The best practice is to set the lease period to a longer duration (for example, 8 days). For devices such as CallManager servers, Unity, application servers, conferencing, transcoding, and voice gateways, assign the static IP addresses.

Before you choose Option 66 to pass the TFTP server information to the phones, make sure that you are not using that option in your network. Many other vendors already use the TFTP Boot Host 66 record for other purposes (netbooting X Windows workstations). If you are already using Option 66 for such purposes, you should use DHCP custom Option 150. If you use Option 66, you have to use a fully qualified name to specify the DHCP server, which requires relying on the DNS server to resolve the DHCP server name to an IP address before IP Phones can send out the DHCP request. By comparison, DHCP custom Option 150 allows you to configure the IP address for the DHCP server and to specify an array of IP addresses instead of just one. IPT endpoints such as Cisco IP Phones can receive the multiple TFTP server to provide the TFTP server redundancy and no need to relay on the DNS server.

The behavior of the IP phones as far as DHCP is concerned is the same as the behavior of any other DHCP client. When an IP phone boots, it sends a DHCPREQUEST, if it previously had a valid lease. The DHCP server responds with a DHCPACK message, if the phone can continue to use the same address. If the phone moves to another subnet, it gets a DHCPNACK, which forces the phone to do a DHCPDISCOVER and get a new lease. The lease should not expire, because the IP phone will make renewal attempts over the course of the lease time at certain intervals according to the DHCP specification (RFC 2131 and RFC 2132). Having a longer DHCP lease period helps the functioning of the IPT network, even if the DHCP server is down for more than one or two days.

You can use CallManager Publisher as a DHCP server for smaller IPT deployments of up to 250 phones. In a large network, the best practice is to deploy DHCP and TFTP servers on the same server. The following URL explains configuring Windows 2000 Server as a DHCP server:

http://www.cisco.com/en/US/partner/products/sw/voicesw/ps556/products_tech_note09186a00800942f4.shtml

The DHCP Export Import Tool from Microsoft comes in handy when you are upgrading server hardware or moving the DHCP server to a different machine. You can download the tool from the Microsoft website:

http://www.microsoft.com/downloads/details.aspx?familyid=3603ae26-81f0-478a-836c-b31ed463af5e&displaylang=en

You can always use any other DHCP server, or even a router, as long as you can configure Option 150 to give out the TFTP server address as part of the DHCP request to the IP Phones.

Typically, companies use a centralized DHCP server that resides on the data network subnet that leases out the addresses for IP Phones and for user workstations. In this case, you should configure the **ip helper-address** IP address of the DHCP server on the routing interface (the routing interface acts as a relay agent) or set up a separate DHCP relay agent to convert the DHCP broadcast requests into unicast and forward them to the DHCP server and vice versa.

# Optimization Tips

You can use some of the tools discussed earlier to fine-tune the network and optimize it for better performance. This section includes some tips to optimize the IPT network.

## Time Synchronization

You should synchronize with a centralized network time server the clock on all the IPT devices, such as CallManager, Unity, and other application servers and gateways. This ensures that all the trace events that are logged in trace files and Event Viewer have a consistent date and time stamp. When troubleshooting a problem, you often need to collect the traces logs from multiple devices. Having the same time synchronization source helps you to accurately correlate the information from multiple devices so that you can identify the sequence of events that occurred based on the date and time the problem occurred. For more information on procedures to synchronize the clock, refer to the following document:

http://www.cisco.com/en/US/partner/products/sw/voicesw/ps556/
products_configuration_example09186a008009470f.shtml

## CallManager Services

Turn off unnecessary services on CallManager; activate only the services that are absolutely needed. This frees up more memory for the other processes. For example, if you are not using the software media resources such as conference, transcoding, and Music on Hold, you can turn off the Cisco IP voice Media streaming application. In addition, because the Publisher database is the only read/write database, you can make changes and view the configurations if you have the access to the CallManager Administration and Serviceability pages on the Publisher server. Hence, you can set the IIS service to Manual start on the subscriber servers.

## Name Resolution

Use the local name resolution methods by employing hosts and LMHOSTS files (located in the C:\Winnt\System32\drivers\etc directory on all the servers) to resolve the names to IP addresses. Update these files if you add or remove any servers in the cluster. The local resolution helps to keep up the communication between the servers if the DNS server in the network fails. Do not enable the DNS service on CallManager or any other application servers, because this service consumes a considerable amount of CPU resources in answering the DNS resolution requests received from various endpoints. Use an existing DNS server in your network to provide the DNS service.

## IP Addressing

Use the IP address instead of the host name to define the server in the CallManager Administration page. If you use CallManager server names here, the configuration files that are generated for IP phones will have DNS names instead of IP addresses. Hence, IP phones will have to contact the DNS server and resolve the name of the server before proceeding to the registration. If the DNS server does not respond to the queries from IP phones, the IP phones cannot complete the registration process.

## Subnetting and VLANs

Create different VLANs for the CallManager servers in the cluster. This prevents the following:

- A broadcast storm caused by a faulty NIC bringing down the servers in the same broadcast domain; using different VLANs for the servers in a cluster prevents this scenario.

- Spread of viruses from one server to another.

## Proactive Problem Identification and Resolution

Study the reports generated by RTMT. Analyze them carefully and take proactive measures to prevent repetition of the top issues. For example, Figure 9-14 shows various alerts generated in a day. The graph shows 26 CriticalServiceDown alerts in a day, which is not a good indication. You should check the details of those alerts from the RTMT alert logs and check which services had the problems.

**Figure 9-14** *RTMT Top 10 Alerts from Alert Report*

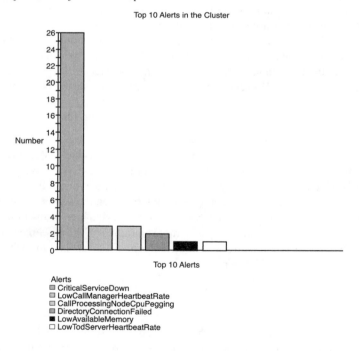

The Device Statistics report in RTMT gives the information about the number of registered phones, H.323 gateways, and MGCP gateways per CallManager node. Monitor these numbers regularly to ensure that you have not exceeded the device weight and dial plan weights recommended per server. Refer to Chapter 1, "Cisco IP Telephony Solution Overview," for information on dial plan weights and device weights.

## Duplex and Speed Settings

When deploying Cisco IP Phones, use the Auto setting to negotiate the duplex and speed with the connected switches. By default, the switch port and the PC port on the IP phone are set to do auto-negotiation to configure the speed and duplex. Hence, no manual configuration on the IP phones is required.

You should configure the Ethernet port on the closet switch and the NIC setting on the PC to do auto-negotiation. This configuration approach avoids negotiating mismatched speed and duplex settings and prevents voice-quality problems caused by interface buffer overflows and device connection timeouts with CallManager. Hard-code the NIC setting on the servers and on switch ports that connect the servers to 100/FULL. After you perform any upgrades on the servers, ensure that the configuration settings of the NIC on the servers are not changed.

## Dial Plan Optimization

When you are designing the dial plan, keep it as simple as possible by following the tips recommended next to optimize the performance of CallManager.

### Route Pattern Design

When implementing the dial plan, you can use explicit route patterns such as 9.[2-9]XX[2-9]XXXXXX or route patterns with the @ wildcard character along with route filters. Recall from Chapter 6, "Design of Call Processing Infrastructure and Applications," that the @ wildcard character is a macro that comprises many route patterns, depending on the dial plan loaded in CallManager. By default, CallManager understands only the North American Numbering Plan (NANP). Beginning with CallManager 3.3.4, support for international dial plans has been added. Refer to the following document on Cisco.com for more information on supported international dial plans:

http://www.cisco.com/en/US/partner/products/sw/voicesw/ps556/
prod_configuration_guide09186a0080292f3d.html

If you are deploying CallManager in a country outside North America, you can download the country-specific International Dial Plan file from the following URL and install it on all the servers in the cluster:

http://www.cisco.com/cgi-bin/tablebuild.pl/IDP

The dial plan definition files are stored on the CallManager servers under the C:\Program Files\Cisco\DialPlan directory. By default, the NANP file contains the various route patterns that comprise NANP. For example, if you install an Australian Numbering Plan on the

CallManager servers, you see an additional file called AUNP under the same directory. After you install the international dial plan, when defining the route patterns, you can choose which numbering plan the route pattern should use, as shown in Figure 9-15.

**Figure 9-15** *Choosing Numbering Plan for Route Pattern*

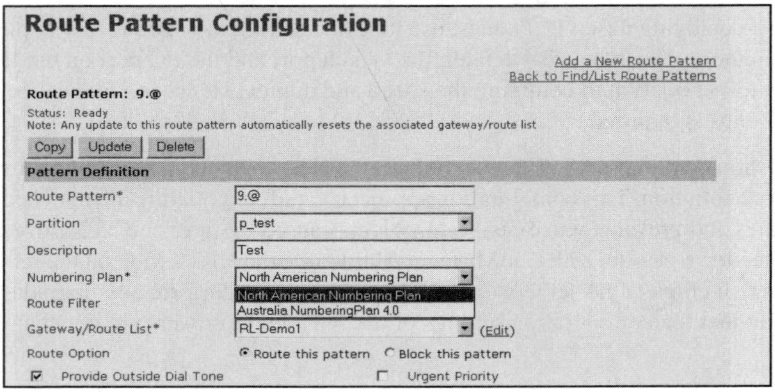

For inexperienced users, designing the dial plan using explicit route patterns without the use of route filters is easy and simple to understand. However, there are some instances in which using route filters can be beneficial, particularly when a single route pattern with the @ macro can replace multiple route patterns.

To emphasize this point, consider the example of defining the toll-free numbers in the United States. Calling toll-free numbers commonly is allowed from lobby phones and common areas. The toll-free numbers are part of the long-distance dial pattern of 1 + ten digits. They should be defined in the dial plan and assigned to a class of service. The five area codes for toll-free numbers are 800, 855, 866, 877, and 888. Instead of defining five route patterns, you can use a 9.@ route pattern with the following route filter to group all five area codes. The following is the definition of the route filter:

(LONG-DISTANCE-DIRECT-DIAL EXISTS AND

AREA-CODE == 800 AND

TRANSIT-NETWORK DOES-NOT-EXIST)

OR

(LONG-DISTANCE-DIRECT-DIAL EXISTS AND

AREA-CODE == 855 AND

TRANSIT-NETWORK DOES-NOT-EXIST)

OR

(LONG-DISTANCE-DIRECT-DIAL EXISTS AND

AREA-CODE == 866 AND

TRANSIT-NETWORK DOES-NOT-EXIST)

OR

(LONG-DISTANCE-DIRECT-DIAL EXISTS AND

AREA-CODE == 877 AND

TRANSIT-NETWORK DOES-NOT-EXIST)

OR

(LONG-DISTANCE-DIRECT-DIAL EXISTS AND

AREA-CODE == 888 AND

TRANSIT-NETWORK DOES-NOT-EXIST)

In the preceding example, the LONG-DISTANCE-DIRECT-DIAL clause is included to force the use of 1. Also, we have to exclude the TRANSIT-NETWORK to prevent the user from dialing the transit network escape code of 1010XXX.

## Partition Rules

When you create a directory number, route pattern, translation pattern, CTI port, or CTI route points, CallManager puts them in a <none> partition. It is a good practice to place all of them in their own partition. Leaving them in a <none> partition leaves room for toll fraud. Assume that you have a route pattern of 9.1[2-9]XX[2-9]XXXXXX in a null partition. All the IP phones, including lobby phones, have access to this route pattern and thus can make long-distance calls. This breaks your Class of Restriction policies. It also allows users to set Call Forward All to long-distance numbers and thus misuse the telephony network.

## Calling Search Space Rules

Minimize the number of partitions and the length of the partitions as much as possible, because the number of characters allowed in the calling search space (CSS) is limited to 512 characters. As you know, the CSS is a list of partitions. Hence, lengthy partition names or a large number of partitions limits the number of partitions that you can have in the CSS. Also, shorter partition names improve performance because of faster string matches.

In a multisite centralized CallManager deployment model, you can use the alternate Calling Search Space Design described in Chapter 6, "Design of Call-Processing Infrastructure and Applications." This uses the CSS on the line level and the device level to determine the effective calling restrictions on the IPT devices.

## Prefixing the Digits in Missed and Received Calls

When an IP phone user receives an incoming call from the PSTN, the phone displays the digits sent by the PSTN in the missed and received calls options. This number does not include the access code (for example, 9 or 0) that is required if the user dials the external number. You can prefix the access codes and the long-distance access codes easily by using the following new advanced service parameters (under Clusterwide Parameters [Device - PRI and MGCP Gateway] section) for CallManager service, introduced in CallManager 3.3.3:

- National Number Prefix
- International Number Prefix
- Unknown Number Prefix
- Subscriber Number Prefix

CallManager adds the prefix values defined in the service parameters to numbers in the missed and received calls directories based on the inbound Q.931 call type value.

For example, in North America, for international numbers, you can prefix 9011 by configuring "9011" in the International Number Prefix parameter, and for national numbers, you can prefix 91 by configuring "91" in the National Number Prefix parameter. You likely want to keep the prefix for subscriber and unknown numbers blank. One limiting factor is that (at least in North America) Q.931 call types do not distinguish between local and long-distance numbers, so ten-digit local numbers will be dialed with a 91 long-distance prefix. Again, this is normally a nonissue because if you want to avoid the long-distance rates for the local calls, you can create an outbound translation pattern for the area codes that do not require you to dial 1 and remove 91 before sending the call to the PSTN.

# Securing the Servers

It is critical to secure the call-processing servers and other application servers from viruses, worms, and denial of service (DoS) attacks. Chapter 6. discusses the best security practices. This section gives operational best practices to keep the servers up to date to prevent them from becoming potential targets for security attacks.

## Operating System Hardening

Apply the operating system service packs and critical hot fixes regularly to prevent security attacks and thus harden the operating system. Upgrade the antivirus software on the servers as and when new versions are available.

Cisco bundled a security script CCM-OS-OptionalSecurity.cmd beginning with CallManager operating system release version 2.6. The script is available in the C:\Utils\SecurityTemplates directory on the CallManager servers. You can optionally run this script only on the CallManager servers to harden the operating system.

| CAUTION | Be aware that running this script on the CallManager servers that are integrated with other applications, such as Cisco IP-IVR and Cisco IPCC Express, is not supported. Refer to the Readme file in the C:\Utils\SecurityTemplates directory before making a decision to run this optional security script. |
|---|---|

## Cisco Security Agent

CSA is a distributed security software solution that helps prevent malicious behavior on CallManager and other application servers. The CSA solution is composed of several elements:

- **CSA Software Agent**—Core endpoint technology that resides on servers and autonomously enforces local policies that prevent attacks
- **CSA Management Console**—Core management application that provides a central means of defining and distributing policies, providing software updates, and maintaining communications to the agents
- **CSA Profiler**—Plug-in management application that provides the capability to build custom policies to protect new applications and tune and modify existing policies in live environments

You should install the CSA Software Agent on all CallManager servers as well as other application servers such as Unity, IPCC Express and so forth. You can download the CSA Software Agent for CallManager at no charge from the following URL:

http://www.cisco.com/cgi-bin/tablebuild.pl/cmva-3des

Similarly you can download the CSA Software Agent for Unity from the following URL:

http://www.cisco.com/cgi-bin/tablebuild.pl/unity3d

Remember that each Cisco IPT application has it's own version of CSA Software Agent. Hence, make sure that you download and install the version that is specific to your product.

# Service and Enterprise Parameter Fine-Tuning

Sometimes you have to fine-tune the CallManager service and Enterprise parameters, based on the size of your network and your requirements. The service parameters are stored in the SQL database and are replicated between the CallManager servers in the cluster. The default values are stored in the ProcessConfigDefault table, and running values are stored in the ProcessConfig table in the SQL database. However, some parameters are specific to a given CallManager server, and others are cluster-wide parameters. Changing a cluster-wide parameter affects the whole cluster operation. Previous chapters and this chapter discussed some of these service parameters in detail. Table 9-4 lists the other commonly changed service parameters. To access the service parameters, from the CallManager Administration page, go to **Service > Service Parameters,** and then select the desired service to display the associated service parameters.

Some of the services have advanced service parameters that are not displayed by default. To view them, click the Advanced button on the Service Parameters page.

**Table 9-4**    *Commonly Changed Service Parameters*

| Service Name | Service Parameter Name | Value (Default in Bold) | Purpose |
|---|---|---|---|
| CallManager Service | CDR Enabled Flag | **False**/True | Set to True to enable logging of CDRs. |
| | Call Diagnostics Enabled | **False**/True | Set to True to enable logging of CMR records. CMR records help you to generate the reports through CAR, which helps you to troubleshoot the voice-quality issues such as delay and jitter. |
| | Digit Analysis Complexity | **Standard**/ Translation Pattern and Alternate Analysis | To troubleshoot dial plan issues, change to Translational Pattern and Alternate Analysis. Setting this option creates detailed digit analysis in CCM traces. |
| | Unknown Caller ID Flag | **True**/False | The Unknown Caller ID Flag parameter enables the parameter enables the Unknown Caller ID and Unknown Caller ID Text parameters. If this parameter is set to True, the information provided in the Unknown Caller ID and Unknown Caller ID Text parameters is displayed to called parties for inbound calls that are received without caller ID information. |
| | Unknown Caller ID | Blank | |
| | Unknown Caller ID Text | Blank | |
| | Caller ID | Blank | This parameter affects the caller ID sent to the PSTN from the CallManager for outgoing calls for all gateways. If you set this parameter to 4082349999, the external callers see this number when you make outbound calls from any device configured in the CallManager. This setting overrides any digit manipulation performed for the calling party number at the route pattern or route list level. Changing this parameter requires a restart of CallManager Service. |

**Table 9-4**  *Commonly Changed Service Parameters (Continued)*

| Service Name | Service Parameter Name | Value (Default in Bold) | Purpose |
|---|---|---|---|
| | Change B-Channel Maintenance Status 1 to 5 | Blank | You can use these five parameters to take one or more B channels in a T1 PRI/E1 PRI circuit. This might be required when doing maintenance on the gateways or circuits. Click the "i" button on the Service parameters page to obtain more information on using these parameters. |
| | H323 Network Location OffNet | **False**/True | Set this to True if incoming calls come via an H.323 gateway and require IP phones to ring differently when receiving internal calls and external calls. |
| | MGCP Network Location OffNet | **False**/True | Set this to True if incoming calls come via MGCP FXS/ FXO ports and require IP phones to ring differently when receiving internal calls and external calls. |
| | MGCP Network Location OffNet for E1 and T1 | **False**/True | Set this to True if incoming calls come via an MGCP T1/ E1 and require IP phones to ring differently when receiving internal calls and external calls. |
| | Automated Alternate Routing Enable Flag | **False**/True | Set this parameter to True to enable AAR. |
| Database Layer Monitor Service | Max CDR Records | **1500000** | By default, 1.5 million records are stored in CDR before purging the data. Changing this value is not required often. However, if you need to store more records, you can change this parameter. Note: Increasing this value increases the size of the CDR database, which then occupies more hard disk space and increases the amount of time required to complete the backup operation. |
| Extension Mobility | Enforce Maximum Login Time | **False**/True | Use the Extension Mobility parameters to control the behavior of the Extension Mobility feature. Set this parameter to True to specify the duration, a user session can be active on an IP Phone. The value of the duration is specified in the Maximum Login Time parameter. |
| | Maximum Login Time (Hours:Minutes) | **8:00** | Use this parameter to specify the duration of the user session. |
| | Maximum Concurrent Requests | **3** | |
| | Multiple Login Behavior | **Multiple Logins Not Allowed**/Auto Logout/ Multiple Logins Allowed | This parameter specifies the maximum number of login or logout operations that can occur simultaneously. This maximum prevents the Extension Mobility service from consuming excessive system resources. Depending on the the number of users, you can set this parameter to any value between 1 and 100. |

*continues*

**Table 9-4** *Commonly Changed Service Parameters (Continued)*

| Service Name | Service Parameter Name | Value (Default in Bold) | Purpose |
|---|---|---|---|
| | Alphanumeric User ID | **True**/False | This parameter specifies whether the user ID to be used is alphanumeric or numeric. Valid values specify True (user ID is alphanumeric) or False (user ID is numeric). You must restart the Cisco Tomcat Service for any changes to this parameter to take effect. |
| | Remember the Last User Logged In | True/**False** | This parameter specifies whether the user ID of the last user logged in on an IP phone is remembered by the extension mobility application. <br><br> For security reasons, you might want to leave this field to it's default value False. |
| Cisco TFTP | Alternate File Location 1 to 10 | Blank | If you have multiple TFTP servers in your network, you can configure these locations so that CallManager can direct the end devices to look into these locations when downloading the configuration and firmware loads. |
| | Enable Caching of Configuration Files | **True**/False | By default, for greater performance, the TFTP server does not write the files into the hard drive. It caches the files into the memory. However, when you are troubleshooting device registration issues, you can set Enable Caching of Configuration Files to False to write the files to hard disk. |
| Cisco Messaging Interface | Backup CallManager Name | **None** | CMI service enables you integrate with a voice-mail system via SMDI. Configuration of some or all of the parameters is required to enable successful integration. |
| | CallManager Name | **None** | |
| | Data Bits | **7** | |
| | Stop Bits | **1** | |
| | Serial Ports | **COM1** | |
| | Voice Mail DN | **None** | |
| | Voice Mail Partition | **None** | |

**Table 9-4**    *Commonly Changed Service Parameters (Continued)*

| Service Name | Service Parameter Name | Value (Default in Bold) | Purpose |
|---|---|---|---|
| Cisco IP Voice Media Streaming App | Supported MoH Codecs | **G.711mulaw**/ G.711alaw/ G.729 Annex a/ Wideband | If you want to stream the MoH audio streams in other formats (such as G.729 Annex a), you need to make the selection here. For example, select both G.711mulaw and G.729 Annex a if you are using a centralized MoH server and want to stream the audio files in G.729 Annex a format to remote branches and G.711mulaw format within the local network. |
| | Run Flag | **True**/False | The Run Flag service parameter is available for Annunciator (ANN), Conference Bridge, Media Termination Point (MTP) functions. Cisco IP Voice Media Streaming App service provides all three services plus MoH functionality. If you do not want to use MTP or Conference Bridge services, for example set the Run Flag to False. |

As the name implies, the service parameters are associated with a service, and changing the values affects the behavior of the corresponding service. In addition to the service parameters, CallManager provides another set of parameters called enterprise parameters. Changing the values of enterprise parameters affects all the devices and services within the CallManager cluster. To access the enterprise parameters, from the CallManager Administration screen, select **System > Enterprise Parameters**. In most cases, you do not have to change any of these values. Table 9-5 lists some commonly changed Enterprise Parameters and their effects on the cluster operation.

**Table 9-5**    *CallManager Enterprise Parameters*

| Enterprise Parameter Name | Value | Purpose |
|---|---|---|
| Cluster ID | StandAloneCluster | The CDRs and CallManager trace files contain this string. If you have multiple CallManager clusters, give a meaningful name to each cluster, which helps you to identify which cluster the CDR information and trace files are sourced from. |
| URL Directories | http://<CCMNAME/ CCMCIP/xmldirectory.asp | By default, when users press the Directories button on the phone, CallManager looks up the DC Directory. If you have a corporate directory and would like to send the directory lookups against the corporate directory server, you can change this URL to point to a server that is hosting the directory lookup service. |

*continues*

**Table 9-5**    *CallManager Enterprise Parameters (Continued)*

| Enterprise Parameter Name | Value | Purpose |
|---|---|---|
| URL Services | http://CCMNAME/CCMCIP/ getservicesmenu.asp | If you have a dedicated services server to host the IP Phone services, you can change this URL to point to that server. When users press the Services button on the IP phone, they are directed to the services server. |
| Show Ring Settings | False | Enabling this lets users choose how they want their phone to ring when it is idle and when it is in use. Users can go to the CCMUSER pages and configure their settings. |

## Deployments Involving Shared Lines

Deploying an IPT network with shared lines increases the dial plan weight on the CallManager servers. Hence, you must carefully size the servers and memory requirements in shared-line deployments. If you are using shared lines on many IP phones, a single directory number can appear on 300 devices. Therefore, if you have two different directory numbers, you can share them on two different sets of 300 phones, with shared line 1 on the first 300 phones and shared line 2 on the other 300 phones, for a total of 600 devices with shared lines. In practical deployments, no one requires such a large number.

## Call Detail Records

If you have enabled CDRs, the call activities are stored in the CallManager CDR database in the SQL server. If you leave the CDR database untouched, over a period, the number of records stored in the database becomes substantial and occupies a lot of hard disk space. Having a large CDR database increases the amount of time to complete the backup and restore process and results in high usage of memory and CPU by SQL service whenever you run queries or generate reports through CAR. To avoid these issues, you should routinely purge the CDR database.

You can use the CAR tool to schedule the purge of CDRs periodically. To configure automatic purge of the CDR and CMR records from the CAR application, select **System > Database > Configure Automatic Purge**.

If you do not want to install CAR, you can manually purge the CDR data by using the procedure described in the following document:

http://www.cisco.com/en/US/partner/products/sw/voicesw/ps556/
products_tech_note09186a0080100566.shtml

# CallManager Traces

Leave the CallManager trace level to its default and enable detailed tracing only when troubleshooting. Configure the trace settings back to their default values after you complete the troubleshooting. Enabling detailed tracing involves a lot of disk writing cycles and occupies hard disk space.

Another approach is to enable detailed tracing only for CallManager Service, Cisco Database Layer Monitor Service, and Cisco RIS Data Collector Service and leave the trace settings on other services to Error level. When you enable detailed tracing, you can limit the number of files and the size of each trace file to the minimum required. CallManager overwrites the trace information, beginning with the first file, when the file limit is reached, and moves to the next file when the number of lines in the current file reaches the specified threshold.

# Firmware Loads

Always use the same phone loads or gateway loads throughout the cluster. This ensures that whenever you upgrade the CallManager, all the devices get a new load. Otherwise, over a period of time, you will have a few phones and gateways that are left with old device loads in the network. Use BAT to query for the phones and gateways that have different loads and remove the device-specific load information from the configuration pages.

# Cluster Guidelines

This section discusses some operational best practices in configuring and managing the CallManager cluster.

## Removing a Subscriber

If you remove a subscriber server from a cluster, also remove the server name from the CallManager Server page. Do not just power off the server. If you leave the removed server name on the CallManager Server page, the Publisher server still views the server as part of the cluster even though you powered off the server. Hence, the Publisher server tries to contact the server in the back end, which is a waste of CPU resources.

## Auto-Registration

Auto-registration in CallManager enables the phone to register automatically and get a directory number. This feature is helpful during the implementation phase when used along with BAT and TAPS, as discussed in Chapter 8, However, you should either turn off this feature after you complete the implementation or use the following method to forward all the calls from auto-registered phones to a security operator number as soon as they go off-hook. That way, even if someone successfully registers the "rogue phone" to the cluster, the call will always reach the security operator.

**Step 1**   Create two partitions: pt_autoregphone and pt_fwdsecurity.

**Step 2**   Create a CSS css_fwdsecurity and include pt_fwdsecurity partition.

**Step 3**   Create a CSS css_allphones and include pt_internal partition (the partition assigned to all IP phone directory numbers).

**Step 4**   Create a <none> Translational pattern whose partition is pt_fwdsecurity and CSS is css_allphones. In the Called Party transformation mask, put the directory number of the security operator phone.

**Step 5**   From the CallManager Administration page to **System > Cisco CallManager**, select a primary CallManager subscriber, uncheck the Auto-registration Disabled on this CallManager option, and select the auto-registration partition pt_autoregphone from the list box.

**Step 6**   Pick the device pool in which the CallManager you selected in Step 5 is the primary CallManager Subscriber. On the Device Pool Configuration page, set the Calling Search Space for Auto-registration field to **css_fwdsecurity**, as shown in Figure 9-16.

**Figure 9-16**   *Setting the CSS for the Auto-Registered Phones*

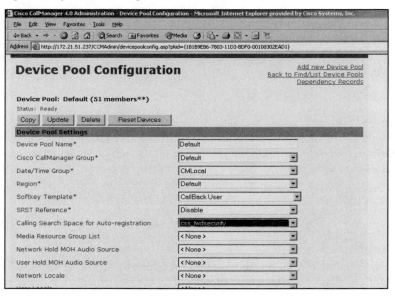

The preceding configuration forwards the calls to the security operator as soon as an auto-registered phone goes off-hook and thus allows you to prevent the misuse of the IPT network by auto-registered phones, as shown in Figure 9-17.

**Figure 9-17**  *Call Flow for an Auto-Registered Phone Forwarding to Security Operator*

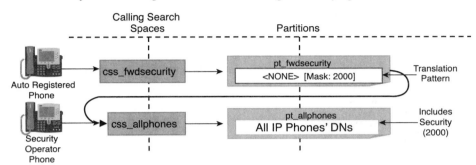

## Installing Third-Party Software Applications

Do not install unsupported third-party applications on any of the IPT application servers, to avoid issues such as memory leaks in those applications that affect the CPU and the availability of memory resources on the servers.

### Changing Session Timeout for CallManager

The session timeout for CCMAdmin and CCMService pages is set to 20 minutes by default. The steps to increase or decrease this setting are as follows:

**Step 1**  From the CallManager server, select **Start > Program > Administrative Tools > Internet Services Manager**.

**Step 2**  Click the server name and then click + to expand the Default Web Site selection, as shown on the left in Figure 9-18.

**Step 3**  Right-click **CCMAdmin** and select **Properties**.

**Step 4**  Click the **Configuration** button to open the Application Configuration dialog box, shown on the right side of Figure 9-18.

**Step 5**  Select the **App Options** tab.

**Step 6**  Check the Enable Session State option (if it is unchecked) and change **Session Timeout** to the desired value.

**Step 7**  To change the session timeout for the CallManager Serviceability pages, follow the preceding procedure but right-click CCMService rather than CCMAdmin in Step 3.

**Figure 9-18** *Changing the Session Timeout*

 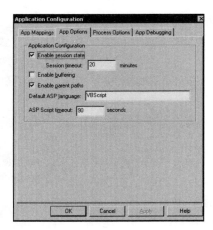

## Cisco Unity Operations

As discussed in Chapter 7, "Voice-Mail System Design," Cisco Unity uses an underlying messaging network for proper functioning. The messaging store could be either Microsoft Exchange or IBM Lotus Domino. If you are following Microsoft's or IBM's best practices for monitoring and maintaining Exchange, Windows, or Domino, it is unlikely that you will encounter issues regarding these messaging products. Using Exchange or Domino to store and retrieve voice messages, break down distribution lists to addresses, and then route SMTP messages is basic mail technology that Exchange and Domino have a solid track record of handling. If you maintain the message store servers properly, the weakest point between Unity and the message stores will be the network connection between them. If there are network latency issues between the Unity and message store servers, it can manifest itself as telephone user interface (TUI) delays in the Unity conversation that the end user will hear.

Refer to the Cisco Unity Maintenance Guide on Cisco.com for recommendations on how to maintain the Unity systems:

http://www.cisco.com/univercd/cc/td/doc/product/voice/c_unity/unity40/maint/maint403/ex/index.htm

# Day 2 Monitoring and Management Tasks

You now have an understanding of the various day-to-day operations and the optimization techniques and tools that are available to execute those operations. This section lists the recommended tasks that CallManager system administrations should follow to perform some of the major operational activities. The individual tasks within each operational activity refer to the tools described earlier in the chapter. Specifically, this section discusses the tasks involved in the following major operational activities:

- CallManager day-to-day monitoring tasks
- CallManager pre-upgrade tasks
- CallManager post-upgrade tasks

## CallManager Day-to-Day Monitoring Task List

Table 9-6 summarizes the day-to-day monitoring tasks that are recommended to achieve the high availability of IPT networks. The tasks listed in Table 9-6 are centered on CallManager. However, you can develop similar tasks for other application servers, depending on your network.

**Table 9-6**    *CallManager Day-to-Day Monitoring Task List*

| Task | Frequency | Notes |
|---|---|---|
| Upgrade OSs | Monthly | This task applies to CallManager and other Cisco AVVID application servers. This ensures that the OS version is up to date and minimizes system failures caused by faults in the OS. |
| | | Subscribe to the Cisco Voice Technology Group Subscription tool: |
| | | http://www.cisco.com/cgi-bin/Software/Newsbuilder/Builder/VOICE.cgi |
| | | Whenever you perform an OS upgrade on CallManager servers, upgrade the other servers that are not MCS OS based, such as Cisco Unity and IP Phone services server. |
| Apply critical hot fixes | As soon as available | Same as previous. |
| Scan for viruses | Daily | This task applies to CallManager and other Cisco AVVID application servers and ensures that systems are clean from viruses. |
| Update virus definition files | Weekly | Check for the updated virus definition files and update the CallManager and other application servers. If any critical releases are released, perform the update immediately. |
| Back up | Daily | Back up to a tape drive or a network location. The next business day, verify that the backup is successful the next business day. |
| Restore | Bi-weekly | Use the backup data to rebuild the CallManager subscriber in the lab every two weeks and verify that the restore operation successfully recovers the CallManager and other application data. |

*continues*

**Table 9-6**  *CallManager Day-to-Day Monitoring Task List (Continued)*

| Task | Frequency | Notes |
|------|-----------|-------|
| Monitor | Daily | Monitor the health of CallManager and other servers. |
| | | Set up the alerts and notifications. Monitor registered phones, registered gateways, service status, CPU and memory usage, heartbeat, and disk space. Include the performance counters (listed in the "Document Registered Device Counts" section discussed earlier in this chapter) listed in Table 9-1 into your monitoring list. |
| | | Review the reports generated by RTMT and perform detailed analysis. If you observe any abnormalities, take immediate preventative measures. |
| Upgrade CallManager | As and when required | Check the release notes. If you see any new features or critical defects that affect your network, develop an upgrade plan and then perform the upgrade. |
| Work with Cisco TAC or other Cisco engineers | As and when required | This might be required to resolve some product issues or to get design assistance from Cisco. |
| Generate reports | Weekly/monthly | Use the CAR tool to generate the reports for management review purposes. |
| Handle escalated end-user issues | Daily | Some issues reported by end users might require additional configuration or research. Use the various tools described in this chapter to troubleshoot problems. |
| Plan for future network growth and new features | Monthly | Plan for the IPT network expansion, new product deployment, and enabling new features in the existing products. |

# CallManager Pre-Upgrade Task List

Table 9-7 summarizes the list of high-level checks that you should perform before you upgrade the CallManager servers. Depending on your network and IPT components, your list could be shorter or longer. You might have to perform some additional tasks, depending on the CallManager version that you are running in your network.. Read the release notes and the upgrade guide thoroughly before you make an upgrade.

**Table 9-7**  *CallManager Pre-Upgrade Task List*

| Task | Notes |
|------|-------|
| Decide which CallManager version to use. | Review the release notes to check which defects been resolved before making a decision on the upgrade. |
| Check the Compatibility Matrix. | If you have other application servers, check the Compatibility Matrix at the following URL: http://www.cisco.com/univercd/cc/td/doc/product/voice/c_callmg/ccmcomp.htm |

**Table 9-7**    *CallManager Pre-Upgrade Task List (Continued)*

| Task | Notes |
|---|---|
| Remove CallManager servers from the domain. | If CallManager servers are part of the Windows NT/ Windows 2000 server domain, remove them from the domain before the upgrade. |
| Stop antivirus software, third-party applications, and CSA. | Follow the steps described earlier in this chapter. |
| Inform the management, NOC staff, and end users about the possible interruptions to call processing. | Follow your organization's configuration change request procedures. |
| Note the number of registered gateways and phones, gatekeepers, and media resource devices. | Use RTMT or performance counter application. Refer to Table 9-1 and note the values of the counters for the Cisco CallManager object. |
| Note the device loads currently deployed. | On the CallManager Administration page, select **System > Device Defaults** to get a list of device loads for various devices. |

## CallManager Post-Upgrade Task List

Table 9-8 summarizes the list of high-level checks that you should perform after an upgrade on the CallManager servers. Depending on your network and IPT components, your list could be shorter or longer.

**Table 9-8**    *CallManager Post-Upgrade Task List*

| Task | Notes |
|---|---|
| Upgrade the JTAPI plug-in and TSP drivers. | If you have applications that use JTAPI, download the new plug-in from the CallManager Administration page and update it. Do the same for the TSP drivers. |
| Check the CallManager OS version on all servers. | From the CallManager server, select **Start > Programs > Cisco OS Version**. |
| Check the CallManager version on all servers. | From the CallManager Administration page, click the **Details** button. |
| Check the SQL version on all CallManager servers. | From the CallManager server, select **Start > Programs > Microsoft SQL Server > Query Analyzer** and type in the command **select @@version**.<br><br>Or, use the DBL Helper tool by running dblhelper.exe from the command line. |
| Check the SQL subscription. | Same as the preceding note. |
| Check the number of registered gateways and phones, gatekeepers, and media resource devices. | Use RTMT to ensure that the device count is the same before and after the upgrade. |
| Check the health of CallManager services. | Use RTMT. |
| Check Event Viewer. | Check Windows 2000 Event Viewer for any critical errors. |

*continues*

**Table 9-8** *CallManager Post-Upgrade Task List (Continued)*

| Task | Notes |
|------|-------|
| Search for users. | From the CallManager Administration page, select **User > Global Directory** and search for users. Ensure that the search is successful. This check verifies whether the directory services are working. |
| Access CCM user pages. | Access the CCMuser pages at http://IPADDRofCCM/ccmuser and ensure that you can log in successfully. |
| Check the functionality of voice mail and MWI. | Check that access to voice mail works and that MWIs are functional. |
| Check the functionality of other features. | Make sure that the following features are functioning properly:<br><br>MoH for internal and external calls<br><br>Emergency calling<br><br>Call forwarding<br><br>Call transfer<br><br>Call hold<br><br>Conference calling<br><br>Meet-Me<br><br>Pick-up groups<br><br>IP Phone services<br><br>Speed dials<br><br>Fast dials<br><br>Personal Address Book<br><br>Incoming and outgoing calls<br><br>Calls to IP-IVR/AA systems<br><br>Access to voice-mail systems from PSTN<br><br>Sending/receiving Fax messages if enabled<br>Receiving Calling Name and Caller ID<br><br>Integrations with legacy voice mail and PBX<br><br>Intercluster calls if multiple CallManager clusters are deployed |

# IPT Network Management Tools

Cisco IPT rides on top of the existing network infrastructure. The IPT solution includes main components such as CallManager, IP Phones, gateways, and application servers. The network infrastructure includes routers and switches. It is imperative to track the health of both IPT and network infrastructure components.

The CallManager server in a cluster handles the call-processing requests; adding IPT management software should not complicate the equation. You should select management software that can proactively monitor the voice components and generate alerts to prevent potential problems. The management software should not affect CallManager operation.

## CiscoWorks and IP Telephony Environment Monitor

CiscoWorks IP Telephony Environment Monitor (ITEM) is a suite of tools that aids you in monitoring the health of your IPT system. ITEM runs on Microsoft Windows 2000 Server and Professional platforms. The main components of ITEM are CiscoWorks and IP Telephony Monitor. The plug-in modules Gateway Statistics Utility (GSU), IP Phone Information Utility (IPIU), and IP Phone Help Desk Utility (IPHDU) complete the suite of products in ITEM to monitor all the components in your IPT network. The following are the benefits of ITEM:

- Proactively monitors all the voice components
- Provides real-time fault information about the underlying IP fabric
- Assists in gateway capacity planning
- Monitors the availability of critical services using confidence testing to simulate features such as Off-Hook, TFTP, conference, phone registration, end-to-end call, Message Waiting Indicator, and emergency call test

ITEM monitors various IPT components via Simple Network Management Protocol (SNMP) MIB polling, SNMP trap reception HTTP and ICMP polling to collect information from different components. ITEM does not require installation of a polling or data collection agent on the CallManager. This not only eases troubleshooting CallManager issues but also provides stability to CallManager. ITEM correlates the information received, intelligently reports critical problems, and identifies whether several events from the same device are related. This reduces the number of alerts.

You can perform the device configurations, define thresholds, set or modify alerts, generate reports, and monitor gateway performances via the ITEM GUI. To access the ITEM GUI, type http://IP address:1741/login.html in your browser of choice (where IP address is the IP address of the ITEM server). Figure 9-19 shows the ITEM GUI interface.

**Figure 9-19**   *IPT Environment Monitor*

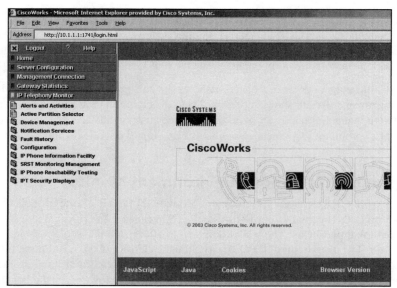

The ITEM GUI has two important components:

- IP Telephony Monitor (ITM)
- Gateway Statistics

These two components appear on the left side of the browser after you log in. You have to install the GSU plug-in component for the Gateway Statistics component to show up on the ITEM GUI. The ITEM software contains the ITM component by default. The ITM component gives you the following options to choose from:

- Alerts and Activities
- Active Partition Selector
- Device Management
- Notification Services
- Fault History
- Configuration
- IP Phone Information Facility (IPIF)
- SRST Monitoring Management
- IP Phone Reachability Testing
- IPT Security Displays

As shown in Figure 9-19, some of the previous items have multiple options that you can choose to perform a variety of tasks. For example, the Notification Services option has two suboptions: SNMP Trap Notification and E-Mail Notification.

This section briefly covers the aforementioned options in ITM and highlights how you can use the information provided by ITM to manage your IPT network. To obtain detailed information about features and functionality in the ITM, refer to the ITM user guide on CCO:

http://www.cisco.com/en/US/products/sw/cscowork/ps5431/products_user_guide_book091 86a00801c1bd5.html

The next section covers the following two other optional items in ITEM:

- IPHDU
- GSU

## Alerts and Activities

The Alerts and Activities option displays the list of alerts generated by the devices that are currently monitored by ITM, as shown in Figure 9-20. This feature is similar to the Alert Central window in RTMT (as discussed earlier in the "RTMT Alerts" section). The alerts are summarized by device. Click on any alert to see a complete list of events associated with that alert.

**Figure 9-20**   *ITM - Alerts and Activities*

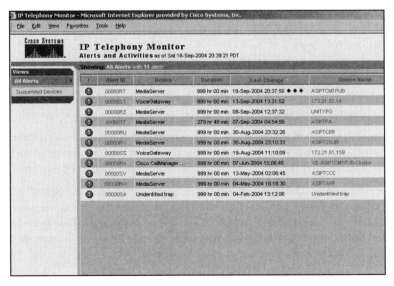

## Active Partition Selector

ITM allows you to group devices into multiple partitions. If you have numerous devices in your IPT network, you will likely want to use this feature. For example, if you have two CallManager clusters managed by two different groups of users, you might want to create two partitions and place the devices in different partitions according their cluster association. You can then set up user groups and give permissions in such a way that each group can control its own cluster.

## Device Management

Device Management allows you to add, delete, and modify all devices that ITM monitors. It also allows you to view the device state and provides an interface to change the credentials such as SNMP community string, username, and password for the servers. You can add a single device or import devices by using a comma separated value (CSV) file. You can enter two types of devices in the ITM. One is a Network Device and the other is a Media Server. The Network device consists of all routers and switches, and the Media server consists of CallManager, Unity, Personal Assistant, CER, and CCC servers. After you add all the network devices that need to be monitored by ITM, you can use View Discovery Status to find the state of the device.

## Notification Services

The Alerts and Activities option contains information on alerts that are generated because of an event. You can forward such alert information to other systems and users. There are two types of notifications:

- SNMP Trap notification
- E-mail notification

In configuring either notification type, you need to select the list of devices for which you want to enable the notification. As shown in Figure 9-21, you can select individual devices or a group of servers (for example, All Cisco Gateways). You can also choose to send the alert only if a critical alarm is generated from the selected device or group of devices.

By choosing different combination of these parameters, you can control the information that is sent to the individuals who are responsible for different components of the network. In other words, you can filter the information based on the job function of each recipient.

When configuring SNMP trap notification, you need to enter the SNMP trap recipient, which is the DNS name or IP address of the server that receives the trap notification. In case of E-Mail notification, the recipient information is the e-mail addresses of the intended persons to send the alert notification. You also need to specify the SMTP server information to communicate with the E-Mail server.

**Figure 9-21**  *ITM - Notification Services*

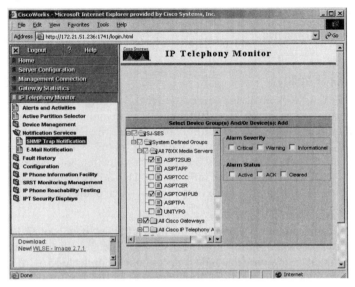

## Fault History

Fault History allows you to view the alerts and events generated by devices that are monitored by ITM for the past 30 days. Based on the fault history, you can tell if the event or the alert is recurring or not. If you see a recurring event in the fault history, you need to analyze the reason for that event and take the appropriate steps to resolve the issue.

## Configuration

Configuration allows you to configure the thresholds for various events, polling intervals, and other configuration parameters that apply to ITM. Within the Configuration display, one useful option is Confidence Testing, which is discussed in the following section.

### Confidence Testing

In confidence testing, a group of synthetic traffic simulates network activity related to IPT functionality. The data collected during these tests helps you to maintain the availability of IPT; these tests provide insight into the following areas:

- IP availability
- SNMP availability
- Application availability

- Operational availability (ability of phones to connect)
- Server interface availability
- MWI performance

## IP Phone Information Facility

In a complex network involving several switches, keeping track of the switch port to which the IP phone connects becomes hard. IPIF helps ITM to monitor, track, and maintain the phone information in the network. This utility provides information about the phone extension, IP address of the phone, MAC address of the phone, status of the phone, type of phone, protocol, SRST mode, CallManager address, switch address, switch port, switch port status, VLAN name, VLAN ID, and SRST router information. This utility helps in troubleshooting issues with phone registration when the phone moves. The switch details are populated for those switches that are managed by ITM.

Using IPIF, you can find IP Phones in the network, view details of IP Phones, schedule phone discovery, and view the status of phone discovery. You can generate individual reports of all phones in the network, unregistered suspect phones, duplicate MAC/IP address IP Phones, phone audit, phone move, and IPT applications. The IPT Applications display provides information for all IPT applications that are registered with CallManager.

## SRST Monitoring Management

As discussed in Chapter 1, "Survivable Remote Site Telephony (SRST)" section, the SRST feature provides backup call processing for the IPT endpoints in the branch sites in case of connectivity failure with the CallManager at the central site.

The SRST Monitoring Management in ITM monitors the WAN link between the central site router and the branch site router configured for SRST. When the WAN link goes down, ITM sends an alert informing that IPT endpoints such as Cisco IP Phones in the branch site are in SRST mode. By viewing this alert, you can check the status of the remote WAN link and resolve the issue to restore the WAN link.

## IP Phone Reachability Testing

This testing assists you in proactively monitoring the status of the IP phones. It also provides information about the availability of the intermediate network among the IP Phone, ITM, and SAA (Service Assurance Agent) router. This testing requires a router to run SAA. The SAA router sends SAA-based pings to all key phones; you can optionally configure the ITM server to send an ITM ping in addition to the SAA ping. You can use the Phone Reachability Testing Manager page to add, configure, delete, and view reachability tests.

## IPT Security Displays

IPT Security Displays provides the following views:

- **Unregistered/Suspect IP Phones**—Provides information about the unregistered phone in the CallManager cluster and the phone that has made an unsuccessful attempt to register.

- **Duplicate MAC/IP Address IP Phones**—Provides information about the phones that have a duplicate MAC address or a duplicate IP address. A phone with a duplicate MAC address has the same MAC address as another IP phone in the network but a different IP address. A phone with a duplicate IP address has the same IP address as another phone in the network but a different MAC address. This report is useful during implementation and during day-to-day operations to find out configuration errors for MAC addresses.

- **IP Phone Audit**—Provides information about the addition and deletion of IP phones in the cluster and provides information about the phones when the status changes, such as when a phone becomes unregistered with CallManager.

- **IP Phone Move**—Provides information about the phones that have physically moved within the cluster and the phones that have moved between clusters. The IP Phone Movement Tracking process runs every 5 minutes to collect this information, which is stored in the database for 30 days and then purged. This interval cannot be changed.

The information collected from IPT Security Displays assists in the inventory of all phones, troubleshooting issues with call routing, and the identification of phone theft. The report contains attributes such as the phone extension, IP address of the phone, MAC address of the phone, switch address, switch port details, and the CallManager address.

## IP Phone Help Desk Utility

The combination of IPHDU and IPIF constitutes a great tool for help desk personnel to troubleshoot problems with a phone. IPHDU allows help desk personnel to access IPIF without requiring them to have complete access to ITEM. IPHDU is an optional component that you can install IPHDU on any Windows platform. The help desk personnel can obtain information about the phone by using the phone extension, IP address of the phone, or MAC address of the phone. IPHDU provides the following information:

- Extension number
- IP address
- MAC address
- Switch IP address
- Switch port number on that switch
- Cisco CallManager IP address
- VLAN information on the switch

## Gateway Statistics Utility

GSU assists in collecting performance and capacity statistics from CallManagers and gateways. GSU is an optional web-based plug-in that can be installed on top of ITEM.

GSU communicates with CallManager and collects information about registered MGCP gateways. You can use GSU to schedule a study, which is a task to collect device statistics of MGCP gateways from CallManager. A study can be scheduled to run once or over a period of time; you can perform trending analyses based on the data collected over the time period.

GSU polls the Performance Monitor counters and provides the following performance statistics:

- Active calls on the gateways in a cluster
- FXS, FXO, T1 CAS, and T1/E1 PRI port utilization for MGCP gateways in the cluster
- Channel utilization of PRIs on MGCP gateways

# Summary

This chapter described the various tasks involved in the operations and optimization phase and provided some guidelines to establish a process and develop the support teams to support the converged network. In addition, this chapter presented the various tools that are available, explained when and how to use them, provided best practices for upgrades, and outlined recommended day-to-day maintenance.

You should read the system administrator and serviceability guides from time to time to discover what new tools and features are available in various products. Cisco.com has an excellent collection of information on commonly faced problems and corresponding resolution procedures.

Cisco CallManager TAC support:

http://www.cisco.com/cgi-bin/Support/browse/psp_view.pl?p=Software:Cisco_Call_Manager

Cisco Unity TAC support:

http://www.cisco.com/cgi-bin/Support/browse/psp_view.pl?p=Software:Unity

Cisco Voice Applications TAC support:

http://www.cisco.com/cgi-bin/Support/browse/index.pl?i=Software&f=2755

If you still have problems with your IPT system after referring to the information contained in this URL, you can contact Cisco TAC by opening the service request from the following URL:

http://www.cisco.com/warp/customer/687/Directory/DirTAC.shtml

PART III

# Appendixes

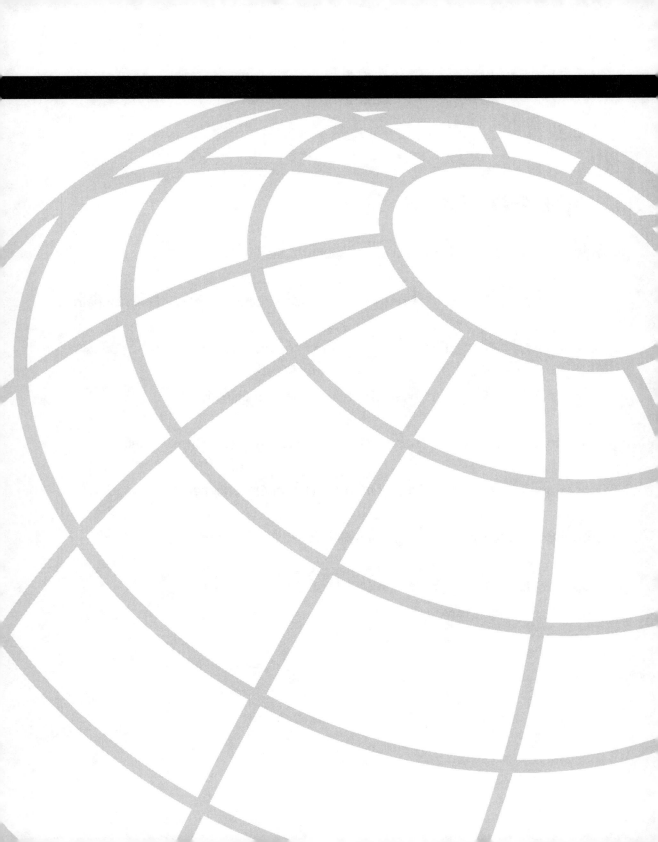

# APPENDIX **A**

# Cisco IP Phone Models and Selection Criteria

Table A-1 summarizes the features and the selection criteria for the Cisco IP Phones. Figure A-1 displays various Cisco IP Phone models.

**Figure A-1**   *Cisco IP Phone Models*

**Table A-1** *Overview of Cisco IP Phone Models*

| IP Phone Model | Description/Features | Where to Deploy |
|---|---|---|
| Cisco IP Phone 7902G | Single line<br>No integral switch<br>No LCD display<br>No programmable (soft) keys<br>6 fixed feature keys<br>No advanced features<br>No hands-free support<br>No headset port<br>SCCP<br>Codecs: G.711, G.729a<br>Americans with Disabilities Act (ADA) compliant | Lobby, break rooms |
| Cisco IP Phone 7905G | Single line<br>No integral switch<br>Pixel-based display (monochrome)<br>4 programmable (soft) keys<br>2 fixed feature keys<br>Advanced features: softkeys support<br>No hands-free support<br>No headset port<br>SCCP, H.323, SIP<br>Codecs: G.711, G.729a<br>ADA compliant | Lobby, break rooms |
| Cisco IP Phone 7912G | Single line<br>Integral switch<br>6 programmable (soft) keys<br>6 fixed feature keys<br>No advanced features<br>No hands-free support<br>No headset port<br>SCCP, SIP<br>Codecs: G.711 and G.729a<br>ADA compliant | Employees' desks, lobby, break rooms |

**Table A-1**    *Overview of Cisco IP Phone Models (Continued)*

| IP Phone Model | Description/Features | Where to Deploy |
|---|---|---|
| Cisco IP Phone 7940G | Two lines<br>Integral switch<br>Pixel based (grayscale)<br>6 programmable (soft) keys<br>8 fixed feature keys<br>Support for 7914 expansion module<br>Hands-free support<br>Headset port<br>SCCP, MGCP, SIP<br>Codecs: G.711, G.729a<br>ADA compliant | Employees' desks |
| Cisco IP Phone 7960G | Six lines<br>Integral switch<br>Pixel based (grayscale)<br>6 programmable (soft) keys<br>8 fixed feature keys<br>Support for 7914 expansion module<br>Hands-free support<br>Headset port<br>SCCP, MGCP, SIP<br>Codecs: G.711, G.729a<br>ADA compliant | Managers',<br>executives', or<br>employees' Desks |
| Cisco IP Conference Station 7936 | Single line<br>No integral switch<br>Pixel based<br>3 programmable (soft) keys<br>8 fixed feature keys<br>Conference phone, high-quality speaker phone<br>Hands-free support<br>No headset port<br>SCCP<br>Codecs: G.711, G.729a<br>External microphone port<br><br>Note: 7936 is an enhanced version of the 7935 phone with improved LCD display and external microphone port. | Conference room,<br>executive suites |

*continues*

**Table A-1**   *Overview of Cisco IP Phone Models (Continued)*

| IP Phone Model | Description/Features | Where to Deploy |
|---|---|---|
| Cisco Wireless IP Phone 7920 | Wireless LAN phone<br>Single line<br>2 soft keys<br>Pixel-based display<br>Headset support<br>IEEE 802.11b<br>Frequency range: 2.4–2.497 GHz<br>Range: 500–1000 ft indoors<br>SCCP<br>Codecs: G.711, G.729a | Mobile professionals in warehouse, sales floor, call center, nurses, doctors, educators, IT personnel, etc. |
| Cisco IP Phone 7970G | Eight lines<br>Integral switch<br>Color pixel display<br>Touch-screen feature<br>6 programmable (soft) keys<br>Hands-free support<br>Headset port<br>SCCP<br>Codecs: G.711, G.729a<br>Supports IEEE 802.3af Power over Ethernet (PoE) standard<br>ADA compliant | Managers, employees, executive desks |
| Cisco IP Communicator | Software-based application that runs on the PC<br>SCCP<br>Supports XML applications<br>Emulates the Cisco IP Phone 7970<br>Ability to select the RTP port range to be used<br>VPN support | Telecommuters or even for general deployment across the organization because of the scalability |

**Table A-1**    *Overview of Cisco IP Phone Models (Continued)*

| IP Phone Model | Description/Features | Where to Deploy |
|---|---|---|
| Cisco IP SoftPhone | Software-based application that runs on the PC<br><br>Uses CTI to communicate with CallManager<br><br>Drag-and-drop dialing<br><br>VPN support<br><br>Ability to control the physical IP phone<br><br>Third-party application integration (Microsoft NetMeeting, Microsoft Outlook, and other collaboration applications)<br><br>Codecs: G.711, G.723, G.729a | Telecommuters |
| Cisco IP Phone 7914 Expansion Module | Add-on module to Cisco IP Phone 7960G that provides an additional 14 programmable buttons per module (see Figure A-1)<br><br>Two 7914 expansion modules can be added to the 7960G phone, enabling users to program 28 buttons as lines or speed dial | Useful for deploying at administrative assistants' desks or at receptionists' desk to handle multiple calls or to support multiple executives |

All models have Message Waiting Indication (MWI) except for the 7936 models. XML applications developed by third parties are available only for 7940G, 7970G, and 7960G Cisco IP Phones.

**NOTE**    Cisco has released Cisco IP Phone 7971G-GE, which is the second IP Phone model in the Cisco IP Phone 7970 executive series. The main difference between Cisco IP Phone 7970G and Cisco IP Phone 7971G-GE is that the later model has a 10/100/1000 Mbps switch daughter card that offers Gigabit Ethernet connectivity to the upstream switch and to the attached PC.

# IPT Planning Phase: Network Infrastructure Analysis Questionnaire

The purpose of this questionnaire is to help you collect the information that you need about a customer's existing network infrastructure to provide to that customer a Cisco IP telephony (IPT) solution. To obtain the answers to this questionnaire, you can either take this questionnaire and meet with the customer or e-mail the questionnaire to the customer and have them complete it. Customers usually provide some part of the information requested in this questionnaire in their Request for Proposal (RFP).

After you obtain from the customer all the information requested in this questionnaire, you must ensure that the network infrastructure adheres to the Cisco AVVID infrastructure recommendations, presented in Chapter 4, "Planning Phase." If you encounter deviations from the best practices, you must communicate this to the customer and recommend a solution before proceeding with the IPT deployment.

---

**NOTE**     Some parts of this questionnaire are available on Cisco.com as part of the IP Telephony Network Readiness Assessment tool, at http://tools.cisco.com/Assessments/jsp/welcome.jsp?asmt=VOIP.

---

The following is an outline of the sections in the Network Infrastructure Analysis Questionnaire:

- Customer Business and Technical Expectations
    - Company Overview
    - Company Vision
    - 3- to 5-Year Plan
    - Solution Expectations
    - Project Expectations
    - Deployment Time-frame
    - Financial Expectations

- Network Design
  - — Hierarchy
  - — Modularity
  - — Layer 2 Design—Core Layer
  - — Layer 2 Design—Distribution Layer
  - — Layer 2 Design—Access Layer
  - — Wide-Area Network
    - WAN Design and High Availability
    - WAN—Network Baseline
    - WAN—Capacity Planning
  - — Routed Network—Layer 3 Design
    - IP Addressing
    - Routing Protocol
    - IP Hot Standby Routing Protocol
    - Quality of Service
- Network Services
  - — DNS
  - — DHCP
  - — NTP
  - — Directories
  - — Messaging System
- Cabling and Network Links
- Hardware Scalability
- Software
- Power Protection and Environmental Condition
  - — Power Protection
  - — Environmental Condition
  - — Power Calculations
- Security

Some sections might not be applicable to the network that you are planning, so skip any such sections.

# Customer Business and Technical Expectations

At the beginning of the planning phase, you must summarize the customer's business, techinical expectations, requirements, and future growth plans to accommodate the increasing demands of the customer in terms of supporting additional IP phones, supporting new features, or adding more applications.

## Company Overview

Table B-1 provides the questions that you should ask a customer to get an overview of the customer's company.

**Table B-1**   *Company Overview*

| No. | Question | Answer |
|---|---|---|
| 1 | What is the customer name? | |
| 2 | Briefly describe the customer's business. | |
| 3 | Provide a brief overview of the services and applications that the customer is running on the network. | |
| 4 | Identify whether the deployment is a "green field" (new network) opportunity. If it is not, give a brief overview of the current network. | |

## Company Vision

What is the company's proposed goals and expected growth in the next 3 to 5 years?

## 3- to 5-Year Plan

What is the company's 3- to 5-year plan for both voice (telephony) and data networks?

## Solution Expectations

What are the company's upper management expectations and requirements for the completed solution, including service levels, features, and functionalities?

## Project Expectations

What are the company's upper management expectations and requirements regarding the project (timelines, priority deployment sites, success criteria, cost expectations, and so forth)?

## Deployment Timeframe

The objective of this section is to collect answers to the following questions:

- What expectations does the customer have for the deployment of the IPT solution?
- What timeline does the customer have for the deployment of the IPT solution?
- Should you give any sites, departments, or users priority for deployment?

Use Table B-2 to provide the timeline and description of various phases.

**Table B-2**   *Deployment Timelines*

| Target | Start Date | End Date | Brief Description of the Phase |
|---|---|---|---|
| Successful rollout of IPT for entire organization | | | Marks the complete IPT rollout in the entire organization |
| Phase 1 | | | Includes IPT rollout at Headquarters |
| Phase 2 | | | Includes IPT rollout at branch sites |
| Phase 3 | | | Deploy additional IPT applications |
| Add additional phases as needed | | | |

Typically, large-scale deployments divide the complete IPT deployment into smaller phases. For example, Phase 1 might be to roll out IPT to a group of users who are located at Headquarters, Phase 2 might be to roll out IPT at some branch sites, Phase 3 might be to deploy additional IPT applications, and so forth. You need to expand Table B-2 and clearly specify how you want to prioritize the deployment to achieve your final goal of converting your customer's network to end-to-end IPT.

## Financial Expectations

What are the company's upper management expectations regarding the new solution's return on investment (RoI)?

# Network Design

The questions provided in this section will help you to gather detailed information on the customer's network infrastructure.

## Hierarchy

Network hierarchy and modularity are perhaps the two most important aspects of network design. A hierarchical network is easier to understand and easier to support because consistent, expected data flows for all applications occur on the network over similar access, distribution, and backbone layers. This reduces the overall management requirements of the network, increases understanding and supportability of the network, and often results in decreased traffic-flow problems, congestion issues, and troubleshooting requirements. Having a network hierarchy also improves the scalability of the network by allowing it to grow without requiring major network changes. Finally, a hierarchical network promotes address summarization, which is important in larger IP routing environments.

Table B-3 provides the questions that you should ask a customer to understand if the network design follows a hierarchical model.

**Table B-3**   *Network Design—Hierarchy*

| No. | Question | Answer |
|-----|----------|--------|
| 1 | Does the network have separate core, distribution, and access layers that are appropriate for the number of campus users? | ❑ Yes<br>❑ No |
| 2 | Are users, servers, and WAN services connected to the access layer for all campus environments? | ❑ Yes<br>❑ No |
| 3 | If a distributed campus environment exists, does the network support a hierarchical and modular WAN core with defined core, distribution, and access connectivity? | ❑ Yes<br>❑ No |

Notes/Comments

In this section, you need to collect the customer's LAN architecture diagram for all sites that require the IPT deployment. Based on the answers to the questions in Table B-3 and after studying the network layout, you need to document the strengths and weaknesses in the network and provide the recommendations to the customer to make the infrastructure ready to run IPT for this area of the network.

# Modularity

A modular network uses consistent network modules for the access, core, and distribution layers. Using a consistent "model" for each layer of the network improves the supportability because it becomes much easier to properly test modules, create troubleshooting procedures, document network components, train support staff, and quickly replace broken components.

Table B-4 provides the questions that you should ask a customer to understand if the network is designed following the modular approach guidelines.

**Table B-4**   *Network Design—Modularity*

| No. | Question | Answer |
|-----|----------|--------|
| 1 | Does the network have consistent hardware and software modules deployed for the LAN server and user access? | ❏ Yes<br>❏ No |
| 2 | Does the network have consistent hardware and software modules deployed for the LAN distribution and core layers? | ❏ Yes<br>❏ No |
| 3 | Does the network have consistent hardware and software modules deployed for access and distribution layer WAN services? | ❏ Yes<br>❏ No |

# Notes/Comments

In this section, you need to obtain information about the router and switch hardware deployed at the core, distribution, and access layers. Use Table B-5 to gather the information, which will be helpful later to do the following:

- Determine whether the routers and switches are capable of supporting inline power.

- Determine whether the routers and switches have hardware or software revisions or versions that are required to run specific IPT features.

- Calculate the number of inline power modules required to provide the power to IP phones.

- Calculate the power supply requirements for modular switches.

**Table B-5**   *Network Design—Hardware List Example*

| Layer | Vendor, Product Family | Installed Modules | Part Number | IOS/CatOS Version Number |
|-------|------------------------|-------------------|-------------|--------------------------|
| Core | Cisco Catalyst 6509 | 1000BASE-X Supervisor<br>Multilayer Switch Feature<br>Multilayer Switch Feature | WS-X6K-SUP1A-2GE<br>WS-F6K-MSFC2<br>WS-X6348-RJ-45 | CatOS 8.1.(3)<br>12.1.20E2 |

**Table B-5**    *Network Design—Hardware List Example (Continued)*

| Layer | Vendor, Product Family | Installed Modules | Part Number | IOS/CatOS Version Number |
|---|---|---|---|---|
| Distribution | Cisco Catalyst 6509 | 1000BASE-X Supervisor Multilayer Switch Feature 10/100BASE-TX Ethernet | WS-X6K-SUP2-2GE WS-F6K-MSFC2 WS-X6348-RJ-45 | CatOS 8.1.(3) 12.1.20E2 |
| Access | Cisco Catalyst 3550 | 48 inline power Ethernet 2 Gigabit Ethernet ports | WS-C3550-48-EMI | 12.1.20-EA1 |

# Layer 2 Design—Core Layer

This section looks at design and configuration considerations for the core layer for larger campus deployments. Smaller organizations might have more of a collapsed model, with the distribution and core layer functionalities combined in the same device.

## Core Layer Performance

Table B-6 provides a list of questions that you should ask a customer to understand the current core layer performance characteristics.

**Table B-6**    *Network Design—Core Layer Performance*

| No. | Question | Answer |
|---|---|---|
| 1 | Is it possible to increase the core capacity? | ❏ Yes ❏ No |
| 2 | Do core layer devices have the required system resources, including backplane utilization, packet forwarding capability, CPU and memory to support redundant core failover, and fast Layer 2 and Layer 3 convergence? | ❏ Yes ❏ No |
| 3 | If a Layer 2 core is used, will the Layer 3 neighbor count scale to the required growth? | ❏ Yes ❏ No |

## Notes/Comments

Describe the extent to which it is possible to increase the capacity of the core, either with existing hardware or by upgrading the hardware. Also, highlight any hardware limitations.

## Core Layer High Availability

Table B-7 provides a list of questions that you should ask a customer to understand the current core layer high-availability characteristics.

**Table B-7**    *Network Design—Core Layer High Availability*

| No. | Question | Answer |
|-----|----------|--------|
| 1 | Does the campus core support redundant and modular core layer devices? | ❏ Yes<br>❏ No |
| 2 | Do Layer 3 equal-cost paths exist through the campus core for optimal routing convergence? | ❏ Yes<br>❏ No |
| 3 | Are core layer devices environmentally controlled and power protected for higher availability? | ❏ Yes<br>❏ No |

### Notes/Comments

Highlight any configuration problem that is not in line with best practices for the configuration of core switches.

## Core Layer Configuration

Table B-8 provides a list of questions that you should ask a customer to understand the current core layer configuration characteristics.

**Table B-8**    *Network Design—Core Layer Configuration*

| No. | Question | Answer |
|-----|----------|--------|
| 1 | Are links between core layer devices and distribution layer devices hard configured for matching speed and duplex settings? | ❏ Yes<br>❏ No |
| 2 | If a Layer 3 core is used, are the interfaces configured with point-to-point subnets? | ❏ Yes<br>❏ No |
| 3 | Is ISL trunking or 802.1Q trunking eliminated from core layer devices? | ❏ Yes<br>❏ No |

### Notes/Comments

Highlight any configuration problem that is not in line with best practices for the configuration of core switches.

# Layer 2 Design—Distribution Layer

This section reviews the distribution layer architecture, high-availability considerations, and configuration of the distribution layer in a large campus environment. Smaller organizations might have a collapsed architecture. In smaller environments, for high availability, Cisco recommends combining the distribution and core layers and placing the servers on the access layer.

## Distribution Layer Performance

Table B-9 provides a list of questions that you should ask a customer to understand the current distribution layer performance characteristics.

**Table B-9**    *Network Design—Distribution Layer Performance*

| No. | Question | Answer |
|-----|----------|--------|
| 1 | Does the distribution layer have increased bandwidth to handle access scalability, access aggregation, and distribution failover? | ❏ Yes<br>❏ No |
| 2 | Do the distribution layer devices have sufficient backplane, CPU, and memory resources for the required multilayer switching and features (including Hot Standby Routing Protocol [HSRP])? | ❏ Yes<br>❏ No |
| 3 | Do distribution layer devices have the required resources to support LAN campus QoS parameters deployed at the distribution layer? | ❏ Yes<br>❏ No |

### Notes/Comments

Highlight any configuration problem that is not in line with best practices for the configuration of distribution switches.

## Distribution Layer High Availability

Table B-10 provides a list of questions that you should ask a customer to understand the current core layer high-availability characteristics.

**Table B-10**    *Network Design—Distribution Layer High Availability*

| No. | Question | Answer |
|-----|----------|--------|
| 1 | Does the distribution layer have redundant devices that can handle bandwidth requirements when alternate or primary distribution connectivity is unavailable? | ❏ Yes<br>❏ No |
| 2 | Has the organization anticipated failover and recovery scenarios with the chosen routing protocol, HSRP, and spanning-tree configuration? | ❏ Yes<br>❏ No |
| 3 | Is trunking between distribution layer devices configured only for VLANs where high-availability server access is needed for multiple access switches? | ❏ Yes<br>❏ No |

### Notes/Comments

Highlight any configuration problem that is not in line with best practices for configuration of distribution switches.

## Distribution Layer VLAN Architecture

Use Table B-11 to collect the VLAN architecture information at distribution layer switches in the campus network.

**Table B-11**    *Network Design—Distribution Layer VLAN Architecture*

| No. | Question | Answer |
|-----|----------|--------|
| 1 | In general, are VLANs maintained on two distribution layer switches and one access layer switch only, and not carried on any link between the distribution layer switches? | ❏ Yes<br>❏ No |
| 2 | Are VLANs limited to two distribution layer devices and two access layer devices where high-availability access is needed? | ❏ Yes<br>❏ No |
| 3 | Are management VLANs separated from user VLANs at the distribution and access layers? | ❏ Yes<br>❏ No |

### Notes/Comments

Highlight any configuration problem that is not in line with best practices for configuration of distribution switches.

## Distribution Layer Configuration

Table B-12 provides a list of questions that you should ask a customer to get an overview of the current distribution layer configuration.

**Table B-12**    *Network Design—Distribution Layer Configuration*

| No. | Question | Answer |
|-----|----------|--------|
| 1 | Is spanning tree configured on distribution switches, even when loops are not planned? | ❏ Yes<br>❏ No |
| 2 | Are the two distribution switches configured as alternating roots and secondary roots for alternating VLANs, with corresponding HSRP active and HSRP standby routers, for load balancing and redundancy? | ❏ Yes<br>❏ No |
| 3 | Has Backbone Fast been set for all distribution switches? | ❏ Yes<br>❏ No |
| 4 | Do links between access and distribution layer devices have hard-coded matching speed and full-duplex settings? | ❏ Yes<br>❏ No |

**Table B-12**   *Network Design—Distribution Layer Configuration (Continued)*

| No. | Question | Answer |
| --- | --- | --- |
| 5 | Has trunk mode been set explicitly to on for trunking ports? | ❑ Yes<br>❑ No |
| 6 | Has channel mode been set to desirable for port channels? | ❑ Yes<br>❑ No |
| 7 | Is Uni-Directional Link Detection (UDLD) configured for switch-to-switch connections? | ❑ Yes<br>❑ No |

## Notes/Comments

Highlight any configuration problem that is not in line with best practices for configuration of distribution switches.

# Layer 2 Design—Access Layer

## Access Layer Characteristics

Table B-13 provides a list of questions that you should ask a customer to get an overview of current access layer characteristics.

**Table B-13**   *Network Design—Access Layer Characteristics*

| No. | Question | Answer |
| --- | --- | --- |
| 1 | Does the access layer support 10/100-Mbps switched connections for all user end stations? | ❑ Yes<br>❑ No |
| 2 | Does the access layer support 100- or 1000-Mbps switched connections for all server and distribution connections? | ❑ Yes<br>❑ No |
| 3 | Does the access layer device support multiple queues to prioritize voice traffic where needed? | ❑ Yes<br>❑ No |
| 4 | Can the access layer devices handle peak utilization from servers and clients? | ❑ Yes<br>❑ No |

## Notes/Comments

Highlight your findings on the access layer characteristics.

## Access Layer High Availability

Table B-14 provides a list of questions that you should ask a customer to understand the current access layer high-availability characteristics.

**Table B-14**   *Network Design—Access Layer High Availability*

| No. | Question | Answer |
|-----|----------|--------|
| 1 | Do access switches have redundant trunking to two distribution switches and only to the distribution switches? | ❑ Yes<br>❑ No |
| 2 | Do critical access switches have redundant processors and power supplies? | ❑ Yes<br>❑ No |
| 3 | Do high-availability servers have redundant connections to a single VLAN on two access switches? | ❑ Yes<br>❑ No |
| 4 | Is auto-negotiation configured for clients? | ❑ Yes<br>❑ No |
| 5 | Has duplex and speed been matched for server connections? | ❑ Yes<br>❑ No |
| 6 | Is PortFast configured on client/server ports? | ❑ Yes<br>❑ No |
| 7 | Is UplinkFast configured on switches that support high-availability servers, where forwarding and blocking VLAN trunks exist on the access switch? | ❑ Yes<br>❑ No |

### Notes/Comments

Highlight any configuration or design problems that are not in line with best practices for configuration of access layer switches.

## Wide Area Network

This section looks at hub-and-spoke design considerations in Frame Relay hub-and-spoke environments.

## WAN Design and High Availability

Table B-15 provides a list of questions that you should ask a customer to understand how the WAN links are provisioned, current link utilizations and configured QoS parameters.

**Table B-15**   *Network Design—WAN Design and High Availability*

| No. | Question | Answer |
|-----|----------|--------|
| 1 | Do you have a hub-and-spoke topology network? | ❏ Yes<br>❏ No |
| 2 | Will the WAN have redundant links to support high availability across the WAN? | ❏ Yes<br>❏ No |

### Notes/Comments

In this section, you need to obtain the following information pertaining to the customer's WAN architecture:

- The customer's WAN diagram
- A description of the overall WAN architecture
- A list of the overall WAN strengths and weaknesses

## WAN—Network Baseline

This section examines whether the organization has properly planned for the addition of IP telephony traffic in terms of the existing traffic and the addition of RTP voice streams. This starts with a baseline of busy-hour or peak data traffic on trunk ports and extends to resource utilization for LAN devices, including buffers, memory, and CPU utilization on devices. Table B-16 provides a list of questions that you should ask the customer to gather the WAN base line information.

**Table B-16**   *Network Design—WAN Baseline*

| No. | Question | Answer |
|-----|----------|--------|
| 1 | Do you collect a baseline for your WAN (intended to support Cisco IP Telephony) that includes link utilization, queue depth, end-to-end packet delay, CPU, and memory? | ❏ Yes<br>❏ No |
| 2 | Has the organization determined the potential impact of Voice over IP (VoIP) traffic in the WAN in terms of bandwidth utilization and system resources? | ❏ Yes<br>❏ No |
| 3 | Does the current baseline and added traffic suggest that utilization and system resources are well within network capabilities, including peak link utilization below 75 percent and WAN links with a minimum of 128 kbps? | ❏ Yes<br>❏ No |

### Notes/Comments

Use this section to document the data for link utilization, end-to-end packet delay, and CPU usage for the WAN link. Also collect and document the information about memory that is installed on the router at the main location and at the branches.

Highlight any potential problems for IPT deployment.

## WAN—Capacity Planning

You should ask the questions given in Table B-17 to analyze the capacity of the existing WAN and determine how much extra bandwidth is required to run the voice traffic along with the data traffic on the same links.

**Table B-17**    *Network Design—WAN Capacity Planning*

| No. | Question | Answer |
|-----|----------|--------|
| 1 | Will the WAN be upgraded to support Cisco IPT solutions to help ensure consistent voice performance? | ❏ Yes ❏ No |
| 2 | Will WAN links that support voice traffic meet minimum bandwidth requirements for Cisco IPT deployments? (64-kbps frame, 64-kbps leased line, or 768-kbps ATM or ATM/Frame Relay is required.) | ❏ Yes ❏ No |
| 3 | In Frame Relay environments, will the organization have committed information rate (CIR) in the Frame Relay network for voice and configure traffic shaping to the CIR to guarantee voice traffic within the Frame Relay network? | ❏ Yes ❏ No |
| 4 | In ATM environments, will the organization use ATM traffic classes such as constant bit rate (CBR) or variable bit rate real time (VBR-rt) to guarantee critical voice traffic across the ATM network and shape ATM traffic to the guaranteed bandwidth? | ❏ Yes ❏ No |
| 5 | Will the WAN have adequate bandwidth to support peak voice usage across the WAN? | ❏ Yes ❏ No |

### Notes/Comments

Overall, is the network ready to run the voice traffic over the data network?

# Routed Network—Layer 3 Design

This section reviews the current IP addressing scheme and information on routing/routed protocols that are deployed in the data network.

## IP Addressing

Use Table B-18 to gather the information on the currently deployed IP addressing scheme for the data network and the customer's plans for assigning the IP addresses to IPT devices such as IP phones, voice gateways, call processing servers, etc.

**Table B-18**    *Network Design—IP Addressing*

| No. | Question | Answer |
|---|---|---|
| 1 | Provide the information on current IP addressing scheme. | |
| 2 | Does your organization have an IP addressing plan for integrating IP phones into the network? | ❏ Yes<br>❏ No |
| 3 | Does the organization have plans to implement RFC 1918 for private addressing? | ❏ Yes<br>❏ No |
| 4 | Does the IP addressing plan support IP address summarization? | ❏ Yes<br>❏ No |

### Notes/Comments

Use this section to document the currently deployed IP addressing scheme along with VLAN ID assignments, VLAN naming and numbering conventions followed.

## Routing Protocol

Use table B-19 to analyze the current IP routing design and configurations deployed in the network.

**Table B-19**    *Network Design—IP Routing Protocol*

| No. | Question | Answer |
|---|---|---|
| 1 | Has the organization implemented Open Shortest Path First (OSPF) or Enhanced Interior Gateway Routing Protocol (EIGRP) for improved network convergence? | ❏ Yes<br>❏ No |
| 2 | Does the organization use any other routing protocols that redistribute to/from the primary EIGRP or OSPF autonomous system? | ❏ Yes<br>❏ No |
| 3 | Does the organization maintain standard routing protocol configurations for all routers in the network? | ❏ Yes<br>❏ No |
| 4 | Are static routes confined to network edges for partner connectivity or ISDN backup? | ❏ Yes<br>❏ No |
| 5 | Has the organization implemented IP summarization toward the core to reduce routing protocol overhead and ensure IP scalability? | ❏ Yes<br>❏ No |

*continues*

**Table B-19**    *Network Design—IP Routing Protocol (Continued)*

| No. | Question | Answer |
|-----|----------|--------|
| 6 | Has the organization implemented stub or default routing in WAN hub-and-spoke environments to reduce routing protocol traffic overhead on WAN links? | ❑ Yes<br>❑ No |
| 7 | Has the organization reviewed routing protocol impact and scalability based on device types, number of routes, and IP routing protocol neighbors? | ❑ Yes<br>❑ No |
| 8 | Is routing disabled on user and server LAN interfaces to prevent core routing through user LANs? | ❑ Yes<br>❑ No |
| 9 | Is routing filtered on access site WAN interfaces to advertise only WAN site information? | ❑ Yes<br>❑ No |
| 10 | What other interior routing protocols are used in the network other than IP? | List: |

## Notes/Comments

Describe the overall routing design.

Provide network maps and diagrams for the Layer 3 design.

# IP Hot Standby Routing Protocol

This section looks at HSRP considerations with respect to the common infrastructure model. Table B-20 provides the questions that you should ask a customer to understand how the HSRP is designed in the network.

**Table B-20**    *Network Design—IP HSRP*

| No. | Question | Answer |
|-----|----------|--------|
| 1 | Does the network use HSRP for redundant default gateway support? | ❑ Yes<br>❑ No |
| 2 | Does the organization understand convergence issues given the number of HSRP groups supported on the device? | ❑ Yes<br>❑ No |
| 3 | Does the network use the HSRP preempt feature to return control to the primary gateway, closely associated with the spanning-tree root for the VLAN? | ❑ Yes<br>❑ No |
| 4 | Has the organization considered the HSRP track feature that is used to track backbone or WAN connectivity from the primary HSRP gateway? | ❑ Yes<br>❑ No |

Notes/Comments

Describe how and where HSRP is deployed in each part of the network. HSRP design might be complex when it is deployed in Layer 2 switches with internal and chassis redundancy.

## Quality of Service

You should use the questions provided in Table B-21 to analyze whether the network devices have the quality of service (QoS) capabilities to support IPT.

**Table B-21**   *QoS*

| No. | Question | Answer |
|-----|----------|--------|
| 1 | Can auxiliary VLANs with 802.1Q/p be used for voice? | ❑ Yes<br>❑ No |
| 2 | Can the voice bearer streams be marked as EF (Expedited Forwarding) and voice control streams as AF31 (Assured Forwarding 31)/CS3 (Class Selector 3)? | ❑ Yes<br>❑ No |
| 3 | Is QoS configurable on devices where buffers might be reaching capacity? | ❑ Yes<br>❑ No |
| 4 | Is Low Latency Queuing (LLQ) configurable on all WAN interfaces? | ❑ Yes<br>❑ No |
| 5 | Is Link Fragmentation and Interleaving (LFI) configurable on all links where speed is below 768 kbps? | ❑ Yes<br>❑ No |
| 6 | Do you have any mission-critical traffic besides voice (e.g., video, DLSW, etc.)? If yes, please specify the traffic types and how they are currently classified in your network. | ❑ Yes<br>❑ No |

Notes/Comments

Describe the QoS strategy in place and highlight any potential problems when deploying voice over the data network.

# Network Services

Network services are included because they are critical to the overall functionality of IP telephony environments. The major services are Domain Name Service (DNS), Dynamic Host Configuration Protocol (DHCP) and Network Time Protocol (NTP). This section looks at the configuration and resiliency of these services for high availability, overall manageability, and functionality requirements in the IP telephony environment.

# DNS

DNS is an important network service. Table B-22 provides a list of questions that you should ask customers to evaluate configuration and resiliency of DNS in terms of network devices.

**Table B-22**   *DNS*

| No. | Question | Answer |
|-----|----------|--------|
| 1 | Does the organization have a resilient DNS architecture with primary and secondary DNS servers? | ❑ Yes<br>❑ No |
| 2 | Provide the DNS server IP addresses and your fully qualified domain name. | ❑ DNS 1<br><br>❑ DNS 2<br><br>❑ FQDN |

## Notes/Comments

DNS is not mandatory for deployment of IPT. However, it provides load balancing and redundancy for accessing IPT XML services.

# DHCP

DHCP is an important network service for large-scale IP telephone provisioning. All IP telephony implementations should implement DHCP for phone provisioning otherwise, manual phone configuration is required. The DHCP service should support option 150 (to support Cisco IPT implementations), which is one of the custom options that can be configured in the DHCP servers. These custom options allow the DHCP servers to provide additional information to the DHCP clients and, in case of IPT networks, the IP phones and the gateways. Option 150 in Cisco IPT networks provides the TFTP server information to the IPT endpoints. Use the questions in Table B-23 to get information about customer DHCP implementation.

**Table B-23**   *DHCP Implementation Details*

| No. | Question | Answer |
|-----|----------|--------|
| 1 | Does the organization use DHCP services to provide the IP addressing for clients? | ❑ Yes<br>❑ No |
| 2 | What DHCP software (including version number) is in use? | ❑ MS DHCP<br>❑ Lucent QIP<br>❑ Other<br>❑ Specify |
| 3 | Will the DHCP server support the configuration of customized options? (IP phones accept the TFTP server information in DHCP option 150 or 66.) | ❑ Yes<br>❑ No |

**Table B-23** *DHCP Implementation Details (Continued)*

| No. | Question | Answer |
|---|---|---|
| 4 | If the answer to question 3 is yes, can the IPT network use your existing DHCP server to provide the IP addresses to IPT endpoints such as IP Phones and voice gateways? | ❏ Yes<br>❏ No |
| 5 | Is the DHCP service resilient with configuration backups and disk mirroring? | ❏ Yes<br>❏ No |
| 6 | Do you use a centralized DHCP server for the entire organization? | ❏ Yes<br>❏ No |
| 7 | If you have distributed DHCP services at the remote branches, does the router provide the DHCP services, or do you have a separate DHCP server for each branch office? | Provide details in the "Notes/Comments" section. |

## Notes/Comments

Add any additional information about the customer's DHCP implementation.

# Network Time Protocol

The use of NTP services in the network ensures that all the devices in the network use the same time source to synchronize their clocks. Use Table B-24 to evaluate the existing NTP configuration and setup in the customer's network.

**Table B-24** *NTP*

| No. | Question | Answer |
|---|---|---|
| 1 | Does the organization currently use NTP? | ❏ Yes<br>❏ No |
| 2 | If the answer to question 1 is yes, what are the NTP IP addresses of the NTP sources? | ❏ Source 1<br><br>❏ Source 2 |
| 3 | Do you want to configure the IPT devices to synchronize their clocks with NTP servers? | ❏ Yes<br>❏ No |

## Notes/Comments

Understand how NTP is implemented today in the network and use the information gathered in Table B-24 to implement NTP in the voice devices, such as CallManager servers, IPT application servers, and gateways.

# Directories

Organizations use directories to store employee-related information such as e-mail ID, phone numbers, location, user ID, authentication information, etc. Table B-25 provides the list of questions that you should ask the customer to understand the currently deployed directory.

**Table B-25**    *Directory*

| No. | Question | Answer |
|-----|----------|--------|
| 1 | What directory service is currently deployed in the organization? | ❏ Microsoft AD<br>❏ Netscape<br>❏ Sun One<br>❏ iPlanet<br>❏ Version |
| 2 | Is there a requirement to integrate the IPT applications with your existing corporate directory? | ❏ Yes<br>❏ No |
| 3 | If directory integration is not a requirement, are you looking at providing the corporate directory access lookup from IP Phones? | ❏ Yes<br>❏ No |

## Notes/Comments

Cisco IPT applications such as Cisco CallManager use an embedded directory (DC Directory) to store user information such as password, PIN number, phone number, speed dials, and so forth. If the customer's organization has deployed a directory, Cisco IPT applications can integrate with it, without the embedded directory. This reduces the administrative overhead and provides a single repository for all the applications. Careful planning is required for the successful integration of IPT applications with the existing corporate directory.

## Messaging System

Use Table B-26 to gather the information about customer's current existing messaging system.

**Table B-26**   *Messaging System*

| No. | Question | Answer |
|---|---|---|
| 1 | What is the current e-mail messaging environment used in the organization? | ❏ MS Exchange<br>❏ Lotus Domino<br>❏ Other<br>❏ Version<br>_____ |
| 2 | Does the organization intend to deploy unified messaging along with the IP telephony deployment? | ❏ Yes<br>❏ No |

### Notes/Comments

If the customer decides to use unified messaging, you should obtain some preliminary information on its messaging architecture. You can collect detailed information using the Voice-Mail Design Questionnaire in Appendix G.

## Cabling and Network Links

Use Table B-27 to analyze if your customer network uses the industry standard copper/fiber cabling systems, redundancy, and diversity for riser, interbuilding, and long-distance WAN connections.

**Table B-27**   *Cabling and Network Links*

| No. | Question | Answer |
|---|---|---|
| 1 | Does the organization follow common guidelines for twisted-pair Category 5 cabling installations? | ❏ Yes<br>❏ No |
| 2 | Does the organization maintain well-organized patch cords and cable labeling for WAN cables, fiber, and copper? | ❏ Yes<br>❏ No |
| 3 | Does the organization follow common guidelines for building or interbuilding campus fiber installations? | ❏ Yes<br>❏ No |
| 4 | Is the fiber and copper cabling tested? | ❏ Yes<br>❏ No |
| 5 | Does the organization have non-Ethernet segments in the network? | ❏ Yes<br>❏ No |

## Notes/Comments

The information that you collect from Table B-27 helps you to analyze the existing cabling infrastructure and provide recommendations.

# Hardware Scalability

This section reviews the hardware that is deployed in the network to ensure that feature requirements, scalability, and hardware resources will meet IPT requirements. The process of hardware replacement is also critical to higher availability. Table B-28 provides a list of questions that you should ask customers to analyze whether the existing hardware in the network supports the IPT deployment: If not, you can suggest the modifications required to support the IPT deployment.

**Table B-28**    *Hardware Scalability*

| No. | Question | Answer |
|---|---|---|
| 1 | Are there any non-Cisco switches at the access layer in the network? | ❑ Yes<br>❑ No |
| 2 | Do you need to connect the Cisco IP Phones to the non-Cisco access switches? | ❑ Yes<br>❑ No |
| 3 | If you have non-Cisco switches, do they support 802.1Q/p? | ❑ Yes<br>❑ No |
| 4 | Which Power over Ethernet (PoE) standard does the organization want to use? | ❑ Cisco PoE<br>❑ IEEE 802.3af |
| 5 | Can the other Cisco switches in the access layer be field upgraded to support inline power? | ❑ Yes<br>❑ No |
| 6 | Will the hardware scale to support the IPT endpoints, such as IP phones and gateways? | ❑ Yes<br>❑ No |
| 7 | Does the organization have chassis redundancy where appropriate? | ❑ Yes<br>❑ No |
| 8 | Does the organization have module redundancy where appropriate? | ❑ Yes<br>❑ No |
| 9 | Does the organization keep spare hardware parts onsite? | ❑ Yes<br>❑ No |
| 10 | Does the organization have a service contract with the hardware vendor to replace the defective parts? If yes, what is the agreed response time? | ❑ Yes<br>❑ No<br>❑ Response Time |

## Notes/Comments

You must determine the hardware scalability section for every site in the network. Key things to note are whether the access layer switches are Cisco or non-Cisco switches and the support of 802.1Q/p protocol, because these determine the QoS capabilities of access layer switches and which PoE standard the organization uses.

# Software

This section looks at infrastructure software to help ensure that the software versions used will support features required by IP telephony, are tested, and are standardized within the organization. Table B-29 provides a list of questions that you should ask customer to understand the software certification processes that exist in the organization.

**Table B-29** *Software*

| No. | Question | Answer |
|---|---|---|
| 1 | Does the organization create and maintain software standards for the network? | ❑ Yes<br>❑ No |
| 2 | Does the organization have a software certification process in place? | ❑ Yes<br>❑ No |
| 3 | Is software tested before it is deployed on the production network? | ❑ Yes<br>❑ No |
| 4 | Does the organization standardize on general deployment software where possible? | ❑ Yes<br>❑ No |
| 5 | Does the organization maintain standard global software configurations? | ❑ Yes<br>❑ No |

## Notes/Comments

Provide the versions of Cisco IOS and Catalyst OS running on the network.

# Power Protection and Environmental Condition

This section looks at power and environment to help ensure that the organization has a power protection strategy for infrastructure components that support IP telephony. The organization should also perform environmental planning to ensure devices are properly environmentally conditioned for temperature and humidity. The equipment should also be located in physically secure locations, accessible only to networking staff.

# Power Protection

Table B-30 provides a list of questions that you should ask customer to understand the current power protection strategy implemented in the network.

**Table B-30** *Power Protection*

| No. | Question | Answer |
|---|---|---|
| 1 | Are core and distribution layer devices that serve multiple buildings or sites power protected with UPS and generator backup? | ❏ Yes<br>❏ No |
| 2 | Are access switches backed up with UPS or a generator where power-protected network access or IP telephony is required? | ❏ Yes<br>❏ No |
| 3 | Does the organization use network components that support redundant power supplies? | ❏ Yes<br>❏ No |
| 4 | Does the organization perform periodic maintenance on UPS and generator systems to ensure system availability? | ❏ Yes<br>❏ No |

## Notes/Comments

When you deploy IPT and use an inline power method to deliver the power to IP Phones, delivering uninterruptible power is necessary to achieve high availability. It is especially important for the access layer switches to include redundant power supplies. Based on your observations collected from Table B-30, provide your recommendations in this section.

# Environmental Condition

This section examines the processes followed in the organization to monitor and maintain the stable environmental condition for various components to function properly. Table B-31 provides a list of questions you should ask the customer to understand the current measures that are implemented for environmental conditioning.

**Table B-31** *Environmental Condition*

| No. | Question | Answer |
|---|---|---|
| 1 | Does the organization investigate heat dissipation, temperature, and humidity information for new product implementations? | ❏ Yes<br>❏ No |
| 2 | Does the organization provide uninterrupted ventilation and cooling to network devices to maintain a consistent operating temperature and environment? | ❏ Yes<br>❏ No |
| 3 | Does the organization use environmental monitoring systems for critical equipment locations? | ❏ Yes<br>❏ No |
| 4 | Does the server room where you are planning to house the IPT servers, switches, and gateways have enough rack space? | ❏ Yes<br>❏ No |

**Table B-31**   *Environmental Condition (Continued)*

| No. | Question | Answer |
|---|---|---|
| 5 | Do you have adequate power outlets to support the additional devices? | ❏ Yes<br>❏ No |
| 6 | What is the current capacity of the UPS system? | Capacity _____ |
| 7 | Can the existing UPS system handle the additional load to support the new IPT servers, gateways, and switches? | ❏ Yes<br>❏ No |

## Notes/Comments

Based on the answers to the questions in Table B-31, you can provide the recommendations to the customer on the importance of constant checking of environmental conditions for power backup systems to ensure uninterruptible functioning of the IPT system.

# Power Calculations

As part of the infrastructure analysis, you need to collect the information as per Table B-32. You will not know the type of Cisco IP phone models at the time of the planning phase. However, you need to determine the switch hardware and line card information so that you can size the power supply capacities on the switches correctly after you decide on the phone models. Typically, you decide on the phone model selection during the design phase. You need to come back to this table during the design phase and input your phone quantities selected phone models in Table B-32. (Refer to Table B-5 to get hardware information on the switches that are deployed in the network.)

**Table B-32**   *Power Calculations*

| Switch Name, Location, Product Family, Chassis Type | Line Cards Installed | Input Voltage | Cisco IP Phone Model | Quantity | Recommendations from Cisco Power Calculator |
|---|---|---|---|---|---|
| | | | 7960G<br>7970G<br>7940G | | |
| | | | 7960G<br>7970G<br>7940G | | |
| | | | 7960G<br>7970G<br>7940G | | |

## Notes/Comments

You can input the information collected in Table B-32 in the Cisco Power Calculator (CPC), available on Cisco.com at http://tools.cisco.com/cpc/launch.jsp, to complete the power calculations.

In Table B-32, in the "Recommendations from Cisco Power Calculator" column, you can put the output of the CPC, such as whether the system can support the specified number of IP phones, whether the system requires additional power supply, etc.

# Security

This section looks at general security practices followed in the organization. Table B-33 provides a list of questions you should ask the customer to gather this information.

**Table B-33**    *Security*

| No. | Question | Answer |
|---|---|---|
| 1 | Has the organization developed a security policy regarding access to network devices, monitoring, privacy, and protection of information assets? | ❑ Yes <br> ❑ No |
| 2 | Has the organization implemented basic security measures such as strong passwords and password encryption to control access to the devices via network? | ❑ Yes <br> ❑ No |
| 3 | Are the network devices in a secure and locked location that requires authorization for physical access? | ❑ Yes <br> ❑ No |
| 4 | Is there a mechanism employed to authenticate users, control access to network devices, and provide accounting information for audit purposes? | ❑ Yes <br> ❑ No |
| 5 | What antivirus software does the organization use currently to protect the servers and workstations from viruses? | ❑ McAfee <br> ❑ Symantec <br> ❑ Trend Micro <br> ❑ Other <br><br> ——————— <br> ❑ Version No <br> ——————— |

**Table B-33**   *Security*

| No. | Question | Answer |
|---|---|---|
| 6 | Does the organization currently use any host-based intrusion detection/ prevention software? If yes, provide the name of the product and vendor. | ❑ Yes<br>❑ No<br>❑ Product<br><br>❑ Vendor |
| 7 | Does the organization have a defined policy for applying the security hot fixes and operating system patches to critical servers? If yes, describe it in the "Notes/Comments" section. Include information such as how long it would take to apply a critical hot fix, what testing/certification procedures are followed, etc. | ❑ Yes<br>❑ No |

# Notes/Comments

Based on the information in Table B-33, you can provide the recommendations, if necessary, to secure the IP telephony infrastructure components.

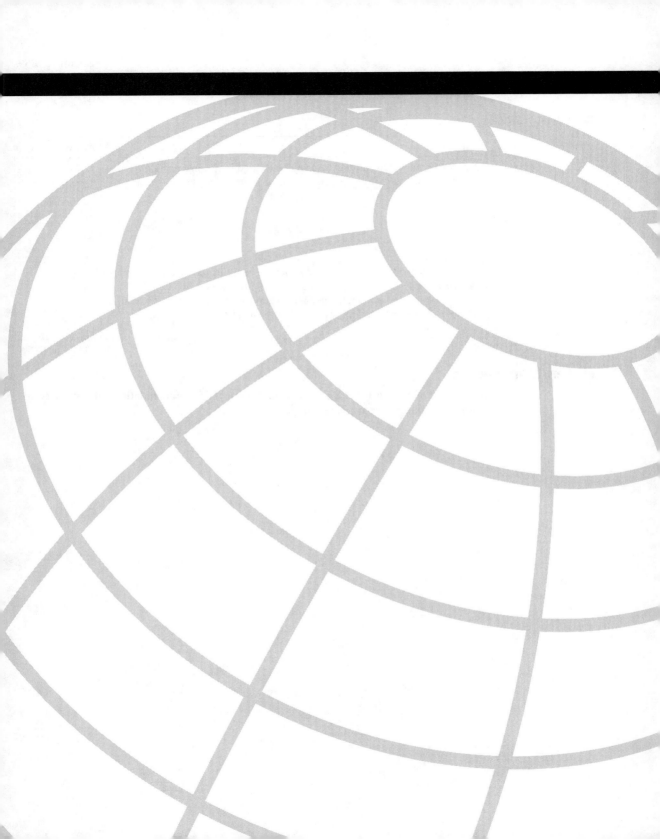

# IPT Planning Phase: Telecom Infrastructure Analysis Questionnaire

The purpose of this questionnaire is to help you collect the information that you need about a customer's existing telecom network infrastructure to provide that customer with Cisco IP telephony (IPT) solution. To obtain the answers to this questionnaire, you can either take this questionnaire and meet with the customer or e-mail the questionnaire to the customer and have them complete it. Customers usually provide some part of the information requested in this questionnaire in their Request for Proposal (RFP).

The following is an outline of the sections in the Telecom Infrastructure Analysis Questionnaire:

- PBX Infrastructure

- Analog Device Information (Fax/Modem)

- Trunk Sizing

- Telephony Numbering Plan

- Voice-Mail Infrastructure

- Telephony Features and Applications

- Applications Security

- Operations and Maintenance

  — Network Management System

  — Remote Network Monitoring/Management

  — Maintenance and Support Contract

Some sections might not be applicable to your customer's telecom network needs. In that case, continue to the next section.

# PBX Infrastructure

A plethora of hardware (PBXs, key systems, processor modules, line modules), software, and signaling protocols (Primary Rate Interface [PRI], Q.SIG, and channel-associated signaling [CAS]) exist to facilitate call control. For interaction or replacement of these systems with IP telephony systems to take place, you must start preparation and planning early in the deployment cycle. This section takes you through the first step of surveying the components that exist to facilitate this initial planning and helps you to determine an overall level of effort or risk given the impending deployment of IP telephony. Use the questions provided in Table C-1 to gather information on existing PBX deployments at your customer network.

**Table C-1**  *Details of the PBX in the Existing Network*

| No. | Question | Answer |
|---|---|---|
| **Basic PBX Information** | | |
| 1 | What are the site details and location of the PBX? | Location Name: <br> Site Address: <br> City/State/ZIP: <br> PBX Room No.: <br> Floor: |
| 2 | Who is the PBX contact representative at this site? | Name: <br> Phone: <br> E-Mail: |
| 3 | Is this PBX leased or owned? If it is leased, what is the lease expiration date? | ☐ Leased <br> ☐ Owned <br> Lease Expiration Date: |
| 4 | If the vendor maintains the PBX, what is the vendor contact information? | Name: <br> Phone: <br> Alternate Phone: <br> E-Mail: <br> Pager: |
| 5 | Who are the vendors and their corresponding models of the PBX at this site? | Location : <br> Vendor: <br> Model: <br> SW Release: <br> Signaling Protocol: <br> Location: <br> Vendor: <br> Model: <br> SW Release: <br> Signaling Protocol: |

**Table C-1**    *Details of the PBX in the Existing Network (Continued)*

| No. | Question | Answer |
|-----|----------|--------|
| 6 | Are you planning to replace this PBX or integrate it with the IPT system? | ☐  Replace<br>☐  Integrate |
| 7 | If you are replacing the PBX, do you want to do a flash-cut migration to the new IPT system or a phased migration? | ☐  Flash-Cut Migration<br>☐  Phased Migration |
| 8 | If you plan to do a phased migration, what are your plans? | |
| 9 | What link types provide network-side (trunk) access to the PSTN? | ☐  Digital<br>☐  Analog |
| 10 | What is the existing PRI/T1/E1 trunk capacity, and how many trunks are in use? | Capacity:<br>Trunks Used: |
| 11 | What is the existing analog trunk capacity and how many trunks are in use? | Capacity:<br>Trunks Used: |
| 12 | What is the existing recEive and transMit (E&M) trunk capacity, and how many trunks are in use? | Capacity:<br>Trunks Used: |
| 13 | What are the signaling protocols that connect to the PSTN?<br>If analog is used, is it Foreign Exchange Office (FXO), Foreign Exchange Station (FXS), E&M, or Direct Inward Dial (DID)? | ☐  PRI<br>☐  E1R2<br>☐  BRI<br>☐  Analog<br>☐  SS7 |
| **Voice Circuit Characteristics** | | |
| 14 | What is the name of the service provider, and what is the circuit ID? | Service Provider:<br>Circuit ID: |
| 15 | What are the framing type, encoding type, and D-channel locations? | Framing        ☐  ESF<br>                    ☐  SF<br>                    ☐  G.704<br><br>Line Code      ☐  B8ZS<br>                    ☐  AMI<br>                    ☐  CRC-4<br>                    ☐  HDB3<br><br>D-Channel Location   ☐  Ch24<br>                    ☐  Ch1 |

*continues*

**Table C-1**   *Details of the PBX in the Existing Network (Continued)*

| No. | Question | Answer |
|-----|----------|--------|
| 16 | What is the central office switch type? | ☐  DMS 100<br>☐  DMS 250<br>☐  DMS 500<br>☐  5ESS<br>☐  NI2<br>☐  Other |
| 17 | What is the trunk's hunt sequence? | ☐  Top Down<br>☐  Bottom Up<br>☐  Least Idle |
| 18 | How many digits are out-pulsed? | Digits: |
| **PBX Interconnection Between Sites** | | |
| 19 | Is this PBX interconnected to other PBXs at other sites? | ☐  Yes<br>☐  No |
| 20 | What link type interconnects the PBXs? | ☐  Q.SIG BC<br>☐  Q.SIG NA<br>☐  Q.SIG GF<br>☐  Other |
| 21 | Are any special or proprietary PBX features enabled on these links?<br>If yes, describe them in the "Notes/Comments" section. | ☐  Yes<br>☐  No |
| **PBX Integration—Hardware Specifications** | | |
| 22 | Are there available ports on the PBX for connecting to Cisco voice gateways? | ☐  Yes<br>☐  No |
| 23 | What signaling type is available on the ports to communicate with Cisco voice gateways? | ☐  PRI<br>☐  E1<br>☐  BRI<br>☐  FXO<br>☐  E&M |
| **PBX High Availability and Traffic Statistics** | | |
| 24 | Is redundancy deployed where possible in the PBXs? | ☐  Yes<br>☐  No |
| 25 | What are the busy hour and busy hour traffic at this location? | Busy Hour:<br>No. of Calls: |
| 26 | What percentage of total calls are the fax calls? | |

**Table C-1**   *Details of the PBX in the Existing Network (Continued)*

| No. | Question | Answer |
|---|---|---|
| **PBX Support for Emergency Call Routing and Advanced Features** | | |
| 27 | (Specific to U.S. and Canada) Do all the PSTN trunks support 911 emergency call routing and send the caller information to the public safety answering point (PSAP)? | ☐  Yes<br>☐  No |
| 28 | Does your existing PBX system support E911 functionality? If yes, explain in the "Notes/Comments" section how this functionality is provided in the PBX. | ☐  Yes<br>☐  No |
| 29 | (Specific to U.S. and Canada) Does your state or province regulation require you to comply with E911 regulations? | ☐  Yes<br>☐  No |
| 30 | Are advanced carrier services, such as AT&T's Software Defined Network (SDN), in use? | ☐  Yes<br>☐  No |
| 31 | What is the range of extensions that is currently configured on this PBX? | Use the "Notes/Comments" section to provide the list of configured extensions. |
| 32 | What are the DID number ranges assigned to this site, and over which trunk interface are these DIDs delivered? | DID delivered via:    ☐  PRI E1/T1<br>    ☐  Analog<br>    ☐  E&M |

## Notes/Comments

You have to collect the information given in Table C-1 for each site. You will use the information that you collect through this table during the design and implementation of the IPT project. During the design and implementation phase, configuration changes are required on the PBX systems to migrate the users to the IPT system. The PBX representatives are the personnel who have authority to make these configuration changes on the PBX. Provide details such as how and when you will move users and Public Switched Telephone Network (PSTN) trunks from the legacy PBX to the new IPT system.

# Analog Device Information (Fax/Modem)

The information that you collect in Table C-2 provides the location of fax/modem devices, the number of fax/modem lines, and other information that is related to fax and modems.

**Table C-2**    *Analog Device Information*

| Site Name | Fax/Modem | Building Number/Location | Number of Fax/ Modem Lines | Is This a Device Off of PBX/ PSTN? | Are These Modem Pool Members? |
|---|---|---|---|---|---|
|  |  |  |  |  |  |
|  |  |  |  |  |  |
|  |  |  |  |  |  |
|  |  |  |  |  |  |
|  |  |  |  |  |  |

## Notes/Comments

The information that you collect in Table C-2 is useful to plan for the number of analog ports required in the IPT deployment.

# Trunk Sizing

The information that you collect in Table C-3 sizes the trunks required from each site and designs the call admission control (CAC) for voice calls.

**Table C-3**    *Trunk Sizing*

| Site Name | On-Net Minutes per Month | Off-Net Minutes per Month | Number of Users | Total Minutes | Trunk Size Required[1] |
|---|---|---|---|---|---|
|  |  |  |  |  |  |
|  |  |  |  |  |  |
|  |  |  |  |  |  |
|  |  |  |  |  |  |
|  |  |  |  |  |  |

1. The trunk size required is derived from the rest of the data.

## Notes/Comments

The information that you collect in Table C-3 is helpful in sizing the PSTN trunks.

---

**NOTE**    On-Net refers to calls that originate from and terminate on an IP endpoint. An On-Net call never requires a connection to a PSTN and uses only IP for the entire duration. Off-Net refers to a call that requires the connection to a PSTN network to complete the call.

---

# Telephony Numbering Plan

The dial plan or telephony numbering plan describes how voice calls are routed within the network and explains the site numbering plan and site-to-site dialing instructions. To replace or integrate the legacy PBX systems with the IP telephony systems, you should ask the customer the questions listed in Table C-4 to get an understanding of the current dial plan. If the requirement is to use toll bypass or Tail-End Hop-Off (TEHO) to save the communication costs, you need to obtain the local area calling information for each site. This helps in designing the call routing in the IPT system.

**Table C-4**    *Telephony Network Design and Dial Plan*

| No. | Question | Answer | |
|-----|----------|--------|---|
| 1 | Does documentation exist to describe the overall dial plan? If yes, provide it by using Tables C-5 and C-6. | ☐ | Yes |
| | | ☐ | No |
| 2 | Does documentation exist to describe the overall PBX-to-PBX and PBX-to-PSTN connectivity? <br><br> If yes, provide the information in the "Notes/Comments" section. | ☐ | Yes |
| | | ☐ | No |
| 3 | Has the organization developed a new dial plan for the IPT deployment? | ☐ | Yes |
| | | ☐ | No |
| 4 | Has the organization determined gateway-specific requirements, including protocol-supported and supplementary services (such as call hold, park, and conferencing)? | ☐ | Yes |
| | | ☐ | No |
| 5 | Has the organization determined gateway site-specific requirements such as encoding, calling line ID (CLID), DID support, analog or digital support, and fax relay? | ☐ | Yes |
| | | ☐ | No |
| 6 | Has the organization decided to implement TEHO? If yes, obtain the toll-bypass information in Table C-7. | ☐ | Yes |
| | | ☐ | No |

# Notes/Comments

Use Table C-5 to document the current numbering plan in the organization, the current number of users, and the estimated growth in the number of users at each site. You need to use the estimated growth in the number of users when sizing the call-processing servers and voice gateways to accommodate the future growth.

**Table C-5**    *Existing Numbering Plan*

| Site Name | On-Net Site Access Code | No. of Digits in Station Numbering Plan | DID Ranges | Station DN Numbering Ranges | Station Intercom Numbering Range | Voice-Mail Numbering Range | Current Number of Users | Expected Growth of Users in Next 3 Years |
|---|---|---|---|---|---|---|---|---|
| | | | | | | | | |
| | | | | | | | | |
| | | | | | | | | |

Use Table C-6 to describe currently implemented Class of Restrictions (COR) groups in the PBX. Table C-6 shows some sample information that helps you to understand the type of information that you need to collect. Use the information collected in Table C-6 to define the calling search space and partitions in the CallManager.

**Table C-6**    *Class of Restrictions Groups*

| COR Group | Phone Types | Type of Access Granted |
|---|---|---|
| COR 1 | Assigned to lobby phones | Local calls, emergency calls, toll-free calls, service calls such as directory assistance, and calls to other sites |
| COR 2 | Employee phones | All access given to lobby phones plus long-distance calling |
| COR 3 | Executive phones | All access given to lobby and employee phones plus international dialing |

If toll-bypass or TEHO implementation is required, you need to obtain the information listed in Table C-7 on a per-site basis.

**Table C-7**    *Local Calling Area List for Implementing Toll Bypass*

| Site Name, PSTN Access Code | DID Extension Range | Local Calling | In-State Toll Calling | In-State Toll Calling | |
|---|---|---|---|---|---|
| | | Area Codes/ Exchange | Number of Digits Dialing | Area Codes/ Exchange | Number of Digits Dialing |
| | | | | | |
| | | | | | |
| | | | | | |
| | | | | | |
| | | | | | |

# Voice-Mail Infrastructure

In this section, you can use the questions listed in Table C-8 to collect information regarding the existing voice-mail infrastructure from your customer.

**Table C-8**    *Voice-Mail Infrastructure*

| No. | Question | Answer |
|---|---|---|
| 1 | What hardware/software platform provides voice-mail functions for the organization? | Vendor:<br>Model:<br>SW Revision: |
| 2 | How is the voice-mail system integrated with the existing PBX systems? Give information about trunk types, signaling, and how the MWI is lighted. | ☐ SMDI<br>☐ Proprietary |
| 3 | If you have multiple voice-mail platforms, are they interconnected? What protocols are used? | ☐ Yes  ☐ AMIS<br>☐ No  ☐ VPIM<br>  ☐ Other |
| 4 | Are slots available on your existing voice-mail platforms for voice and signaling? | ☐ Yes<br>☐ No |
| 5 | Do you want to integrate the voice-mail system with the new IPT system? | ☐ Yes<br>☐ No |

*continues*

**Table C-8**    *Voice-Mail Infrastructure (Continued)*

| No. | Question | Answer |
| --- | --- | --- |
| 6 | What types of IP integration methods are available on the voice-mail system? (Refer to the "Notes/Comments" section for the full names of the acronyms.) | ☐  TSP<br>☐  TAPI<br>☐  SCCP<br>☐  JTAPI<br>Other: |
| 7 | What is the pilot number that accesses the voice-mail system from internal extensions? | Voice-Mail Pilot No. |
| 8 | What number do employees use to access the voice-mail system from the PSTN? | Voice-Mail Access No. |
| 9 | What is your current messaging environment? | ☐  Exchange 5.5<br>☐  Exchange 2000<br>☐  Exchange 2003<br>☐  Lotus Domino<br>☐  Domino Version |
| 10 | Do all users in the organization use the existing message store? | ☐  Yes<br>☐  No |

## Notes/Comments

The following methods are available to integrate the voice-mail systems with the IPT system. You need to know which type of IP integration the voice-mail system supports so that you can design the CallManager system to work properly with the voice-mail system.

- TSP—Telephony Service Provider
- TAPI—Telephone Application Programming Interface
- SCCP—Skinny Client Control Protocol
- JTAPI—Java Telephony Application Programming Interface

The information that you collect in Table C-8 is useful during the design and implementation of the IPT system to integrate it with the existing voice-mail system.

# Telephony Features and Applications

Telephony applications provide extended capabilities such as voice mail and Automatic Attendant. Specialized applications such as loud ringing and overhead paging also exist in many environments. In addition, you can find applications such as Predictive Dialing, Automatic Call Distribution (ACD), Interactive Voice Response (IVR), and Computer

Telephony Integration (CTI) to support small subsets of an organization in scaled-down implementations. Use the questions listed in Table C-9 to collect the information on currently deployed telephony features and applications.

**Table C-9**    *Telephony Features and Applications*

| No | Question | Answer |
|----|----------|--------|
| 1 | What hardware and software platform provide AA functionality? | Vendor:<br>Model:<br>SW Revision: |
| 2 | What is the integration method of AA with PBX? | ☐ Analog<br>☐ Digital E/PRI<br>☐ Other: |
| 3 | Does the AA system support customizing the opening greetings based on the time of day and holiday schedules? | ☐ Yes<br>☐ No |
| 4 | What hardware and software platform provide overhead paging functionality? | Vendor:<br>Model:<br>SW Revision: |
| 5 | What is the integration method of the overhead paging system with PBX? | ☐ Analog<br>☐ Digital E/PRI<br>☐ Other: |
| 6 | What hardware and software platform provide ACD functionality? | Vendor:<br>Model:<br>SW Revision: |
| 7 | What is the integration method of the ACD system with PBX? | ☐ Analog<br>☐ Digital E/PRI<br>☐ Other: |
| 8 | Do you have multiple ACD systems? If yes, explain how these systems are interconnected. | ☐ Yes<br>☐ No |
| 9 | How many agents and supervisors are configured per ACD? | Agents:<br>Supervisors: |
| 10 | What hardware and software platforms provide CTI functions for the organization? | Vendor:<br>Model:<br>SW Revision: |
| 11 | What is the integration method of CTI applications with PBX? | ☐ Analog<br>☐ Digital E/PRI<br>☐ Other: |

*continues*

**Table C-9** *Telephony Features and Applications (Continued)*

| No | Question | Answer |
|----|----------|--------|
| 12 | Are any other telephony applications currently in use or being considered for future deployment? If so, describe them. | ☐ Yes<br>☐ No |
| 13 | Does documentation exist to describe how the organization uses these telephony applications? If yes, please provide the information along with information on call flow. | ☐ Yes<br>☐ No |
| 14 | What is the envisioned interaction between these applications and the IPT system in the near term? | Provide your answer in the "Notes/Comments" section. |
| 15 | What is the envisioned interaction between these applications and the IPT system in the long term? | Provide your answer in the "Notes/Comments" section. |
| 16 | What is the main number that customers call to reach your organization, and how is the call routed? | Provide the call-flow diagrams in the "Notes/Comments" section. |
| 17 | When callers reach the company general number or the call center group, do they hear music or announcements while they are waiting in the queue (Music on Hold [MoH] feature)? | ☐ Yes<br>☐ No |
| 18 | What hardware and software platform provide MoH functionality? | Vendor:<br>Model:<br>SW Revision:<br>Interface to PBX: |
| 19 | What do callers hear when they call during out-of-office hours or during holiday periods? | Provide details in the "Notes/Comments" section. |
| 20 | What other PBX features are implemented in the network? Use the "Notes/Comments" section to describe how each feature works in the current system. | ☐ MWI for voice mail<br>☐ Call pick-up<br>☐ Call park<br>☐ System speed dials<br>☐ Account codes<br>☐ User hunt groups<br>☐ Advanced call forwarding<br>☐ Feature access codes[1] |
| 21 | How do administrative assistants cover calls for managers? | |
| 22 | What headsets do phone users use? You need this information to check the compatibility of the currently used headsets with IP phones. | Vendor:<br>Model:<br>SW Revision: |

**Table C-9**    *Telephony Features and Applications (Continued)*

| No. | Question | Answer |
|-----|----------|--------|
| 23 | Does the PBX system support conferencing? | ☐ Yes<br>☐ No |
| 24 | What is the maximum number of participants in a single conference call and the maximum number of participants supported on the system? | Maximum per Call:<br>Total No.: |

1. Feature access codes (FACs) are typically two- or three-digit codes that activate or cancel certain features such as call park and call pick-up from the phones.

## Notes/Comments

The information that you collected using the Table C-9 is useful in identifying the type of features that need to be enabled on the new IPT system and whether additional applications are required. Include how the manager's lines appear on the assistant's phone, what buttons are used, and what the call flow is.

# Applications Security

Use the questions listed in Table C-10 to evaluate the current security policies and practices that are implemented in the network.

**Table C-10**    *Applications Security*

| No. | Question | Answer |
|-----|----------|--------|
| 1 | Does the organization want the IPT application servers to be part of the corporate directory domain? | ☐ Yes<br>☐ No |
| 2 | Do you have a global security policy for adding new servers to your network? Provide the details in the "Notes/Comments" section. | ☐ Yes<br>☐ No |
| 3 | Do you require encrypted communication between the Cisco IP Phones? | ☐ Yes<br>☐ No |
| 4 | Do you want Cisco IP Phones and other devices to authenticate to the call-processing servers before registration? | ☐ Yes<br>☐ No |
| 5 | Do all the applications have antivirus software installed? | ☐ Yes<br>☐ No |

## Notes/Comments

By using the information collected in Table C-10, you should be able to design an IPT system that meets the organization's security requirements.

# Operations and Maintenance

A stated plan for ongoing operations of an IPT network ensures maximum availability and quick problem resolution. This section is a preliminary check and covers the presence and foundation that built (or will build) the operations plan.

## Network Management System

This section reviews the existing network management systems (NMSs) and procedures used to manage the current network in the customer organization by asking the questions listed in Table C-11. This information will be useful when proposing the NMS to manage the IPT system.

**Table C-11**    *Network Management System*

| No. | Question | Answer | |
|-----|----------|--------|---|
| 1 | Does the organization use a network management product(s) to monitor the existing PBX, voice-mail systems, routers, and switches? If so, specify the product name and version number of each. | ☐ Yes<br>☐ No<br>Product:<br>Version:<br>Used For: | |
| 2 | Which hardware and software platforms do the network management products use? | Hardware | ☐ Dell<br>☐ HP/Compaq<br>☐ Sun<br>☐ Other |
| | | Software | ☐ Windows 2000<br>☐ Solaris<br>☐ Linux<br>☐ Other |
| 3 | What is the envisioned interaction between these NMS products and the IPT system in the near term? | Use the "Notes/Comments" section to specify whether you would like to use the same NMS products to manage the IPT network or have some other requirement. | |

**Table C-11**    *Network Management System (Continued)*

| No. | Question | Answer |
|-----|----------|--------|
| 4 | If you have multiple NMS products, do they integrate with any other system or product to provide a single view of the complete network? | ☐ Yes<br>☐ No<br>Product:<br>Version: |
| 5 | What kind of reports would you like the IPT system to generate? | Use the "Notes/Comments" section to provide details of the reports, sample formats, and how often the reports are to be generated. |
| 6 | Do you want the IPT system to generate billing records? | ☐ Yes<br>☐ No |
| 7 | Do you currently use billing software to generate the billing records? If yes, give the details about this product in the "Notes/Comments" section. | ☐ Yes<br>☐ No |
| 8 | Do you have an external partner who provides the billing reports? | ☐ Yes<br>☐ No |
| 9 | If the answer to question 8 is yes, how does this process work? | Use the "Notes/Comments" section to provide details such as how you provide your current Call Detail Records (CDRs) to the external billing vendors and attach the sample billing report format. |
| 10 | What is the organization's process for submitting and approving change management requests? | |
| 11 | What is the average turn-around time for submitted change management requests to be approved or denied? | |

## Notes/Comments

The following are examples of some management and operational reports:

- Device utilization
- Trunk utilization
- System availability reports
    — Call-processing server availability
    — Voice-mail system availability
    — Application server availability

— IP phone availability

— Branch availability

- Summary of critical outages
- Summary of critical events generated
- Summary of problems reported and resolution times

# Remote Network Monitoring/Management

Many customers are opting for Remote Network Monitoring/Management (RNM) service, which is provided by third-party vendors to remotely monitor various network devices 24 hours a day, 7 days a week. RNM service generates alerts to customer personnel when critical events occur and instructs them in which proactive corrective measures to take. RNM service allows customers to offload their internal staff from monitoring the network status, thus saving money. Use the questions listed in Table C-12 to understand your customer's current network management provider and plans with the deployment of IPT.

**Table C-12**   *Remote Network Monitoring/Management*

| No. | Question | Answer |
|-----|----------|--------|
| 1 | Does the organization have a monitoring system in place? | ☐  Yes<br>☐  No |
| 2 | Does the organization use an external vendor to provide remote network monitoring? | ☐  Yes<br>☐  No |
| 3 | If the answer to question 2 is yes, how is the vendor provided access to your network? | ☐  Dial-up<br>☐  Leased<br>☐  VPN<br>☐  Other: |
| 4 | Do you want to outsource the network management of the IPT system to an external vendor? | ☐  Yes<br>☐  No |
| 5 | What are the requirements and standards for a third party to be an RNM provider for your network? | Use the "Notes/Comments" section to provide the requirements and standards that vendors must meet to be your RNM provider. |
| 6 | Where do you want the network operations center (NOC) to be located—your premises or the vendor's premises? | ☐  Own<br>☐  Vendor |
| 7 | Is the fault management system capable of notifying operations personnel if soft failures occur? | ☐  Yes<br>☐  No |

## Notes/Comments

The information that you collect in this section helps you understand whether the customer already uses an RNM service provider to monitor the existing network. Also, if the customer's requirement is to outsource the monitoring of the IPT network to the RNM service provider, you need to understand how the current RNM service provider accesses the network, polls the device status information, etc. You also need to engage the RNM service provider from the beginning of the IPT project, so that it can plan for the monitoring equipment and staff to manage the new IPT network. Some of the tasks that an RNM vendor can provide to a customer are as follows:

- Manage IPT call-processing servers and other application servers.
- Provide proactive and reactive support of QoS on the IPT network (LAN and WAN).
- Perform logical (soft) moves, adds, and configuration changes.
- Provide a single point of contact in response to trouble calls and tickets.
- Generate web-based reports and ticket notification.
- Remotely perform software upgrades and patches.
- Follow up with product vendors for replacement of defective hardware components.
- Perform routine backup operations.
- Ticket, track, and escalate carrier outages to the service provider.
- Coordinate with telephone service providers.

## Maintenance/Support Contract

This section analyzes the current maintenance and support model in the organization. Use the questions listed in Table C-13 to gather this information for your customer.

**Table C-13**  *Maintenance/Support Contract*

| No. | Question | Answer |
|---|---|---|
| 1 | Does the organization have a support contract with an external vendor to provide day 2 support for the existing data and voice network, or is it self managed? | ☐  Vendor<br>☐  Self<br>Vendor Details: |
| 2 | Does the organization have plans to outsource the day 2 support of the IPT network to external vendors? | ☐  Yes<br>☐  No |
| 3 | What is the trouble ticket management system in use? | |
| 4 | Does the organization have a documented escalation procedure that begins at a certain time in the life of a trouble ticket? | ☐  Yes<br>☐  No |

*continues*

**Table C-13**  *Maintenance/Support Contract (Continued)*

| No. | Question | Answer |
|---|---|---|
| 5 | Does the organization have a process in place to manage changes to the network? | ☐  Yes<br>☐  No |
| 6 | What are your expectations regarding the following change management requests? | Phone/User Moves, Adds and Changes (MAC):<br><br>New Branch Provisioning:<br><br>Installing New Trunks:<br><br>Voice-Mail Change:<br><br>Other: |
| 7 | What are the organization's plans for training the administrators who support the proposed IPT network? | |
| 8 | What are the organization's expectations in providing training to end users? | |

## Notes/Comments

Use the information obtained through Table C-13 to clearly understand the customer organization's current support strategy and propose the support requirements for the new IPT solution.

# IPT Design Phase: IP Phone Selection Questionnaire

The purpose of this questionnaire is to help you collect the information that you need about a customer's end user phone requirements to provide to that customer a Cisco IPT solution. To obtain the answers to this questionnaire, you can either take this questionnaire and meet with the customer or e-mail the questionnaire to the customer and have them complete it. Customers usually provide some part of the information requested in this questionnaire in their Request for Proposal (RFP).

After you obtain from the customer all the information that is requested in this questionnaire, you should check the available Cisco IP Phone models (a current list of models and features is provided in Appendix A, "IP Phone Models and Selection Criteria,") and identify which models suit the end users' needs. Based on the number of users and user types at each location, you can calculate the number of phones required for the total IPT rollout.

## User Requirements for Phone Features

This section evaluates the end users' requirements for the Cisco IP Phones. Appendix A lists the currently available Cisco IP Phone models and describes the features that are available in each model. The cost of the Cisco IP Phones ranges from $100 to $1000 depending on the model. It is important to choose the right model because the purchase price has a direct impact on the total cost of the project.

Limiting the number of IP Phone models to one or two in the network reduces operational overhead. If you deploy varying phone models, operational staff has to be trained to support the varying phone models.

The questions in Table D-1 will help you to gather the end users' requirements and decide on the IP Phone model and features to enable for each user group. Use the employees' business functions to place them into user groups. For example, the following classification is commonly used:

- Employee phones (User Group 1)

- Manager phones (User Group 2)

- Assistant/operator phones (User Group 3)

- Lobby/break room phones (User Group 4)

- Conference room phones (User Group 5)

Some of the common requirements of the preceding groups are as follows:

- Employee, manager, and assistant phones require PC connectivity.

- Lobby phones and conference room phones do not require the Call Forward to Voice Mail, Call Forward Busy to Voice Mail feature enabled on the CallManager.

- Managers and assistants require more lines on the phones than do employees.

- Lobby phones and conference room phones generally do not require multiple lines on the phone.

**Table D-1**    *IP Phone Requirements*

| No. | Question | User Group 1 | User Group 2 | User Group 3 |
|-----|----------|--------------|--------------|--------------|
| 1 | Do you require support for Cisco Power over Ethernet (PoE) or IEEE 802.3af inline power? This decision has to be made globally and should not depend on the user groups. | ☐  Cisco PoE<br>☐  IEEE 802.3af PoE<br>☐  Both | | |
| **Basic Phone Features** | | | | |
| 2 | Place calls using handset | ☐  Yes<br>☐  No | ☐  Yes<br>☐  No | ☐  Yes<br>☐  No |
| 3 | Support for external headset | ☐  Yes<br>☐  No | ☐  Yes<br>☐  No | ☐  Yes<br>☐  No |
| 4 | Speaker phone support | ☐  Yes<br>☐  No | ☐  Yes<br>☐  No | ☐  Yes<br>☐  No |
| 5 | Set Call Forward All to another number from the IP Phone | ☐  Yes<br>☐  No | ☐  Yes<br>☐  No | ☐  Yes<br>☐  No |
| 6 | Redial the last number dialed | ☐  Yes<br>☐  No | ☐  Yes<br>☐  No | ☐  Yes<br>☐  No |
| 7 | View list of previously dialed numbers | ☐  Yes<br>☐  No | ☐  Yes<br>☐  No | ☐  Yes<br>☐  No |
| 8 | View list of missed calls | ☐  Yes<br>☐  No | ☐  Yes<br>☐  No | ☐  Yes<br>☐  No |
| 9 | View list of received calls | ☐  Yes<br>☐  No | ☐  Yes<br>☐  No | ☐  Yes<br>☐  No |

**Table D-1**    *IP Phone Requirements (Continued)*

| No. | Question | User Group 1 | User Group 2 | User Group 3 |
|-----|----------|--------------|--------------|--------------|
| 10 | MWI to indicate new voice-mail messages | ☐ Yes<br>☐ No | ☐ Yes<br>☐ No | ☐ Yes<br>☐ No |
| 11 | Number of lines required on the phone | | | |
| 12 | Number of calls required per line | | | |
| 13 | Supplementary features such as Hold, Conference, and Transfer | ☐ Yes<br>☐ No | ☐ Yes<br>☐ No | ☐ Yes<br>☐ No |
| 14 | Call Park | ☐ Yes<br>☐ No | ☐ Yes<br>☐ No | ☐ Yes<br>☐ No |
| 15 | Meet-Me | ☐ Yes<br>☐ No | ☐ Yes<br>☐ No | ☐ Yes<br>☐ No |
| 16 | Call Pickup and Group Pickup | ☐ Yes<br>☐ No | ☐ Yes<br>☐ No | ☐ Yes<br>☐ No |
| 17 | Call Waiting | ☐ Yes<br>☐ No | ☐ Yes<br>☐ No | ☐ Yes<br>☐ No |
| 18 | Call Forward Busy (CFB) to Voice Mail | ☐ Yes<br>☐ No | ☐ Yes<br>☐ No | ☐ Yes<br>☐ No |
| 19 | Call Forward No Answer (CFNA) to Voice Mail | ☐ Yes<br>☐ No | ☐ Yes<br>☐ No | ☐ Yes<br>☐ No |
| 20 | Auto Answer | ☐ Yes<br>☐ No | ☐ Yes<br>☐ No | ☐ Yes<br>☐ No |
| 21 | Display the calling party number and name | ☐ Yes<br>☐ No | ☐ Yes<br>☐ No | ☐ Yes<br>☐ No |
| 22 | Number of speed dials required on the IP Phone | | | |
| **Advanced Features** | | | | |
| 23 | PC connectivity required from the IP Phone | ☐ Yes<br>☐ No | ☐ Yes<br>☐ No | ☐ Yes<br>☐ No |
| 24 | Support of XML services on the IP Phone, such as Personal Address Book (PAB), Fast Dials, corporate directory lookup, etc. | ☐ Yes<br>☐ No | ☐ Yes<br>☐ No | ☐ Yes<br>☐ No |
| 25 | Support of Cisco IPMA feature on the IP Phone | ☐ Yes<br>☐ No | ☐ Yes<br>☐ No | ☐ Yes<br>☐ No |
| 26 | Call Back | ☐ Yes<br>☐ No | ☐ Yes<br>☐ No | ☐ Yes<br>☐ No |

*continues*

**Table D-1**     *IP Phone Requirements (Continued)*

| No. | Question | User Group 1 | User Group 2 | User Group 3 |
|-----|----------|--------------|--------------|--------------|
| 27 | Extension Mobility feature support | ☐ Yes<br>☐ No | ☐ Yes<br>☐ No | ☐ Yes<br>☐ No |
| 28 | Wireless support | ☐ Yes<br>☐ No | ☐ Yes<br>☐ No | ☐ Yes<br>☐ No |
| 29 | Customized ring tones on IP Phones | ☐ Yes<br>☐ No | ☐ Yes<br>☐ No | ☐ Yes<br>☐ No |
| 30 | Color display or black-and-white display on the IP Phone | ☐ Color<br>☐ B&W | ☐ Color<br>☐ B&W | ☐ Color<br>☐ B&W |
| 31 | Touch-screen display functionality on the IP Phone | ☐ Yes<br>☐ No | ☐ Yes<br>☐ No | ☐ Yes<br>☐ No |
| 32 | Is Gigabit Ethernet connectivity to the upstream LAN switch and to the PC a requirement? | ☐ Yes<br>☐ No | ☐ Yes<br>☐ No | ☐ Yes<br>☐ No |

# IPT Design Phase: IPT Requirement Analysis Questionnaire

The purpose of this questionnaire is to help you collect the customer's information that you need to design the customer's IP Telephony (IPT) network. You need to collect this information for each site. To obtain the answers to this questionnaire, you can either take it and meet with the customer or e-mail it to the customer and have the customer complete it. Customers usually provide some part of the information requested in this questionnaire in their Request for Proposal (RFP).

After you obtain from the customer all the information requested in this questionnaire, you can start the design process. Refer to Chapter 6, "Design of Call Processing Infrastructure and Applications," to review the example of how the information collected in this questionnaire for XYZ, Inc., was used in its IPT network design.

The following is an outline of the sections in the IPT Requirement Analysis Questionnaire:

- IP Telephony Deployment Model
- Codec Selection
- Legacy Voice-Mail Integration Requirements
- Legacy PBX Integration Requirements
- Sizing the CallManager Cluster
- Branch Office IPT Requirements
- Class of Restriction Requirements
- Call-Routing and Dial Plan Requirements
- Sizing the PSTN/Gateway Trunks
- Power Requirements (Per Site/Per Switch Specific)
- Call Admission Control Considerations
- Corporate Directory Requirements
- Conferencing, Transcoding, and MTP Requirements for Central Sites
- Music on Hold Requirements

Some sections might not be applicable to the network that you are designing, so skip any such sections.

# IP Telephony Deployment Model

The type of deployment model that you should choose depends on, among many other factors, your customer's needs, users, geographical distribution of users and devices, call-processing volume at each location, and disaster-recovery plans.

You have four choices of deployment models, which are numbered for easy reference in this questionnaire:

1  Single site with centralized call processing

2  Multisite WAN with centralized call processing

3  Multisite WAN with distributed call processing

4  Clustering over the WAN

Use Table E-1 to identify the chosen deployment model.

**Table E-1**  *IP Telephony Deployment Model*

| No. | Question | Answer |
|---|---|---|
| 1 | What IPT deployment model are you adopting? | ❑ 1<br>❑ 2<br>❑ 3<br>❑ 4<br>(Refer to the previous list for the model name) |
| 2 | If you have selected option 4, what is the round-trip time (RTT) between the sites hosting the servers belonging to the same cluster? | RTT _____ ms |

# Notes/Comments

The choice of IPT deployment depends on your network architecture and requirements. Refer to the section "IP Telephony Deployment Architectures" in Chapter 1, "Cisco IP Telephony Solution Overview," to choose the right deployment model.

# Codec Selection

The selection of codec affects the amount of bandwidth that needs to be provisioned on the WAN links. Table E-2 provides a list of questions that you need to collect from the customer regarding its codec choice.

**Table E-2**    *Codec Selection for LAN/WAN*

| No. | Question | Answer |
|---|---|---|
| 1 | What codec do you want to use? | ❑ LAN (G.711)<br>❑ LAN (G.729)<br>❑ LAN (G.723)<br>❑ LAN (WideBand)<br><br>❑ WAN (G.711)<br>❑ WAN (G.729)<br>❑ WAN (G.723)<br>❑ WAN (WideBand) |
| 2 | Do the VoIP calls require compressed RTP when being sent over the WAN? | ❑ Yes<br>❑ No |

## Notes/Comments

You need to collect this information for each site. In case of a centralized call-processing deployment with multiple remote branch sites, you need to identify the type of codec to be used between the central site and each remote site.

# Legacy Voice-Mail Integration Requirements

If the integration of CallManager with a legacy voice-mail system is a requirement, provide the information detailed in Table E-3.

**Table E-3**    *Legacy Voice-Mail Integration Requirements*

| Site Name | Voice-Mail System Type, Version, Ports Configured | Number of Users | Integration Method with CallManager | Is Integration with Existing PBX Required? | Type of Gateway Required from Cisco |
|---|---|---|---|---|---|
| | | | | | |
| | | | | | |
| | | | | | |

## Notes/Comments

Some of the major supported integration methods are the following:

- Skinny Client Control Protocol (SCCP) with Cisco Unity

- Simplified Message Desk Interface (SMDI)-capable voice-mail system with CallManager through a Media Gateway Control Protocol (MGCP) gateway or with a VG-248

- Cisco Digital PBX Adapter (DPA) integration for Octel or Nortel Meridian voice mail systems

- CTI/TSP integration for other systems

After you collect the information about the legacy voice-mail system, you can determine the type of integration required to integrate the voice-mail system with the IPT system.

# Legacy PBX Integration Requirements

If integration of CallManager with a legacy PBX system is a requirement, obtain the information detailed in Table E-4. Table E-4 shows some sample data that will help you to understand the type of information that needs to be gathered.

**Table E-4**  *Legacy PBX Integration Requirements*

| Site Name | PBX Type/ Software version | IPT Transformation— Integration/Full Migration? | IPT Users/ PBX Users | Integration Trunk Type/ Number of Trunks | Type of Gateway Required from Cisco/Software Version for Integration |
|---|---|---|---|---|---|
| Detroit | Definity | Integration | 200 (IPT)/100 (PBX) | T1-PRI/1 | WS-X-6608-T1/ PCG00000 |
| New York | Siemens | Full Migration | 300 (IPT)/0 (PBX) | Not Applicable | Not Applicable |

## Notes/Comments

You can use the information collected from Table C-1 in Appendix C, "IPT Planning Phase: Telecom Infrastructure Analysis Questionnaire," to fill out part of Table E-4. After you have the PBX details for each site, you can decide on the voice gateway model and the appropriate software version required on the voice gateway for successful integration. In case of integration with an IPT system, the existing trunks currently terminating on the PBX will be divided between the PBX and the voice gateway according to the user split ratio to preserve busy hour call attempts (BHCA).

For example, in Table E-4, for the Detroit site, the Definity PBX system needs to be integrated with the IPT system. Out of 300 users, 200 users will be migrated to the IPT system, and 100 users will be retained on the PBX system. Currently, the PBX has three T1-PRI trunks interfacing the PSTN. To preserve BHCA, during integration, two trunks will be moved to the voice gateway interfacing the PSTN.

You need to determine the approximate call volume between the users on the IPT system and the users remaining on the PBX system. This information is useful to size the trunks required between the PBX system and the voice gateway. The sample Detroit site information provided in Table E-4 uses one PRI trunk.

# Sizing the CallManager Cluster

CallManager servers can be grouped together to form a cluster. A cluster can contain a maximum of eight CallManager servers doing the call processing. There can be other servers in the cluster to perform dedicated functions, such as a Publisher server that hosts a read/write database, a dedicated TFTP/DHCP server, a dedicated Music on Hold (MoH) server, and so forth. The publisher database is used as a single point of administration for the cluster configuration changes and to produce Call Detail Records (CDRs). The TFTP server facilitates the download of configuration files, device loads (operating code), and ring types.

The information in Table E-5 needs to be collected on a per-site basis to determine the number of clusters, the number of CallManager servers per cluster, and the type of hardware platform required per cluster.

**Table E-5**    *CallManager Clustering Requirements*

| Site Name | IP Phones with Model Numbers | Voice-Mail Ports | TAPI/JTAPI Interfaces | Voice Gateways Include the Model and Number of DS0s | Conferencing, Transcoding, MTP, MoH Resources |
|---|---|---|---|---|---|
| | | | | | |
| | | | | | |
| | | | | | |
| | | | | | |

## Notes/Comments

A CallManager cluster consists of two or more CallManager servers. The number of devices that can be supported by a single CallManager server depends on the quantity of device types that need to be registered, such as IP Phones and gateways. To correctly size the CallManager cluster, you need to collect the information given in Table E-5 and follow the CallManager cluster-sizing guidelines given in Cisco IP Telephony Solution Reference Network Design (SRND) at http://www.cisco.com/go/srnd to decide on the hardware platform and number of servers in the cluster.

# Branch Office IPT Requirements

When connecting regional offices (branch office) to the main site, Survivable Remote Site Telephony (SRST) or Cisco CallManager Express (CCME) features are used. Use Table E-6 to collect the information needed to determine whether SRST and Cisco CCME should be implemented. Table E-6 is applicable for CallManager deployment models 2, 3, or 4 (refer to Table E-1 for model definitions).

**Table E-6**    *Requirements for SRST/CCME*

| 1 | 2 | 3 | 4 | 5 | 6 | 7 | 8 | 9 | 10 | 11 | 12 | 13 | 14 | 15 | 16 | 17 | 18 | 19 |
|---|---|---|---|---|---|---|---|---|----|----|----|----|----|----|----|----|----|----|
|   |   |   |   |   |   |   |   |   |    |    |    |    |    |    |    |    |    |    |
|   |   |   |   |   |   |   |   |   |    |    |    |    |    |    |    |    |    |    |    |
|   |   |   |   |   |   |   |   |   |    |    |    |    |    |    |    |    |    |    |    |

1   Branch Office Name, Address

2   Member of CallManager Cluster

3   Bandwidth from the Hub, Type of Link (FR/Leased/ATM), Current Link Utilization

4   Number of IP Phones Planned

5   Number of IP Phones with Single Line Appearance

6   Number of IP Phones with Multiple Line Appearances

7   Current Branch Router Model, Memory, IOS Version

8   Codec, G.711, G.729, G.723, and WideBand

9   Direct Inward Dial (DID) or Calling Line ID (CLID) Requirements

10   Supplementary Services Requirements

11   Gateway Protocol, MGCP, or H.323

12   Gateway Trunk Type, Number of Trunks

13   Does This Branch Require Conferencing, Transcoding, MoH Resources?
     If Yes, Specify the Location of the Resources (Local/Remote)

14   Number of Analog Ports Required

15   Class of Restriction Requirements

16   BHCA Across the WAN Links

17   Number of Voice Mail Boxes

18   Centralized/Local Voice Mail

19   Recommended Branch Hardware, Software Upgrades

## Notes/Comments

Information collected using Table E-6 is helpful in making the following determinations:

- If a given branch site is being transformed as a standalone site using the CCME feature, that site will not be a part of the Cisco CallManager cluster. Hence, in Table E-6, for such sites, the second column is not applicable.

- Collecting the information about current router hardware and software details is helpful in determining whether new hardware or software is required based on the number of phones connected in the branch site.

- The choice of codec and the location of conferencing endpoints affect the amount of bandwidth required on the WAN links and the DSP resources required on the router.

- BHCA affects the WAN bandwidth requirements.

- The analog ports are typically used in branch sites to connect fax machines. These analog ports can also be used as backup lines to route calls to the PSTN if a primary connection fails.

# Class of Restriction Requirements

Table E-7 gives typical class of restriction (CoR) definitions commonly deployed in telephony networks. You need to collect your choice of CoRs for the IP Phones.

**Table E-7**    *Class of Restriction Requirements*

| Service Level | Allows Calls To |
|---|---|
| 1 (Lobby phones) | All IP Phones; 911 and other services such as 411, 611, local calls (7- or 10-digit dialing based on the site); toll-free numbers; voice mail; block 900 numbers; access to all other customer locations; access to toll calls from other locations |
| 2 (Employee phones) | Level 1 access; plus long-distance calls |
| 3 (Executives phone) | Level 2 access; plus international calling |

## Notes/Comments

The CoR feature is enabled by configuring partitions and calling search spaces (CSSs) in CallManager. By configuring different levels of CSS for the IP Phones or for the directory numbers, you can provide different levels of access to the PSTN from IP Phones.

# Call-Routing and Dial Plan Requirements

Gathering call-routing and dial plan requirements is an important step in the IPT design phase. The requirements collected here dictate how to plan for route patterns, partitions, route groups, and route list designs in CallManager.

The first step is to gather the information on the existing numbering plan, as shown in Tables E-8 through E-10. If you have collected this information earlier, you can use that information; otherwise, gather this information before starting the dial plan design on the CallManager.

**Table E-8** *Existing Numbering Plan*

| Site Name | On-Net Site Access Code | No. of Digits in Station Numbering Plan | DID Ranges | Station Directory Numbering Ranges | Telephony Feature Pilot Numbers | Site-Level DID | No. of CoRs Required |
|---|---|---|---|---|---|---|---|
| | | | | | | | |
| | | | | | | | |
| | | | | | | | |

**Table E-9** *Dial Plan Requirements*

| No. | Question | Answer |
|---|---|---|
| 1 | Are there any conflicts with current legacy numbering ranges? If yes, identify them and work on the dial plan to resolve them. | ❏ Yes <br> ❏ No |
| 2 | Do you have any conflicts of dialing plans with other locations? <br><br> When you are migrating from a distributed PBX or key system (A key system is a multiline phone system with basic features such as conferencing, transfer, or intercom. You can think of the key system as a scaled down version of the PBX system.) deployment to a centralized IPT deployment, you need to identify how many digits are used in each site for local dialing. If there is a conflict in the numbering plans between the sites, you should consider increasing the number of digits required to avoid the overlapped numbering ranges. | ❏ Yes <br> ❏ No |
| 3 | Do you want to retain the existing dialing behavior? | ❏ Yes <br> ❏ No |

**Table E-9**    *Dial Plan Requirements (Continued)*

| No. | Question | Answer |
|---|---|---|
| 4 | Is digit translation needed? (Example: Prefix digits, discard digits, append digits, changing the calling party/called party number and so on.) | ❏ Yes<br>❏ No<br><br>Specify: |
| 5 | Do you have a toll-free number requirement? | ❏ Yes<br>❏ No<br><br>Specify: |

**Table E-10**    *Call-Routing Requirements for Site 1*

| No. | Type of Calls | Call-Routing Preferences, in Order of Priority |
|---|---|---|
| 1 | Local | 1. Local gateway<br>2. Central site gateway via IP WAN |
| | Emergency | Local gateways only |
| | Long distance | 1. Local gateway<br>2. Central site gateway via IP WAN |
| | International | 1. Central site gateway via IP WAN<br>2. Local gateway<br>3. Remote site 2 gateways |
| | Toll bypass | 1. Central site gateway via IP WAN<br>2. Site 2 gateways<br>3. Local gateway |
| | To international offices | 1. Central site gateway via IP WAN<br>2. Local gateway |

# Notes/Comments

List the DID requirements. DID is a PBX or Centrex feature that permits outside calls to be placed directly to a station line without use of an operator.

# Sizing the PSTN/Gateway Trunks

If you are sizing the number of PSTN/gateway trunks for a new deployment or are planning to estimate the number of PSTN/gateway trunks required, use the Erlang-B calculator, as discussed in Chapter 6. The information requested in Table E-11 is required to estimate the number of trunks. In an existing network, you can obtain this information from the statistics available in the PBX.

**Table E-11** *Sizing the PSTN Trunks*

| No. | Question | Answer |
|-----|----------|--------|
| 1 | What is the BHCA? | BHCA: |
| 2 | What is the AHT? | AHT: |
| 3 | What is the BHT? | BHT = (BHCA × AHT / 3600): |
| 4 | What is the GoS? | GoS: |

## Notes/Comments

The following list explains the terms used in Table E-11:

- **Busy hour call attempts (BHCA)**—Number of calls attempted during the busiest interval. This could be any interval, such as the "busy hour," a half-hour interval, or any other interval.

- **Average handle time (AHT)**—The average duration (talk time) of the call.

- **Busy hour traffic (BHT)**—Measure of the traffic load during your network's busiest hour, which represents the maximum traffic load that your network must support.

- **Grade of service (GoS)**—The percent of calls that will receive busy tone (no trunks available on gateway/PSTN) during the busy hour (also called percent blockage). A 1-percent blockage means 99 percent of all calls from the PSTN attempted during the interval will have a trunk port available on the gateway/PSTN to reach the user.

# Power Requirements (Per Site/Per Switch Specific)

This section describes the questions that the customer needs to answer related to its network's power infrastructure. This information is important to select the correct types of switches deployed in the IPT network and to design a highly available IPT network. Tables E-12 and E-13 help you to determine your strategy in providing power to IP Phones and whether the closet switches require additional power to provide the inline power to IP Phones.

**Table E-12**     *Power Requirements*

| No. | Question | Answer |
|---|---|---|
| 1 | How do you want to provide the power to the IP Phones? | ❑ Inline<br>❑ Local power<br>❑ External power panel |
| 2 | If you are using the inline power option, provide the information requested in Table E-13. | |

**Table E-13**     *Evaluating Inline Power Requirements*

| No. | Site Name, Bldg., Floor | Switch Model, Number of Power Supplies, Wattage, Power Type | Phones Types, Count | Backup Power Available? Yes/No |
|---|---|---|---|---|
| 1 | Site 1, Bldg. J, 3$^{rd}$ Floor | Cat 6506, 2 power supplies, 2200W, AC | 7960, 50<br>7940, 10<br>7935, 5 | |
| 2 | | | | |
| | | | | |
| | | | | |

# Call Admission Control Considerations

While designing the IPT network, you need to collect the traffic patterns to better engineer the traffic flows. The information listed in Table E-14 is needed for call admission control (CAC) and related design considerations for each site.

**Table E-14**     *CAC Design*

| No. | Question | Answer |
|---|---|---|
| 1 | Has a review been done to analyze the on-net call volume traffic among the sites that are going to be served by the same CallManager cluster? | ❑ Yes<br>❑ No |
| 2 | Does your IPT deployment follow a hub-and-spoke topology? (Applicable for models 2, 3, 4; refer to Table E-1.)<br>For the CAC mechanism to function properly, the WAN topology should follow the hub-and-spoke model. | ❑ Yes<br>❑ No |

*continues*

**Table E-14**   *CAC Design (Continued)*

| No. | Question | Answer |
|---|---|---|
| 3 | What type of CAC mechanism will be deployed? | ❑ CallManager locations CAC<br><br>❑ Gatekeeper CAC |
| 4 | If deploying gatekeeper CAC, how many CallManager clusters are interconnected via the gatekeeper? | Number of clusters<br><br>_____ |
| 5 | What is the estimated number of calls per second (CPS) that the gatekeeper needs to process?<br>This determines the gatekeeper hardware to be deployed. | CPS<br><br>_____ |
| 6 | What is the number of gatekeepers required in the network and gatekeeper network design? (Identify the requirements for the directory gatekeeper.) | Number of Gatekeepers<br><br>_____ |
| 7 | Which type of gatekeeper deployment will be used? | ❑ HSRP<br>❑ Cluster |

Table E-15 lists the on-net call requirements and call volumes from remote sites to central sites.

**Table E-15**    *CAC Bandwidth Values for WAN Links*

| No. | On-Net Call Path | On-Net Calls Allowed | |
|-----|------------------|----------------------|---|
| 1 | Central site – Site 1 | Voice | ❑ G.729<br>❑ G.711<br>❑ G.723<br>❑ Other _____<br><br>Number of calls ____ |
| | | Fax | ❑ G.711<br><br>❑ Other _____<br>Number of calls ____ |
| | | MoH | ❑ G.729<br>❑ G.711<br><br>❑ Other _____<br><br>Number of calls ____ |
| | | RTP compression? | ❑ Yes<br>❑ No |
| | | Does this site use location CAC or gatekeeper CAC? | ❑ Location CAC<br>❑ Gatekeeper CAC |
| | | Total bandwidth that needs to be reserved for this site | _____ kbps |

# Notes/Comments

When you are sizing the WAN bandwidth and the CAC, you need to determine the number of calls that traverse the WAN links. You need to take into consideration the fax and MoH streams in addition to voice calls. The choice of codec for each type of call also has an effect on the total bandwidth required on the WAN links.

# Corporate Directory Requirements

Two requirements exist when discussing the corporate directory and CallManager:

- Directory access
- Directory integration

Table E-16 helps you to gather these requirements and design your customer's IPT network. After collecting the basic information from Table E-16, if your client's network is going to include directory access, obtain the information requested in Table E-17. For corporate directory integration, obtain the information requested in Table E-18.

**Table E-16**    *Information About Existing Corporate Directory*

| No. | Question | Answer |
|-----|----------|--------|
| 1 | If your enterprise has a corporate directory deployed, what type of corporate directory is it? | ❏ AD<br>❏ Netscape<br>Specify the versions of the directory:<br><br><br>(Example: AD 2000, AD 2003, Netscape 4.x, and so on.) |
| 2 | Do you require corporate directory access from IP Phones or integration of CallManager with the corporate directory? | ❏ Access<br>❏ Integration |
| 3 | Do you have full redundancy for your directory? | ❏ Yes<br>❏ No |

# Directory Access Requirements

Meet with the corporate directory team to obtain the information requested in Table E-17. Directory access refers to when a user presses the Directory button on the IP Phone, the LDAP queries are sent to an external server hosting the Directory Lookup service and then forwarded to the corporate directory server.

**Table E-17**    *Directory Access Requirements*

| No. | Question | Answer |
|-----|----------|--------|
| 1 | Do you have a server on which to install the Cisco IP Phone Services SDK? | ❏ Yes<br>❏ No |
| 2 | What are the configuration details of the IP Phone service server on which the SDK is installed?<br><br>The Cisco IP Phone Services SDK runs only on a Microsoft Windows 2000 or 2003 platform and uses ASP (Active Server Pages) scripts. If you plan to use any OS other than these, you have to develop your own scripts. | OS version:<br>Service pack level:<br>DNS name:<br>IP Addr.: |
| 3 | What URL needs to be configured on the CallManager to provide the directory access to the IP Phones?<br><br>This depends on how you have configured the virtual directories on the IIS on the IP Phone service server. | URL<br>Example:<br>http://<IP address of IP Phone services server>/ldapsearch/ldapsearch.asp |
| 4 | What is the DNS name/IP address of the corporate directory server that IP Phones can access to get the directory list? | DNS name/IP address: |
| 5 | What is the username and password required to access the directory for lookup? | Username<br>Password<br><br>Example:<br>Cn=diruser,<br>ou=users,dc=Cisco,dc=com |
| 6 | What is the user search base? | User search base:<br><br>Example:<br>ou=users, dc=Cisco,dc=com |

## Notes/Comments

Directory access is simple compared to directory integration. Refer to Chapter 8, "Implementation," for instructions on implementing directory access on IP Phones using Microsoft Active Directory as the corporate directory.

## Directory Integration

Integrating the CallManager with an external corporate directory such as Microsoft AD or Netscape Directory Server stores all the CallManager-related information in the corporate directory rather than in the CallManager default DC directory. Collect the information requested in Table E-18 to understand the requirements of CallManager integration with an existing corporate directory.

**Table E-18**   *Directory Integration Requirements*

| No. | Question | Answer | |
|-----|----------|--------|--|
| 1 | Who are the contacts in your corporate directory team? | Name:<br>Role:<br>Phone:<br>E-mail:<br><br>Name:<br>Role:<br>Phone:<br>E-mail:<br><br>Name:<br>Role:<br>Phone:<br>E-mail: | |
| 2 | How many CallManager clusters exist in your network? | Number of CallManager Clusters: | |
| 3 | Do all the CallManager clusters run the same version of CallManager, or do they run different versions? If different, list them. | CallManager Versions: | |
| 4 | Are any other Cisco telephony applications deployed or planned to be deployed in the network? | CCC<br>CER<br>PA<br>CRS<br>Unity | Version:<br>Version:<br>Version:<br>Version:<br>Version: |

**Table E-18**    *Directory Integration Requirements (Continued)*

| No. | Question | Answer | |
|---|---|---|---|
| 5 | Do any other applications currently use your directory? | App. 1:<br>App. 2:<br>App. 3:<br>App. 4: | Details: |
| 6 | The following type of information needs to be obtained from the directory team for the existing directory architecture. The questions to ask depend on the directory being used. For example, if AD is deployed, you need to ask the following regarding the AD architecture:<br>What is the number of forests?<br>What is the number of domains?<br>Where are domains located?<br>Do you have multiple sites?<br>Do you have multiple name spaces?<br>What are the replication latency times?<br>Do you have users created under multiple OUs or under a single OU? | Attach the architecture diagrams, documents that describe the directory deployment. | |
| 7 | Does the corporate directory team understand how the CallManager directory integration works? Do they have all the information about schema changes and possible increases in the size of the directory database?<br><br>If the answer is no, do not proceed. Go back and clear up all the concerns that the directory team has regarding this whole process. | ❑ Yes<br>❑ No | |
| 8 | Who has the schema master right to modify the schema on the directory? | Name:<br>Role:<br>Phone:<br>E-mail: | |
| 9 | Do you want to use the account that has schema master permission for CallManager to use, or do you want to give a separate account with only required permissions? | | |
| 10 | If you are creating a separate CCMdiruser account, what are the account name, password, and permissions given to this user? | Username (FQDN):<br>Password:<br>Permissions: | |

*continues*

**Table E-18**    *Directory Integration Requirements (Continued)*

| No. | Question | Answer |
|-----|----------|--------|
| 11 | What is the IP address/DNS name of the schema master, and what is the LDAP port number? | IP Address:<br>LDAP port |
| 12 | Where do you want the Cisco directory tree to be created in your directory structure? (This is referred to as the Cisco Configuration DN in CallManager.) | Example:<br>OU=CISCOCCM_DIT,dc=Cisco,dc=com |
| 13 | CallManager requires that a few user accounts be created in the directory for its operations. What is the user creation base? | Example:<br>ou=users, dc=Cisco,dc=com |

## Notes/Comments

When you are proposing CallManager directory integration with a corporate directory, you must inform the corporate directory team about the schema changes that will be done on the corporate directory and address all of their questions and concerns before moving forward with directory integration.

# Conferencing, Transcoding, and MTP Requirements for Central Sites

Collect the information requested in Table E-19 to determine the conferencing, transcoding, and MTP requirements for the planned IPT network. These questions will help you to determine the hardware required at the central and remote sites for these media resources and to group these media resources in the CallManager by properly configuring the media resource groups (MRGs) and MRG lists (MRGLs) as per these requirements.

**Table E-19**    *Conference, Transcoding, and MTP Requirements*

| No. | Question | Answer |
|-----|----------|--------|
| 1 | What is the maximum number of participants per conference call? | Max. participants: |
| 2 | What is the maximum number of conference sessions required? If you have multiple sites, list them in the table form as shown as follows. | Max. sessions: |

**Table E-19**   *Conference, Transcoding, and MTP Requirements*

| No. | Question | Answer |
|---|---|---|
| 3 | Are you deploying multiple codecs in the IPT network? | ❑ Yes<br>❑ No<br>List of codecs: |
| 4 | Do you plan to deploy applications such as CRS and Unity in the network? | ❑ Yes<br>❑ No<br>List the applications and codec configured for these applications: |
| 5 | Do you plan to provide the conferencing and transcoding resources at each remote site, deploy all the resources at the central site, or use the distributed model? | ❑ Central<br>❑ Remote<br>❑ Distributed |
| 6 | Do you want to use the conferencing, transcoding, and MTP resources on the CallManager servers that are part of the cluster? | ❑ Yes<br>❑ No<br>Specify the CallManager server names where these features are enabled: |
| 7 | Do you plan to dedicate a server to provide the media resources in software? | ❑ Yes<br>❑ No<br>Specify the number of servers and physical locations of the servers: |
| 8 | Do you plan to deploy hardware media resources rather than use the resources on the CallManager servers or use a dedicated server, or do you want to deploy a combination of both? | ❑ Hardware<br>❑ Software<br>❑ Both<br>Fill in table E-20 with details. |
| 9 | Do you have any non–Cisco H.323 endpoints that do not support Empty capabilities set? | Yes<br>No<br>Specify the endpoints and their locations: |

## Notes/Comments

List the site-wide requirements for conferencing, transcoding, and MTP. To assist you, Table E-20 shows examples of the XYZ, Inc. network requirements.

**Table E-20** *XYZ Conferencing, Transcoding, and MoH Requirements*

| Site Name | Codec Used | Media Resources Required Hardware or Software | Preference for Accessing These Resources | Hardware at the Site |
|---|---|---|---|---|
| San Jose | G.711 | Conferencing, transcoding, and MTP required<br><br>Use hardware<br><br>Disable the resources on CallManager | All San Jose users use the central site resources | Ad Hoc Conferencing and Transcoding (ACT) port adapter on CMM on 6500 switches |
| Seattle | G.711 Local;<br><br>G.729 on WAN | Conferencing, transcoding, and MTP required<br><br>Use hardware | Seattle users use local resources first and then the resources at San Jose | DSPs on the NM-HDV modules on the Seattle router |
| Dallas | G.711 Local;<br><br>G.729 on WAN | Conferencing, transcoding, and MTP required<br><br>Use hardware | Dallas users use San Jose resources | No DSP resources are available for media services on the local router |

# Music on Hold Requirements

Collect the information requested in Table E-21 to determine the MoH requirements for the planned IPT network.

**Table E-21** *MoH Requirements*

| No. | Question | Answer |
|---|---|---|
| 1 | What is the total number of IP Phones deployed in the cluster? | Number of IP Phones: |
| 2 | Is a dedicated MoH server or a collocated MoH server required?<br><br>This depends on the size of the network. | ❏ Collocated<br>❏ Dedicated |
| 3 | Do you plan to use a fixed audio source?<br><br>Using a fixed audio source allows the stream to be played from CD. | ❏ Yes<br>❏ No<br>Name of the server on which the sound card will be installed: |
| 4 | How many streams do you plan to use?<br><br>This is the number of different audio files. | Number of streams: |

**Table E-21**   *MoH Requirements (Continued)*

| No. | Question | Answer |
| --- | --- | --- |
| 5 | How important is redundancy for the MoH server? If the MoH server fails, users hear tones instead of music. | ❑ Redundancy<br>❑ No redundancy |
| 6 | Do you have a multisite deployment model? If yes, do you want MoH to be streamed from the central site? | ❑ Yes<br>❑ No<br><br>❑ Yes<br>❑ No |
| 7 | Do you have multiple codecs configured in your network (for example, G711 for LAN or G729 for WAN)? | ❑ Yes<br>❑ No<br>List the codecs used: |
| 8 | Is multicast enabled and supported on your network? If not, do you plan to support multicast on your network in the future? | ❑ Yes<br>❑ No |
| 9 | Is there any requirement to play certain music for a particular group and different music for others?<br><br>For example, marketing might require a particular stream to be played to callers during the hold, engineering might require a different stream, and so on. If you have such requirements, you can configure different audio sources for these groups. | ❑ Yes<br>❑ No<br>Specify the number of different groups that require different streams: |
| 10 | Do you want MoH to be streamed to all the sites? If not, list which sites need MoH, which sites use a local MoH feature on the routers, and which sites use the Tone on Hold feature. | Provide the attachment. |
| 11 | Do you want to enable the multicast MoH on the MoH server? If yes, list the range of multicast group addresses that can be used by the MoH server to assign it to the audio streams.<br><br>Ensure that these addresses are unique and not already in use in the network. | ❑ Yes<br>❑ No<br>Range of multicast addresses: |

## Notes/Comments

MoH, as the name implies, provides music to callers when they are put on hold. There are various ways you can provide MoH to users. The information gathered by using Table E-21 will assist you in determining the organizational needs in providing MoH and assist you in designing the MoH services in the IPT network.

# APPENDIX F

# Ordering T1/E1 PRI from the Carrier Questionnaire

The purpose of this questionnaire is to help you to order new T1/E1 lines or inform the carrier to make changes to the existing T1/E1 circuits to support deployment of the new IP Telephony (IPT) system. You can collect the information in this questionnaire from the customer and use it to place an order with the customer's carrier for new T1/E1 circuits or to make changes to the existing circuits. If you have T1/E1 circuits with multiple carriers, you have to place the order with each carrier.

Table F-1 provides the list of questions that carriers typically ask when someone is placing an order for T1/E1 PRI circuits. Some carriers might require additional information. Check with your customer's carrier and provide additional information if required.

**Table F-1** *Information Required by Carriers to Provision a New T1/E1 Circuit*

| No. | Question | Answer |
|-----|----------|--------|
| 1 | What are the vendor name and the server version of the PBX system? | Organization: <br> Location: <br> Vendor: <br> Model: <br> SW revision: <br><br> Example: <br> Organization: XYZ, Inc. <br> Location: San Jose <br> Vendor: Cisco Systems <br> Model: CallManager <br> SW revision: 4.0 |

*continues*

**Table F-1**    *Information Required by Carriers to Provision a New T1/E1 Circuit (Continued)*

| No. | Question | Answer |
|-----|----------|--------|
| 2 | Which jack type are you going to use for PRI? | ☐ RJ-48<br>☐ SmartJack<br><br>Note:<br>Describe how you wire the cable from the termination jack to voice gateways and write the distance.<br><br>Example:<br>Terminate the circuit to SmartJack.<br>XYZ runs RJ45 from SmartJack to the Cisco WS-X6608/CMM module in the Cisco Catalyst 6506 switch. |
| 3 | What is the ISDN configuration requested?<br><br>If NFAS, do you need 23B+D or 23B+D+D? | ☐ FAS<br>☐ NFAS<br><br>☐ 23B+D<br>☐ 23B+D+D |
| 4 | Which signaling type is required? | ☐ ISDN PRI<br>☐ MFCR2<br>☐ CAS—E&M immediate start<br><br>CAS—E&M wink start<br>☐ Ground start<br>☐ Loop start |
| 5 | What is the ISDN type—national or custom? | ☐ National<br>☐ Custom<br>☐ Unknown<br>☐ ISDN |
| 6 | What is the B-channel glare? | ☐ CPE yields<br>☐ CPE controls |
| 7 | What is the CPE type? | ☐ PBX<br>☐ MUX |

**Table F-1**    *Information Required by Carriers to Provision a New T1/E1 Circuit (Continued)*

| No. | Question | Answer |
|---|---|---|
| 8 | How many DID digits do you need from the service provider? | Number of Digits:<br>Note: Specify how many digits you want to receive from the carrier. The number needed depends on how you set up the gateways in the CallManager. You can receive full digits from the carrier, and you can discard the common digits and use the rest of the digits to do call routing within your network. |
| 9 | What is the channel protocol for E&M CAS trunks? | ☐  Wink<br>☐  Delay<br>☐  Immediate |
| 10 | What is the pulse type? | ☐  DTMF<br>☐  MF<br>☐  DP |
| 11 | What is the framing and encoding format? | Framing<br>☐  ESF<br>☐  SF (D4)<br>☐  MF<br><br>Line code<br>☐  B8ZS<br>☐  AMI<br>☐  HDB3 |
| 12 | What is the circuit direction? | ☐  Inbound only<br>☐  Outbound only<br>☐  Two way |
| 13 | What is the hunt type? | ☐  High to low<br>☐  Low to high<br>☐  Most idle |
| 14 | What is the CoS? Do you want to be able to make international calls or just local and domestic long-distance calls? | ☐  Local only<br>☐  Domestic only<br>☐  International only Local and domestic<br>☐  All |

*continues*

**Table F-1** *Information Required by Carriers to Provision a New T1/E1 Circuit (Continued)*

| No. | Question | Answer |
|-----|----------|--------|
| 15 | Do you want inbound caller ID? If so, do you want to see the number only or the name and number? | ☐ Number only<br>☐ Name only<br>☐ Name and number<br>☐ None |
| 16 | Do you want the name to be transmitted for the outgoing calls? If so, give the name (maximum of 15 characters). | ☐ Yes<br>☐ No<br><br>Name to be transmitted:<br><br>Example: XYZ, Inc.<br><br>Notes: You can control what number to transmit when making outgoing calls in the CallManager. Take into account that this information will be overwritten by the provider if it is not agreed upon beforehand. |
| 17 | Do you want these phone numbers to be listed in directory listings? If so, in which type(s) of pages?<br>You need to supply the name and phone number that you want listed. | ☐ Yes<br>☐ No<br>☐ Blue pages<br>☐ Yellow pages<br>☐ Standard pages<br><br>Number to be listed:<br>Name to be listed: |
| 18 | (For U.S and Canada only) Do you want this T1/E1 PRI to support E-911 ? If yes, what is the callback number and name to be delivered to PSAP? | ☐ Yes<br>☐ No<br>Callback number:_____<br><br>Name :_____ |

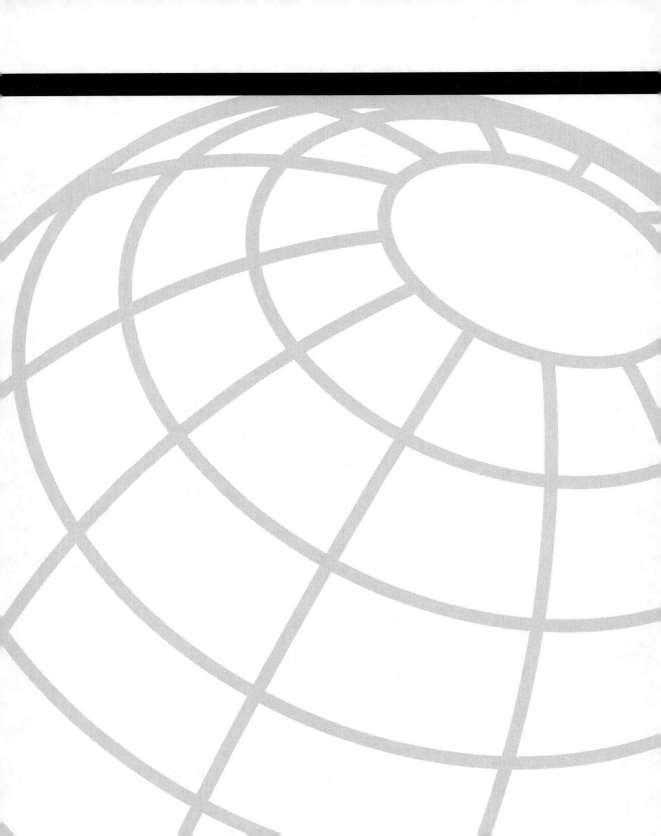

# Voice-Mail Design Questionnaire

The purpose of this questionnaire is to help you to collect from the customer the information that you need to design and customize the Cisco Unity voice-mail system in the customer's network. To obtain the answers to this questionnaire, you can either take this questionnaire and meet with the customer or e-mail the questionnaire to the customer and have the customer complete it. Customers usually provide some part of the information requested in this questionnaire in their Request for Proposal (RFP).

After you obtain from the customer all the information requested in this questionnaire, you can start the design process. Refer to Chapter 7, "Voice-Mail System Design," to review the example of how the information collected in this questionnaire for XYZ, Inc. was used in its network design.

This questionnaire is divided into the following sections:

- Voice-Mail Requirements
- Messaging and Directory Architecture
- Infrastructure Requirements for Unity Deployment
- Sizing the Unity Server
- Unity Integration with PBX/CallManager
- Unity Networking with Other Voice-Mail Systems

Some sections might not be applicable to the network that you are designing, so skip any such sections.

## Voice-Mail Requirements

Use the questions in Table G-1 to obtain the requirements to design the Unity voice-mail system.

**Table G-1**    *Voice-Mail Requirements*

| No. | Question | Answer |
|---|---|---|
| 1 | Customer Name | Name: |
| 2 | Who are the contacts in your enterprise messaging team? | Name:<br>Role:<br>Phone:<br>E-mail:<br><br>Name:<br>Role:<br>Phone:<br>E-mail: |
| 3 | Who are the contacts in your enterprise directory team? | Name:<br>Role:<br>Phone:<br>E-mail:<br><br>Name:<br>Role:<br>Phone:<br>E-mail: |
| 4 | Who are the contacts in your enterprise security team? | Name:<br>Role:<br>Phone:<br>E-mail:<br><br>Name:<br>Role:<br>Phone:<br>E-mail: |
| 5 | Do you intend to deploy Cisco Unity in a Unified Messaging (UM) configuration or voice mail–only configuration? | ☐ UM<br>☐ Voice mail |
| 6 | If this is a UM deployment, is it a new installation, a migration, or a partial integration? | ☐ **New installation:** Considered a fresh install into an environment where no messaging previously existed.<br>☐ **Migration:** Considered a full deployment of Unity to replace an existing legacy voice-messaging infrastructure.<br>☐ **Partial integration:** Installation of Unity into an existing environment where other messaging systems will continue to operate. |

**Table G-1** *Voice-Mail Requirements (Continued)*

| No. | Question | Answer |
|---|---|---|
| 7 | If this is a voice mail–only deployment, is it a new installation, a migration, or a partial integration? | ☐ **New installation:** Considered a fresh install into an environment where no messaging previously existed.<br>☐ **Migration:** Considered a full deployment of Unity to replace an existing legacy voice-messaging infrastructure.<br>☐ **Partial integration:** Installation of Unity into an existing environment where other messaging systems will continue to operate. |
| 8 | Do you require Unity to integrate with your fax server? If yes, list the type of integreation, the fax server software vendor, and the version number. | ☐ Yes<br>☐ No<br>Vendor:<br>Version: |
| 9 | Which special features do you want to use in Unity? | ☐ Auto Attendant<br>☐ Text to Speech (TTS)_____ sessions<br>☐ Cisco Personal Communications Assistant (Cisco PCA)<br>☐ License Pooling<br>☐ RSA (Rivest, Shamir, and Adelman)<br>☐ Dual Switch Integration<br>☐ IP PBX Media Gateway (PIMG)<br>☐ Voice Profile for Internet Mail (VPIM)<br>☐ Unity Bridge<br>☐ Others (Specify) |
| 10 | Do you need Unity support of any language other than U.S. English? If yes, specify the language(s) for each category. | ☐ Yes<br>☐ No<br><br>TTS languages:<br>Telephony User Interface (TUI) languages:<br><br>Graphical User Interface (GUI) languages: |

## Notes/Comments

The information collected using Table G-1 helps you to understand the scope of the voice-mail deployment.

# Messaging and Directory Architecture

Table G-2 includes the questions to ask the customer related to the existing messaging and directory architecture. It is critical to understand the existing architecture so that you can decide which Unity deployment model to use and where to locate the Unity servers.

**Table G-2**    *Messaging and Directory Architecture*

| No. | Question | Answer |
|---|---|---|
| 1 | What is your messaging platform? | ☐  Exchange<br>☐  Domino |
| 2 | If Active Directory (AD) is deployed, what is the AD version? | ☐  AD 2000<br>☐  AD 2003<br>☐  N/A |
| 3 | If Microsoft Exchange is deployed, what is the version? Give details about installed service packs and hot fixes. If you currently have an older version of Exchange deployed in your network, please provide the time frame to migrate to newer versions of Exchange. | ☐  5.5<br>☐  2000<br>☐  2003<br>☐  Mixed Mode<br><br>Service Pack Level<br><br>Hot Fixes<br><br>Time Frame for Migration |
| 4 | If Microsoft Exchange is deployed in a mixed mode, which different Exchange versions are deployed in the messaging network? | ☐  5.5<br>☐  2000<br>☐  2003 |
| 5 | Specify the operating system on which you are running the Exchange servers. | ☐  Windows 2000<br>☐  Windows 2003 |
| 6 | Do you run the Standard or Enterprise version of Exchange? | ☐  Standard<br>☐  Enterprise |
| 7 | If you have an existing Exchange/Domino network, do you plan to use the existing servers to store voice mails for Cisco Unity subscribers, or do you plan to have a separate Exchange/Domino server? | ☐  New<br>☐  Existing |

**Table G-2**    *Messaging and Directory Architecture (Continued)*

| No. | Question | Answer |
|-----|----------|--------|
| 8 | If your message store is Domino, what is the Domino version? If you currently have an older version of Domino installed in your network, please provide the time frame for migrating to a newer version of Domino. | Version number:<br><br>Time frame to migrate: |
| 9 | Is your messaging store centralized or distributed? | ☐ Centralized<br>☐ Distributed |
| 10 | Provide diagrams that show your existing messaging architecture.<br>The architecture details should have the following information:<br>AD architecture<br>Forests<br>Root domains, child domains<br>Location and details, such as IP addresses and names of domain controllers and global catalog servers<br>Exchange site topology<br>Exchange routing groups<br>Bridgehead servers<br>Locations where Exchange servers are located<br><br>For Domino:<br>Domino domains<br>Domino clusters<br>Locations where Domino servers are located | Attach the diagrams that represent the active directory domain topology, exchange/domino topology, and necessary documents describing the overall architecture. |
| 11 | If you have an existing AD, do you want to deploy Cisco Unity in a separate domain or have it join the existing domain?<br>Sometimes there will be different management groups within the organization that manage the corporate domain and other special domains. Sometimes, for security reasons, no permissions will be given to access the corporate domain. | ☐ New domain<br>☐ Join existing domain |
| 12 | If you are creating a new domain for Unity servers, are there plans in the future to make this new domain a part of corporate domain? | ☐ Yes<br>☐ No |

*continues*

**Table G-2** *Messaging and Directory Architecture (Continued)*

| No. | Question | Answer |
|-----|----------|--------|
| 13 | How many users currently use the Exchange or Domino messaging system? | Number of users |
| 14 | What is average number of users per Exchange or Domino server? | Average number of users |
| 15 | What is the average size of the user's mailbox in megabytes? | Average size of user's mailbox _____megabytes |
| 16 | What is the expected growth in the next 6–12 months? | Growth in terms of number of users |
| 17 | Provide the total number of Unity subscribers. | Number of Unity subscribers |
| 18 | Which e-mail clients are used to retrieve e-mail? | ☐ Outlook<br>☐ Eudora<br>☐ Others (specify)<br>Version |
| 19 | Which operating systems do these e-mail clients currently run? | ☐ Windows 95<br>☐ Windows 98<br>☐ Windows 2000<br>☐ Windows XP<br>☐ Macintosh<br>☐ UNIX<br>☐ Linux<br>☐ Others (specify) |
| 20 | Which client protocol is used to retrieve e-mail? | ☐ POP3<br>☐ IMAP<br>☐ Others (specify) |
| 21 | Which backup software do you currently use to back up your messaging data? | ☐ ARCserve<br>☐ Legato<br>☐ VERITAS<br>☐ Others (specify) |

**Table G-2**    *Messaging and Directory Architecture (Continued)*

| No. | Question | Answer |
|-----|----------|--------|
| 22 | What is your current message store licensing policy? | ☐   Client access licenses<br><br>☐   Server-based licenses<br><br>☐   Others (specify) |
| 23 | Which current software packages and utilities monitor the current messaging infrastructure? | List of monitoring tools and utilities: |
| 24 | What antivirus software does the organization use to protect the messaging servers from viruses? | ☐   McAfee<br>☐   Symantec<br>☐   Trend Micro<br>Other vendor (specify)<br><br>Version no. |
| 25 | Provide the DNS server information. | Primary DNS server details<br>Secondary DNS server details<br><br>Name:<br><br>IP address:<br><br>Name:<br><br>IP address: |
| 26 | Provide details on enterprise security policies relative to user account management, service account management, and general access policies. | Attach the details: |

*continues*

**Table G-2**    *Messaging and Directory Architecture (Continued)*

| No. | Question | Answer |
| --- | --- | --- |
| 27 | If your message store is Domino, provide the details about Domino deployment . | Domino version<br><br>Admin server name |
| | Is Domino clustering used? | ☐  Yes<br>☐  No |
| | Specify the number of nodes per cluster | |
| | Specify the number of databases per cluster | |
| | Is Notes installed on the Domino server? | ☐  Yes<br>☐  No |
| | Is names.nsf used as the primary directory? | ☐  Yes<br>☐  No |
| | Specify the operating system on which Domino servers are installed. | ☐  Windows 2000<br>☐  Windows 2003 |
| | What is the Lotus Notes version? | |
| | What is the Lotus Domino version? | |
| | What is the Domino server operating system version? | |

## Comments/Notes

The information collected from Table G-2 is critical to ensure successful integration of the Unity system with the current corporate directory and messaging systems.

# Infrastructure Requirements for Unity Deployment

Unity uses AD when deployed in the Exchange messaging environment. The corporate directory administrator must understand the implications of this before proceeding with actual deployment. Table G-3 includes the questions to ask the corporate directory administrator to ensure that the customer understands the infrastructure requirements to deploy Unity.

**Table G-3**    *Infrastructure Requirements*

| No. | Question | Answer |
|---|---|---|
| 1 | Deploying Unity in the existing AD requires schema extensions. Is your corporate directory team aware of this change and approve it?<br><br>To see the list of schema extensions that Unity makes to the AD schema, refer to the following URL:<br><br>http://www.cisco.com/en/US/partner/products/sw/voicesw/ps2237/products_white_paper09186a00800875c5.shtml | ☐  Yes<br>☐  No |
| 2 | Extending the AD schema increases the size of the AD database. Did you plan for the extra size of the database?<br><br>Refer to the following URL for information on AD capacity planning:<br><br>http://www.cisco.com/en/US/partner/products/sw/voicesw/ps2237/products_white_paper09186a00800e4535.shtml | ☐  Yes<br>☐  No |
| 3 | Who has the schema master right to modify the schema on the directory? | Name:<br>Role:<br>Phone:<br>E-mail: |
| 4 | Did you integrate the CallManager directory with this AD? | ☐  Yes<br>☐  No |
| 5 | Will the Unity system be collocated with the Exchange servers? | ☐  Yes<br>☐  No |
| 6 | How many users require remote access or other special access to Unity via a VPN, a dial-up connection, or another method?<br><br>For instance, traveling users with laptops generally sync up with their messaging system via remote dialup, which makes streaming an issue because of bandwidth constraints. Indicate the number of mobile users who will use Unity. | VPN<br><br>Dial-up<br><br>Others |
| 7 | If you plan to deploy Unity at a central location, do you have remote sites that access Unity at the central site? If yes, what are the typical bandwidths? | ☐  Yes<br>☐  No<br><br>Bandwidth |
| 8 | Specify on what operating system you want to install Unity. | ☐  Microsoft Windows 2000<br>☐  Microsoft Windows 2003 |

## Comments/Notes

When you deploy Unity into an existing messaging network, you need to work with the corporate directory and messaging teams and brief them about Unity's dependency on the existing directory and messaging infrastructure.

# Sizing the Unity Server

The Unity server has many features that are licensed. Hence, sizing the Unity server is required so that you can buy the right number of licenses and decide on the right server platform to support the number of users required and the storage requirements. Table G-4 includes the questions to ask the customer to help you size the Unity server.

**Table G-4**   *Sizing the Unity Server*

| No. | Question | Answer |
|-----|----------|--------|
| 1 | Has a study been done on traffic patterns for accessing voice mail within the existing system? <br> If not, you should perform the study because this information is helpful in determining the number of ports/sessions required on the Unity system. You need the following information: | ☐   Yes <br> ☐   No |
| | Average calls per hour to the voice-mail system <br> The duration of the call | _____ calls <br> _____ seconds |
| 2 | What is the existing policy or the policy to be enforced on the voice-mail system? | Archive voice mail: <br> (days) |
| | This information, along with the codec selection, is required to size the hard disk space required for Unity. | Record opening greeting: <br> (seconds) |
| | | Record the message: <br> (seconds) |
| | | Keep deleted voice mail? <br> ☐   Yes <br> ☐   No |
| | | How long do you want to keep the deleted mail? <br> (days) |

**Table G-4**    *Sizing the Unity Server*

| No. | Question | Answer |
|---|---|---|
| 3 | Do you currently have Outcall notification configured on the voice-mail system?<br><br>Outcall Notification notifies the user at their cell and home phone numbers about new voice-mail messages they have received. | ☐ Yes<br>☐ No |
| 4 | What is your choice of codec?<br><br>To get more information on codecs and the bandwidth used per codec, refer to the following URL:<br><br>http://www.cisco.com/en/US/partner/products/sw/voicesw/ps2237/products_white_paper09186a00800875b7.shtml | ☐ G.711<br>☐ G.729a<br>☐ ADPCM 8kbps<br>☐ ADPCM 6kbps<br>☐ GSM 6.0<br>☐ G.726 |
| 5 | Do you want redundancy (failover) for Unity servers? | ☐ Yes<br>☐ No |

## Comments/Notes

The user might be notified about new voice-mail messages by receiving a pager message or a call on a configured external phone number. Enabling these features on the Unity system not only uses the Unity ports but also requires you to provide additional infrastructure, such as telephone lines. The requirement for the number of Unity port licenses increases depending on the number of users who need these features.

The selection of codec has a direct impact on the hard disk size and network bandwidth requirements. The information collected in Table G-4 helps you to size the Unity server by determining the hardware and number of ports required. Chapter 7 covers the sizing of hard disks based on the codec selection.

# Unity Integration with PBX/CallManager

Unity support for dual integration means that it can integrate simultaneously with the existing PBX and with CallManager. Understanding the integration requirements helps you in the design. Table G-5 includes the questions to ask the customer to determine the integration requirements for Unity.

**Table G-5**    *Unity Integration Requirements*

| No. | Question | Answer |
|---|---|---|
| 1 | What are the details of the existing PBX systems? | Vendor:<br>Model:<br>Software version:<br><br>Vendor:<br>Model:<br>Software version:<br><br>Vendor:<br>Model:<br>Software version: |
| 2 | How will Unity be integrated with PBX?<br>Unity integrates with CallManager using SCCP. | ☐ DTMF<br>☐ Serial (SMDI)<br>☐ SCCP |
| 3 | Do you want to do a dual integration of Cisco Unity? In other words, will Unity integrate with CallManager and PBX system? | ☐ Yes<br>☐ No |
| 4 | If you want to integrate Unity with PBX, you need to have slots available on the PBX to plug in the interface card required (for example, an analog interface card for DTMF integration and an SMDI interface card for serial integration). Do you have available slots on the PBX system? Do you have the hardware available? | ☐ Yes<br>☐ No |
| 5 | What voice-mail integration protocols does your PBX system support? | ☐ SMDI<br>☐ SIP<br>☐ DTMF |
| 6 | Does your PBX system require you to purchase additional software licenses to enable the voice-mail integration protocols? | ☐ Yes<br>☐ No |
| 7 | What is the physical distance between the PBX system and the Unity server? | Distance |
| 8 | How many CallManager clusters do you have in the network, and what are the version numbers? | Number of clusters:<br><br>CallManager version numbers: |
| 9 | Do you want Unity to integrate with multiple CallManager clusters? | ☐ Yes<br>☐ No |

**Table G-5**    *Unity Integration Requirements (Continued)*

| No. | Question | Answer |
|-----|----------|--------|
| 10 | What are the MWI On/Off numbers? If you have multiple CallManager clusters, you need to have unique numbers for each cluster. | Cluster 1: MWI On: MWI Off: <br><br> Cluster 2: MWI On: MWI Off: |
| 11 | What is the voice-mail pilot number that users dial to check their voice-mail? | Pilot number |

## Comments/Notes

The answers to the questions collected via Table G-5 give you the information required to integrate the Unity system with a legacy PBX system or with CallManager systems.

# Unity Networking with Other Voice-Mail Systems

Unity can network with other voice-mail systems if they coexist in the network. Understanding the existing voice-mail systems and the support of networking protocols helps you to design the system such that it meets the customer requirements. Use Table G-6 to collect information about the existing voice-mail system and networking requirements.

**Table G-6**    *Unity Networking Requirements*

| No. | Question | Answer |
|-----|----------|--------|
| 1 | What are your existing voice-mail systems? | Vendor: Model: Software version: Site: License expiration date: <br><br> Number of ports/sessions: <br><br> Number of subscribers: <br><br> Vendor: Model: Software version: Site: License expiration date: |

*continues*

**Table G-6**    *Unity Networking Requirements (Continued)*

| No. | Question | Answer |
|-----|----------|--------|
| 2 | Are these voice-mail systems currently networked? If yes, what is the protocol used for networking? | ☐  VPIM<br>Version:<br>☐  AMIS<br>Version:<br>☐   Analog OctelNet<br>Version:<br>☐   Avaya Interchange<br>Version:<br>☐   Other:<br>Version: |
| 3 | If you have an Avaya/Octel voice-mail system, do you want to network between the Unity system and the Avaya/Octel system? | ☐   Yes<br>☐   No |
| 4 | If you have multiple sites, where will Unity be deployed? In which locations will the Octel system continue to exist?<br><br>This information helps you to identify the Unity Bridge server location. Unity Bridge is required to enable the networking between the Unity system and an Avaya/Octel system. Having Unity Bridge nearer to Octel reduces the communication costs incurred in transferring the voice-mail messages between the two systems. | Provide the attachment. |
| 5 | Provide the networking configuration information for the existing voice-mail systems. | VPIM node IDs:<br>AMIS node IDs:<br>OctelNet node IDs:<br>Avaya Interchange node IDs: |
| 6 | Provide the number of subscribers in each voice-mail node. | VPIM subscribers<br>AMIS subscribers<br>OctelNet subscribers<br>Avaya Interchange subscribers<br><br>Internet subscribers |

## Comments/Notes

When you are deploying a new voice-mail system into an existing network, the customer often wants to network the legacy and new voice-mail systems so users from either system can address messages to users on the other system. You can use Table G-7 to capture the Unity networking requirements.

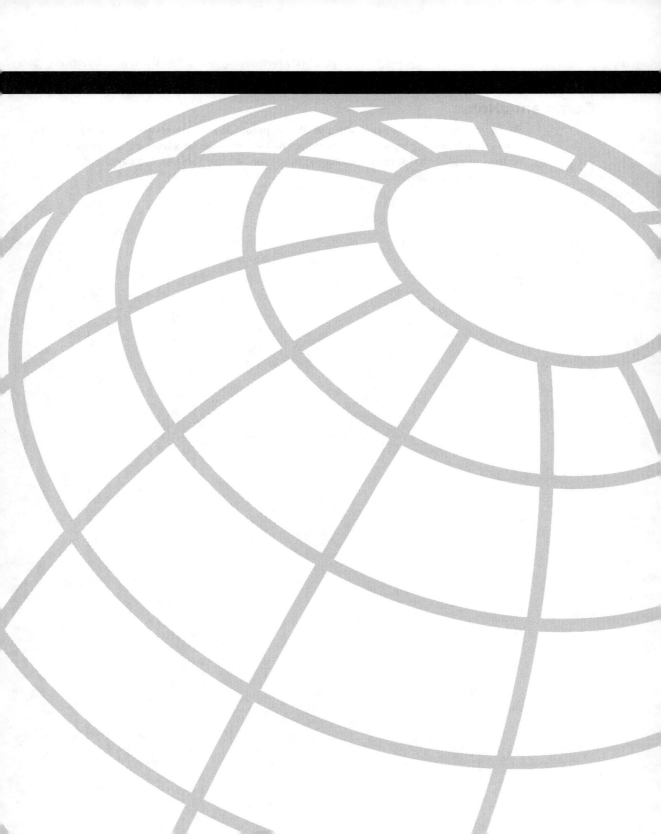

# IPT Implementation Checklist

This appendix contains several checklists to help you and the IP Telephony (IPT) deployment team collect and check all the preliminary customer information before deploying IP Phones, switches, gateways, and other IPT components. To obtain the answers to this questionnaire, you can take this questionnaire to the site where you are deploying IPT, or you can ask the customer to complete it. Completing this checklist ensures that all the prerequisite steps are completed before you start the deployment of IPT components.

## Preimplementation Tasks

This section contains checks to ensure that the following high-level preimplementation tasks are completed before you start deploying the IPT solution:

- Project plan
- Site information
- Implementation team

## Project Plan

The project manager who is assigned to the deployment project develops the project plan for implementing the IPT solution. You should contact the project manager to obtain the project plan and ensure that, at minimum, the high-level tasks listed in Table H-1 are included in the project plan.

**Table H-1**  *Project Plan Tasks Verification*

| No. | Task Category | Included in the Project Plan? |
|-----|---------------|-------------------------------|
| 1 | Preimplementation preparations: procure all required equipment, establish the right contacts, and so on. | ☐ Yes <br> ☐ No |
| 2 | Site survey tasks: check the readiness of the site | ☐ Yes <br> ☐ No |

*continues*

**Table H-1**    *Project Plan Tasks Verification (Continued)*

| No. | Task Category | Included in the Project Plan? |
|-----|---------------|-------------------------------|
| 3 | IPT implementation procedure: actual implementation of IPT components | ☐  Yes<br>☐  No |
| 4 | IPT add-on feature implementation: complete the implementation of additional applications such as AutoAttendant, Unity, and features in CallManager such as extension mobility and IP Manager Assistant (IPMA) | ☐  Yes<br>☐  No |
| 5 | Acceptance tests: test-case scenarios that need to be successfully executed on the deployed solution | ☐  Yes<br>☐  No |
| 6 | Post-implementation documentation: document the network topology and configurations | ☐  Yes<br>☐  No |
| 7 | Customer acceptance: sign-off process in which the customer acknowledges project completion | ☐  Yes<br>☐  No |

# Site Information

Collecting the site information ahead of time helps you to obtain the necessary permissions for the implementation staff to enter the buildings within the sites beforehand (see Table H-2). In addition, if the deployment involves multiple sites, the project manager can plan for the additional remote resources required to perform the implementation at these sites.

**Table H-2**    *Site Information*

| No. | Question | Answer |
|-----|----------|--------|
| 1 | What is the company name? | Company name: |
| 2 | What is the site address? | Street:<br>City:<br>State:<br>Country:<br>Zip code:<br>Phone:<br>Fax: |
| 3 | Is building access approval required? | ☐  Yes<br>☐  No |
| 4 | Does everyone in the deployment team have access to the building and the server rooms? | ☐  Yes<br>☐  No |
| 5 | What are the normal hours of operation in the building? | Working hours: |

**Table H-2**    *Site Information (Continued)*

| No. | Question | Answer |
|-----|----------|--------|
| 6 | Are any special access permissions required to work after hours? | ☐  Yes<br>☐  No |
| 7 | Who is the site coordinator contact? | Name:<br>Work phone:<br>Cell phone:<br>E-mail:<br>Pager: |
| 8 | Which room is designated for the equipment staging? | Room location: |
| 9 | Does the project team have an office space in which to work, equipped with office supplies, printers, and network connectivity at all the site locations? | ☐  Yes<br>☐  No |

# Implementation Team

An implementation team is the key to the successful deployment of the IPT network. Table H-3 lists the team members required for the implementation.

**Table H-3**    *Implementation Team*

| No. | Team Member | Answer |
|-----|-------------|--------|
| 1 | Project manager | Name:<br>Work phone:<br>Cell phone:<br>E-mail:<br>Pager: |
| 2 | Project engineer(s) | Name:<br>Work phone:<br>Cell phone:<br>E-mail:<br>Pager:<br><br>Name:<br>Work phone:<br>Cell phone:<br>E-mail:<br>Pager: |

*continues*

**Table H-3**　　*Implementation Team (Continued)*

| No. | Team Member | Answer |
|-----|-------------|--------|
| 3 | IPT design engineer(s) | Name:<br>Work phone:<br>Cell phone:<br>E-mail:<br>Pager:<br><br>Name:<br>Work phone:<br>Cell phone:<br>E-mail:<br>Pager: |
| 4 | IPT implementation engineer | Name:<br>Work phone:<br>Cell phone:<br>E-mail:<br>Pager: |

# Implementation Readiness Analysis

The implementation readiness analysis includes four categories:

- Site readiness
- Voice network readiness
- Data network readiness
- IPT readiness

The following sections cover the checks required for each category before proceeding with the IPT deployment.

## Site Readiness Analysis

The site readiness analysis includes the checks to ensure that all the information is available to begin deploying the IPT endpoints (see Table H-4). The site readiness analysis includes tasks to do the following:

- Identify equipment placement and termination points
- Ensure that rack space is available to mount the equipment

- Ensure that necessary cables and connectors are available

- Check the power availability and stable environmental conditions

**Table H-4**    *Site Readiness Analysis Checklist*

| No. | Question | Answer |
|---|---|---|
| **I. Equipment Placement and Termination** | | |
| 1 | Do you have all the network topology diagrams available? | ☐  Yes<br>☐  No<br>Attach list. |
| 2 | Do you have a list of termination points for the IP Phones available?<br>Get a list of the buildings and floors where IP Phones need to be deployed. | ☐  Yes<br>☐  No<br>Attach list. |
| 3 | Do you have a list of termination points for the voice gateways? | ☐  Yes<br>☐  No<br>Attach list. |
| 4 | What is the contact information for the local telephone company for each site? | Name of carrier:<br>Contact phone:<br>Phone number:<br>E-mail:<br>Contract number to be supplied when reporting problems: |
| 5 | Do you have a list of IP addressing/VLAN assignment information? | ☐  Yes<br>☐  No<br>Attach list. |
| **II. Rack Space Requirements**<br>You should make sure that all IPT components have required rack space available for the installation. The rack space requirement varies depending on the type of server, switch, or router. You should obtain the number of rack units required to mount each hardware device. Refer to the vendors' product documentation to obtain this information. | | |
| 1 | Do you have enough rack space to rack mount the CallManager servers? | ☐  Yes<br>☐  No<br>Number of servers:<br><br>Rack space units required per server: |

*continues*

**Table H-4**    *Site Readiness Analysis Checklist (Continued)*

| No. | Question | Answer |
|---|---|---|
| 2 | Do you have enough rack space to rack mount the Unity servers? | ☐ Yes<br>☐ No<br>Number of servers:<br><br>Rack space units required per server: |
| 3 | Do you have enough rack space to rack mount the Unity Bridge servers? | ☐ Yes<br>☐ No<br>Number of servers:<br><br>Rack space units required per server: |
| 4 | Do you have enough rack space to rack mount the voice gateways? | ☐ Yes<br>☐ No<br>Number of gateways:<br><br>Rack space units required per gateway: |
| 5 | Do you have enough rack space to rack mount the gatekeeper? | ☐ Yes<br>☐ No<br>Number of gatekeepers:<br><br>Rack space units required per gatekeeper: |
| 6 | Do you have enough rack space to rack mount the application servers? | ☐ Yes<br>☐ No<br>Number of application servers:<br><br>Rack space units required per application server: |

**Table H-4**    *Site Readiness Analysis Checklist (Continued)*

| No. | Question | Answer |
|-----|----------|--------|
| **III. Cabling and Termination Points** | | |
| Different types of cables are required for implementing the IPT network in different parts of the network. | | |
| 1 | What type of cabling is used within the LAN? | ☐  Cat 3<br>☐  Cat 5 |
| 2 | What are the T1/E1 line terminations for connecting the voice circuits? | Site:<br>Building:<br>Floor: |
| 3 | What are the locations of analog line terminations? | Site:<br>Building:<br>Floor: |
| 4 | Is distance between the telco termination and the voice gateway in acceptable range? | ☐  Yes<br>☐  No<br>Distance in feet: |
| **IV. Power and HVAC Requirements** | | |
| 1 | Are the power requirements met, as evaluated in the planning phase?<br><br>Power calculator:<br>http://www.cisco.com/go/powercalculator | ☐  Yes<br>☐  No |
| 2 | Can HVAC systems take the additional load of the equipment? | ☐  Yes<br>☐  No |
| 3 | Does the site have proper grounding for the equipment? | ☐  Yes<br>☐  No |

# Voice Network Readiness

The voice network readiness analysis includes checks to ensure that the customer has taken all the necessary steps required to integrate, if required, the newly deployed IPT system with legacy PBX, voice-mail, and Automated Call Distribution (ACD) systems. See Table H-5.

**Table H-5**     *Voice Network Readiness Analysis Checklist*

| No. | Question | Answer |
|---|---|---|
| **I. Voice Circuit Analysis** | | |
| 1 | Is the interfacing equipment required for integration of PBX, voice-mail, and ACD systems with CallManager available? | ☐   Yes <br> ☐   No |
| 2 | Do the software versions that run on the PBX, voice mail, and other equipment requiring integration support CallManager? | ☐   Yes <br> ☐   No |
| 3 | If moving the PSTN circuits from the PBX to the IPT system, does a different telco interface need to be requested? | ☐   Yes <br> ☐   No |
| 4 | Who are the contacts for the PBX, voice-mail, and ACD systems? You might have to obtain a list of additional contacts, depending on need. This staff should have access rights to make configurations changes. | PBX system contact name: <br> Work phone: <br> E-mail: <br> Cell phone: <br><br> Voice mail system contact name: <br> Work phone: <br> E-mail: <br> Cell phone: <br><br> ACD system contact name: <br><br> Work phone: <br> E-mail: <br> Cell phone: |
| 5 | Did you place the order with the telco to terminate the new voice circuits? | ☐   Yes <br> ☐   No |
| 6 | If you plan to migrate users from the PBX system to the IPT system, have you grouped the identified users? | ☐   Yes <br> ☐   No |

# Data Network Readiness

The data network readiness analysis includes checks to ensure that the customer data network is ready to carry the voice traffic (see Table H-6). In this analysis, you check whether the customer has followed your recommendations to fill the gaps in the infrastructure that were identified during the planning phase.

**Table H-6**   *Data Network Readiness Analysis Checklist*

| No. | Question | Answer | |
|-----|----------|--------|--|
| **I. LAN Analysis** | | | |
| 1 | Are the switch ports on the LAN switches enabled? | ☐ Yes | ☐ No |
| | Are required QoS configurations—such as auxiliary VLAN, port trusts, speed/duplex, inline power, and recommended software versions—completed to connect the IP Phones, servers, and voice gateways? | ☐ Yes | ☐ No |
| 2 | Is the DHCP server configured with all the scopes, correct default gateways, DHCP option 150 or 66, and DNS values? | ☐ Yes | ☐ No |
| 3 | Is the IP helper address configuration that was completed on the routed interface pointing to the right DHCP server for each IP Phone VLAN segment? | ☐ Yes | ☐ No |
| 4 | Did you provide the list of server names and IP addresses to the administrators of the DNS servers? This is required so that DNS servers can resolve the names of the voice servers properly. It is always better to do this in advance because the DNS replication process takes a few hours to replicate the information to all the servers in the network. | ☐ Yes | ☐ No |
| **II. WAN Analysis** | | | |
| 1 | Are the WAN routers running the right Cisco IOS software to support the required QoS feature set? | ☐ Yes | ☐ No |
| 2 | Is the configuration on the WAN routers in accordance with QoS recommendations to transport the voice traffic in the priority queue? | ☐ Yes | ☐ No |
| 3 | If a gatekeeper is required for CAC, is it rack mounted, loaded with the right Cisco IOS software, and configured? | ☐ Yes | ☐ No |
| 4 | Do the WAN routers have sufficient DRAM? | ☐ Yes | ☐ No |
| 5 | Are the route-trip delay times between the central and branch sites within the acceptable range to achieve good quality on voice calls? | ☐ Yes | ☐ No |

# IPT Readiness Analysis

The IPT readiness analysis is intended to ensure that the detailed design tasks such as call-processing design, dial plan design, and decisions on the software versions to be deployed in the network are completed and all the necessary software and licenses are available. See Table H-7.

**Table H-7**    *IPT Readiness Analysis Checklist*

| No. | Question | Answer |
|---|---|---|
| **I. IPT Readiness Analysis** | | |
| 1 | Have you completed a detailed design for call-processing servers, dial plan, gateway selection, and sizing ? | ☐ Yes<br>☐ No |
| 2 | If you are deploying Cisco Unity, do you have a detailed design to deploy? | ☐ Yes<br>☐ No |
| 3 | Have you completed the design of the CRS/IPCC Express servers and other application servers? | ☐ Yes<br>☐ No |
| 4 | Have you completed the design of IPT features, such as AutoAttendant, IVR, Web Dialer, SoftPhone, Cisco IP Communicator, IPMA, and Extension Mobility? | ☐ Yes<br>☐ No |
| 5 | Do you have all the servers rack mounted and ready to start the installation of the software? | ☐ Yes<br>☐ No |
| 6 | Do you have all the available software disks and licenses? | ☐ Yes<br>☐ No |
| 7 | Do you have information on all the latest operating system service releases that need to be applied to servers? | ☐ Yes<br>☐ No |

# Configuration Checklist for Installation of CallManager and Other Application Servers

Use Table H-8 to list the name and role of each server and where to connect the servers in the network.

**Table H-8**    *Summary of Servers in the Network*

| Server Name | Role | Location of Servers Site/Building/Floor | Connected to Switch Name/ Slot/Port/VLAN ID |
|---|---|---|---|
| CCMSJPUB | CallManager publisher | | |
| CCMSJSUB1 | CallManager subscriber 1 | | |
| CCMSJSUB2 | CallManager subscriber 2 | | |
| CRASJ1 | CRA primary server | | |
| CRASJ2 | CRA backup server | | |

**Table H-8**  *Summary of Servers in the Network (Continued)*

| Server Name | Role | Location of Servers Site/Building/Floor | Connected to Switch Name/ Slot/Port/VLAN ID |
|---|---|---|---|
| UNITYSJ1 | Unity primary server | | |
| UNITYSJ2 | Unity backup server | | |
| IPSVCSSJ1 | IPT services server | | |
| TFTPDHCPSJ | TFTP and DHCP server | | |

# Server OS Installation Configuration Parameters

Table H-9 lists the basic information you need to have while installing the basic operating system on any Cisco Architecture for Voice, Video and Integrated Data (AVVID) application servers.

**Table H-9**  *Server OS Installation Configuration Parameters*

| No. | Configuration | Input |
|---|---|---|
| 1 | Cisco product key | |
| 2 | Username (this is just for registration) | |
| 3 | Name of the organization | |
| 4 | Computer name<br><br>Changing the server name is not possible after CallManager installation. Choose a descriptive name that makes it easier to identify the server by role; for example, CCMSJPUB, CCMSJSUB1. | |
| 5 | DNS domain suffix | |
| 6 | Workgroup | |
| 7 | Current time zone, date, and time | Time zone:<br>Date:<br>Time: |
| 8 | TCP/IP properties (do not use DHCP for server IP addressing) | IP address<br>Subnet mask<br>Default gateway |
| 9 | DNS servers (optional) | DNS server 1<br>DNS server 2 |

*continues*

**Table H-9**   *Server OS Installation Configuration Parameters (Continued)*

| No. | Configuration | Input |
|---|---|---|
| 10 | WINS servers (optional) | WINS server 1 |
|  |  | WINS server 2 |
| 11 | LMHOST information |  |
| 12 | Administrator password |  |
| 13 | NIC configuration<br><br>Speed/duplex settings<br>Check the settings that are configured on the switch port and match them accordingly. | ☐   Auto/Auto<br>☐   10 Mbps/FULL<br>☐   100 Mbps/FULL |

## CallManager Server Installation Parameters

Table H-10 lists the information required to install the CallManager servers after you have completed the basic OS installation configurations specified in Table H-9.

**Table H-10**   *CallManager Installation Parameters*

| No. | Configuration | Input |
|---|---|---|
| 1 | Server type | ☐   Publisher<br>☐   Subscriber |
| 2 | Backup server type | ☐   Backup server<br>☐   Backup target |
| 3 | Password phrase<br>The password phrase is used to generate the passwords for the other service accounts. |  |
| 4 | DC directory administrator password |  |
| 5 | Administrator password |  |

# Acceptance Tests

Table H-11 organizes the acceptance tests into the following categories:

- CallManager check
- General IP Phone and feature tests
- Centralized call processing with remote branches
- Distributed call processing with multiple CallManager clusters
- Advanced IPT tests

You might have to add more test cases depending on the complexity and types of integrations involved in your network. In addition, you should perform the tests outlined in Table H-11 after every upgrade on the CallManager and any other application servers to ensure that the system is functioning properly and that nothing ceased to function because of the upgrade.

**Table H-11**    *IPT Implementation Acceptance Tests*

| Test Category: CallManager Check | | |
|---|---|---|
| **No.** | **Test Case** | **How to Perform** |
| 1 | CallManager service status | Use the Real-Time Monitoring Tool (RTMT) to check whether all the services are up and running. |
| 2 | CallManager configuration | Check that the dial plan is configured according to the design. |
| 3 | CallManager device default configuration | Check whether the IP Phones and gateways are loaded with the right loads. |
| 4 | CallManager gateway | Place outgoing and incoming calls and verify that call routing is successful. |
| 5 | CallManager voice-mail integration | Access the voice-mail system and verify that it recognizes the IP Phone extensions. Leave a voice mail and check whether the MWI light comes up. Listen to the new voice mails and ensure that the MWI is off. |
| 6 | Class of Restriction (CoR) | Configure the IP Phones with different Calling Search Spaces based on their CoR category. For example, the CoR category is the lobby phone, employee phone, executive phone, and so forth. Make test calls from each IP Phone and verify that users can make permitted calls and that all other calls are denied. |
| Test Category: General IP Phone and Feature Tests | | |
| 1 | Basic IP Phone | Make a phone call from IP Phone A to IP Phone B and ensure that two-way audio is established. |
| 2 | Call on-hold and retrieval | Press the Hold softkey on IP Phone A during the call and verify that the IP Phone user at IP Phone B is on hold. If Music on Hold (MoH) is configured, verify that the party on hold (IP Phone B user) hears the music. If MoH is not configured, verify that the user on hold hears beeps. |
| 3 | Call park | Make a phone call from IP Phone A to IP Phone B. Park the call at a different number and try to retrieve the call by dialing the call park number. |
| 4 | Group pickup | Make a phone call from IP Phone A to IP Phone B and pick up the call from IP Phone C by dialing the group pickup number. |

*continues*

**Table H-11**  *IPT Implementation Acceptance Tests (Continued)*

| No. | Test Case | How to Perform |
|-----|-----------|----------------|
| 5 | Call transfer to an off-net IP Phone | Make a phone call from IP Phone A to IP Phone B and answer the call. Press the Transfer softkey on IP Phone B, dial an external PSTN phone number, and verify that the call is established between IP Phone A and the PSTN phone. |
| 6 | Call transfer to an on-net IP Phone | Make a phone call from IP Phone A to IP Phone B and answer the call. Press the Transfer softkey on IP Phone B and dial IP Phone C. Verify that the call is established between IP Phone A and IP Phone C. |
| 7 | Call forward to an off-net IP Phone | From IP Phone A, press the CFwdALL softkey and enter a PSTN number. Make a phone call from IP Phone B to IP Phone A and verify that the call is forwarded to the PSTN number. |
| 8 | Call forward to an on-net IP Phone | From IP Phone A, press the CFwdALL softkey and enter the phone number of IP Phone C. Make a phone call from IP Phone B to IP Phone A and verify that the call is forwarded to IP Phone C. |
| 9 | Ad Hoc conference | Make a phone call from IP Phone A to IP Phone B and answer the call. Press the Confrn softkey on IP Phone A and dial the extension of IP Phone C. Answer the call at IP Phone C. Press the Confrn softkey on IP Phone A to set up the Ad Hoc conference between all three IP Phones. Verify that all three phone users can hear each other. |
| **Test Category: Centralized Call Processing** | | |
| 1 | Phone-to-phone dial-up to a remote site | Make a phone call from IP Phone A at the central site to IP Phone X at the branch site and verify that two-way audio is established. Also during the call, press the i button twice on the Cisco IP Phone and check that the phones are using the configured codec. |
| 2 | Call transfer to an IP Phone in a remote site | Make a phone call from IP Phone A to IP Phone B and answer the call. Press the Transfer softkey on IP Phone A and dial the extension of IP Phone X at the remote site. Verify that the call is established between IP Phone A and IP Phone X. |
| 3 | Call forward to an IP Phone in a remote site | From IP Phone A, press the CFwdALL softkey and enter the phone number of IP Phone X at the remote site. Make a phone call from IP Phone B to IP Phone A and verify that the call is forwarded to IP Phone X. |

**Table H-11**    *IPT Implementation Acceptance Tests (Continued)*

| No. | Test Case | How to Perform |
|---|---|---|
| 4 | Ad Hoc conference over WAN link | Make a phone call from IP Phone A to IP Phone B and answer the call. Press the Confrn softkey on IP Phone A and dial the extension of IP Phone X at the remote branch. Answer the call at IP Phone X. Press the Confrn softkey on IP Phone A to set up Ad Hoc Conferencing between all three IP Phones and verify that all three phone users can hear each other. Also during the call, press the i button twice on the IP Phone and check that the phones are using the configured codec. You can use Performance Monitor to monitor performance objects for conferencing and transcoding resources (Refer to the "Document Registered Device Counts" section of Chapter 9, "Operations and Optimization," for more information on doing this.) |
| **Test Category: Distributed Call Processing** | | |
| 1 | Phone-to-phone dial-up test in different cluster | Make a phone call from IP Phone A in cluster 1 to IP Phone B in cluster 2 and verify that two-way audio is established. |
| 2 | Call transfer to an IP Phone in another cluster | Make a phone call from IP Phone A in cluster 1 to IP Phone B in cluster 2 and answer the call. Press the Transfer softkey on IP Phone A and dial the extension of IP Phone C in cluster 2. Verify that the call is established between IP Phone A and IP Phone C. |
| 3 | Call forward to an IP Phone in another cluster | From IP Phone A in cluster 1, press the CFwdALL softkey and enter the phone number of IP Phone B in cluster 2. Make a phone call from IP Phone C in cluster 1 to IP Phone A and verify that the call is forwarded to IP Phone B in cluster 2 and that the call is successful. |
| **Test Category: Advanced IPT Tests** | | |
| 1 | Fax to fax | Send a fax message from one fax station to another fax station and verify that the fax transmission is successful. |
| 2 | CallManager failover | Stop the CallManager service on the primary subscriber. Verify that phones fail over to the backup subscriber and that all functionality is retained. Unplug the network cable for the primary subscriber. Verify that phones fail over to the backup subscriber and that all functionality is retained. |

*continues*

**Table H-11**  *IPT Implementation Acceptance Tests (Continued)*

| No. | Test Case | How to Perform |
|-----|-----------|----------------|
| **Test Category: Dial Plan Testing** | | |
| 1 | Local call routing | Make local calls and check that the called party receives the right caller ID and calling name. |
| 2 | Long-distance call routing | Make long-distance calls and make sure that they go via the right gateway. |
| 3 | On-net call routing | Make on-net calls to other locations. |
| 4 | Off-net call routing | Make off-net calls. |
| 5 | E911 or emergency call routing | Call the emergency number and inform the person that this is a test call. Verify that the public safety access point (PSAP) gets the right phone number and address. |

# INDEX

## A

AA (Active Assistant), 287
AA (Auto Attendant), 396
    configuration of, 303
    implementation, 399–406
AAR (Automated Alternate Routing), 259
    CallManager locations, 201
    CSS, 261
    group configuration, 261
acceptance tests, 431, 622–626
access
    CALs, 293
    CMM modules, 388
    directories, 417–418
    levels (MLA), 431
    Octel access numbers, 302
    OWA, 289
    PSTN, 180
    Unity servers, 285, 289
access control lists (ACLs)
    CallManager, 273
    QoS, 155
access layer
    campus networks, 99–100, 102
    Catalyst 6500 switches, 152
Account page (Unity), 328, 341
Account Policy page (Unity), 339
accounts, Unity installation, 296
ACLs (access control lists)
    CallManager, 273
    QoS, 155
ACT (Ad Hoc Conferencing and Transcoding), 182
Active Assistant. *See* AA
Active Directory. *See* AD
AD (Active Directory), 279–283
Ad Hoc conferencing, 182
Ad Hoc Conferencing and Transcoding (ACT), 182
Add New Gateway option, 221
adding
    CSQ, 414
    partitions, 232
    subunits (to CMM modules), 390
addressing options, 357
Admin Utility, 469–470

administration
    BAT, 382
    calls (Unity), 347–356
    MLA, 429–431
    networks (Unity), 356–361
    SA, 320
    systems (Unity), 361–366
    training, 434
    Unity Bridge, 312
agents
    CSA
        installation, 277
        Unity servers, 285
    MTA, 308
    sizing, 193
AHT (average handle time), 193
ALG (Application Layer Gateway), 274
alternate extensions (Unity), 345
Alternate Greeting page (Unity), 335
AMIS-a (Audio Messaging Interchange Specification-analog), 308
analog endpoints, 222
analog signaling, 12
analog terminals, 179
analysis
    DNA, 382, 397–398
    readiness (implementation), 378–380
Application Layer Gateway (ALG), 274
application servers
    implementation, 380–382
    CallManager installation checklist, 620
applications, 179–188, 269–271
    in converged networks, 38–42
    installation, 381
    Microsoft Outlook e-mail, 288
    security, 272–277
    third-party installation, 382
    Unity Bridge, 311
    upgrading, 444–445
application-specific integrated circuit (ASIC), 154
applying policies to interfaces, 155
architecture
    AD, 282
    CallManager, 224
    call-processing, 141, 143
    deployment (with Unity Bridge), 310

MRGs
   assignment, 220–221
   configuration, 216–218
   design, 218–219
partitions (groups), 231
routes, 230, 238
Super User Group, 430
user (MLA), 430
GUI (graphical user interface), 286–287
GUI Languages page (Unity), 364

# H

H.323, 14, 224
hardware
   conferencing, 183
   memory, 450–451
   PBX trunks, 181
   PSTN trunks, 180
   Unity Bridge, 311
   Unity servers, 292
   upgrading, 449
help desk staff training, 434
high availability of Unity servers, 285
high-level IPT design, 179. *See also* design
   analog/fax terminals, 179
   IPT applications, 185–186
   media resources, 181–185
   voice gateways, 180–181
Holidays page (Unity), 365
hops (CallManager), 298
host-based instruction detection, installation of, 277
hybrid Unity servers, 284

# I–K

ICD (Interactive Call Distribution), 228
idapsearch.asp scripts, 420
IETF (Internet Engineering Task Force), 151
IIS (Internet Information Services), 273
implementation, 378. *See also* configuration
   AA, 399–406
   acceptance tests, 431
   checklists
      data network readiness, 618

implementation readiness analysis, 614
   IPT network readiness, 619
   pre-implementation tasks, 611
   voice network readiness, 617
components, 380
   application servers, 380–382
   CallManager, 380–382
day 2 support, 432
dial plans, 397–398
IP CID, 409, 412–415
IP ICD, 406, 409
IP IVR, 415–416
IP Phones, 394
post-implementation documentation, 432
readiness analysis, 378–380
services, 416–424
tools, 425–431
training, 433–435
voice gateways, 382–393
implementation phase of PDIOO methodology, 71–72
implementation readiness analysis, 614, 617
inbound call routing, 258
inboxes, Cisco Unity Inbox, 287
inconsistencies in software versions, 429
Increment Multicast On option, 213
infrastructure
   call-processing architecture, 141
   design
      central site LANs, 150
      central site QoS, 150–159
      central site WAN QoS, 174
      DHCP, 147
      IP addressing/VLAN schemes, 145
      QoS, 145
      remote-site IPT, 159
      remote-site LAN QoS, 161–166
      remote-site WAN QoS, 166–174
      TFTP, 147
   IP Phones, 143–145
   IPT security, 272–277
inline power (IP Phones), 112–113
input queues, 154
installation
   application, 381
   CallManager, 381, 620
   CSA, 277

# U

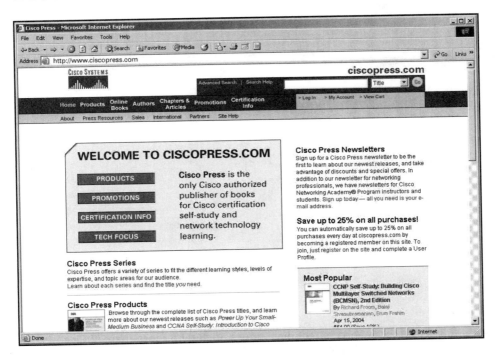
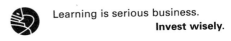

# SEARCH THOUSANDS OF BOOKS FROM LEADING PUBLISHERS

Safari® Bookshelf is a searchable electronic reference library for IT professionals that features more than 2,000 titles from technical publishers, including Cisco Press.

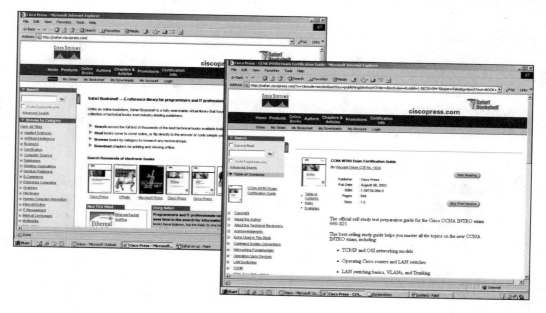

With Safari Bookshelf you can

- **Search** the full text of thousands of technical books, including more than 70 Cisco Press titles from authors such as Wendell Odom, Jeff Doyle, Bill Parkhurst, Sam Halabi, and Karl Solie.

- **Read** the books on My Bookshelf from cover to cover, or just flip to the information you need.

- **Browse** books by category to research any technical topic.

- **Download** chapters for printing and viewing offline.

With a customized library, you'll have access to your books when and where you need them—and all you need is a user name and password.